THE SOCIOLOGY OF
MENTAL DISORDERS

The Sociology of Mental Disorders

ANALYSES AND READINGS IN PSYCHIATRIC SOCIOLOGY

Edited by S. Kirson Weinberg

Aldine Publishing Company / Chicago

First Published 1967 by
ALDINE PUBLISHING COMPANY
320 West Adams Street
Chicago, Illinois 60606

Library of Congress Catalog Card Number 66–23169
Designed by Bernard Schleifer
Printed in the United States of America

Second printing, 1968

For
Mitchell Bergwin
Roger Maynard
Douglas Daniel

PREFACE

T he surge of inquiry during the past twenty years into the social aspects of mental disorders has accrued into considerable but dispersed knowledge of these phenomena. My aim in this book is to present some representative studies in a sequence that would characterize the growing field of psychiatric sociology, with attention focused on (1) the perspective and scope of psychiatric sociology as a branch of sociology; (2) the epidemiological distribution of mental disorders in the socioeconomic structure; (3) the effects of successive groups and associations on the development of disordered persons and the social psychological aspects of the types of disordered behavior; (4) the social definitions of mental disorders as types of deviant behavior; (5) the processes involved in the hospitalization of very disorganized persons; (6) the effects of the mental hospital as an institution in facilitating or retarding the improvement of the patients; (7) the influences that contribute to the post-hospital adjustment of former patients; (8) the plans and personnel in the reduction of mental disorders, particularly from the vantage point of "community psychiatry"; and (9) the cross-cultural influences on the types of disordered behavior and the modes of treatment.

Because the sociologist directs his interests to certain areas, an uneven distribution of studies within the field of psychiatric sociology results. Many studies concentrate on epidemiology and the institutional analysis of the mental hospital, but comparatively few deal with the developmental aspects of disordered behavior. The studies also vary in their emphases. Some papers represent theoretical positions; others are rigorous empirical inquiries; a third group consists of exploratory analysis; and a fourth group contains critical reviews of the literature. All types of papers are necessary for a rounded representation of inquiries in this field.

This edited compilation and analysis varies in emphasis and content from my previous book, *Society and Personality Disorders*. For reasons of space, I have not included some forms of acting-out behavior such as alcoholism or suicide, although these facets of disordered experience could come within the scope of psychiatric sociology. For topics such as the mental hospital, representative studies were selected from an array of excellent studies. The mechanics of publishing contributed to the selection of some articles over others.

I acknowledge with thanks the review and critical comments concerning the outline from Professors H. Warren Dunham and Howard S. Becker and Dr. Lawrence Appleby. Many stimulating intellectual exchanges occurred at the meeting of the Committee on Psychiatric Sociology of the Society for the Study of Social Problems; in these sessions many of these basic problems of psychiatric sociology were discussed and analyzed. I am grateful to Roosevelt University for reducing the hours of my teaching schedule and am very appreciative for the necessary procedural assistance by Esther Brown, Mary Demetro, Cheryl Peskin, Larissa Celewych, Michael Gainer, and Joan Lichterman. I am especially appreciative of the perceptive suggestions and criticisms of my wife, Dr. Rita M. Weinberg. Needless to say, I alone am responsible for whatever limitations or merits this volume has.

S. KIRSON WEINBERG

CONTENTS

ix

PART IV: DISORDERED BEHAVIOR AND SOCIAL DEVIANCE

PART V: THE MENTAL HOSPITAL

part I
APPROACH AND THEORY

PSYCHIATRIC SOCIOLOGY:

THE SOCIOLOGY OF MENTAL DISORDERS*

S. Kirson Weinberg

THE convergence of sociology and psychiatry into a designated field of study may be viewed from two vantage points: the emergent field of inquiry from the sociological perspective that is designated psychiatric sociology[1] and the area of study and social action that, from the psychiatric viewpoint, is called social psychiatry.[2]

Psychiatric sociology is the study of mental disorders as social phenomena. It is concerned with (1) the social factors and social processes that contribute to mental disorders, (2) the social definitions of mental disorders as forms of social deviance, (3) the social facets in the treatment and care of disordered persons, and (4) the social aspects of the prevention of mental disorders.[3]

Its theories and methods stem mainly from sociology, while the objects of its inquiry have been traditionally within psychiatry. Its particular vantage point in studying disordered behavior has contributed a social dimension to the knowledge of this problem that varies from the biomedical and psychobiological dimensions of psychiatry. It has revised the object of study from an organism to a person in a social setting and has contributed to a changed conception and method of studying mental disorder, whether the objects of inquiry are patients in mental hospitals or people in the community. Its orientation is consistent with and basic to "community psychiatry," which aims to extend treatment and preventive methods to groups in the community.[4]

Psychiatric sociology does not mean only a correlation of sociological and psychiatric variables derived from different frames of reference. To maintain a consistent sociological dimension and to build a body of validated theory limits its scope to the social personality, not the total personality, and to the sociocultural environment, not the total environment.

Before the surge of empirical studies of disordered behavior, sociologists were concerned with defining the converging fields of sociology and psychiatry. One version of psychiatric sociology dealt with the correlations between sociological and psychiatric variables.[5] Since many mental disorders were regarded as predominantly biological, the investigators emphasized the social features of these disorders, including their distribution in the socioeconomic structure. The proponents of this version regarded the process of these disorders as reflecting the course of an underlying organic pathology, hence the social stresses were subsidiary to biological influences in the development of these mental disorders.

Another more consistent version of psychiatric sociology—which I advocate—is concerned with the social facets of mental disorders and their care, treatment, and prevention; the etiology of these disorders may be influenced by social processes. The distribution of mental disorders in the socioeconomic structure is one step in determining the relevant social indicators that may causally affect these disorders. From this perspective, the social stresses affecting mental disorders are investigated in terms of their etiological significance, and, therefore, the course of some functional mental disorders are considered results of pathological personality development.

For example, Dunham regarded psychiatric sociology both as the study of psychiatric problems from the viewpoint and techniques of the sociologist and as a research area that correlates disorders or personality maladjustments with social variables.[6] Schermerhorn included in this field the sociocultural dimensions of mental disorder, the social relational aspects of therapy, and the social activities in prevention.[7] The field of psychiatric sociology reflects the perspective, objectives, and problems of the sociologist.

Certain assumptions of personality, socialization, and culture basic to this discipline of psychiatric sociology require elaboration.

The unit of study of mental disorders is a socialized person, not an organism and not a psyche abstracted from the social setting. In the processes of socialization, the infant becomes a symbolic, social participant and develops social relations in his membership and reference groups,

*Written for this volume

3

that can affect his personal stability. Psychiatric sociology focuses on these social influences that disrupt or thwart the person's activities and relationships and contribute to his instability and mental disorder. From this viewpoint, the person's constitutional endowments and physiological dysfunctions are held constant because the objects of concern are the social influences that contribute to his disorder or his mental health.

Mental disorders are conditions of extreme personality disorganization, not extensions of physical illness nor physical dysfunctions, and result from social processes that can lead, at the extreme, to incapacitation. As personality impairments, these disorders are studied as emergents of interpersonal and personal conflicts. Since the social personality rather than the mind alone is affected in disordered behavior, the terminologically accurate designation is "personality disorders," but this designation has already been equated with "acting-out disorders." The connotation, "mental disorders," does not seem as consistent with the theory of contemporary social psychology, because it stems from the psychoanalytic version of the psyche, "the mental life."

The place of stress in personality development as it relates to the analysis of mental disorder derives from a more basic version of personality formation and development. The psychogenetic position emphasizes that personality is formed during early life. Hence the critical experiences in early life are generally considered to determine the degree of basic personal stability. Reactions to stress in later life would be considered subsidiary to or repetitions of earlier anxiety reactions. On the other hand, the predominant sociological position has emphasized that, despite the significance of early experiences in personality formation, stresses in all stages of the person's life cycle may affect his instability and mental disorder. For example, during World War II some soldiers who had relatively stable childhoods experienced neurotic and even psychotic breakdowns, which implied that even relatively stable persons could break down under severe stress.

Because of the prevalence of the psychogenetic view, many studies have concentrated on family influences, especially maternal influences, in the formative processes of disordered behavior. The sociological position that has pointed to the stresses in subsequent life has also encouraged inquiries into the effects of peers, the school, the work situation, marriage, and retirement in senescence upon disordered behavior.

The sociological position raises different problems of mental disorders from those of the psychoanalytic view. It is concerned with shifts in responsibilities and duties for different age roles as these contribute to mild or intense disorders. For example, it is concerned with the increase of mental disorders after age 50, which may develop not only from physical decline but from stresses endured at this period of life. It maintains that each age period requires analysis in terms of its particular stresses.

This sociological position also assumes that stressful situations can contribute to personal conflict regardless of whether the personal conflicts are aggravated by biological deficits or restimulated by previous anxiety experiences.

The difference between objective stress considered inherent in the social situation, and the subjective reaction to stress as it leads to disorders requires clarification. Beaglehole has differentiated between the difficulties of a complex, heterogeneous culture and the conflicts one experiences subjectively.[8] Conceivably, in a complex culture, an individual may pursue a monotonous routine that averts cultural contradictions and intense personal conflicts.[9] On the other hand, it is difficult to see how one can encounter unemployment, downward mobility, bereavement, or being jilted in a love affair without experiencing intense conflicts and anxieties. The objective and subjective aspects of stress have been distinguished by Langner and Michael as stress and strain. They define stress as "the environmental force pressing on the individual" and strain as "a reaction to the external environment."[10] The stresses of a situation that can be ascertained from studying sociocultural conditions, however, represent the bases for personal strains and conflicts.

The epidemiological distributions of mental disorders in the community and socioeconomic structure indicate where the stresses are allocated and what social categories of persons have become emotionally disturbed or mentally disordered in this socioeconomic structure. Although epidemiological studies may not directly indicate etiological processes, sociological inquiries should determine the extent to which social factors indicate social causation.

The pertinence of epidemiological factors to social processes and causal significance has been identified to some degree. By successively isolating the crucial factors as indicators of mental disorders, the causal social processes can become more circumscribed. For example, Gruenberg and Leighton have traced the following factors that may have causal significance for disordered behavior.

At one time it was predicted on the basis of theory that the vicissitudes of adjustment to life in the New World would constitute just those types of strain conducive to psychiatric disorder. Investigation showed that, true enough, the first generation immigrant had a higher mental health risk than his old American counterpart or his peers in the country of origin in Europe. It was further shown that the frequency of psychiatric disorder decreased with the second and third generation. Then the hypothesis of class determination arose, for there were theoretical grounds for supposing that conditions of family and adult life in the lower socioeconomic brackets could produce psychiatric disorders. Empirical studies demonstrated there were indeed marked correlations of risk and class position. This survived controlling age and sex. It was further discovered in the Midtown Study that if one controlled socioeconomic level then the effects of immigration disappeared. The same applied to differences between ethnic groups when socioeconomic factors were controlled.[11]

Socioeconomic factors are fundamental to migration and ethnic subcultures in contributing to the onset of mental disorders. The Stirling County study reported that socioeconomic status was a definite influence on mental disorder and that a high correlation existed between social disintegration and the frequency of psychiatric disorders. When the condition of social disintegration was controlled, the influences of socioeconomic status were minimal. This suggested that social disorganization, not poverty *per se*, was the "effective noxious force" in disordered behavior among people of low socioeconomic status.

The next step in this methodological procedure is to refine the broader category of social disintegration and to isolate the social processes which contribute directly to mental disorder.

PSYCHIATRIC SOCIOLOGY AND SOCIAL PSYCHIATRY

The pervasive definition of social psychiatry pertains to social action and subsumes "community psychiatry," "preventive psychiatry," and social change of psychiatric institutions. The study of social etiology is instrumental to facilitating treatment and care of disordered persons, and, as a consequence, social psychiatry utilizes all available knowledge to deal with or to correct a particular aberrant situation more effectively. Ruesch has differentiated this process in social psychiatry from psychiatric sociology, the social science, as follows:

In contrast to the social scientist who is inclined to study one aspect of behavior at a time—for example, roles intelligence, or value orientations—the social psychiatrist investigates patterns. The emphasis upon patterns as opposed to single aspects is dictated by the necessity for remedial or preventive intervention. When professionals have to act they have to know all there is to know at the moment of the intervention. Time and timing, therefore, is a dimension that all operating disciplines share in common and that distinguishes them from the basic sciences. It follows that when the social psychiatrist wishes to utilize information contributed by the nonapplied sciences he has to simplify the information and add a time dimension.[12]

Thus, one pervasive version of social psychiatry, as defined by Wilmer and Leighton is that of an eclectic and applied discipline used by the psychiatrist in his particular role.[13] Ruesch has regarded social psychiatry in these terms as "a hybrid discipline which attempts to integrate and apply the knowledge derived from the social sciences with the skills of the psychiatrist."[14] He characterized seven of its major areas: (1) population surveys including the epidemiology and ecology of mental disorders; (2) cultures and subcultures relevant to psychiatric conditions such as military, ethnic, and class groups; (3) cultural changes that affect migrants, exiles, prisoners, and mobile persons; (4) the effects of family as well as age and sex groups on the participants; (5) routine situations and critical situations; (6) social learning and social interaction; and (7) the social features of treatment and custody.[15]

As a clinical discipline, social psychiatry is concerned with the diagnosis and treatment of disordered behavior. It is distinct from the biomedical and individualistic approaches to psychiatry because it is concerned with disordered behavior from the perspective of social relations and the group.

Social psychiatry intersects with psychiatric sociology in the social dimension of disordered behavior. The extremes of each discipline, however, clarify their diverse emphases. The sociologists are concerned with the social variables while the psychiatrists are concerned with the psychiatric and individual variables. For example, the sociologists are mainly concerned with the effects of social class on disordered behavior; the psychiatrists are mainly interested in the diagnostic conditions of the persons in the social classes. In differentiating between the two specialists, we are aware that with the persistent cross-fertilization of disciplines, some psychiatrists have acquired research skills to engage in social scientific inquiries, while a few sociologists have acquired clinical skills and have turned to the therapeutic aspects of disordered behavior from a sociological viewpoint.

Psychiatric sociology aims to be a unified discipline even though, as our readings indicate, the works of anthropologists, educators, and other behavioral scientists are included. This multidisciplinary inclusion is consistent because the perspective and methods, not the topics, are consistent. Sociologists and anthropologists do not differ markedly in their perspectives and methods of studying the mental hospital; the comparative studies of disordered behavior, while done largely by anthropologists, have also been done by sociologists. Educators have studied the influence of the school on disordered behavior from a sociological perspective. Because sociology is a basic discipline, its viewpoint has disseminated to other behavioral disciplines.

On the other hand, social psychiatry is not just multidisciplinary, it is a coordinating as well as a general field, because it utilizes the findings of sociology, cultural anthropology, economics, and social psychology, among other disciplines, for psychiatric purposes.

The omnibus view of social psychiatry that is quite prevalent has been developed by both Ruesch and Rennie. Rennie, one of the pioneers in social psychiatry, has contributed to its theoretical formulations and to the coordination of interdisciplinary studies of disordered behavior. He has conceived of social psychiatry as "the study of the etiology and dynamics of persons seen in their total environment, and [as aiming] to determine the significant facts in family and society which affect individual and group adaptation in the natural setting, and [as] concerned with the processes that retard or facilitate adaptation of all persons within the whole framework of contemporary living."[16] This distinction from psychiatric sociology is clear.

PLAN OF THIS BOOK

In this first part of the book, I have described the scope and problems of psychiatric sociology, its differences from social psychiatry, and the convergence of several disciplines to the interactional view of mental disorders. In subsequent parts of this book I present the studies, analyses, and criticisms of the specific areas within this field.

Part II covers the epidemiological inquiries of mental disorders. These studies are concerned with the distribution of disorders in the community and in the socioeconomic structure and with the effects of social mobility on disordered behavior. The subsequent epidemiological problems that are dealt with include the influence of the factors of migration and foreign birth, ethnic affiliation, race, age, sex, and marital status upon disordered behavior.

Part III is concerned with the processes that contribute to disordered behavior by the person's successive groups of participation, beginning with the family and leading to the stresses incurred in the peer group, the school, the work and marital situation, and old age. Persons may behave differently in these situations and groups, but the emphasis is largely upon the stresses encountered in these successive group situations.

Part IV surveys and evaluates the attitudes of psychiatrists and laymen to ascertain how the two groups define disordered behavior as socially deviant behavior. Disordered behavior as social deviance has diverse but consistent meanings among psychiatrists as clinical specialists and the public. The role of the family in defining the behavior of a disordered member becomes significant in his disposition, particularly when that member is psychotic. The reaction of the family in accommodating or not accommodating to his psychosis becomes crucial in determining his hospitalization. The processes of hospital commitment necessitate diagnostic screening and a judicial hearing. The manner of this diagnostic screening and the process of commitment are analyzed critically.

Part V deals with the effects of hospitalization upon the patients, with the organization and functions of the mental hospital as an institution, with the roles and activities of the staff, and with the functions of the hospital organization and ward milieu in facilitating or retarding the improvement of patients.

Part VI describes the theories of post-hospital adjustment of former mental patients with the aim of determining what types of patients remain out and what types of patients are returned to the hospital.

Part VII covers the many facets of out-patient treatment by private therapists as well as in clinics.

Part VIII characterizes the rationale, methods, problems and critique of out-patient rehabilitation of disordered persons and prevention of disordered behavior, holistically called "community psychiatry."

Part IX concentrates upon the culturally comparative or cross-cultural approach to mental disorders and their care, treatment, and prevention. It includes the cross-cultural analyses of the incidence and onset of varied mental disorders and the modes of physical and psychological treatment for these disorders in diverse folk and urban societies.

NOTES

1. The name, "psychiatric sociology," has been the title of the Committee for the Society for the Study of Social Problems and also for the International Sociological Association. The term, "psychiatric sociology," was initially used by Arnold M. Rose who sought a designation that would be distinct from being an adjunct of psychiatry.

2. Viola W. Bernard, "Some Aspects of Training For Community Psychiatry in a University Medical Center," in Stephen Goldston (Ed.), *Concepts of Community Psychiatry*, Public Health Service Publication No. 1319 (Washington D.C.: U.S. Government Printing Office, 1965).

3. See previous comparable syntheses: S. Kirson Weinberg, *Society and Personality Disorders* (Englewood Cliffs, N.J.: Prentice-Hall, 1952); H. Warren Dunham, *Sociological Theory and Mental Disorder* (Detroit: Wayne State University Press, 1959); Arnold M. Rose (Ed.), *Mental Health and Mental Disorder* (New York: W. W. Norton, 1955); Alexander H. Leighton, John A. Clausen, and Robert N. Wilson, *Explorations In Social Psychiatry* (New York: Basic Books, 1957); and Milbank Memorial Fund, *Causes of Mental Disorders* (New York: Milbank Memorial Fund, 1961).

4. *Community Mental Health and Social Psychiatry: A Reference Guide* (Cambridge, Mass.: Harvard University Press, 1962); Stephen E. Goldston (Ed.), *Concepts of Community Psychiatry*, Public Health Service Publication No. 1319 (Washington, D.C.: U.S. Government Printing Office, 1965); and R. Kotinsky and W. L. Witmer (Eds.), *Community Programs for Mental Health: Theory, Practice, Evaluation* (Cambridge, Mass.: Harvard University Press, 1955).

5. L. Guy Brown, "The Field and Problems of Social Psychiatry," in L. L. Bernard (Ed.), *Fields and Methods of Social Psychiatry* (New York: Ray Long and Richard R. Smith, 1934), pp. 129–45; and Joseph K. Folsom, "The Sources and Methods of Social Psychiatry," in L. L. Bernard (Ed.), *op. cit.*, pp. 387–401.

6. H. Warren Dunham, "The Field of Social Psychiatry," *American Sociological Review* (April, 1948), *13*, 183–97.

7. Richard Schermerhorn, "Social Psychiatry," *Antioch Review* (Spring, 1953), *13*, 67–85.

8. Roy R. Grinker and John B. Spiegel, *Men Under Stress* (Philadelphia: Blakiston, 1945), pp. 129–30; and S. Kirson Weinberg, "The Combat Neurosis," *The American Journal of Sociology* (March, 1946), *51*, 465–78.

9. Ernest Beaglehole, "Cultural Complexity and Psychological Problems," *Psychiatry* (August, 1940), *3*, 330–32.

10. Thomas S. Langner and Stanley T. Michael, *Life Stress and Mental Health* (New York: The Free Press of Glencoe, 1963), pp. 6, 7. *See* Harold G. Wolff, "Stressors as a Cause of Disease in Man," in J. M. Tanner (Ed.), *Stress and Psychiatric Disorder* (Oxford: Blackwell Scientific Publications, 1960), pp. 17–30.

11. Ernest M. Gruenberg and Alexander H. Leighton, "Epidemiology and Psychiatric Training," in Stephen E. Goldston (Ed.), *Concepts of Community Psychiatry*, Public Health Service Publications No. 1319 (Washington, D.C.: U.S. Government Printing Office, 1965), pp. 114–15.

12. Jurgen Ruesch, "Social Psychiatry: An Overview," *Archives of General Psychiatry* (May, 1965), *12*, 501–509.

13. H. A. Wilmer, *Social Psychiatry in Action* (Springfield, Ill.: Charles C Thomas, 1958); *see also* M. Jones, *Social Psychiatry in the Community, in Hospitals and in Prisons* (Springfield, Ill.: Charles C. Thomas, 1962); and Alexander Leighton, *et al., Explorations in Social Psychiatry* (New York: Basic Books, 1957), p. 4.

14. Jurgen Ruesch, "Research and Training in Social Psychiatry in the United States," *International Journal of Social Psychiatry* (1961), *7* (2), 87–96.

15. *Ibid.*, pp. 87–88; *see also* E. M. Bluestone, "Social Psychiatry: A Critique," *International Journal of Social Psychiatry* (1959), *4*, 291–95.

16. Thomas A. Rennie, "Social Psychiatry: A Definition," *International Journal of Social Psychiatry* (1955), *1* (1), 5–13.

SOCIAL INTERACTION AS AN ORIENTATION TO MENTAL DISORDERS AMONG THE BEHAVIORAL SCIENCES PRIOR TO 1950*

S. Kirson Weinberg

PSYCHIATRIC sociology has been influenced by several disciplines that intersect at the vantage point of social relationships.

Some psychiatrists and psychologists who took this vantage point in their studies of disordered behavior are hardly distinguishable in perspective on this level from sociologists and social psychologists. After 1950, many interdisciplinary studies of disordered behavior have emerged between sociologists and psychiatrists, such as Srole, Opler, Langner, Rennie and Leighton; Hollingshead and Redlich; Dunham and Gottlieb; and Lefton, Dinitz, and Pasamanick. Many epidemiological and correlative studies involved a division of labor in which the psychiatrists performed the diagnostics while the sociologists devised the research design. Each such study contributed to the merging analysis. These inquiries involved questions of theoretical consistency because the assumption that social influences were operative upon these disorders was implicit in the epidemiological studies.

This relational perspective to mental disorders was stimulated by unsuccessful efforts to explain psychoses in terms of organic pathology only, by the decline of neo-Darwinian doctrines of instincts, and by efforts to find an intersecting area between cultural norms and the biological individual.[1] It was catalyzed by the endeavors to understand explicitly psychotherapeutic relationships and by the growing recognition of the deep effects of social relationships upon human behavior.[2] Within the past three decades, interpersonal relations as a viewpoint have received attention from several disciplines dealing with mental disorders, including sociology, anthropology, psychiatry, psychoanalysis, and psychology.[3]

SOCIOLOGY

Sociologists developed the conception of social interaction at an early time, but their studies were directed to normal persons and groups and seldom to disordered persons. Although sociologists, in the first quarter of the century, were aware of the studies of psychiatrists and psychoanalysts, they did not incorporate or restate their concepts into social psychological terms. Two factors, caused this resistance to apply these conceptions to disordered persons: sociologists for a long time were "academic outsiders" who found difficulty gaining access to data in clinics and mental hospitals, and social pressures within the discipline for a period led to the avoidance of the "tragic and the bizarre" as subjects of inquiry.

By the second decade of this century the sociologists had evolved a sophisticated theory for discerning the influence of social relationships upon personality. This process was especially manifest after World War I with the decline of neo-Darwinism and the credibility of the instinct theory. Social relations then were regarded as levers that contributed to the formation of social personality and influenced motivation. In the first part of the century, Cooley had laid the basis for this developing view of social relations by emphasizing that human nature was an outgrowth of intimate relationships, a phase of the primary group, and seemed to "decay in isolation." George H. Mead also reinforced and elaborated this process by his theories of the dynamic quality of role-taking and the rise of the self in the matrix of social interaction. Prior to the end of World War I, Thomas and Znaniecki set the empirical groundwork in their studies of personal disorganization and social deviation.[4]

Deviant types—such as the criminal, the juvenile delinquent, the prostitute, and the suicide—were investigated as manifestations of an urban process or as members of variant cultures.[5]

*Written for this volume.

When the individual variant was analyzed as a person, as the suicide, or as the disorganized Polish peasant, in terms of his "career" of attitudes or wishes, self-conceptions, and status, the theoretical beginnings for studying personal disorders were discerned. The analysis of the unique variant was further expressed in the investigation of urban rooming-house areas, where cultural patterns were mingled and confused and where a marked degree of anonymity prevailed; the isolated inhabitants could not be studied as the subjective impress of the local "spurious" culture. The perspective of interaction had to be implemented in order to discern the isolated individual inhabitant. Zorbaugh said:

'More frequently the person accommodates himself to the life of the rooming house world by an individuation of behavior. Old associations are cut. Under the strain of isolation with no group associations or public opinion to hold one, living in complete anonymity, old standards disintegrate and life is reduced to a more individualistic basis. The person has to live and comes to live in ways strange to the conventional world. The person tends to act without reference to social definition. Behavior is individualized—impulsive rather than social.[6]

Yet this recognition of individuated behavior was viewed more as a phase of a broad urban process than as an aspect of personality disorder.

From another vantage point, the different explanations of juvenile delinquency by sociologists and psychiatrists serve to illustrate their disparate ways in applying social relations to understanding this form of deviant behavior. The sociologists regarded the delinquent as a cultural type, as one who was acculturated into a variant peer group through systematic permissive relationships within a local community.[7] The psychiatrists, Healy and Bronner, considered the delinquent an individual whose hostile and rebellious attitudes arose from repressive and dissatisfying family relations.[8] On the one hand, delinquency was an acquisition from interaction; on the other, disturbed social relationships threw the person back upon himself, prompting personality defenses that could emerge into variant behavior by the selection of delinquent companions. Both types of responses were products of social relationships, yet knowledge of the person's private and unique responses that estranged him from the family and impelled him to seek delinquent associates was essential for an understanding of disordered behavior. For disordered behavior is in a sense the antithesis of acculturated behavior.

This interest in maladjusted and disordered

behavior was evident in the study of the family. It was indicated in the personality development of the child, in the influence of the parental attachments on adjustment during engagement as well as upon marital relations generally. These sociological studies led increasingly to the restatement of psychoanalytic concepts within the framework of sociology.[9]

Studies of mental hygiene and of psychoses, neuroses, and psychopathy laid the bases for an intersecting area between sociology and psychiatry. Ecological studies initiated by Faris and Dunham preceded studies of schizophrenia.[10] Schizophrenics were studied within the context of the local urban area. For example, paranoids in the rooming house areas had a minimum of informal, personal relationships, and young male catatonics who clustered in high-rate delinquency areas presumably were unable to find congenial companions from the surrounding play groups. In both instances the personal isolation engendered was a function of the modes of relationships within the local community. Concomitant and subsequent studies were made of the social personality of the schizophrenic as an emergent of his social relationships.[11] The studies of the neuroses and of psychopathy during and since the war years have also pursued this line of inquiry.[12] It has more recently been evident in the study of the mental hospital, which was analyzed in terms of interpersonal relationships.

In the general area of personality and culture or the individual and the group, psychiatrists and sociologists have emphasized different phases of personal development. Psychiatrists have emphasized the import of early relationships upon personal disorders, while sociologists have stressed the juvenile, adolescent, and adult relationships upon these disorders. In assessing this distinction as manifested in personal disorganization and social disorganization generally, and in neurotic reactions specifically, Blumer wrote:

One thing that sociological studies do point to is the condition of individuals seemingly well adjusted during childhood who become quite disorganized under certain social conditions. I refer especially to the marginal man in the generic sense of that type.

An individual who seems to have made normal adjustments during the early part of his life may be placed in a situation where he is subject to conflicting demands and appeals of a fundamental sort, and suffers distressing confusion as a result. But even more important than such social or cultural conflict is the acute and disturbing self-consciousness which such an individual may experience owing to the fact that his conception of himself is markedly disjointed from the actual status which he occupies.[13]

In brief, before 1950 sociologists had extended their concepts to cover the individual variant and had directed attention to the personal relationships and social experiences that affected disordered behavior. They usually studied the variant within the neighborhood and community, but their studies were not confined to these contexts.

SOCIAL ANTHROPOLOGY

The anthropologists who are mainly concerned with objective cultural patterns, practices, and functions of nonliterates were almost "anti-psychological" in their approach before 1920, and some remain so. Although some biographies and personal documents had been published before that time, and some ethnologists had taken cognizance of certain types of abnormal behavior in their inquiries, the concerted efforts to implement psychiatric and psychoanalytic concepts to nonliterate groups came after Freud's venture into anthropology, particularly in *Totem and Taboo*.[14]

The Freudians, influenced by the English anthropologists, adopted an evolutionary approach to society and sought to parallel societal development with the stages of individual growth. Their views, which were non-historic, were founded on very little evidence and became so congealed that the criticisms of anthropologists had little if any effect. In fact, both psychoanalysts and anthropologists talked past each other, until recently. In spite of the aloofness of psychoanalysts, the very provocative nature of their theories began to effect the views of anthropologists.[15] For example, Kroeber had castigated Freud's work for its flimsy and distorted evidence, but agreed nonetheless that the work contained significant insights.[16] Such field anthropologists as Malinowski, Margaret Mead, and D. Eggan endeavored to test or to apply certain Freudian hypotheses, such as the Oedipal attachment, in their investigations of nonliterate societies.[17] The net effect of these and other inquiries was to direct attention to social relationships, particularly parent-child relationships, in their more dynamic aspects in other cultures. They emphasized also the relativity of intrafamily relations, which varied with the family structure and with roles of the respective members. This approach, in part, paved the way for discerning the nonliterate person as a distinct individual rather than as one with a cultural impress similar or identical to others in his homogenous group.

From a theoretical line of attack, Sapir, who was familiar with anthropology, sociology, and psychiatry, attempted to find a midpoint between individual psychiatry and cultural anthropology. This middle area, as Sapir clearly stated, resided within the field of social psychology and the sphere of social relationships. He said:

As we follow tangible problems of behavior rather than the selected problems set by recognized disciplines, we discover the field of social psychology, which is not a whit more social than it is individual and which is, or should be, the mother science from which stem both the abstracted impersonal problems as phrased by the cultural anthropologists and the almost impertinently realistic explorations which are the province of the psychiatrist.[18]

In characterizing this culture-personality nexus, Sapir saw this area essentially composed of the emergent meanings of interpersonal relations, as George Mead did earlier in social psychology. From this point of view, the emergence of the distinct and unique personality became inevitable, because of the unique as well as the common interpretations that each individual gave and derived in the process of interpersonal relations.[19]

Though this approach was not always pursued in empirical inquiry of disordered persons, there have been field researches in which the different meanings arising from personal relationships could contribute to disorders. This was evident in the works by Cooper, Hallowell, and Landis. Opler traced the mode of therapeutic relationships between the shaman and the disordered person among the Apache. And Beaglehole has indicated how a gross superorganic or objective view of culture complexity was misleading in understanding mental disorders.[20]

From a culturological viewpoint, Benedict, Fortune, and others have shown clearly the relativity of abnormality.[21] Within this framework Fortune, for example, was able to depict both the individual variant in the Dobuan society and the relations of the Dobuans to him. Kardiner, Linton, and their associates, in an integration of psychoanalysis and cultural anthropology, have shown that the value systems within the culture are patterns of interpersonal relationships and that these patterns are the most conspicuous features of the culture. The most significant feature of their contributions has been to show the effects of early parent-child relationships upon the personality structure and the function of this personality structure in sustaining the existent mode of relations within the culture. From this standpoint, a closer inspection of the imbalances within the personality could be analyzed. They have thus distinguished between a "modal personality" common to the culture and the individual personality structure.[22]

Davis, Warner, and their associates studied the influence of human relations on personality in the varied socioeconomic levels of contemporary society and have taken account of the personal conflicts and the deviant and aberrant personalities in these social classes.[23] Since personality differences were noted in the social classes, it was assumed that the types of mental disorders might also vary among these groups. As yet there has been no definitive study of the relationship between the social structure and disordered behavior except possibly for the development of anxiety, which presumably concentrated among the middle class. As a point of fact, the ecological distributions of certain types of psychotic disorders, as schizophrenia and manic-depression reflect differences for different socioeconomic groups. Yet these different distributions are at best indices to the types of social relationships which obtain in areas of different income levels. From an operational standpoint, Chapple has attempted to classify persons on the basis of their mode of interpersonal relations and he has extended this theory to the differentiation of the personally disordered from the normal.[24]

In brief, many anthropologists veered from superorganic or super-personal approach to an interpersonal approach to culture. Their chief contributions have been to point out and elaborate the relativity of modes of social relations in diverse cultures and in different socioeconomic groups and the varying effects of these relationships in contributing to the onset and therapy of mental disorders.

PSYCHIATRY

Psychiatry as a branch of medicine was concerned with the diagnosis, understanding and treatment of "mental disease." From its biomedical vantage point it regarded personality as a biological being; psychiatrists dealt with hospitalized and nonhospitalized psychotics from this biological viewpoint. During the first quarter of the twentieth century when the influence of psychobiology and of psychoanalysis began to make headway against a powerful Kraepelinian tradition, the social phases of personality began to become more explicit and to receive more interest.

The psychobiological school recognized the patient as a dynamic being in a total environment rather than as a static organism. From this holistic emphasis, the social aspect of personality was one facet that had to be studied.[25] Adolph Meyer wrote in this connection:

Much is gained by the frank recognition that man is fundamentally a social being. There are reactions in us which only contacts and relations with other human beings can bring out. We must study men as mutual reagents in personal affections and aversions and their conflicts; in the desires and satisfactions of the simpler appetites for food and personal necessities; in the natural inter-play of anticipation and fulfillment of their desires and their occasional frustration; in the selection of companionship which works helpfully or otherwise—for the moment or more lastingly throughout the many vicissitudes of life.[26]

In attempting to understand the disordered person as a dynamic social being instead of as a pathological organism or as an isolated individual within the clinic, the psychiatrists had to acknowledge the influence of the social relationships upon the patient's disordered condition. This was particularly true for psychiatrists who dealt with children's problems. Bunker indicated that "the futility of studying the individual as an isolated unit instead of as an integrated part of the social group was less easy to overlook in the case of the child than in the adult's."[27]

This notion of the person in the social context became more crystallized, not only among specialists in child guidance and in mental hygiene, but also among psychiatrists who were influenced directly by the social sciences such as T. Burrow, W. A. White, and H. Adler.[28] White, for example, recognized the significance of psychoanalysis, and was among the first psychiatrists to attribute more importance to social relationships as a means of understanding the social personality. He considered "social psychiatry as a discipline which deals with man as a social being in his relations to his fellows."[29] In 1934, Bentley maintained that a comparison of the psychiatric approach one generation ago and at that time would have shown the increased emphasis upon the "socialization of the subject. Then the patient was an afflicted organism; now (1934) he is a disturbed, distorted and unadjusted member of a family and a community; in this sense, he is a disordered person."[30] Later, Plant gave systematic expression to this tendency, when he regarded the personality as operating in life situations. In criticizing the medical or classical psychiatric approach to personal disorders, Plant stated:

The classical psychiatric approach—preoccupied with the structure of the individual in vacuo—thus seems to us inadequate to a situation facing frankly the sociological forces. The approach rigidly adhered to would predict nothing but rapid and widespread mental breakdown throughout our area. We are suspicious that psychiatric theory demands considerable reformulation after it has had a much more extensive experience with individuals actually adjusting in a certain milieu. As long as we center our interest in hospitals—and will study our patients at ten, twenty, or hundreds of miles away from their actual homes, psychiatric theory must suffer from a certain parochial sort of individualism that quite lacks realism.[31]

Plant explicitly considered the influences of the social matrix upon the person and the importance of social relationships within this matrix and in this sense anticipated the broad approach of "community psychiatry."

Sullivan, a psychoanalyst, was even more definite in his analyses of the effects of interpersonal relations upon personal disorders which he regarded as the essential subject matter of psychiatry. Perhaps more than any other psychiatrist Sullivan was instrumental in giving currency to the term "interpersonal relationships." By emphasizing the effects of the interpersonal or social above the instinctively sexual, as conceived by orthodox psychoanalysts, he explored the emergent derivatives of these relationships in meanings, language, and the self. He divided experience and interpersonal relations into three types: the prototaxic, the parataxic, and the syntaxic. The protaxic relations include the early, presymbolic modes of interaction. The parataxic relations consist of unwitting and personalized meanings that enter into social relationships. The syntaxic relations are viewed as sharing processes that lead to agreement among the interactants.[32]

Sullivan investigated the modes of social relationships which contribute to anxiety, schizophrenia and other disorders. He defined the interpersonal processes between patient and therapist, called attention to the disruptive and singular meanings as well as common meanings that arise in communication, and emphasized the influences of interpersonal relationships upon personality development, especially during the formative years of early life which he felt were not explored sufficiently. He tried to incorporate the other approaches to personality into the study of interpersonal relations and to implement various disciplines in this study. He stated:

The elucidation of the fundamental characteristics of interpersonal relations ("personality processes") in the forms of scientific laws requires the extended collaboration of investigators along many approaches. These investigators must be relatively free from the more serious inhibitions of their alertness in the interpersonal relations that supply the data; and significant freedom from inhibitions of alertness is but rarely the outcome of personality as it is likely to occur among us. In other words, it has usually to be acquired by way of special training in interpersonal relations by methods related to the best of current psychoanalytic practices . . .[33]

Not only Sullivan's followers but psychiatrists generally were influenced by his theory of personal relationships in personality development and in mental disorders. As they attempted to fit his views within their own conceptual schemes, they inadvertently had to modify their theoretical frameworks and especially their conceptions of the personality from an afflicted organism or an isolated individual to a disordered person in a social context. "Psychiatry is the study of processes that involve or go on between people," Sullivan wrote. "The field of psychiatry is the field of inter-personal relations, under any and all circumstances in which these relations exist. It was seen that a personality can never be isolated from the complex of inter-personal relations in which the person lives and has his being."[37]

From this viewpoint, many facets of disordered personality that were hitherto neglected began to receive more research scrutiny. The constellation of relationships the psychotic had experienced to the time of his breakdown, the unique and often uncommunicative meanings he expressed, and his general modes of relationships became objects of interest and of research. In this way the psychotic became a less forbidding person and was viewed as a product of social relationships as was the normal person.

PSYCHOANALYSIS

Although psychoanalysis has become accepted in large or small part by many psychiatrists, it differs from psychiatry proper because its concentrated concern has been with the neuroses and because it has developed a specific body of theory and specific psychotherapeutic methods and techniques. Recently it has extended its theory and therapeutic techniques to the psychoses, especially schizophrenia, and to psychosomatic disorders.[35] In spite of its instinctual bias and its individual-genetic approach to culture, psychoanalysis is chiefly concerned with psychodynamics. It is not unexpected then, that Freud regarded the dynamism of repression as one keystone of his conceptual framework. In interpreting the formation of these dynamisms, the psychoanalysts have begun to attribute more importance to the social matrices within which these dynamisms were formed and expressed. The explicit recognition of the influence of interpersonal relations upon human behavior arose from two sources: it was affected by the challenging questions offered by the social scientists, and it was stimulated and clarified by the increasing awareness of the interpersonal process between the therapist and the patient.

It is not surprising that women, notably Karen Horney and Clara Thompson, were among the neoFreudians who rejected some of Freud's early formulations.[36] They rejected the notions of the innate psychological differences between men and women and the seeming inferiority of women. Instead, they pointed out that many psychological differences between the sexes resulted from their respective roles in society and that woman's supposed inferiority merely reflected her social role. They correctly maintained that Freud universalized the social position of the woman in the middle and upper-middle classes of Austria. With this vantage point, Horney particularly placed increasing emphasis upon the culture and upon the modes of relationships within the culture as the bases for understanding the disturbed and disordered personality. Hence she adopted a virtual sociological perspective instead of an instinctivistic physio-anatomical view to personality. Horney wrote:

My conviction...is that psychoanalysis should outgrow the limitations set by its being an instinctivistic and genetic psychology. Thus the analysis of the actual character structure moves into the foreground of attention...when character trends are no longer explained as the ultimate outcome of instinctual drives, modified only by the environment, the entire emphasis falls upon life conditions molding the character and we have to search anew for the environmental factors responsible for creating neurotic conflicts; thus disturbances in human relationships become the crucial factor in the genesis of the neuroses. A prevailing sociological orientation then takes the place of a prevailingly anatomical-physiological one.[37]

Horney, Fromm, Thompson, FrommReichmann, and others have also attributed the genesis of neuroses to faulty early relationships and have revised or disposed of many of the ontogenetic complexes to which many orthodox Freudians adhered.[38] Fromm scrutinized the relationships between the authority figure and the child, and in another study showed how the context of relationships has differentiated "modern man" from other historic types.[39] Even the psychoanalysts who have not veered far from Freud have concentrated more attention upon the ego or the self and therefore have attributed more importance to the sphere of interaction. For example, Alexander and his associates have come to regard neurosis as "the result of emotional experiences in human relations which the patient could not deal with adequately in the past."[40]

In reappraising the patient-therapist relationships, some psychoanalysts have become more sharply aware of the effects of this mode of interaction upon the patient's condition. Ferenzci and Rank were among the first to call attention to the "emotional experience of the patient in his relationships to the physician which is the main therapeutic factor and that recovery of forgotten events is not an essential part of the treatment."[41] This notion has since been developed by psychoanalysts in both prolonged and brief psychotherapy.[42] In addition, they recognized that clinical relationships are an integral segment of the total web of the patient's relationships. The relationships that the patient experienced between treatment sessions—in the family, in the office, among his friends—could hinder or facilitate the therapeutic outcome. The cautious therapist, therefore, became aware of the problems confronting the patient in his diverse contemporary groups. Because of this interest, the patient's impersonal and competitive associations had to be examined, and these competitive contacts revealed a somewhat different dimension of relationships than were encountered in the family. As a matter of fact, these competitive relationships of the impersonal community became a distinct means by which psychoanalysts could interpret our culture.

But the psychoanalysts also were concerned with the affects of the patient-therapist relationship in the treatment process. Horney reinterpreted the importance of the transference process and recognized the importance of human relationships in understanding and in treating neurotic behavior.[43] She maintained that the knowledge of human psychology was in essence based upon comprehending the processes inherent in social relationships and that the therapist, by his knowledge and skillful use of these relationships as expressed specifically in transference, could make the treatment far more effective.[44] We find that with the increasing recognition and understanding of the intimate processes of social interaction, psychoanalysts also became more occupied with those aspects of personality which emerge from social interaction. This resulted in a tendency to shift from an emphasis upon the libidinal phases of behavior to a more intense interest in the "self," "attitude," and in other aspects of the social personality.

But the psychoanalysts retained a certain rigidity concerning the function of social relations in disordered behavior and became somewhat isolated from the confluence of interests between psychiatrists and social scientists. Except for those psychoanalysts who incorporated these conceptual trends of a social interaction approach such as the Washington School of Psychiatry, the concentration of psychoanalytic interest was at best focused on the therapeutic process.

PSYCHOLOGY

Although early psychologists recognized the social influences upon personality, the increasing shift toward social relationships as a central interest in psychology became manifest with the influences of dynamics of the neo-Freudians, the group dynamics of field theory, the preoccupation with the counseling-client relationship, and the interaction between examiner and the tested subject,[45] as well as with the use of social psychological concepts to explain the dynamic processes as represented in projective tests and the formulation of comparative norms of behavior for the use of projective tests in different societies.[46]

The neo-Freudian influences strived to reconcile Freudian and field concepts in disordered behavior and placed more emphasis upon social forces. Social interaction was also used to analyze client-counselor relationships in the explicit definition of the counselor's role and the client's role and was intensified in the interest in the dynamics of group therapy and milieu therapy.

Social psychological concepts were increasingly used to explain the protocols of projective techniques. It was found that the subject's relationships with his parents and authority figures or his siblings and peers, his general attitudes toward the opposite sex, and his general orientation to himself in the social orbit could be discerned from these tests, especially from the Thematic Apperception Test. Although these aspects of content were more difficult to uncover in the Rorschach Test, the subject's conception of himself could be learned from the "M" or movement responses and his relationships with his mother from card VII; his degree of self-tolerance and social tolerance could also be discerned.

Studies of persons in different cultural settings showed different norms of behavior. Bleuler found that the inhabitants of Morocco concentrated on the trivial details of the Rorschach cards. Their responses would be considered indicative of schizophrenia. Among Western Europeans Rorschach himself found variations in the typical responses of subjects in different sections of Switzerland. Oberholzer interpreted the Rorschach protocols among the Alorese. These variations in norms can be interpreted in two ways: the personal stability among varied groups or variations of the norms for interpretation among different cultures.

Psychologists have attempted to correlate personal stability and opinions toward social issues. Despite the limitations of these studies, the interest has been upon the relationships of disturbed and disordered persons to specific minority groups. In brief, psychology has increasingly recognized social relationships as a crucial dimension in human behavior and has applied this concept to the understanding of the counseling interview.

CONCLUSIONS AND INTERPRETATIONS

We have pointed out the directions from which the construct of interpersonal relations has converged as a viewpoint to disordered behavior. This viewpoint had come to the forefront of attention for a variety of reasons: (1) certain disorders could not be explained adequately on the basis of biological and instinctual factors; (2) the analysis of individually contained dynamisms isolated from a complex social milieu was frequently felt to be incomplete; (3) the therapist-patient relationship had to be made explicit in order to understand the treatment process more thoroughly; and (4) the cultural forms and the biological individual had to have an area of reconciliation.

Consequently, psychiatrists have shifted from a static, classical approach to a dynamic view of personality. Some psychoanalysts, psychologists, and psychiatric social workers have become more sharply aware of the influence of the social process, and some social anthropologists and sociologists have extended their theoretical scheme to account for the individual variant.

But the overall inclusive concept of interpersonal relations, nonetheless, has divergent emphases, and these emphases result not only from the different frameworks of the respective disciplines, but also from the study of different types of subjects. Initially, psychiatrists were concerned with psychotics, especially hospitalized psychotics, who were not always or necessarily communicative but more or less cut off from relations with real people, used language to reveal their individualized conflicts or unique wishes rather than to communicate with others.

Those psychiatrists who had considered patients as afflicted organisms regarded their conversations as symptomatic of profounder physiological and anatomical pathologies. Though this was undoubtedly true of organic personality disturbances, many psychotics with personality disturbances expressed delusions and hallucinations which arose from their psychotic condition. It was only when these conversations were considered indicative of certain conflicts and related to the disorder that some psychiatrists tried to make meaning out of nonsense in the expressions of the patients; this interest paved the way for some form of communication to proceed eventually between the patients and therapists. The mode as well as content of this communicative process led to revealing clues about the previous social relationships and the unique conflicts of the patients.

The psychoanalysts initially dealt with chronic neurotics of middle and upper socioeconomic status. The homogeneity of their patients made it congenial to apply their clinical theories, which were developed during a period when the influence of the biological sciences on the psychological and social sciences was very great. But in the past few decades, as psychoanalysts emerged from their isolation, they have become more aware of the social process. At the same time they have devoted more attention to the patient-therapist interaction as a factor in controlling and improving the treatment process. This, in turn, has led to increasing interest in the social aspects of personal growth and in the character of the universe of relationships in which the patient participated and of which the clinic was an integral part. This has resulted in a revised emphasis upon the patient's personality characteristics and in a greater interest in his present and past social relationships.

Sociologists and anthropologists usually dealt with the normal and socialized persons whom they saw as members of a cultural series. Anthropologists, though initially concerned with the nonliterate in a homogeneous culture, began also to study the person in modern society and became more concerned with the subconscious phases of behavior resultant from a person's relationships and experiences within the context of his culture. Sociologists, who were generally interested in the common and shared aspects of interpersonal relations, had to inquire into the unique and private phases of experiences in order to understand the individual variant.

There were also disparate aims and methods in these inquiries. Clinicians—as psychiatrists, psychoanalysts, psychologists, and psychiatric social workers—were usually oriented to diagnostic and/or therapeutic ends. Researchers, who had less contact with the clinic, were preoccupied with studies of patients in the community or in institutions. However, many clinicians are also researchers and some researchers also have therapeutic ends along with their research. The convergence in this direction is evident, though differences remain.

The different aims of research and clinical work as practiced by social scientists and psychiatrists have developed, as we have emphasized, from their distinct professional roles.

NOTES

1. Edward Sapir, "The Contribution of Psychiatry to an Understanding of Behavior in Society," *American Journal of Sociology*, (May, 1937) *XLII* (6), 870. S. Kirson Weinberg, *Society and Personality Disorders* (Englewood Cliffs, W.J. Prentice-Hall Inc., 1952) Chapter 3.

2. Such collaborative efforts have developed among a number of research groups (as Kardiner, Linton and DuBois; Kluckhohn and Murray; the Wm. Alanson White Foundation; Aginsky and Wilbur; Chapple and Lindeman; Levy and the Henrys; Mirsky and Bunzel), and it is also evident in the cooperative interdepartmental influences in the universities and among the clinical teams in the neuropsychiatric clinics. See Clyde Kluckhohn, "Psychiatry and Anthropology," *One Hundred Years of American Psychiatry* (New York: Columbia University Press,

1944); Clyde Kluckhohn and Henry A. Murray (Eds.), *Personality in Nature Society and Culture* (New York: Alfred A. Knopf, 1949); Patrick Mullahy (Ed.), *A Study of Interpersonal Relations* (New York: Hermitage Press, 1949), and S. Stansfeld Sargent and Marian W. Smith (Eds.), *Culture and Personality* (New York: The Viking Fund, 1949).

3. This approach begins sometimes with the general concept of adjustment, because adjustment starts with the individual rather than the person as an integral part of the group. It does not denote specifically the emergence of the social personality as a result of social relationships. This view has been generally advocated by psychologists. See the section on psychology in this chapter. For a comprehensive summary of the literature, see Verne Wright, "Summary of the Literature on Social Adjustment," *American Sociological Review* (June, 1942), 7 (3), 407–422.

4. Charles Cooley, *Human Nature and the Social Order* (New

York: Charles Scribner's Sons, 1902); George H. Mead, *Mind, Self and Society* (Chicago: University of Chicago Press, 1937); and William I. Thomas and Florian Znaniecki; *The Polish Peasant in Europe and America* (New York: Alfred A. Knopf, Inc., 1927).

5. Frederick M. Thrasher, *The Gang* (Chicago: University of Chicago Press, 1927); Clifford R. Shaw, *The Jackroller* (Chicago: University of Chicago Press, 1930); Walter C. Reckless, *Vice in Chicago* (Chicago: University of Chicago Press, 1934); and Ruth S. Cavan, *Suicide* (Chicago: University of Chicago Press, 1928).

6. Harvey W. Zorbaugh, "The Dweller in Furnished Rooms: An Urban Type," in Ernest W. Burgess (Ed.), *The Urban Community* (Chicago: University of Chicago Press, 1926), pp. 98–105.

7. See Clifford R. Shaw, *op. cit.,* Burgess states: "[The case of Stanley] is typical . . . in the same way that every case is representative of its type or species. This case is a member of the criminal species and so must bear the impress of the characteristics and experience of the criminal" ("Discussion," *The Jackroller*, pp. 185–86).

8. Healy and Bronner state: "It appears that at some varying distance up stream in the sequence of delinquent causation there are almost deeply felt discomforts arising from unsatisfying human relationships. Herein we have found the answer to one of our prime questions: why living under the same environmental conditions, often inimical, is one child nondelinquent and the other delinquent? The latter we almost universally found to be one at some stage in his development to be blocked in his needs for satisfying relationships in his family circle" {*New Light on Delinquency and Its Treatment*, (New Haven: Yale University Press, 1936, p. 201).

9. Willard Waller, *The Family: A Dynamic Interpretation* (New York: Gordon, 1938), and Kimball Young, *Personality and Problems of Adjustment* (New York: F. S. Crofts, 1940), Part II.

10. Robert E. L. Faris and H. Warren Dunham, *Mental Disorders in Urban Areas* (Chicago: University of Chicago Press, 1939).

11. H. Warren Dunham, "The Social Personality of the Catatonic-Schizophrene," *American Journal of Sociology* (May, 1944), *XLIX,* 508–518, and Robert E. L. Faris, "Cultural Isolation and the Schizophrenic Personality," *American Journal of Sociology* (September, 1937), *XL,* pp.   .

12. S. Kirson Weinberg, "The Combat Neuroses," *American Journal of Sociology*, (March, 1946), *LI* (5), 465–78.

13. Herbert Blumer, "Social and Individual Disorganization," *American Journal of Sociology* (May, 1937), *XLII,* 876.

14. Clyde Kluckhohn, "Psychiatry and Anthropology," *One Hundred Years of American Psychiatry* (New York: Columbia University Press, 1944), p. 591. Sapir and Kluckhohn attribute this resistance to psychiatry in part to the particular types of personalities who are attracted to anthropology.

Alfred L. Kroeber in 1906, Paul Radin in 1913, and Elsie Clew Parsons in 1922 collected personalized sketches of nonliterates.

Sigmund Freud, *Totem and Taboo* (New York: Dodd Mean, 1918).

15. In 1925 Goldenweiser stated: "Whatever may be said in criticism of Freudian and other such mechanisms, the fact remains that we know more today about the urge of sex, about repression, conflicts, compensations and sublimations than we did yesterday and we hope for an even richer harvest tomorrow" ("Psychology and Culture," *Publications of the American Sociological Society*, XIX, 15–24).

16. Alfred L. Kroeber, "Totem and Taboo: An Ethnologic Psychoanalysis," *American Anthropologists* (1920), *XX,* 48–55.

17. Bronislaw Malinowski, *Sex and Repression in Savage Societies* (New York: Harcourt Brace & Company, 1927); Margaret Mead, *Sex and Temperment in Three Primitive Societies* (New York: W. W. Morrow, 1935); and Dorothy Eggan, "The General Problem of Hopi Adjustment," *American Anthropologist* (1943), *XLV,* 357–73.

18. Edward Sapir, "Cultural Anthropology and Psychiatry," *Journal of Abnormal and Social Psychology* (1932), *XXVII,* 236–37.

19. Edward Sapir, "The Emergence of the Concept of Personality in the Study of Cultures," *Journal of Social Psychology* (June, 1934), *V,* 408–415, and Ernest Beaglehole, "Interpersonal Theory and Social Psychology," in Patrick Mullakny (Ed.), *A Study of Inter-personal Relations* (New York: Hermitage House, 1949), pp. 50–79.

20. John M. Cooper, "Mental Disease Situations in Certain Cultures," *Journal of Abnormal and Social Psychology* (April–March, 1934–35), *XXIX,* 1–9. A. Irving Hallowell, "Culture and Mental Disorder," *Journal of Abnormal and Social Psychology* (1938), *XXXIII,* 195–225. Edward M. Opler, "Some Points of Comparison and Contrast Between the Treatment of Functional Disorders by Apache Shamans and Modern Psychiatric Practice," *American Journal of Psychiatry* (1930), *XCII,* 1371–87; and Ernest Beaglehole, "Cultural Complexity and Psychological Problems," *Psychiatry* (August, 1940), *III,* 335–37.

21. Ruth Benedict, *Patterns of Culture* (New York: Houghton Mifflin, 1935), and Reo Fortune, The Sorcerers of Dobu (New York: Little Brown, 1932).

22. Abram Kardiner and Associates, *The Individual and His Society* (New York: Columbia University Press, 1939) and *Psychological Frontiers of Society* (New York: Columbia University Press, 1945).

23. Allison Davis and Robert R. Havighurst, *Father of the Man* (New York: Houghton Mifflin, 1948), and W. Lloyd Warner, "The Society, the Individual and His Mental Disorders," *American Journal of Psychiatry* (1937), *XCIV,* 275–84.

24. Eliot D. Chapple and Carelton S. Coon, *Principles of Anthropology* (New York: Henry Holt, 1942), pp. 58–62.

25. Alfred Lief, (Ed.), *The Commonsense Psychiatry of Dr. Adolph Meyer* (New York: McGraw-Hill, 1948), and W. Muncie, *Psychobiology and Psychiatry* (St. Louis: C. V. Mosby, 1939).

26. Adolph Meyer, "The Contributions of Psychiatry to the Understanding of Life Problems," address delivered at the Celebration of the One Hundredth Anniversary of Bloomingdale Hospital (Privately printed, Society of the New York Hospital, 1921).

27. Henry Alden Bunker, "Psychiatry as a Speciality," in Kluckhohn, *op. cit.,* p. 497.

28. Trigant A. Burrow, "So-called 'Normal' Social Relationships Expressed in the Individual and the Group, and their Bearing upon Neurotic Discharmonies," *Publications of the American Sociological Society,* XXIV: 2L192, pp. 285–286; William A. White, "Psychiatry and the Social Sciences," *American Journal of Psychiatry* (March, 1938), *VII* (5); and Herman Adler, "The Relation Between Psychiatry and the Social Sciences," *American Journal of Psychiatry* (April, 1927), *VI,* 661–670.

29. William A. White, *Forty Years of Psychiatry* (Washington, D.C.: Nervous and Mental Disease Publishing Co., 1933), pp. 83–84.

30. Madison Bentley, "General and Experimental Psychology," in Madison Bentley and E. V. Cowdrey (Eds.), *The Problem of Mental Disorder* (New York: McGraw-Hill, 1934), p. 294.

31. James S. Plant, *Personality and the Cultural Pattern* (New York: The Commonwealth Fund, 1937), p. 143.

32. Harry Stack Sullivan, "Multidisciplined Coordination of Interpersonal Data," in S. Stansfeld Sargent and Marian W. Smith (Eds.), *Culture and Personality* (New York: The Viking Fund, 1949), pp. 175–94; *see also* Sullivan, "The Study of Psychiatry," *Psychiatry* (1947), *10,* 355–71.

33. Harry Stack Sullivan, "A Note on the Implications of Psychiatry: The Study of Interpersonal Relations for Investigations in the Social Sciences," *American Journal of Sociology* (May, 1937), *XLII* (6), 852.

34. Harry Stack Sullivan, "Conceptions of Modern Psychiatry," *Psychiatry* (February, 1940), *3,* 4–5.

35. John N. Rosen, "The Treatment of Schizophrenic Psychosis by Direct Analytic Therapy," *Psychiatric Quarterly* (January, 1947), *21* (1), 1–37; Freida Fromm-Reichmann, "Remarks on the Philosophy of Mental Disorder," in Patrick Mullahy (Ed.), *A Study of Interpersonal Relations* (New York: *Heritage House,* 1949), pp. 162–91; and Freida Fromm-Reichmann. "Transference Problems in Schizophrenics," in Sylvanus S. Tompkins (Ed.), *Contemporary Psychopathology* (Cambridge, Mass.: Harvard University Press, 1947), pp. 371–380.

36. Karen Horney, *New Ways in Psychoanalysis* (New York: W. W. Norton, 1939), and Clara Thompson, *Psychoanalysis: Evolution and Development* (New York: *Hermitage House*, 1950).

37. Karen Horney, *op. cit.,* p. 9.

38. Karen Horney, *Our Inner Conflicts* (New York: W. W. Norton, 1945), and Erich Fromm, "Individual and Social Origins of Neurosis," *American Sociological Review* (June, 1944), *V*, 380–84.

39. Erich Fromm, "Sozial Psychologische Teil," in M. Horkheimer (Ed.), *Studien Uber Authorite und Familie* (Paris: Felix Alcan, 1936), and Erich Fromm, *Escape from Freedom* (New York: Farrar and Rinehart, 1941).

40. Franz Alexander, "Introduction," *Proceedings of the Third Psychoanalytic Council* (Chicago: Institute for Psychoanalysis, 1946), p. 13; *see also* Paul Schilder, "The Sociological Implications of the Neuroses," *Journal of Social Psychology* (1942), *15*, 3-21.

41. Sander Ferenczi and Otto Rank, *The Development of Psychoanalysis* (New York: Nervous and Mental Disease Publishing Co. 1925), p. 21.

42. *Proceedings of the Third Psychoanalytic Council* (Chicago: Institute for Psychoanalysis, 1946); *see also* Franz Alexander, *Our age of Unreason* (Philadelphia: J. B. Lippincott, 1942).

43. Franz Alexander and Thomas French, *Psychoanalytic Therapy* (New York: Ronald Press, 1946).

44. Karen Horney, *New Ways in Psychoanalysis*, *op. cit.*, pp. 34–35, 154–57.

45. *See* William James, *Principles of Psychology* (New York: Longmans Green, 1890); Morton Prince, *The Unconscious* (New York: Macmillan, 1924); James M. Baldwin, *Mental Development in the Child and the Race.* (New York: Macmillan, 1895); William McDougall, *Introduction to Social Psychology* (London: Methuen, 1908); Carl R. Rogers, *Counseling and Psychotherapy* (New York: Houghton Mifflin, 1942); and Carl R. Rogers, *Client Centered Therapy* (New York: Houghton Mifflin, 1951).

46. *See* W. Joel, "The Interpersonal Equation in Projective Methods," *Rorschach Research Exchange and Journal of Projective Techniques* (December, 1949) *8* (4), 479–82; Lawrence K. Frank, *Projective Methods*, (Springfield, Ill.: Charles C. Thomas, 1948); and William E. Henry, "The Thematic Apperception Technique in the Study of Culture and Personality Relations," *Genetic Psychology Monographs*, (1947), *35*, 3–135.

part II
EPIDEMIOLOGY

SECTION 1

COMMUNITY, SOCIAL CLASS, AND SOCIAL MOBILITY

THE epidemiology of mental disorders and mental health, perhaps the most fully studied aspect of psychiatric sociology, deals with the distribution of mental disorders in the social structure as well as with the influence of social and personal factors upon these disorders. The interrelated points of departure which we consider highly significant in analyzing the distribution of mental disorders in the social structure are the community, socioeconomic status or social class, and social mobility. The community in turn has been analyzed primarily in terms of socioeconomic status, although the criterion of isolation has also been used to differentiate the degree of community influence on disordered behavior. Despite variations in the types of subjects studied and the methods used, one persistent finding has been the existance of an inverse relationship between socioeconomic status and rates of schizophrenia. But qualifications exist even for schizophrenia, depending on the criteria of socioeconomic status. Thus the influence of the socioeconomic factor on disordered behavior is neither simple nor conclusive. For purposes of rigorous comparison, similar types of disorder and similar criteria of social class or socioeconomic status would have to be studied.

Faris and Dunham have demonstrated that an inverse relationship exists between socioeconomic status as determined by median rentals and rates of schizophrenia.[1] On the other hand, manic-depressives are distributed randomly in the urban community, indicating that manic-depressives are not concentrated among persons in the lower socioeconomic status. Hollingshead, Kirby, and Ellis have based their class framework on the previous studies of Hollingshead and Redlich, who found that an inverse relationship exists between socioeconomic status and rates of schizophrenia but that this inverse relationship to socioeconomic status does not apply to psychoneurosis.

Dunham, in his paper, "Social Class and Schizophrenia," scrutinized the first admissions to all psychiatric facilities for two contrasting communities with high and low rates of schizophrenic disorders. He then used a five-class system, which was devised from the two-factor index of education and occupation, a variation of the Hollingshead and Redlich index, for ascertaining the socioeconomic status of schizophrenics and other psychotics. He found that while schizophrenia and other diagnostic types were concentrated in the lowest socioeconomic stratum, namely class V, for both communities, the rates of schizophrenia for the other classes tended toward parity.

The findings of Srole, Langner, and their associates in their study of "Mental Health in Midtown Manhattan" are consistent with the other inquiries, but their subjects are a sample of the general Midtown population and differ from hospitalized or severely disturbed persons who were the subjects of other studies. The authors found that the mild and moderate categories of stability for persons in the different socioeconomic groups are remarkably uniform but that the well or symptom-free category of persons correlates positively with socioeconomic status, while the impaired category correlates inversely.

As these studies indicate, socioeconomic level has a definite influence on personal stability generally and on schizophrenia particularly as well as on susceptibility to hospitalization. In brief, the person in the lowest socioeconomic group, class V, appears to have a greater tendency to be unstable, to become schizophrenic, and to be hospitalized for his disorder than persons in other socioeconomic strata. These differences seemingly are not conclusive for persons in other social classes. Although more persons in the higher social classes generally exhibit personal stability than persons in the lower social classes, this finding of personal stability may possibly indicate the class bias of the investigators whose criteria of personal stability incline to the middle class. On the other hand, socioeconomic status does seemingly influence modes of participation and the process of social relations which would perhaps directly affect the processes leading to disordered behavior.

Mobility is the dynamism within an open-class society that differs from the static position of socioeconomic status and social class. The initial ecological studies strived to explain aspects of the residential distribution of psychotics in terms of downward "drift" from higher socioeconomic levels. The downward drift concept, however, was not verified from the ecological studies. Thus it was not known whether the indigenous forces within the local communities influenced the precipitation of the disorder or whether predisposed individuals drifted into the areas because of socioeconomic failure and the desire of some to secure privacy amid a context of social anonymity. Clausen and Kohn found that the men in rooming houses tended to drift there for purposes of securing anonymity.[2] It was also found that suicide accompanied downward drift, because men who had experienced this downward mobility had recourse to suicide as a way out of their predicament. On the other hand, Jaco pointed out that the indigenous conditions indicative of inducing isolation within given communities may be precipitants of schizophrenia.[3] Dunham and Faris also found some indicators of the stress of social isolation within several areas that they studied, such as high rates of schizophrenia in low socioeconomic areas of high residential mobility, ethnic groups residing amid different ethnic groups, and slum-residing, foreign-born people.[4] Perhaps the terms "predisposing" and "precipitating" are too dichotomous and require modification because contributing stresses in combination along the course of an individual's life can develop into a given disorder. Although the ecological findings concerning the processes of drift for manic-depressives and for types of schizophrenics remained inconclusive, the ecological investigators pointed to the problems of drift as relevant to disordered behavior.

Dunham, in his comparative study of two communities in Detroit, reported that the schizophrenics in his sample "showed no significant downward or upward mobility patterns" despite the high incidence rate of schizophrenia in the lowest socioeconomic status, class V. In a later study, however, Dunham, Phillips, and Srinavasan pointed out that male schizophrenics are in the lowest socioeconomic stratum because they are unable to achieve an occupation commensurate with their education. By comparing the occupation and education of male schizophrenics, their fathers, nonschizophrenic patients, and residual patients who were composed mainly of psychopaths and undiagnosed types, Dunham and his colleagues hypothesized that "it is the nature of the disease which determines the class position of the schizophrenic and that it is not the class position which influences the nature of the disease".[5]

Srole and Langner in their study of a sample of the general population of Midtown Manhattan reported that the nonmobile subjects were evenly balanced in numbers of well and impaired persons. The upwardly mobile or "climbers" included more persons who were well than persons who were impaired by a ratio of 3:2; the downwardly mobile or "descenders" had more impaired persons than well persons in their midst by a ratio of 5:2. Despite qualifications to these findings, more upwardly mobile persons than downwardly mobile persons tended toward personal stability or mental health.

In the study of "Social Mobility and Mental Illness" Hollingshead, Ellis, and Kirby compare the effects of mobility on selected groups of neurotics, schizophrenics, and nonpatient controls in classes III and V. Class III individuals, both patients and nonpatients, were predominantly upwardly mobile; nonpatients were lowest in achieved mobility and schizophrenics were highest in achieved mobility, as determined by level of education and type of occupation. This suggests that in class III a relationship exists between social mobility and mental disorders. In class V, nonpatients and schizophrenics were on a par in terms of achieved mobility, but neurotics were significantly higher than persons in the other two categories. Neurotics and schizophrenics in classes III and V respectively indicated that their aspirations markedly exceeded their achievements. Thus their frustrations accrued from status-striving, which may be a contributing factor to disordered behavior.

This general problem of status-striving, and the discrepancy between achievement and aspiration, is aptly analyzed by Kleiner and Parker in their thorough review of "Goal-Striving: Social Status and Mental Disorder; A Research Review." One of their significant and relevant conclusions is that groups of disordered persons usually have larger discrepancies between achievement and aspirations than do comparable control groups of normal persons.

REFERENCES

1. Robert E. L. Faris and H. Warren Dunham, *Mental Disorders in Urban Areas* (Chicago: University of Chicago Press, 1939).

2. John Clausen and Melvin L. Kohn, "Social Relations and Schizophrenia," in Don Jackson (Ed.), *Etiology of Schizophrenia* (New York: Basic Books, 1960).

3. E. Gartly Jaco, "The Social Isolation Hypothesis and Schizophrenia," *American Sociological Review* (October, 1954), *19*(5), 567–77.

4. Faris and Dunham, *op. cit.*

5. H. Warren Dunham, Patricia Phillips, and Barbara Srinivasan, "A Research Note on Diagnosed Mental Illness and Social Class," *American Sociological Review* (April, 1966), *31*(2), 223–27.

URBAN AREAS AND HOSPITALIZED PSYCHOTICS*

S. Kirson Weinberg

ALTHOUGH few studies have been made of the residential distributions of neurotics in the urban community, many inquiries have traced the residential patterns of hospitalized psychotics, particularly of schizophrenics and manic-depressives. These inquiries have demonstrated a relationship between the residential distribution of hospitalized psychoses generally and of schizophrenia particularly and the organization and growth of the urban community. Faris and Dunham initiated ecological studies of these psychotic types mainly for Chicago and for Providence, Rhode Island.[1] They have had their pioneer conclusions corroborated, with slight variations, by other studies of St. Louis, Cleveland, Omaha, Kansas City, Milwaukee, and Peoria.[2] Since these ecological patterns of residential distribution in the urban community prevailed before the extensive rehabilitation of deteriorated areas around the center of the city and before the building of high-rise, low-cost housing throughout the city, the relative decline of the neighborhood, and the movement to the suburbs, their inquiries characterized the patterned distribution for an urban community of a past era. In addition the ethnic composition of the city has changed with the rising influx of Negroes, Southern whites, and Puerto Ricans as first settlers into the city.

Despite these changes, the enduring features of these studies pertain to their determination of the positive relationships between low rental and disorganized urban areas and rates of schizophrenia, and of the randomly distributed urban residential pattern for manic-depression. In their ecological study Dunham and Faris analyzed 28,763 cases from four state mental hospitals; these cases represented all persons committed to these institutions between 1922 and 1934. Their findings confirmed the hypothesis that the residential distributions of hospitalized psychoses, like other detected social deviants, fit the conventional pattern of distribution in the unplanned urban community. These rates of disorders are highest near the center of the city and tend to decline toward the circumference of the city.

Schizophrenics, the first of the psychoses to be analyzed ecologically, is characterized by blunt mood, by delusional and at times hallucinatory behavior, by emotional and social withdrawal, by impaired judgement in the area of personal conflict, and generally by the substitution of private for shared versions of social reality.

The ecological findings concerning the residential distributions of schizophrenics in the urban community include: (1) The rates for hospitalized schizophrenics in the different zones of the urban community are consistent with the rates for all mental disorders: highest near the center of the city and declining as one moves toward the periphery of the city. (2) The highest rates for schizophrenia are concentrated in very disorganized, lower-income communities, but most communities have low rates of schizophrenics except for the few with high rates. (3) The rates for male and female schizophrenics separately reveal similar residential concentrations. (4) The rates for schizophrenia for the foreign born by total number and by sex in the urban community indicate that differences between rates result from other factors than varying proportions of foreign born. (5) The upper quartile of the communities contained 40 per cent of the cases but only 24 per cent of the population. (6) The rates of schizophrenia by race and nativity in different areas of the city showed consistently high rates in the extremely disorganized parts of the city. (8) The rates of schizophrenia for whites are highest in areas where Negroes are in the majority, although the rates of schizophrenia for Negroes in all-Negro areas tend to be lower than in racially mixed areas.

Manic-depressives, characterized by an extremely elated mood or an extremely depressed mood, or a circulation of moods, in contrast with the residential distribution of schizophrenics, have a random residential distribution in the city. Although the highest rates are in the first zone, the rates do not decline with the distance from the center of the city. In all other zones, the difference between rates is so small that it lacks statistical significance.

Therefore, we may conclude: (1) The rates of urban residential distribution for manic-depressives

* Written for this volume.

are neither high nor low in any systematic way. (2) The distributions of rates for male and female manic-depressives separately show similar random patterns. (3) The distributions of rates of cases from private and state hospitals reveal a similar randomness. (4) The rates for manic and depressed types separately are distributed randomly. (5) The manic-depressive rates show that approximately similar numbers of communities had high and low rates. (6) Since the percentages in each quartile are similar for manics and for depressives, no definite concentration of cases exists. (7) The rates for manic-depression distributed according to nativity and race by housing areas lack a residential distribution pattern.

From comparing the residential distributions of schizophrenics and manic-depressives, we may conclude as follows: (1) Distributions of rates of schizophrenics and manic-depressives differ in almost every way. (2) The schizophrenic rates which have this conventional distributive pattern are concentrated in the disorganized and poverty-ridden urban areas. (3) Seemingly, manic-depressives come from a higher socioeconomic stratum than do schizophrenics. (4) The ratio for manic-depressives according to race and nativity in different areas of the city lack consistency but rates for schizophrenics for a given nativity group increase in areas which are not populated primarily by members of that group.

These findings have been supported by Schroeder for five midwestern cities. Dee reported that in St. Louis no correlation exists between distributions of schizophrenia and of manic-depression. Ruess found that in Milwaukee distributions of manic-depression although more random than distributions of schizophrenia concentrate in areas in the down-town and river valley sections. Mowrer found from his studies in Chicago that distributions of manic-depression, while not random, had little in common with distributions of other psychoses. Mowrer claimed too that "the same concentric pattern exists for manic-depression as for schizophrenia but with a break in the upper four-fifths of the range," and that this diagnostic type did not necessarily come from a relatively high socio-economic status.[3]

These results have a similarity to the findings of Hollingshead and Redlich who studied the prevalence of treated mental disorders in New Haven, Connecticut. Using the criteria of occupation, education, and place of residence for class stratification, they reported that schizophrenia had a frequency in the lowest social class stratum almost ten times that of the highest two social classes.[4]

INTERPRETATION OF THE DISTRIBUTIONS

These findings can be viewed as reflecting the results of urban ecological processes and as indices of the influences affecting the etiology of these disorders.[5] Our concern is with the latter problem.

We can say at the outset that these ecological distributions as epidemiological indicators of presumed social or biogenetic processes of etiological significance have not been demonstrated. At best the ecological distributions provide clues for further and more definitive inquiry. The interpretations of these distributions when made from the biogenetic viewpoint would emphasize the genetic predisposition and constitutional vulnerability of those who have incurred schizophrenic or manic-depressive disorders. Despite the works of Kallman and others concerning the influence of heredity on schizophrenia and other disorders, these findings have not been related to the ecological distributions. Furthermore even assuming greater genetic vulnerability in this social selection process among the lower socioeconomic strata to schizophrenia, we would still have to assume a certain constancy of the social environment because persons in the lower strata seem to experience a more stressful social reality than do persons in the middle classes. We would also have to assume that persons genetically predisposed to manic-depression are randomly distributed in the class structure.[6]

Krout, from a psychoanalytic viewpoint, has read into these distributions, differences of childhood training.[7] The schizophrenics, who predominated in the lower socioeconomic levels, had an arrested development at the oral stage of infancy because of feeding difficulties. But the manic-depressives, who more frequently come from the higher socioeconomic levels, had an arrested development in the anal stage of growth because of defective toilet training. First, it has not been ascertained empirically that these respective differences in feeding and toilet training hold for the lower and higher socioeconomic levels, respectively. Second, there is no definite evidence that frustrations in these different erogenous zones of the body are causally correlated with schizophrenia and manic-depression, respectively. In short, as stated in this specific psychoanalytic manner this contention may seem untenable. But early emotional deprivation may affect the subsequent adaptation of the individual in his competitive process and in his bid for occupational success and hence may contribute to his immobility within the communities with low rentals. This kind of interpretation would be relevant for the interpretations of the distributions of schizophrenia. Since many persons in the lowest stratum have not drifted downward, they may have been impeded in their early personality development because of the excessively high rates of schizophrenia among this socioeconomic category.

The other interpretation is that some schizophrenics drift or remain in or near the center of the city and thus are a selected group. This interpretation implied at the time of the study, that foreign-born white and Negro groups would have a greater tendency to schizophrenic disorders than native groups. Faris and Dunham, however, found that the rates for the foreign-born populations divided by the total foreign-born population are distributed similarly to the rates for all cases.[8] Rates for Negroes are high in areas not populated entirely by Negroes but low in areas inhabited predominantly or entirely by Negroes. [9] Although this evidence is not sufficient to invalidate the drift hypothesis, it makes the validity of the hypothesis unlikely.

The other problem concerns the downward mobility of some schizophrenics and the upward mobility of some manic-depressives, particularly manics.[10] As we have pointed out, the schizophrenics most likely to drift would be the paranoids and hebephrenics who inhabit the "hobohemian" sections of the city. But these "hobohemian" areas comprise only a small proportion of the total cases. In addition, some schizophrenics have been born and reared in family slum areas adjacent to the central business district and may possibly have been influenced by the local neighborhood and class subculture. The "drift" hypothesis does not explain the allocation of schizophrenia only by a social selective process resulting from personal and economic maladjustment. This has been affirmed by H. Warren Dunham in his study of "Social Class and Schizophrenia."

The other side of the coin emphasizes the influences inherent within the community. There are those who claim that communities with high rates of mobility tend to have high rates of disordered persons.[11] This may mean that the downwardly mobile persons are more likely predisposed to psychotic disorders than are the immobile. It can be argued that excessive personal mobility may create personal instability which may contribute to an eventual breakdown. On the other hand, it may be contended that, in areas of very marked mobility, the anonymity and isolation among the residents would deprive each person of those intimate social relations that are necessary for sustaining an ordered condition and may contribute to the precipitation of schizophrenia. The function of the anomic condition of the community may be an essential influence on the onset of disordered behavior. Lander found from his factorial analysis of community criteria affecting delinquency that the anomic condition rather than the low income was instrumental to the rise of delinquency. Perhaps there is a generic quality of social disorganization that may contribute to the deviant or the delinquent as it does to the onset of schizophrenia.[12]

In "family" slum neighborhoods, relationships are claimed to be harsh. Since social difficulties are presumably more harsh than in middle-class areas, the individual resident adjusts with difficulty. But it is not known whether this factor is crucial. Indeed, before they break down, prepsychotic persons from lower-income groups have experiences in different groups through their jobs. Hence, a psychotic breakdown cannot be attributed merely to the social relationships within the community, at least not for all cases. Catatonics who are committed at a relatively early age may be influenced by a manipulating mother rather than by the play patterns and the modes of relationships with juvenile and adolescent groups who may contribute to the onset of their personal disorders.[13] Nonetheless, despite these relationships among lower-income groups, these groups do not practice exclusion as intensely as the same age groups do in upper-middle socioeconomic levels.

The different value judgments and the reasons for committing disordered persons to mental institutions in different communities may also affect the ecological distributions. Are there uniform criteria in this commitment process in all types of communities? Owen maintains that certain types of disorders may lead to commitment in one community but not in another.[14] Faris contends that the persons committed to mental hospitals are so "extremely insane" that few families would be wealthy enough to care for them outside the hospital.[15] Very likely most schizophrenics and manic-depressives may be committed to mental hospitals, but it is also known that some cases are reported long after the breakdown has occurred, or they may not be reported at all.[16]

Lemkau, Tietze, and Cooper, in a survey of a Baltimore community, found that 367 psychotics were hospitalized and that 73 psychotics were not hospitalized. Age and sex seemed to influence the commitment of psychotics in this community. Nonhospitalized patients were somewhat older than the hospitalized—median age, 51 against 43— and were more often females—59 per cent against 46 per cent. The racial distribution was the same for both groups.[17]

In general, ecological distributions are significant in showing the communities where the varied disorders are concentrated and where the disorders are sparse. From these facts, we can analyze more intensively the social influences upon the persons within these communities. The disparate concentrations of these disorders in different communities, however, are only indices to the whole universe of personal relationships which disordered persons experienced until they broke down and were then committed by others to mental hospitals.

The circular nature of the variables is such

that the geneticists and biological determinists claim that preexisting predisposition to disorder influence socioeconomic position of residence as it would socioeconomic status. On the other hand, the sociologists claim that the stresses within the varied communities would exert a contributing causal influence upon the onset of disordered behavior. Srole and his associates in their study of Midtown Manhattan found an inverse relationship between their subjects' symptoms or degree of mental health and the socioeconomic status of the subjects' parents. From this they infer that emotional deprivation in childhood and downward intergenerational mobility may have contributed to this inverse relationship. But this relationship had not as yet been demonstrated for schizophrenia and manic depression. (See subsequent chapter by Srole and Langner). Perhaps there is no single general inference to be made concerning the influence of the community on disorders, especially schizophrenia. Perhaps some predisposed individuals may gravitate to certain areas. Other persons may be affected markedly by the local community which represents a network of stressful influences and which in turn can contribute markedly to the onset of schizophrenia.[18]

NOTES

1. Robert E. L. Faris and H. Warren Dunham, *Mental Disorders in Urban Areas* (Chicago: University of Chicago Press, 1938).

2. Stuart A. Queen, "The Ecological Study of Mental Disorder," *American Sociological Review* (April, 1940), V, 201–209; Howard W. Green, *Persons Admitted to the Cleveland State Hospital, 1928–1937* (Cleveland: Cleveland Health Council, 1939); Clarence W. Schroeder, "Mental Disorders in Cities," *American Journal of Sociology* (July, 1942), XLVIII, pp. 40–47; Ernest W. Mowrer, *Disorganization: Personal and Social* (New York: J. B. Lippincott, 1942), chapters 15 and 16; and E. E. Hadley et al., "Military Psychiatry: An Ecological Note," *Psychiatry* (Nov., 1944), VII, 379–407.

3. Schroeder, *op. cit.*, pp. 40–47, and Mowrer, *op. cit.*

4. August B. Hollingshead and Fredrich C. Redlich, "Social Stratification and Psychiatric Disorders," *American Sociological Review* (April, 1953), 18, 163–169.

5. There have been some criticisms of the validity of these findings. One criticism has been that the number of cases initially used for the manic-depressive group were too few. The second criticism is that the differences between the rates in the communities were due to chance and were not significant.

Melvin L. Kohn and John A. Clausen, "The Ecological Approach in Social Psychiatry," *American Journal of Sociology* (September, 1954), 60, 140–151.

6. For an analysis of the status of the ecological approach to personal disorders, see H. Warren Dunham, "Current Status of Ecological Research in Mental Disorder," *Social Forces* (March, 1947), XXV (3), 321–326.

Franz J. Kallman, *Heredity in Health and Mental Disorder* (New York: W. W. Norton, 1953).

7. Maurice H. Krout, "A Note on Dunham's Contribution to the Ecology of the Psychoses," *American Sociological Review* (April, 1938), III, 209–212.

8. Robert E. L. Faris and H. Warren Dunham, *Mental Disorders in Urban Areas*, p. 169.

9. *Ibid.*, pp. 164–169. Faris and Dunham studied catatonics and paranoids separately between 15 and 29 and those 30 and over. They found that the younger cases of paranoids, who did not have time to drift, were concentrated in central areas as were the older cases. The younger catatonic cases had a slightly different distribution than the other cases. Seemingly, the catatonics showed a tendency to drift from the slum residential areas to the hobo areas. See Robert E. L. Faris, *Social Disorganization* (New York: Ronald Press, 1948), p. 231, footnote.

10 See Morris S. Schwartz, "The Economic and Spatial Mobility of Paranoid Schizophrenics and Manic Depressives" (University of Chicago: unpublished master's thesis, August, 1946).

11. Christopher Tietze, Paul Lemkau, and Marcia Cooper, "Personal Disorders and Spatial Mobility," *American Journal of Sociology* (July, 1942), XLIII, 29–39.

Bruce P. Dohrenwend, "Social Status and Psychological Disorder: An Issue of Substance and An Issue of Method," *American Sociological Review* (February, 1966), 31 (1), 14–34.

12. Bernard Lander, *Towards An Understanding of Juvenile Delinquency* (New York: Columbia University Press, 1954).

13. H. Warren Dunham, "The Social Personality of the Catatonic-Schizophrenic," *American Journal of Sociology* (May, 1944), 49, 508–518.

14. Mary Bess Owen, "Alternative Hypotheses for the Explanation of Some of Faris' and Dunham's Results," *American Journal of Sociology* (July, 1941), 47, 48–51.

15. Robert E. Faris, *Social Disorganization* (New York: Ronald Press, 1948), pp. 230–231.

16. Robert White, *The Abnormal Personality* (New York: Ronald Press, 1948), pp. 564–565.

17. Paul Lemkau, Christopher Tietze, and Marcia Cooper, "Mental Hygiene Problems in an Urban District," *Mental Hygiene* (1942), 26, 275–288.

18. See H. Warren Dunham, "Social Structures and Mental Disorders: Competing Hypotheses of Explanation," *Causes of* *Mental Disorders: A Review of Epidemiological Knowledge, 1959* (New York: Milbank Memorial Fund, 1961), pp. 227–265.

SOCIAL CLASS AND SCHIZOPHRENIA

H. Warren Dunham

THIS PAPER reports certain findings concerning social class and the incidence of schizophrenia within two subcommunities of sharp cultural contrast, within the city of Detroit. It is part of a large-scale epidemiological study of this disorder in these two subcommunities. Several previous studies, notably Stein,[7] Morris,[5] Srole *et al.*,[6] and Hollingshead and Redlich,[1] have examined the significance of the social class factor in relation to mental disease and psychiatric symptoms, in general, but no epidemiological study has focused, as has this one, on one particular mental disorder. It is true that Stein reports a class gradient in relation to schizophrenia in two culturally contrasting boroughs of London, but she is uncertain as to the interpretation; and Morris, from London, reports briefly about an earlier study in progress that shows an inverse relationship between occupational class and schizophrenia for a sample of male patients but reports an even distribution over the occupational structure for the fathers of those patients. Srole, *et al.*, for their sample in mid-Manhattan, show a greater percentage of persons with psychiatric symptoms in the lowest socioeconomic category than in the highest. Hollingshead and Redlich have demonstrated, on the basis of their careful analysis of a six-month's total coverage of treated psychiatric cases from New Haven, that the prevalence rate for psychosis varies inversely with social class and also that the incidence rate for schizophrenia varies inversely with social class. By this we mean that they have shown that the prevalence and incidence rates increase as the socioeconomic level declines. We will return to this study for comparison with our own findings as we report them.

These studies taken together raise numerous questions with respect to both methods and results. It would seem that the issue that should be settled in a more definitive fashion is that of whether, for a given mental disorder or for mental disorder in general, there is a true variation in its incidence in the different social classes for a given society.

Reprinted from *American Journal of Orthopsychiatry* (July, 1964), 34(4), 634–42. Copyright by the American Orthopsychiatric Association and used by permission.

It is this issue that the present study has attempted to resolve in one way or another for the schizophrenic disorder. Consequently, in this paper we have been concerned with the following questions.

1. Do incidence rates of schizophrenia vary inversely with social class?

2. If they do, can these incidence rates of schizophrenia in the various social classes of our two subcommunities be accepted as reliable and valid?

3. Are there reliable and valid differences in the incidence of schizophrenia with respect to vertical mobility?

4 What is the most plausible interpretation of incidence rate differences by social class that may be found from the examination of our data?

METHODS OF PROCEDURE

It is well recognized by those of us who have worked in this field that numerous obstacles, some seeming almost insurmountable, confront the investigator who expects to conduct an epidemiological study. A detailed analysis of these obstacles is not possible here, but some will be recognized as the discussion proceeds, for in this investigation we faced all of them, even though we may not have been able to surmount them all. Our basic procedure was as follows: We made two studies of the distribution of first-admissions from Detroit who had been diagnosed as schizophrenic at the state hospitals. These two distributions were separated by 20 years, one in 1936 to 1938 and the other in 1956 to 1958. The distributions were quite similar in terms of the concentration of cases, even though the physical topography of Detroit had changed markedly during the 20 years. There was a tendency for the later distribution of the rates in the 51 subcommunities of Detroit to form a normal curve, while, in the earlier distributions, the rates were quite skewed to the right. On the basis of the later distribution we made a demographic analysis of ten subcommunities having high rates and ten subcommunities having low rates. By this analysis we selected a high-rate and a low-rate subcommunity, trying to obtain a similarity with respect to age, sex, nativity, race and mobility. We were fairly successful in this on all factors except race. The changing racial composition of the city, speeded by certain Supreme Court decisions, makes it practically impossible to select an all-white subcommunity that has a high rate of schizophrenia. Anyway, as one well recognizes in this type of research, we were stuck with our decisions and had to proceed with our analysis.

The next step was to screen all the psychiatric facilities in southeastern Michigan, to select out all of those cases with functional disorders that came originally from our two subcommunities. Psychiatric facilities fall into eight categories: federal hospitals, state hospitals, city and county hospitals, private mental hospitals, private general hospitals with psychiatric wards, outpatient clinics, diagnostic centers and private psychiatrists. Some conception of the magnitude of the task is gained by noting that we screened 176 psychiatric facilities (131 of which were private psychiatrists representing 81 per cent of all those practicing in the metropolitan area of Detroit), and picked up 3,086 psychiatric cases coming from our two subcommunities and covering a period of time roughly from 1950 to 1960. For the years 1956, 1957 and 1958, the screening was complete. For the base year, 1958, the screening was intensive. This means that a psychiatrist and a sociologist personally attempted to make contact with all of the cases in the year 1958, for the purposes of making a clinical examination and collecting certain social background data on each case. Further, each case was examined carefully to determine if the person's admission in 1958 was the first time he had had contact with any type of psychiatric facility. This meant further that all cases found in one facility were checked carefully against the cases found in all the other facilities, to spot any duplicated admissions.

The psychiatric cases from our two subcommunities that were located in the various facilities

fell into three diagnostic groups: (1) all cases of schizophrenia, (2) the nonschizophrenics—affective disorders, the psychoneuroses and schizoid personalities, and (3) all additional psychiatric cases, which included, for the most part, character disturbances and the acting-out disorders. Our focus, of course, was on schizophrenia; the other two diagnostic groupings are presented for comparative purposes.

As stated above, a psychiatrist attempted to get in touch with all schizophrenics that had a first admission to psychiatric facilities from our two subcommunities in 1958 and saw also the majority of the cases in our second diagnostic grouping to determine if, in his judgment, they possessed a schizophrenic disorder. Thus, in 1958, we had certain cases that the psychiatrist claimed were not schizophrenics even though the facility had diagnosed them as such. This amounted to five cases in the high-rate and four cases in the low-rate subcommunity. However, the following data are based on all cases that were diagnosed as schizophrenic by a facility and that entered a facility for the first time during 1958 from residence in our subcommunities. The results obtained by personal contact by the psychiatrist and sociologist for all cases found in our two subcommunities for 1958 are shown in Table I.

Our next step was to work out the class structure in our two subcommunities. This was done by employing the method utilized by Hollingshead and Redlich in determining the class structure for New Haven. Here, however, we used their Two-Factor Index and determined class on the basis of combining the respective weights for occupation and education of the heads of the households. These percentages were then applied to the population in each Census tract of our two subcommunities and the combining of these figures for each Census tract resulted in a class structure* for each subcommunity. It is of some interest to compare our picture of the class structure in the

TABLE 1.   Case Count of First Contacts from Screening 176* Psychiatric Facilities in Southeastern Michigan by Diagnostic Grouping and Patient Contact

Patient Contact	Cass			Conner-Burbank		
	Schiz.	onschiz.	Additional	Schiz.	Nonschiz.	Additional
Contacted	37	40	37	24	42	29
Not located	6	13	187		1	3
Moved out of city	3	6	12		2	
Refusals		4	1		3	1
Deceased			1			2
Total	46	63	238	24	48	35

* Federal hospitals 4, State hospitals 7, City and county hospitals 2, Private sanitaria 10, Private general hospitals 8, Outpatient clinics 10, Diagnostic centers 3, Private psychiatrists 131.

two subcommunities of Detroit with that of New Haven. The results are almost identical, although the percentage distribution of psychiatric patients from our two subcommunities shows a greater concentration in Class V than does the. New Haven Data. The shift is due almost entirely to the different distribution of patients in Class IV and V in our subcommunities as compared to New Haven.

ANALYSIS OF DATA AND FINDINGS

With our psychiatric cases screened, checked for duplications and interviewed for psychiatric and sociological study, and the class structure for the two subcommunities delineated, we were in a position to examine in detail any relationship that might be found between schizophrenia and class structure, utilizing the data from our base year of 1958. We then proceeded to distribute the cases for the three diagnostic groups and for the groups with and without psychosis in the five social classes. The results of the analyses, that is, for the three diagnostic groups, are shown in Figure 1.

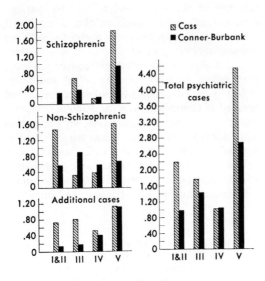

FIGURE 1. Incidence rates (per 1,000 total population) of all psychiatric cases by social class in two subcommunities of Detroit, 1958.

While this analysis was based upon the Hollingshead and Redlich scheme for determining class, we also made a comparable analysis based upon the census categories for determining class. The results were very much the same although the

census scheme tended to make for somewhat higher rates in the upper four classes. A careful inspection of these rate distributions by social class points to the following findings.

1. The rates for each diagnostic grouping in both subcommunities, with the exception of the additional cases in Conner-Burbank, do not vary inversely with social class.

2. This absence of an inverse relationship is also seen in the distribution of rates for the combined cases from the two subcommunities.

3. In all diagnostic groupings—as well as in the total cases for both subcommunities the rates are highest in Class V, again with one exception: The nonschizophrenic group in Conner-Burbank has a lower rate in Class V than in Class III.

4. Again, there is an absence of an inverse relationship between the rates for both psychotic and nonpsychotic cases and the class structure. This holds particularly in utilizing the Hollingshead-Redlich index.

5. Utilizing this scheme, the highest rate appears in Class V for both subcommunities for the group with psychosis but not for the group without psychosis, in which the highest rate is in Class II for Cass.

6. Utilizing the Census scheme tends, as we have already noted, to provide larger rates for the upper four classes, with the result that the highest rate is never found in Class V.

These analyses of incidence rates for the social classes in the two subcommunities and for the three diagnostic groups hardly provide any confidence of a class variable in relation to the incidence of functional mental disorder. We note this particularly with respect to our schizophrenic rates on the various class levels because they represent the central focus of our inquiry. Even when we combined the schizophrenic cases in our two subcommunities and computed rates for the various classes we noted that a pattern emerges similar to that of the subcommunities when considered separately. We next used a statistical test to determine if there were any significant differences between schizophrenic rates in the various classes for each subcommunity and for New Haven.

Here, we noted, using a critical ratio of three, that the only significant differences are between Class V and the other three classes for New Haven, while in the Detroit data the only significant differences are between Class IV and V for Cass. The small number of cases in the upper four classes raises a question as to their reliability for both the Detroit and New Haven data. We can, of course, do nothing about this except to point out that despite the general small size of the population in the first three classes we find a small number of cases from these classes. We have used this test on all of our rates in the various classes and for the three diagnostic groups and while we are not presenting them here we wish to point out that, out of 45 comparisons between the rates, there were only five significant differences, all centered in a comparison of the rate of Class V with that of the other four classes. Because of the small number of cases we also combined the cases in our two subcommunities and, again, in testing for the significance of the difference between them, the only significant differences are between Class V and the other three classes for the schizophrenic and additional diagnostic groups. In the non-schizophrenic grouping the only significant difference was between Class IV and Class V.

These findings do not serve to substantiate any claim that there is an inverse relationship between incidence rates of schizophrenia and the class structure. This general finding seems to be the same for the other two diagnostic groups as well. Thus, insofar as the incidence rates for schizophrenia are at a parity in the upper four classes, the problem centers around determining the best explanation for the concentration of the large percentage of schizophrenic cases in Class V. Does a population in the lowest class actually produce more persons who develop schizophrenia than the upper four classes do, or is the concentration of schizophrenic cases in Class V caused by the procedure used to determine the class of the patient in combination with the operation of some unknown selective process?

Some clues for answering this question can be obtained by examining vertical mobility patterns in relation to psychiatric illness. There has been frequent discussion in the literature of the vertical mobility patterns of the mentally ill. In fact, some literature in the 1930s went so far as to suggest that neuroses and perhaps more acute mental disturbances might be related to the striving and competitive tendencies within our culture, resulting in increased frustrations, mounting anxiety, hostility and ambivalence.[2, 8] The Hollingshead-Redlich study[1] attempted to show that the prevalence rates for treated psychiatric cases could not be explained in terms of either upward or downward social mobility. Lystad[3] reports that middle-class, white females who have been through grammar school and are not mentally ill achieve higher status than do schizophrenic patients with these characteristics. In contrast, lower-class,

Negro males who are not mentally ill and have less than grammar school education achieve no higher status than do schizophrenics with these characteristics. Finally, Michael and Langner,[4] utilizing data from the Midtown Manhattan study, examined various diagnostic types and psychiatric symptoms in relation to vertical mobility. From the symptom groups of epileptic, retarded, alcoholic, senile, dissocial, depressed, frigid, suspicious and schizophrenic, they found significant evidences of downward mobility. They conclude that their data can hardly be interpreted as meaning that experiences on a low socioeconomic level cause psychiatric symptoms, particularly because Freudian theory hypothesizes that these character deviations have presumably been established in early childhood. Rather, they lean to the more plausible interpretation that these various psychiatric symptoms interfere with the life adjustment of the person and hence, lead to downward mobility.

These findings suggested that in an analysis of the vertical mobility patterns for our sample of psychiatric cases, broken down by diagnostic grouping and subcommunity, downward mobility would be expected. Vertical mobility was measured by the discrepancy between the occupational category of the father and that of the patient. For married female patients, the occupational category of the husband was contrasted with the occupational category of the patient-wife's father. The mobility of students (only college students, high school students were excluded) was determined by the educational level that the student had reached in contrast to the occupation of the father and the level of education such an occupation demanded. By this device it was possible then to determine from our sample of cases those that were upwardly mobile and those that were downwardly mobile. These data, as organized for the combined subcommunities in each diagnostic group, are

TABLE 2. DISTRIBUTION OF FIRST CONTACT CASES
BY VERTICAL MOBILITY PATTERN AND
DIAGNOSTIC GROUPING, 1958*
Both Sub-Communities

Mobility	Schizo-phrenics	Nonschizo-phrenics	Additional	Total
Upwardly mobile	17	27	16	60
Nonmobile	19	21	21	61
Downwardly mobile	16	21	17	54
Total	52	69	54	175

*$\chi^2 = 1.6051$; p > .05; N.S.

shown in Table 2. Using a chi square test we find that there are no significant differences in mobility patterns among the three groups. It is only when we combine all diagnostic groups and compare the distribution of cases in the two subcommunities with respect to vertical mobility that we obtain a chi square of significance at the 5 per cent level. The same result emerges when the mobility distributions in the two subcommunities are compared, utilizing only schizophrenic and nonschizophrenic cases. This suggests a tendency for the more upwardly mobile cases to be more prevalent in Conner-Burbank, thus inferentially supporting Lystad's findings.

While this analysis suggests that the vertical mobility patterns in all three diagnostic groups in both subcommunities are similar, it provides no basis for asserting that schizophrenic persons are more likely to be downwardly than upwardly mobile, although this is what might be expected. Rather we find that the subcommunities, as might be expected, conform to the vertical mobility patterns of the psychiatric patients residing in them, irrespective of diagnosis.

This finding that the schizophrenics in our sample, for each subcommunity and the combined subcommunities, showed no significant downward or upward mobility patterns is doubly surprizing in the light of the previous finding that the schizophrenic incidence rate was higher in Class V and that the rate here, in some instances, differed significantly from the rates in any of the other classes.

METHOD OF INTERPRETATION

This analysis of the incidence of schizophrenia in relation to the class structure has pointed up two questions.

1. Why are the highest incidence rates for schizophrenia, as well as the other diagnostic groupings, always found in Class V for both subcommunities, while the rates in the other four classes tend toward a parity?

2. Why do the schizophrenic cases, as well as the other diagnostic groupings, show a parity with respect to their vertical mobility pattern?

To initiate an answer to these questions, we note that the schizophrenic rates in the upper four classes show no significant variation for either subcommunity or for the two subcommunities combined. This finding, consequently, is critical of any assertion that the incidence of schizophrenia is inversely related to the class structure. The heavy concentration of cases in Class V has three possible explanations if analyzed from the point of view of the social system: (1) Although the fathers of some schizophrenic cases found in Class V were in a higher class, the off-spring failed in their educational and occupational efforts and consequently were recorded as members of the lowest class; (2) among those in the sample who left their parental home, their developing schizophrenic condition prevented them from realizing their occupational goal, so they were recorded as members of Class V; and (3) more persons in this class than in the other classes have a genetic structure that prevents them from competing on equal terms with other persons and thus are relegated to Class V through the operation of the social process.

Now, it should be recognized that all these hypothetical explanations emphasize geographical or vertical mobility patterns, which are so characteristic of the American culture. The first and second hypotheses may appear to contain similar elements; they do not. The first hypothesis emphasizes that the schizophrenic experienced a decline in class status because of his underlying schizophrenic proneness. The second points to a salient characteristic of American culture, namely, the tendency at a certain age to leave home to seek one's fortune and in general try to better one's self by means of the personality and skills that one possesses. Thus, the second hypothesis states that those schizophrenics that left their parental homes, no matter what the social class status of the home was, failed to realize their ambitions and hence found themselves with educational and occupational status that marked them for Class V.

Currently, we have been engaged in the reexamination of some of our data to determine which of these hypotheses is the most plausible. An examination of the age factor and the previous address of the patient in relation to social class revealed nothing of significance. We analyzed the social class of the father in contrast to the social class of the patient and found that the incidence rates of schizophrenia, by father's social class, tend to be about equal for all the classes with the highest rate being in Class II, while, as we have seen, the patients on the basis of their own social class tend to concentrate in Class V. This suggests our second hypothesis, that the development of the schizophrenic condition actually prevented patients from realizing their occupational goals, and indicates that the psychiatric condition of the patient appears to determine his social class rather than his social class determining or influencing his disorder. This interpretation, thus, is similar to the one Michael and Langner favored.

The second question with respect to the parity for vertical mobility patterns suggests no readily plausible hypothesis. It may be, however, that these mobility patterns as measured by the discrepancy between the occupational class of the father and that of the son tell us nothing about the behavior of schizophrenic patients but reflect, rather, a basic theme in American society—the attitude that sons should raise their social level above that of their fathers. Then, the vertical mobility patterns of schizophrenia, as we have found them, would show only that schizophrenics, like nonschizophrenics in the society, also tend to raise their social status. On a broad, general level, the patterns may also be a symptom of the affluent society.

Finally, if we should examine social stratification in our two subcommunities from a functional viewpoint, we would face up to the following propositions. Every human society, as well as animal societies, has been found to have some type of stratification structure. This structure has the function of distributing persons in any society into several differential status positions. The principle governing such a distribution will vary between societies and may be based on birth, achievement, personality, education, influence or something else. This structure functions to locate every member of the society in a hierarchical arrangement. In an open, democratic society that rewards individual achievement to a high degree, the central process becomes personal competition, both legitimate and illegitimate, and the chief selective agency becomes the educational system. It would be expected that under such a system the genetically defective, the physically handicapped, the chronically sick, the rebels, the criminals, the vice-ridden and persons with unacceptable personality traits would experience difficulty in fitting into the hierarchy, except at the lowest status positions. If this analysis is valid, it would be natural to expect that in our type of society many persons destined for schizophrenia would be placed in the lowest status position unless their respective families provided the fortress to protect them from the cruel judgments of the outside competitive world. Thus, they would be protected and sheltered by the humanistic quality of our culture but not from the consequences of the ranking process.

REFERENCES

1. Hollingshead, A. B. and F. C. Redlich. *1958*. Social Class and Mental Illness. John Wiley & Sons, Inc. New York, N.Y.

2. Horney, K. *1937*. The Neurotic Personality of Our Time. W. W. Norton & Company. New York, N.Y.

3. Lystad, M. H. *1957*. Social mobility among selected groups of Schizophrenic patients. Amer. Sociological Review. (3): 288–292.

4. Michael, S. T. and T. S. Langner. *1963*. Social mobility and psychiatric symptoms. Dis. Ner. Syst. Supp. *24* (4).

5. Morris, J. N. *1959*. Health and social class. The Lancet. (February): 303–305.

6. Srole, L., T. S. Langner, S. T. Michael, M. K. Opler and T. A. C. Rennie. *1962*. Mental Health in the Metropolis: The Midtown Manhattan Study, vol. 1. McGraw-Hill Book Company, Inc. New York, N.Y.

7. Stein, L. *1957*. Social class gradient in schizophrenia. Brit. J. Prev. Soc. Med. *2*(4): 181–195.

8. Warner, L. *1937*. The society, the individual and his mental disorders. Amer. J. Psychiat. *94*(2): 275–284.

SOCIOECONOMIC STATUS GROUPS:
THEIR MENTAL HEALTH COMPOSITION

Leo Srole and Thomas Langner

INTRODUCTION: THE SETTING IN MIDTOWN MANHATTAN   S. Kirson Weinberg

MIDTOWN Manhattan is amid the most urbanized areas in the United States, the "New York–Northeastern New Jersey urban complex," which has 13 million people crammed into 4000 square miles. Comprising about 172,000 people, Midtown New York City adjoins the central business district of Manhattan and represents its residential center.[1]

Midtown combines the features of a "Gold Coast and slum." Family incomes range from $300 to $50 weekly, but the largest occupational group, about 60 per cent of the gainfully employed, are white-collar workers ranging from executives and proprietors down to salesmen and clerks. About one-third of its inhabitants are native New Yorkers, another one-third have migrated from small towns in the United States, and one-third are foreign born who, comprise largely German, Austrian, Irish Italian, Russian, Czech, British, and Hungarian.

About one-half of the people are Catholic, who are predominantly among the lower and middle classes; of the remainder, one-third are Protestants and one-sixth are Jewish, chiefly among the middle and upper classes. Of the many religious institutions in the area, there are thirty Protestant churches, about twenty Catholic parishes, and several synagogues.

Educational attainment ranges from about 12.8 per cent of the inhabitants who did not complete grammar school to 18·3 per cent of the residents who graduated from college and had professional training. Like other large cities, Midtown is congested, noisy, impersonal, status-striving, and fraught with personal isolation. It is multicultural from its ethnic and class groups and is embroiled in rapid social change and intense mobility. Its physical topography consists of little grass and trees, considerable asphalt, innumerable automobiles, and lack of sunshine.

From *Mental Health in the Metropolis: The Midtown Manhattan Study*, Vol. 1, By Leo Srole, Thomas S. Langner, Stanley T. Michael, Marvin K. Opler and Thomas A. C. Rennie. Copyright 1962 McGraw-Hill Book Company. Used by permission.

The structure of Midtown is mainly residential and although adjacent to the main shopping section of Manhattan, Midtowners patronize local small shops and independent stores; there are few chain stores. Most Midtowners work in the office section of Manhattan except for the doctors who practice in the Midtown area.

Many single adults and childless couples live alone and are relatively isolated in rooming houses. But the many Midtown families have the typical nuclear American family consisting of parents and children. Although a three-generation household characterizes lower status immigrants, the younger generations are veering towards the two-generation nuclear family.

Midtown is more socially disorganized than the other boroughs of New York. It's infant mortality rate is one-fourth greater than the other boroughs, in spite of greater access to medical services. It has higher rates of mortality from alcoholism and from non-vehicular accidents, and twice the rates of active cases of tuberculosis. Its juvenile delinquency rates is half again as high as most other comparable districts of New York city. These high death and morbidity rates in Midtown reveal a social pathology because of the inadequate use of the available medical services by the residents.

To survey the mental health of this relatively large community, the authors first narrowed their range to that of prime adulthood, ages 20 to 59. This reduced the population from 175,000 to 110,000 people, whom of 1,660 persons were selected at random as a representative cross-section of the population.

One aim in studying this sample was to determine concentrations of mental disorders and psycholothology in divergent socio-economic subgroups. In terms of status, the crucial criteria are socio-economic differentiation.[2]

Three major strata emerged: 1) the wealthy or upper class, 2) the middle or white-collar class and 3) the lower or blue-collar class. Each stratum in turn was composed of an upper and lower sub-

TABLE 1. DISTRIBUTION OF 1660 RESPONDENTS ACCORDING TO
SEVERITY OF SYMPTOMS AND ASSOCIATED IMPAIRMENT

Category	Mental Health Ratings	Percent Rating I	Percent Rating II
Well	0– 1	18.8	18.5
Mild Symptoms	2– 3	41.6	36.3
Moderate Symptoms	4– 5	21.3	21.8
Impaired	6–12	18.3	23.4
Marked Symptoms	6– 7	10.7	13.2
Severe Symptoms	8– 9	6.2	7.5
Incapacitated	10–12	1.4	2.7
(N = 100 per cent)		1660	1660

stratum. Subsequently, this social stratum was reformulated into socioeconomic status based upon the occupation and income of the subjects and of their parents.

In order to determine the mental health rating of these persons by socioeconomic status, each subject was interviewed for about two hours. The one hundred symptoms of the pretested questionaire were derived from items in the army's Neuropsychiatric adjunct, from the Minnesota Multiphasic Inventory, and from the clinicians' own extensive experience.

This rating scale consisted of these categories of mental disorder or mental health as indicated by symptoms: (1) severe or impairing symptoms, (2) moderate symptoms, (3) mild symptoms, and (4) symptom-free or well. The severe or impaired category of symptoms was in turn subdivided into (1) marked symptoms, (2) severe symptoms, and (3) incapacitating symptoms.

Kirkpatrick and Michael made independent psychiatric evaluations of each of the 1660 respondents on a seven-point scale of impairment. Because each psychiatrist assigned a rating from 0 to 6, each respondent had two ratings. These ratings were combined to form a composite thirteen-point scale (0–12). This scale in turn was "collapsed," yielding final distributions of Ratings I and II (see Table I).

In terms of Mental Health Rating II, based upon the larger amount of data, less than one-fifth of the population in Midtown is well, while about three-fifths have some form of mental disorder, and over one-fifth are morbid or sick. In other words,

at least 23.4 per cent of the Midtown sample manifest some personal impairment in their behavior. This impaired category of the Midtown sample, according to Dr. Rennie, corresponds roughly to the range of impaired patients who visit psychiatric clinics, and hospitals.

The sample of subjects of Midtown revealed no differences in the influence of city and country background upon their mental health. Their socioeconomic status is the most important criterion in mental health and mental disorder; it is associated more closely with mental disturbance than any other factor and was basic in its influence to the group's urban or rural background. The socioeconomic status of the parents as determined by the father's occupation and education is a definite correlate to their mental health. The physical and mental health of the parents also are contributing influences upon the mental health of the residents. The subjects are apparently affected by their parents' physical and mental health, by the frequency with which their parents quarrelled, and by the death or divorce of their parents before the subjects were age 6.

Srole and Langner have hypothesized that status mobility is related to mental health; they have traced this relationship in the discussion to follow between upward and downward social mobility and mental disorders.

[1] Thomas S. Langner and Stanley T. Michael, *Life Stress and Mental Health* (New York: The Free Press, 1963), pp. 66–73.
[2] Thomas A. C. Rennie, Leo Srole, Marvin K. Opler, and Thomas S. Langner, "Urban Life and Mental Health," *American Journal of Psychiatry* (March 1957), *113* (9), 831–36.

CHANGE as it may, socioeconomic status is a life-long motif in the individual's web of daily experience. One of the dominating designs in the vast tapestry of the nation's culture, it also weaves itself into the dreams, calculations, strivings, triumphs, and defeats of many Americans from childhood on.

Accordingly, the hypothesis linking frequency of mental illness to SES differences was inevitable, and indeed has drawn the attention of numerous investigations. Their reports provide convenient points of departure for the present chapter.

In largest numbers these researchers chose to test the hypothesis by the relatively simple ex-pedient of enumerating psychiatric patients recorded on treatment rosters as their measure of the extent of mental morbidity. With several notable exceptions, these efforts did not explicitly distinguish between *treated* frequency and *over-all* (untreated and treated) frequency of mental illness as very different yardsticks of morbidity. They therefore applied the former but fell into the error of drawing generalizations as if they had measured the latter.

We hold that socioeconomic status linked on one hand to over-all frequency of mental illness and on the other to frequency of psychiatric treatment *among the sick* presents rather different situations that require discrete hypotheses and separate testing. In the next chapter we take up the SES-and-treatment hypothesis, where the previous studies of patient populations can claim direct relevance. To our top-priority hypothesis connecting status and *over-all* mental morbidity, these limited studies do not offer tests that satisfy the criterion of relevance.

Potentially offering a more adequate test of the latter hypothesis are the investigations that have looked beyond patients appearing on institutional records and, in search of both untreated and treated cases of illness, reached with a far wider, albeit crude, net into the lifestream of a general popul-ation at large. Relatively few in number, these published studies deserve brief examination for any light they can throw on the present state of know-ledge bearing on this particular hypothesis.

Probably the first and the largest of these was the National Health Survey conducted in 1936 under Federal auspices. Using the interview method and covering, in one of its aspects, a sample of 703,092 households (2,502,391 individuals) in 83 cities,[1] this study included a wide range of medical disabilities reported active on the day of interview. Included was the category "nervous and mental diseases," specifically "neurasthenia, nervous breakdown, epilepsy, chorea, locomotor ataxia, paresis, other diseases of the nervous system." Occupation was the SES indicator (among the employed in the age range 15 to 64) and was dichotomized on the line of the white-collar and blue-collar distinction. In frequencies of nervous and mental disease the data for employed females revealed no difference by occupation category. Among males, on the other hand, the white-collar rate of nervous and mental disease exceeded that of the blue-collar category by about 3:2.

A check of the latter finding is at hand in several wartime studies of Selective Service male registrants, with rejections for "mental and per-sonality disorders" as the criterion of morbidity. One of these investigations involved a national sample clinically examined during November-December, 1943, with occupation again the status indicator.[2] With the exclusion of farmers, students, and the unemployed, no significant differences in psychiatric rejection rates were found among the several occupational categories there defined.

A second Selective Service study was conducted with 60,000 male registrants examined at the Boston Area Induction Station in 1942.[3] The Boston psy-chiatric rejection rates by socioeconomic level of registrants, as indexed by area of residence, were as follows:

Socioeconomic level	Rejected in each level
A (highest)	7.3%
B	9.2
C	9.4
D	10.0
E	12.7
F (lowest)	16.6

The most recent study relevant here is that conducted in Baltimore.[4] From our discussion in Chapter 8 it will be remembered that this inves-tigation involved a clinical examination and evalua-tion of a sample of 809 men and women (approximately 30% of these were nonwhites) and covered a broad spectrum of some 30 somatic dis-orders. The mental disorder rates by income level are reported only for whites and nonwhites com-bined. If we assume that the nonwhites of Baltimore, as elsewhere, are highly concentrated in the lowest of the four income brackets defined, then the other income groups, inferred to be predominantly white, have mental disorder rates reported as follows:

Income level	Disorders in each level
$6,000 and over	13.6%
$4,000-$5,999	8.9
$2,000-$3,999	8.9

The four inquiries just considered had in common the relatively rare feature of covering a general population rather than an aggregate of patients. However, on the issue of a connection between SES and over-all prevalence of psychiatric disability, the findings of these studies point in almost all possible directions. In the national Selective Service investigation the correlation was practically zero; in the Boston Selective Service survey it was inverse, i.e., the lower the SES level, the higher the morbidity rate; among the Baltimore sample whites it was apparently positive, i.e., highest morbidity rate in the top-income category; and in the National Health Survey the correlation was zero among females and positive among males.

Although the four inquiries used different SES indicators—occupation, area of residence, or income—these are standard measures that are known to be highly correlated with and predictive of each other. Accordingly, it is unlikely that the contradictory findings arise from the different socioeconomic yardsticks applied. Note in particular that the same index, occupation, was used in the two national investigations, yet divergent morbidity trends were obtained for the males in the two samples.

In the absence of sufficient evidence to explain or reconcile the inconsistent yields in the four studies reviewed,[5] the suggested hypothesis linking socioeconomic status and over-all mental morbidity in the general population can be viewed as an open question.

PARENTAL SES: MENTAL HEALTH DISTRIBUTIONS

During childhood, the individual shares the socioeconomic status of his parents and its many fateful consequences. This factor of SES origin we postulate to be an independent precondition related inversely to variations in adult mental health. We look to the Midtown Home Survey and its sample, representing some 110,000 adult "in residence" Midtowners, for a test of this hypothesis.[6] From the previous chapter it will be remembered that respondents' SES origins are distributed among six strata according to composite scores derived from their fathers' schooling and occupational level. With the SES-origin strata designated A through F in a sequence from highest to lowest position, Table 12-1 arranges the Midtown sample adults in each stratum as they are distributed on the gradient classification of mental health assigned by the Study psychiatrists.

Reading Table 12-1 horizontally from left to right in order to discern the nature of the trends, we might direct first attention to the Mild and Moderate categories. It is readily apparent that the frequencies of these two mental health conditions are remarkably uniform across the entire SES-origin range. These categories, it will be remembered, encompass more or less adequate functioning in the adult life spheres, although some signs and symptoms of mental disturbance in presumably subclinical forms are present. Equally prevalent along the entire continuum of parental SES, these two mental health types emerge here as generalized phenomena, much as they did with the age variable in Chapter 9.

TABLE 12–1. HOME SURVEY SAMPLE (AGE 20–59), DISTRIBUTIONS OF RESPONDENTS ON MENTAL HEALTH CLASSIFICATION BY PARENTAL-SES STRATA

Parental-SES strata

Mental health categories	A (highest)	B	C	D	E	F (lowest)
Well	24.4%		19.9%	18.8%	13.6%	9.7%
Mild symptom formation	36.0	38.3	36.6	36.6	36.6	32.7
Moderate symptom formation	22.1	22.0	22.6	20.1	20.4	24.9
Impaired*	17.5	16.4	20.9	24.5	29.4	32.7
Marked symptom formation	11.8	8.6	11.8	13.3	16.2	18.0
Severe symptom formation	3.8	4.5	8.1	8.3	10.2	10.1
Incapacitated	1.9	3.3	1.0	2.9	3.0	4.6
N = 100%	(262)	(245)	(287)	(384)	(265)	(217)

*$x^2 = 28.81$, $5 df$, $p < .001$.

We also note in the above table that around these numerically stable mental health categories the Well and Impaired frequencies vary on the SES-origin scale in diametrically opposite directions. From the highest (A) to the lowest (F) of the status groups the Well proportions recede gradually from 24.4 to 9.7%, whereas the Impaired rate mounts from about one in every six (17.5%) to almost one in every three (32.7%).[7]

These countertrends can be more efficiently communicated by converting them into a single standard value that expresses the number of Impaired cases accompanying every 100 Well people in a given group. In the Midtown sample as a whole, this Sick-Well ratio[8] emerges with a value of 127, a norm available for comparative uses in the pages to come. In bar chart form Figure 1 presents the Sick-Well values translated from Table 12-1.

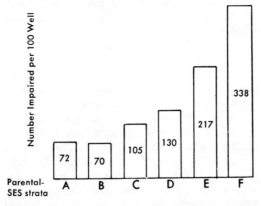

FIGURE 1. Home Survey Sample (ages 20 to 59). Sick-Well ratios of parental-SES strata.

With the top SES-origin levels (A and B) as our points of comparison, we observe in Figure 1 that the Sick-Well ratio is half again larger in the adjoining group C, almost twice higher in the D stratum, three times greater in the E level, and at a point of five-power magnification in the bottom (F) group. Phrased somewhat differently, the two highest strata (A and B) taken together constitute about 30% of the sample but account for 40% of the Well and for only 22% of the Impaired. On the other hand, the two lowest strata (E and F) taken together constitute 29% of the sample but account for only 19% of the Well and for fully 39% of the Impaired.[9] Through these variously expressed data a connection seems to be apparent between parental SES and mental health in Midtown's adults.

But before we accept such a conclusion, we must give precautionary consideration to this question: Could not the above differences be the result of biasing factors that intruded in the research process? Four major points of potential intrusion can be identified, namely, (1) selection of a sample unrepresentative in SES composition, (2) bias on the part of the interviewing staff, (3) status-linked differences in reporting symptoms on the part of respondents, and (4) preconceptions about social class held by the Study psychiatrists. These error potentials are too serious to be briefly dismissed and too technical for lengthy digression here. Accordingly, they are being held for evaluation in Appendix H. In fine, that evaluation presents firm evidence indicating that two of the four potential sources of bias (1, 4) had left no discernible traces of intrusion. Another possible source (2) is unlikely to have contributed significantly to such error, and the fourth (3) probably operated in a direction to *understate* the SES differences seen in Table 12-1. On balance, therefore, the chances seem large that the connection observed between SES origin and adult mental health is authentic rather than a spurious consequence of biases brought out by the research process. If so, the data reported appear to offer an adequate test of the following hypothesis as originally stated: Parental socioeconomic status during childhood is an independent variable that is *inversely* related to the prevalence of mental morbidity among Midtown adults. However, the data produced do not support the hypothesis in its original form. Instead, they force its modification into a three-part proposition: the stated independent variable of parental SES is related (1) inversely to the frequency of the Impaired condition of mental health, (2) directly to the frequency of the Well state, and (3) not at all to the frequencies of the Mild and Moderate types of symptom formation.

The first part of this proposition asserts that successively lower parental status carries for the child progressively *larger* risk of impaired mental health during adulthood. For those who may hold reservations about the clinical identity of the Impaired category of mental health, the second part of the proposition refers to the asymptomatic state as beyond cavil the minimal form of good mental health; and it asserts that successively lower parental SES tends to carry for the child progressively *smaller* chances of achieving the Well state during adulthood.[10]

The above proposition attributes some share of responsibility for adult mental health to differences in family socioeconomic status during childhood. Notwithstanding respondents' real differences in parental SES, however, it is altogether possible that the decisive factors influencing their current mental health had occurred not during childhood but since they have become adults.

The only approximate test of this possibility open to us here is to isolate the sample segment that has most recently turned adult, i.e., the age 20 to 29 respondents, who, on the average, are only five years removed from the end point of the teen-age phase. If childhood factors associated with parental socioeconomic status carry little weight for adult mental health, then we would expect that among these youngest sample respondents the parental-SES subgroups will emerge with relatively minor differences in Impaired and Well rates. For each of the three parental-SES "classes"[11] among the age 20 to 29 respondents the actual frequencies and the Sick-Well ratio are seen in Table 12–2.

Table 12-2 shows that the theoretical possibility defined is not fulfilled. On the contrary, among these young people recently out of adolescence,[12] significant differences in Well-Impaired weightings are plainly tied to variations in SES origin. We can therefore plausibly infer that these differences were predominantly implanted during the preadult stage of dependency upon parents and were brought into early adulthood rather than initially generated there.

STATUS MOBILITY AND MENTAL HEALTH

We have thus far concentrated attention on *parental* socioeconomic status, postulated as embracing overarching constellations of different life conditions during childhood. However, there is a generalized cultural mandate binding all social classes in American society. Rising from impoverished immigrant parents to the summit of an industrial empire, Andrew Carnegie gave utterance to this mandate in ringing words: "Be a King in your dreams. Say to yourself 'My place is at the top.'"[13]

A more realistic injunction and one more widely accepted is this: Whatever your status inheritance from parents as a point of departure, strive to "do better," i.e., advance beyond it. In due course, the adult settles into his own position, at a level that may be higher, lower, or more or less the same as his father's. These three parent-offspring sequences are technically designated as the variable of *intergeneration status mobility*. The status mobility variable circumscribes an extremely complicated and dynamic set of processes that operate in the individual's life history between childhood under the roof of parental-SES conditions and his own status shelter built in adulthood for his spouse and children.

What light does published research shed on the mental health aspects of such mobility differences? In their recent literature-synthesizing book *Social Mobility in Industrial Society*, Lipset and Bendix[14] devote separate sections to (1) "the consequences of social mobility" for the individual and (2) varying individual orientations that spur different directions of status change. In the former discussion they conclude that "studies of mental illness have suggested that people moving up in America are more likely to have mental breakdowns than the non-mobile." An examination of the New Haven study used as the principal source of this inference shows that Lipset and Bendix appear to have misread the evidence. The New Haven reports[15] on status mobility covered 847 schizophrenics in treatment, who were found to be 88% nonmobile, about 4% upward-mobile, and 1.2% downward-mobile. (The remainder were in the category of "insufficient family history.") Contrary to the Lipset-Bendix reading, these data do not suggest a picture of upward mobility as a major trend among the New Haven cases. More important, even if their reading were correct, trends among treated schizophrenics, whatever their direction, can hardly be generalized to apply to treated nonschizophrenics (unreported

TABLE 12–2. HOME SURVEY SAMPLE (AGE 20–59), DISTRIBUTIONS ON MENTAL HEALTH CLASSIFICATION OF AGE 20–29 RESPONDENTS BY PARENTAL-SES CLASSES

Mental health categories	Parental-SES classes		
	Upper (A–B)	Middle (C–D)	Lower (E–F)
Well	34.1%	21.4%	12.9%
Mild symptom formation	35.5	38.1	39.6
Moderate symptom formation	20.5	23.7	27.7
Impaired	9.9*	16.8	19.8*
N = 100%	(132)	(132)	(101)
Sick-Well ratio	29	82	154

*$t = 2.1$ (.05 level of confidence).

in the New Haven publications), or to untreated schizophrenics, or to the untreated with other disorders. Above all, these trends cannot be extrapolated, as Lipset and Bendix have done, to "mental breakdown" trends in the universe of "people moving up in America" as compared with trends in the universe of nonmobile Americans. In point of fact, there is now some question whether it is possible to extrapolate from the New Haven treated schizophrenics to schizophrenic patients generally. In a recent New Orleans study,[16] such patients were reported to be predominantly (45.7%) downward-mobile—in striking contrast with the New Haven cases.

In further fact, single point-of-time studies, whether of treated or over-all mental morbidity, offer no basis for the inference that status mobility "may cause difficulties in personal adjustment."[17] Such investigations cannot parcel out the discrete mental health *consequences* of individual changes in socioeconomic status from the specific personality *preconditions* of different self-determined mobility paths.

However, citing the *same* New Haven treated schizophrenic rates, Lipset and Bendix assert[18] in their later section on differential motivations for mobility that "mental illness rates would seem to provide additional data for the notion that the upwardly mobile [population] tend to be deprived psychodynamically." In its context, this statement seems to suggest that psychic deprivation tends to induce status climbing. But clearly no study of patients can tell us about the psychically deprived and nondeprived segments of the nonpatient population and their respective mobility tendencies.

In a relevant research paper,[19] Douvan and Adelson preface their data report with the observation that in the large literature on social mobility

...only limited attention has been given to studying the motivational sources of mobility. What we do find is a general disposition to treat *upward* mobility in a vaguely invidious fashion. It would seem that, in this country, the Horatio Alger tradition and the "dream of success" motif have been pervasive and distasteful enough to have alienated, among others, a good many social scientists. The upwardly aspiring individual has apparently become associated with the pathetic seeker after success or with the ruthless tycoon. This image of success is, much of it, implicit—assumption and attitude, and not quite conviction—but it seems to have dominated the thinking of our intellectual community.

In their insightful study of a national cross-section sample of 1,000 age 14 to 16 boys, Douvan and Adelson set out to test their ego-theory conceptualizations on personality determinants of precareer mobility aspirations. To draw on the summary of their findings:

The upward aspiring boy is characterized by a high energy level, the presence of autonomy, and a relatively advanced social maturity. These attributes may be viewed as derivatives of a generally effective ego organization. [In the] downward mobile boys . . . we see an apparent blocking or impoverishment of energy which should ideally be available to the ego. There is a relatively poor articulation among the psychic systems; impulses threaten the ego's integrity; the superego seems overly severe and yet incompletely incorporated. These boys seem humorless, gauche, disorganized—relatively so, at least. Perhaps the most telling and poignant datum which the study locates is their response to the possibility of personal change, their tendency to want to change intractable aspects of the self, and the degree of alienation revealed by their desire to modify major and fundamental personal qualities.

The study just reviewed was focused on mobility aspirations, among a general sample of adolescents, and their personality corollaries. As contrast to this prospective approach to adult developments, in the Midtown sample of adults we are focusing retrospectively on status mobility, completed or in process, and current mental health. In the planning phase of the Study we were clear that from the latter we could not dissect (1) what the level of mental health had been at the threshold of the respondent's career and (2) what increments of mental health change were subsequently added as a specific result of engagement in the struggle for own SES.

Nevertheless, in his 1952 proposals for the Midtown Home Interview Survey the senior author formulated a series of hypotheses[20] bearing retrospectively for each sample adult on the following nexus of forces: (1) respondent's choice of parental identification figure during childhood; (2) parents' agreement or disagreement in occupational hopes for and pressures on the respondent; (3) respondent's own occupational aspirations (upon completion of schooling) relative to the level of parental hopes; (4) respondent's current occupation relative to his end-of-schooling aspirations; (5) respondent's feeling of fitness for and strain in his occupation; etc. Although these dynamic dimensions of status mobility were all covered in the sample interviews for their relevance to mental health, they form a network too complex and specialized to have been incorporated in the analytic design of the present monograph. Accordingly, they are being reserved for future treatment in a separate publication by the senior writer:

On a more encompassable plane, we also postulated as follows:

1. Upward mobility requires not only appropriate aspirations but also efficient personal mobilization, such that to actually "make the grade," sound mental health is a decided preparatory asset and impaired health is not. Downward mobility, on the other hand, is culturally so deviant from group and self-expectations that it can only happen under some initial, predisposing handicap in physical or mental health.

2. In turn, given adequate preparation in the preadult stage, accomplished upward mobility and its rewards tend to have constructive consequences for subsequent adult mental health[21]; whereas the consequences of downward mobility and its deprivations would tend to be in the opposite direction.

3. However, countervailing tendencies also operate. For some people, status climbing may have costly pathogenic effects that would have been avoided had they remained stationary, i.e., nonmobile, relative to father. Similarly, downward mobility may conserve or stabilize mental health in certain special, limited circumstances, when other courses would have been taxing or damaging to the individual.

As to the relative importance of these postulated elements in the resultant current mental health of sample respondents, we believe that those subsumed under hypothesis 3 are relatively rare and partially offset those suggested in hypothesis 2. The latter, in our view, are secondary to the dominant contribution of the forces emphasized in hypothesis 1, namely, the psychosocial selection of different kinds of preadult mental health for adult replication, advance, or retreat from parental status.

In testing the relationship of status mobility, as a reciprocal-type variable, to current adult mental health, we faced a number of alternatives in choosing a common yardstick to measure SES of both the respondent and his father. The decision finally taken was that for this specific purpose occupation level by itself, though not accounting for all socioeconomic variability, is more useful in identifying specific father-offspring sequences than any two status indicators arithmetically averaged. From the previous chapter it will be remembered that a series of three questions was used with each respondent to elicit (1) the nature of his own work and (2) that of his father when the respondent was age 18. On the basis of these data, father and respondent were separately placed within the identical occupational framework of six levels, numerically scored 1 to 6. Where respondent and father have a like score, the former is classified nonmobile. If the respondent has a higher score, he is classified upward-mobile, and if a lower score, downward-mobile.

It can now be reported of the 911 sample males and never-married females[22] who could be placed in terms of both father's and own occupation that their distribution among the three forms of mobility approximates a 1:1:1 ratio. However, the mental health compositions of these three groups present significant differences in the hypothesized direction, as Table 12-3 reveals.

We note first in Table 12-3 that the stable nonmobile group presents an even balance in its number of Impaired and Well members. With this as a point of comparison, we further observe that among the "climbers" there is an imbalance, with the Well outnumbering the Impaired by about 3:2. Finally, among the "descenders" the imbalance is tipped sharply to the other side, the Impaired exceeding the Well by almost 5:2.[23]

Two qualifications must be weighed for these trends. First, the relationship between occupational mobility and mental health would be at least partially spurious if the up-moving people were largely younger adults of higher status origins and those moving in the opposite direction were principally

TABLE 12-3. HOME SURVEY SAMPLE (AGE 20–59), RESPONDENT DISTRIBUTIONS ON MENTAL HEALTH CLASSIFICATION OF MEN AND SINGLE WOMEN BY OCCUPATIONAL MOBILITY TYPES

Mental health categories	Mobility types		
	Up	Stable	Down
Well	21.0%	22.6%	12.7%
Mild symptom formation	41.6	37.0	33.8
Moderate symptom formation	23.8	16.8	23.4
Impaired*	13.6	23.6	30.1
N = 100%	(315)	(297)	(299)
Sick-Well ratio	65	104	235

*$x^2 = 24.57$, $2df$, $p < .001$.

older adults of lower parental SES. The fact is that the climbers are split below and above the 40-year line exactly 50-50, whereas the descenders are split 40-60. Decidedly, the descenders *are* the older group. On the other hand, the climbers are predominantly (67%) from blue-collar fathers, whereas the descenders are mainly (55%) from white-collar fathers. Thus, the two potentially masking factors approximately serve to cancel each other out.

Second, our data may actually understate the strength of the relationship. An optimal test would focus on self-supporting adults at an age when occupational change is largely over, i.e., beyond the age of 40. Among younger adults, particularly in bureaucratic organizations, further reaches of work upgrading may still lie ahead. If so, mobility tendencies among younger adults would expectedly have a lesser linkage with mental health than among older poeple. This inference is actually supported by a comparison of the younger (age 20 to 39) and older (age 40 to 59) male and single women respondents. That is, the contrast in Impaired-Well balance between the upward- and downward-mobile types is considerably sharper in the senior than in the junior group.

We can look more closely at the character of the changes by focusing down to the 442 U.S.-born male respondents known in terms both of own and of father's occupation. This particular segment of the population is of purified relevance because it excludes the single women, who are limited in their occupational movements by an intracultural bias. Also excluded are the foreign-born males, whose mobility can be measured only by their occupational place in the American economy as compared with their father's occupational level in the economy of the homeland. Here various intercultural biases probably operate.

We might start with the high white-collar level of business executives and professionals. Sixty-three fathers had been in this stratum. Of their 63 sampled sons, 33 established themselves in the some occupational bracket; the other 30 dropped to lower levels—several in fact to the bottom of the blue-collar range. However, more than offsetting the latter were 65 men who climbed into this stratum from fathers in lower occupations. (Fifteen of these men had blue-collar fathers.) Now let us consider the respondent mental health differences selectively carried in these shifts. To be emphasized is that the number of cases involved is small and accordingly the Sick-Well values are to be regarded as suggestive only. In Figure 2 the arrow indicates the direction of mobility (horizontal arrow signifies nonmobility), and the number

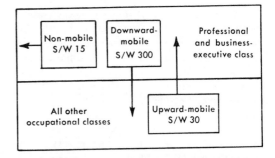

FIGURE 2. **Home Survey Sample (ages 20 to 59). Sick-Well ratios of sons originating in or ascending into the top occupational class.**

in the circle attached represents the Sick-Well ratio of the men who moved in that direction.

As Figure 2 indicates, the healthier sons replicated their father's top occupational position. On the other hand, the less healthy sons more often moved down, to be replaced by far healthier men ascending from fathers at lower levels. Thus, all 63 sons of top-level fathers present a Sick-Well value of 70, whereas for all 98 men *now* in that occupational bracket the corresponding value is 24.

At the opposite pole is the unskilled class of blue-collar occupations. Fifty of our U.S.-born male respondents were from fathers at this level. Of these sons, 14 remain in the same kind of occupation; 6 of these have impaired mental health, 3 are well. Thirty-six other sons have climbed to higher points—14 to the low and middle white-collar strata, 6 to the executive-professional ranks—and have an approximate balance in number of Impaired and Well respondents (Sick-Well ratio of 120). Replacing these climbers are 37 descenders from fathers in higher positions.[24] With the out-climbers healthier in composition than the nonmobile men and the in-descenders least favorable of all in mental health (Sick-Well ratio of 240), the 51 men now in the unskilled class have a Sick-Well ratio of 225. This compares with a value of 150 for the group of 50 offspring of unskilled fathers.

In the intervening occupational levels the mobility traffic is at once more balanced and more complicated. For example, there are 135 male respondents with fathers in the middle (managerial and semiprofessional) white-collar stratum. Of the sons, 65 (48%) were nonmobile, 46 (34%) were climbers, and 24 (18%) descenders. However, the latter two types of out-movers from the class were replaced by two types of in-movers, namely, 43 climbers from fathers of lower occupational standing and 26 descenders from executive-professional fathers. As net effect of these four-way counter-balancing movements, the mental health composition of American-born male respondents who *are themselves* in the middle white-collar category is little different from that of the group of men *deriving* from fathers who had been in this category.

We would emphasize again that the mental health differences reported for the three mobility types of respondents probably represent the convergence of two sets of factors: (1) original (preadult) mental health differences among those carried in different own-SES directions and (2) subsequent mental health shifts along the several mobility courses.

A longitudinal study design will be required to bridge the Douvan-Adelson data from adolescents and our own from Midtown adults. To such a prospective study, both sets of data offer the hypothesis that on the whole healthier adolescents tend to be more heavily drawn into the traffic of upward-moving adults, whereas more disturbed adolescents tend to be shunted into the downward traffic. We suggest the further hypothesis that on the whole those in the ascending traffic stream are subsequently less likely to show exogenous deterioration in mental health than those in the descending stream.

It may be asked how these hypotheses are to be articulated to the postulates in the previous chapter bearing on the child of low-status families. Among sample respondents derived from blue-collar fathers we know that about two in every five have been upward-mobile on our six-level occupation scale. Whether or not these Midtowners are in this respect typical of blue-collar offspring elsewhere is not yet known; but from evidence presented in Chapter 6 there are intimations that they may be more upward-oriented than their occupation peers elsewhere seem to be. Even here, however, the nonclimbers outnumber the ascenders. That there are climbers at all would seem to reflect two factors: (1) The dynamic New York economy has open places at the requisite occupational levels, and (2) the objective goals to escape to a more comfortable and respected style of life probably sort out the climbers from the nonclimbers along such personality dimensions as were delineated in the Douvan-Adelson study and were briefly sketched earlier in this chapter. The latter inference raises the further question whether differences in lower-class families yield personality variations among their offspring which issue in status-mobility divergences. It is this question which will be separately addressed by the Study's unanalyzed focus, outlined above, on the nexus

of child-parent identifications and of congruences and conflicts in parent-child career aspirations.

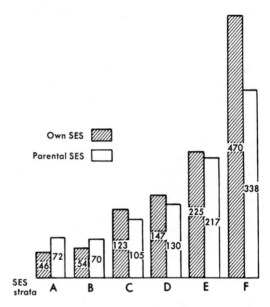

FIGURE 3. **Home Survey Sample (ages 20 to 59). Sick-Well ratios of own SES and parental-SES strata.**

OWN SES AND MENTAL HEALTH

From the unraveling of father-son occupational changes we can better grasp the results when the entire Midtown sample of adults are examined for mental health compostion as classified on the scale of own socioeconomic status. In Figure 1 we charted the Sick-Well ratios of the sample arranged by SES origin as indexed by father's schooling and occupation. These are reproduced in Figure 3, but they now accompany bars representing the Sick-Well values of the entire sample when sorted by own SES as indexed by respondent's own education and own occupation.[25]

Reflecting the greater tendency of the Well to move upward and the Impaired downward, Figure 3 for the first time reveals that own SES stands to adult mental health in a relationship even more sharply accentuated than does parental SES. In other words, if parental socioeconomic status plays any contributory part in mental health determination, own SES tends to overstate the magnitude of that contribution.

For purposes of strict comparison of SES origin and own SES, we were compelled to apply to respondents the same two socioeconomic indicators as were available for their fathers. In

TABLE 12-4. HOME SURVEY SAMPLE (AGE 20–59), RESPONDENT DISTRIBUTIONS ON MENTAL HEALTH
CLASSIFICATION OF TOP AND BOTTOM STRATA IN EXPANDED OWN-SES RANGE

Mental health categories	Highest stratum	Lowest stratum
Well	30.0%	4.6%
Mild symptom formation	37.5	25.0
Moderate symptom formation	20.0	23.1
Impaired	12.5*	47.3*
Marked symptom formation	6.7	16.7
Severe symptom formation	5.8	21.3
Incapacitated	0.0	9.3
N = 100%	(120)	(108)
Sick-Well ratio	42	1,020

*$t = 6.0$ (.001 level of confidence).

order to obtain a more refined differentiation of respondent's own SES, we inquired about his family income and household rent as well as his education and occupation. From the sum of the scores on these four indicators, the sample was divided into 12 own-SES strata, as nearly equal in numbers of respondents as possible.

In the strata at the top and bottom extremes of this expanded range are 7.0 and 6.5% of the sample, respectively. Table 12-4 gives the complete distributions of these two sets of respondents on the Study psychiatrists' classification of mental health.

The Moderate and Mild categories of symptom formation aside, the mental health contrast between the top and bottom strata could hardly be more sharply drawn. The story is partially told in their Severe and Incapacitated totals (5.8 and 30.6%, respectively) and above all in their Sick-Well ratios.

Of even larger interest perhaps is the shape of the Sick-Well trend line across the entire range of the expanded own-SES continuum. This is profiled in Figure 4.

Confronting the data that gave Figure 4, some investigators would defer to a statistical device (like chi square) for a yes-or-no dictum about the existence of a relationship between two variables, beyond that producible by chance, and consider their work done if the answer is "yes" at a given level of confidence. Since such an answer conveys nothing whatever about the relative strength or weakness of the relationship so affirmed, other investigators apply more specialized statistical devices to measure closeness of the correlation.

However, both kinds of statistical yardsticks are completely insensitive to something potentially important in the data which are given in Figure 4. That is, on the over-all spread of the trend there is a wide socioeconomic span (strata 1–4) devoid of any notable differences in mental health composition until a line of change is crossed. Rising to the 125 to 130 level at this crossing point, the Sick-Well ratio next remains in a flat trend across another broad span of own-SES differences (strata 5–10). These two large plateaus are followed toward the bottom of the own-SES range by two Sick-Well peaks (strata 11 and 12).

The precise extent to which Midtown's mental health distributions statistically vary with differences in own socioeconomic status is of negligible moment compared to this demand of sheer curiosity: Given that each of the graph's four SES zones has its own inner similitude of mental health composition, how can these segments be concretely identified? We have already

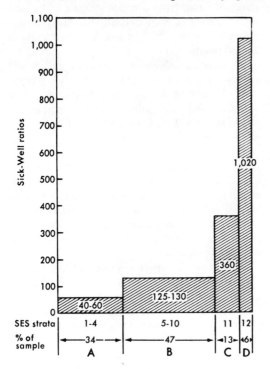

FIGURE 4. Home Survey Sample (ages 20 to 59). Sick-Well ratios of expanded own-SES strata.

seen that the adult own-SES groupings are the residues of rise and fall of status around the parental-SES points of departure. However, our present interest in identifying the four own-SES zones is directed not to their past but rather to their present life circumstances. These are large contemporary "worlds", we can assume, that are the scene or the source of morbidity-precipitating events for the more vulnerable people in their midst. On the basis of data culled for this volume we can indicate the approximate boundaries of these four worlds only in the most elementary economic terms.

In order of size, the largest zone B, embracing strata 5 to 10 and roughly half of the entire sample. These six strata are quite uniform in mental health composition, with Sick-Well ratios that stand near the whole sample's value of 127. They are broadly spread across the lesser ranks of the middle managerial and semiprofessional occupations, through the lower white-collar, the skilled blue-collar, and the higher-wage ranks of the semiskilled factory workers. The family income span, in 1954 dollars, was in the main from $3,000 to $6,000, permitting a tolerable but hardly ample standard of consumption and certainly not permitting the accumulation of any significant reserve funds. With this "tightrope" living standard as the foundation of their claim to respectability, these respondents are close to the line of insecurity. When family crises jeopardize the economic supports of this way of life, the strain placed upon personality resources may be great.

Since these people are numerically the dominant and psychosocially the pivotal segment in the Midtown population, they have a potentially large influence on the mental health climate of the community, above all at times of collective crisis.[26]

Noteworthy also is the large representation of blue-collar respondents in this zone. In recent decades they have caught up with the lower white-collar class[27] in both income and level of consumption and now also match their mental health composition. A tantalizing question they pose is this: Has their documented economic and social progress through these decades been accompanied by an unobserved improvement in mental health, i.e., improvement sufficient to close what had previously been an unfavorable difference? A ready source of evidence to answer the question is not directly apparent. However, the historical implications of a positive answer *are* immediately apparent, matters to which we will return in Chapter 18.

Second in sample representation (34%) are zone

A's own-SES strata 1 to 4, covering the more affluent managerial and professional classes. Here we cross into a world characterized by a more secure, expansive, and ego-nurturing style of life with larger buffers or cushions against the inevitable abrasions and hard knocks of human existence. It is striking that above roughly $6,000 annual income further increments toward $15,000 and far beyond, with all the accompanying socio-economic corollaries, do not appear to register any further gains in group mental health composition. However, it can be hypothesized that without the common denominator "prophylactics" of these strata their latent store of mental pathology would probably emerge in more overt and impairing forms.

At the other side of the own-SES range we find that zone C absorbs a relatively narrow 13% segment of the Midtown sample. Occupationally they are semiskilled workers in the City's newer, marginal low-wage industries and workers in the more stable forms of unskilled labor, e.g., domestics, sweepers, window washers, and janitors. Weekly family income may at times reach the $60 point but more often hovers around $50. Here, we move into a zone of "struggle to keep head above water." The entire style and tone of life bear the marks of strain from constant struggle at the edge of poverty. The mental health situation here is suggested by the spike in the Sick-Well ratio to the 360 point.

In zone D there is breakthrough to still another psychosocial realm, namely, poverty itself. Stemming in the main from parents in unskilled and semiskilled manual occupations, people in zone D are in or near the bottom bracket on every one of our four status indicators. Probably of first significance is that most of them did not complete elementary school. For some respondents this default doubtless was determined by such exogenous barriers as extreme poverty, a disabled or departed parent, or an otherwise acutely deprived family; for other respondents the default may reflect childhood endogenous disabilities, physical or mental.

Whatever the specific source of the barrier, subminimals schooling on its own account sets off a chain of other restrictions: (1) restriction largely to marginal, temporary forms of unskilled labor; (2) restriction to a low, unstable income[28] that at best is beneath the minimal necessary to shelter, clothe, and feed a family (total income in zone D households almost without exception was in a range between $15 to $40 weekly); (3) restriction to cramped quarters in the most deteriorated slum tenements.

Such noxious life burdens, together with inadequate or vulnerable personalities developed in childhood, often combine to produce a break in the intolerable struggle. Chronic poverty has brought almost all zone D respondents to the City Welfare Department for financial assistance; and many belong to "multiproblem" families that are known to the police, courts, private social agencies, and mental hospitals.

From this group's mental health distribution reported in Table 12-4 above, it is seen that exceedingly few are Well (4.6%) and nearly half (47.3%) are Impaired. Segregated with others in like circumstances and mental health conditions, the numerically dominant Impaired of zone D doubtless help to create a "sick" slum community that often carries its own pathogenic "contagion," in particular for the children in its midst. It is hardly surprising, therefore, to hear of a 1956 New York City Youth Board Survey that covered 825 children of needy families and reported that 40% of these children manifest "serious behavior problems." It was predicted that another 10%, principally in the youngest segment of the sample, would likely develop such problems.

Here the frequency of adult mental pathology is probably of unprecedented proportions. And here the environmental contamination of children very likely ensures that the epidemic shall continue to reproduce itself in the generation ahead, as it apparently has from the generation preceding.

Reviewing the four zones observed in Figure 4, we can infer that certain turning points in the quality and weight of adult life conditions emerge along the status continuum represented in our expanded own-SES scale.

SUMMARY

In this sweep across the front defined by socioeconomic status with its multiform salients, we probed a number of discrete hypotheses with the following returns:

1. On the parental-SES range the frequency of impairment varies inversely and the Well rate varies directly.

2. This trend in Impaired-Well balance also characterizes those in the sample's youngest age group, who only recently have crossed the threshold from adolescence. It was thus possible to reject the hypothesis that SES-origin differentials in mental health had almost entirely been generated during adult life.

3. Among the several SES-origin groups no significant differences appear in the frequency of

schizophrenic signs, anxiety-tension symptoms, or excessive intake behaviors. In all other pathognomonic dimensions covered, however, there is an *inverse* correlation with parental SES. These dimensions included disturbances in intellectual, affective, somatic, characterological, and interpersonal functioning.

4. Simultaneous analysis of age and status-origin against respondent mental health revealed that *both* demographic variables are related to mental health, each in its own right. This suggested first that parental-SES differences had implanted varying mental health potentialities among sample respondents during childhood; and second, that during the temporal course of adolescence and adulthood, precipitating factors had provoked overt morbidity among the more vulnerable people from all SES-origin strata. The combined power of these two demographic variables, as reflected in the index of Sick-Well magnitudes, is substantial.

5. The hypothesis was suggested that this triad of age, parental SES, and adult mental health was specific to the kinds of people who choose to live in an area like Midtown. That is, the identified nexus lacked wider currency in the American population. Evidence from three radically different populations indicated rejection of this hypothesis. Positively stated, the complex triad isolated in the Midtown sample may well characterize larger reaches of the American people.

6. Intergeneration status mobility, as read in a single point-of-time study, is a reciprocal factor relative to adult mental health. In the Midtown sample's coverage of three mobility types, the climbers had the smallest Sick-Well values and the descenders had the largest by far. For prospective longitudinal studies these data suggested the two-part hypothesis: (*a*) Preadult personality differences partially determine directions of status change in adulthood; (*b*) *on the whole*, upward status mobility is rewarding psychically as well as materially, whereas downward status mobility is depriving in both respects.

7. Reflecting the selective escalator effects of status mobility, own-SES shows an even stronger relationship to adult mental health than does respondent status origin.

8. Using four status indicators it is possible to divide the own-SES range into 12 finer strata. Revealed in these strata are four mental health zones, or contemporary worlds, seemingly marked at their boundaries by breakthrough points of differences in the size and security of economic underpinnings, in styles of life, in ego nurturance, and in their psychosocial atmospheres. In zones

C and D, at or near the poverty level, we discern particularly heavy pathogenic weights currently bearing on the especially vulnerable people.

For targeting of social policy, Midtown zones C and D, and likely their psychosocioeconomic counterparts elsewhere on the national scene, convey highest priority claims for milieu therapy in its broadest sense. Ultimately indicated here may be interventions into the downward spiral of compounded tragedy, wherein those handicapped in personality or social assets from childhood on are trapped as adults at or near the poverty level, there to find themselves enmeshed in a web of burdens that tend to precipitate (or intensify) mental and somatic morbidity; in turn, such precipitations propel the descent deeper into chronic, personality-crushing indigency. Here, we would suggest, is America's own displaced-persons problem.

For basic research, the joint evidence of this chapter and of several collateral studies of general populations here reviewed highlights the status system as an apparatus that differentially sows, reaps, sifts, and redistributes the community's crops of mental morbidity and of sound personalities.

In no way have we claimed that the mental health effects produced by this apparatus are determined by sociocultural processes alone.

Nevertheless, in line with our field of professional competence and responsibility to future investigators, we have advanced a number of hypotheses that implicate certain specific forms of sociocultural processes operating within the framework of the social class system. These hypotheses focus on the four mental health zones we have found dividing Midtown's SES range. Distinguishing these zones, the hypotheses suggest, are economic factors linked to mechanisms of invidious discrimination that pervade the zones' respective way-of-life constellations. These postulates hold that toward one pole of the status range, in both preadult and adult life, such processes tend to penetrate the family unit with eugenic or prophylactic effects for personality development, whereas toward the opposite pole they more often work with pathogenic or precipitating effects.

These hypotheses chart paths of further necessary exploration. They can thereby lay reasonable claim to the attention of the several sciences that are joined in the "crash" research program of social psychiatry.

NOTES

1. David E. Hailman, *The Prevalence of Illness among Male and Female Workers and Housewives*, Public Health Bulletin, 260, United States Public Health Service, 1941.

2. L. G. Rowntree, K. H. McGill, and L. P. Hellman, "Mental and Personality Disorders in Selective Service Registrants," *J. Am. Med. Assoc.*, vol. 128, no. 15, pp. 1084–1087, Aug. 11, 1945.

3. R. W. Hyde and L. V. Kingsley, "Studies in Medical Sociology: The Relation of Mental Disorder to the Community Socioeconomic Level," *New Eng. J. Med.*, vol. 231, pp. 543–548, Oct. 19, 1944. Subjects were classified by place of residence, the residential unit being "the area under the jurisdiction of each local selection board." Each area was rated by criteria of "attractiveness as a residential section." The highest (A) of the six rating categories covered "wealthy suburban communities" and the lowest (F) covered "the worst Boston slums."

4. Reported in *Chronic Illness in a Large City: The Baltimore Study*, 1957. The SES indicator employed was annual family income, as classified in four categories: Under $2,000, $2,000–$3,999, $4,000–$5,999, $6,000 and over.

5. It should be observed that the four investigations had a second common characteristic; namely, psychiatric evaluation of the sample individuals was quite peripheral in emphasis to a physical examination. In the Boston Selective Service investigation, Hyde and Kingsley report that each psychiatrist examined about 50 men in a five-hour day, averaging in fact a few minutes per man. In the Baltimore study, a large number of chronic and acute somatic conditions were in the purview of the examining internists, who also made the psychiatric evaluation—if they were so inclined and scarce time permitted. Thus, the possibilities of judgmental error in the mental morbidity rates of all four studies loom large. Further-

more, when enmeshed in a variable like socioeconomic status, such an element of error can unwittingly work to bias the findings in various directions among different studies.

We can assume that reliability of mental health determination in a general population study partially depends on primacy of the psychiatric focus in the research design and also upon measures for controlling potential bias in the classification process.

6. This hypothesis, it must be emphasized, cannot be tested in the patient aggregate counted by the Midtown Treatment Census nor in the patient aggregate enumerated by the earlier, parallel New Haven Psychiatric Census conducted by Hollingshead and Redlich. Both sets of patients are being held for later discussion of the treatment variable in the chapter that follows.

7. To be sure, the trend in incapacitation rates—except between the extreme strata—is not altogether consistent. It should be remembered, however, that Midtown's mental hospital patients have been drawn principally from the incapacitated group. These patients were excluded from the Home Interview Survey but were included in the Midtown Treatment Census. In the latter operation, we could determine only own SES of patients, in a form allowing delineation of three status levels. As we shall see presently, the hospitalization rates in the upper, middle, and lower of these levels are 0.2, 0.4, and 0.7%, respectively. Accordingly, we can infer that if the hospitalized patients could be added to the several columns in Table 12-1, the trend in incapacitation rates on the SES-origin scale would probably be somewhat smoother and sharper than now appears to be the case.

In any event, the smaller the frequency values in a distribution, the more prone they are to magnify chance fluctuations due to sampling. Thus, with small frequencies some irregularity of trend is a negligible matter if the over-all direction of the trend is clear. Such a trend is discernible in the above incapacitation rates, especially when corrected for the hospitalized patients.

8. Needless to say, this measure carries no claim to a place in the armamentarium of statistics. It is a supplementary reporting device for arithmetical summary of two rates and is employed for the convenience of the reader when intergroup comparisons of such paired rates become too complicated and cumbersome to juggle.

It will be recognized that the term "Sick" is paired with "Well" only as a short substitute designation for the sample's Impaired respondents.

9. The intermediate (C and D) levels number 41% of the sample and account for 41 and 39% of the Well and Impaired categories, respectively.

10. Thus, parenthetically, our findings do not rest entirely on the impairment band of the Study's mental health spectrum. The frequency of impairment usually varies in a counterpoise congruence with the Well category, in such a way that a generalization about one category often applies in reverse to the other. This seesaw bond seems to reinforce the apparent significance of both mental health types.

11. The three classes are mergers of the six SES-origin strata and carry their original A to F notations. Only by such merger can the progressive shrinkage of cases in subgroups be partially compensated. The price paid, of course, is reduction in the range of SES differences.

12. Of the four age groups in the sample it will be remembered that this is also by far the most favored in mental health composition (cf. Chap. 9).

13. Quoted by R. K. Merton, *Social Theory and Social Structure*, 1949, p. 132.

So ingrained is the emphasis upon status change in the *upward* direction that it can operate as a reflex in seemingly unrelated kinds of spatial situations. Referring to changes in tenancy, for example, a prominent New York realtor reports that in Manhattan "many tenants, commercial as well as residential, have a great reluctance to move down. When they move to new quarters, the space *must be* [italics added] on a higher floor than that which they leave" (*The New York Times*, Apr. 27, 1958). Because of street noises and lack of vistas, avoidance of quarters at low floors is of course utilitarian. However, this rationale is hardly involved in upward changes from quarters on the higher floors of Manhattan's skyscraper apartment houses and office buildings. The penthouse and the executive suite at the crown of the tower are of course physical embodiments symbolizing Carnegie's phrase, "My place is at the top."

14. S. M. Lipset and R. Bendix, *Social Mobility in Industrial Society*, 1959, pp. 65, 251.

15. A. B. Hollingshead and F. C. Redlich, "Schizophrenia and Social Structure," *Am. J. Psychiat.*, vol. 110, no. 9, pp. 695–701, March, 1954.

16. M. H. Lystad, "Social Mobility among Selected Groups of Schizophrenic Patients," *Am. Sociological Rev.*, vol. 22, no. 3, pp. 288–292, June, 1957.

17. Lipset and Bendix, *op. cit.*, p. 65.

18. *Ibid.*, pp. 251–252.

19. E. Douvan and J. Adelson, "The Psychodynamics of Social Mobility in Adolescent Boys." *J. Abnormal and Social Psychol.*, vol. 56, no. 1, pp. 31–44, January, 1958.

20. These hypotheses had been influenced by the promising conceptualizations of Ruesch bearing on (1) mobility motivations as emergents from "attitudes toward one's parents" and (2) the distinction between "climbers," and "strainers" as the upward aspiring who did not quite succeed. Ruesch, *op. cit.*, p. 125.

21. Some writers, Ruesch included, tend to view the consequences of upward mobility in terms of stresses that we can subsume under the concept of role discontinuity. As employed in Chap. 9 above, this concept refers to the disjunctive predicament enveloping an individual when he acquires a rather new kind of role without adequate preparation of the requisite psychic defenses and social skills. This concept would probably apply in the main to the relatively rare instances of individuals who rise for economically in a relatively short period of time. However, our observations suggest that in most cases status mobility tendencies go back to the child's socialization in family, age-peer, and school settings. In such instances, furthermore, adolescence tends to be a period of informal apprenticeship in developing skills for the higher-status goal envisaged. Indeed, one of the major functions of high school and college life is to offer just such an apprenticeship. Thus, the usual gradual transition from parental SES to higher own status seems to us to be rather more continuous than discontinuous.

22. Married women were excluded from this analysis because intergeneration status mobility was accomplished in their case through their choice of husband. The wife's effect on his status movement was expected to be secondary to his own personality determinants. Indeed, when we classify wives according to occupational differences between their father and their husband, we find relatively small variations in mental health composition among the three mobility types.

23. The schizophrenic-process respondents form only a small fraction of the down-mobile group.

24. Nine of the latter fathers were in the white-collar category and two in the executive-professional class. If the latter sons represent the extreme type of downward mobility, the six sons who rose from unskilled fathers to top-drawer careers exemplify maximal upward mobility. In this particular sample of American-born males such "rags-to-riches" movement occurred once in every 75 men. It is a plausible guess that the latter is an exceptionally high rate, probably to be found in few populations outside of New York City.

25. In the case of married women, the indicators used were own education and husband's occupation.

26. As evidence of one possible facet in this crisis potentiality, the history of collective pathology is not likely to minimize the significance of industrial Germany's Nazi period.

27. It is not to be assumed that this group has been economically static. Reflecting not unionization but shortages in the local white-collar labor market, city-wide data on clerical office workers indicate that between 1949 and 1959 their salaries increased 59% in dollars and 21% in buying power.

28. Applying as a criterion the frequency of *steady* employment during the minor economic recession of 1958, a national survey revealed a frequency of only 50% among workers with less than nine years schooling, 75% among high school graduates, and 90% among holders of a college degree. Unpublished study by the University of Michigan Survey Research Center and United States Census Bureau.

SOCIAL MOBILITY AND MENTAL ILLNESS

A. B. Hollingshead, R. A. Ellis, and E. C. Kirby

THE idea that an individual's movement in the social structure is associated with the development of psychiatric difficulties has been expressed both by psychiatrists[1] and sociologists.[2] Some empirical research has been done on the question,[3] but psychiatrists and sociologists have not worked together[4] previously to determine if psychiatric patients are more or less mobile socially than comparable non-patients. The research reported here has attempted to do this.[5] However, before the findings are presented, the methodological procedures involved in the study will be outlined.

RESEARCH DESIGN

This research was designed so that class position, on the one hand, and the presence or absence of diagnosed functional mental illness, on the other, could be controlled. It was reasoned that by holding each of these factors constant, premised interrelationships between social mobility and mental illness could be found. To achieve this objective, sub-samples of psycho-neurotic and schizophrenic patients in classes III and V were drawn from the psychiatric population[6] of the New Haven community. Comparable control sub-samples of non-patients from classes III and V were drawn from the general population.[7]

The sub-samples were selected from non-adjacent classes because we believed that the influence of class factors could be determined more easily in persons from distinctly different classes than in persons from adjacent classes. Classes III and V were selected for the following reasons: *first*, these classes have sharply different prevalence rates for treated schizophrenia and psychoneurosis; *second*, they have not been studied carefully in previous psychiatric research; and *third*, they comprise approximately 40 per cent of the population of the New Haven community.

Each class may be characterized briefly as follows: Class III is composed of proprietors of small businesses, white-collar workers, and skilled

Reprinted from *American Sociological Review* (1954), *19*, 577–584, by permission of the American Sociological Association.

manual workers who are, for the most part, high-school graduates. These people live in apartments, flats, and single family dwellings in widely-scattered residential areas. Class V is composed almost exclusively of unskilled and semi-skilled workers who typically have an elementary education or less and who live in the most crowded slum areas of the city.

The combination of patients from two different diagnostic categories and two social classes, with non-patients from the same classes, produced the six cell research design presented in Table 1. A glance at Table 1 will show that each of the four cells for patients is filled with a minimum of 12 cases; each cell for non-patients is populated with 30 individuals.

TABLE 1. NUMBER OF PATIENTS AND NON-PATIENTS STUDIED BY CLASS

	Patients		Non-Patients
Social Classes	Neurotics	Schizo-phrenics	Controls
III	13	13	30
V	12	12	30
Total	25	25	60

All individuals in the study, patients and non-patients, are white and between the ages of 22 and 44. These age limits were imposed because attention was focused upon patients who presumably had reached adult responsibility and adjustment, but who had not entered the involutional period. The ages of the non-patients were held to the same limits so comparisons could be made between the two groups.

Detailed data were collected on each patient by the psychiatrist and sociologists with a 128-page schedule.[8] While the data were being assembled on the patients, the sociologists interviewed the non-patients with a shorter schedule.

The representativeness of the sub-samples of patients and non-patients to their appropriate universes was crucial to the research. This was complicated by the differences in the ways the two sub-samples were obtained. Patients who met the requirements of the research design were selected individually. The non-patients, on the other hand, were selected at random from the 5 per cent systematic sample of the community's population used in earlier phases of the research. Representativeness of the non-patients was determined by comparing them with the systematic sample of the general population on the following variables: age, sex, religion, ethnic origin, and class score. The patients were compared with the psychoneurotics and schizophrenics in the psychiatric population[9] on the same variables. No significant difference was found at the 5 per cent level of confidence on any variable when the two groups were compared with their parent universes.[10] In short, the patients were representative of all psychiatric patients in their appropriate age, sex, class, and diagnostic groups, and the non-patients were representative of the New Haven population in their age, sex, and class groups. When the representativeness of the two sub-samples was established, assumed interrelations between class position, mobility factors, and mental illness were tested.

The general proposition under study hypothesizes that in the several social classes, interrelationships exist between mobility factors and diagnosed psychoneurosis and schizophrenia. Data on only two types of mobility factors are reported here. They are: (1) achieved social mobility, and (2) discrepancies between an individual's achievements and his aspirations. A specific proposition on each factor was stated as follows:

(1) A differential relationship exists in the amount of social mobility achieved by non-patients in comparison with psychoneurotics, or schizophrenics, in classes III and V.
(2) A significant discrepancy exists between a class III, or a class V, psychoneurotic's or schizophrenic's achievements and his aspirations.

The first proposition grew out of analyses the team had made of different aspects of mobility among 847 schizophrenics in an extensive study reported elsewhere.[11] That work indicated that the originally hypothesized relationship between status striving and mental disorders was probably different in the several classes. The second proposition was formulated after preliminary analysis of the data on mobility indicated interrelationships between the disorders of the psychoneurotic and schizophrenic patients and their efforts to realize their aspirations. Unfortunately, we were unable to make the same analyses in the non-patient group, because the data were not identical for the patients and non-patients.

THE FINDINGS

Proposition One: Achieved Social Mobility. Statistical tests of the first proposition were dependent upon the measurement of achieved social mobility. It was measured by the use of Hollingshead's two factor *Index of Social Position*. This *Index* is based upon education and occupation. To use it, the number of years of school the individual has completed is scored on an educational scale; likewise, his occupation is scored on an occupational scale.[12] Then, the scale value for education is multiplied by a weight of six, and the scale value for occupation by a weight of eight. The resulting calculated score is assumed to be a measure of the individual's position in the community's class structure.[13]

Two *index* scores were computed on each patient and non-patient. The first was the score of the individual's parental family; the second was the score of the individual being studied. The difference between the score of the parental family and the score of the individual in the study, whether positive or negative, was used as the measure of the individual's achieved social mobility. If the difference was positive, the individual was considered to be upward mobile; if negative, he was viewed as downward mobile.[14]

When achieved social mobility had been defined, the crucial question was: Have the psychoneurotics or the schizophrenics in either class III or class V been significantly more mobile or less mobile than the non-patients? Answers to this question were sought by making a series of comparisons of social mobility scores of the non-patients with the patients.[15]

Achieved Social Mobility in Class III.

Class III individuals, both patients and non-patients, were far more mobile than class V individuals.[16] As we expected, achieved social mobility in class III was almost entirely upward. Only three individuals were downward mobile by as many as 10 points; one was a non-patient, one was a psychoneurotic, and one was a schizophrenic. All others were upward mobile by varying amounts. Three patients moved upward more than 50 points. All were females; one was a psychoneurotic; the others were schizophrenics.

The amounts of mobility achieved by the non-patients, the psychoneurotics, and the schizophrenics, are summarized in Table 2. Table 2 shows that, in comparison with their parental families, the non-patients moved upward 20 points, the psychoneurotics 27 points, and the schizophrenics 36 points on the *Index of Social Position*. The differences in achieved upward mobility between both the psychoneurotics and the non-patients, and the schizophrenics and the non-patients, are striking.[17] These data indicate a definite inter-relationship between social mobility and mental illness. The controls have been the least mobile, and the schizophrenics the most mobile of the three groups. This suggests a correlation between the extent of a class III individual's achieved mobility and the severity of his illness.[18]

TABLE 2. MEAN NUMBER OF MOBILITY POINTS ACHIEVED BY THE NON-PATIENTS, THE PSYCHONEUROTICS, AND THE SCHIZOPHRENICS BY CLASS

Group	Points Achieved in Each Class	
	III	V
Non-patients	20	8
Psychoneurotics	27	12
Schizophrenics	36	8

Since the achieved mobility scores were calculated by comparing the scores of the present generation with the parental generation, the next step was to determine if the non-patients, the psychoneurotics, and the schizophrenics had the same, or different, parental base lines. Components included in the base line were: (1) the *Index of Social Position* of the family or orientation; (2) ethnic origins, and the number of generations in the United States; (3) religious affiliation; and (4) community of origin. No significant differences were found on any of these factors,[19] when the non-patients in class III were compared with the psychoneurotics and schizophrenics. Two conclusions were clear from these comparisons: first, that the three groups, non-patients, psychoneurotics, and schizophrenics, had come from an essentially homogeneous social and cultural base; any differences that existed were of a random order; second, that the demonstrated differences in achieved social mobility in the present generation were produced by the differential efforts of the individuals in the study to attain more education and to get better jobs than their parents had had. In addition, the inference may be made that the psychoneurotics, and especially the schizophrenics, were over-achievers.

Achieved Social Mobility in Class V.[20]

The average achieved social mobility for each group in class V is summarized also in Table 2. A glance at Table 2 will show that the non-patients, on the average, moved upward 8 points. The schizophrenics also moved upward 8 points, but the psychoneurotics made a 12 point gain. The amount of upward mobility achieved by the psychoneurotics, is significantly more than by the non-patients; obviously, there is no difference between the non-patients and the schizophrenics.[21]

The analysis of the data on the family base lines of the class V's showed that there were no significant differences between the patients and the non-patients on ethnic origins and the number of generations in the United States, religion, or community of origin. However, the psychoneurotics came from families with lower scores on the *Index of Social Position* than the non-patients. This difference was not significant, but the tendency was strong. The schizophrenic patients came from a significantly lower base line than the non-patients. In fact, *all* of the schizophrenics came from families with the lowest possible scores on the *Index of Social Position*. This fact needs to be taken into consideration in any interpretation of the amount of achieved mobility among these patients.

The demonstrated relationship between upward mobility and psychoneurosis in both class III and class V, is in accordance with the first proposition; but, the data on the schizophrenics only partially support it. In class III, the schizophrenic patients are significantly more mobile than the non-patients; in class V there are no differences on the amount of mobility achieved by the schizophrenics and the non-patient's. However, the data on the patients and the non-patients in class III, and in class V, are consonant with the assumption that achieved social mobility is a function of an individual's position in the class system. Stated otherwise, the data show that the class III individual is in a position to achieve a considerable measure of upward mobility, but the class V individual does not have the same kinds or types of opportunity.

Proposition Two: Discrepancies Between Achievement and Aspiration.

The attempt to assess the meaning that education and occupation had for the patients gave rise to the second proposition, regarding meaningful inter-relationships between what the patients had achieved and what they had hoped to achieve. Achievement was defined, in accordance with proposition one, as the position a patient had attained educationally and occupationally. What he said he wanted to achieve in each area was defined as aspiration. The difference between what was attained and what was hoped for was defined as discrepancy. The discrepancy, if any, between achievement and aspiration was assumed to be a stress vector in the patient's life.

Throughout this phase of the analysis we were concerned with the question: Are the aspirations expressed by these patients an integral part of their personality structures or are they merely scenery on the stages of their make-believe worlds? In order to answer this question, each patient's history was studied to determine if evidence supported his statements of his aspirations. If his pre-morbid behavior indicated he had made more or less consistent efforts to bridge the gap between his claimed aspirations and his actual achievements, it was inferred that verbalized statements of his hopes were meaningful elements in his personality.

Educational Discrepancies—Class III.

The data on educational achievement, aspiration, and discrepancies in class III are summarized in Table 3. This tabulation shows that the average

TABLE 3. MEAN EDUCATIONAL ACHIEVEMENT AND ASPIRATIONS MEASURED IN YEARS OF SCHOOL FOR CLASS III PSYCHONEUROTICS AND SCHIZOPHRENICS

Educational	Years of School	
	Psychoneurotics	Schizophrenics
Achievement	13.3	14.1
Aspiration	16.1	16.4
Discrepancy	2.8	2.3
	$F = 8.688$, 1/25	$F = 6.988$, 1/25
	p less than .01	p less than .05

class III psychoneurotic completed slightly more than one year of college, but he aspired to a college degree. The average class III schizophrenic completed two years of college, and he too, wanted to finish college. The discrepancy between educational achievement and aspiration among the class III psychoneurotics and schizophrenics is significant.

Twelve of the 13 psychoneurotics in class III were dissatisfied with the amount of education they received. One of the 12 summed up these feelings of educational inadequacy when he said with reference to his hopes for his children's education: "Parents today want their children to have the amount of education that the parents themselves wanted to receive." This man had worked his way through two years to college, and he was eager to see his children realize the hopes he had once held for himself. This man was typical, for all these patients had worked hard to achieve their educations. Moreover, they viewed education as the area of activity that would enable them to realize their goals in life.

In class III, schizophrenics emphasized educa-

tion more strongly than the psychoneurotics; and they implemented their desires by going to school a year longer, on the average. Every schizophrenic had put forth great personal efforts to obtain his education. He was usually a good student; and he enjoyed school. Typically his problem was to get enough education to prepare him for the job he wanted. He worked upon the premise that if he could get enough education he would get the desired job, then he would be accepted socially, and his problems would be ended. Finally, he looked upon education as a panacea for his personal and social problems.

Apparently these patients did not recognize that factors other than education are involved in the realization of successful aspirations. For example, one patient with an I.Q. of 140 graduated in 1936 from high school at the age of 16, with an "A" average. He intensely desired to enter an Ivy League university, but his family was on relief. He took examinations for the United States Military Academy, but did not pass the physical examination. At this point in his career he had a schizophrenic break with a remission of symptoms. He went to work instead of to college, and his dream of a college education appeared to be but a memory. However, World War II came and he joined the Army. While he was overseas he had another psychiatric break and was hospitalized. After the war he married, had a family, and applied for educational benefits under the G.I. Bill, entered college, but not in the Ivy League, and began upon the realization of his educational dream. He worked nights to supplement his G.I. benefits and to support his family, and completed the work for his bachelor's degree in the usual four years. However, he discovered to his dismay, that his college education had not fitted him for a particular job he desired. He was frustrated, angry, and misunderstood. His wife could not understand why he could not step out and command a job commensurate with his education so that she could be supported in the style she had dreamed of in the years he was in college. His parents could not see why their son did not get the kind of job they thought a college man should have. He did not realize that he was ten years older than the usual college graduate, and that employers were more interested in this fact than in his education. In short, this man, like the other class III schizophrenics who had over-aspired and over-achieved in the educational sphere, was not able to consolidate his educational achievement. The net result was excruciating anxiety over his failure to realize his job and status aspirations.

Class V.

Educational achievements and aspirations among the class V patients are summarized in Table 4. This tabulation shows that the discrepancy

TABLE 4. MEAN EDUCATIONAL ACHIEVEMENT AND ASPIRATIONS MEASURED IN YEARS OF SCHOOL FOR CLASS V PSYCHONEUROTICS AND SCHIZOPHRENICS

| Educational | Years of School | |
	Psychoneurotics	Schizophrenics
Achievement	8.9	7.3
Aspiration	13.8	10.6
Discrepancy	4.8	3.3
	$F = 14.158, 1/23$	$F = 6.462, 1/23$
	p less than .01	p less than .05

between achievement and aspiration is significant for both the psychoneurotics and the schizophrenics.

The class V psychoneurotics believed they could have had skilled jobs, or clerical positions, if only they had been able to finish high school and had received specialized vocational training. They stated their aspirations largely in terms of a better job, and they looked retrospectively to education to solve their economic problems. The function of education, as they looked back upon it, was to prepare an individual for a good job. A good job meant a higher standard of living, and, if one lived well, what other problems could one have?

The class V schizophrenics all encountered educational frustrations. Most of them were compelled to leave elementary school, at the earliest legal age, by a combination of economic circumstances and parental indifference, if not hostility, toward education. As adults they regretted their lack of an education, and they were aware that they could not improve their positions without more education, but they felt incapable of obtaining it.

Occupational Discrepancies—Class III.

When we turn from the educational to the occupational area, we find a definite discrepancy between the actual and the idealized. However, there are no differences in the occupations engaged in by the class III psychoneurotics in comparison with the class III schizophrenics. Both groups have moved in this generation from manual work into work that requires specialized training and reasonably smooth interpersonal relations. The men are employed as clerks, salesmen, and supervisors; the women are employed, or they were before marriage, as secretaries, elementary teachers,

nurses, and technicians. Although the occupational achievements of both sexes have been substantial, their aspirations are far above their accomplishments. The men would like to be professionals, or in business for themselves; the women would prefer to be professionals, or married to professional men. The occupational reference groups of the patients include lawyers, doctors, professors, engineers, artists, musicians, and business executives.

Only two class III patients—both female—were satisfied occupationally; one was a psychoneurotic and the other was a schizophrenic. The story of the schizophrenic will be outlined to illustrate how this woman's aspirations were linked with her emotional problems. She struggled, over a seven-year period, to work her way through college and a year of graduate school. She obtained a job as a research assistant as soon as she finished her studies. She liked her job, but she was very dissatisfied with the pay and the fact that she saw books, not people. She was forced, by her low salary, to live with several girls, when she desired an apartment of her own, social life, and male friends. She realized her educational and occupational goals, but they did not provide her with the things she thought they would. She became anxiety-ridden when she saw that the social goals she had hoped to attain through her long struggle for an education were beyond her reach. Shortly after she realized that her education and her job did not solve her personal-emotional problems, her ego structure collapsed, and she experienced a psychotic episode.

This woman felt throughout her life that she was handicapped severely by her family background. She aspired to a higher status than the one ascribed to her by her family of orientation, and she struggled to achieve a desired social position through education. In the end, she was trapped by her failure to utilize her educational achievement to solve her emotional needs in the social sphere.

Class V.

The class V patients, both psychoneurotics and schizophrenics, were either semi-skilled or unskilled workers. They felt their jobs were unsatisfactory; they worried about how long they would last, the nature of the work, that they did not pay enough to meet the needs of their families, that there was no advancement, that the job carried no status, and so on through a long series of specific irritations.

The jobs they aspired to were relatively modest ones, such as stationary engineer, machinist, a foremanship, clerical work. Significantly, not a single class V patient realized his occupational aspirations.

As a group, they were aware of the connection between good jobs, steady jobs, jobs that paid a living wage, and a dreamed-of standard of living. Occupational aspirations were stronger among the class V women, both patients and spouses of patients, than among the men. Apparently, they visualized the connection between education, jobs, and mobility better than the men. About one-half of the men hoped for a steady, semi-skilled factory job; the remainder dreamed of skilled jobs. Their wives, however, wanted more money, shorter hours, higher status jobs for their husbands, and a "better shake for the kids."

DISCUSSION

Vertical mobility has been shown to be a factor of significance in both schizophrenia and psychoneurosis, in the representative samples of two classes of the New Haven population. This does not necessarily mean that mobility is the only, or even the principal, causative factor. Nor is there any information here concerning how this factor may contribute to mental abnormality. It seems clear, however, that the relations between status striving, anxiety, and mental health, deserve further intensive investigation.

NOTES

* Paper read at the annual meeting of the Eastern Sociological Society, April 3–4, 1954. The research reported here is supported by a grant from the National Institute of Mental Health of the United States Public Health Service to Yale University under the direction of Dr. F. C. Redlich, Chairman, Department of Psychiatry, and Professor August B. Hollingshead, Department of Sociology.

1. Sigmund Freud, *Collected Papers,* Vol. III, No. 4, Psychoanalytic Notes Upon an Autobiographical Account of a Case of Paranoia (Dementia Paranoides), pp. 445 ff; Karen Horney, *The Neurotic Personality of Our Time,* New York: Norton and Co., Inc., 1937, pp. 80–82, 178–179; Abraham Myerson, "Review of *Mental Disorders in Urban Areas,*" *American Journal of Psychiatry,* 96 (January, 1940), pp. 995–997.

2. Pitirim Sorokin, *Social Mobility,* New York: Harper and Brothers, 1927, especially, pp. 510–511, 515, 522–525; W. L. Warner, "The Society, The Individual and His Mental Disorders," *American Journal of Psychiatry,* 94 (September, 1937), pp. 275–284; R. K. Merton and Alice S. Kitt, "Reference Group Theory and Social Mobility," in R. K. Merton and Paul F. Lazarsfeld, *Studies in the Scope and Method of "The American Soldier,"* Glencoe, Illinois: The Free Press, 1950, pp. 84–88.

3. J. Ruesch and others, *Chronic Disease and Psychological Invalidism,* New York: American Society for Research in Psychosomatic Problems, 1946; J. Ruesch, Annemarie Jacobson, and Martin B. Loeb, "Acculturation and Illness," *Psychological Monographs: General and Applied,* 62 (1948), Whole No. 292; John Dollard, "The Life History in Community Studies," *American Sociological Review,* 3 (October, 1938), pp. 724–737; John Dollard and Neal Miller, *Personality and Psychotherapy,* New York: McGraw-Hill, 1950; Evelyn Ellis, "Social Psychological Correlates of Upward Social Mobility Among Unmarried Career Women," *American Sociological Review,* 17 (October, 1952), pp. 558–563.

4. The present research team is composed of two psychiatrists, Drs. F. C. Redlich and B. H. Roberts, and two sociologists, A. B. Hollingshead and J. K. Myers.

5. For earlier reports on this research see: A. B. Hollingshead and F. C. Redlich, "Social Stratification and Psychiatric Disorders," *American Sociological Review,* 18 (April, 1953), pp. 163–169; F. C. Redlich, A. B. Hollingshead, *et al.,* "Social Structure and Psychiatric Disorders," *American Journal of Psychiatry,* 109 (April, 1953), pp. 729–734; H. A. Robinson, F. C. Redlich and J. K. Myers, "Social Structure and Psychiatric Treatment," *American Journal of Orthopsychiatry* (April, 1954).

6. A *Psychiatric Census* of patients in the New Haven community on December 1, 1950, was taken by the Research Team. For a report of this activity, see A. B. Hollingshead and F. C. Redlich, "Social Stratification and Psychiatric Disorders," *op. cit.,* p. 166.

7. A systematic 5 per cent sample of the population of the

New Haven community in November, 1950, was interviewed by the Research Team. This is reported in *ibid.*

8. The schedule was divided into four parts. The first part was filled out by a psychiatrist in interviews with the patient; the second was filled out by a psychiatrist in an interview with the patient's therapist. The third and fourth parts were filled out by a sociologist in interviews with members of the patient's family of orientation and his family of procreation. In addition, considerable material came from the clinical record and the clinical interview that Dr. Redlich had with each patient at the end of the interviewing process. As a last step, the team developed two assessment schedules to evaluate the data systematically. The schedule covered the following areas: psychopathological history, history of physical illnesses, attitude toward psychiatry and psychiatric treatment, social identification, family dynamics, education, religion, ethnicity, recreation, occupation, housing, and social class.

9. The patients in the *Psychiatric Census* mentioned in Footnote 6 are referred to here.

10. Chi-square, the *t-test,* and analysis of variance were used on appropriate variables to determine whether the subsample under test varied significantly from its parent universe.

11. A. B. Hollingshead and F. C. Redlich, "Social Stratification and Schizophrenia," *American Sociological Review,* 19 (June, 1954); A. B. Hollingshead and F. C. Redlich, "Schizophrenia and Social Structure," *American Journal of Psychiatry,* 110 (March, 1954), pp. 695–701.

12. The occupational rating used here was the last job the patient held before he entered treatment. His father's occupation was the one he followed in his mature years.

13. The scores on this *Index* range from 14 to 98. A score 14 represents the highest position an individual could reach by a combination of outstanding educational and occupational achievements and 98 the lowest position. To receive a score of 14 an individual has to have a graduate professional degree, and be engaged in a profession, or be a high executive in a large business. A score of 98 is assigned to an individual with less than seven years of schooling, who is an unskilled laborer. All degrees of education and types of jobs fall within these extremes.

14. Difference in scores between the parental and the present generation could be a consequence, either of the increased amount of education received by the present generation, or changes in the occupational structure that have occurred over a generation. A third possibility is that they are a combination of both. Although this point is of general interest it is not germane to this discussion, because changes in the educational and occupational areas of the culture have been controlled by the research design.

15. The *t-test* was relied upon in each comparison to determine significance of the differences between the mobility scores of the control and the patient groups.

16. This finding was in accord with the general assumption

that class III represents one sub-cultural group, and class V a distinctly different one. Comparisons of social mobility between class III and class V controls, schizophrenics, and psychoneurotics produced 2-tailed t-test values that were significant beyond the .005 level of confidence.

17. Differences between (a) the psychoneurotics and the non-patients are significant beyond the 10 per cent level of confidence; (b) the schizophrenics and the non-patients beyond 5 per cent level of confidence. Interpretation of these levels of significance requires a word of explanation. The t-test was used to test significance of differences. When this test is used on relatively small samples with large variances the degree of significance that may be expected is limited. Since our samples were small and the variances were large, the significance of the differences stated here is conservative.

18. When the distinct relationship had been found between achieved social mobility and both psychoneurosis and schizophrenia, social mobility scores were computed on the patients' adult brothers and sisters to see if they had been as mobile as the patients. This operation showed that the psychoneurotic and schizophrenic patients in class III had been significantly more mobile than their siblings. The one-tailed *sign test* was used. Probability was less than 2 per cent for the psychoneurotics,

and less than 5 per cent for the schizophrenics in comparison with the median of their adult siblings.

19. The t-test was used to test significance of difference on the *Index of Social Position* between the families of orientation of the non-patients in comparison with the psychoneurotics, and the schizophrenics; chi-square was used to test significance on the other factors in the base lines.

20. Achieved social mobility patterns are very different in class V from those in class III. Class V individuals are not as mobile as the class III's, but the general tendency is upward. Surprisingly enough, no class V individual was downward mobile and only one, a schizophrenic, was upward mobile by as many as 20 points. These figures indicate that there is much less variance in class V than in class III.

21. When the achieved mobility data of the patients were compared with those of their adult brothers and sisters, no significant difference was found between the mobility scores of the psychoneurotics and their siblings. The schizophrenics, however, had significantly lower mobility scores than their brothers and sisters. They appeared to be under-achievers within the sibling group. However, the differences between the schizophrenic patients and their non-patient siblings were small.

GOAL-STRIVING, SOCIAL STATUS, AND MENTAL

DISORDER: A RESEARCH REVIEW

Robert J. Kleiner and Seymour Parker

IN both the professional and the popular literature, one frequently encounters the idea that excessive goal striving and frustration because of failure to reach desired goals are responsible for mental illness. Merton,[1] for instance, has stimulated considerable research in this area by his suggestive work concerning the relationship of anomie, status striving, and deviant behavior (e.g., crime, mental illness, alcholism, etc.). Also some of the theorizing and experimental research of Lewin, Festinger, and their associates[2] on the determinants of goal-striving behavior is related to this problem.

This paper attempts to review some of the research on the relationship of status position, social mobility, and mobility orientation (i.e., discrepancy between achievement and aspiration) to mental illness. Although work on the periphery of this problem is considerable, the connection among these phenomena has been insufficiently explored. These three independent variables link both sociological and psychological factors to each other and to mental disorder. Most of the studies in this field correlate *either* one or the other of these concepts with mental disorder. In reviewing the literature, the authors were impressed with the need to bring together in one review some of the disparate findings, and to suggest the possible interrelationship of the data. This attempt also provides an opportunity to discuss some of the methodological problems that arise in this research.

The central theme of the review will be the relationship between goal-striving behavior and mental disorder. The first of the variables mentioned above, status position, is intimately related to various aspects of goal striving. The position an individual has achieved will affect the nature of his aspirations, will limit his potential for social mobility, and will affect his preception of his chances of obtaining his goals. The second variable, social mobility, is related to the social distance a person has moved, from a point of time in the past,

Reprinted from *American Sociological Review* (April, 1963), *28* (2), 169–203, by permission of the American Sociological Association.

to his present level of achievement. One may assume that the individual who has experienced a high degree of upward status mobility feels successful and is thus psychiatrically relatively healthy. On the other hand, it is also possible that status mobility is accompanied by shifting reference groups and concomitant interpersonal disturbances. The third independent variable, mobility orientation, is a major source, and probably a more direct measure, of frustration. Although the review will be limited to the above-mentioned variables, there is no implication that they represent either the only, or the most important, factors in mental disorder.

"Mental illness" is difficult to define. However, without defining the term, we may still delimit the kinds of data to be included under this rubric. The studies to be reviewed embrace mental illness and emotional instability as diagnosed by judgments of qualified medical and non-medical personnel, making use of clinical interviews, psychological tests, and scores on questionnaire check-lists of psychosomatic and neurotic symptoms. Although "casting such a wide net" raises many problems of its own, the existing level of knowledge concerning the nature and limits of "mental illness" (and mental health) does not warrant a constriction of the definition to include only medically diagnosed cases. In addition to the problem of inadequate knowledge of the nature of these disorders, recent studies by Leighton, Rennie, Pasamanick, and others, show that large numbers of undiagnosed and untreated "cases" exist in the community population, imposing limits on the generalizing value of incidence and prevalence studies of medically diagnosed cases.

STATUS POSITION AND MENTAL DISORDER

The research findings concerning the relationship between socio-economic status and mental illness are both numerous and confusing. Confusion is sometimes compounded by failure to distinguish between incidence and prevalence studies. Incidence is generally defined as the number of *new* cases appearing within a given interval of time, while prevalence refers to *all* cases active during a given interval. Prevalence rates, which include re-entries (or re-admissions), continuations, and first admissions, provide valuable information with regard to the frequency of disease in general. When interest is focused on etiological factors, however, incidence studies are superior because the new case is closer in time to the precipitating conditions.

A number of studies have indicated that a high *incidence* of schizophrenia is associated with low socio-economic status. Faris and Dunham,[3] in their studies of the distribution of mental hospital first admissions in the Chicago area during the 1930's, found that the low status areas of the city sent much larger proportions of their residents to the mental hospitals than did those areas designated as middle or upper status. Although schizophrenia conformed to this pattern, manic-depressive psychoses showed a relatively uniform distribution throughout the various status groups. Similar findings have subsequently been reported for a number of different areas. Titze, Lemkau, and Cooper[4] found that high rates of schizophrenia in Baltimore were associated with lower class status. Manic-depressive disorders were slightly more common in upper class groups. The earlier findings in Chicago (with respect to both types of disorders) were also confirmed in a subsequent study in that city by Clark.[5] Kaplan, Reed, and Richardson[6] reported a higher incidence of undifferentiated hospitalized psychoses in a lower and lower-middle class area of Boston than in an upper and upper-middle class section. The inverse relationship between the incidence of schizophrenia and social class was also found in England and Wales.[7]

Hollingshead and Redlich[8] carefully studied treated mental disorder in New Haven. Incidence rates revealed a slightly different picture than the studies previously mentioned. While rates of psychoses were highest for Class V (lower-class), there was but little differentiation from Class I-II to Class IV. For schizophrenia, there was a linear increase from Class I-II to Class V. Neuroses, on the other hand, showed no relationship to social class.

Clausen and Kohn[9] found no relationship between the incidence of schizophrenia and socio-economic position in a small city in Maryland. Jaco[10] reported a curvilinear relationship between the incidence of all psychoses and social status in the state of Texas. Incidence rates were high among those who had the lowest and the highest

occupational and educational statuses, and were low among those in medium status positions. In a study of the Negro population of Philadelphia, Parker, Kleiner, and Eskin[11] reported that the incidence rates of schizophrenia, character disorder, and total mental illness were not linear in this population. There was a direct increase in these rates from Class I (high) to Class III, with a relatively small drop in the lowest status group (Class IV). Neuroses showed no social class differences. Kleiner, Tuckman, and Lavell[12] showed that Catholics in Pennsylvania (1951–1956) had significantly higher incidence rates of schizophrenia than Protestants, despite the similarity of their status positions (as measured by occupation and education). These investigators also found no relationship between occupational status and incidence of schizophrenia among Negroes (in Pennsylvania, 1951–1956), but there was some evidence of an inverse relationship among white patients.[13] Incidence studies in Australia,[14] in Norway,[15] and in England[16] also failed to confirm the inverse relationship between status and schizophrenia, manic-depressive psychoses, or psychoneuroses. The research cited in this section indicates that the stability of socio-economic position in predicting mental disorder is open to question. However, further conceptual clarification, both of the independent variable of status position and the dependent variable of mental disorder, is necessary before a definitive conclusion can be reached.

In a report of *prevalence* rates, Hollingshead and Redlich[17] found that the rates of treated (undifferentiated) psychiatric illness were highest in the lowest social class (Class V). However, patients were actually under-represented in Classes I through IV.[18] Furthermore, this under-representation increased from Classes I to IV. If socio-economic status and treated psychiatric illness were inversely related, under-representation should have decreased. There were no significant differences in morbidity rates of Classes I through IV; the reported inverse relationship was due to a marked over-representation of patients in Class V. While the prevalence of psychoses was inversely related to status position, neurotic disorders varied directly with socio-economic status. In examining the separate components of prevalence (i.e., incidence, re-entry, and continuations), it was found that these two relationships could be largely accounted for by one of these elements— continuations.

All of the previously mentioned studies deal with diagnosed mental disorder. It is generally recognized that many undiagnosed "cases" do not come to the attention of the medical profession and continue to live in the community. Because of the possibly biased picture presented by hospital statistics, there is widespread interest in whether the inverse relationship would be confirmed in studies of the distribution of mental disorder outside the mental hospital. Attempts to answer this question must deal with the complex problem of how to identify mental disorder in the general population. It is impossible to diagnose even a sample of the community population by accepted psychiatric diagnostic procedures—hence the development and use of various questionnaire methods designed to obtain information on such things as psychosomatic and other psychopathological symptoms.[19] In an extensive prevalence survey of the non-hospitalized population in an area of New York City, Srole, Langner, Michael, Opler, and Rennie[20] reported that, when the severity of psychiatric disturbance was considered, the usual inverse relationship was found. High status individuals had fewer representatives in the "impaired" group and more in the "well" group. In a preliminary study, Rennie, Srole, Opler, and Langner[21] found that 75 per cent of the entire community sample showed "significant" (pathological) anxiety. The proportion of anxious individuals was about the same in the lower, middle, and upper status groups. It is interesting that when all the respondents were classified according to diagnostic "types," the "psychotic type" was inversely related to class status, the "neurotic type" was directly related, and the "neurotic type with prominent symptoms" varied independently of class position.

Still another prevalence study of psychiatric disorder in a representative sample of the non-hopitalized population was conducted in Baltimore by Pasamanick, Roberts, Lemkau, and Krueger.[22] The majority of respondents were examined by (non-psychiatric) physicians and a diagnosis arrived at by clinical evaluation procedures. When the population was divided into five status groups, it was found that, except for the lowest group, psychotic disorders generally decreased as income increased. The exception was explained by the fact that Negroes, who had lower rates of psychoses than their white counterparts, were concentrated in this group. For neurotic disorders, there was a U-shaped curve, the rates being high in the low status group, declining in the middle status group, and rising once more in the highest status group. There was a direct relationship between the prevalence of psychosomatic complaints and

economic status. Primrose[23] failed to find any significant relationship between prevalence of psychoses or neuroses and social class in a community in Northern Scotland. Character disorders, however, showed a greater concentration in the lowest status group. A combination of neuroses and "some" character disorders revealed a U-shaped distribution—higher prevalence rates both in the highest and lowest classes.

Several investigators attempted to determine incidence rates in non-hospitalized populations. Hyde and Kingsley[24] gathered statistics on a large number of inductees rejected by the armed services for psychiatric reasons. The number of psychiatric rejections varied inversely with the economic status of the communities from which the inductees came. Kaplan, Reed, and Richardson[25] reported the rates of non-hospitalized psychoses to be greater in an upper class community. This conclusion was based on information gathered from "sophisticated" informants in the community. Lin[26] also failed to confirm the inverse relationship between mental disorder and socioeconomic status in three Formosan communities.

Sewell and Haller[27] administered a questionnaire to 1,462 elementary school children. This instrument was designed to explore the relationship between class position (of the family) and symptoms of nervousness and anxiety. The children were placed either in an upper or lower status group. Lower status students scored higher than those in the upper group, both for nervous symptoms and general anxiety. This finding seems consistent with Auld's comprehensive review of the literature[28] dealing with the relationship of status position and neurotic symptoms as gauged by the Rorschach, the T.A.T., the M.M.P.I., and other psychological tests. He noted that almost all of the studies showed either a significant inverse relationship or a tendency in this direction. In no study was there a direct relationship between class and neuroticism.

Although there is no consistent inverse relationship between mental illness and status position, it appears from these findings that, for treated schizophrenia and total psychoses, there exists an excess of illness in the lower status groups. In spite of some contradictory evidence, this tendency appears more pronounced in the incidence studies. Notwithstanding the impressive results of Hollingshead and Redlich, it is difficult to generalize with any confidence about results of the prevalence studies (of treated cases) noted in this paper. For manic-depressive psychosis, psychoneurosis, and psychosomatic symptoms, the data are even more inconclusive. However, these conditions tend to show a more even class distribution than schizophrenia, and, in some cases, a slightly higher rate in the upper status groups. In the non-hospitalized population, most of the evidence again indicates more serious pathology in the lower status groups.

An overview of the results presented in this section indicates that the relationship between status and mental disorder is by no means a simple one and may be complicated by varying definitions of mental disorder, different case-finding methods. and the nature of the class system in the community being studied. In a recent article on social status, Jackson[29] concluded that the components of social status commonly used (e.g., education, occupation, etc.) were experienced psychologically as "separate and distinct status dimensions in America today." This investigator raised serious questions about the advisability of determining an overall status rank by averaging the various disparate status ranks of an individual. It is possible that, even if the same components of status position are used and the same weights assigned to them (which is not usual), the psychological meaning and social concomitants of a given status position may vary in different types of communities. The finding of Clausen and Kohn[30] that the usual inverse relationship did not hold for a small urban community is suggestive in this regard. The studies reported by Pasamanick, and his associates,[31] and by Kleiner, Tuckman, and Lavell[32] indicate that the status dimension, as it applies to mental disorder, may operate differently for whites and Negroes. Further exploration of this phenomenon necessitates a more precise delineation of the character of the populations and the communities in which the findings are made, and an understanding of the more subtle intervening variables in these gross epidemiological relationships.

A study pertinent to this problem of intervening variables was recently reported by Tuckman and Kleiner.[33] These investigators found that, by applying an index of discrepancy (between education as an indicator of aspiration, and occupation as an indicator of achievement) to various social groups, they could predict rates of schizophrenia with greater accuracy than by using conventional criteria of social status position. In addition, their method provides an explicit theoretical rationale for the predictions, clearly related to the unifying theme of this review. The paper by Tuckman and Kleiner suggested a relationship between a high discrepancy in goal-striving behavior, and mental disorder. If this intervening variable is pertinent to the discussion of status position and mental disorder, it is important to establish a link between status position and discrepancy. A number of studies enable us to do this. Gould[34] found that, in a sample of 81 college students, those from a lower socio-economic background tended to have higher discrepancies between actual performance and aspiration on experimentally created tasks. Empey[35] reported that, while the absolute occupational status aspirations of lower class senior high school students were lower than those either of the middle or upper class, their *relative* occupational aspirations (i.e., distance between their fathers' occupations and their own occupational aspirations) were higher than either of the two other groups. The idea of a relatively larger discrepancy between achievement and aspiration in the lower class was also supported in a study by Centers and Cantril[36] concerning "income satisfaction and income aspiration." They found that the lower a person's income, the more likely he was to be dissatisfied with his current earnings, and the more he desired a proportionally larger increase. In a recent paper,[37] the authors of this review reported that a low status group with a high rate of mental illness also showed greater goal discrepancies than a high status group with a low rate of illness. Possibly, inconsistencies in previously mentioned studies relating status position to mental disorder can be accounted for by this social-psychological intervening variable (i.e., goal discrepancy). In another paper,[38] the authors reported that native-born Philadelphia Negroes had a higher rate of mental illness than in-migrants from the South. The native-born, who have the higher rate, also occupying higher status positions and show larger goal-striving discrepancies than the in-migrants.

The findings reported in this section have a bearing on whether neurotic and psychotic conditions vary together on one continuum, or are (qualitatively) distinct phenomena that vary independently. It appears that there is no consistent tendency for the relative rates of the neuroses and the psychoses to be similar when comparing different population segments. No clear relationship between social class and these two illness categories is evident in the findings. Even within the psychoses, population groups differ considerably in their relative amounts of schizophrenia and manic-depressive illness. When the variables of psychosomatic symptoms and generalized anxiety are considered, the picture becomes even more confused. As explorations of mental disorder in the general community proceed, it will become increasingly important to examine the relationship between various indices (that are being used) of mental disorder, such as psychosomatic symptoms and anxiety, and diagnosed psychiatric illness. A study conducted by Gurin, Veroff, and Feld[39] showed that the relationship between level of anxiety and nervous symptoms (both obtained by self-reports) is by no means clear. It may be either that the degree of anxiety is causally unrelated to mental disorder, or that certain types of anxiety are more psychopathogenic than others. A start in the investigation of this question has been made by Myers and Roberts.[40]

Another suggestive line of research[41] indicated that the degree to which a given level of discomfort and anxiety motivates an individual to "go to the doctor" is crucially influenced by "the tendency to take the sick role." Thus, before we can properly evaluate the epidemiological evidence on psychiatric disorder, we need to know more about the distribution of the social-psychological factors in the population that influence "the tendency to take the sick role." Research in the behavioral sciences strongly indicates that the course of an illness is influenced by factors other than those thought to be inherently related to the endogenous disease processes.

In summary, the studies reviewed in this section point to the potential value of the discrepancy between achievement and aspirations as an intervening social-psychological variable between status position and mental disorder. Considerable research has been done along these lines, and these studies will be more fully reviewed in a later section.

STATUS MOBILITY AND MENTAL DISORDER

This section deals with changes in the status level of an individual from a baseline of the status position of his parental family, or of his own adult status at an earlier point in time. Research in this area has been concerned mainly with two questions: (1) Can the high rates of mental disorder, often reported for the lower socio-economic groups, be explained by the "downward drift" of sick individuals into a lower socio-economic position? (2) Can social mobility itself (regardless of direction), and degree of such mobility, differentiate between normals and the mentally ill, or between subgroups of the ill population, or between both?

With regard to the first question, if the high rates in the lower class can be explained on this "downward drift" basis, then the factors associated with lower-class life per se, might have little relevance for mental disorder. This question has been discussed many times since the early study of Faris and Durham.[42] Tietze, Lemkau, and Cooper[43] reported that the inverse relationship between schizophrenia and social class could not be explained by pre-psychotic mobility into the lower socio-economic class. Using "place of residence" as a criterion of status position, Lapouse[4] also found evidence that "for first admissions of schizophrenics to state hospitals from Buffalo, the concentration in the low economic areas is not the result of downward drift from higher areas. Nor is there any evidence that the concentration in the poor areas is the result of a recent migration into those areas of mobile men who live alone." More recent studies by Hollingshead and Redlich[45] and Clausen and Kohn[46] support these findings.

Although there is impressive evidence tending to refute the "downward drift" hypothesis, other studies tend to support this hypothesis. Lystad[47] found that schizophrenic patients tended to be significantly more downwardly mobile than a comparable group of non-mentally ill individuals. In their study of a non-hospitalized population in New York City, Srole and his associates,[48] reported that a relatively high proportion of the interviewees having severe psychiatric symptoms have been downwardly mobile. Jaco[4] investigated social mobility in communities yielding different rates of mental disorder and noted more downward mobility (compared to achievement of the parental generation) in communities with high rates of mental illness. In a study carried out in England, Morris[50] reported a heavy concentration of schizophrenic patients in his low status group but noted that the fathers of these patients were randomly distributed throughout all classes. He referred to a downward "drop" as opposed to "drift," observing that the schizophrenics in his sample appeared in Class V immediately after leaving school.

With regard to the second question, there is considerable theorizing to the effect that individuals who have experienced social mobility are more prone to be confused as to their referent groups and their self-identity, thus experiencing concomitant interpersonal difficulties.[51] Ruesch[52] and Ruesch, Jacobson, and Loeb[53] reported that people who had been "social climbers" tended to be more subject to chronic psychosomatic disorders than those who had not been socially mobile, or who had been downwardly mobile. Both Sorokin[54] and Warner[55] speculated that high social mobility in our society was related to mental illness. The data presented by Srole and his associates[56] indicated that, in the non-hospitalized population, 30 per cent of the downwardly mobile individuals were in the severely impaired category, while 23 per cent of the non-mobile individuals, and only 14 per cent of the upwardly mobile, were in this group. This suggests that downward mobility, rather than mobility per se, may be related to the severity of psychiatric symptoms.

The evidence concerning the relationship of social mobility and class position within the mentally ill population is not clear. Hollingshead and Redlich[57] reported that in Class III, using parental achievement as the baseline, schizophrenics had experienced the most upward mobility, neurotics less, and a group of normal controls even less. In addition, the schizophrenics and neurotics in this class had experienced more upward mobility than their siblings. These authors concluded that the mentally ill (especially schizophrenics) in Class III were "over-achievers." However, in Class V, the schizophrenics and normals had the same social mobility relative to parental achievement, while the psychoneurotics were slightly higher. The psychoneurotics showed no difference compared to their siblings, but the schizophrenics showed less upward mobility. This study pointed out that, in general, psychiatric patients showed more upward mobility than normals, and certainly more upward than downward mobility.

Research carried out by Lystad[58] in New Orleans confirmed the Hollingshead and Redlich finding that schizophrenic patients and community controls in the lowest socio-economic group showed the same amount of social mobility, relative to the father's achievement. However, she also found that middle-class community controls showed more upward social mobility than did schizophrenics. These data do not support the findings of Hollingshead and Redlich.

The research reported above does not permit generalizations in this area. It seems that if social mobility is involved in the etiology of mental disorder at all, its relative influence probably differs within the various social class groups. One problem in evaluating the research results in this area stems from the lack of "longitudinal" studies. We need to know more about the temporal relationship between social mobility and the onset of mental illness in order to understand its etiological relevance. Finally, the most serious difficulty is that there is little consensus of opinion in defining and identifying a "case" of mental illness.

MOBILITY ORIENTATION AND MENTAL DISORDER

The research in this area is primarily concerned with the discrepancy between achievement and aspiration and its relation to mental illness. This discrepancy will be referred to as "mobility orientation." There are many assertions in the literature about the relationship between mobility orientation and mental disorder. These are usually based on clinical experience. Such well-known clinicians as Horney[59] and Kardiner[60] emphasize that our society makes status achievement an important element in self-evaluation and self-esteem. Failure to achieve desired goals leads to feelings of worthlessness, and, in some cases, to mental disorder. Kardiner found, in his study of Negroes, that achievement striving was an important etiological factor in the middle class psychopathology, but not in that of the lower class. Studies of mental illness in immigrant populations also maintain that the discrepancy between expected (and desired) and actual achievement frequently leads to mental disorder.[61]

Hollingshead, Ellis, and Kirby[62] investigated this problem in New Haven and found that the mentally ill, both in the lower and middle class, had large discrepancies between their occupational and educational achievements and their aspirations in these areas. These authors concluded that vertical mobility striving and frustrations in both classes were significant in schizophrenia and neurosis, and that these factors merited intensive investigation. Myers and Roberts[63] studied intensively a small sample of psychiatric patients and their families and found that equally large discrepancies existed between the aspirations and achievements of patients both in Class III (middle) and Class V (lower). However, the authors felt that these discrepancies were psychologically significant only in Class III because, while patients in this class spent a great deal of energy striving to narrow the gap between their achievement and aspirations, Class V patients appeared to be more reconciled to the low probability of achieving their aspired goals. In Class III, the prevailing belief was that if a person worked diligently, he would be successful; therefore, the failure of a middle class individual to reach his goals led to a drop in self-esteem and to feelings of depression.

Related to the finding of differences in the emphasis on achievement striving between Class III and Class V individuals are studies of the importance of this factor in various psychiatric diagnostic groups. Controlling for class, schizophrenic patients showed higher discrepancies compared to their siblings than did neurotics.[64] Becker[65] compared the achievement-related characteristics of a small group of manic-depressive patients to a comparable number of normal controls. The psychiatric patients placed significantly more emphasis than the normal controls on achievement values. Since manic-depressive psychosis is significantly associated with middle class status, this indirectly confirms the findings of Myers and Roberts. However, the patients did not score higher than the controls in "need for achievement," as measured by the T.A.T. The author concluded that in manic-depressive patients the high achievement values and conformity behavior seemed to have as a goal the gaining of approval of others rather than satisfying internalized standards. Eysenck and Himmelweit[66] compared goal-striving behavior of two groups of psychiatric patients—those who manifested affective symptoms (i.e., introvert-dysthymic group) and hysterics. They found a marked tendency in the affective group to neglect the reality of their past achievement performance and to be dominated instead by subjective factors. The affective group tended to depreciate their past performances and to over-value (unrealistically) their future possibilities. In his intensive social-psychological study of the "schizophrenic type," Weinberg[67] found that the inability of such patients "to assess their own limitations and/or limitations of a given situation in which they participated was one direct contributing factor in their subsequent breakdowns." He also noted their deep need for approval, leading to intense over-compensatory aspirations. Dunham[68] confirmed this in a study of catatonic schizophrenia.

Hinkle and Wolff[69] found in a large sample (of predominantly working-class persons) that those individuals who were most frustrated in their aspirations and disappointed in their accomplishments also had the highest incidence of illness and showed more disturbances of mood, thought, and behavior than those who came nearer to reaching their aspirations. Sewell and Haller[70] also found a direct relationship between achievement frustration and psychiatric symptoms in a study of 1,462 elementary school children. On the California Test of Personality, lower class children scored as more maladjusted than children in the middle class, and also had significantly more concern over achievement. In addition to showing a direct relationship between concern about achievement and symptoms of maladjustment, this study tended to question the frequently reported finding that socialization in lower socio-economic groups results in a reduction of achievement striving and achievement anxiety.[71] The authors of this review[72] found (for Negro and white populations) that when occupational achievement was controlled, groups with higher educational achievement yielded relatively higher rates of schizophrenia than those with less education. Assuming educational achievement to be an index of level of aspiration, it was inferred that the discrepancies were larger for those with high rates of schizophrenia. In the two previously cited papers by the authors,[73] high rates of mental disorder (including all diagnostic categories) were significantly correlated with large discrepancies between aspiration and achievement. In these studies, the discrepancies were measured directly from data obtained in interviews.

The studies in this section suggest that mobility orientation is a significant factor in mental disorder. In addition, the data indicate that larger discrepancies between achievement and aspiration may be more prevalent among individuals in lower socio-economic groups. However, Myers and Roberts[74] showed that middle class individuals were more psychologically involved in their aspirations. This points to the need for studies of the psychological effects of the individual's subjective probability of goal attainment and the importance of the goal area to him. These variables are suggested by the goal-striving theory of Lewin, Festinger, and their associates.[75]

SMALL GROUP STUDIES OF ACHIEVEMENT-RELATED BEHAVIOR AND MENTAL DISORDER

The studies reported in this section are concerned mainly with small group research, using experimentally created tasks. Although some of these studies were carried out with medically diagnosed psychiatric cases, others employed various measures of maladjustment and anxiety.

A large body of research indicates that persons showing some evidence of maladjustment also tend to select experimentally created tasks that have either a very high or very low probability of being successfully completed. The discrepancies between their actual performances and their aspirations tend to be either extremely high or low (but predominantly high) compared to more "normal" subjects.[76] In a study of the achievement behavior of a group of college students, Atkinson, Bastian, Earl, and Litwin[77] found that individuals who had high needs to avoid failure (as determined by the T.A.T.) tended to avoid tasks having intermediate risks and selected those having either high or low probabilities of success. In a group of 50 neurotic patients, Cohen[78] attempted to determine the relationship between goal-setting behavior, and feelings of self-rejection, as determined by the Rorschach Test. He found that both very high and very low goal settings were significantly related to a high degree of self-rejection. A low degree of self-rejection was related both to medium-high and medium-low goal settings. On the other hand, self-acceptance was found to be associated with low positive or low negative aspirations. Atkinson[79] showed that those with high aspirations also had large discrepancies between their actual and their ideal self-images.

Individuals in need of psychotherapy also had large discrepancies between their perceptions of what they were and what they would like to be.[80] Pauline Sears[81] found a definite relationship between various personality traits and achievement behavior on experimentally created tasks. Students who had negative discrepancies (i.e., goal levels lower than past performances) tended to find it anxiety-provoking to admit that they were striving for more than they were able to achieve. These students had very low tolerance for failure. Consequently, after even one failure, they quickly dropped their levels of aspiration to points below their previous performances. Students with low positive discrepancies between their performances and aspired goals were relatively confident and secure. Those with high positive discrepancies also had high fears of failure but were able to admit failure without too much damage to their self-esteem. Klugman[82] investigated the relationship between aspiration on contrived tasks and emotional stability in a group of 30 native-born white subjects. His results indicated that the more stable subjects tended to have narrower ranges of discrepancy between attainment and aspiration than did the less stable ones. Those who were more emotionally stable tended to be flexible and to shift their goals moderately in response to their previous attainments. However, those in the less stable group were more inclined either to maintain their aspirations rigidly, or to show extreme

changes. Mahone[83] attempted to apply some of the findings reported above to a situation in which the respondent was asked to select socially relevant goals instead of an aspiration on a contrived laboratory task. He administered vocational interest questionnaires and anxiety scales to a sample of 135 college students. As predicted, he found that those students who had high "debilitating anxiety" were unrealistically high in their occupational aspirations. In addition, these individuals were also least accurate in placing themselves in rank order of achievement in their class. They had difficulty in giving a realistic estimate of their own abilities.

Many of the laboratory experiments with individuals showing definite psychopathology indicate that these individuals are characterized by relatively high discrepancies. Himmelweit[84] compared psychoneurotic individuals with normals and found that the former had high "D" scores (i.e., discrepancy scores). Jost[85] noted that the same was true of schizophrenic patients, as compared to a normal group. Children diagnosed as emotionally disturbed showed higher discrepancy scores than did their normal peers.[86] Such high discrepancy scores between aspiration and achievement on laboratory tasks were also found in those with multiple psychosomatic symptoms,[87] asthma,[88] and peptic ulcer.[89]

The evidence cited above points to a tendency for emotionally disturbed subjects either to over- or under-aspire, compared to those who have made a better adjustment. The dominant tendency in these studies, however, is for over-aspiring in the maladjusted and pathological groups. Generally, two lines of reasoning have been advanced to explain this phenomenon. One argument is that maladjusted subjects have high anxiety and high fear of failure, compared to others. They attempt to minimize anxiety by selecting a task that is so easy that they cannot fail, or one which is so difficult that failure would be no cause for self-blame.[90] The other explanation advanced is that the high level of anxiety experienced by maladjusted subjects prevents them from accurately evaluating their own abilities relative to the realistic difficulties in reaching certain goals.[91]

Although most of the studies in the field support the idea that maladjusted subjects select either very high or very low levels of aspiration, not all research in the area confirms this finding. The level of aspiration may be a function of personality type. Chance[92] selected a group of maladjusted (as determined by the M.M.P.I.) college students and divided them into depressives and repressors. She hypothesized that the former would under-aspire because they would tend to minimize their past achievements. On the other hand, the repressors, who generally denied their failure, would tend to over-aspire. After subjecting both groups to an experimentally contrived failure situation, she found that students of the depressive type lowered their aspirations considerably; however, the repressors maintained their old goals or reduced them only slightly. Davids and White[93] studied 30 normal children and a matched sample of 30 who were diagnosed as emotionally disturbed. Prior to the experience of experimental success or failure, the disturbed children showed larger discrepancies between achievement and aspiration on the tasks. After the experimentally produced success, both the normals and the disturbed group increased their aspirations; the increase for the normals was higher. After experimentally produced failure, the disturbed group decreased their aspirations significantly more than the normals did. In addition, the disturbed children showed much more heterogeneity in their responses after failure than did the normal children. These results indicate that the maladjusted group only selected (relatively) extreme aspirations after a failure situation.

The hypothesis has been advanced, with some supporting evidence, that schizophrenics are minimally responsive to external environmental stimuli in their achievement behavior, and tend to raise or lower their aspirations indiscriminately either after success or failure situations.[94] Olson[95] investigated this question, using a sample of 45 male schizophrenics between the ages 20–40 and a comparable group of normal subjects. This investigator was interested in the reactions of the two groups to three kinds of experimentally created situations. In one situation, the investigator approved their performances by telling them that they had done well, better than others, etc. In the second situation, he told them that their performances had been poor. With the third group, he remained neutral and gave neither positive nor negative reactions. There was no way for the subjects in this situation to evaluate their performances realistically. After mild disapproval of their performances, the subsequent achievement of the normals improved, but that of the schizophrenics remained relatively the same. Members of the ill group showed the greatest subsequent improvement after their performances were approved by the investigator. This study lends little support to the idea that schizophrenics are not responsive to external environmental stimuli.

It also shows that praise is a more effective enhancer for these individuals than even mild disapproval. Thus, there is some evidence for hypersensitivity to failure among disturbed subjects.

The research reviewed in this section shows that the "emotionally disturbed" are not uniform in their goal-oriented behavior. There is considerable variation among personality types and diagnostic categories. Little is known at this point about the applicability of the theory concerning achievement behavior in "real life" situations. Assuming that it is relevant, an interesting methodological problem arises. In previous sections of this paper, we reviewed research concerned with the etiological relevance of achievement-related behavior for mental illness. For example, attempts were made to see whether the magnitude of the discrepancy between achievement and aspiration was related to mental illness. However, some of the small-group research suggests the possibility that the size of this discrepancy may arise as a defense against emotional disturbance rather than act as a cause of it. Achievement-related behavior may be relevant *both* as a cause and an effect of mental disorder. It is thus crucial for any research in this area to determine carefully the temporal relationship between the onset of mental illness and changes in achievement-related behavior. Only in this way will it be possible to separate the role of achievement behavior either as an antecedent or as a consequence of mental disorder.

CONCLUSIONS

Although the present state of the research on status position, social mobility, and mental disorder does not permit firm generalizations, it seems likely that the social psychology of goal-striving behavior provides such a unifying thread. Notwithstanding the conceptual and methodological problems in this area of endeavor, the empirical studies focusing directly on mobility orientation, and the inferences that were drawn from related research, justify this belief.

The methodological problems characterizing these studies have been discussed at various points in the review. These problems, which apply both to the dependent (i.e., mental disorder) and the independent (i.e., sociological factors) variables, make comparisons of the different studies difficult and limit the extent to which generalizations can be made. Some problems result from a lack of clarity or a lack of consensus concerning the nature of the concepts used, while in other cases the difficulty is not conceptual clarity, but rather the use of different operational definitions for a given construct.

One of the most serious methodological problems encountered in this review stems from the concept of "mental disorder." Because of varying definitions of this condition and a limited understanding of the factors involved, either in its etiology or current dynamics, there is a need for research to help clarify and delineate this concept.

Another problem besetting attempts to compare the various studies in the field arises from variations in case-finding methods. In some instances, the investigator does not provide a full and precise explanation of the methods he uses. Where such explanations *are* furnished, it is frequently not valid to compare results; the same inferences and the same conclusions should not be made from incidence and prevalence studies.

The essential point of this discussion is that the present status of our knowledge of mental disorder may impair its usefulness as a variable in sociological research. It is necessary to pursue further research on the nature of the disease processes involved in order to define variables that are genotypically homogeneous.

While the use of mental disorder as a research variable presents considerable problems, the various sociological variables mentioned in this review also present some methodological difficulties. In a previous section we noted that Jackson[96] seriously questioned the advisability of averaging the ranks of the various status components to obtain a mean status position. It is also possible that the psychological meaningfulness of using such a procedure varies according to the nature of the population (e.g., racial composition) or the community being studied (e.g., rural or urban community).

Another problem associated with the concept of status position and its relationship to mental disorder arises from the question of which point

in a patient's career should be used to determine his achieved rank. The previous review of studies exploring the drift hypothesis indicated that there was little agreement about the relative social mobility of psychiatric patients and normal control groups. It is clear that, at least in some instances, the status distribution of patients will differ, depending on whether the investigator has chosen the achievement level at the time of entering treatment, or another point in time that would be a closer approximation to the patient's pre-morbid achievement. If the aim is the focus on the etiological factors in mental disorder, rather than on its effects, it is important to use the latter point.

With regard to the discrepancy (between aspiration and achievement) concept, studies have utilized various methods of determining the level of aspiration. Some investigators asked their subjects about the goals they expected to reach, while others inquired about the desired goals. Research shows that the expected and the desired goals are quite different. It is sometimes felt that expected goals will be more realistic and psychologically meaningful than desired goals. However, it may also be true that expected goals represent a painful compromise and will fail to give a true picture of a subject's degree of striving and frustration.

This review has brought into clear relief some of the theoretical and methodological problems in the sociological and psychological studies of psychopathology. There has been little effort to utilize theoretical schemes to explain inconsistencies. Despite the methodological problems noted above, we are impressed with the agreement of the findings on the relationship between mobility orientation and mental disorder. This points to the importance of exploring social-psychological concepts as intervening variables. They can serve to further our understanding of the relationship between sociological variables and mental disorder and also help to explain apparent inconsistencies in the data.

NOTES

*Supported by Research Grant M–3047. National Institutes of Health, Public Health Service, Bethesda, Maryland. The authors wish to acknowledge the assistance of Miss Rochelle Eskin in the preparation of this paper.

1. Robert K. Merton, *Social Theory and Social Structure*, Glencoe, Ill: The Free Press, 1949, pp. 125–149.

2. Kurt Lewin, Tamara Dembo, Leon Festinger, and Pauline Sears, "Level of Aspiration," in J. McV. Hunt, editor, *Personality and the Behavior Disorders*, Volume I, New York: The Ronald Press Company, 1944, pp. 333–378.

3. Robert E. L. Faris and H. Warren Dunham, *Mental Disorders in Urban Areas*, Chicago: University of Chicago Press, 1939.

4. Christopher Tietze, Paul Lemkau, and Marcia Cooper, "Schizophrenia, Manic-Depressive Psychosis, and Social-Economic Status," *American Journal of Sociology*, 47 (September, 1941), pp. 167–175.

5. Robert E. Clark, "Psychoses, Income, and Occupational Prestige," *American Journal of Sociology*, 54 (March, 1949), pp. 433–440.

6. Bert Kaplan, Robert Reed, and Wyman Richardson, "A Comparison of the Incidence of Hospitalized and Non-

Hospitalized Cases of Psychosis in Two Communities," *American Sociological Review*, 21 (August, 1956), pp. 472–479.

7. J. N. Morris, "Health and Social Class," *Lancet*, 1 (February, 1959), pp. 303–305.

8. August B. Hollingshead and Frederick C. Redlich, *Social Class and Mental Illness*, New York: John Wiley and Sons, Inc., 1958, pp. 194–249.

9. John A. Clausen and Melvin L. Kohn, "Social Relations and Schizophrenia: A Research Report and a Perspective," in Don D. Jackson, editor, *The Etiology of Schizophrenia*, New York: Basic Books, Inc., 1960, pp. 295–320.

10. E. Gartley Jaco, *The Social Epidemiology of Mental Disorders*, New York: Russell Sage Foundation, 1960, p. 178.

11. Seymour Parker, Robert J. Kleiner, and Rochelle M. Eskin, *Social Status and Psychopathology*, paper presented at the annual meeting of the Society of Physical Anthropology, Philadelphia, April, 1962.

12. Robert J. Kleiner, Jacob Tuckman, and Martha Lavell, "Mental Disorder and Status Based on Religious Affiliation," *Human Relations*, 12 (September, 1959), pp. 273–276.

13. Robert J. Kleiner, Jacob Tuckman, and Martha Lavell, "Mental Disorder and Status Based on Race," *Psychiatry*, 23 (August, 1960), pp. 271–274.

14. J.F.J. Cade, "The Aetiology of Schizophrenia," *Medical Journal of Australia*, 2 (July, 1956), pp. 135–139.

15. Johan Bremer, "A Social Psychiatric Investigation of a Small Community in Northern Norway," *Acta Psychiatrica et Neurologica*, 1951, Supplementum 62; Ornulv Odegaard, "The Incidence of Psychoses in Various Occupations," *International Journal of Social Psychiatry*, 2 (Autumn, 1956), pp. 85–104.

16. Lilli Stein, "Social Class' Gradient in Schizophrenia," *British Journal of Preventive and Social Medicine*, 11 (October, 1957), pp. 181–195.

17. Hollingshead and Redlich, *Social Class and Mental Illness, op. cit.*, p. 210.

18. *Ibid.*, p. 199.

19. Allister M. Macmillan, "A Survey Technique for Estimating the Prevalence of Psychoneurotic and Related Types of Disorders in Communities," in Benjamin Pasamanick, editor, *Epidemiology of Mental Disorder*, Washington, D.C.: American Association for the Advancement of Science, 1959, pp. 203–228.

20. Leo Srole, Thomas S. Langner, Stanley T. Michael, Marvin K. Opler, and Thomas A. C. Rennie, *Mental Health in the Metropolis: The Midtown Manhattan Study*, New York: McGraw-Hill Book Co., 1962, p. 230.

21. Thomas A. C. Rennie, Leo Srole, Marvin K. Opler, and Thomas S. Langner, "Urban Life and Mental Health," *American Journal of Psychiatry*, 113 (March, 1957), pp. 831–836.

22. Benjamin Pasamanick, Dean W. Roberts, Paul W. Lemkau, and Dean B. Krueger, "A Survey of Mental Disease in an Urban Population: Prevalence by Race and Income," in Benjamin Pasamanick, editor, *Epidemiology of Mental Disorder*, Washington D.C.: American Association for the Advancement of Science, 1939, pp. 183–201.

23. E. J. R. Primrose, "Psychological Illness: A Community Study," *Mind and Medicine Monographs, 3: Psychological Illness*, London: Tavistock Publications, pp. 17–35.

24. Robert W. Hyde and Lowell V. Kingsley, "Studies in Medical Sociology I: The Relation of Mental Disorders to the Community Socioeconomic Level," *New England Journal of Medicine*, 231 (October, 1944), pp. 543–548.

25. Kaplan, Reed, and Richardson, *op. cit.*

26. Tsung-yi Lin, "A Study of the Incidence of Mental Disorder in Chinese and Other Cultures," *Psychiatry*, 16 (November, 1953), pp. 313–336.

27. William H. Sewell and A. O. Haller, "Factors in the Relationship between Social Status and the Personality Adjustment of the Child," *American Sociological Review*, 24 (August, 1959), pp. 511–520.

28. Frank Auld, Jr., "Influence of Social Class on Personality Test Responses," *Psychological Bulletin*, 49 (July, 1952), pp. 318–332.

29. Elton F. Jackson, "Status Consistency and Symptoms

of Stress," *American Sociological Review*, 27 (August, 1962), pp. 469–480.

30. Clausen and Kohn, in *The Etiology of Schizophrenia, op. cit.*

31. Pasamanick, Roberts, Lemkau, and Krueger, *op. cit.*

32. Kleiner, Tuckman, and Lavell, *Psychiatry, op. cit.*

33. Jacob Tuckman and Robert J. Kleiner, "Discrepancy between Aspiration and Achievement as a Predictor of Schizophrenia," *Behavioral Science*, 7 (October, 1962), pp. 443–447.

34. Rosalind Gould, "Some Sociological Determinants of Goal Strivings," *Journal of Social Psychology*, 13 (May, 1941), pp. 461–473.

35. LaMar T. Empey, "Social Class and Occupational Aspiration: A Comparison of Absolute and Relative Measurement," *American Sociological Review*, 21 (December, 1956), pp. 703–709.

36. Richard Centers and Hadley Cantril, "Income Satisfaction and Income Aspiration," *Journal of Abnormal and Social Psychology*, 41 (January, 1946), pp. 64–69.

37. Robert J. Kleiner and Seymour Parker, *Occupational Status, Goal Striving Behavior, and Mental Disorder*, paper presented at the annual meeting of the American Psychological Association, St. Louis, September, 1962.

38. Robert J. Kleiner, Seymour Parker, and Hayward G. Taylor, *Goal Striving and Psychosomatic Symptoms in a Migrant and Non-Migrant Population*, paper presented at the meeting of the World Federation for Mental Health, Paris, September, 1961.

39. Gerald Gurin, Joseph Veroff, and Shiela Feld, *Americans View Their Mental Health:* A Nationwide Interview Survey, New York: Basic Books, 1960, p. 193.

40. Jerome K. Myers and Bertram H. Roberts, *Family and Class Dynamics in Mental Illness*, New York: John Wiley and Sons, Inc., 1959.

41. David Mechanic and Edmund H. Volkart, "Stress, Illness Behavior, and the Sick Role," *American Sociological Review*, 26 (February, 1961), pp. 51–58.

42. Faris and Dunham, *op. cit.*

43. Tietze, Lemkau, and Cooper, *op. cit.*

44. Rema Lapouse, Mary A. Monk, and Milton Terris, "The Drift Hypothesis and Socio-Economic Differentials in Schizophrenia," *American Journal of Public Health*, 46 (August, 1956), pp. 978–986.

45. August B. Hollingshead and Frederick C. Redlich, "Social Mobility and Mental Illness," *American Journal of Psychiatry*, 112 (September, 1955), pp. 179–185.

46. John A. Clausen and Melvin L. Kohn, "Relation of Schizophrenia to the Social Structure of a Small City," in Benjamin Pasamanick, editor, *Epidemiology of Mental Disorder*, Washington, D.C.: American Association for the Advancement of Science, 1959, pp. 69–94.

47. Mary H. Lystad, "Social Mobility Among Selected Groups of Schizophrenic Patients," *American Sociological Review*, 22 (June, 1957), pp. 288–292.

48. Srole, Langner, Michael, Opler, and Rennie, *op. cit.*, p. 226.

49. E. Gartley Jaco, "Social Stress and Mental Illness in the Community," in Marvin B. Sussman, editor, *Community Structure and Analysis*, New York: Thomas Y. Crowell Co., 1959, pp. 388–409.

50. Morris, *op. cit.*

51. Peter M. Blau, "Social Mobility and Interpersonal Relations," *American Sociological Review*, 21 (June, 1956), pp. 290–295.

52. Jurgen Ruesch, *Chronic Disease and Psychological Invalidism: A Psychosomatic Study*, New York: American Society for Research in Psychosomatic Problems, 1946, pp. 104–124; Jurgen Ruesch, "Social Technique, Social Status, and Social Change in Illness," in Clyde Kluckhohn, Henry A. Murray, and David M. Schneider, editors, *Personality in Nature, Society, and Culture*, New York: Alfred A. Knopf, 1956, pp. 123–136.

53. Jurgen Ruesch, Annemarie Jacobson, and Martin B. Loeb, "Acculturation and Illness," *Psychological Monographs: General and Applied*, Vol. 62, No. 5, Whole No. 292,

1948, Washington, D.C.: The American Psychological Association.

54. Pitirim Sorokin, *Social Mobility*, New York: Harper and Bros., 1927, p. 510.

55. Lloyd W. Warner, "The Society, the Individual, and His Mental Disorders," *American Journal of Psychiatry*, 94 (September, 1937), pp. 274–284.

56. Srole, Langner, Michael, Opler, and Rennie, *op. cit.*, p. 226.

57. Hollingshead and Redlich, *American Journal of Psychiatry*, *op. cit.*

58. Lystad, *op. cit.*

59. Karen Horney, *The Neurotic Personality of Our Time*, New York: W. W. Norton and Company, Inc., 1937, pp. 162 ff, 172 ff.

60. Abram Kardiner and Lionel Ovesey, *The Mark of Oppression: A Psychosocial Study of the American Negro*, New York: W. W. Norton and Company, Inc., 1951, p. 315.

61. Abraham A. Weinberg, "Problems of Adjustment of New Immigrants to Israel," *World Mental Health*, Part I, 5 (May, 1953), pp. 57–63; Part II, 5 (August, 1953), pp. 129–135; Abraham A. Weinberg, "Mental Health Aspects of Voluntary Migration," *Mental Hygiene*, 39 (July, 1955), pp. 450–464; J. M. Last, "The Health of Immigrants: Some Observations from General Practice," *Medical Journal of Australia*, 1 (January, 1960), pp. 158–162.

62. August B. Hollingshead, Robert Ellis, and E. Kirby, "Social Mobility and Mental Illness," *American Sociological Review*, 19 (October, 1954), pp. 577–584.

63. Myers and Roberts, *op. cit.*, pp. 133–137.

64. *Ibid.*, p. 162.

65. Joseph Becker, "Achievement Related Characteristics of Manic-Depressives," *Journal of Abnormal and Social Psychology*, 60 (May, 1960), pp. 334–339.

66. H. J. Eysenck and Hilda T. Himmelweit, "An Experimental Study of the Reactions of Neurotics to Experiences of Success and Failure," *Journal of General Psychology*, 35 (July, 1946), pp. 59–75.

67. S. Kirson Weinberg, "A Sociological Analysis of a Schizophrenic Type," in Arnold M. Rose, editor, *Mental Health and Mental Disorder*, New York: W. W. Norton and Company, Inc., 1955, pp. 240–257; S. Kirson Weinberg, "Social Psychological Aspects of Schizophrenia," in L. Appleby, Jordan M. Scher, and John Cumming, editors, *Chronic Schizophrenia*, Glencoe, Ill.: The Free Press, 1960, pp. 68–88.

68. H. Warren Dunham, *Sociological Theory and Mental Disorder*, Detroit: Wayne State University Press, 1959, pp. 157–174.

69. Lawrence E. Hinkle and Harold G. Wolff, "Health and the Social Environment: Experimental Investigations," in Alexander H. Leighton, John A. Clausen, and Robert N. Wilson, editors, *Explorations in Social Psychiatry*, New York: Basic Books, 1957, pp. 105–137.

70. Sewell and Haller, *op. cit.*

71. Allison Davis, "Socialization and Adolescent Personality," in Theodore M. Newcomb and Eugene L. Hartley, editors, *Readings in Social Psychology*, New York: Henry Holt, 1947, pp. 139–150; Herbert H. Hyman, "The Value System of Different Classes: A Social Psychological Contribution to the Analysis of Stratification," in Reinhard Bendix and Seymour M. Lipset, editors, *Class, Status, and Power*, Glencoe, Ill.: The Free Press, 1953, pp. 426–442; Hollingshead and Redlich, *Social Class and Mental Illness, op. cit.*, pp. 114–135.

72. Seymour Parker, Robert J. Kleiner, and Hayward G. Taylor, "Level of Aspiration and Mental Disorder: A Research Proposal," *Annals of the New York Academy of Sciences*, 84 (December, 1960), pp. 878–886.

73. Kleiner and Parker, paper presented at the annual meeting of the Psychological Association, *op. cit.*; Kleiner, Parker, and Taylor, paper presented at the meeting of the World Federation for Mental Health, *op. cit.*

74. Myers and Roberts, *op. cit.*

75. Lewin, Dembo, Festinger, and Sears, *op. cit.*

76. John W. Atkinson, "Motivational Determinants of Risk-Taking Behavior," *Psychological Review*, 64 (November, 1957), pp. 359–372.

77. John W. Atkinson, Jarvis R. Bastian, Robert W. Earl, and George H. Litwin, "The Achievement Motive, Goal Setting, and Probability Preferences," *Journal of Abnormal and Social Psychology*, 60 (January, 1960), pp. 27–36.

78. Louis D. Cohen, "Level-of-Aspiration Behavior and Feelings of Adequacy and Self-Acceptance," *Journal of Abnormal and Social Psychology*, 49 (January, 1954), pp. 84–86.

79. John W. Atkinson, "Explorations Using Imaginative Thought to Assess the Strength of Human Motives," in M. R. Jones, editor, *Nebraska Symposium on Motivation, 1954*, Lincoln: University of Nebraska Press, 1954, pp. 58–112.

80. Ralph H. Turner and Richard H. Vanderlipp, "Self Ideal Congruence as an Index of Adjustment," *Journal of Abnormal and Social Psychology*, 57 (September, 1958), pp. 202–207; J. M. Butler and G. V. Haigh, "Changes in the Relation between Self Concepts and Ideal Concepts Consequent upon Client Centered Counseling," in C. R. Rogers and Rosalind F. Dymond, editors, *Psychotherapy and Personality Change*, Chicago: University of Chicago Press, 1954, pp. 55–75.

81. Pauline Snedden Sears, "Level of Aspiration in Relation to Some Variables of Personality: Clinical Studies," *Journal of Social Psychology*, 14 (November, 1941), pp. 311–336.

82. Samuel F. Klugman, "Emotional Stability and Level of Aspiration," *Journal of General Psychology*, 38 (January, 1948), pp. 101–118.

83. Charles H. Mahone, "Fear of Failure and Unrealistic Vocational Aspiration," *Journal of Abnormal and Social Psychology*, 60 (March, 1960), pp. 253–261.

84. Hilda Himmelweit, "A Comparative Study of the Level of Aspiration of Normal and Neurotic Persons," *British Journal of Psychology*, 37 (January, 1947), pp. 41–59.

85. Kenneth C. Jost, "The Level of Aspiration of Schizophrenic and Normal Subjects," *Journal of Abnormal and Social Psychology*, 50 (May, 1955), pp. 315–320.

86. Eva D. Ferguson, "The Effect of Sibling Competition and Alliance on Level of Aspiration, Expectation, and Performance," *Journal of Abnormal and Social Psychology*, 56 (March, 1958), pp. 213–223.

87. Samuel F. Klugman, "Relationship between Performance on the Rotter Aspiration Board and Various Types of Tests," *Journal of Psychology*, 23 (January, 1947), pp. 51–54; Klugman, *Journal of General Psychology, op. cit.*

88. Sue W. Little and Louis D. Cohen, "Goal Setting Behavior of Asthmatic Children and of Their Mothers for Them," *Journal of Personality*, 19 (June, 1951), pp. 376–389.

89. Irving Raifman, "Level of Aspiration in a Group of Peptic Ulcer Patients," *Journal of Consulting Psychology*, 21 (June, 1957), pp. 229–231.

90. Atkinson, *Psychological Review, op. cit.*

91. Mahone, *op. cit.*

92. June Elizabeth Chance, "Personality Differences and Level of Aspiration," *Journal of Consulting Psychology*, 24 (April, 1960), pp. 111–115.

93. Anthony Davids and Augustus A. White, "Effects of Success, Failure, and Social Facilitation on Level of Aspiration in Emotionally Disturbed and Normal Children," *Journal of Personality*, 26 (March, 1958), pp. 77–93.

94. M. F. Hausmann, "A Test to Evaluate Some Personality Traits," *Journal of General Psychology*, 9 (July, 1933), pp. 179–189.

95. Gordon W. Olson, "Failure and the Subsequent Performance of Schizophrenics," *Journal of Abnormal and Social Psychology*, 57 (November, 1958), pp. 310–314.

96. Jackson, *op. cit.*

part II
EPIDEMIOLOGY

SECTION 2

OTHER SOCIAL FACTORS

DESPITE the seemingly prime influence by the socio-economic factor, other variables have also had definite influences on disordered behavior.

In "Religion, National Origin, Immigration, and Mental Illness," Roberts and Myers surveyed the prevalence of patients in New Haven, Connecticut, according to religion, national origin, and immigration. They found that neuroses were very high among Jews, that alcoholism was very prevalent among Irish Catholics, but that the rate of paresis declined among Negroes. Senile and affective disorders were more prevalent among foreign born, while neuroses were more frequent among native born. In comparing their study with past inquiries, they attempted to explain their statistical findings in terms of the discrepant social processes.

"Social Psychological Correlates of Mental Illness and Mental Health," by Scott, critically reviews the theories and research on the influence of the environmental and interpersonal factors on disorders with the intent of showing their correlations as well as their differences. Racial and ethnic differences, group membership ties, and diverse intergroup relations as they influence types of disorders are selected from this presentation.

RELIGION, NATIONAL ORIGIN, IMMIGRATION, AND MENTAL ILLNESS[1]

Bertram H. Roberts and Jerome K. Myers[2]

IN the midst of the current dynamic orientation in psychiatric theory, the investigators in this study have reapproached some of the major social variables that have been part of the basic etiological data of clinical psychiatry. These are long-standing regularities which must either be included in psychodynamic theory or dismissed as artefacts. The distribution of mental illness among religious and nationality groups is a subject of special interest since these factors undoubtedly create a great deal of personal conflict. People still tend to type themselves according to these labels even though this form of differentiation is very much discredited in the American ideology. Beyond this rejection based upon our system of values the scientist cannot disregard certain empirical findings in the distribution of mental illness which have turned up with considerable regularity.

It has been pointed out in previous studies that the diagnostic categories of mental illness are not proportionately distributed among the religious and nationality groups; also, that immigration into the United States has a determining effect upon the occurrence of mental illness. Most of the preceding investigations have dealt with the numbers of first admissions to mental hospitals(2, 6, 7). There have also been surveys of Selective Service examinations which represent random samples of the male population within certain age limits(4). In this study, we have examined the distribution of psychiatric illness according to religion, national origin, and immigration in an urban center with a population of approximately 250,000. Since the previous studies were carried out 10 to 30 years ago, our findings can be expected to reflect some of the trends brought about by advancement in psychiatric treatment and also some of the effects of changing social conditions.

Reprinted from *American Journal of Psychiatry* (April, 1954), *110*, 759–764, by permission of the American Psychiatric Association.

DESIGN OF THE SURVEY

A survey was made of all patients with residence in the metropolitan area of New Haven under the treatment of a psychiatrist on December 1, 1950. For each patient a schedule was addressed to his psychiatrist or filled out from his record in a mental hospital or outpatient clinic. The effort to cover the entire population under psychiatric treatment on this particular date involved contacting all the practitioners, clinics, and hospitals in the state and nearby regions, as well as national hospitals treating New Haven patients. In the total, 1,963 cases were found with 1,393 located in public hospitals, 37 in private hospitals, 159 in clinics, and 374 being treated by private practitioners.

A direct inquiry was made about the patient's place of birth, rearing, and religion; also the nationality of his parents in order to determine his national origin. The psychiatric diagnosis proposed by the practitioner or the record was converted into the Veterans Administration diagnostic scheme after agreement with the opinion of members of our psychiatric team.[3] Since consensus was difficult in certain of the sub-categories, the differences were resolved by combining the subcategories under a more general heading. This was necessary for the psychoneurotic, psychosomatic, and character disorders. Alcohol and drug addictions were grouped together as were the affective disorders and the illnesses of senescence. The small number of organic mental illnesses necessitated their inclusion under one heading. The final form of the diagnostic scheme which has been carried through the entire study is presented in Table 1.

FINDINGS

Religion and Mental Illness.

The analysis of the population broken down into 3 major religious groupings is shown in Table 1. Comparison of this psychiatric population with a

TABLE 1.   Distribution of Psychiatric and General Population According to Diagnosis and Religious Affiliation

	Catholic		Protestant		Jewish	
	No.	%	No.	%	No.	%
General population	6,736	57.5	3,869	33.0	1,108	9.5
Total psychiatric population	1,059	57.0	576	31.0	223	12.0
Psychoneurotic and character disorder	189	46.2	122	29.8	98	24.0
Alcohol and drug addiction	61	68.5	28	31.5	0	0.0
Schizophrenia	506	60.8	245	29.4	81	9.7
Affective disorders	86	55.1	53	34.0	17	10.9
Psychosis with mental deficiency	56	61.5	23	25.3	12	13.2
Disorders of senescence	100	55.9	67	37.4	12	6.8
Epilepsy	25	71.5	9	25.7	1	2.9
Other organic	36	53.8	29	43.4	2	2.8

control group consisting of a 5% systematic sample of the general population reveals a significant statistical difference in the distribution of total mental illness, the psychoneurotic disorders, and alcohol and drug addiction among the religious groups.[4] In addition, significance is approached in the distribution of the organic illnesses. However, it was found that schizophrenia, the affective disorders, psychosis with mental deficiency and illnesses of senescence were distributed in the same proportions as in the general population. Since it was found in a previous analysis that social class is also a determining factor in the distribution of mental illness, this possibility was checked in all of the significant findings in this study (8). This was of importance in the finding that psychoneurotic disorder among Jews was 2½ times above expectation. Our check brought out that social class accounted for this skewed religious distribution in the lowest socio-economic level; however, only 10% of the neurotic patients were in this level. The Catholic group was found to be inordinately high for alcohol and drug addiction, and it is remarkable that there were no Jews with this form of illness. Social class was of no importance in this instance.

Our findings have been compared with those of Malzberg and Dayton, using first hospital admissions (2, 6). As would be expected, our rates were higher for psychoneurotic disorders since we had included ambulatory patients. In all other categories our findings are substantially the same as those of other investigators. In contrast to what is stated in 2 textbooks of psychiatry (3, 9), we did not find a higher rate of affective disorders among Jews. This observation was also made by Malzberg (5) in 1930.

National Origin and Mental Illness.

The response to the question regarding national origin cannot be taken as an entirely valid indication of nationality. It is merely the respondent's subjective impression of the patient's origin. Since our data on this item were crudely defined, analysis was limited to 4 categories representing relatively distinct groups—the Irish, Italian, Negro, and Jewish.[5] As national origin of the parents differed in only 10% of the cases, that of the father was used as the index. As there are no general population figures dealing with national origin, it was necessary to compare the distribution of diagnoses within each nationality group (See Table 2).

Significant differences were found in the distribution of mental illness among these groups. Within the individual groups Jews were high for psychoneurotic disorder (Table 1). The Italians

TABLE 2.   Distribution of Psychiatric Population According to Selected Ethnic Groups and Diagnosis

	Irish		Italian		Jewish		Negro	
	No.	%	No.	%	No.	%	No.	%
Psychoneurotic and character disorders	50	15.5	93	23.4	98	43.9	10	11.1
Alcohol and drug addictions	35	10.9	3	0.8	0	0.0	8	8.9
Schizophrenia	153	47.5	192	48.4	81	36.3	50	55.6
Affective disorders	23	7.1	35	8.8	17	7.6	1	1.1
Psychosis with mental deficiency	12	3.7	21	5.3	12	5.4	3	3.3
Disorders of senescence	42	13.0	36	9.1	12	5.4	9	10.0
Epilepsy	0	0.0	3	0.8	1	0.4	1	1.1
Other organic	7	2.2	14	3.5	2	0.9	8	8.9
Total	322	99.9	397	100.1	223	99.9	90	100.0

were low for alcohol and drug addiction while the Irish were high. Clearly the high rate of alcoholism among Catholics mentioned previously actually is to be found in the Irish group since these 2 nationalities make up the majority of Catholics in this city. A unique finding is that Negroes were extremely low in their proportion of affective disorders (10). Six of the 8 Negroes with organic disease had general paresis; however, this represents a dramatic decline in total numbers in comparison with earlier studies (2, 6). All other findings are substantially the same as previously presented.

Immigration and Mental Illness.

Since immigration into the United States has been very low during the last 2 decades, the average age of the foreign-born population is considerably higher than the native-born. For this reason, analysis was limited to a comparison of the psychiatric and general population over 21 years of age.[6] These findings are presented in Table 3. There is a

TABLE 3. DISTRIBUTION OF PSYCHIATRIC AND GENERAL POPULATION, 21 YEARS OF AGE AND OVER, BY NATIVITY AND PSYCHIATRIC DIAGNOSIS

	Native-Born		Foreign-Born	
	No.	%	No.	%
General population	135,568	79.5	34,900	20.5
Total psychiatric population	1,363	77.0	408	23.0
Psychoneurotic and character disorders	313	93.2	23	6.8
Alcohol and drug addictions	70	85.4	12	14.6
Schizophrenia	643	76.9	193	23.1
Affective disorders	102	65.4	54	34.6
Psychosis with mental deficiency	67	84.8	12	15.2
Disorders of senescence	91	50.3	90	49.7
Epilepsy	32	91.4	3	8.6
Other organic	45	68.2	21	31.8

significant difference in the distribution of native- and foreign-born with a higher proportion of foreign-born in the total psychiatric population and in the diagnostic categories of affective disorder, illnesses of senescence, and the organic illnesses. A significantly higher occurrence of psychoneurosis is found among the native-born. In the remaining diagnostic categories there are no significant differences between the native- and foreign-born. The similarity between these findings and those of Dayton (2) is remarkable if neurosis is excluded from the computation.

The foreign-born population was broken down into specific national groups (Table 4). It was found that the Italians were high for affective disorders and illnesses of senescence. The Irish were high for illnesses of senescence and the addictions but devoid of any psychoneurotic disorders. Northwest Europe was high for illnesses of senescence; Poland and Russia for affective disorders and schizophrenia. These findings show the same relative trend reported by other investigators.

GENERAL DISCUSSION

It is important to note that this survey is not a true prevalency study of psychiatric illness: it is limited to those people with mental illness who are under the treatment of a psychiatrist. It would be inaccurate to infer that the distribution found here is a direct reflection of what might be found if the community were surveyed on a random door-to-door basis since the present findings refer to a selected population. It is therefore necessary to speculate on factors that might differentiate this psychiatric population from such a prevalency sample. For example, there may be significant differences among the religious and nationality groups in their recognition of psychiatric symptoms. A similar exclusion from psychiatric treatment would arise from a difference between the cultural groups with regard to their acceptance of psychiatry as the optimal treatment for mental symptoms. These general implications of this treated prevalency sample must be held in mind in reviewing the details of this study.

The negative findings are of some interest; for example the social variables under consideration had no effect on the distribution of schizophrenia or psychosis with mental deficiency. Among the positive findings this investigation showed an increased frequency of psychoneurotic disorders. Part of this can be immediately credited to the inclusion of ambulatory patients. The acceptance of psychiatry and psychotherapeutic treatment, however, is undoubtedly a growing trend in the United States. As a new development requiring some informed intellectual comprehension, it would be expected that the better educated would have first exposure to the trend. This would explain the higher rate of psychoneurotic disorder among the native-born who have reached a higher educational level.

It is our opinion that the acceptance of psychiatry probably accounts for the inordinately high rate of psychoneurosis among Jews. The explanation for this must be considered in terms of

TABLE 4. DISTRIBUTION OF PSYCHIATRIC AND GENERAL POPULATION, 21 YEARS OF AGE AND OVER, BY COUNTRY OF BIRTH AND PSYCHIATRIC DIAGNOSIS

	Italy		Ireland		N.W. Europe		Poland and Russia		Other For.-Born		Native Born	
	No.	%	No.	%	No.	%	No.	%	No.	%	No.	%
General population	13,369	7.8	3,357	2.0	5,723	3.4	7,252	4.3	5,199	3.0	135,568	79.5
Total psychiatric population	135	7.6	51	2.9	64	3.6	97	5.5	6	3.4	1,363	77.0
Psychoneurotic and character disorder	5	1.5	0	0.0	6	1.8	5	1.5	7	2.1	313	93.2
Alcohol and drug addictions	1	1.2	4	4.9	3	3.7	2	2.4	2	2.4	70	85.4
Schizophrenia	56	6.7	23	2.8	27	3.2	60	7.2	27	3.2	643	76.9
Affective disorders	25	16.0	5	3.2	6	3.8	14	9.0	4	2.6	102	65.4
Psychosis with mental deficiency	6	7.6	0	0.0	1	1.3	1	1.3	4	5.1	67	84.8
Disorders of senescence	35	19.3	16	8.8	16	8.8	10	5.5	13	7.2	91	50.3
Epilepsy	1	2.9	1	2.9	1	2.9	0	0.0	0	0.0	32	91.4
Other organic	6	9.1	2	3.0	4	6.1	5	7.6	4	6.1	45	68.2

the ethnic structure and the tradition of the Jewish group in addition to its religious organization. Among Jews it is generally accepted that there is no conflict between religious doctrine and psychoanalytic theory. This is in contrast to a partially supported opposition among Catholics. From the standpoint of community attitude, the Jews exhibit a high level of acceptance of psychoanalytic psychiatry with a minimum of disturbance of their social values. The Jewish attitude is widely divergent from the Irish as is substantiated by our finding that not a single patient of Irish birth was receiving psychotherapy for psychoneurosis. Although this explanation of the rates of psychoneurosis in terms of the acceptance of modern psychiatry appears plausible, we cannot definitely state that the actual occurence of the illness is not higher among Jews.

In this study there was found a general diminution in organic mental disease. Probably this is due to the fact that general paresis is a vanishing clinical entity as a result of improved chemotherapy. This trend also is dependent upon an enlightened acceptance of modern medicine. Our findings show that this has particularly benefitted the Negro group. Considering the mental illnesses of senescence among foreign-born, it would be our speculation that this might be explained by the specific type of deficiency caused by this illness. The loss of recent memory erases the skill, learned later in life, essential to an adjustment in the American culture. This would create a more prevading difficulty for those who have immigrated to this country than for those reared in its practices.

The high rate of alcoholism among the Irish population and its absence among Jews has repeatedly been found (1). If this finding is compared with the rates of psychoneurosis it appears that there is some kind of cultural determination in the formation of symptoms. This poses a challenging question to the conceptual framework of psychodynamic theory. A second finding of similar challenge is in the distribution of affective disorder. This illness was found to be higher among the foreign-born and apparently of diminishing frequency in the Jewish group. The trend in affective illness, which is one of the major forms of psychosis, is not easily explained in terms of our knowledge of etiological factors.

The explanation for these cultural psychological phenomena must be in terms of the manner in which the external environment impinges upon the psychological mechanism. There are two important junctures at which this is conceived to occur. The first is the manner in which social factors color the childhood experiences, and the second is in terms of the ego's reaction to external reality. The conception of the ego's relationship with external reality implies its capacity to control the social manifestations of internal impulses in deference to external pressures. Just as behavior is modified in this way, it can be expected that neurotic symptoms which are also interpersonal communications will be influenced by social pressures. There is considerable acceptance by the Irish of alcohol as a means of tension relaxation. From the psychodynamic standpoint, it is remarkable that the Irish can find an outlet for many diverse forms of psychic conflict in this single form of escape. On the other hand, the Jewish disapproval of inebriety precludes this means for the Jewish neurotic. Our findings represent an example of cultural conditions expressing a suppressive and displacing effect upon the symptomatic manifestations of psychic disorder.

To explain the distribution of affective disorder we must seek it in the direction of the developmental process. According to psychoanalytic theory, the affective illness is based upon a fixation in the first four years of life. Hence, if social forces have some effect upon the formation of this illness, it must be that they are brought to bear upon the dynamics of the family. More concretely, this would mean the role and responsibility assumed by various members of the family and the quality of the parent-child relationship. If this is the case, it is conceivable that since the American family structure differs from the European there would be a different etiological force operating to produce affective illness. This is plausible since early childhood experience in America differs from other cultures. It has been suggested elsewhere that the accentuation of feeding has been an important factor in the causation of affective illness among Jews. The acculturation of the Jewish family to America has tended to play down this practice. We can only speculate that such changes as these operating within the family dynamics have brought about the diminution of affective illness among Jews and native-born Americans.

SUMMARY

A survey of the prevalency of patients with mental illness who were under treatment in New Haven was analyzed according to religion, national origin, and immigrational status. It was found that psychoneurotic disorders were more frequent among Jews whereas the rate of affective disorder in this group had fallen to the average of the population. Alcoholism is most prevalent among the Irish Catholics. There has been a general fall in the rate of organic mental disease, particularly in that of general paresis among Negroes. The illness of senescence and the affective illnesses are higher in the foreign-born while psychoneurotic disorders are more frequent in the native-born. Schizophrenia and psychosis with mental deficiency are not related to the social variables.

Comparisons were made between these findings and previous studies. Speculative explanations are offered to explain the trends and disproportions.

NOTES

1. Read at the 109th annual meeting of The American Psychiatric Association, Los Angeles, Calif. May 4–8, 1953.
2. From the Yale University Departments of Psychiatry and Sociology, aided by USPHS Mental Health Act Grant MH 263 (R), "Relationship of Psychiatric Disorder to Social Structure." Also participating in this research were F. C. Redlich, A. B. Hollingshead, H. A. Robinson, and L. Z. Freedman.

3. Adapted from the Veterans Administration Nomenclature: TB 10A–78.
4. The Chi Square test for difference was utilized in all calculations in this paper and significance is defined at the .05 level, although in most cases it was less than .01.
5. Negroes are included although strictly speaking they represent a racial group.
6. The data on the country of birth of the general population were obtained in 1950 United States Census reports.

REFERENCES

1. Bacon, S. D., et al. Studies of Drinking in Jewish Culture. New Haven: Laboratory of Applied Physiology, Yale University, 1951.
2. Dayton, A. N. New Facts on Mental Disorders. Springfield: Charles C. Thomas, 1940.
3. Henderson, D. K., and Gillespie, R. D. A Textbook of Psychiatry, 7th ed. London: Oxford University Press, 1950.
4. Hyde, R. M., and Chisholm, R. M. Studies in medical sociology, III: The relation of mental disorder to race and nationality. New England J. of Med., 23:612, 1944.
5. Malzberg, B. The prevalence of mental disease among Jews, Ment. Hyg., 14: 926, 1930.

6. Malzberg, B. Social and Biological Aspects of Mental Disease. Utica: State Hospital Press, 1940.
7. Pollock, H. M., et al. Hereditary and Environmental Factors in the Causation of Manicdepressive Psychoses and Dementia Praecox, Utica: State Hospital Press, 1939.
8. Redlich, F. C., et al. Social structure and psychiatric disorder. Am. J. Psychiat., 109: 729, Apr. 1953.
9. Rosanoff, A. J. Manual of Psychiatry and Mental Hygiene, 7th ed. New York: John Wiley and Sons, Inc., 1944.
10. Tooth, G. Studies in Mental Illness in the Gold Coast, Colonial Research Publications (No. 6). London: His Majesty's Stationery Office, 1950.

SOCIAL PSYCHOLOGICAL CORRELATES OF MENTAL ILLNESS AND MENTAL HEALTH*

William A. Scott

THEORIES and empirical findings concerning the etiology of mental illness come from a variety of scientific disciplines representing a wide range of levels of analysis, from the biochemical to the historico-cultural. The data and hypotheses are so disparate as to defy incorporation within a single comprehensive theory or research program. It is common practice for each researcher to work, relatively independently of others, within the scope of variables encompassed by his particular scientific discipline. This inevitably restricts the possibilities for interrelating of findings and for interpreting the facts discovered by one researcher within the theoretical framework of another. A further major impediment to the integration of research findings on mental illness and health is the diversity of definitions of these phenomena employed by various researchers (54). In many cases it is not known in what manner mental illness defined by one criterion relates to mental illness defined by another.

Yet from diverse approaches have come hypotheses and facts that conceivably bear relationships to one another, so that an imaginative researcher of the future might well combine them into a more general interpretation of the phenomena of mental illness and health . . . . The purpose of the present paper is to critically review theories and research from the level of analysis—. . . of the interpersonal—with the aim of suggesting interrelations where possible, or of leaving a confusion of disparate results where necessary.

Racial and Ethnic Differences

It is generally reported, on the basis of hospital admissions statistics, that psychoses, especially schizophrenia and manic-depressive psychoses, show higher incidence among Negroes than among whites (41, 50). However, there are some reversals of this difference (50), and it is not clear to what extent the general tendency is due to socioeconomic differences between the two races. No study has come to hand which compares incidence rates for the racial groups, while holding socioeconomic status constant.

A group of studies reported by Rose and Stub (50) indicate that Jews have lower incidences than non-Jews for all of the psychoses enumerated: schizophrenia, manic-depressive psychosis, alcoholic psychosis, general paresis, senile psychosis, psychosis with cerebral arteriosclerosis, and paranoia. A parallel difference does not hold for psychoneuroses under treatment, which may be somewhat higher among Jews than non-Jews.

There is an apparent interactional effect of race on the relationship of mental illness to other factors, similar to that discussed above for sex. Clark (3) reports that the (negative) correlation between occupational prestige and incidence of psychosis is less pronounced for Negroes than for whites. Similarly, Henry and Short (23) indicate that the relations of suicide and homicide rates to the business cycle are different for Negroes than for whites. In the case of suicide, the Negro tendency is in the same direction as that for the majority group, but simply weaker. For homicide, however, the directions of relationship are opposed: homicides of whites increase during business contraction, while those of Negroes decrease.

Explanations for the differential rates of mental illness among the different racial and ethnic groups tend to be more speculative than empirically demonstrated. In addition to the problem of controlling socioeconomic status when making interethnic and interracial comparisons, there is the likelihood that differential willingness to care for psychotics within the family, rather than within institutions, might be responsible for some of the apparent differences in incidence. Once such potentially confounding influences have been eliminated it might be worthwhile to explore the possibility that any remaining group differences be due to variations in subgroup norms or to differential security of the minority members within their own groups and within the larger society.

Reprinted from *Psychological Bulletin* (March, 1958), 55 (2), 65, 72–87, by permission of the American Psychological Association.

INTER-PERSONAL CORRELATES OF MENTAL HEALTH AND MENTAL ILLNESS

We shall consider certain factors in mental health that have been explicitly defined in terms of group interaction processes. The causative nature of such factors has been implied in many of the explanations mentioned above for the various demographic differences reported. But in the previous section, explanations in terms of group norms or other social processes have generally been offered as attempts to explain at a more basic level, and after the fact, relationships which had already been observed at a higher, or more superficial, level of analysis. The formulations to be considered here are more of a predictive sort, and imply that the presumably causative characteristics of all social interaction systems will have similar implications for mental illness or mental health, regardless of the specific demographic factors in which they happen to be manifest.

Though the determining characteristics of social processes to be discussed here are better formulated theoretically, there are frequently large gaps in the empirical data required to support them. Consequently, instead of being faced with large numbers of inadequately explained empirical correlations, as was frequently the case in the demographic sections, the reader may often find here intriguing theoretical formulations for which there is virtually no evidence.

In reviewing a number of studies and theories concerning the relation of sociological factors to mental health, Schneider (51) observed that nearly all their hypotheses could be subsumed under a small number of categories. Mental disturbance was seen variously as stemming from (*a*) the individual's inability to meet role demands, (*b*) membership in some underprivileged group, (*c*) a forced abrupt transition from one social situation to another, (*d*) disorganization of a social system, (*e*) inability to attain social acceptance, (*f*) subjective or objective mobility in the class structure, (*g*) incompatible values, and (*h*) social isolation.

Here we shall discuss these and other factors presumed to affect mental health under three headings: First, there are factors reflecting the degree to which the individual maintains group membership ties, or the relative strength of those ties. Second, there are factors which describe the nature of the intragroup relations in which he is involved. Finally, there are factors relating to conflict or compatibility among the various groups of which he is, simultaneously or successively, a member. Each of these categories of supposedly determining characteristics will be discussed in turn.

Extent of Group Membership Ties

It has been maintained by some (11, 37) that social isolation, in and of itself, is a causative factor in the development of mental disorder, especially schizophrenia. From a contemporary analysis, the hypothesis may be stated as follows: low participation in social interaction, either through isolation from one's membership and reference groups or through rapid mobility, results in socially deviant behavior and accompanying disorganization of psychological processes (5). Or, formulated developmentally, if a child's interaction with his peer group is restricted by his parents, his understanding of other people's reactions never develops; consequently his own responses to social situations are inappropriate (11).

A number of cross-sectional correlations have been reported which are consistent with this formulation, but they are not specific to schizophrenia. Faris and Dunham (6, 12), in their original ecological study of Chicago, found admission rates for schizophrenia to be disproportionately high among persons from areas which were not primarily populated by members of their own ethnic or racial groups. That is, admissions rates tended to be higher for minority members of a community than for members of the dominant group. Lemert (37) found in rural Michigan a negative correlation between the incidence of hospitalized psychosis (undifferentiated) among foreign-born people and the number of foreign-born of that nationality living in the county. Gruenberg (20) reports that Norwegian immigrants in Minnesota had higher admissions rates than native-born in the same area, and higher rates than Norwegians who stayed in Norway. Also that the native white rate of admissions is higher in a predominately Negro area than the rate for Negroes in the same area, while the Negro rate in a dominant white area is higher than the white rate.

In his study of the distribution of senile psychoses (admitted to hospitals) in Syracuse, Gruenberg (19) found that the number of people living alone in a particular area was a better predictor of incidence than was the socioeconomic status of the area. Similar correlations with both of these factors were also found for all other admitted psychoses (undifferentiated).

With respect to suicide rates, a social isolation interpretation is also applicable. Suicide occurs more frequently among unmarried persons, especially divorced, than among married persons (10, p. 147). Immigrants are said to have higher suicide rates than natives, and higher rates than persons who did not emigrate from their nation (10, pp. 148, 161).

Finally, certain neurotic anxiety symptoms were found by Halmos (21) to be associated significantly, though moderately, with reported difficulties in social interaction and with actual indices of the extent of the subject's social participation.

It is difficult to evaluate the etiological significance of social isolation on the basis of these correlational findings, because of the large number of uncontrolled factors. Since the immigrant population is largely self-selected, it may differ systematically from native-born and nonemigrants in their own countries with respect to factors predisposing to mental illness. And the choice of place of residence—whether with people of one's own ethnic group or not—is to a certain degree a matter of self-selection, so the direction of the relationship between isolation and proclivity to mental disorder is hard to determine. Moreover, since social isolation of various sorts has been found associated with a variety of mental disturbances—schizophrenia, senile psychosis, suicide, and anxiety symptoms—the specificity of such an etiology to schizophrenia is hardly established.

Two available studies attempted to distinguish schizophrenia from manic-depressive psychosis in regard to social interaction correlates. They lead to opposite conclusions concerning the specificity of social isolation as a causative factor in schizophrenia Jaco (29) determined the incidence rates of the two disorders in 15 census tracts in Austin on the basis of commitments to a local public mental hospital. He then selected the two tracts which were highest for each disorder, and compared them, respectively, with the two tracts lowest for each disorder on a number of social characteristics such as anonymity, spatial mobility, social participation. These characteristics for the tracts were determined either from census data or from systematic sample interview surveys within them. With respect to some of the indices the high and low manic-depressive tracts were found to differ significantly in the same directions as the high and low schizophrenia tracts. When such parallel differences occurred, the significance of the difference between differences was tested (high vs. low schizophrenia areas minus high vs. low manic-depressive areas). Those indices of

social isolation which differentiated residents of the high and low schizophrenia areas to a greater degree than the high and low manic-depressive areas were: (a) likelihood of knowing the names of one's neighbors, (b) number of friends, (c) number of acquaintances, (d) membership in lodges and fraternal organizations, (e) unemployment rate, (f) number of jobs held previously, (g) number of visits to central business district, (h) number of visits with friends, (i) number of visits to other areas of the city, (j) number of trips out of town, (k) amount of intercity migration (high schizophrenia tracts showed less), (l) number of friends in remote areas (high schizophrenia areas less). Differences specific to schizophrenia rates were *not* found for the following characteristics of the tracts: (a) church membership, (b) voting in previous election, (c) frequency of discharge from, or quitting of, jobs.

These general differences among the census tracts are interpreted by Jaco as evidence in favor of the specific applicability of the social isolation hypothesis to schizophrenia. Yet there is a statistical flaw in the study which may have contributed to spurious differences, and hence renders the interpretation questionable. When comparing high- and low-incidence tracts, significance tests were based on the size of the sample of respondents, with no correction for homogeneity of people with tracts. The appropriate test would have been to consider the sample as a multistage sample of people within tracts, and base the significance tests on the number of clusters, i.e., two high-rate tracts and two low-rate tracts. Since the wrong statistical tests were employed, it is reasonable to infer that significance levels were overstated—this assumes positive intraclass correlations for the traits measured. (For a discussion of multistage sampling and the effects of clustering, see Kish [31]).

This criticism may be rephrased in nonstatistical language as follows: The four tracts compared on the social isolation characteristics were not selected in random fashion from larger populations of high and low schizophrenia tracts. Hence, other differences among the tracts, besides those relevant to the hypothesis, cannot be assumed to be randomly distributed. One does not know, then, to what degree the differences in incidence of schizophrenia are associated with the designated characteristics and to what degree with contaminating factors. Thus, although people in the two selected high-incidence tracts differed significantly in certain respects from people in the two low-incidence tracts, it is not possible to generalize these differences beyond the four particular tracts included in the sample. Whether or not these obtained differences are critical to the incidence of schizophrenia in other communities—even within Austin—is not ascertainable from this study.

Kohn and Clausen (33) obtained interview data from 45 schizophrenic and 13 manic-depressive patients from Hagerstown, Maryland, who were hospitalized between 1940 and 1952. This was a nearly complete population, rather than a sample; exclusion of people from the interviewed group was due to inaccessibility (physical or psychological), rather than to random selection. These 58 patients and ex-patients were matched, subject for subject, with a normal sample, on the basis of age, sex, and occupation. Both the schizophrenic and manic-depressive groups were more likely than matched normals to have been relatively isolated at age 13–14 (that is, larger proportions of them played primarily alone at that age). But the schizophrenic and manic-depressive patients did not differ from each other in this respect. Moreover, the interview data yielded no significant differences between patients' and normals' reports of their parents and of inter-personal relations within their families of orientation. Specifically, there was no evidence that social isolation resulted from parental restrictions. The authors are led by these findings to propose an alternative explanation to the standard social isolation hypothesis: As a result of inadequacies in social relationships, certain individuals come to feel that they do not belong to their peer groups. This may lead to withdrawal, but not necessarily; it may also lead to compulsive inter-action of the kind engaged in by some manic patients.

In assessing the adequacy of this study's findings for its conclusions, two features of the design may be considered (aside from the restriction of the sample to the particular hospital and time period). First, it should be noted that the samples were quite small (13 manic-depressives, 45 schizophrenics), so that small differences between these groups were not likely to appear statistically significant. Second, there is a difficulty inherent in ex post facto matching. Since it is not possible to match on the basis of all possibly relevant variables, one cannot be sure that differences between patients and normals did not result from some contaminating factor which was not controlled. In this particular instance, a crucial contaminating factor might have been the distortion of recall concerning the patients' childhood play relationships. Thus the results of this study serve rather to suggest hypotheses for more systematic exploration than to test in unambiguous fashion previously established hypotheses.

The strength of group membership ties can be assessed on bases other than simple social isolation. Some groups, by virtue of strong normative forces, exert more pressure toward conformity on their members than do other groups. Durkheim observed this in his interpretation of differing suicide rates in different membership groups (8). Henry and Short (23) have generalized and extended this interpretation in attempting to account for differing suicide and homicide rates among various demographic groups, and for differing magnitudes of correlation with the business cycle of suicide and homicide rates in these groups. Their formulation is intriguing and exceedingly general, though it gains only suggestive, rather than conclusive, support from the demographic data brought to bear on it.

Assumptions of Henry and Short's interpretation are that: (a) the basic and primary target of aggression is another person rather than the self; (b) the degree to which aggression is directed against others varies with the degree to which other-oriented aggression is defined as legitimate by the aggressor. Self-oriented aggression thus becomes a residual category—aggression for which outward expression is denied legitimacy. Proceeding from these assumptions, they theorize that, when behavior is required to conform rigidly to the demands and expectations of others (i.e., when external restraints are strong), the expression of aggression against others tends to be legitimized. When external restraints are weak, other-oriented aggression consequent to frustration fails to be legitimized, and aggression is directed against the self.

This reasoning suggests the hypotheses that the tendency toward suicide should vary inversely with the strength of external restraint over behavior, while the tendency toward homicide should vary directly with the strength of such restraint. Two principal sources of external restraint are posited: low social status and a strong relational system. Thus a low status person's response to frustration is more likely to be homicide than suicide; this differential proclivity is reversed for high status persons (e.g., white, male, young, wealthy). Also for people in groups with strong relational systems (e.g., nuclear family, Catholic church) the tendency toward homicide as a response to frustration should be greater than that toward suicide; while the reverse should be true for members of weak relational systems.

Such an interpretation helps to rationalize a number of diverse empirical relations between suicide and homicide rates on the one hand, and certain environmental and demographic factors on the other. For instance, suicide rates tend to increase during periods of business contraction (suicide representing a high status response to frustration). This correlation is stronger for high status groups—males, whites, younger persons, and residents of high rent areas—than for low status persons. Homicide rates of whites tend to increase during business contraction (external restraints are increased for the dominant group), while those for Negroes tend to decrease (external restraints are decreased for the outgroup).

This model is intriguing for its generality and simplicity, yet one should bear in mind that it was developed largely as an attempt to explain already existing data. Hypotheses using new indices of the major variables (status and strength of relational system) will be required to establish its predictive validity. Moreover, while the theory refers to interaction processes (degree of external restraint over behavior), the data brought to bear on it come from higher units of analysis—census tracts and other demographic categories. So one is left with questions similar to those applicable to the ecological studies reviewed earlier: Have the presumed causal relations been directly tested? (Apparently not.) Can the empirical results be attributed to genotype factors other than those specified by the thoery? (Probably so.)

The strength of group membership ties may be regarded as a function of the rigidity of group norms, but the degree to which these impinge on the individual will also be a function of his degree of identification with the group. Accordingly, one might expect various indices of mental health to be lower for transitory or highly mobile members of a community than for the more stable members. Such has been found to be the case in at least two studies of treated psychoses. Tietze et al. (60) report higher rates of mental disturbances in the Baltimore Eastern Health District among people who move most frequently (holds for intracity migrants only). Hollingshead et al. (24) found more upward social mobility among their Class III (middle class) schizophrenic patients than in the cross-sectional sample of New Haven. (Class V patients—lower class—did not differ from the total community in this respect.)

In the realm of nonpsychotic mental disorders, Ellis (9) reports a similar relation between upward mobility and evidence of emotional maladjustment. She analyzed data from 27 single working women

in Montgomery, Alabama, whose occupational prestige ratings were higher than their fathers' (upwardly mobile), in comparison with 33 single working women whose occupational prestige ratings were the same as, or lower than, their fathers' (nonmobile). Larger proportions of the upwardly mobile reported experiences of community and parental rejection in childhood and of parental preference for a sibling. They tended more often to report their own attachment to parents as "less than average." At the time of the study, these upwardly mobile women had fewer intimate friends and a shorter average duration of friendships than the stable group. More of them kept pets and more manifested psychosomatic symptoms. There was no difference between the groups in self-report of happiness.

Ellis' conclusion is that "The evidence is consistent with the theory that upward social mobility is likely to be an outgrowth of basically neurotic drives resulting from unsatisfactory early primary group relations, and that mobility leads to a continuation of superficial, impersonal primary group relations and other overt manifestations of emotional maladjustment" (9, p. 563).

This interpretation explicitly posits a mutually reinforcing relation between mental disturbance and mobility, and does not assign causation exclusively in one direction. A similar circular effect may be presumed to hold for the psychoses. As Dunham (7) has pointed out, whether schizophrenically disposed persons move frequently or whether frequently moving persons are more prone to develop schizophrenia is an open question.

One might expect that the disruptive effects of status mobility could be counteracted by enduring primary group ties for the mobile individual. Thus there should be less difference in the mental health of mobile and nonmobile married persons. Mangus' study of personality changes in adolescents over a 10-year period (42) showed relative deterioration among children from broken homes, but relative improvement among children of upwardly mobile families. The latter findings might be interpreted to suggest either that the upwardly mobile parents were *more* healthy than average or that they were less likely than others to transmit their maladjustments to their offspring. However, since Ellis' and Mangus' studies employed rather different criteria for mental health, a comparison of their findings is inconclusive with regard to the interactive influences of primary group ties and status mobility.

The effect of group membership ties in restoring

mental health, as well as maintaining it, is suggested by Straus (57), who describes the experience of the Blue Hills Hospital (Connecticut) in its outpatient treatment of alcoholics. Patients who were both married and employed were twice as likely to continue therapy following hospitalization as were those who were neither married nor employed.

The implication of many of the foregoing theories and data regarding the effect of group membership ties on mental health appears to be that membership per se contributes to sound mental health. The over-generality of such a conclusion is apparent if one considers that the norms of certain groups may be such as to impair mental health, either from the standpoint of adjustment within the wider society of which the group is part, or from the standpoint of certain "absolute" standards of mental health which the researcher may espouse. It has been noted by sociologists and social psychologists (40, 45, 58, 62) that delinquency and criminal behavior are supported by the norms of deviant groups with which the individual identifies. Knowledge and beliefs in this area are based more on anecdotes and case history studies than on empirical testing of systematic hypotheses. One is thus left, at present, with the rather trite generalization that the degree to which group membership contributes to mental health depends in part on the relation of the norms of the particular group to the criteria for mental health which one adopts.

Another limiting consideration is suggested by Jahoda (30), to the effect that the degree to which membership in any group promotes mental health is a function of the broader community structure within which that group operates. She hypothesizes that if a community is organized so as to favor mutually exclusive voluntary group memberships, the dependency of the individual on the one group to which he belongs will be excessive. By contrast, when an individual can belong to several groups which put less exclusive claim on his loyalty, so that his identity will not be threatened when he leaves the group, membership in it will enhance his mental health. The evaluative implication of this hypothesis is that, while group membership may contribute to the security and ego identity of the individual, these aspects of his self should not be totally dependent on a single group. Such an implication appears completely appropriate to the kinds of criteria for mental health which Jahoda has proposed, namely "active adjustment," "need-free perception," and "integration of personality." It may well be relevant to mental health as defined by other criteria as well, but data bearing directly on this hypothesis are not available at present.

Such considerations as these force recognition of the possibilities that whether, and to what degree, group membership enhances or impedes mental health depends on: (a) the nature of the group and its relation to the wider social structure, (b) the manner in which group membership is maintained by the individual, and (c) the particular criteria for mental health chosen. Further systematic elaboration and testing of these notions would appear fruitful.

The Nature of Intragroup Relations

Certain propositions concerning the effects of group structure on mental health have been advanced, both at a general level and with reference to a specific group, the family of orientation. Data on the general propositions are hard to come by, and those relating to the specific propositions are inconclusive.

At the general level, it had been maintained, on the one hand, that the degree of adjustment to roles is a function of the degree of clarity with which they are defined (30). Somewhat the same idea is involved in the proposition stemming from Durkheim (8): Where roles are infinitely extensible, disorientation (anomie) occurs, because no limits are set to human desires. On the other hand, where roles are nonextensible, disorientation may occur through a failure of the role to absorb more than a small portion of the personality; the personality is thereby blocked and thwarted (51). This is stated somewhat more specifically by Jahoda in the hypothesis: If a single type of behavior is rewarded, the pressures for conformity—that is, passive acceptance, rather than active adjustment—will be great, resulting in mental illness by her definition (30). Thus, the likelihood of breaking down under a specific role may be expected to vary inversely with the number of roles one plays in a given system (28, p. 46).

Combining these two sets of propositions, one might propose that poor role definition promotes maladjustment (at least within the particular social system in which the role occurs; not necessarily within a different, or more inclusive, social system), while overprecise role definition, if not accompanied by available alternative roles, may lead to mental illness, not from the point of view of adjustment to the particular social system, but from the standpoint of some other, system-free, criterion of mental health. Thus optimum mental health, by both kinds of criteria—social and psychological—might be expected to occur to the extent that roles are clearly defined, but in a way which does not demand exclusive absorption of the person within them.

At a level more amenable to empirical testing, hypotheses regarding the effect of intrafamily relations on children's mental health have been proposed. Wahl (61) suggests an intrafamilial etiology of schizophrenia as follows: The child's attitude toward himself is a function of his parents' relations with him. In large families, children are more frequently ignored than in smaller families, thereby engendering feelings of worthlessness, presumably a predisposing factor in schizophrenia. This is suggested as an explanation for data presented by Wahl to the effect that a sample of schizophrenics in Elgin State hospital came from families averaging 4.1 children, in comparison with the U.S. average of 2.2 children per family. A major shortcoming of these data in reference to the hypothesis is that they fail to take into account differences in social class distribution between the patients and the general population. Schizophrenics appear to come preponderantly from the lower classes, for reasons not yet clearly understood. Perhaps the relatively large family size in these groups is a crucial factor but, if so, then the relationship between family size and prevalence of schizophrenia should be tested *within* each social class, rather than within the total population at once. A partial correlation between family size and prevalence of schizophrenia, with social class held constant, would provide more convincing evidence in favor of the hypothesis.

Failure to control for social class differences might lead to unwarranted conclusions with regard to another characteristic of family structure, the locus of parental authority. In a study by Kohn and Clausen (34), comparing 45 schizophrenic patients and ex-patients from Hagerstown, Maryland, with a "normal" group matched on age, sex, and occupation, more of the schizophrenics reported that their mothers played a dominant role in the family decision-making process. But when socioeconomic status was controlled by testing this relationship within each of three social class groups, the difference between schizophrenics and normals disappeared, except for the higher SES group. It is probably not justified, on the basis of this analysis, to conclude that maternal dominance plays any role whatsoever in the etiology of schizophrenia, even in the upper class group, for singling out one significant relationship among the three tested tends to capitalize on chance variation to a greater degree than is indicated by the reported level of significance.

A study in near-publication stage, by Miller and Swanson (43), is expected to shed some light on the social psychological mechanisms underlying social class differences in mental disorders. These investigators proceeded from the assumption that differences between middle and lower class child rearing practices would produce differential preference for defense mechanisms relevant to manifestations of mental illness. Thus a conceptual link is made from characteristics of social structure, through interpersonal relations, to psychological mechanisms.

In the Yorkville community mental health study (48) the following aspects of relations within the respondent's family of orientation were assessed in the interview: (a) the degree of interparental accord or discord, (b) parental anxiety level, (c) degree of affectional acceptance or rejection from parents, (d) parents' predictability in punishing misdeeds, (e) parents' pressures on the responent for goal achievement, and (f) extent of sibling rivalry. Hypotheses concerning the influence of such factors on mental health are only implicit in reports of this study to date. Results of their testing are scheduled for publication in the near future.

A recently completed investigation (15, 16, 17) of the relation between parental attitudes and children's adjustment in St. Louis has yielded negative findings in this regard. Employing a battery of questions similar to those previously validated by Shoben (56) in his study of juvenile delinquents, Gildea, Glidewell, et al. attempted to relate mothers' attitudes toward child rearing to the level of adjustment shown in their children's classroom behaviors. No correlation appeared between responses to Shoben's items and emotional disturbance of the children. There was, however, a substantial relation between social class and these child-rearing attitudes. Moreover, certain other parental attitudes which were previously believed by these researchers to relate directly to the children's mental health—such as acceptance of responsibility for behavior of one's children—were subsequently found to be highly related to socioeconomic status. When the latter variable was held constant, the predicted correlation between mother's attitude and child's behavior vanished (15).

Caution must be exercised in interpreting these findings to indicate that child-rearing practices related to these attitudes have no effect on children's adjustments independent of social class. It is evident that the attitudes expressed in response to the questionnaire items may in many cases bear scant resemblance to the actual nature of the parent-child relationships. The fact that upper and middle class respondents give more "acceptable" answers to the questions may indicate, more than anything else, that they know what sorts of responses a middle class interviewer will approve.

A similar kind of limitation of their own interview study has been considered by Sears et al. (55). They minimize its importance, on the basis of internal evidence from their data, and suggest a number of relations between child-rearing practices and emotional disturbance in infants. Among them are the following: severity of weaning and toilet training are associated, respectively, with the extent of the child's upset over weaning and toilet training. The latter response is *not* associated with more general training practices, such as severity of restrictions or achievement demands. Retarded bladder control in children is associated with a combination of severe toilet training, high maternal sex anxiety, and "cold personality" in the mother. Excessive feeding problems were found with a combination of severe toilet training, physical punishment, and maternal "coldness." All data on both training practices and emotional disturbance were obtained from the same interview with mothers several years after many of the relevant events had occurred. Thus, while they provide important information concerning interrelations among contemporary attitudes, perceptions, and remembrances, they offer less clear evidence concerning the effects of early family relationships on later personality patterns. Definitive studies in this area would probably have to combine direct observation of child-rearing practices with a subsequent independent assessment of the child's level of mental health.

Compatibility among Norms and Roles of Different Groups

It is generally maintained by social psychologists that the individual's personality is largely created through his performance of prescribed or idiosyncratic roles in the various groups in which he participates.

Insofar as socially important roles form a portion of the personality system and insofar as action within these socially important roles is motivated by the interiorization of certain cognitions, beliefs, values, and attitudes, personality system and social system may be said to "mesh" or be oriented (51, p. 35).

Disorientation between the personality and society is thus defined by Schneider as a failure of the individual's motives, attitudes, beliefs, values, etc., to mesh with the needs of certain socially important roles (51, p. 36).

Such a failure of congruence may be attributed to the fact that the system of norms and roles within which the personality was formed is frequently quite different from that to which the person is required to adapt in adult life. Presumably slight or moderate changes in the individual's social system will not lead to incongruence, for the personality is capable of becoming adapted, through learning mechanisms, to a reward structure somewhat different from that to which it has been accustomed. However, extreme discontinuities requiring adaptation to a diametrically opposed set of norms may produce such violent disruption of expectations that new learning fails to occur. Some exceedingly basic and general dimensions of role definition have been described by Parsons (46); Schneider applies these to a theoretical formulation of some possible sources of disorientation between the personality and the social system.

Disorientation may be expected to occur when: (*a*) the individual's need for affection and response are not met within the cold impersonality of many of the institutional roles of the large-scale society; (*b*) a personality incorporating dominant collectivity-oriented motivation is unable to meet the demands of ruthlessly individualistic roles; (*c*) a personality which has been formed within the framework of ascribed roles is unable to adjust to the demands of achievement; (*d*) a personality which has been formed largely within particularistically oriented roles, which accentuate affectional needs and emotional dependence, meets the universalistic roles of an industrial urban society. More specifically, Schneider hypothesizes that:

1. Occupations in which competition is exceptionally severe and judgments of attainment highly impersonal (e.g., bureaucracy) will be marked by high incidence of mental disorder.

2. Mental disorder will result when an affectively oriented person encounters severely oriented roles.

3. Mental disorder will occur when the support of affectively charged relations is suddenly removed, for example, by a broken home or a disrupted love affair.

4. Mental disorder will occur when members of a minority group encounter severe amounts of hatred or discrimination, especially when their personalities predispose them to feel the same type of prejudice against their own group that they themselves are experiencing.

It is generally assumed that, in Western society,

the nuclear family and other primary groups contributing to socialization of the child partake of the Gemeinschaft characteristics—affectivity, collectivity-orientation, ascription, particularism, and diffuseness—while the secondary groups of later life display the opposite, Gesellschaft characteristics—affective neutrality, self-orientation, achievement, universalism, and specificity. In a folk society, where Gemeinschaft characteristics are more prevalent in all roles, discontinuity would presumably not be a dominant source of mental disorder (51, p. 48).

The implication of Schneider's formulation would appear to be that nearly all members (or at least male members) of this society, reared as they are within primary groups, would be expected to experience some degree of disorientation to certain of the social roles they are expected to perform as adults. "Disorientation" seems to be regarded by Schneider as equivalent to mental disorder, and in this sense the formulation appears exteme. While disorientation may give rise to mental disorder (in the more common senses of the term), the latter should not be regarded as either synonymous with, or a necessary concomitant of, the former. Human beings have mechanisms for handling disorientaion, not the least prevalent of which is the kind of "active adaptation" to which Jahoda refers (30).

One is tempted to suggest that there are more exceptions than corroborations of the propositions put forth by Schneider. In fact, one might expect that incumbents of the complex, competitive, impersonal roles typified by bureaucracy would have developed a correspondingly complex set of defensive or adaptive mechanisms which serve to maintain personality integration in the "normal stressful situation" (22) encountered in such roles. Perhaps the roles themselves are a source of adaptive mechanisms as well as stresses. Thus a more complex set of propositions is called for: The likelihood of disorientation varies as a function of discontinuities in role expectation along the dimensions suggested by Schneider, but mental disorder as a response to such disorientation is likely only to the extent that adaptive mechanisms are not either already available to the person or acquired by him in the course of role performance. From this point of view, the crucial factor in mental disorder is not so much the fact of disorientation between the personality and social system, as it is the manner in which such disorientation is handled by the personality.

Jahoda (30) has advanced two hypotheses concerning the learning of adaptive mechanisms through the socialization process:

1. The correct perception of reality will increase through frequent changes of environment; this will, at the same time, be conducive to passive acceptance, rather than active adjustment, unless the original "home" environment has enhanced the integration of personality.

2. The greater the chance to practice active adjustment and to reject passive acceptance at an early stage, the less is the likelihood that environmental changes will produce passive acceptance.

SUMMARY

This review of interpersonal correlates has included a number of theories and some empirical findings concerning the significance of social interaction processes in the development of mental disorder. A variety of operational definitions of mental illness have been used in these studies, but the one which appears conceptually appropriate to most of the formulations is that of maladjustment, or deviance from social norms. Thus the researcher who would coordinate theory and empirical data within and between these two levels of analysis is faced with the problem of determining the relation between social maladjustment and exposure to psychiatric treatment—two distinct definitions of mental illness. Though some correspondence between these two kinds of criteria has been indicated (54), it is not clear that inclusion by one necessarily requires inclusion by the other.

If we assume what has yet to be demonstrated, that social maladjustment will eventuate in mental disturbance diagnosable by other criteria, it is possible to speculate regarding a possible correspondence between some of the demographic-environmental correlates and some of the interpersonal correlates of mental illness. Specifically, we may interpret certain empirical relations in the former category in terms of concepts utilized in the latter. It is possible, for example, to regard major cultural events, such as war, depression, and technological advancement as having potential effects on the society's mental health through the widespread role dislocations and disruption of primary group ties which accompany them. Similarly, it is possible to seek explanations for the geographic, socioeconomic, race, and sex differences in rates of mental illness in certain interpersonal characteristics of the ecological and demographic situations. Possibly relevant dimensions of the interactional processes have been suggested; social isolation, the degree of involvement of individuals within a particular social system, and differences in socialization procedures employed by various groups.

Such interpretations as these are speculative and vaguely formulated at present. It is by no means clear that the interpersonal level of analysis is the most appropriate level at which to seek explanations of mental disorder. Nevertheless, it appears likely that a reformulation of some of the macro-societal differences in micro-social terms will suggest genotypes which are not readily discernible at the grosser levels of empirical correlation. Even if these do not provide causal explanations for many of the psychological manifestations which accompany mental disorder, they may at least expand the field of inquiry in directions which could eventually yield more basic understanding of the nature of mental health and mental illness.

NOTES

*This review was prepared for the Survey Research Center, University of Michigan, as background material for that organization's national survey of mental health, sponsored by the Joint Commission on Mental Illness and Health. The writer is indebted to Gerald Gurin of the Survey Research Center, and to Fillmore Sanford, formerly of the Joint Commission, for their contributions to the ideas presented here. Also appreciation is due the following researchers for their suggestions and for data from current studies which they provided: Harry Beilin, John Clausen, Benjamin Darsky, John Glidewell, Marie Jahoda, Morton Kramer, Thomas Langner, Charles Metzner, M. Brewster Smith, and Shirley Star.

1. Auld, F. Influences of social class on personality test responses. *Psychol. Bull.*, 1952, **49**, 318–332.
2. Belknap, I. V., & Jaco, E. G. The epidemiology of mental disorders in a political-type city, 1946–1952. In *Interrelations between the social environment and psychiatric disorders*. N. Y.: Milbank Memorial Fund, 1953.
3. Clark, R. E. Psychoses, income, and occupational prestige. *Amer. J. Sociol.*, 1949, **54**, 433–440.
4. Clausen, J. A. *Sociology and the field of mental health.* N. Y.: Russell Sage Foundation, 1956.
5. Clausen, J. A., & Kohn, M. L. The ecological approach in social psychiatry. *Amer. J. Sociol.*, 1954, **60**, 140–151.
6. Dunham, H. W. Current status of ecological research in mental disorder. *Soc. Forces*, 1947, **25**, 321–326.
7. Dunham, H. W. Some persistent problems in the epidemiology of mental disorders. *Amer. J. Psychiat.*, 1953, **109**, 567–575.
8. Durkheim, E. *Le suicide.* Paris: F. Alcan, 1897. (English translation, Glencoe, Ill.: Free Press, 1951.)
9. Ellis, Evelyn. Social psychological correlates of upward social mobility among unmarried career women. *Amer. sociol. Rev.*, 1952, **17**, 558–563.
10. *Epidemiology of mental disorder.* N. Y.: Milbank Memorial Fund, 1950.
11. Faris, R. E. L. Ecological factors in human behavior. In J. McV. Hunt (Ed.), *Personality and the behavior disorders.* N. Y.: Ronald, 1944.
12. Faris, R. E. L., & Dunham, H. W. *Mental disorders in urban areas.* Chicago: Univer. of Chicago Press, 1939.
13. Francis, T. Evaluation of this material. In *Epidemiology of Mental Disorder.* N. Y.: Milbank Memorial Fund, 1950.
14. Frumkin, R. M. Occupation and major mental disorders. In A. M. Rose (Ed.), *Mental health and mental disorder.* N. Y.: Norton, 1955.
15. Gildea, Margaret C., Domke, H. C., Mensh, I. N., Buchmueller, A. D., Glidewell, J. C., & Kantor, Mildred. Community mental health research: findings after three years. Paper read at Amer. Psychiat. Ass., Chicago, May, 1957.
16. Glidewell, J. C., Mensh, I. N., & Gildea, Margaret C. Behavior symptoms in children and degree of sickness. *Amer. J. Psychiat.*, 1957, **114**, 47–53.

17. Glidewell, J. C., Mensh, I. N., Domke, H. R., Gildea, Margaret C., & Buchmueller, A. D. Methods for community mental health research. *Amer. J. Orthopsychiat.*, 1957, **27**, 38–54.
18. Goldhamer, H., & Marshall, A. *Psychosis and civilization.* Glencoe, Ill.: Free Press, 1953.
19. Gruenberg, E. M. Community conditions and psychoses of the elderly. *Amer. J. Psychiat.*, 1954, **110**, 888–896.
20. Gruenberg, E. M., Major disorders. In *Epidemiology of mental disorder.* N. Y.: Milbank Memorial Fund, 1950.
21. Halmos, P. *Solitude and privacy.* London: Routledge & Kegan Paul, 1952.
22. Henry, W. E. Psychology. In *Interrelations between the social environment and psychiatric disorders.* N. Y.: Milbank Memorial Fund, 1953.
23. Henry. A. F., & Short, J. *Suicide and homicide.* Glencoe, Ill.: Free Press, 1954.
24. Hollingshead, A. B., Ellis, R., & Kirby, E. Social mobility and mental illness. *Amer. social. Rev.*, 1954, **19**, 577–591.
25. Hollingshead, A. B., & Redlich, F. C. Social stratification and psychiatric disorders. *Amer. social. Rev.*, 1953, **18**, 163–169.
26. Hollingshead, A. B., & Redlich, F. C. Schizophrenia and social structure. *Amer. J. Psychiat.*, 1954, **110**, 695–701.
27. Hyde, P. W., & Kingsley, L. V. Studies in medical sociology. I: The relation of mental disorders to the community socio-economic level. *New England J. Med.*, 1944, **231**, 543–548.
28. *Interrelations between the social environment and psychiatric disorders.* N. Y.: Milbank Memorial Fund, 1953.
29. Jaco, E. G. The social isolation hypothesis and schizophrenia. *Amer. social. Rev.*, 1954, **19**, 567–577.
30. Jahoda, Marie. Toward a social psychology of mental health. In A. M. Rose (Ed.), *Mental health and mental disorder.* N. Y.: Norton, 1955.
31. Kish, L. Selection of the sample. In L. Festinger & D. Katz (Eds.), *Research methods in the behavioral sciences.* N. Y.: Dryden, 1953.
32. Kohn, M. L. A discussion of prevalence and incidence. Bethesda, Md.: Biometrics Branch, NIMH (Mimeographed, no date).
33. Kohn, M. L., & Clausen, J. A. Social isolation and schizophrenia. *Amer. social. Rev.*, 1955, **20**, 265–273.
34. Kohn, M. L., & Clausen, J. A. Parental authority behavior and schizophrenia. *Amer. J. Orthopsychiat.*, 1956, **26**, 297–313.
35. Krout, M. H. A note on Dunham's contribution to the ecology of the functional psychoses. *Amer. Sociol. Rev.*, 1938, **3**, 209–212.
36. Leighton, A. H. A proposal for research in the epidemiology of psychiatric disorders. In *Epidemiology of mental disorder.* N. Y.: Milbank Memorial Fund, 1950.
37. Lemert, E. M. An exploratory study of mental disorders in a rural problem area. *Rural Sociol.*, 1948, **13**, 48–64.
38. Lemkau, P. Tietze, C., & Cooper, M. A survey of statistical studies on the prevalence and incidence of mental disorders in sample populations. *Publ. Hlth Rep.*, 1943, **58**, 1909–1927.

39. Lindemann, E., Et Al. Minor disorders. In *Epidemiology of mental disorders*. N. Y.: Milbank Memorial Fund, 1950.

40. Lindesmith, A. S., & Strauss, A. L. *Social psychology*. N. Y.: Dryden, 1956.

41. Malzberg, B. *Social and biological aspects of mental disease*. Utica: State Hosp. Press, 1940.

42. Mangus, A. P. Personaity change in adolescents. *Publ. Hlth Rep.*, 1957, **72**, 576–578.

43. Miller, D. R., & Swanson, G. E. A proposed study of the learning of techniques for resolving conflicts of impulses. In *Interrelations between the social environment and psychiatric disorders*. N. Y.: Milbank Memorial Fund, 1953.

44. Myers, J. K., & Schaffer, L. Social stratification and psychiatric practice: A study of an out-patient clinic. *Amer. sociol. Rev.*, 1945, **19**, 307–310.

45. Newcomb, T. M. *Social psychology*. N. Y. Dryden, 1950.

46. Parsons, T., & Shils, E. *Toward a general theory of action*. Cambridge: Harvard Univer. Press, 1951.

47. Paul, B. D. Mental disorder and self-regulating processes in culture: A Guatemalan illustration. In *Interrelations between the social environement and psychiatric disorders*. N. Y.: Milbank Memorial Fund, 1953.

48. Rennie, T. A. C. The Yorkville community mental health research study. In *Interrelations between the social environment and psychiatric disorders*. N. Y.: Milbank Memorial Fund, 1953.

49. Robinson, W. Ecological correlations and the behavior of individuals. *Amer. sociol. Rev.*, 1950, **15**, 351–357.

50. Rose, A. M., & Stub, H. R. Summary of studies on the incidence of mental disorders. In A. M. Rose (Ed.), *Mental health and mental disorder*. N. Y.: Norton, 1955.

51. Schneider, E. V. Sociological concepts and psychiatric research. In *Interrelations between the social environment and psychiatric disorders*. N. Y.: Milbank Memorial Fund, 1953.

52. Schroeder, C. W. Mental disorders in cities. *Amer. J. Sociol.*, 1942, **48**, 40–47.

53. Schroeder, C. W., & Beegle, J. A. Suicide: An instance of high rural rates. In A. M. Rose (Ed.), *Mental health and mental disorder*. N. Y.: Norton, 1955.

54. Scott, W. A. Research definitions of mental health and mental illness. *Psychol. Bull.*, 1958, **55**, 29–45.

55. Sears, R. R., Maccoby, Eleanor, & Levin, H. *Patterns of child-rearing*. Evanston: Row, Peterson, 1957.

56. Shoben, E. J. The assessment of parental attitudes in relation to child adjustment. *Genet. Psychol. Monogr.*, 1949, **39**, 101–148.

57. Straus, R. Alcoholism. In A. M. Rose (Ed.), *Mental health and mental disorder*. N. Y.: Norton, 1955.

58. Sutherland, E. H. *The professional thief*. Chicago: Univer. of Chicago Press, 1937.

59. Tietze, C., Lemkau, P., & Cooper, M. Schizophrenia, manic-depressive psychosis, and socio-economic status. *Amer. J. Sociol.*, 1941, **47**, 167–175.

60. Tietze, C., Lemkau, P., & Cooper, M. Personal disorder and spatial mobility. *Amer. J. Sociol.*, 1942, **48**, 29–39.

61. Wahl, C. W. Antecedent factors in schizophrenia. *Amer. J. Sociol.*, 1941, **47**, 167–175.

62. Whyte, W. F. *Street corner society*. Chicago: Univer. of Chicago Press, 1955.

part III
PERSONALITY DEVELOPMENT AND MENTAL DISORDERS

SECTION 1

SOCIAL INFLUENCES ON MENTAL DISORDERS

ONE general approach to the social development of disordered behavior refers to the sequences of social influences that have contributed to the disordered behavior of the afflicted person. This is distinct from the physical maturational approach to disordered behavior, which would emphasize the influence of organic changes and dysfunctions on social behavior, and from the psychogenetic position, which claims that disordered behavior is based upon experiences in early formative years and that subsequent stresses tend to exacerbate or manifest a basically predisposed condition of the personality.

From the viewpoint expressed in this book, experiences in early life are significant in personality formation and frequently are determinants of severe mental disorders. The stresses encountered in subsequent experiences tend to sustain a continuity of personal strain which can eventuate into mild or severe mental disorders. Formative influences in early life or even constitutional deficits may contribute to the predisposition of the severe disorders. But many disorders can arise from the combined sequence of stressful influences in early and later life, and some disorders can emerge from stresses in adolescence and later, despite a seemingly stable childhood.

The readings concern the kinds of experiences disordered persons had, prior to their breakdowns, in successive groups such as the family, peer group, school, work, marriage, and old age. In the characterization of the familial influences on disordered behavior, we include the analyses dealing with patterns of family organization and the modes of parent-child relations, especially mother-child relations, which may affect disordered behavior generally and schizophrenia particularly.

Since schizophrenia has been investigated intensively and offers the most thorough and consistent information, several papers deal with this psychotic condition. But the kinds of pathological influences that contribute to schizophrenia are evident in some measure in other disorders. For example, Block and her associates in using the Rorschach Inkblot Test, the Minnesota Multiphasic Personality Inventory, and the Thematic Apperception Test reported no differences in test results between the parents of neurotic and the parents of schizophrenic children, except for extreme items.[1] At the extreme level, the neurotogenic mother seemingly was a highly tentative person pervaded by guilt and worry, one who required continual reassurance. In close communication with her emotional life, she readily manifested her feelings. Submissive and uncertain in her social relations, she herself sought parental figures for her own emotional protection. The schizophrenogenic mother by contrast is completely Machiavellian and very egocentric. She uses other people including her child to serve her needs and ends. She then could exploit, ignore, or manipulate others for her own purposes. Her power orientation represented a basic defense against her own anxiety.

This general effort to determine personality differences and types as contributory or causal influences upon a given disorder reduces the dynamic dimension of the interaction between parents and children to static personality traits, which in action presumably contribute to disordered behavior, specifically schizophrenic behavior. The sociological approach regards parental traits as indicators of relations but aims to ascertain the modes of interaction and the social conditions which contribute to the type of disordered behavior.

The source of the data also is a criterion of the scope and validity of the results for a particular study. If the source consists of hospital records, these data may not be as thorough nor as profound as interviews. Second, the types of schizophrenics

are taken to be of uniform diagnosis and hence of a uniform personality condition. But the duration of the disorder and the degree of personality disorganization among schizophrenics vary, and hence the modes of influence may be expected to vary.

In her paper, "Contradictory Parental Expectations in Schizophrenia," Lu compares the effects of parental relationships on fifty schizophrenic subjects and fifty nonschizophrenic siblings. The schizophrenics were more dependent upon their parents and more responsible in achievement generally and in doing specific tasks than the nonschizophrenics were. They strived for perfection but remained uncritically dependent upon their parents. The siblings were less perfectionistic, less dependent, and more realistic in their goals.

Kohn and Clausen, in "Social Isolation and Schizophrenia," inquire into the extent to which the lack of peer associations is a predisposing influence in schizophrenia. They compared matched groups of schizophrenics and controls as well as small groups of manic-depressives and controls. They found that isolation from peers in early adolescence was not predisposing to schizophrenia or manic-depression, because only one-third of the subjects were isolated, and even these did not appear predisposed to psychosis as a direct consequence of the isolation. Although social isolation is symptomatic of deep personal conflicts among many schizophrenics, only some schizophrenics have been traumatized by the rejection and ostracism of their peers.

Leavy and Freedman, in their paper "Psychoneurosis and Economic Life," describe the effects of economic activities on neurotic behavior. But economic influences are not easily disentangled from social influences. Economic insecurity creates emotional insecurity in the processes of obtaining and keeping a job and of maintaining social status by acquiring the goods from one's earnings. But economic and emotional insecurity in childhood, from the developmental viewpoint, can affect economic pursuits and reactions to economic insecurity in later life.

Persons in the lower classes encounter basic stress because of job dissatisfaction and the inability to earn a living. But persons in the middle classes experience intense stress when economic mobility is blocked. Lack of job satisfaction and the discrepancy between the type of job one has and the job one wants can also contribute to anxiety and frustration for these people. Furthermore, persons in the different classes define and react differently to disordered behavior. This

[1] Jeanne Block, Virginia Patterson, Jack Block, and Don D. Jackson, "A Study of the Parents of Schizophrenic and Neurotic Children," *Psychiatry* (1958), *21*, 387–97.

discrepancy is consistent with the frustration experienced between occupational attainment and occupational aspiration.

Lowenthal traces the relationship between "Social Isolation and Mental Illness in Old Age" from a sample of four subgroups of 1,200 institutionalized and noninstitutionalized persons. She analyzes the social, physical, and psychological characteristics. From her data, she summarizes that lifelong isolation and alienation are not necessarily conducive to the development of the kinds of mental disorders that bring people to the psychiatric hospital in old age. She claims instead that in later life isolation may be more a consequence than a cause of a disordered condition. Marginal social adjustment, however, does contribute to the development of disordered behavior.

TYPES OF FAMILY PATTERNS THAT CONTRIBUTE TO MENTAL DISORDERS

S. Kirson Weinberg

THERE is no single, social path to schizophrenia because biological endowments as well as modes of family relations among schizophrenics vary. Except in extreme cases, it is often difficult to predict that a given family's relationships will create schizophrenia among its members. Schizophrenia combines a series of influences that can be understood as a configuration; this will be seen in the following discussion of (1) the ingrown family, (2) parental traits and parent-child relationships, and (3) *folie à deux*.

THE INGROWN FAMILY

In the "ingrown family," the members' relationships and attachments are confined to the family. More or less isolated socially, they become estranged from the practices and expectations of the community, and they are considered "queer" or "different" by the neighbors.[1]

Within this ingrown family, the dominant and significant parent, usually the mother, subjugates the rest of the family and forbids them to cultivate outside relationships. Children experience extreme difficulty in transitional adjustment to the outside community. At this juncture, they are personally retarded and cannot develop outside relations. In brief, the families that approximate this type contribute to personal immaturity and possibly lay the groundwork for disordered behavior among the children.[2]

PARENTAL TRAITS AND PARENT-CHILD RELATIONSHIPS

To understand the interacting process between parents and preschizophrenic children, two considerations must be stressed. First, these relationships are a dynamic, continuous sequence rather

Part of this paper appeared previously in S. Kirson Weinberg, *Society and Personality Disorders* (Englewood Cliffs, N. J.; Prentice-Hall, 1952).

than a static, terminal affair; hence, all participants are affected. Second, unwitting and unconscious aspects of the interacting process are usually as effective, if not more so, in influencing the children than overt and direct types of expressions because these modes of interaction are less understood by the participants and are more difficult to control or to revise. In general, parental relationships with preschizophrenic children tend to be conflict-creating at an earlier age than parental relationships with neurotics and more intense in their effects upon the lowered self-evaluation of the preschizophrenics, although some schizophrenics seem outwardly "normal" during childhood. As pointers to understanding parent-child relations, the personalities of the parents become relevant because their traits may be static indicators of their dynamic relationships with their children.

Despite the variety of personality differences among the parents of schizophrenics, instability and harsh or subtle domination stand out as being among the most significant characteristics. Lidz and Lidz found that only five out of fifty schizophrenics came from reasonably stable families in which parents were relatively balanced and compatible. The parents of the other 45 were unstable or incompatible.[3]

The mother usually is the more influential parent, but this does not necessarily follow. Friedlander found that the parents were markedly inconsistent in their relations with their children. The fathers were austere and strict, while the mothers were indulgent.[4] Despert found that in 19 out of 29 cases the mothers were aggressive, oversolicitous, and overanxious about the children, but the fathers were docile and understanding.[5] Wittman and Huffman found that, though the mothers were unstable, oversolicitous, and overprotective, the fathers were more or less normal.[6] In a study of 100 schizophrenics, Terry found that 58 mothers or mother substitutes were domineering, possessive, oversolicitous, overindulgent, neurotic, eccentric, or psychotic. She found that many mothers and fathers fell into the roles demanded by the children who eventually broke down.[7] During adolescence and adulthood, the offspring retained intense attachments to and dependency upon the parents, especially the mothers. Sometimes, the children's behavior aggravated the parents' instability because they did not turn out as the parents had hoped.

In comparing the parental reactions of schizophrenic, neurotic, and normal subjects whose ages were over 12 and under 32 years, McKeown found that the parents of the schizophrenic children were more "demanding-antagonistic" and more "discouraging" than were the parents of normal children, but that their reactions were somewhat similar to the parents of neurotic children.[8]

Despite variations in personalities, the parents tended to make the children very dependent upon them, to suppress their initiative, and to impose their own distorted goals upon their children. Hence, many preschizophrenic children lived for their parents and could not evaluate themselves in terms of their own needs. When the children did not measure up to parental demands, the children were frequently taunted, ridiculed, or made to feel very guilty.

Many parents encouraged immaturity in the children. One schizophrenic recalled that when she got into difficulty with her father and went into a tantrum, the father would "forgive and forget." When she tried to behave maturely by accepting responsibility after some mistake, the father became ruthless in his reprimands and persisted in nagging allusions weeks after the incident occurred. Consequently, she continued with these tantrums until late adolescence because that was the only way she could absolve herself from difficulties.

In a study of 25 mothers of schizophrenics, Tietze found that almost all of them were domineering, but that their techniques of domination were of two general kinds—open and subtle. Of the two types, the subtle domination was more harmful because the mother's activity was not clear to the children and hence did not lead to open defiance and rebellion. For example, one mother dominated her three daughters in a subtle manner; two became schizophrenic and one was afflicted with ulcerative colitis. When displeased or angry, this mother did not shout or raise her voice; she cried, had headaches and fainting spells, and eventually took to bed when these sick spells came on. Her sick spells occurred conveniently, when her daughters wanted to go to a party or have "some fun." The mother then insisted that the daughters stay home and care for her. Consequently, the daughters despaired of planning for "any fun."[9]

The most harmful types of parent-child relationships were those in which the children were rejected very early in life. In these instances, the children, feeling unwanted, unloved, and despised, often despaired of obtaining affection from other persons. In a gesture of protective avoidance, they turned inward and became distant and isolated from others. These extremely rejecting relationships occurred in few cases, but many other parents expressed unwitting feelings of rejection and hostility; then they tried to cover up these attitudes and to compensate for them by oversolicitousness for which they expected the gratitude of the children.

Finally, the parents seemed to contribute to the psychosexual retardation of the preschizophrenic children. They instilled deep feelings of guilt over masturbation and relationships with the opposite sex. In general these parental influences led to the preshizophrenics' isolation from the conventional patterns of the peer group, to a denial of their sexual roles as demanded by the peer group, and to a lowering of their self-esteem.

The preschizophrenic may have been the youngest or eldest sibling, the only boy, or the only girl. He may have been estranged from other family members because of age, differential ability, or physical condition. Sometimes his isolation from other family members intensified his attachment to the mother.[10]

FOLIE À DEUX: "DISORDER OF TWO"

Folie à deux means that one person who becomes disordered is influenced by intimate relationships with another person who is disordered or disturbed. This disorder is not necessarily confined to two persons only, but may extend to three persons, *folie à trois*, or to four persons, *folie à quatre*. Though occuring chiefly among family members, this disorder sometimes is found among intimate friends.[11] Gralnick, in an intensive review of the literature, classifies these disorders, chiefly by mode of relationships and by mode of onset, into four types: (1) simultaneous, (2) communicated, (3) imposed, and (4) induced.[12]

The simultaneous type refers to identical psychotic conditions of two or more family members at the same time. The communicated type means that one person, despite his resistance, acquires the delusional ideas of another. The imposed type refers to the acquisition of similar delusions and mannerisms by a person, who may himself be ordered but also submissive and dependent upon a domineering, disordered person. When the two persons are separated, the submissive person tends to improve. The induced type refers to the acquisition of new delusions by a disordered person who is influenced by another disordered person.

All these disorders result from direct learning by at least one of the disordered persons. Although these disordered expressions may vary, the paranoid schizophrenic form is the most frequent. Of the types of *folie à deux*, the "imposed" form occurs most frequently. Among the schizophrenics, Gralnick found that 38 cases were imposed, eighteen communicated, three simultaneous, and one induced. Of the family combinations, seventeen were sister combinations, thirteen mother-child, fifteen husband-wife, five brother, one father-daughter, and one sister-brother. One case was between two friends, and two involved three sisters.[13]

Since these types of breakdown are influenced directly or indirectly by family relationships, many important phases of family life can be illuminated by the extreme character of the cases. In the instance of the Carrington family, compiled by Gralnick, the entire family of four broke down, but at different times. The mother, Anne, was the initially disordered person, a paranoid, and the dominant member of the family. Because of her influence, the husband and the two children also became psychotic, and her influence upon her two children was especially evident.[14]

THE FAMILY AND SCHIZOPHRENIA

Thus, the modes of socialization among pre-schizophrenic children are definitely affected by parents (especially the mother) who tend to be unstable, domineering, and demanding. These parents try to control the lives of their children, to retard their development and emotional independence, and to isolate them from the peer group. Although schizophrenia is not definitely related to order of birth among the children, the preschizophrenic tends to be isolated from the other siblings because of age or physique or his general personality, which makes him more dependent upon the parents. The ingrown family tends to influence children in this direction, and the presence of an irrational, domineering parent can create the phenomenon of *folie à deux* in which more than one person in the family becomes afflicted.

Although these familial influences are predominant, there is no single type of family from which schizophrenia arises. The family types are many, as are the parental types, and these family and parental types require more definitive analysis. Moreover, little is known of the siblings of schizophrenics. The study by Lu does add to the knowledge of the family life of the schizophrenic and indicates why one sibling breaks down and others do not.

NOTES

1. S. Kirson Weinberg, *Incest Behavior* (New York: Citadel Press, 1955).
2. *Ibid.*
3. Ruth W. Lidz and Theodore Lidz, "The Family Environment of Schizophrenic patients," *American Journal of Psychiatry* (November, 1949), *106* (5), 343.
See also Theodore Lidz *et al.*, *Schizophrenia and the Family*, (New York: International University Press, 1965).
4. Dorothy Friedlander, "Personality Development of 27 Children Who Later Became Psychotic," *Journal of Abnormal and Social Psychology* (1945), *40*, 330–35.
5. Louise J. Despert, "Schizophrenia in Children," *Psychiatric Quarterly* (1938), *12*, 336–71.
6. M. Phyllis Wittman and A. V. Huffman, "A Comparative Study of Developmental Adjusted Teen-Aged Youths," *Elgin State Hospital Papers* (December, 1944), *5*, 228–37.
7. Described in Leo Kanner, *Child Psychiatry* (Springfield, Ill: Charles C. Thomas, 1942), p. 492.
8. James Edward McKeown, "The Behavior of Parents of Schizophrenic, Neurotic, and Normal Children," *American Journal of Sociology* (September, 1950), *56* (2), 175–79. Since the neurotic subjects in this study were children, it is possible that these children may incur a schizophrenic disorder in later life.
9. Trude Tietze, "A Study of Mothers of Schizophrenic Patients," *Psychiatry* (February, 1949), *12*, 55–56. *See also* Joseph Kasanin, E. Knight, and P. Sage "The Parent-Child Relationship in Schizophrenia," *Journal of Nervous and Mental Disease* (1940), *79*, 249–63.
10. Nicholas J. Demerath, "Adolescent Status Demands and the Student Experiences of twenty Schizophrenics," *American Sociological Review* (1943), *8*, 513–18.
11. Alexander Gralnick, "Folie à Deux—The Psychosis of Association: A Review of 103 Cases and the Entire English Literature," *Psychiatric Quarterly* (April, 1942), *16* (2), 491–520.
12. *Ibid.*, p. 3.
13. *Ibid.*, pp. 4–7.
14. Alexander Gralnick, "The Carrington Family: A Psychiatric and Social Study Illustrating the Psychoses of Association or Folie à Deux," *Psychiatric Quarterly* (April, 1943), *17*, 32.

CONTRADICTORY PARENTAL EXPECTATIONS IN SCHIZOPHRENIA: DEPENDENCE AND RESPONSIBILITIES

Yi-chuang Lu

THIS PAPER reports some preliminary findings of one aspect of a research on schizophrenic patients and their families. Previous investigations such as the works of Lidz,[12-16] Hill,[6] Wynne,[21] Bowen,[2,3] Bateson,[1] and Jackson[8] have indicated that parental pathology or pathological patterns of interpersonal relationships in the family are of etiological significance to the development of schizophrenia. Most of these studies have concentrated on the patients' families. In comparing parental or parent-child relations in the schizophrenics' families with those in the nonschizophrenics' families, other investigators use "normals" or "psychoneurotics" as controls. The pieces of research by Kohn,[10] Clausen,[4] and Myers and Roberts[18] are examples of this type. These later researches have shown the prevalence of certain patterns of parental authority structure in the schizophrenics' families which are different from those in the nonschizophrenic families, at least among families in a certain socioeconomic class.

While the existing investigations on schizophrenia revealed the significance of parental or family pathology or parental authority structure,[8] one question remains to be answered: "Why does one child in a family develop schizophrenia, while another child, presumably exposed to similar parental or family pathology or parental authority structure, does not?" This question suggests that merely studying parental or family pathology or parental authority structure in the family alone is not enough to explain the development of schizophrenia. To seek an answer, it is necessary to compare the parents' relationships with the preschizophrenics and the parents' relationships with the nonschizophrenic siblings of the patients. In the present research, therefore, the nonschizophrenic siblings are used as controls. The objective here is to discover the specific patterns, if any, of parent-child interactions that are related to the development of schizophrenia. An attempt is also

Reprinted from the *Archives of General Psychiatry* (March, 1962), Vol. 6, pp. 219–35. Copyright 1962 by the American Medical Association.

made to ascertain other significant life experiences of the preschizophrenics which are different from those of the nonschizophrenic siblings and which are related to the development of schizophrenia.

METHOD OF RESEARCH

The sample of this research consisted of 50 schizophrenic patients who are part of the patient population in a male-female chronic schizophrenic research unit at the Manteno State Hospital, Illinois. Only those schizophrenic patients who had a nonschizophrenic sibling, preferably of the same sex and near in age and whose parents, particularly the mothers, were available for interviews, were included in the sample. Other criteria for selection of cases included: no organic brain disease or mental deficiency, young (preferably under 35), white, with minimum grade school education, families from lower socioeconomic strata, preferably with parents who live in Chicago.

The data of this project were obtained by my interviewing the patients intensively and observing their behavior in the schizophrenic research unit of the hospital in the last 5 years. Intensive interviews were also conducted by me with the patients' fathers, mothers, siblings, and other significant persons in the patients' life. All these interviews were recorded verbatim and conducted for research purposes. The length of an interview with the schizophrenic patients varied. It ranged from half an hour to 2 hours or sometimes longer, depending on the mood, mental condition of the patients, or their desires to express themselves at the time of the interview. The first interview with a parent or sibling, particularly with the mother, often lasted up to about 4 hours or more. Most of the family members spoke spontaneously and freely. The mothers in particular tended to confide their particular feelings and report the interpersonal relationships in the family. In addition to interviews by appointment, casual interviews with and observations of family members were also made during their visits with the patients on the hospital ground. The reliability and validity of the interview data were tested by comparing the patients' statements with those of their parents and siblings. In addition to interviews, a schedule was constructed. Therefore, this project combines the use of both qualitative and quantitative data.

The preliminary findings to be presented in this paper are based on analysis of the life histories of 24 out of the total of 50 cases in this sample. A detailed statistical presentation of all data will be deferred to the future when the schedule data of all 50 cases are completely analyzed. At the time of the investigation, most of the subjects reported in this paper were 35 years of age or under. They were white; 15 males and 9 females. The majority of them completed at least their grade school education; 10 of them attended college. Nine of the subjects are from families of lower-lower and 10 from upper-lower socioeconomic classes, 4 from lower-middle and 1 from upper-middle classes; immigrant backgrounds and diverse ethnic groups were predominant. The majority of the patients were Catholics, and some of the parents' marriages were of mixed religious faith. The ages at the first schizophrenic break range from 16 to 30; the median age of the first break is 20.

CONTRADICTORY PARENTAL EXPECTATIONS OF DEPENDENCE AND RESPONSIBILITY

A comparison between the parents' relationships with the preschizophrenic child and the parents' relationships with the nonschizophrenic sibling shows that they are quite different with respect to the parents' contradictory expectations for the child's dependence and responsibility and the child's efforts to fulfill these expectations. In this section, the terms "dependence" and "responsibility" will be defined; the differences between the role patterns of the preschizophrenic child and the nonschizophrenic sibling in relation to their parents will be presented and discussed; and case excerpts will be used to illustrate these differences. In the next section, an attempt will be made to show how later specific social situations acting on the previously developed relational role pattern of the preschizophrenic child precipitate the schizophrenic break. The third section will trace the different role patterns of the preschizophrenic child and the nonschizophrenic sibling to the different social, familial, and personal situations confronting them at their birth and infancy. Finally,

the implications of these preliminary findings for a theory of schizophrenia will be discussed.

1. Dependence.

The term dependence is used here to refer to one's reliance upon others for emotional support (response, recognition, security, appreciation, encouragement, and reassurance), for protection, and/or for care. In the preschizophrenic's relations with his parents, dependence also implies the former's sensitivity to the latter's feelings and expectations for obedience and submission—the parents' approval and acceptance being vital to his emotional survival. It also denotes the persistent efforts on the part of the offspring to please his parents and conform to their wishes and demands at the cost of his personal autonomy. Dependence is the opposite of independence or autonomy in decision-making or assuming responsibility.

The data in this sample indicate that although the parents attempted to exercise authority over both the preschizophrenic child and his nonschizophrenic sibling since their childhood, the parents expected a higher degree of obedience, submission and dependence from the preschizophrenic than from the nonschizophrenic child. Twenty-two out of the 24 cases have reported such a difference. On his part, the preschizophrenic child was much more obedient, submissive to and dependent on the parents than the nonschizophrenic child, while the nonschizophrenic child got away from parental control and strove for independence. Of the 24 cases, 23 cases reported such a difference. The 22 patients whose parents had higher expectations for their dependence are also the patients who became more dependent on their parents.

The following excerpts shows the differences between the preschizophrenic child and the nonschizophrenic sibling in regard to their dependent relationships with their parents.

A 19-year-old female patient with grade school education reported: "My parents are strict on their children. I think they are more strict on me and they punished me more (than other kids in the family). I always broke my arms since I was 2 years old. Both my mother and father took care of me on account of it. This made me more dependent on them. But other kids in the family had not been sick (physically). They were on their own. Both Sandra and Cathy (sisters) like to do things for themselves. But I like to depend on someone else to do things for me. I am much more dependent on my mother than Sandra and Cathy. I always told my mother everything.

"Before I was mentally sick, I tried to please my parents by running errands for them, doing the things my mother asked me to do. But still they didn't appreciate it. I cared more about my parents' feelings than Sandra and Cathy.—At the age of 13, I went to work for a family to help take care of their children and their house. But it lasted only a couple of weeks because I was too tied to my mom and dad's apron strings. I was so used to my mom and dad that I couldn't be on my own. When I worked for this family, I lived in their house. But I called my mom every day. When I called her, she answered the phone right away. Apparently she was sitting there waiting for my call. She had protected me more than other kids at home. Sandra and Cathy were not tied to my mother's apron strings."

Another patient, aged 24, a male college student, said: "My mother babied me. Sometimes maybe she made me feel like a baby, like I was afraid to leave my home for the army, or something like that. I still feel I am dependent because I can't hold a job. I am dependent on my mother and father. Dependence means that they cook for me, they take care of the house, and they pay for my room and board. They just told me to cut the lawn, to go to the store, maybe to dust the furniture. I have never really taken care of myself. But Philip (brother) is very able to take care of himself than I of myself. He is able to hold a job. I was real close to my parents. I was closer to my father and mother than my brothers were. I confided in them about everything."

2. Responsibility.

While the parents expected the preschizophrenic child to be more dependent than they expected the nonschizophrenic sibling, they at the same time entertained a conflicting expectation that the preschizophrenic child assume *responsibility for achievement and perfection*. In this paper, the term "responsibility" is used to refer to 2 different categories of role demands. The first category is responsibility for the fulfillment of certain *generalized and often abstract demands*, such as high aspirations for achievement, striving for social mobility, and striving for perfection. The second is responsibility for performing certain *concrete, specific, and immediate tasks* such as financial responsibility and household functions, particularly those relating to adult roles in the American society.

In this section, we are concerned only with the first category of responsibility—the more *generalized* expectations. In 19 out of 24 cases, the parents had, since the preschizophrenics' childhood, higher expectations for their achievements and for their striving for social mobility and perfection than for the patients' nonschizophrenic siblings. Although the parents who themselves were often perfectionists had great desires for the success of both the preschizophrenic and the nonschizophrenic sibling, it was the preschizophrenic in whom the parents constantly instilled such high expectations. The schizophrenics, their parents, and siblings often reported that the

parents always expected and even insisted that their preschizophrenic children be perfect, be the best, and be on the top among their peers either educationally, occupationally, socially, or as a person.

The mother of a single, 24-year-old student who studied in a theological seminary to be a priest at the time of his schizophrenic break reported: "My husband, who was a foreman, was a perfectionist. I am also a perfectionist. I was a school teacher and I am a very ambitious person. Since Gordon (the patient) was a child and began to go to school, I expected him to be a scholar. I expected Fred (the nonschizophrenic sibling) to be successful, but I had never expected him as much as Gordon. When Gordon was at the eighth grade, his class prophecy of him was Professor Smith. I had always expected him to be a scholarly person. If he could be one, I would be satisfied. He always had good grades in school. If they could do it, of course you would expect them to. But I did not expect Fred as much, because he had not done so well in school. I wanted Gordon to go to the township high school because I wanted him to learn speech in order to study to be a priest. Gordon tried to please me much more than Fred. Since childhood, Gordon was much more dependent on me than Fred."

A 25-year-old college student whose father was a policeman said: "Before I was sick, my parents drove me very hard. My mother always told us to be better than we were and to do better. But she hasn't driven my brother so hard. My mother expected me to become a lawyer or some kind like that. It means that I will also be doubly important than I am. I mean, she could do it herself and do me no harm. What I do for myself is much better for myself than for anyone else. Mother always wanted me to do what she wanted. Even when I was a big boy at the age of twenty, she told me what to do. She always insisted on me to do what she wanted me to do. She would order me around while I wanted to do my own thinking."

On their part, the preschizophrenics had also attempted desperately to live up to the parental expectations, although some might complain about the parental drives for their success and perfection. In this sample, it was found that in 18 out of 24 cases the preschizophrenics had a much higher mobility aspiration and desire for achievement and perfection than the nonschizophrenic siblings. Seventeen cases in this group are the same cases among the 19 cases where the parents had higher expectations for the preschizophrenics' achievements and perfection than for the nonschizophrenic siblings. In other words, in almost all the cases where parents had higher expectations for the preschizophrenics' achievement and perfection than for the nonschizophrenic siblings, the preschizophrenics also tried harder to live up to that expectation than the nonschizophrenic siblings.

In many cases, the preschizophrenics' initial efforts and aspirations for achievement did actually result in their success as the best students in grade school, and, for many, even in high school. The parents, siblings, and the schizophrenic patients themselves frequently reported that the preschizo-phrenics obtained the highest grades in their classes. Many were honor students, scholarship holders, and were valedictorians for their gradua-ting class at grade school. Although many non-schizophrenic siblings had done well, they were seldom such top students at these early student periods. The preschizophrenics had not only striven for achievements; they also attempted to be perfect as defined by their parents, often vaguely, such as being "the best," "good," "nice," etc. Not infrequently they were extremely religious and obedient. In contrast, the nonschizophrenic siblings had not taken these parental expecta-tions so seriously. They tried as much as possible to go out with their friends.

Take, for example, the case of Gordon, a student at a theological seminary who has been discussed in the first part of this section. The widowed mother gave the following description of her preschizophrenic and nonschizophrenic children:

"Gordon was too much of a perfectionist. He wanted everything in perfect order. But Fred is not a perfectionist at all. He is just the opposite of Gordon. Gordon was a very ambitious boy. But with Fred, I had to push him. Gordon's marks started falling down in the second year of theological seminary. He took too many courses in the second year, because he wanted to get into Novitiate. In one of the courses, he was in the class with younger students. They threw papers over him. He could do nothing about it, because he wanted to have 100 points in his conduct course. If he threw papers back to them, then he couldn't get it. He was too much of a perfectionist. He took things too seriously. Gordon was interested to work very much. You don't have to tell him to clean the basement, to mow the lawn, or to clean the house. He just kept everything beautifully at home. But Fred never did anything. Gordon worked so hard might be because he wanted to please me. He was so wonderful to me before he was sick. Naturally I praised him a lot for it. So he might want to please me even more. I never missed a birthday or a Mother's Day without a gift from Gordon. But Fred doesn't even know when my birthday is."

The patient, Gordon, also reported: "I think I am the favorite of my mother among all the boys in the family. You know, I have been the closest one to her. I had always tried to make her happy. But my brothers never cared about her like I did. My 2 older brothers graduated from high school and then went to work. I am the only one in the family who went to college; I think I was the smartest among my brothers at that time. I got the second honor in my class at the fourth grade and I got the first honor in my class at the sixth grade. As to

high school, at first I also got good grades. But I didn't get good grades in the last 2 years. But they let me graduate anyway. I think I am the most ambitious one among my brothers. They wanted to do well too. But since they couldn't do it, they went to work. Now they are pretty successful in their work. My 2 older brothers are married now. My mother and I were the most religious persons in the family. I always wanted to be a priest and I still want to be one now. But my brothers never wanted to be priests and they never have been so religious. I always wanted to be good. My younger brother doesn't listen to my mother as I do."

The preschizophrenic's effort in conforming to parental expectations for success and perfection, together with its results, can also be seen in the following excerpt.

The parent of a single, 26-year-old ex-newspaper delivery boy said: "Graham (patient) used to like to jump on high things. But his brother did not care. Graham was extremely ambitious. He was the only one among my kids who always wanted to make something of himself. He always wanted to make the home better. He got a big citation and a medal from Mayor Kelly when he was 13 for collecting the largest amount of scrap paper during the wartime. He was also the one who made the speech for the graduating class in grade school. He got so many medals but he never put them on. Other kids would be proud of this and put them on. But Graham never did. He wanted to be the best. But not my other kids."

The type of responsibility which the above interview excerpts bring out refers to the fulfillment of obligation or "duty" of a more generalized or abstract nature. This first category of respons-ibility is more or less a long-range goal to be achieved. It played a more prominent role in the preschizophrenic's life *long* before the appearance of schizophrenic symptoms. It is to be distinguished from the second category of responsibility which plays a definite role as a factor in *precipitating* the schizophrenic symptoms to be discussed later in this paper. This second category of respons-ibility is related to the performance of more specific, concrete, and immediate tasks.

So far, the data on parental expectations for dependence and for responsibility, and the data on their children's attempt to fulfill them, have been presented separately. Now it is necessary to see how many parents had entertained higher expectations for their preschizophrenic children than for their nonschizophrenic children to play *both* the role of dependence *and* the role of assum-ing responsibility for achievement and perfection, and how many preschizophrenics had made greater efforts than their nonschizophrenic siblings to play these contradictory roles. For the parents to expect the preschizophrenics to play the contradictory roles of dependence and responsibility is to involve the preschizophrenics in a dilemma. An examination of the data shows that in 19 out of 24 cases, the parents had expected their preschizophrenic children to play these contradictory roles of dependence and responsibility for achievement and perfection much more than they expected their nonschizophrenic children. Again, 17 out of the 24 preschizophrenics had persistently made greater efforts than their nonschizophrenic siblings to fulfill these contradictory parental expectations of dependence and responsibility for achievement and perfection. These 17 cases are among the 19 cases where there were higher contradictory parental expectations for the preschizophrenics than for the nonschizophrenics. Since these have been illustrated in the interview excerpts presented above, no more quotations will be given here.

Closely related to the contradictory parental expectations of responsibility and dependence is another set of contradictions in parental expectation and attitudes or behavior which merits a brief discussion here. This is the contradiction between parental expectation of the child's high achievement and perfection on one hand, and, on the other, the parents' competition with the preschizophrenic child for status, power, and possession. It seems that whenever the child performed adequately according to the parental expectation of achievement, the parents would feel that their power and status were threatened. On the other hand, the preschizophrenic also competed with the parents while attempting desperately to fulfill parental expectations at the same time. Such parental expectations of the preschizophrenic's achievement and parent-child competition often began to occur when the preschizophrenic child was in high school. In comparison, the parents expected less from the nonschizophrenic sibling and were less competitive with him than with the preschizophrenic child. The preschizophrenic child also took them more seriously than the nonschizophrenic sibling. The following excerpt illustrates one aspect of such parental contradiction and the schizophrenic child's responses to them.

A 25-year-old single football player who won a football scholarship to a university reported: "My father and mother expected me to amount to something much more than they expected of my brother. I think I was more ambitious than my brother. My father especially expected me to do well in the football field, because all through his life he had wanted to be a football coach. But he had to support his family and so he had to give it up. Therefore he wanted me to be a coach. I feel I took what my parents said as real, and seriously, but my brother didn't. Whenever I played football with other kids in high school, my father used to come and insist on coaching me. My friends all laughed at me on account of it. But whenever I did play real well, my father would get mad at me. He wanted to feel he was better than me. I think he competes with me more than he with my brother."

3. Discrepancy between Aspiration and Self-Evaluation.

In 14 out of the 24 cases in the data, the discrepancy between the preschizophrenic's aspiration for achievement, perfection, and his self-evaluation is greater than the discrepancy between those of the nonschizophrenic sibling.

As the preschizophrenics grew older, the fulfillment of contradictory parental expectations for dependence and responsibility of achievement and perfection became increasingly difficult for them, for the American culture deplores dependence and values increasing independence from parents as one enters adolescence and approaches adulthood. Moreover, competition during childhood among a small group of children was less keen than competition with peers on higher educational levels, who were a more selected group. In high school or college, the preschizophrenics' chance to remain at the top was decreased. Furthermore, there were some preschizophrenics who attended larger high schools and colleges than their nonschizophrenic siblings. The latter reported that it was much more difficult for the preschizophrenics to be on the top level than themselves, because of keeper competition in larger schools. Consequently the preschizophrenics could not remain on the top as before. From the time they were in high schools or colleges, the preschizophrenics began to fall behind, but the nonschizophrenic siblings became much more successful than the preschizophrenics. Therefore it became increasingly difficult for the preschizophrenics to fulfill their parents' contradictory expectations for perfection and dependence. An adverse self-conception was thus formed when the preschizophrenics were not able to maintain their level of achievement and to obtain the same degree of parental approval and acceptance. While their self-evaluation became increasingly lower, their aspirations for achievement and perfection remained as high as before. Thus, there was great discrepancy between the preschizophrenics' aspiration for success and their self-evaluation. In contrast, the nonschizophrenic siblings became more insistent on independence from their parents as they grew older. And they were also much more realistic in setting the goals of their lives and were much more flexible in changing them. Since their goals were comparatively easier to reach than those of the preschizophrenics, and since their self-conceptions did not depend as much on parental approval, their self-evaluation was much higher than that of the preschizophrenics. Furthermore, as they became more successful in their endeavor, they gained more praise and approval from their parents which further lowered the preschizophrenics' self-evaluation. Thus the preschizophrenics felt they were incompetent. They lacked self-confidence. They had a sense of failure, especially after the parents' comparison of their "failure" with the nonschizophrenic siblings' "success." They were very jealous of their nonschizophrenic siblings, whom they greatly admired at the same time. They did not want to be themselves. They wanted to be like others, especially their siblings, while the nonschizophrenic siblings learned to accept themselves and not try to be somebody else. The following interview data illustrate the preschizophrenic's high aspirations for success and how his low self-evaluation was developed after he once lost out in the competition.

A 26-year-old unmarried high school student whose father had never been regularly employed and whose family had been on relief ever since the patient's childhood reported: "I was more ambitious than my brother because I was the valedictorian of my graduating class in grade school. I felt I was like Abraham Lincoln. But I wasn't proud of it; neither were my parents. When I spoke for my class, my girl was there. I felt I was somebody important. When I was about 12 years old, I thought I was in the brink of confidence and success.—As a child, I did want to be a drummer. I wanted to be successful in everything. My ambition was to be a doctor at that time. But then something went wrong. When I was 16, I competed and I was supposed to be the leader in the drum section in high school. Then one of my friends was made the drum section leader. I couldn't see how he was chosen, because he never had the training I had had. That was a great disappointment.— Well, my brother didn't have any ambition when he was a child. Now he goes to junior college, so he has ambition now. He is also married. But I am good at nothing."

The nonschizophrenic siblings' more realistic approach in setting the goals of their lives and their being more flexible to change them can be seen in the following statement.

A nonschizophrenic sibling whose widowed mother worked as an unskilled laborer to support both the patient and the nonschizophrenic sibling said: "I want very much to continue my college education. But judging from the financial condition of the family, I know it's impossible for me to do so. Now I realize I couldn't have it, so I don't insist on it. Now I just enjoy working."

The parent's comparison of the nonschizophrenic sibling's success with the preschizophrenic's failure and the preschizophrenic's jealousy over the former's success is shown in the following statements.

The father said: "Jerome (patient) always wanted to be better than others. But Carl and Francis (the nonschizophrenic siblings) don't care. My wife wanted Jerome to go to college in order to get better, so Jerome went to college. My wife also wanted the other 2 boys to go to college, but they didn't want to go. My wife always praised Carl and Francis, because they worked and made so much money. But Jerome didn't like it. He said, 'How come any time I get a new job, they always fire me?' What bothered Jerome most is that my wife always said the other two boys made so much money, nice money. She implied that Jerome didn't make so much money."

The patient, Jerome, also reported: "I am jealous of my younger brother, Francis, because he is able to hold a job."

THE SOCIAL SITUATIONS PRECIPITATING THE SCHIZOPHRENIC BREAK

So far, some background factors related to the development of schizophrenia have been discussed. Now it is time to turn to the question: "When or under what social situations did the schizophrenic symptoms first appear?" The data tend to indicate that schizophrenic symptoms first appeared after the preschizophrenic was confronted with the combination of 2 social situations which heightened to the critical point the dilemma between dependence and responsibility.

The first of the 2 social situations is *sudden explicit expression* by the significant others[17] that the patient should assume *concrete* adult responsibility, or *sudden* pressure on the patient to assume *increased concrete* adult responsibility. This means that the preschizophrenic who had never been expected to bear financial, household, or other responsibility since childhood was now suddenly expected to take up this adult responsibility or to play the adult role. In other cases, the preschizophrenic who had taken up some such responsibility before was now subject to sudden pressure to assume an increased financial, household, or other responsibility.

The second social situation is the loss or lack of intimate relations with members of a peer group or persons on whom the patient could depend for emotional support. The group or persons are those the preschizophrenic looked up to and wished to identify himself with. Twenty-one out of 24 preschizophrenics were confronted with both of these social situations before their schizophrenic breaks. And among these 21, 15 are also the same patients who had, long before the schizophrenic breaks, persistently made greater efforts than their nonschizophrenic siblings to fulfill contradictory parental expectations of dependence and responsibility for achievement and perfection.

In general, when the situation suddenly called for someone in the family to take up responsibility, it was always the preschizophrenic who was expected to play that role. During adolescence and early adulthood most preschizophrenics had been struggling to meet the demands to accept concrete adult responsibilities. These responsibilities were particulary burdensome to them, for they had been extremely dependent all their lives. It was not uncommon that not long before the schizophrenic breaks, the preschizophrenics had attempted to work excessively hard. Besides going to school, they often took a full-time job plus a part-time job, or several part-time jobs. Such extreme compulsion to work was not found in the nonschizophrenic siblings. There are some cases where the onset of schizophrenic psychoses were followed by the death of the father which resulted in the sudden expectation or pressure for the preschizophrenics to take up the deceased father's role of providing for the family. In other cases, before the schizophrenic breaks, the preschizophrenics were suddenly expected to take up heavy household responsibilities or, in the case of some female patients, to assume the increased responsibility of bringing up or bearing children.

This sudden increase in parental pressure for the preschizophrenics to take up adult responsibility took place simultaneously with such events as the loss of friends who went into the services, or the moving of the families to new neighborhoods, or the preschizophrenics' change to a new or large school where it was difficult for them to establish peer relationships. Although many expectations for the preschizophrenics' assuming responsibility often came from the parents and close relatives, they may sometimes be reflections of the "generalized others"[17]—the expectations of the community or society in general. Or they may simply be a necessity because of the financial condition of the lower-class family.

The data on social participation indicate that although many preschizophrenics had been shy and passive in interpersonal relations, they managed all along to have friends and belong to some peer groups. At least there was someone besides their parents on whom they could depend. The schizophrenic breaks might be avoided as long as they were not expected to take up suddenly increased concrete responsibility, and as long as their dependence on their parents could be transferred to members of their peer, social, or occupational group, or to a sibling, or to the spouse. Some patients reported that just before they were mentally sick, they could no longer get the support of the members of their peer groups. They said that they needed encouragement from friends to give them self-confidence. But the parents of some patients increasingly insisted that they go to work instead of hanging around the street corners with their friends.

In contrast, the nonschizophrenic siblings were reported to be the ones who were not so dependent on their parents, who always had more friends. When the situation called for responsibility, they either shouldered it readily, or avoided it by leaving their parents and finding a life of their own.

The following excerpt will show how the onset of schizophrenic symptons was preceded by the combination of these 2 factors: first, sudden pressure on the patient to assume increased concrete adult responsibility caused by the death of the father; and, second, the loss or lack of peer group or persons on whom the patient could depend for emotional support.

The elder sister for a patient reported: "Bob had the nervous breakdown after my father's death. Not soon after my father's death, my sister, brother and I all got married and left home. Bob was the only one left with my mother. He felt the responsibility to take care of her. As a matter of fact, he was the only one who was responsible for her financial support after my father's death. He felt he failed everybody. He is so dependent on my mother. He always needs someone. He needed young people. My mother was not enough. After my father's death, not only all of us left home and he had no one to hold on to, but all of his friends also went into the services. He had to take care of my mother."

Sometimes the sudden explicit expression of parental expectation for the patient to take up the adult role or responsibility might be prompted by the patient's sudden physical growth from boyhood to manhood.

The schizophrenic break of a 17-year-old student occurred after his widowed mother persistently insisted on his finding a job after the family moved to a new neighborhood where the patient could find no friends. The sibling reported: "After we moved to the Cermak Street address when Ernest was 17, my mother began to want him to get a job. That was just before he was mentally sick. At that time he was growing fast. He *suddenly* grew up to be real tall. Before that he was just a small boy and my mother never expected him to work before. But then my mother *suddenly* began to try to put more ambition in him. She said to him, 'You are such a big man now. You should go and find a job to help the family out.' But at the same time, my mother still continued to treat him like a little boy. She always did things for him, practically dressed for him. She got shoes for him and polished the shoes for him and did almost everything for him. Before we moved to the Cermak Street address and before he was transferred to the new school, everything was nice with him. But after we moved, it seems that he felt no one was interested in him. He really didn't get any attention from us. I was busy with my outside activities. But before we moved, Ernest and I were real companions then. He was close to me."

The following case of a manual laborer illustrates the effect of the sudden pressure on the preschizophrenic to assume immediate increased financial responsibility in the family due to his parents' divorce, in combination with the preschizophrenic's separation from his peer group and elder sibling from whom he used to acquire emotional support.

The patient reported: "I had my first breakdown; I guess it's because I was overworked. It happened when I was about 16 or 17 after my father and mother were divorced. And my grandmother also died around this time. After my grandmother's death, my mother was ordered by the court to pay her sister some $2,000 to $3,000. My brother went into the service at about the same time. So I was the only one left to support my family. It was too much for me. After my parents' divorce, not only I had to support my mother, but also she needed a lot more money because she had to pay her sister. So I overworked. All I needed was to have a rest. Now I got my rest. So I am all right. Before my first breakdown at the age of 17, I used to run with a gang in the neighborhood. We grew up together. But just before my first breakdown, most of them went into the service. My brother also went into the service. I also passed both my physical and mental examinations. But I couldn't go because I had to support my mother. Then I got sick."

A 26-year-old young mother became schizophrenic when she was pregnant for her fifth child and after her husband on whom she had been extremely dependent began to spend both day and night outside of the home on business and paid no attention to her. The patient said: "The first time I was (mentally) sick was at the time I discovered I was 4 months pregnant with my fifth child. I worried a great deal. Because at that time *suddenly* there was too much work for me. I just couldn't take it. You see, besides taking care of the 4 kids and the housework, I had to redecorate the whole house over, from inside to outside of the house. I wanted to do a *perfect* job. I was very ambitious about it. And yet I had to do everything *alone*. Therefore when I learned I was pregnant again, I thought I couldn't take in any more responsibility. This also happened after 6 months my husband began to have a business of his own. And he became extremely busy. He had to go out at 4 o'clock in the morning and wouldn't finish his work until 9 or 10 in the evening. We could hardly talk to each other. That was too much for me. I needed to leave home and go somewhere else where I didn't have to take so much responsibility. But my husband wouldn't agree on this. Then I became sick."

The presentation of the above data shows that the kind of responsibility expected of the preschizophrenics which precipitated their schizophrenic symptoms differs from the relatively general, abstract, long-range expectation for achievement and perfection which the preschizophrenics had attempted to live up to since childhood. The former was a more specific, definite, immediate and sudden responsibility pressed on the preschizophrenics. Although they had attempted all their lives to fulfill contradictory parental expectations of dependence and responsibility for perfection and achievement, this more specific, immediate, and sudden increased responsibility became far more difficult for them to cope with. For one thing, this suddenly increased responsibility was naturally beyond the ability of the habitually dependent and inflexible persons to bear. Moreover, it consisted of specific tasks which had to be performed immediately. Therefore, to the preschizophrenics, success or failure would be determined within a relatively short time, and the "verdict" would be "pronounced" almost at once. Thus, the performance of concrete, specific and immediate tasks was in principle different from the previous effort in achieving those general, abstract, and long-range objectives. To the preschizophrenics, it served as an immediate test of their adequacy and competence, and therefore affected their immediate self-conception and self-evaluation. Furthermore, the preschizophrenics were also aware of the cultural expectation for adults or persons approaching adulthood to assume increased specific responsibilities. At a time when there was the extra burden of assuming the suddenly increased responsibility, the deprivation of emotional support from peers further increased their anxieties because now they had to shoulder the heavy responsibility alone. Thus, the combination of the 2 social "pressures" heightened critically to a breaking point their dilemma between dependence and responsibility (independence) and precipitated the development of schizophrenic symptoms.

THE SOCIAL, FAMILIAL, AND PERSONAL SITUATIONS AT BIRTH AND INFANCY

Now the question arises as to why the parents expected more from the preschizophrenic than from the nonschizophrenic child and why the preschizophrenic child tried much harder than his nonschizophrenic sibling to fulfill contradictory parental expectations. The process of such parents-preschizophrenic interaction and emotional entanglement seems to begin as early as the period of the patient's birth and infancy. It is necessary, therefore, to reconstruct the experiences of the parents and the infant at this period. It is expected that the social, familial, or personal situations confronting the preschizophrenic children at the time of their birth and infancy are different from those confronting the nonschizophrenic children.

The parents, often the mothers had paid more attention to the preschizophrenic child or given him more protection than the nonschizophrenic child because of one of the following 2 reasons: One consists of such unusual circumstances as the preschizophrenic child's being sick as an infant, or an unusually big infant, or the only male child to carry the family name, or being the oldest or the youngest child, etc. The second reason is that the tension between father and mother or the parents' hardships and frustration at the time of the birth or infancy of the preschizophrenic child was much more intense than at that of the birth or infancy of the nonschizophrenic sibling. These tensions and frustrations often arose out of the much more adverse financial condition at the time of the birth and infancy of the preschizophrenic child, or sexual difficulty between father and mother because of the fear of being pregnant again, or the mother's living and having difficulties with in-laws, or disappointment in the sex of the infant, or the mother's difficulty in the labor of the infant, etc. Out of the 24 cases there are 17 cases where the parents reporting either such unusual circumstances mentioned above or heightened tension between the parents at the time of the birth or infancy of the preschizophrenics, but not at the time of the birth or infancy of the nonschizophrenic siblings.

Another interesting fact about the difference between the preschizophrenic infant and the nonschizophrenic sibling is the personal situation confronting them at the time of their birth. Out of the 14 cases where information is available, 10 cases have been reported by the mothers that the preschizophrenics were more passive or slower than the nonschizophrenic siblings after they were born. One may expect that the mother would give the child more protection or pay him more attention if he were more passive and needed more help from adults.

The following excerpt may serve to illustrate the differences in the social and familial situations confronting the preschizophrenic at birth and infancy and those confronting the nonschizophrenic sibling.

The mother said: "David (patient) was not a planned baby but Paul (nonschizophrenic sibling) was. David was born right after my husband was demoted in his work because of bad business conditions. Definitely among all my children David was born at a time where the financial condition of the family was the worst. There was too much tension between my husband and me. I definitely worried much more when David was born than at the birth of Paul and the other boys. After David was born, my sexual relations with my husband were not good, because I worried about having more babies. We did not use contraceptives. I am a Catholic and my husband was a Protestant. But after Paul was born, we didn't worry about it. Maybe it's because the financial condition was better. And when David was born, he was a big baby—9 lbs. That was my hardest delivery among all. But Paul was a smaller baby than David. Another thing is that before David was born, both my husband and I wanted a girl so much, and therefore we were greatly disappointed. After we learned it was a boy, I didn't want to see David and my husband's face also turned white. But when Paul was born, I didn't care whether it was a boy or a girl. I took more care of David than Paul when they were babies. I stayed home more and I might have spent more time with David than Paul and made David dependent on me when they were young."

COMPARISON WITH OTHER RELATED INVESTIGATIONS

The preliminary findings presented in this paper raise some interesting questions in regard to some related studies in this area.

1. Relation to Double-Bind Theory.

The comparison between the preschizophrenics and their nonschizophrenic siblings in this paper shows how contradictory parental expectations of dependence and responsibility (independence) on the one hand, and the child's persistent efforts to fulfill these expectations, on the other, are related to the development of schizophrenia These preliminary findings call attention to a closely related theory, the double-bind theory advanced by Bateson and his associates.[1] In general, the double-bind theory is consistent with the preliminary findings presented in this paper. For in a sense this theory also implies that schizophrenic symptoms may develop if in an intense relationship a person is caught in a persistently unresolved contradictory or dilemma situation. The preliminary findings presented here, however, differ from the double-bind theory in several ways. First, while Bateson's theory emphasizes the mother's general ambivalence toward the preschizophrenic child as indicated by the incongruent messages of hostile (or withdrawing) and loving (or approaching) behavior that she communicates to him, the writer focuses on a more specific pair of contradictory expectations of the parent (or parents). The writer's data suggest that as far as the American families (from lower socioeconomic strata) are concerned, one of the most striking sets of contradictory expectations relates to the parents' expecting at the same time the child's dependence and independence (or responsibility, decision-making, etc.). They tend to indicate that in the American culture which is dominated by the value orientation of independence, responsibility, achievement (work), and personal autonomy in adulthood, the persistently unresolved emotional conflict arising out of pressure to play the independent role and the dependent role at the same time is among the severest strains which seem to be related to the development of schizophrenic symptoms in this group of lower socioeconomic classes of families. In other words, those contradictory expectations which affect the preschizophrenic child's ability to fulfill the social expectations of his adult roles in his subculture are one of the most conspicuous sets of contradictory expectations experienced by preschizophrenics. Implicit in this analysis is the idea that not every pair of "double-bind" messages or expectations is of equal significance in the development of schizophrenic symptoms.

Second, while Bateson and associates stress the double-bind situation "created" by the mother's (and/or father's) simultaneously expressing 2 or multiple orders of messages to the child, or her one-way ambivalence as the most important etiological factor in the genesis of schizophrenia, the writer stresses the *2-way interaction* between the preschizophrenic child and the parent(s) as one of the factors related to the development of schizophrenic symptoms. To me, not only the contradictory *parental* expectations, but also the *extreme dependence* of the *preschizophrenic child* on his parent(s) or his persistent efforts to fulfill

contradictory parental expectations play a significant role in promoting the "double-bind" relationships between the parent(s) and the child.

In other words, the double-bind theory seems to have emphasized the mother's active role and the preschizophrenic's passive role in such relationships. The data of the present research, however, show that the child also plays a role[17] in the promotion of such parent-child entanglement relationship. The possibility of a child avoiding "being caught" in a double-bind situation "created" by the mother is seen in the nonschizophrenic sibling's insistence to be independent from his parents and his refusal to take the contradictory parental expectations seriously. Therefore, without the preschizophrenic's part in promoting such a role pattern in the parent-child interaction, the mother's simultaneous expression of multiple levels of messages probably would not result in the double-bind relationship which is described by Bateson and his associates. Since the publication of Bateson's paper on double-bind theory, his position has been qualified by Weakland, one of Bateson's associates. Weakland acknowledged that potentially the child could "escape" the double-bind situation by establishing more satisfactory communication elsewhere and that the unavailability of such an escape is usually an outcome of the preschizophrenic's dependence on his parent.[19] This qualification points to a direction which parallels the writer's preliminary findings. But the question remains whether the role of the preschizophrenic child in such parent-child relational formation can be considered so subordinate to the contradictory messages or expectations of the parents, especially as implied by the term "double-bind" and whether the child's dependence and "unavailability of avenue of escape" from the double-bind situation merely assist in forming such relational pattern. For in the parent-child reciprocal role relations such as those observed in the schizophrenic families, it is extremely difficult to determine which role, the parents' or the child's, is the independent variable. Stated positively, the question is whether the preschizophrenic child's extreme dependence on the parent is in itself also a *form of active participation* in the process of *promoting* such mutual role formation. This significant question must be answered in any attempt to push forward the frontier of our knowledge. To raise this question poignantly and to direct empirical research in an endeavor to seek an answer, the writer proposes, in lieu of the double-bind theory, the concept of "*quadruple-bind*": on the one hand,

the parent(s) entertained contradictory expectations of dependence and independence (responsibility) and, on the other hand, the child attempts
persistently to fulfill such contradictory expectations. This hypothesis of "quadruple-bind"
then has the advantage of leaving open for future
researchers to tackle the question of the relative
importance of the child's role in promoting such
parent-child role patterns.

Furthermore, while the writer agrees with
Bateson and his associates on the extreme importance of the communication factor, she also takes
into account the social-situational or milieu factor
in precipitating the onset of schizophrenic behavior,
which factor does not seem to have been sufficiently taken into consideration by Bateson. For it
seems that communication alone does not explain
how the preschizophrenics lose their ability to
interpret and discriminate social reality validly,
which many seem to have possessed before their
schizophrenic breaks, and why the schizophrenic
symptoms occur at that particular time.

2. Relation to Social Class Research.

The ecological research such as that by Faris and
Dunham[5] and the social class research by Hollingshead and Redlich[7] suggest the inverse relationship
between socioeconomic status and rates of schizophrenia. The social-psychological significance of
low socioeconomic status for the development of
schizophrenia in the American culture has also
been somewhat reflected in the intensive studies
presented in his paper. For the hardships and, thus,
the tensions of the parents at the time of the birth or
during the infancy of the preschizophrenic infant
are, among other factors, related to the parents'
ultimate emotional entanglement with the preschizophrenic which consequently gives rise to the
special role assigned to the preschizophrenic infant
in the family. Furthermore, the necessity for the
children in the lower socioeconomic strata to
assume heavier family responsibilities and the
value of striving for upward social mobility is a
reality in the daily struggle for existence in the
American lower class families. Therefore it seems
that certain conditions in the life of the lower
socioeconomic strata are ultimately more conducive to the development of schizophrenia than
those prevailing among the higher strata. However,
one question which can be raised here is whether
the contradictory parental expectations emerge
from (*a*) a contradiction inherent in the value
system prevalent among groups of lower socioeconomic status, or (*b*) the presence of a strong
middle class orientation in these lower class families. In the sample of this research, many mothers

had married downward* either educationally,
occupationally, or socioeconomically and had
placed much emphasis on the achievement of the
children. At the same time, facing the hardships
of life in the lower socioeconomic levels, the
parents took over many values appropriate to such
an existence. One of these values is the children's
obedience and dependence.[11] Some children in this
sample may have faced a contradiction between
middle class norms of achievement, responsibility,
independence on the one hand; and on the other,
lower class values of obedience and dependence.
Sometimes the contradiction confronting the preschizophrenic children may have been due to the
mixed religious marriages or the immigrant backgrounds of the fathers and the mothers, or even
due to contradictory values within a parent himself
or herself.

CONCLUDING COMMENTS

The preliminary findings presented in this
paper suggest that although the preschizophrenics
and the nonschizophrenic siblings are reared in
the same family, they may not be exposed to the
same social and psychological conditions in different periods of their lives. First of all, the
data tend to indicate that the social, familial, and
personal situations confronting the preschizophrenics and the nonschizophrenic siblings at the
time of their respective birth and infancy may not
be the same. The special circumstances surrounding the preschizophrenic's birth or infancy define
the special role which the infant is to occupy in
the total family constellation, as well as the special
role which he is to play in relation to his parents.
This initial definition of the special role for the
preschizophrenic infant may on the other hand
assist the nonschizophrenic child to avoid playing
that role in the family. Furthermore, the continuous reciprocal process of interaction between the
parent and the preschizophrenic child throughout
the latter's childhood and adolescence leads to
a role pattern which is characterized by contradictory parental expectations coupled with the
preschizophrenic's persistent efforts to fulfill them.
This role relation differs from that between the
parent and the nonschizophrenic sibling. In view
of the possibility that the preschizophrenic child
as well as the parent(s) participates in the formation
of this specific relational pattern of contradictory
parental expectations and the child's performance,
the writer proposes the use of the concept
"quadruple-bind" for future research. In addition

to this basic difference between the preschizophrenic and the nonschizophrenic sibling, there might, due to contingencies, also be differences in other significant experiences later in life, such as those related to peer groups, schools, and occupations. The lack of support from these social groups may further reinforce the preschizophrenic's tendency to continue the original role pattern of complying with contradictory expectations of the parent(s), while the support the nonschizophrenic sibling gained from such groups may increase the latter's independence from the parent(s).

The presentation in this paper indicates that among other factors, the interplay of 3 conditions seems to be contributory to the development of schizophrenic symptoms in this sample of American lower-class families: (1) contradictory parental expectations regarding dependence and independence (responsibility, etc.), coupled with the preschizophrenic child's persistent efforts in compliance with both expectations; (2) certain experiences at birth or during infancy that incline both the parents and the preschizophrenic child to interact in the contradictory ways as described; and (3) certain sociocultural situations which heightened to the critical point the dilemma between dependence and independence to which the schizophrenic symptoms may be considered as a response.

Finally, it must be pointed out that these preliminary findings which are based on part of the data in the sample are not conclusive. The hypotheses remain to be tested statistically when the schedule data of all the 50 cases are completely analyzed.

NOTES

This research is supported by a grant from the Psychiatric Training and Research Fund of the Department of Mental Health, State of Illinois. This is an expanded version of a paper read at the 55th Annual Meeting of the American Sociological Association, Aug. 31, 1960, in New York City, as part of the program on "Sociology and Mental Health: Familial and Social Relationships and Schizophrenia."

Acknowledgment is made to Nathaniel S. Apter, M.D., chief of the chronic schizophrenia research unit at the Manteno State Hospital, Illinois State Department of Mental Health, Richard Graff, M.D., Superintendent. I am indebted to Dr. Ernest W. Burgess of the University of Chicago, Dr. Robert Dentler of Dartmouth College, Dr. Bernard Farber of the University of Illinois, and Dr. Bingham Dai of Duke University for their criticisms and suggestions.

REFERENCES

1. Bateson, G., et al.: Toward a Theory of Schizophrenia, Behav. Sci. 1:251–264 (Oct.) 1956.

2. Bowen, M.: Family Relationships in Schizophrenia, in Schizophrenia, edited by Alfred Auerback, New York, The Ronald Press Company, 1959, pp. 147–178.

3. Bowen, M.: A Family Concept of Schizophrenia, in The Etiology of Schizophrenia, edited by Don D. Jackson, New York, Basic Books, Inc., 1960, pp. 346–372.

4. Clausen, J. A., and Kohn, M. L.: Social Relations and Schizophrenia: A Research Report and a Perspective, in The Etiology of Schizophrenia, edited by Don D. Jackson, New York, Basic Books, Inc., 1960, pp. 295–320.

5 Faris, R. E. L., and Dunham, H. W.: Mental Disorders in Urban Areas, Chicago, University of Chicago Press, 1939.

6. Hill, L.: Psychotherapeutic Intervention in Schizophrenia, Chicago, University of Chicago Press, 1955.

7. Hollingshead, A. B., and Redlich, F. C., Social Class and Mental Illness, New York, John Wiley & Sons, Inc., 1958.

8. Jackson, D. D.: Conjoint Family Therapy, Some Considerations on Theory, Technique and Results, Psychiatry (Suppl.) 24:30–45, 1961.

9. Klebanoff, L. B.: Parental Attitudes of Mothers of Schizophrenic, Brain-Injured and Retarded and Normal Children, Amer. J. Orthopsychiat. 29:445–454 (May) 1959.

10. Kohn, M. L., and Clausen, J. A.: Parental Authority Behavior and Schizophrenia, Amer. J. Orthopsychiat. 26:297–313 (April) 1956.

11. Kohn, M. L.: Social Class and Parental Values, Amer. J. Sociol. 64:337–351, 1959.

12. Lidz, T., et al.: The Role of the Father in the Family Environment of the Schizophrenic Patients, Amer. J. Psychiat. 113:126–132 (Aug.) 1956.

13. Lidz, T., et al.: The Intrafamilial Environment of the Schizophrenic Patients: II. Marital Schism and Marital Skew, Amer. J. Psychiat. 114:241–248 (Sept.) 1957.

14. Lidz, T., et al.: The Intrafamilial Environment of the Schizophrenic Patient: I. The Father, Psychiatry 20:329–342 (Nov.) 1957.

15. Lidz, T.: Schizophrenia and the Family, Psychiatry 21:21–27 (Feb) 1958.

16. Lidz, T., et al.: Intrafamilial Environment of the Schizophrenic Patients: VI. The Transmission of Irrationality, A.M.A. Arch. Neurol. Psychiat. 79:305–316 (March) 1958.

17. Lu, Y. C.: Mother-Child Role Relations in Schizophrenia: A Comparison of Schizophrenic Patients with Nonschizophrenic Siblings, Psychiatry 24:133–142 (May) 1961.

18. Myers, J. K., and Roberts, B. H.: Family and Class Dynamics in Mental Illness, New York, John Wiley & Sons, Inc., 1959.

19. Weakland, J. H.: "The Double-Bind" Hypothesis of Schizophrenia and Three Party Interaction, in the Etiology of Schizophrenia, edited by Don D. Jackson, New York, Basic Books, Inc., 1961, pp. 373–388.

20. Warner, W. L., and associates: Social Class in America: A Manual of Procedure for the Measurement of Social Status, Chicago, Science Research Associates, Inc., 1949.

21. Wynne, L. C., et al.: Pseudo-Mutuality in the Family Relations of Schizophrenics, Psychiatry 21:205–220 (May) 1958.

SOCIAL ISOLATION AND SCHIZOPHRENIA*

Melvin L. Kohn and John A. Clausen

OF the several hypotheses relating the frequency of mental disorders to social conditions, none has been more persistently enunciated that that which proposes that schizophrenia is the outgrowth of social isolation. First stated by Faris in 1934,[1] this hypothesis subsequently seemed consistent with, and indeed explanatory of, the findings of Faris and Dunham's classic ecological study of mental disorder. Faris and Dunham ascertained that high rates of first hospital admissions for schizophrenia are found in areas of the city characterized by high residential mobility and low socioeconomic status, among ethnic group persons living in non-ethnic areas, and among the foreign-born populations of the slums.[2] All of these indices were regarded as reflecting tendencies toward the social isolation of certain segments of the population.

In earlier statements of the hypothesis, Faris suggested that "any form of isolation that cuts the person off from intimate social relations for an extended period of time may possibly lead to this form of mental disorder."[3] More recent statements have suggested that isolation is a result of in-congruent intra-familial and extra-familial orientations toward the child and represents a stage in a "typical process" for schizophrenics. Briefly this typical process is said to involve the following stages:

(1) "Parental oversolicitude produces the 'spoiled child' type of personality," and leads to

(2) "a certain isolation from all but the intimates within the family."

(3) "The next stage is persecution, discrimination or exclusion by children outside the family."

(4) "The most usual reaction to this persecution is to feel unhappy but with no immediate depreciation of establishing friendships."

(5) "Often the children try for years to make friends.... Eventually there is a resignation—a withdrawal from a hopeless goal ... From this time on their interest in sociability declines and they slowly develop the seclusive personality that is characteristic of the schizophrenic."

(6) Finally, the symptoms of schizophrenia are ascribed to the lack of social experience in the person

Reprinted from American Sociological Review (June, 1955), *20*, (3), 265–73, by permission of the American Sociological Association.

so isolated: "Not being experienced in intimate personal contacts with a larger number of other persons he is deficient in his understanding of the reactions of others, and responds unconventionally and inappropriately to them."[4]

This view holds that social isolation—that is, the diminution or total absence of social interaction with peers—enters the schizophrenic process as a directly predisposing or "causative" factor. The bizarre behavior of the schizophrenic is attributed to social inexperience stemming from isolation. Presumably then, such isolation should underlie all schizophrenic disorders. Supporting evidence for this hypothesis was provided in a study by Dunham of the early social experience of catatonic schizophrenes who grew up in areas of high delinquency rates.[5] On the other hand, Weinberg found little evidence of social isolation in the childhood histories of a sample of acute schizophrenics (called by him transient schizophrenics), more than half of whom were catatonics.[6]

The present paper reports findings of a study designed to ascertain the extent and significance of social isolation in adolescence in a sample group of schizophrenic patients and a matched group of normal controls. A small group of manic-depressive patients, together with controls for these patients, was also studied.

SAMPLE AND METHOD OF DATA COLLECTION

The sample of patients interviewed consists of 45 schizophrenic and 13 manic-depressive patients who were first admitted to mental hospitals in Maryland during the period 1940–1952. These comprise 58 out of a total of 79 first admissions from Hagerstown, Maryland, who were diagnosed either schizophrenic or manic-depressive during this period. Of the 21 patients not interviewed, at the time of the research, 11 were too ill, 6 had moved too far from the site of the research, and 4 refused to be interviewed. Thus interviews were secured with 73 per cent of the total sample and 94 per cent of those patients who can be regarded as having been physically and psychologically accessible. In 15 of the 21 cases where an interview with the patient was not possible, we were able to interview a close relative. Analysis of these interviews demonstrates that the non-interviewed patients do not differ appreciably from the interviewed patients with respect to their social participation as adolescents.

Controls were individually paired with the patients of the basis of age, sex, and occupation (or father's occupation), using records derived from Public Health Service morbidity studies conducted periodically in Hagerstown since 1921. By this method it was possible to accomplish matching as of a period well before the onset of illness—on the average, 16 years before hospitalization. In roughly half of the cases the patient and his control had attended the same class in public schools. In addition to individual matching on the characteristics mentioned overall frequencies were balanced with respect to family composition and area of residence.[7]

The interview schedule covered the following topics: residential and occupational history, relationships in the parental family, friendship and activity patterns in early adolescence, dating patterns, social participation as an adult, and a brief psychosomatic inventory.

All interviews with patients were conducted by one of the authors, as were approximately one-fifth of the interviews with controls. The balance of the controls were interviewed by another staff member after a period of training and with careful check to insure comparability of approach.

EXTENT OF SOCIAL ISOLATION AMONG SCHIZOPHRENICS

Assessment of social isolation was accomplished by the use of an index of social participation based upon the respondents' answers to two types of questions. The first ascertained *with whom* the respondent played when he was 13–14 years old, the second *what types* of activities he engaged in at that age.[8] We first asked:

"(When you were 13 or 14 years old) did you usually hang out with a crowd, with one or two close friends, with your brothers or sisters, or did you stay by yourself most of the time?"

Both schizophrenic and manic-depressive patients more frequently than their controls replied that they stayed by themselves, controls that they played with a crowd or with close friends.[9]

TABLE 1.   Usual Play Patterns of Patients and Controls in Adolescence

Usually Played	Schiz.	Con-trols	Manic-Dep.	Con-trols
With crowd or close friends	20	37	6	11
With siblings	5	6	1	2
Alone	8	1	4	–
Primarily alone, but occasionally with crowd, close friends, or siblings	12	1	2	–
Total	45	45	13	13

To determine the *types* of social activities in which respondents engaged, we asked a series of questions:

(1) What were your favorite activities or pastimes when you were 13 or 14 years old?

(2) What sorts of things did you and your friends do together?

(3) What were the types of things you most enjoyed doing *alone* when you were 13 or 14?

(4) Did you enjoy (the things you did alone) as much as you enjoyed playing with other children?

(5) Thinking back to whomever it was you considered your closest friend about the time you were 13 or 14, can you tell me what sorts of things you most enjoyed doing together?

(6) Did you belong to the scouts, the "Y", or any clubs in school, or Sunday School? Which clubs?

This material was then coded without knowledge of any respondent's replies to other questions, or whether the respondent was a patient or a control.[10] Four categories were used: (a) activities primarily social, with few or no solitary activities; (b) both social and solitary activities; (c) activities primarily solitary, with few or no social activities; and (d) ambiguous cases.

Finally, these two aspects of social participation—*with whom* the individual played and the *types* of activities in which he engaged—were combined to form a single index. In schematic form, this *Index of Social Participation*[11] is as follows:

TABLE 2a.   Types of Activities Participated in by Patients and Controls in Adolescence

	Schiz.	Con-trols	Manic-Dep.	Con-trols
Activities primarily social, few or no solitary activities	15	21	4	5
Both social and solitary activities	19	20	6	6
Activities primarily solitary, few or no social activities	9	3	3	1
Ambiguous cases	2	1	0	1
Total	45	45	13	13

TABLE 2b.   PATTERN OF ASSOCIATION IN PLAY ACTIVITIES (AT AGE 13–14)

Types of Activities	"Alone"	"Alone, but Occasionally with Friends or Crowd"	"With Siblings," or "Alone, but Occasionally with Siblings"	"With Close Friends" or "Crowd"
Social	X	X		
Both social and solitary	X	Partial isolates	Played only with siblings	Non-isolates
Solitary	Isolates	X	X	X

(X = Ambiguous classification)

Comparing patients to controls on the basis of this Index, we find a significantly larger proportion of both the schizophrenics and the manic-depressives than of the controls have been isolates or partial-isolates. However, this is by no means true of all patients—only one-third of the schizophrenics and one-third of the manic-depressives had been isolated or partially-isolated at this age. Finally, patients and controls do *not* differ with respect to the proportion who played only with siblings.[12] For two-thirds of the patients, then, retrospective reports show no discernible social isolation in early adolescence.

In the present state of psychiatric knowledge, there is considerable question whether either schizophrenia or manic-depressive psychosis is a single disease of common etiology or a group of similar appearing diseases of differing etiology. For this reason, even though two-thirds of the patients were not isolated as adolescents, there remains the possibility that isolation was a predisposing factor for the remaining one-third; these may constitute a distinct sub-group whose etiology differs from that of the other patients. If so, this sub-group cannot be defined according to the usual diagnostic criteria. Schizophrenics are no more likely to have been isolates than are manic-depressives: the proportion of manic-depressives who were classified as having been isolates or partial isolates is 38 per cent, the proportion of schizophrenics 34 per cent. Similarly, within the schizophrenic group the proportion of isolates is approximately the same among

paranoids (42 per cent) as it is among catatonics (31 per cent).[13]

Therefore, it appears that, for the cases here studied, social isolation in early adolescence is not a necessary condition for any subtype of schizophrenia. There remains, however, the task of examining the conditions leading up to isolation and the consequences of isolation. We turn to a direct comparison of the adolescent social experiences of the isolated and the non-isolated patients. Because the proportion of isolates and partial-isolates among the manic-depressives is so similar to the proportion among schizophrenics, the two diagnostic groups will be considered together. The results that will be presented are almost precisely the same as those for the schizophrenic group alone, because empirically the manic-depressive isolates and partial-isolates behaved similarly to the schizophrenic isolates and partial-isolates, and the manic-depressive non-isolates behaved similarly to the schizophrenic non-isolates.

CONDITIONS LEADING TO ISOLATION

There are several possible reasons why the isolates might have been prevented from playing with other children—for example, childhood illness, living on out-of-the-way farms, great residential mobility. But a systematic comparison shows that these factors were no more applicable to the isolated and partially isolated patients

TABLE 3.   CLASSIFICATION OF SOCIAL PARTICIPATION OF PATIENTS AND CONTROLS

	Schizophrenics Number Per Cent		Controls Number Per Cent		Manic-Depres. Number Per Cent		Controls Number Per Cent	
Isolates	7	16	1	2	3	23	0	0
Partial-isolates	8	18	1	2	2	15	0	0
Played only with siblings	9	20	6	14	1	8	2	15
Non-isolates	19	42	36	80	6	46	9	70
Ambiguous cases	2	4	1	2	1	8	2	15
Total	45	100	45	100	13	100	13	100

TABLE 4. NUMBER OF CHILDREN OF SIMILAR AGE
REPORTED TO HAVE BEEN LIVING IN THE
NEIGHBORHOOD WHEN PATIENT WAS
13–14 YEARS OLD

	Isolated and Partially-Isolated Patients*	Non-Isolated Patients†
	(20)	(25)
	Per Cent	Per Cent
None	5	0
One or two	10	4
Three to five	15	4
More than five	70	88
Can't say	0	4
	100	100

* Isolated and partially-isolated patients have been combined
in all tables because empirically they behaved almost identically.

† Ambiguous cases and persons who played only with their
siblings are excluded from these comparisons. The isolates and
partial-isolates are compared only to the clear-cut non-isolated
cases.

than to the non-isolated patients. A slightly higher
proportion of the isolates report fewer than five
available playmates, but the difference does not
approach statistical significance and even among
the isolates 14 in 20 report there were five or more
children of their age living in the neighborhood.

The isolates were not prevented by serious
illness from playing with other children: isolates
and partial-isolates do not differ significantly
from non-isolates with respect to the proportion
who report having been very sickly or rather sickly,
either in the first decade of life or as a teenager.[14]

Finally, the isolates were not prevented by
excessive residential mobility from interacting
with other children: isolates and partial-isolates
do not differ significantly from non-isolates with
respect to the proportions who lived in five or more
residences, four or more neighborhoods, or four or
more cities up to the age of fifteen.[1]

These factors, then, do not explain why the
isolates became isolated. Non-isolates and controls
who lived on out-of-the-way farms apparently
managed to play in the school yard after school
hours or to have their classmates visit them at
home. The isolates did not do this. Non-isolates

TABLE 5. RECOLLECTIONS OF PARENTAL BEHAVIOR
BY PATIENTS AND CONTROLS*

Respondent Recalls Mother As	Patients	Controls
	(52)	(52)
	Per Cent	Per Cent
More easily angered than father	50	17
More dominating than father	46	19
More likely to restrict the children's freedom than father	38	6

* Excludes those patients and controls raised by only one
parent.

and controls whose families moved around
frequently nevertheless managed to find playmates
where they moved; isolates did not.

Nor is social isolation the result of parental
restrictions upon the activities of the child: no
greater proportion of isolates and partial-isolates
than of non-isolates report parental restrictions
either on physical activities or on choice of friends.

ISOLATION AND FAMILY RELATIONSHIPS

How about the patterning of familial relationships? Let us state, first, that a larger proportion
of *patients* than of *controls* recall their mothers as
having been more easily angered, more dominating, more anxious for the children to get ahead,
less likely to be satisfied with the children's
behavior, and more restrictive than their fathers.
Correspondingly, a larger proportion of patients
recall their fathers as having been more likely in
case of disagreement to give in, less certain of
themselves and less strict than their mothers.[16]

We present a comparison of patients to controls
on three of these items as an illustration: a larger
proportion of patients than of controls recall their
mothers as having been more easily angered, more
dominating, and more restrictive than their fathers.

But *isolated* and *partially-isolated* patients do
not differ significantly from *non-isolated* patients in
their comparisons of mother to father on these
same items. (See Table 6.)

The same is true of all other aspects of family
functioning that the patients report differently
from the controls: in no case do the isolated and
partially-isolated patients differ from the non-
isolated patients. This is true, for example, of their
perceptions of how well their parents got along;
how close they felt to each of their parents; to
which parent they turned when in trouble; and
which parent made the day-to-day decisions, the
major decisions, and the decisions that particularly
affected the children. Nor do isolated patients
differ from non-isolated patients on a number of
other aspects of family structure and functioning
with respect to which patients do not differ from
controls—such as family composition; deaths,
illnesses, or divorce of parents; occupations of
parents; parental aspirations for the children; or
the respondents' relations with their siblings. In
summary we find no evidence that the social isolation of one third of the patients was a resultant
of, or even a correlate of, the familial relationships
studied.

TABLE 6.   RECOLLECTIONS OF PARENTAL BEHAVIOR BY ISOLATED AND NON-ISOLATED PATIENTS

Respondent Recalls Mother As	Isolated and Partially-Isolated Patients *(18)* Per Cent	Non-Isolated Patients *(23)* Per Cent
More easily angered than father	44	48
More dominating than father	49	40
More likely to restrict the children's freedom than father	32	43

TABLE 7.   AGE AT FIRST HOSPITALIZATION

	Isolated and Partially-Isolated Patients *(20)* Per Cent	Non-Isolated Patients *(25)* Per Cent
Under 25	15	28
25–34	40	28
35–44	40	36
45–49	5	8
	100	100

ISOLATION AND WITHDRAWAL

We have been unable to find any evidence that the isolates have been prevented from social participation because of lack of available playmates, residential mobility, illness, or parental restrictions. Nor have we been able to find any evidence that the isolation of one third of the patients resulted from the particular nature of their family relationships. Did the isolates and partial-isolates become isolated, then, because they withdrew from social relationships? Here our primary sources of information are the hospital case-records, based on interviews with family respondents, together with supplementary research interviews that we have conducted with the siblings of still hospitalized patients.

Information indicating that the patient's isolation could be viewed as an expression of his shy, timid, or fearful personality was reported for seven of the ten persons whom we have classified as *isolates*. The pattern is quite different for those patients classified as partial-isolates: family respondents almost uniformly stated that these patients appeared normal and sociable at age 13 or 14. This was true also of the patients classified as *non-isolates*, none of whose case-records gives evidence that his relatives considered him shy, withdrawn, or at all disturbed at age 13–14. But relatives of three of these patients state that subsequent to that age the patients definitely withdrew from normal social participation.

It would seem, then, that the patients whom we have classified as *isolates* had already manifested signs of personality disturbance sufficient to be noted by family respondents by the time they were 13 or 14 years old. Patients whom we have classified as *partial-isolates* appeared normal to their relatives at that age, even though they report that they had already begun to withdraw from social

activities by that age. Presumably the isolation process had not proceeded as far. This process had proceeded least far for the patients classified as *non-isolates*.

THE SIGNIFICANCE OF SOCIAL ISOLATION

We had anticipated that patients who had been isolated from an early age would either have been hospitalized earlier than other patients or would have suffered a more long-lasting illness. Neither of these is the case. Isolates and partial-isolates were hospitalized at approximately the same ages as were non-isolates.

Nor did the isolates and partial-isolates require longer hospitalization, or respond less adequately to hospitalization, than did the non-isolates.

At the time of the research interview, we were unable to discern any important differences in the current functioning of the two groups of patients. Furthermore the two groups do not differ with respect to their current patterns of social relationships—how they spend leisure time, whether or not they belong to formal groups, and how frequently they get together informally with friends. These data all lead to the conclusion that social isolation in this early period does not seem to have appreciably influenced the development of the illness.

SUMMARY AND THEORETICAL IMPLICATIONS

We may summarize our findings as follows: (a) approximately one-third of the schizophrenic and manic-depressive patients give evidence of having been socially-isolated at age 13–14, whereas appreciably none of the normal controls gives evidence of having been isolated at that age; (b) we have been unable to find any evidence that the

TABLE 8. Status of Isolated and Non-Isolated Patients at Yearly Intervals
Following Date of First Admission*

| | ONE YEAR | | TWO YEARS | | THREE YEARS | |
	Isolated and Partially-Isolated Patients	Non-Isolated Patients	Isolated and Partially-Isolated Patients	Non-Isolated Patients	Isolated and Partially-Isolated Patients	Non-Isolated Patients
	(20)	*(25)*	*(19)*	*(22)*	*(17)*	*(18)*
	Per Cent	*Per Cent*	*Per Cent*	*Per Cent*	*Per Cent*	*Per Cent*
Patient resident in a mental hospital	30	16	26	22	18	22
Patient discharged, occupation similar to that prior to illness	45	60	48	60	47	56
Patient discharged, functioning at markedly reduced level	20	24	26	18	29	22
Patient discharged, but no data available as to level on which he is operating	5	0	0	0	6	0
	100	100	100	100	100	100

*The number of patients included beyond the first year decreases because some of the patients had been admitted to the hospital less than two years prior to the time of data collection.

isolated patients had been prevented from interacting with their peers because of a lack of available playmates, excessive residential mobility, severe illness, or parental restrictions; (c) we have been unable to find any evidence of a correlation between social isolation and familial relationships—that is, we have been unable to ascertain any appreciable difference between the perceptions of their relationships with parents and siblings held by the isolated patients and those held by the non-isolated patients.

These data, it must be recognized, are based on the retrospective impressions of a group of persons who have undergone the severely disorienting experience of psychosis. But a systematic comparison of the research interviews with the patients to prior hospital interviews with their relatives shows a high level of consistency for 26 of the 30 patients whose hospital records contain data on this topic.

Our general conclusion must be, then, that for the group here studied the data do not support the hypothesis that social isolation in adolescence is a predisposing factor in either schizophrenia or manic-depressive psychosis. Only a third of the patients were isolated in adolescent life, and even for them isolation does not seem to have been instrumental in predisposing them to psychosis. Nor does it seem to increase the duration of hospitalization.

In early statements of the social isolation hypothesis, it was posited that isolation of any person for an extended period of time results in schizophrenia. Later the process was seen as far more complex: a particular type of person, living in a particular social setting, becomes rebuffed

and rejected by his peers; after fruitless attempts to gain acceptance, he finally withdraws into a shell of isolation.

One wonders why, if this complex series of events is seen as necessary to the schizophrenic process, isolation is seized upon as the crucial element that leads to schizophrenia. Why was the individual rebuffed in the first place? Why did he react so extremely to rebuff as to withdraw from all social interaction? Does not his behavior before he became isolated indicate that his personality development was already quite abnormal? A far simpler explanation of the isolation experience was afforded by Bleuler as long ago as 1908 in his classic volume on schizophrenia: "The overt symptomatology certainly represents the expression of a more or less successful attempt to find a way out of an intolerable situation."[17]

An interpretation in harmony with the findings of this study is that as a result of inadequacies in their social relationships, both within and outside the family, certain individuals come to feel that they do not really belong to their peer-groups— that is, they become *alienated* from their peers. Under severe enough conditions, alienation may lead to a withdrawal from social interaction, that is, to isolation. But it need not do so; it might lead, for example, to compulsive interaction such as that engaged in by some manic patients, or it might not lead to abnormal behavior at all. In any case, isolation does not seem to be the crucial experience in predisposing the individual to illness.

Thus, in terms of process, social isolation is to be viewed as a sign that the individual's interpersonal difficulties have become so great that he is no longer capable of functioning in interpersonal relationships. The question of how he got that way is not a question of social isolation, *per se*. It is rather a series of problems, starting with the question of what are the conditions that produce

alienation, and continuing with the processes by which subsequent interpersonal experiences transform this base of interpersonal difficulty into interpersonal failure.

NOTES

*Paper read at the annual meeting of the American Sociological Society, September, 1954. The authors are indebted to the Maryland State Department of Mental Hygiene, and its Commissioner, Dr. Clifton Perkins, for making available its patient-files, granting access to patients at State hospitals, and aiding our research with a grant-in-aid; to the hospitals of the State of Maryland, especially Springfield State Hospital and Brooklane Farm Hospital for contributing their case records, and enabling us to interview their patients and former patients; to the physicians of Washington County for aid in arranging interviews and in providing valuable data; and to the Public Health Methods Division of the USPHS (especially Dr. Philip Lawrence, Chief of the Familial Studies Unit in Hagerstown) for granting access to their files of Morbidity Studies (basic to our control-group selection) and for valuable suggestions and aid in the field work.

1. Robert E. L. Faris, "Cultural Isolation and the Schizophrenic Personality," *American Journal of Sociology*, XL (September, 1934), pp. 155–164.

2. Robert E. L. Faris and H. Warren Dunham, *Mental Disorders in Urban Areas*, Chicago: University of Chicago Press, 1939. In this volume, Faris and Dunham base the case for the social isolation hypothesis primarily on the findings of high rates in areas of high residential mobility and among ethnic group persons living in non-ethnic neighborhoods (*ibid.*, pp. 173–177). Faris' hypothesis that peer-group rejection leads to isolation and consequent psychosis is developed in his chapter, "Ecological Factors in Human Behavior," in J. McV. Hunt (ed.,) *Personality and the Behavior Disorders*, 2 vol. New York: Ronald Press, 1944, II, pp. 736–757; and in *Social Psychology*, New York: Ronald Press, 1952, especially pages 338–365. Dunham has further hypothesized that the harsh, competitive character of life in the foreign-born slum communities, particularly for persons already sensitive, self-conscious, or timid, is productive of isolation and thus of schizophrenia. See H. Warren Dunham, "The Current Status of Ecological Research in Mental Disorder," *Social Forces*, 25 (March, 1947), pp. 321–326. We have discussed a number of questions relating to interpretations made in these studies and to the clarification of the concept, social isolation, in "The Ecological Approach in Social Psychiatry," *American Journal of Sociology*, LX (September, 1954), pp. 140–151.

3. Faris, "Cultural Isolation and the Schizophrenic Personality," *op. cit.*, p. 157.

4. This statement of Faris' hypothesis of a typical process is abstracted from "Ecological Factors in Human Behavior," *op. cit.*, pp. 752–753.

5. H. Warren Dunham, "The Social Personality of the Catatonic-Schizophrene," *American Journal of Sociology*, XLIX (May, 1944), pp. 508–518.

6. S. Kirson Weinberg, "A Sociological Analysis of a Schizophrenic Type," *American Sociological Review*, XV (October, 1950), pp. 600–610.

7. Our intent in pairing patients and controls on some variables and balancing frequencies on others was to hold constant several variables known to relate significantly to the frequency of schizophrenia, and then to examine the relationship between presence or absence of this illness and other characteristics or experiences of the two groups, especially with reference to social isolation. This is, of course, quite different from the intent and assumptions involved in matching for an experimental design entailing "before" and "after" measures.

8. It was necessary to delimit the time period about which we asked in order to secure reasonably comparable data from all respondents. It was difficult to determine, however, which time period was most important. In all probability the crucial phases of personality development do not occur at the same age for all

persons. It is also probable that some important events in the individual's relations with his peers occur at so early an age that we cannot expect an adult to remember them. Thus, our selection had to be to some degree arbitrary. Age 13–14 had the two virtues of being a period of high peer-group activity and of being quite definitely marked in the respondent's memory by virtue of the transition from grade school to high school.

We shall show, later in this paper, that the age range selected affects the number of isolates we distinguish in a group of patients, but that it does not affect the question of the possible etiological importance of isolation.

9. The significance of differences between the patient and control groups has been tested by the method suggested by McNemar for comparisons between samples whose means are intercorrelated. See Quinn McNemar, *Psychological Statistics*, New York: John Wiley and Sons, 1949, pp. 71–82. The chi-square test was used for testing the significance of differences between the proportions of isolated and non-isolated patient groups. The five per cent level has been used as the criterion of significance.

10. The answers to these particular questions were transcribed onto separate sheets of paper, without identifying information and without the answers to any other questions. Patients and controls were randomly interspersed. Two coders working independently agreed 94 per cent of the time on the categories in which they would place respondents. We attempted to code this same material along several other continua (for example, physical-sedentary, competitive-non-competitive, structured-non-structured) but coding reliability was too low, approximating only 60 per cent. Interviewing specifications had not been drawn up with such dimensions clearly envisaged.

11. Evidence on the consistency of responses to items in this index with related items not included in the index is provided by the answers to the question, "(At the age of 13–14) did you spend more or less time alone than most other children your age did (or did you spend the same amount of time alone?)" The isolates without exception replied, "more time alone." Nine of the eleven partial-isolates replied "more time alone" and the other two replied, "The same amount of time as the average." Among the non-isolates, eight replied that they spent more time alone, 35 that they spent the average time alone, and 27 that they spent less time alone than other children their age.

12. The most important fact about the person who played only with siblings is that all of the patients and all but one of the controls in this category are female.

13. Though the number of cases on which these percentages are based is small, the consistency is so striking that it seems justified to conclude that there are no appreciable differences in the proportion of isolates and partial-isolates in these diagnostic groups. (These percentages are based on 26 cases of paranoid schizophrenia and 16 cases of catatonic schizophrenia.) Nor is isolation a sex-linked phenomenon: the proportion of females among isolates is 55 per cent, among non-isolates, 64 per cent. (Based on 20 male cases and 38 female cases.)

14. Furthermore, those patients who had been included in the Public Health morbidity records did not differ from their controls with respect to the number of days they were absent from school.

15. Comparisons of residential mobility are based upon complete residential histories secured from all patients. These histories were checked against past Hagerstown City Directories and found to be highly consistent with Directory listings.

16. We have analyzed these data in detail in "Parental Authority Behavior and Schizophrenia," *American Journal of Orthopsychiatry*, in press.

17. Eugen Bleuler, *Domentia Praecox, or the Group of Schizophrenias*, English edition translated by Joseph Zinken, New York: International Universities Press, 1950, p. 460.

PSYCHONEUROSIS AND ECONOMIC LIFE*

Stanley A. Leavy and Lawrence Z. Freedman

WHEN the psychiatrist ventures into studying the economic and social lives of his patients, it is in order to increase his understanding of their illness. Emotional illness is all-pervasive in the lives of those who suffer it. Economic activity of one kind or another is universal. Everyone in the society, whether or not he is directly engaged in getting a living, has been subjected to economic influence. As a child he experiences the economic life of his family, including sometimes deprivation and neglect. Adults engage in the economic activities of acquisition and consumption, in the effort to maintain a secure economic status and in competition with others.

The psychiatrist is prompted to inquire how economic activities and emotional condition may have interacted or be interacting in anyone who comes to him for help. The question may be looked at from two aspects: how do the activities and changes of economic life affect the development of emotional illness or health, and how does emotional illness or health affect the economic life? It is through the focusing lens of illness that all the psychiatrist's observations on these questions must be made. Illness is what brings his patients to him and illness is what he is trained to treat. Through the study of illness he may be able to make observations which are applicable outside the range of the pathological.

Most of the adverse circumstances of childhood take place within the little society of the family. The world outside is known primarily through the medium of the family. It is especially of importance to us that through the family are also transmitted the social values that are integrated into the life of the individual child as part of one of the elementary systems of his personality—the system of sanctions and restrictions known as the superego. Economic attitudes are among the values taken in by the developing child, and these attitudes as well as the adaptive capacities in general are subjected to such influences as, for example, the impact of the experience of poverty or of economic change in either an upward or downward direction.

Reprinted from *Social Problems* (July, 1956), *4* (1), 55–67.

We may ask whether experiences of adult life related to getting a living have a determinative effect in the appearance of neurotic symptoms. We may also ask whether neurotic people show their neurotic symptoms in specific ways in their economic life. These primary questions lie behind the study from which this paper is derived. They are pursued in greater detail with regard to various subdivisions of what we have defined as economic life, and particularly into the problems of competition and prestige, of insecurity, and of work—all in relation to their causal significance in neurosis and to their functions as theatres for the enacting of neurotic behavior.

ECONOMIC INSECURITY

With respect to economic insecurity, the question was asked to what extent our patients' early experience of poverty and the hazards of employment and fluctuations of income which they later experienced may have affected their emotional lives.

We found it difficult, if not impossible, to separate the factors making for economic insecurity from those that produced other unhappy tensions of family life. We may cite as an example of the influence of long-continued poverty and insecurity the case of a young man, D., who had withdrawn from association with his friends into a life of almost total isolation because of his shame and guilt at not having a job during a period of full employment. The neurotic cause of his inability to work lay in the intense anxiety which he experienced in looking for work, when fears of being rejected and humiliated were paramount. In the background was a lifetime of economic insecurity. The most serious episode occurred during the economic depression when D. was in his early adolescence and his father was bankrupt. His father had been the least successful member of his own family and for this was derided by the boy's mother. Deeply attached as the boy was to his mother, he was unable to find any community of interest or understanding with his unsuccessful, disappointed father. Although there was no frank deprivation of the necessities of life, D. did not get many of the things which his friends had. Characteristically, he responded to this deprivation with the reactive attitude that they were probably not worth having anyhow, and in addition that he, at least, was not worthy of having them. We cannot find within the economic situation alone the determinants of the withdrawal from economic life that characterized this boy's neurosis. Conversely, we cannot abstract the deeper dynamic determinants of this illness from the economic insecurity in which he grew up.

In the cases of other persons, the recurring economic insecurity of the environment provoked the deeper insecurity in their personal lives. Another one of our patients was a thirty-eight-year-old woman, L., whose depressive ideas centered around the fear that she and her husband would be unable to maintain the situation of relative security which they had reached. She likewise felt that her children did not have the material advantages which her neighbors' children had, but particularly she feared that her husband would not be able to keep his present satisfactory job. It is interesting to correlate these symptoms with L.'s actual economic experience. Her father, of whom she had been very fond, deserted the family in her early adolescence and the financial situation which had previously been secure became precarious. She had to leave school early because of financial difficulties and when quite young was obliged to work in a store at night. She was married during the economic depression and for a while she and her husband were in serious financial straits. They had to live with her mother, with whom her relationship had been most unsatisfactory since her father's death. Economic requirements made them move away to a strange city, where they began to be more successful and in a few years reached financial independence. At the time of the onset of her illness, this had become imperiled once more by her husband's physical ill health. L. remembered that all during her life she had the fear of repeating the experiences of insecurity of her early childhood. The actual experience was one of virtual repetition of the early disaster.

Depressive patients very often express their fears in economic terms as one sector of the symptoms of their illness. Such patients complain, for example, that business has been bad, that prices are too high, that they have spent too much on the medical case, and so on. They may express strong feelings of guilt that they have not provided better for their families, and may also suffer extreme indecision regarding spending money,

since any purchase requires a restriction of their power to purchase something else. Such ideas may at times assume delusional proportion. In these persons, the deeper fear and guilt indeed surround losses, but not necessarily the loss of money and economic security. It is a loss, or threatened loss, of an object of love. A widow, G., who for many years had centered all of her interest in the progress and education of her daughter, became depressed with fear of destitution when her daughter's engagement was announced. The daughter, who had not been contributing to her mother's support hitherto, was going to marry a wealthy and otherwise acceptable young man. There had been financial reverses in the mother's life years before, but both her social position and her ability to provide for herself and the girl had been in reality fairly secure. At this time, particularly, her daughter's future seemed assured. This kind of illness is more frequently seen in middle life or later when fears of destitution may be backed in reality by the limitation of earning capacity that has taken place. But we do not see such depression with the emphasis on economic loss when the relationships are undisturbed. Moreover, patients of depressive character have all their lives unconsciously required reassurance against the possibility of loss which for them represents total destruction. Economic insecurity is one among several dangers to survival which could threaten them, and the expression of the depressive symptoms in economic terms is a culturally influenced "omnibus" for many fears. The loss of a husband, mother, or lover may be followed by fears of economic disaster. It is the equivalence of economic security with emotional security that is at the core of this problem.

It is of particular interest to us that fear and guilt may be displaced from emotional to economic concerns. This is in part, of course, due to the symbolizations of early life which attach various emotional qualities to money and economic security. Money and what it supplies may become tokens of love. The reliability of parents as sources of comfort may be in part limited by their inability to offer economic security. On the other hand, it is the society that makes such symbols out of economic values by the weight it attaches to them. Money, security, and economic prestige may be of such value in our society that loss or the threat of loss can best be expressed in such terms; or, looking at the matter differently, there may be real danger of economic loss so universally felt that this displacement is easily affected.

Another approach to the question of insecurity is found in the study of the effects of unemployment. Our clinical material did not provide us with direct references to the effects of unemployment, since all the cases studied were seen during a period of full employment. Some of our patients, it is true, did suffer during a period of unemployment during the economic depression and reported something of what the experience had meant to them. Whatever insecurity these patients suffered on an emotional basis was augmented by the indelible impression left upon them in that period.

RELATIONSHIPS TO WORK

We noted that it is not only the threat to subsistence which prevailed, but also the threat to self-esteem. Turning to our clinical material, we must consult a quite different type of economic insecurity than that due to unemployment, namely, that of economic challenge itself. One of our patients, H., was a young man who had hitherto been employed in a small business in which he had occupied a responsible position and had not demonstrated any neurotic symptoms. He was seemingly the most stable member of his family. Within a few days after his opening up a small business venture, in which family funds were invested, H. broke down with symptoms of severe anxiety and depression, withdrew from the new enterprise, and only gradually recovered. It is something not uncommon in psychiatric practice to find that the achievement of an independent occupation or of promotion in status is followed by the precipitation of anxiety. There are many causes of anxiety at such times. A realistic appraisal of the situation may itself reveal that the new task is beyond a man's capacity. The risk may itself be also more than he is prepared to undertake. The responsibility for others' welfare can be too much. On the other hand, another kind of determinant may also exist in patients whose doubts of their adequacy are brought to the surface and underscored once they have attained a position which is unconsciously recognized to be in competition with the parents.

We then wanted to learn how the work in which our patients were engaged was related to the neuroses which they suffered. The questions we asked ourselves were: "Did their work contribute to their neuroses? Did their neuroses affect their work?"

We must start with the observation that in our society a person must work. By this is meant something in addition to the realistic obligation to earn a living important as that is. The need to support one's self and one's dependents, and the urge to provide for the satisfaction of needs and taste beyond the level of subsistence, are not the only powerful pressures that move men to work. A person who does not work is considered to be either sick or bad. This is a socially developed criterion, a derivative of a philosophy of life which has long characterized America.

The psychiatrist, in accord with the conventions of his culture, which sanction work and condemn idleness, assumes as a rule that the person who does not work is ill and that the ability to work once more is evidence of the recovery of mental health. Patients themselves usually recognize this fact and stress as complaints, in many cases, their inability to carry on their work. The contrary patients' excessive preoccupation with work in which their involvement is compulsive. The psychiatric understanding of work as an indication of health is simply that failure to conform in this respect with the social convention is the product of emotional disturbance or the outgrowth of character disorder. This is a fundamental and universal convention, at least within the limited society which we are discussing.

As we have assumed, the concern of the healthy person to work is due in part to his realistic appraisal of his situation—that his living conditions ultimately depend upon work, within the expectations of this society—but it is due also to the social disapproval of inactivity and to the less tangible need for work as itself a satisfaction of emotional needs. Where the feeling of obligation to matic behavior is seen rather in the work is not present, psychiatrists expect to find also that other evidence of situation also exists, in which sympto-illness or character defect. In our cases, such a failure to conform was found only in persons who showed severe defects in the whole sphere of responsibility. A young man who expressed almost all values in terms of money did not accept the obligation to undertake any form of employment; insofar as he did look for work, it was under external compulsion. His various attempts at schooling were defeated, despite his adequate intelligence, by his inability to take seriously any of the scholastic requirements. Persons of this type of character come into constant conflict with their environment because the obligations of the society have never become fully internalized.

Far more frequent is the complaint among our patients that their self-respect is impaired when their symptoms prevent them from working. Not working in a community where nearly everyone works is itself sufficient to arouse feelings of guilt and depression. It stirs up old anxieties, that may have been long latent, concerning one's ability to achieve and maintain independence. The patient who is not working is confronted by the threat of protests from the relatives who are contributing to his support, whether or not these protests are ever actually expressed. He adds to his existing feelings of inadequacy the picture of himself, drawn from reality, as one unable to meet a fundamental demand of the society. To be sure, this complaint, while real enough, is balanced by an unconscious gain in the form of pleasures realized by being allowed to maintain a dependent existence. In such instances, however, the obligation to work is not denied; it is the urgency of the symptoms that prevent participation in the work which is emphasized.

In view of the very common complaint of un-congenial work, we found surprisingly few examples, in our series of patients, of evident connection between the work itself and the development of neurosis. The form of the work might be disturbing because of its actual danger, unhygienic surroundings, offensive administrative measures, or disagreeable associates.

These problems are briefly alluded to in the histories we studied. The unfriendly dictatorial boss was a threat to the security of some of our patients, who saw in this situation a repetition of childhood struggles with authority. Perhaps because we did not see many factory workers, there were no specific complaints of dissatisfaction with the fragmentary nature of the tasks they performed. It is likely that workers today are not aware at first hand of the loss of satisfaction that was once present in the making of a finished product. On the other hand, a group of our patients who had to continue the management of family busi-nesses expressed detestation for this work. This appeared to be a matter of personal preference rather than of actually unfavorable surroundings.

Of the three general economic problems, insecurity, competition, and work, which we studied in investigating our patients, the type of work was the least apparent source of neurotic disturbance. It is tempting, however, to speculate about this. If work was not pointed to in a positive way, it may also be that in a large group of persons, apart from those fortunate enough to be able to express their needs by means of their work, the occupation provided insufficient gratification and was hence negatively a cause.

The second question is asked, "Did t neuroses affect their work?" Here our finding indicate that the occupation provides a significant field for the operation of neurotic behavior. The enactment of neurotic feelings may, indeed, account for some of the problems of business. On the other hand, when neurotic feelings are controlled, work appears to be very important as a partially sublimated or elevated expression of emotional needs. This was true even in the cases of some patients who professed no particular interest in their jobs.

For example, G. worked as a draftsman in a plant for nearly twenty years. He was too insecure ever to assert himself to his superiors and he believed that his present wage was the maximum he could attain. His personal interests, aside from his absorbing work, were expressed entirely out-side the plant. His neurosis, however, included obsessions and compulsions that drove him to extremes in scrupulous adherence to rule and routines. Outside the job, he was always in danger of anxiety because the hours of leisure could not be governed automatically enough and the threat of ungratifiable wishes was constant. He particularly hated Sundays. At work he was contented most of the time because his needs for submission to an inflexible authority and for systematic routine were amply gratified. He welcomed overtime employment and obviously enjoyed the inventory periods that required his presence at the plant over weekends. In addition, this man enjoyed his work because part of it enabled him to exercise domination over other employees. Within this framework, the situation was provided for a really timid, retiring man to indulge in the acting out of a fantasy of grandiose character.

Persons whose work is excessively demanding and who seem to accept the situation whole-heartedly are often suffering from serious neurotic symptoms, but their drive to work accords so satisfactorily with the accepted conventions of society that the illness may not be evident. A plant manager who developed symptoms of frankly aggressive impulses—directed consciously against members of his family, whom he feared he might injure—lived all his waking life with the ideal of high ambition and "getting to the top." He had a large staff of subordinates whom he treated as a potentially mutinous crew, but he also did not spare himself. He rarely relaxed from the pressure and put in a lot of overtime. He accounted for this by his desire to get for his family the advantages he had had himself. It was when he

y of an approaching advancement
l severely from his obsession by
pulses. Previously his intense
l barely been kept in check.

terest that, in these patients,
on the whole was put to constructive ends, although the degree of damage to others in their personal relationships can only be guessed. Of course, ambition and energy at work are not generally symptomatic. At least often, if not as a rule, the urge to produce is experienced as part of a series of pleasurable impulses and is sufficiently integrated with the total personality to make work relationships harmonious.

Apart from these examples of the expression of emotional needs through compulsive work, we saw in our patients other kinds of fulfilment and, of course, other unconscious pressures. There is evidence of the importance of work as a gratification of aims other than self-support or the maintenance of security and status. Our cultural prejudices place favor on such attitudes as "living for one's work," but certain neurotic patients give us further insight into the meaning of this attitude. In those persons whose lives are centered in work, its sublimatory function has at this time failed, but we are able from their histories to reconstruct what the function has hitherto been. Here, as is seen elsewhere in clinical medicine, the pathological state, through its exaggeration of some functions at the expense of others, throws light on the healthy processes.

Some types of work more than others afford this gratification. It is a "consuming interest" and these persons are "in love with" their work. It might be said that all good work has this virtue, since in health the product of one's efforts is potentially a source of pride and satisfaction such as is obtainable in personal relationships. What is loved in it also may be a representation of one's self. On the other hand, in the work of certain school teachers and nurses both the work and the persons who are served may be equally important objects of love.

Two of our patients were very successful women professionally, who enacted in their work the drives which in other spheres of their lives ended in unmanageable conflicts that precipitated a neurosis. One, a school teacher, succeeded in directing her strongly aggressive trends productively in her own schooling and later on as a teacher. Socially, she was unsuccessful and unhappy. The second woman, an artist, was a very extravagant and flamboyant person, who showed these char-

acteristics in her work and also in the financial dealings related to her work. It would be impossible to separate these characteristics from the work itself and from her success in it, but they were connected also with her periods of extreme financial insecurity and the neurotic relationships with others in which she was involved.

Not all of the patients could express their need so satisfactorily, however, in their work. In other cases, we saw the influence of the neurosis rather in the steady deterioration of the work as their anxiety increased. This, indeed, is the more common situation. Satisfaction also progressively diminished, and what had been, in some cases, a refuge from intolerable personal conflicts failed to provide further help.

COMPETITION AND PRESTIGE

We have already referred to the significance of economic competition as one of the possible factors involved in the genesis and precipitation of neurosis. This topic has particular interest because of its intimate association with other elements in the development of neurosis. The attainment of individual ascendency through competition is not limited to the economic sphere; traditionally, this is a major value in other activities such as war, sport, artistic production, and religion. Economic achievement, however, at least in our culture, holds an important position as a demonstration of individual superiority.

We have also emphasized the importance to the healthy individual of conformity to the ideal of participation in useful work, and we have described a mechanism whereby social values are acquired. The expected "social role" of the person in the culture includes certain proprieties, among which is success, which may have a fundamentally economic coloring. Achieving, attaining, obtaining, and displaying may be demonstrations of personal superiority, all of which imply competition with other persons engaged in the same pursuit. The possession of wealth and economic status is regarded as valuable in itself for the personal enjoyment provided, that is, comforts and luxuries and guarantees of security. Maintaining the economic proprieties is an act of allegiance to social values, conscious or unconscious, the outcroppings of which are rationally covered by references to material needs, taste, and preferences, as well as security.

One of our patients was a salesman, T., in a highly competitive business who had obsessing fears of being unable to produce a large enough volume of sales. These fears spread to all-pervasive doubts of his ability to function and support his family, with ensuing profound depression. An immediate stress precipitating this illness occurred when a fellow salesman whom he had previously assisted now had a superior position and, having passed by him, had forgotten his indebtedness. There were additional complications. T. had remained in this business largely because it was one owned by a relative. He felt in some ways more secure here because there was no danger of losing his job, and he was protected to a certain extent from competition. However, he was intensely envious of the owner's success and was often aware of frank wishes to defeat and destroy him. This was not unprovoked, since the owner of the business made and did not fulfil promises of advancement.

But deeper study of this patient's conflict revealed interesting connections. The basic repeated theme in his feelings was his shame at being "not a man." Doubts of his virility were present throughout his adult life, and he reacted to these doubts with promiscuity as well as with his intense need to succeed in his work. In business, as in the instinct life, he had a constant need to overcome this feeling, but he could never succeed in developing adequate conviction of his masculinity. His doubts of his virility in turn were traceable to his early failure of identification with his father or other suitable masculine figures. Even in childhood, he showed reactions, ancipatory of his later behavior, in the development of minor delinquent activities.

At this time, economic insecurity may have played a part in establishing an unhealthy family setting. His family's poverty contributed toward separating him from his father, who had this reason to be absorbed in business, leaving the boy with his mother, toward whom he was deeply attached and overdependent. This childhood relationship with his mother, with all of its dangers to his development of independence, was further reflected in his attitude toward women generally. His promiscuous behavior was determined not only by his attempts to deny his doubts about his masculinity, but also by his need to keep sexual gratification apart from his relation with any woman with whom he could have the emotional satisfaction he had earlier experienced with his mother.

The interweaving of instinctive conflict with the opportunity for its practice in economic life is well illustrated by this case. More specifically, it connects strivings toward the representation of masculine behavior with economic competition.

This is not the only instinctive problem which may find its issue in competition. A series of our patients presented neurotic symptoms in which the economic problem involved was their participation in an inherited business. There was in these no obvious precipitation of the illness through economic insecurity or through unusual striving for the attainment of wealth and prestige. The competitiveness which could be recognized as of neurotic significance in these patients arose from their earliest familial relationship, which the business continued to represent long after the maturity of the patient had been reached.

J., a man of forty, was depressed and preoccupied with bodily symptoms for which no organic cause could be found. He attributed his illness in part to his dissatisfaction with his business, which was very successful, but which he insisted did not interest him, and which he had made a number of attempt to dispose of, always desisting because the firm meant so much to his mother. His father, who had founded it, had died when the patient was a boy, and his mother had never allowed him to consider seriously any other occupation than that of maintaining the firm. He conformed to her will in the matter, but within himself there was a persistent struggle between his efforts at rebelling and his inability to disagree openly with his mother. He had never been able to feel that this was his own responsibility. Because he had inherited it and he looked upon his own success as merely a continuation of his father's, he felt frustrated by the persistent power of his father's influence. His close although ambivalent relationship with his mother, together with the material advantages gained by continuing the inherited business, actually removed him from the field of competing on equal terms with others. At the same time, his dislike of the work and his diminished self-esteem were closely connected with the fact that he was engaged in hopeless competition with his dead father. Implicit here was his requirement, derived from values of the society, that he achieve success independently. He injured his self-esteem by maintaining this business, in which he felt he was denied any really independent expression, but he refrained from selling it because of the economic security it provided and the bond with his mother which it involved.

Our patients' histories prevent us from attributing their problems of competition solely to the overevaluation of success and prestige which our society makes. These social values are incorporated at an early age, since the assumptions on which the parents' lives are organized and which therefore modify what they say to and do with the child include acceptance of the values of competition. Our evidence is that such indoctrination falls on prepared soil. Competitiveness exists by the very nature of the organization of the family. The demand of the child for exclusive possession of one or both parents and the actual or potential rivalry between siblings are the primary sources of competitiveness in the life of the individual. Some societies, such as our own, may be more adjusted than others to invoke the competitiveness that is ultimately grounded in the family. The clinical importance of this can be recognized when we recall that in many patients competitiveness as a neurotic symptom has only incidental economic appearance and is more readily detectable in, for example, the sexual life.

Thus far, our cases have illustrated for the most part the drive toward economic success as a value in itself. Others of our patients in whom economic strivings were intimately related with the neurotic behavior were overconcerned with economic matters because of their great need for social prestige. Although there are exceptions to the rule, namely, in traditionally upper-class families and in some intellectual circles, it is generally true that social status in America is closely geared to economic position. Therefore, where there are intense needs to improve social status there will be, in many persons, a corresponding need for money. A related condition is that in which the maintenance of social prestige is imperiled by economic insecurity.

A young woman, E., who had been brought up by a family that tried to live up to certain aristocratic social ideals, was faced from early childhood by the marked discrepancy that existed between her economic capacity and the social position she had learned to expect. E.'s family was severely affected by the economic depression, but apparently even before that her father's financial irresponsibility kept them in financial straits. Her mother particularly suffered from the deprivation of social position that resulted. On the other hand, there was also the loss of luxuries and comforts that had been so highly valued by them, although it does not appear that they were ever in want.

In her marriage, E.'s husband's lack of conspicuous success as an earner was doubly disturbing to her because she had tastes for expensive things she could not afford and also needed to regain the lost social position of her childhood. It is interesting that in the course of her treatment E., in addition to gaining a degree of insight into the conflicts, also showed a favorable response when her husband's

earning improved so that she could to some extent gratify her economic needs.

We saw a rather similar situation in another patient, S., whose upper-class mother had married far below her class. S. seemed all her life to be attempting to overcome this disgrace. She abandoned a lover for a man of more "respectable" position, whom she married and by whom she expected at last to be given economic self-sufficiency and restoration to the social class to which she felt she belonged. It was a very disturbing experience for her when she was disappointed in both. This woman had a ceaseless preoccupation with money, which for her seemed to have the principal meaning of insuring social respectability. Without it she had to see herself in the image of her disreputable father on whom her mother had "thrown herself away."

The connection between money and social desirability may be recognized quite early in life. Some of our patients remembered humiliating experiences in childhood when they were made aware that their lack of wealth somehow made them less esteemed people than wealthier neighbors. The patient R., who was mentioned at an earlier point because of his unusual lack of a sense of responsibility to work, was also aware in childhood of this distinction. At the age of six, he contrasted his family with the neighbors and felt that his family did not live in a good enough house. His striving for upper-class living seemed to have begun then and remained primary motivation throughout his life; spending large amounts of money was his major satisfaction. Actually, R.'s family was rather well-to-do, and the usual response of his parents throughout his life was to give him money and other material objects. This man, whom we have seen to be psychopathically irresponsible, could apparently recognize a relationship only in terms of the money involved in it. Obviously, this was not the only cause of his irresponsibility, but we are able to see through this, understanding that behind the fanatical interest in money lay an attempt to establish some lasting relationship with other human beings. His social snobbery in turn was predicted upon his contempt for his parents.

All three (E., S., R.) demonstrated quite different processes in which the neurotic meaning of money was involved. They could not do without money, much more money than they could readily get, and this not for the purpose of gratifying material needs or obtaining pleasure. In the two women, and to a lesser extent in the man also, the obtaining of money had as a principal aim the overcoming of situations of insufficient social prestige. This problem may also be looked at from the point of view of security. Not only falling in social position may be a threat to emotional security, but also failing to rise, in the case of persons whose morale requires of them that they advance socially. Such an aim in life is, of course, offered by our society to all who enter it at birth, but only in some does it become a neurotically determined need. Our evidence would be to the effect that this need develops in persons whose early character formation encourages striving, envy, and other mechanisms of "getting" and "winning" and "keeping" that have their origin in the revalries of childhood. The fitting of these mechanisms into the framework of social striving is probably the result of certain identifications made in later childhood, when the object of interest and envy is a person with real or fancied social prestige. Because of the connection that exists between economic position and social prestige, money becomes in these persons an intermediate object.

Psychoanalytic studies, however, add to these observations the recognition of deeper needs which are involved in the getting of money. Since, as far as possible, we have kept in this paper to the type of evidence which our own patients have presented, we shall not discuss this at length. It suffices to say that from a wide range of studies there has come abundant evidence that money has other meanings. Depressed persons, as has been suggested at an earlier point, may see in money the symbol of their direct means of sustenance; loss of money is loss of food. In other instances, persons have been studied who need primarily to keep money or its equivalent in the form of valuable objects; in these persons the unconscious drive is one of retention, and had its origin in the primitive instinctive response of the child to retain his feces—as material of fantasied value, because of the significance of the stool during the process of training of the child. Further connections of this anal attitude toward money with other anal attitudes are to be found. Wishes to soil and wishes to hurt likewise proceed from this period of the child's development; correlated as they are with aggressive aims, it is possible to see how the striving to get and keep money may realize many unconscious goals at the same time. Not only is there both real and imagined security in money; having money and getting it by competitive effort are also gratifying to primitive needs of a destructive kind. Conversely, insofar as our society encourages competitive effort (as industrial societies tend to do), it automatically places a high value, in terms of both actual rewards and of esteem, on the working out of destructive impulses in economic life.

CONCLUSIONS

We have ranged widely in this study, examining topics connected with one another only by virtue of their common reference to the interrelationships of economics and neurosis. We have been prompted to do so in following the leads given us by the study of a large number of case records; the application to the records of a broad criterion of what constituted the economic life of the patients encouraged this approach. The patients whom we studied had many different kinds of economic experiences and their responses to them were also greatly varied. We had information about them differing in psychological depth, so that the interpretations which could be made, pertinent to our subject, were not strictly parallel.

A first generalization which work of this kind permits is that economic life can be shown to have great significance as a determinant of neurosis, provided that an adequate investigation of the economic situation is made. In other words, what persons do to earn a living, what kind of experiences they have had as a result of their parents' problems of earning, what kind of economic mores of the community have been imposed on them—such things constitute definable elements in the development of neurosis.

We made the more or less arbitrary division of our subject into inquiries concerning security, work, and competition. The major economic issues in the lives of the patients could be subsumed under these headings and the pertinent literature could also be surveyed in this way.

The level of interpretation as an index to the significance of economic determinants was found to be very important in all the topics under consideration. That is, the role of economic issues in the lives of the patients may be seen in different perspectives, depending on how much is known about other areas of life. On the subject of *security,* for example, some of the literature covering the statistical examination of large populations supports the conclusion that poverty and economic insecurity generate or precipitate neuroses. Here the single determinant is isolated from, among other things, the character trends of the individual person which foster, or defend him against, neurotic experiences. A superficial personal history may similarly isolate the economic from the characterologic problems of the individual. Conversely, the pursuit of psychological depth often obscures evidence of the relative importance of social and economic agencies.

Under more favorable conditions for study, however, the finer type of scrutiny which is permitted by a detailed case history oriented by psychoanalytical psychology sharpens our view of the interweaving of economic factors with conflicts within the individual. Exclusiveness of economic insecurity as instrumental in producing neurotic behavior is not observed; on the other hand, what are presumably personal conflicts unrelated to economic insecurity are seen sometimes to have themselves originated in childhood situations where poverty and deprivation played a part.

Our observations confirm the view of other writers that at least two factors are involved in the generating of neurotic behavior by economic insecurity: not only is the threat to subsistence of serious consequence, but so also is the threat to self-esteem. Greater and lesser degrees of neurotic behavior resulted when insecurity and poverty defeated the individuals' attempt to live up to the expectations they made upon themselves. Furthermore, the psychological correspondence existing between economic insecurity and loss of love was illustrated in our cases.

Work as a stress situation could also be looked at from more than one point of view. References to the occupation as a source of emotional disturbance were not frequent in these cases. When they did occur, the specific meaning of the stress could be found in the transfer of more deeply determined personal conflicts into the work situation. This,

of course, does not diminish the importance of work as a stress, since this part of life accounts for such a large amount of the time of any person's activity in association with others. On the other hand, for some of the patients whom we studied, the employment provided a demonstrable release for energies which were themselves directed by neurotic conflict. Some of the psychological mechanisms whereby this release may have occurred were discussed, and the literature was approached for theoretical explanations. Evidence was further at hand to show how the cultural evaluation of work may provide a screen of acceptability for compulsive overactivity—the neurotic nature of which was evident only after the person became ill.

We were impressed by the importance of *competition* as a force in the histories of some neurotic persons. Economic competition operated as a pathogenic agency in several ways. The struggle for achievement liberated in some patients feelings of hostility which were poorly withstood. In other cases, the culturally prescribed standards of success and prestige presented goals impossible of achievement, which augmented already existing conflicts. In yet others, economic life offered a new arena for the enactment of competitive struggles which had been going on in one guise or another since early childhood. In all these it may be said that the obligation to compete, like economic insecurity, had a double function: it was a direct threat, since failure might again endanger subsistence, and it was also more subtly involved as a social force, invoking the individual's allegiance in the pursuit of a value not open to criticism.

NOTES

*This paper is abstracted from a longer monograph, with review of the literature, prepared at the request of the National Council of Churches as a part of a multidisciplinary study of ethics and economics. It was also supported by the Foundations Fund for Research in Psychiatry. The Comprehensive report includes a discussion of other relevant studies as well as the theoretical contributions to which we are indebted. The cases and conclusions cited here, however, are derived from the present clinical investigation.

The study, of which this report is a partial synopsis, was based on a systematic examination of five hundred case records of patients, half of whom had been seen in a psychiatric dispensary and the other half in a private psychiatric hospital. In addition, records were examined of patients from the private practice of both authors. The dispensary and private patients demonstrated psychoneurotic illness comparable with respect to diagnoses and severity, but were of different economic backgrounds.

SOCIAL ISOLATION AND MENTAL ILLNESS IN OLD AGE

Marjorie Fiske Lowenthal

ALIENATION and isolation have been crucial concepts in studies of mental and emotional disorders ever since Durkheim's pioneering work on suicide.[1] Forty years later, Faris and Dunham showed that rates and types of treated mental disorders were related to the socioeconomic characteristics of urban census tracts, finding that schizophrenia was more frequent in the central districts of cities, while manic-depressive psychoses and the organic psychoses of old age did not reveal such patterns. The organic psychoses of old age, however, did appear to increase with an increase in poverty. These authors hypothesized that persons in the central districts are more likely to be alienated or isolated, and that these social factors are thus related to a high rate of schizophrenia.[2] More recently, the Hollingshead and Redlich study in New Haven showed that the proportion of treated psychoses was highest among the members of the most underprivileged classes,[3] and Myers and Roberts, studying intensively a sub-sample of the same population, related these differences in part to alienation and isolation from the rest of the community and to unsatisfactory interpersonal relations.[4]

Meanwhile, social theorists have gone on to refine and elaborate the concepts of alienation, anomie, and isolation. One of Merton's five modes of individual adaptation was retreatism. He characterized persons adopting this mode as, sociologically speaking, the true "aliens," and Charlie Chaplin's bum was his prototype for this kind of alien.[5] Recently, Seeman has postulated five components of alienation, namely, powerlessness, normlessness, social isolation, meaninglessness, and self-estrangement, and Dean has focused on the first three.[7]

Empirical sociological studies have explored the role of social isolation in the etiology of specific mental disorders, especially schizophrenia.[8] Just as the concepts of alienation and anomie have been refined for theoretical and empirical purposes, so these and other authors have encountered the need

Reprinted from *American Sociological Review* (February, 1964), 29 (1), 54–70, by permission of the American Sociological Association.

for further elaboration of the idea of social isolation apart from the context of objective social deprivation. Peter Townsend, in his study of elderly people in a London district, has underscored the necessity of distinguishing between objective circumstances and subjective states—between isolation and loneliness.[9] Friis and Manniche, in a Copenhagen survey, also point out that being alone is not necessarily correlated with loneliness,[10] and Pagani reports similar findings from a survey in Milan.[11]

Psychiatrists and psychoanalysts have analyzed the role of isolation as defense mechanism and symptom.[12] Frieda Fromm-Reichmann, in one of her last works, explored various subjective states of loneliness, distinguishing between "real loneliness," which she considered disintegrative and incommunicable, and creative isolation. She suggested that more careful study may indicate that loneliness plays an important part in the genesis of mental disorder.[13]

Social isolation has also been specifically postulated as a crucial aspect of the aging process itself. Parsons singles out isolation as a characteristic of the elderly in middle- and upper middle-class urban society.[14] Changes in social roles, involving fewer contacts or a decrease in their intensity, have been explored in a number of empirical studies of aging.[15] In the work of Cumming and Henry, a theory of social disengagement is the major framework for analyzing the aging process, and the authors postulate that the relation between interaction and morale decreases with advancing age.[16]

On the face of it, the relation between isolation and mental illness assumed or demonstrated in many of these works, and the well-establised fact that social contacts decrease with advancing age, together might account for the higher rates of first admissions to mental hospitals among the elderly that have been reported in recent studies.[17] Studies conducted by clinicians have given rise to conjecture about a causal relation between isolation and the incidence of physical and mental disorder,[18] and, more specifically, between isolation or lack of social integration and the development of the senile psychoses and the late schizo-phrenias.[19] But, just as the studies of increasing isolation in relation to aging have pretty much left open the question of voluntary versus involuntary disengagement, so have these left open the question of age-linked (or illness-linked) versus long-standing isolation. At this stage of our knowledge, one is inclined to agree with Hunt that "all things considered . . . it would seem wisest, pending the outcome of further research, to consider the social isolation hypothesis as uncon-firmed (though by no means discredited)."[20]

Early in the research program of which this present exploratory study is a part, it was apparent that the elderly persons in the psychiatric wards of San Francisco General Hospital had lived far more isolated lives just prior to admission than had their peers who remained in the community. The original purpose of this present study was to analyze three degree-of-isolation groups in the hospital sample and an isolated group in the community sample in order to gain further insight into the relation between what had been assumed to be age-linked isolation and mental illness in old age. Some unex-pected results of this analysis prompted a re-exa-mination of the isolates on a case-by-case basis which led in turn to the finding that we were dealing with differences in kind as well as degree. We hope that the resulting typology will constitute a small contribution to the study of isolation which, as Wilensky has pointed out, has remained under-developed, "a casualty of the cost not only to society but to the researcher of reaching the isolate."[21] The immediate practical objective is to develop hypotheses to be tested in ongoing research in geriatric mental illness.

INDICATORS OF ISOLATION

The parent samples from which the sub-groups to be analyzed here were drawn consist of (a) a population of 534 persons 60 years of age and older admitted to the psychiatric screening wards of the San Francisco General Hospital in the calendar year 1959,[22] and (b) a sample of 600 community residents 60 years of age and older, drawn on a stratified random basis from 18 census tracts in San Francisco.[23] The data reported here were gathered during the "baseline" year of 1959, though all surviving and locatable people in both samples were also interviewed twice more, at approximately annual intervals.

The initial screening criteria used for the selection of the subgroups were, for the hospital sample, level of social activity in the two weeks prior to admission, presence or absence of personal others (friends or relatives) in the decision-making process that eventuated in admission to the psych-iatric ward, and the availability of personal others as informants after admission. For the community sample, only the social interaction question was used as an initial screening criterion. Because of the more elaborate criteria available for the hospital sample, it was possible to delineate a group of extreme isolates, whom we shall call "pure" isolates, as well as a group of semi-isolates whose social deprivation was somewhat less extreme. For the community sample, due to the more structured nature of the data, no semi-isolates could definitely be discerned. Groups of social interactors, however, were drawn from both samples.

The 52 *"pure" isolates* located among the hospitalized are people who had no friends or relatives involved in the decision-making process that led to hospitalization, and for whom no such persons could be located after they had been admitted to the psychiatric ward. On the social activity question, these patients reported no contact with a friend or relative in the two weeks prior to admission. In addition, a careful reading of detailed interview transcripts, which include material on current and past social relationships, revealed that they had had no contact of any kind with a friend or a relative for approximately three years. All of them were, not surprisingly, living alone, except for five from a county old age home and 11 who had been living alone but had briefly occupied institutional way-stations (such as jail or a medical ward) en route to the psychiatric screening wards.

Seventy-seven year old Mr. E. is not untypical of those in circumstances of extreme isolation at the time of ad-mission. He has worked mainly as an itinerant laborer and has lived in nearly every state in the union, retiring in 1948 when he became eligible for Social Security. Since that time he has lived in several rooms or small apartments in San Francisco. He has two siblings but does not know where they are, and says he did not marry because he "wanted to be alone." He is a periodic drinker whose landlady found him otherwise "quite normal" (although he was hallucinating at the time of admission). He had arrived on the psychiatric ward from the county jail where he had been sent for breaking some car windows "because I'd had too much beer." His diagnoses were chronic brain syndrome and alcohol addiction. He appeared not at all unhappy about the prospect of state hospitalization. "It doesn't matter where I am because I keep to myself." He was still in the state hospital at the second and third contacts, and had had no visitors except one from his former landlady. Asked whether he corresponded with anyone, his reply was: "I never liked people to mix with. I am just reticent."

The 56 *semi-isolates* were persons who had no friends or relatives involved in the decision-making process and for whom no personal others could be located after hospitalization. They reported some social contacts in the period prior to admission, but a review of their protocols indicated that these were, by and large, both casual and infrequent.

Mrs. C. is a 66 year old retired nurse who has been a widow for 30 years. She went to the psychiatric ward voluntarily because she was "terribly nervous" and feared that she was developing an addiction to barbiturates she had taken since having a partial gastrectomy. Her diagnosis was psychogenic (affective disorder). She said she had no contact with relatives and that "all of my friends are gone." At another point in the interview she said she had seen no one since her gastrectomy a year earlier. Still later, she remarked that she did not want her friends to know she is ill. At any rate, she refused to name friends, and at the second interview a year later, in a state hospital, she said she had spread the word that she was visiting her brother in British Columbia.

All but 12 of the semi-isolates were living alone prior to hospitalization and, of these, five had stayed briefly in institutions. The seven who had lived with others seem to be justifiably classified as semi-isolates: they had no personal others involved in the decision-making process or as collaterals; there is no evidence of relations with persons other than those they lived with; and their housemates appear to have provided little social support. For example, one man lived with a critically disabled spouse; a second, one of the few sex deviants in the sample, lived with a brother but, "We don't talk to each other . . . we just ignore each other"; a third man lived with his 89 year old mother who was hospitalized prior to his admission; a fourth, an alcoholic, lived with "someone I picked up on the street"—evidently another alcoholic.

The 30 *community isolates* were screened out first on the basis of their having reported only casual contacts or no contacts at all within the two weeks prior to the interview. Their protocols were then reviewed, and only persons who gave no evidence of having any recent contact (i.e., within about three years) with a friend or relative were retained for the final sample. The following brief vignettes provide a glimpse of the living styles of these community isolates.

"Bill" (he refused to give his last name and may not know what it is) is an 83 year old single man who still runs his own tobacco-news-candy stand and has no intention of retiring. He is not eligible for Social Security because "I can't prove my birth, I never knew my parents, I don't think I had any brothers or sisters. Tried to find out for years." He talks with his customers, sometimes strikes up conversations in parks or cafeterias, but otherwise has no social contacts. "I'm either working or in my room or having lunch," he explains. He formerly worked as a door-to-door salesman "all over the country" and enjoys living alone. He considers himself very healthy and says he has no problems. His chief pleasure is fishing. Mr. C. is a 72 year old retired Navy watertender who apparently retired because of tuberculosis, but the disease is no longer active. He does not know whether he has any relatives or not, and has no social contacts except "I see the manager once a month about the rent." He is very happy not to be working, and spends his time watching television and reading newspapers and magazines. The interviewer notes that "he seemed pleased with his living arrangement and pretty contented all around."

Social interactors in both samples include all people who had attended a social function or visited friends in the two-week period prior to the interview. There were only 39 such persons among the hospitalized and all but two of them also had relatives or friends involved in the decision-making process or as collaterals (or both). The remainder of the hospital sample mustered personal others, mainly relatives, at the time of crisis, but had no social contacts with friends in the two weeks just prior to admission. They therefore fall between the semi-isolates and the interactors, and will consequently be useful for comparison purposes. Utilizing these same criteria, 417 persons in the community sample were identified as social interactors. Perusal of the protocols of the 39 hospital interactors and of a random 10 per cent subsample of the community interactors satisfied the analyst that these persons were in fact functioning on a high level of social interaction. There was, however, some indication that the community interactors had broader and more numerous social contacts than the hospitalized.

The "remainder" group in the community sample comprises 144 persons who fall between the isolates and the interactors. An indeterminate number of these 144 persons would presumably resemble the hospital semi-isolates in a time of crisis, but as yet no criteria have been developed for pinpointing them. While a column for them appears in the tables, for the sake of completeness in presentation of the data, they have not been included in this analysis.

The focus of this analysis therefore will be five groups:

Hospital Sample

	N
"Pure" isolates	52
Semi-isolates	56
Interactors	39
Total subsample	147
Remainder of hospital sample	387
	534

Community Sample

Isolates	30
Interactors	417
Total subsample	447
Remainder of community sample	144
Unclassifiable	9
	600

Needless to say, the small size of these subgroups earmarks this study as exploratory. We shall first describe these subgroups from the points of view of isolation and old age, and isolation and mental illness in old age, adding a brief note on morale.[24] We shall then re-examine the protocols on a case-by-case basis in the hope of gaining further insight into certain rather unexpected findings.

ISOLATION AND OLD AGE

If the extreme isolation manifest in these subgroups were largely a consequence of the aging process, one would expect to find the hospitalized isolates older than the interactors. Furthermore, since women live longer than men, and since there are many more very old women than very old men among the hospitalized (34 per cent of the women are 80 or older compared with 19 per cent of the men), one would also expect to find more women among the isolates. Actually, however, the pure isolates and the interactors within the hospital sample closely resemble each other in respect to age, and both groups are somewhat younger than the remainder of the hospital sample. Only the semi-isolates correspond to our expectations:

about a third of them are 80 years or older compared with less than a fifth of the interactors. Nor does sex composition bear out an assumption that extreme isolation is necessarily age-linked. Despite the preponderance of very old women among the hospitalized, about three-fourths of the isolates are men while about three-fourths of the interactors are women.[25] The semi-isolates fall in between, but still include proportionately more males than the hospitalized as a whole. Among the community isolates, too, the majority (86 per cent) are men, but sex discrepancies among the non-hospitalized interactors are comparatively slight.

If extreme isolation were largely the result of a decrease in social interaction with advancing years, one would not expect to find great differences between isolates and interactors in regard to life style, but one would expect more age-linked changes, such as widowhood, among the isolates. Again, however, the data do not support the assumption. There are proportionately more widows and widowers among the interactors than there are among the isolates in both the hospitalized and the nonhospitalized samples. Conversely, more than four times as many hospitalized isolates as interactors are single, and the ratio for the community sample is more than three to one. Hospitalized interactors tend to resemble the remainder of the hospitalized in this respect.

Since the interactors include a higher proportion of housewives who never worked, there is, in fact, less change in occupational status among them than among the isolates and semi-isolates. Among those who have ever worked, the vast majority are retired in all three groups, as is true for the hospitalized as a whole.

The age distribution of the community isolates closely resembles that of the hospital isolates, though they are older than the community interactors. In part because they are older, they are

TABLE 1. SUBGROUP BY AGE AND SEX

	Hospital Sample				Community Sample		
	Pure Isolates %	Semi-Isolates %	Inter-actors %	Re-mainder %	Isolates %	Inter-actors %	Re-mainder %
Men							
60–69	29	20	5	18	30	28	20
70–79	35	20	16	19	33	15	15
80+	8	16	5	8	23	5	14
Women							
60–69	11	14	33	12	7	30	17
70–79	6	12	28	23	7	16	17
80+	11	18	13	20	—	6	17
Total	100	100	100	100	100	100	100
(N)	(52)	(56)	(39)	(387)	(30)	(417)	(144)

TABLE 2. SUBGROUP BY MARITAL STATUS

| | Hospital Sample | | | | Community Sample | | |
	Pure Isolates	Semi-Isolates	Inter-actors	Re-mainder	Isolates	Inter actors	Re-mainder
	%	%	%	%	%	%	%
Single	47	29	10	13	63	19	18
Divorced or separated	24	25	18	21	17	13	11
Widowed	29	44	46	38	20	34	44
Married	—	2	26	28	—	34	27
Total	100	100	100	100	100	100	100
(N)*	(49)	(55)	(39)	(381)	(30)	(417)	(143)

*Totals differ from those in Table 1 because persons whose marital status was unknown were omitted.

TABLE 3. SUBGROUP BY SEX AND OCCUPATIONAL STATUS

| | Hospital Sample | | | | Community Sample | | |
	Pure Isolates	Semi-Isolates	Inter-actors	Re-mainder	Isolates	Inter-actors	Re-mainder
	%	%	%	%	%	%	%
Men							
Employed	2	—	3	3	13	23	17
Retired or unemployed	68	55	23	42	73	25	32
Women							
Employed	—	—	5	1	—	—	9
Retired or unemployed	24	30	41	24	7	16	17
Housewife	6	15	28	30	7	25	25
Total	100	100	100	100	100	100	100
(N)*	(50)	(54)	(39)	(382)	(30)	(414)	(144)

*Totals differ from those in Table 1 because persons whose occupational status was unknown were omitted.

TABLE 4. SUBGROUP BY SOCIOECONOMIC STATUS

| | Hospital Sample | | | | Community Sample | | |
Quartile	*Pure Isolates*	*Semi-Isolates*	*Inter-actors*	*Re-mainder*	*Isolates*	*Inter-actors*	*Re-mainder*
	%	%	%	%	%	%	%
1 (High)	—	8	10	9	7	38	20
2	3	4	21	18	7	24	33
3	18	11	38	31	16	19	25
4 (Low)	79	77	31	42	70	19	22
Total	100	100	100	100	100	100	100
(N)*	(38)	(48)	(39)	(351)	(30)	(409)	(143)

*Totals differ from those in Table 1 because persons who could not be scored on at least two of the three components of socioeconomic status were omitted.

TABLE 5. SUBGROUP BY SOCIOECONOMIC STATUS AND DEGREE OF PSYCHIATRIC IMPAIRMENT, COMMUNITY SAMPLE ONLY

| | Isolates | | Interactors | | Remainder | | Total Sample | |
Psychiatric Rating	*High SES*	*Low SES*	*High SES*	*Low SES*	*High SES*	*Low SES*	*High SES*	*Low SES*
	%	%	%	%	%	%	%	%
High	(100)	77	95	80	68	75	89	78
Low	—	23	5	20	32	25	11	22
Total	(100)	100	100	100	100	100	100	100
(N)*	(4)	(26)	(253)	(156)	(75)	(68)	(332)	(250)

*Totals differ from those in Table 1 because persons who were not scored on socioeconomic status were omitted.

also more likely to be retired than the community interactors. Otherwise, being predominantly male and predominantly single, they closely resemble the hospitalized pure isolates.

The frequently imputed relation between low socioeconomic status and isolation is amply supported in both samples: 79 per cent of the extreme isolates in the hospital sample and 70 per cent of those in the community sample fall into the lowest quartile.[26] Conversely, nearly a third of the hospitalized interactors and well over half of the community interactors are in the upper two quartiles. The socioeconomic status of the hospitalized semi-isolates, however, is only slightly higher than that of the extreme isolates. More than two-fifths of both the community and hospital isolates lived in the "south of Market" area which includes San Francisco's Skid Row.

ISOLATION AND MENTAL ILLNESS IN OLD AGE

If extreme isolation were a causative factor in mental illness among the elderly, one would expect to find more pure isolates among the hospitalized than in the community. And indeed, about 10 per cent of the hospitalized are extreme isolates, compared with 5 per cent of the community sample. This difference is misleading, however, because of the high correlation between extreme isolation and very low socioeconomic status. In comparison with the elderly in San Francisco as a whole, the hospital sample considerably over-represents and the community sample moderately under-represents the very lowest socioeconomic groups.[27] If the two samples had identical socioeconomic distributions, they might well include almost identical proportions of pure isolates.

Furthermore, if extreme isolation were correlated with mental disorder in old age, more persons rated disturbed psychiatrically should be found among the community isolates than among the community interactors. This is true, but again we know that, quite apart from the level of social interaction, low socioeconomic status is linked to a higher incidence of psychiatric disorder.[28] In the sample as a whole, over one-fifth of those coming from the lowest socioeconomic strata were rated psychiatrically disturbed, and one-fifth of the isolates were so rated.[29] Though the numbers in some of the subgroups are too small to be definitive, we do find that 20 per cent of the low socioeconomic-status interactors are psychiatrically

disturbed whereas 95 per cent of the high socioeconomic-status interactors are psychiatrically healthy. None of the four isolates of higher socioeconomic status is psychiatrically impaired.

The development of schizophrenia has been linked to isolation for older as well as for younger age groups.[30] If it were linked to the extreme isolation manifested by our subgroups, more psychogenics (particularly paranoids) should appear among the isolates than among the interactors in the hospital sample. Once more, the assumption is not borne out. Forty-four per cent of the interactors have a diagnosis of psychogenic disorder alone or in combination with an organic disorder, compared with 25 per cent of the semi-isolates and 22 per cent of the pure isolates. Inspection of cases indicates that affective outnumber paranoid disorders in all three groups: six interactors, four semi-isolates, and two isolates have diagnoses of paranoid disorders, compared with seven, six, and four, respectively, having affective disorders.

All three subgroups have fewer organic disorders than the remainder of the sample, with the isolates and semi-isolates resembling each other (58 and 54 per cent, respectively) and the interactors having fewest of all (41 per cent, compared with 62 per cent of the remainder of the sample). Alcoholism, alone or in combination with acute or chronic brain syndrome, is somewhat more frequent among the isolates and semi-isolates than it is among interactors, who resemble the remainder of the sample in this respect.

In general, the isolates and the interactors differ more in physical than in psychiatric terms. The pure isolates ranked much lower than the rest of the hospital sample on the physician's rating of physical condition at time of admission, and the interactors considerably higher (elderly persons with psychogenic disorders are in general physically healthier than those suffering from organic brain disease). The semi-isolates, although suffering from as much brain damage as the isolates, are nevertheless physically healthier, closely resembling the remainder of the hospital sample. (Interestingly enough, however, the interactors were just as likely to have physical health problems which they reported as bothersome as were the isolates.) On ratings of degree-of-psychiatric impairment, on the other hand, the three subgroups did not differ greatly from each other nor from the rest of the hospital sample. Similarly, on two Guttman scales measuring, roughly, physical and social self-maintenance,[31] the interactors ranked far higher on physical self-maintenance, whereas discrepancies on social self-maintenance among the three groups were considerably smaller.

Community sample subjects were not examined physically or psychiatrically. On the crude measure of physical disability used in the community,[32] however, isolates and interactors do not differ appreciably.

majority of both isolates and interactors in the community were not depressed and had no sleep problems.

The question of loneliness was not approached directly in the baseline interview, but there were two checklist questions where it could appear—"main current problems" and "inconveniences in

TABLE 6. Subgroup by Diagnosis, Hospital Sample Only

Diagnosis	Pure Isolates	Semi-Isolates	Interactors	Remainder
	%	%	%	%
Psychogenic disorder, alone or in combination with organic disorder	22	25	44	23
Alcohol addiction, alone or in combination with organic disorder	20	21	15	15
Organic disorder only	58	54	41	62
Total	100	100	100	100
(N)*	(50)	(52)	(39)	(384)

*Totals differ from those in Table 1 because persons not diagnosed were omitted.

TABLE 7. Subgroup by Psychiatrist's Physical Rating at Time of Admission, Hospital Sample Only

Physical Rating	Pure Isolates	Semi-Isolates	Interactors	Remainder
	%	%	%	%
No impairment or mildly impaired	8	18	38	17
Moderately impaired	35	39	46	42
Severely impaired	57	43	16	41
Total	100	100	100	100
(N)*	(49)	(51)	(37)	(375)

*Totals differ from those in Table 1 because persons not given a physical rating at time of admission were omitted.

A NOTE ON ISOLATION AND MORALE

That low morale may be an intervening factor between isolation and the development of deviant behavior, including mental illness, is an at least implicit assumption in much of the literature. In fact, the concept of alienation has been variously elaborated as including two or all three of these components (i.e., isolation, low morale, and deviant behavior).[33] If this were true of the extreme isolation among older people in our samples, the three hospitalized groups should form a continuum on various subjective states of morale, and the community isolates should differ from community interactors in the same direction.

Five questions indirectly relating to morale were asked in the baseline interview: opinion of own age, presence or absence of depression, sleep patterns, energy change, and the feeling of loneliness.[34] On none of these items do the hospitalized pure isolates and the interactors represent polar extremes. In fact, on only one of them—energy—do the isolates and interactors differ by more than 12 percentage points from each other. Only on the depression and sleep items do the hospitalized differ dramatically from the non-hospitalized—the

living arrangements." When loneliness was not checked it did not necessarily mean that the person was not lonely, but only that some other problem took priority. In both samples, reports of loneliness were somewhat *less* frequent among the isolates. Among the hospitalized, the semi-isolates resemble the interactors. And in the interview protocols, spontaneous remarks about being lonely were far more likely to be made by the interactors than by the pure isolates, who often went out of their way to protest that they were *not* lonely.

Throughout our analysis we have found less evidence of an even progression from extreme to semi-isolation to interaction than would be expected if we were dealing with a continuum. On demographic items (age, sex, marital status, occupational level, and Tryon Index) the pure isolates among the hospitalized often resemble the community isolates more than they do the hospitalized semi-isolates. Physically, the semi-isolates resemble the remainder of the sample more than they do the isolates. On the morale items pertaining to depression and sleep, the semi-isolates look more like the isolates, but in regard to energy and loneliness they resemble the interactors. These apparent inconsistencies suggest that the pure isolates and the semi-isolates may be different in kind.

A. The "Pure" Isolates (Hospital Sample)

On the basis of their life style patterns and their own remarks, two patterns are discernible among the pure isolates: a lifelong pattern of isolation just as extreme as that noted at the time of admission, and a pattern of social adjustment which is best described as marginal. These two patterns could perhaps both be subsumed under the mode of adjustment that Merton designated as retreatism,[35] but one group seems to have been completely alienated from the start, while the other, having tried and failed, is more aptly described as defeated. Whether these types represent different kinds of psychological adjustment to early social or psychological deprivation or whether their early deprivations differed in kind are questions requiring more life history material than is available for this analysis.

The Alienated (lifelong extreme isolation). The 25 lifelong pure isolates are predominantly men (80 per cent) and predominantly single (84 per cent), the remainder having been divorced or separated very early in life after a short marriage. Three-fifths had had occupations involving either geographic mobility, a predominantly masculine setting, or both, such as seaman, logger, longshoreman, or itinerant laborer. No persons of white-collar status or above were in this group. Three of them had sustained head injuries early in life and nearly half had severe visual or hearing defects at the time of the first interview (it was generally not possible to determine the duration of these defects). A disproportionately high number of the alienated (one-fifth) had a history of tuberculosis. Only seven of the 25 did not have either a history of tuberculosis, an early head injury, or a sensory defect. More than half were born abroad, over two-thirds had a history of alcoholism or a diagnosis of alcohol addiction, and the majority lived on Skid Row or in its environs. They frequently said that they had been lone wolves all their lives and that they liked being alone, and they rarely mentioned loneliness as a problem of their past or current lives. If they did mention an acquaintance, they did not know his last name nor where he lived. Three sociopaths with histories of shoplifting, drug addiction, and sex offenses are in this group; several had been arrested for drinking. Those who were still hospitalized at the first year follow-up were generally observed to be belligerent and hostile on the wards.

Typical of these lifelong isolates is the following European-born former logger, a single man now 77 years old.

Mr. T.'s only known relative is a sister in France with whom he had not been in touch for many years, but who did write to him after his commitment to a state hospital. He was born in Alsace-Lorraine on a farm. His father sent him to a seminary and wanted him to become a priest, but "I wasn't cut out to be a priest. I was too rebellious." He left school at 17 and, after considering the Foreign Legion, finally took odd jobs in Holland, England, Canada, and Australia. "For two years I was in Australia. I was always a tramp. I'm not a criminal. I never was in jail. Oh yes, I was in jail one day in Pasadena a long time ago. They let me go loose and told me to get the hell out of town. I looked like a criminal."

He came to the United States in 1906 and worked in logging camps most of his life until World War II. In between, he tried some farming, with little success. He never married, but occasionally went to a house of prostitution. "If I would be interested in a woman she wouldn't look at me, I never had enough money." While in his sixties, he worked up and down the West Coast as an itinerant laborer and fruit picker. "Nobody traveled with me; I went alone. I am not a man to hang around. I do not drink or gamble and I didn't when I was young. I like the moving pictures, Charlie Chaplin was my pleasure. That's how I passed my time away." At the first year of follow-up he remarked that there was no one in the world that he could ever trust. In response to a question about happy periods in his life, he said that he had known no happiness since leaving home at age 14. "This is the machine age; if you don't fit in, you are out of luck."

The Defeated (lifelong marginal social adjustment). The remaining 22 pure isolates about whom information is available[36] present a different picture. About two-thirds of them are men, and nearly half have had white-collar or skilled blue-collar occupations. Somewhat fewer, though still nearly half, have a diagnosis of alcohol addiction or a history of problem drinking. They are more likely than the alienated to mention loneliness as a problem, and only one of them said that he likes to be alone. For several men and one woman, the development of alcoholism may have constituted a disruptive factor leading to divorce or separation and a consequent withdrawal from society (or their marital problems may have caused an increase in their drinking). For women, early widowhood or divorce often constituted a turning point. Two had abrupt downward shifts in occupation (one without a history of alcoholism). Compared with the alienated, the defeated had initial advantages in terms of education, being born in the United States, and not having any early physical disorders or traumas. In contrast to the alienated, who tended to remain single, these people often had more than one marriage and divorce. Problems having to do with personal losses figure frequently in their protocols, the death of a parent (usually the mother) or a sibling more often than a spouse, but they tend to blame themselves for their poor adjustment. While none of the alienated isolates had ever attempted suicide, three of these people had. Those who went to state hospitals were often observed to be withdrawn on the wards, though they would respond if spoken to.

Rather typical of this group is the following 62 year old man:

Mr. S. was admitted to the psychiatric screening wards because he had tried to commit suicide with chloroform. He was somewhat reticent about his life history, but one is able to piece together the facts that he was trained as a lawyer at an Eastern university, became a career Naval officer, and sometime in middle life, for obscure reasons, was asked to resign from the Navy. At this point, he married a waitress and went to Europe with all of his life savings, some $50,000. The money disappeared quickly and the marriage soon ended in divorce. Since that time he has had innumerable jobs in travel agencies and small businesses. He currently has been trying, without much success, to give language and piano lessons. The only money he has left is $160 a month from a trust fund. Mr. S. reports that the most difficult thing he ever had to face in his life was when the doctor told him that his mother would only live for four months (he had lived with his mother until she died when he was 43, and says he has been depressed ever since).

Unlike the first group, who seem deliberately to have chosen a nonconformist way of life, the majority of these people, somewhere along the line, made attempts at a conventional social adjustment but failed. For most, the extreme isolation apparent at the time of admission seems to be the end-result of the very low level of social inter-action that had persisted throughout their adult lives. The few who sustained an apparently intimate relationship for some time seem to have lived otherwise socially marginal lives, so that the loss of one person resulted in pure isolation. These losses had usually taken place at least three or four years before admission.

B. The Semi-Isolates (Hospital Sample)

The semi-isolates mustered no friends or relatives as participants in the decision for hospitalization or as collaterals to be interviewed after admission to the psychiatric ward. At the same time, either in the question on social contacts within the last two weeks or elsewhere in their interviews, they gave evidence of having had some fairly recent contact with a friend or relative. As we have seen in the review of demographic, social and psychological factors, these semi-isolates sometimes resembled the pure isolates and sometimes the interactors or the remainder of the hospitalized sample. Closer inspection suggests that they are composed primarily of two rather distinct groups (13 are unclassifiable due to paucity of data).

The Blamers (lifelong marginal social adjustment). The 18 people in this group, like the defeated among the pure isolates, give evidence of having made a marginal social adjustment all their lives. If there was a friend or relative somewhere, the relationship was described in instrumental terms: a brother 2000 miles away who handled finances, a friend who brought in groceries. Like the alienated, this group is largely male (16 of the 18). Like the defeated, about half have a history of alcoholism or problem drinking, and they include more skilled and white-collar workers than the alienated. Half are single, and most of the rest were separated or divorced early in life. Like the defeated, too, they mentioned losses or hurts involving others, usually but not always, far in the past. Closer reading, however, reveals that while they felt sorry for themselves as did the defeated, they tended to blame others or circumstances for their suffering. This mechanism may well produce somewhat less withdrawal than does the tendency to blame oneself, thus accounting for the less extreme degree of isolation we find in this group at the time of admission.

Sixty-seven year old Mr. N., a single man who was for nine years an Army private and later an itinterant laborer, has a sister in Monterey and a brother in Chicago, but "never" sees them. He had a diagnosis of alcoholism, but his landlord said he had never seen him drunk. The patient describes himself as "a rover" who was "never a mixer," and "I feel fine about it." He blames it all on his mother who was a tiny woman and "who had a strap around her neck and if you did not obey, you get it, whack, and that is why I wanted to get away from people."

These "blamers," then, like the defeated, differ from the alienated in being likely to have made some attempt at an intimate relationship. They differ from each other mainly in mode of reaction to their isolation and in the degree of their isolation at the time of admission: the defeated had no contacts, the blamers had a few casual ones.

The Late Isolates. The second category of semi-isolates is different in kind, comprising 25 persons whose extreme isolation apparently developed later in life. They are older than the groups whose isolation was lifelong or almost lifelong, half being over 80, whereas among the other groups, between two-fifths and one-half were under 70. There are more women than men among them, they rarely have a history of alcoholism or problem drinking, two-thirds are widowed (they are often childless), and nearly half have had white-collar jobs or better. Some had out-of-town relatives who appeared after their stay on the screening ward. While the state of isolation apparent at the time of admission had usually persisted for a few years, there was no suggestion in their protocols that large stretches of their lives had been solitary. They were much more likely to be diagnosed as having acute brain syndrome than the lifelong isolated groups, possibly because they were not as tough as the lifelong isolates nor as accustomed to looking out for themselves. Most also had underlying chronic brain syndromes of long standing, and a review of their protocols suggests that their isolation may well have developed only after deterioration began. More often than not, there is also a fairly recent history of injury, physical illness, or severe sensory impairment.

The landlord of a 74 year old widow with diagnoses of acute and chronic brain syndromes, and with no friends or relatives except a brother in the Midwest, reports that after her eyesight began to fail two years prior to admission she did not eat properly. Since that time, she had also lost contact socially, and at the time of admission was very concerned about "who's going to take care of me after I'm dead and gone."

Apart from sensory defects and severe injuries, such as broken hips, several of these patients had suffered from heart disease, cancer, or "small strokes."

Omitting the unclassifiable, we now have four instead of two patterns of isolation among the hospitalized:

	Per Cent
A. The *totally isolated* at time of admission, including:	
1. The lifelong alienated (lifelong "extreme" isolation)	28
2. The defeated (lifelong marginal isolation)	24
B. The *semi-isolated* at time of admission, including:	
3. The chronic blamers (lifelong marginal isolation)	20
4. The late isolates	28
	100
	(90)

While some of the 39 interactors among the hospitalized showed signs, at the time of hospitalization, of having defeatist or blaming tendencies, nothing in their reports of themselves or in their collaterals' reports about them indicates a lifelong pattern of this order. Most of them, however, reveal some social withdrawal in comparison with earlier periods of life, thus differing in degree but not necessarily in kind from the late isolates.

Lifelong isolation, or comparative isolation, then, accounts for 72 per cent of the extreme social deprivation noted at the time of admission. The fourth group (the late isolates) differs in kind, and it is, no doubt, this difference among the semi-isolates, between lifelong marginals and late isolates, that accounts for our failure to find a continuum from extreme to semi-isolation. The research question appropriate to the three long-isolated groups would be: "How does lifelong isolation bear on the development of mental illness in old age?" And, for the fourth group: "What does an increase in social isolation, or social deprivation, relative to earlier periods of life, have to do with the development of mental illness in old age?"

Pertinent to exploration of the first question is the pattern of isolation found among the extreme isolates in the community.

THE COMMUNITY ISOLATES

In several ways the community isolates and the pure isolates among the hospitalized closely resemble each other: they are predominantly male, predominantly single, and come from the lowest socioeconomic groups. The community isolates are somewhat older, somewhat less likely to be foreign born, and there are fewer to whom a history of alcoholism can be definitely attributed (though some clearly have a drinking problem). No specific life history data were collected for them, but on the basis of spontaneous comments and answers to open-ended questions, such as those having to do with major problems, self-image, and stressful and pleasant periods, it is possible to roughly categorize the community sample into probable lifelong isolates and others whose extreme isolation apparently developed later.

Over two-thirds of the 30 community pure isolates have, according to their own statements or by implication, quite clearly been extremely isolated all their lives. Six appear not to have become extreme isolates until middle or later life. These changes usually resulted from loss of spouse through death or separation, and one suspects that for such people (predominantly men) the spouse had been the main, if not the only, social contact. Like the blamers and the defeated among the hospitalized, they seem to have made, and to have ostensibly preferred, marginal social adjustments all or most of their lives. None offers any evidence of changes in social contact that might be attributed to the aging process. (Two of the 30 community isolates are unclassifiable.)

Occupationally, though not in terms of socio-economic status, the community isolates differ somewhat from the alienated in the hospital sample. The geographically mobile type of occupation (longshoreman, logger, itinerant laborer) is less conspicuous, though a fifth of them spent most of their working lives in the armed forces. Phrases such as "I'm a lone wolf and always have been" abound. More than a fourth were in jobs involving continual contact with the public, such as hotel and transport workers. Especially conspicuous among the latter were news or tabacco vendors, some of whom were still working when interviewed. Those who were retired said they missed contact with "the public," and those who were working said they would miss it when they did retire.

As a whole, then, the community isolates appear for the most part to be composed, like the alienated, of the "lifelong extremes," with a fifth of them probably representing a "lifelong marginal" social adjustment like the defeated or the blamers. Differences in work history, how-ever, suggest that retreatism is somewhat less common: the hospitalized alienated found a work milieu made up of marginal persons like themselves, whereas the community isolates tended to relate to a "normal," if anonymous, public. Paucity of data makes it difficult to classify them further. They do not appear to be as hostile as many of the alienated among the hospitalized, but this difference may be due to the fact that many of the hospitalized suffered from organic brain diseases which may have triggered release of a hostility the community group represses. And more authori-tarian occupational structures, clearly defined daily goals as provided in the armed services, or continual contact with the public, may have protected them against their own impulses. In any case, on the surface, community lifelong extreme isolates look more like unemotional "avoiders" than like the hostile alienated, the defeated, or the blamers among the hospitalized. Matter-of-factness characterizes their comments:

A 72 year old retired Navy man, *re* relatives and living alone:

"I don't know whether they are alive or not, haven't seen them since the first war.... Living alone is all right, I've done it all my life and it's too late to change. I was a serviceman too long, I've always been alone.... I ain't got nobody to get mad at outside of myself."

An 80 year old retired city transport driver, single:

"I'm a lone wolf. I strictly mind my own business, quiet—that covers it."

A 64 year old news vendor who is still working:

"I like to be independent, I'm not too friendly—usually by myself. Always been the same."

A 70 year old retired Marine corporal:

"I've been alone all my life. Never had any close friends, always went alone."

If these new subgroups were larger, we could now re-run our tables, distinguishing between the lifelong extreme, the lifelong marginal, and the late isolates. As it is, this analysis must rest with the finding that most of the extreme isolates among the aged in the community, as among the hospitalized, have always been that way. Bearing this in mind, as well as the division of the hospi-talized semi-isolates into two groups (the lifelong and the late), we are now in a position to suggest a hypothesis about the relation between lifelong extreme isolation and mental illness, and to refine the research questions bearing on the problem of agelinked isolation.

SUMMARY AND IMPLICATIONS

Lifelong Isolation and Mental Illness

On the basis of screening criteria applied to the time of the interview and a period of a few years before it, groups of extreme or pure isolates were found in both the community and hospital samples. We conjectured that, if economic factors were held constant, the proportions in the hospital sample would be no greater than those found in the community. A more detailed analysis of these two groups showed that among the 52 hospitalized persons characterized as pure isolates at the time of admission, slightly less than half gave evidence of having maintained such a state all or nearly all of their lives. We have called these people the "alienated." Four-fifths of the community group gave similar though not such complete evidence of lifelong extreme isolation, and while they do not appear as hostile as the hospitalized, they too seem to warrant the description "alienated."

Again, if economic factors were held constant, there would doubtless have been as many lifelong alienated in the community at large as among the hospitalized. Furthermore, the community "alienated" were rated (by reviewing psychiatrists) at least as robust psychiatrically as persons of similar socioeconomic status in the rest of the community sample. The conclusion seems justified, then, that this type of lifelong extreme isolation is not necessarily conducive to mental illness in old age. Nor does it seem to be conductive to a particular kind of mental illness in old age, for there were no more paranoid (or other effective) disorders among the hospitalized alienated than among the rest of the sample. While such an alienated life style might in itself be culturally defined as a form of mental illness, lack of interpersonal relationships, which is one of its main characteristics, may help to prevent the development of overt psychogenic disorder (or to prevent its detection if it does develop).

Two additional groups of persons who have led marginal rather than totally isolated existences all or most of their lives also emerged from among the hospitalized. One of these groups, which we have called the defeated, comprised some of those showing extreme or "pure" isolation at the time of admission. These individuals attempted social adjustment, usually in early adulthood, but retreated, often rather quickly. Their tendency was to blame themselves for their "failure" and to feel sorry for themselves. Only a few of the isolates in the community sample revealed this pattern.

The other hospitalized group whose histories gave evidence of lifelong marginal social existences was found among those who were semi-isolated at the time of admission. They resembled the defeated in many ways, but they did not withdraw quite so completely from interpersonal relationships, and their most characteristic tendency was to blame other persons or circumstances, rather than themselves, for their isolation. While one or two of the community isolates gave some hints of this "blaming" pattern, no semi-isolated group of community subjects was definable for this study,

and the question must be left open as to whether such a life style does indeed exist, and to the same degree, among the community as among the hospitalized aged. Further research may well indicate that it is among those who have led marginal social existence, who have tried but failed, so to speak, that a higher incidence of mental illness in old age is found.

The alienated, the defeated, and the blamers differ in kind from the age-linked isolates found among the hospitalized semi-isolates, while the latter appear to differ only in degree from the remainder of the hospitalized sample. This leads us back to the problem that prompted our interest before we encountered the lifelong isolates: namely, isolation relative to earlier periods of life, developed as a result of the death of friends or relatives, of voluntary or involuntary disengagement, or of other changes linked to the aging process. Is there any evidence that such relative social isolation is causally linked with the development of mental illness in old age, and if so, with any particular type of disorder?

Age-Linked Isolation and Mental Illness

The data suggest that there may be no relation between age-linked isolation and types of mental disorder in old age, considering as "types," for the time being, simply the distinction between psychogenic and organic. As we have seen, those who suffered the greatest relative isolation (the 25 late isolates) include far fewer persons with psychogenic disorders than the interactors; conversely, the interactors include proportionately twice as many persons diagnosed as suffering from psychogenic disorders as the more isolated remainder of the sample. Findings of other studies which have linked schizophrenia to isolation for both old and young had, in the beginning, led us to suspect that the interactors would have a predominance of affective disorders whereas the paranoids would be left in the more isolated remainder of the sample. This does not appear to be the case, however, since the interactors include about equal proportions of paranoids and affectives.

Since the late isolates resemble the remainder of the hospital sample both in comparatively greater incidence of organic disorder and in greater isolation than is found among the interactors, one might postulate that relative social isolation is linked to the development of organic rather than psychogenic psychoses in old age. While there certainly are many more organic than psychogenic disorders among these elderly first admissions (12 per cent psychogenic only, 58 per cent organic only, the remainder having both types of diagnosis), this possibility is no more supported by the data than the hypothesized correlation between isolation and psychogenic, particularly paranoid, disorders. The pure organics in the hospital sample as a whole report no more social change (death of a spouse or another close relative, illness of an important other, change in social living arrangements, retirement) than do those with a psychogenic diagnosis, nor are there any appreciable differences between the "pure" psychogenics and the "mixed" (those who also have a diagnosis of organic brain disorder).

This leaves us with the rather obvious conclusion that the interactors' superior physical condition and lack of intellectual deterioration permits them to maintain their comparatively high degree of interaction, and that the generally poor physical condition and greater intellectual deterioration of the organics who constitute the majority of the remainder of the sample have resulted in their greater isolation. Relative isolation, then, may be more of a consequence than a cause of mental illness in old age, and the consequences for psychogenics may be less severe than for organics because of their generally superior physical condition.

Since we know from a companion study now under way that the hospital sample is considerably sicker physically than these people in the community, a corrollary hypothesis is that a physical change preceded and may be causally related to both the relative social isolation and the development of mental disorder. Tentative support for this hypothesis is provided by the following findings.[37]

1. An earlier decision-making analysis of this sample of aged people has shown that, for the majority of the hospitalized, physical factors were among the reasons for admission given by collaterals.

2. In answer to the question on major life-changes since age 50, serious physical illness was reported for about three-fourths of the sample (such illness, incidentally, was just as likely to be found among the pure psychogenics as among the organics).

3. The social interactors differ from the late isolates mainly in respect to their superior physical condition, ranking much higher both in terms of the physician's rating of general health and on the physical self-maintenance scale, and these physical differences far outweigh differences in psychiatric disability.

To summarize briefly, then: lifelong extreme isolation (or alienation) is not necessarily conducive to the development of the kinds of mental disorder that bring persons to the psychiatric ward in their old age; lifelong marginal social adjustment may be conducive to the development of such disorder; late-developing isolation is apparently linked with mental disorder but it is of no greater significance among those with psychogenic disorders than among those with organic disorders, and may be more of a consequence than a cause of mental illness in the elderly; finally, physical illness may be the critical antecedent to both the isolation and the mental illness.

NOTES

* This report is one of a series growing out of a long-range inter-disciplinary research program on geriatric mental illness being conducted at Langley Porter Neuropsychiatric Institute, San Francisco, California. The program is supported by National Institute of Mental Health Grant 3M-9145, and has also received supplementary support from the California Department of Mental Hygiene. Dr. Alexander Simon and Mrs. Marjorie Fiske Lowenthal are co-principal investigators of the program. The author is indebted to the research assistance of Miss Mella Kessler and Mr. Clayton Haven, and to the editorial assistance of Mr. Gerard Brissette. Special thanks are also due to Professor Leo Lowenthal, Dr. Alexander Simon, Dr. Margaret Clark, Dr. Barbara Anderson, and Mr. Ronald Mock for their perceptive reviews of the manuscript.

1. Emile Durkheim, *Suicide*, Glencoe, Ill.: The Free Press, 1960.

2. Robert E. L. Faris and H. Warren Dunham, *Mental Disorders in Urban Areas*, New York: Hafner, 1960.

3. August B. Hollingshead and Frederick C. Redlich *Social Class and Mental Illness: A Community Study*, New York: John Wiley and Sons, 1958.

4. Jerome K. Meyers and Bertram H. Roberts, *Family and Class Dynamics in Mental Illness*, New York: John Wiley and Sons, 1959.

5. Robert K. Merton, *Social Theory and Social Structure*, Glencoe, Ill.: The Free Press, 1949, p. 144.

6. Melvin Seeman, "On the Meaning of Alienation," *American Sociological Review*, 24 (December, 1959), pp. 783–791.

7. Dwight G. Dean, "Alienation: Its Meaning and Measurement," *American Sociological Review*, 26 (October, 1961), pp. 753–758.

8. Melvin L. Kohn and John A. Clausen, "Social Isolation and Schizophrenia," *American Sociological Review*, 20 (June, 1955), pp. 265–273; E. Gartly Jaco, "The Social Isolation Hypothesis and Schizophrenia," *American Sociological Review*, 19 (October, 1954), pp. 567–577; S. Kirson Weinberg, "A Sociological Analysis of a Schizophrenic Type," in Arnold M. Rose (ed.), *Mental Health and Mental Disorder*, New York: W. W. Norton, 1955, pp. 240–257.

9. Peter Townseed, *The Family Life of Old People*, Glencoe, Ill.: The Free Press, 1957.

10. Henning Friis and Erik Manniche, "Old People in a Low-Income Area in Copenhagen," *Socialforskingsinst*, Technisk Forlag, København (1961).

11. Angelo Pagani, "Social Isolation in Destitution," in Clark Tibbitts and Wilma Donahue (eds.), *Social and Psychological Aspects of Aging*, New York: Columbia University Press, 1962, pp. 518–525.

12. K. R. Eissler, M.D., "On Isolation," *The Psychoanalytic*

Study of the Child, New York: International Universities Press, 14 (1959).

13. Frieda Fromm-Reichmann, "Loneliness," *Psychiatry*, 22 (February, 1959), pp. 1–15.

14. Talcott Parsons, "Age and Sex in the Social Structure of the United States," *American Sociological Review*, 7 (October, 1942), pp. 604–616.

15. Zena Smith Blau, "Structural Constraints on Friendship in Old Age," *American Sociological Review*, 26 (June, 1961), pp. 429–439; Seymour S. Bellin, "Relation Among Kindred in Later Years of Life: Parents, Their Siblings and Adult Children," unpublished paper read at the American Sociological Association Meeting, September 1, 1961, St. Louis, Mo.; Bernard S. Phillips, "A Role Theory Approach to Adjustment in Old Age," *American Sociological Review*, 22 (April, 1957), pp. 212–217, and "Role Change, Subjective Age and Adjustment: A Correlational Analysis," *Journal of Gerontology*, 16 (October, 1961), pp. 347–352.

16. Elaine Cumming and William E. Henry, *Growing Old*, New York: Basic Books, 1961, pp. 14ff.

17. Ben Z. Locke, M. Kramer, and Benjamin Pasamanick, M.D., "Mental Diseases of the Senium at Mid-Century: First Admissions to Ohio State Public Mental Hospitals," *American Journal of Public Health*, 50 (July, 1960), pp. 998–1012; Benjamin Malzberg, "A Statistical Review of Mental Disorders in Later Life," in Oscar J. Kaplan (ed.), *Mental Disorders in Later Life*, Stanford, Calif.: Stanford University Press, 1956, pp. 6–25.

18. H. D. Chalke, "Patients Without Relatives," *University of Leeds Medical Journal*, (June 1, 1957); J. Connolly, "The Social and Medical Circumstances of Old People Admitted to a Psychiatric Hospital," *The Medical Officer*, (August, 1962), pp. 95–100; Ernest M. Gruenberg, M.D., "Community Conditions and Psychoses of the Elderly," *The American Journal of Psychiatry*, 110 (June, 1954), pp. 888–896.

19. H. Williams, M.D., *et al.*, "Studies in Senile and Arteriosclerotic Psychoses," *American Journal of Psychiatry*, 98 (March, 1942), pp. 712–715; D. W. K. Kay and Martin Roth, "Environmental and Hereditary Factors in the Schizophrenias of Old Age (Late Paraphrenia) and Their Bearing on the General Problem of Causation in Schizophrenia," *Journal of Mental Science*, 107 (July, 1961), pp. 649–686.

20. Raymond G. Hunt, "Socio-Cultural Factors in Mental Disorder," *Behavioral Science*, 4 (April, 1959), pp. 96–106.

21. Harold L. Wilensky, "Life Cycle, Work Situation, and Participation in Formal Associations," in Robert W. Kleemeier (ed.), *Aging and Leisure*, New York: Oxford University Press, 1961, pp. 213–242.

22. Total admissions in this age group numbered 774, but 240 persons were excluded from the sample because they had had psychiatric admissions prior to age 60 or because they did not meet San Francisco County residence requirements.

23. For a description of the total hospital and community samples from which these subgroups are drawn, see Marjorie Fiske Lowenthal, *Lives in Distress*, New York: Basic Books (publication pending, Spring, 1964). For a description of methods used for drawing the community sample, see Joseph Spaeth, "Community Sample Background and Procedures," Geriatrics Research Project staff memorandum, October 26, 1960 (copies available on request). Stratification variables were sex and social-living arrangements, on which the community and hospital samples resemble each other, and age, on which they do not, the hospitalized being older than the community sample.

24. In the interest of economy of space, several tables on which this analysis is based are not presented in this text. They are available from the author on request.

25. Whether our screening devices excluded extremely isolated women, or whether such women simply do not exist is an open question. One possibility, supported by some hospitalized cases, is that female isolates tend to form symbiotic relationships, usually with a sister, the two constituting an isolated pair.

26. The index of current economic position is based on a combination of monthly rent, annual income, and the Tryon Index of San Francisco census tracts. The Tryon Index, with scores ranging from zero (low) to 10 (high), is based on proportions of persons in professional or managerial occupations, with college education, and self-employed, the proportion of dwelling units with one or fewer persons per room, and the proportion of domestic and service workers (Robert C. Tryon, *Identification of Social Areas by Cluster Analysis*, Berkeley, California: University of California Press, 1955). The lowest quartile consists of incomes under $2,500, rent under $60, and a Tryon score of less than 5. The majority of isolates were far below these cut-off points on all counts. For details about the construction of this index as well as one based on main gainful occupation and education—the Index of Social Position—see Karen Many, "Indices of Socioeconomic Status," Geriatrics Research Project staff memorandum, September 5, 1961 (copies available on request).

27. The moderate over-representativeness of the community sample in this respect maximized the possibility of locating middle- and upper-class psychiatrically disturbed persons who might, because of economic advantages, be maintained in the community. For comparisons between the two samples and elderly San Franciscans as a whole, see Marjorie Fiske Lowenthal, "Characteristics of the Sample," in Alexander Simon, M.D., and Marjorie Fiske Lowenthal (eds.), *Mental Illness of the Elderly*, (working title) New York: Basic Books (publication pending, 1964).

28. Paul Berkman, "Deprivation and Mental Illness Among the Community Aged," (publication pending, 1964).

29. These ratings were made by psychiatrists on the basis of a review of the protocols. For a description of rating procedures, see Marjorie Fiske Lowenthal and Paul Berkman, "The Problem of Rating Psychiatric Disability in a Study of Normal and Abnormal Aging," presented at the annual meeting of the American Sociological Association, September 1962, Washington, D.C., publication pending in *Journal of Health and Human Behavior*.

30. See Kohn and Clausen, *op. cit.*, and Kay and Roth, *op. cit.*

31. The components of these scales include none of the items used as screening criteria. For details on scale development, see Karen Many, "Indices of Social and Physical Self-Maintenance," Geriatrics Research Project staff memorandum, June 14, 1961 (copies available on request).

32. Components of this health scale are: days in bed past year, medical care past month, hospitalizations past 10 years, and serious physical illness past 10 years.

33. See Merton, *op. cit.*, Seeman, *op. cit.*, and Dean, *op. cit.*

34. Additional morale questions include the Srole and Streib-Thompson scales and were asked in the first and second rounds of follow-up. These will be the subject of a future report.

35. Merton, *op. cit.*, pp. 142–144.

36. All five of the remaining pure isolates were inaccessible at the baseline interview and four of these died before the first follow-up; the fifth refused to be interviewed at both rounds of follow-up. Since they also, by definition, lacked informed collaterals, data are too sparse to permit classification.

37. Indirect support for such an hypothesis, linking physical illness with isolation and both with low morale, is also to be found in the work of Kutner and his colleagues in a survey of community aged in New York. Their relative isolates (by no means as extreme as the isolates we have dealt with here) are in poorer health than their nonisolates, and also of poorer means. They postulate that among persons of very low socioeconomic status, isolation is more likely to accompany declining health, and "from illness and isolation arises a sense of futility, cynicism or resignation that expresses itself in a variety of ways." Bernard Kutner, *et al., Five Hundred Over Sixty*, New York: Russell Sage Foundation, 1956, p. 157.

part III
PERSONALITY DEVELOPMENT AND MENTAL DISORDERS

SECTION 2

SOCIAL PSYCHOLOGICAL ASPECTS OF DISORDERED BEHAVIOR

SECTION 1 of Part III traced the personality development of disordered persons in terms of the effects of their participation in successive groups. This section deals with the development of types of disordered persons.

In the first paper, I describe the social psychological aspects of schizophrenia, including behavioral methods in the study of schizophrenia, diverse theories that try to explain the causal aspects of schizophrenia, social influences that contribute to the breakdown, expressions of the onset, and forms of the schizophrenic's identity.

In the second paper, I describe the social psychological aspects of anxiety behavior. Although neurotic anxiety occurs in childhood, severe stresses in later behavior also arouse intensified anxiety and can precipitate a neurotic condition. This paper illustrates this condition for three adult groups: (1) sickness among the Saulteaux Indians, (2) unemployment among miners in a community in Britain, and (3) among soldiers in combat.

The third paper presents the social psychological aspects of acting-out disorders, including psychopathy, acting-out neurosis, and cultural delinquency. The first two types of acting-out disorders indicate basic personality malformations, but the cultural delinquent is a product of a deviant subculture, whether or not he has emotional difficulties. Despite some similar forms of deviations for these acting-out types, their forms of personality development and organization diverge.

SOCIAL PSYCHOLOGICAL ASPECTS OF SCHIZOPHRENIA

S. Kirson Weinberg

THE schizophrenic when characterized as an incapacitated person falls within the province of social psychological inquiry (Weinberg, 1952; Weinberg, 1958a; Grinker, 1957). From this view, the schizophrenic is considered incapacitated because of his extreme personality disorganization which, in turn, arises from his disrupting social relations and his persistent, self-devaluating conflicts. By contrast, the psychobiological view regards schizophrenia as a mental illness, acquired from the pathology and/or dysfunction of the brain or other organs (Conn, 1934; M. Gross, G. Gross, and Wortis, 1940; Heath, 1954; Hoskins, 1946; Nielsen and Thompson, 1947; Noyes, 1953). The social psychological view maintains that mental illness is not limited to impaired problem solving nor to disrupted integrative acts, nor to cognitive dysfunctions, nor even to an impaired abstracted psyche. Instead "mental illness" is considered an aspect of a disorganized person who participates in a series of group contexts, and whose central component is his self or identity. This self, identity, or ego becomes one central focus of study as it is traumatized by anxiety, social isolation, cultural disorientation, and leads to schizophrenic behavior.

Since the group context integrally influences the individual, sociology proper, which deals with the organizational and functional aspects of group life, is related directly to the social psychological study of aberrant behavior. The group's influences upon schizophrenia provide the point of departure for investigating the processes which contribute to the disorders of individuals. On this level, the schizophrenic becomes an afflicted person whose breakdown has meaning to himself and to his associates. His disorder results in a deviation from the expectations of his social roles to the point requiring psychiatric attention and hospital commitment (Merton, 1949; Parsons,

Reprinted from Lawrence Appleby, Jordan Scher, and John Cummings (Eds.), *Chronic Schizophrenia* (New York: The Free Press of Glencoe, 1960), pp. 68–92, by permission. The section, "Onset Process and Social Definition of the Disorder," is reprinted from "Sociological Analysis of a Schizophrenic Type," *American Sociological Review* (October, 1950), *15*, 600–601, by permission of the American Sociological Association.

1951). The schizophrenic disorder, while viewed as a terminal product for analytic purposes, is in reality either a brief or prolonged episode in the person's life-cycle. The schizophrenic, as more than an abstracted cluster of symptoms, is a person in a process of de-socialized change and in consequence, is considered a deviant by his associates, with prospective removal from society (White, 1948; Whitehorn, 1952).

Among the methods used in studying this facet of schizophrenia are the correlative and the molar-developmental. The correlative method relates social factors or indices with the prevalence and frequency of schizophrenia for comparative purposes, whether in diverse groups or in a single group over different time periods. The molar-developmental method deals directly with the influences of the interpersonal processes upon schizophrenias (Weinberg, 1958c). For example, in the lowest social class, rates of schizophrenia are about eleven times higher than the incidence in the highest social class (Clark, 1947; Dunham, 1947; Hollingshead and Redlich, 1953; Scott, 1958). This fact is consistent with the findings that low-rental, disorganized communities, and unskilled occupational categories correlate positively with high rates of schizophrenia. This inverse relationship becomes a descriptive point of departure for determining what influences in this social class contribute to schizophrenia. Several alternative interpretations can be pursued. The higher rates of schizophrenia in the lower classes may result from a greater proportion of constitutionally predisposed persons or from a greater ratio of character-predisposed persons—because of early mother-child relations or from harsh, frustrating experiences in later age-roles; or the high schizophrenic rates may result from the combined experiences of parent-child relations and later peer relations, work relations, and marital relations. Thus the developmental approach is concerned, more than indices, with the person's reactions to his social relationships in the several groups in which he participates as these relationships influence and precipitate the schizophrenic disorder (Leif, 1948; Weinberg, 1952).

SOME HYPOTHESES ABOUT SCHIZOPHRENIA

The following hypotheses which are within a social psychological scope have been advanced to explain schizophrenia:

1. Schizophrenia is a specific reaction to an extremely severe condition of anxiety which has been initially experienced in childhood and which has become reactivated in subsequent age roles by over-whelming trauma (Arieti, 1955; Bellak, 1948).

2. Schizophrenia is a severe reaction to prolonged isolation from intimate social contacts (Faris, 1952).

3. Schizophrenia is a result of the distortions and misinterpretations of interpersonal meanings which culminate into disorientation and private versions of the culture (Devereaux, 1939).

4. Schizophrenia results from a sequence of reactions including (1) the rejection of the self-image and the intense or feeble striving for self-acceptance and social acceptance, (2) the inability to communicate one's conflict because of intense inhibitions and/or the inaccessibility of others to whom these conflicts can be communicated, and (3) the recourse to empathic withdrawal as a medium of self-defense (Weinberg, 1950).

5. Schizophrenia is a product of a double-bind relationship which exists mainly between the mother and the child. When the child is placed in a situation in which he responds to his mother's simulated affection she will punish him to defend herself from social closeness with him. Hence the child is blocked from intimate relationships with the mother. But when the child does not respond, then she will become anxious because she will feel that she is not a loving mother. Thus, whether or not the child responds to the mother, she becomes endangered and anxious and the child is punished. In addition, his escape routes from the mother are severed. The child is caught in a double-bind relationship that may eventuate into schizophrenia (Bateson, Jackson, Haley and Weakland, 1956).

From the vantage point of action, schizophrenia results from an overwhelmingly stressful event or from a series of continuously threatening situations. The explosive schizophrenic reaction appears in severely stressful situations. As a consequence, transient expressions of schizophrenia may occur among relatively stable persons. Combat soldiers who are overwhelmed by stressful stimuli to which they cannot muster adequate defenses, may deteriorate into a schizophrenic-like condition. Grinker and Spiegel (1945) reported that soldiers in this condition lost their capacity to make discriminatory judgments, expressed very bizarre behavior, laughed or wept uncontrollably, ran about aimlessly, and generally lost self-control. In the more insidious courses of schizophrenia, vulnerable individuals who lack attitudes of self-worth and confidence can become schizophrenic by seemingly mild crises. In fact, their anxiety in mild stress, such as leaving home, would be opportunities for growth for stable persons. In other instances of schizophrenic breakdown, the schizoidal reactions to threat may be so imperceptibly gradual as to be almost undetected because the withdrawal defenses have become so fixed (Boisen, 1936; Clausen and Kohn, 1955; Weinberg, 1950; Weinberg, 1952).

The lack of capacity for integrating critical experiences, according to Arieti (1955), has four stages which culminate in the schizophrenic onset. In these stages the individual experiences mounting anxiety, followed by desocialized behavior and by increasingly intense personal disorganization, until he becomes disoriented. Arieti characterizes the effects of anxiety, however, in terms of a seemingly untenable recapitulation theory in which the individual presumably resorts to lower levels or regressive forms of integration to cope with his problems (Cameron, 1938).

From the viewpoint of social interaction, the isolation hypothesis emphasizes that minimal or no intimate contacts are the bases for schizophrenia. This hypothesis has similarities to Durkheim's (1951) hypothesis concerning the relationship between loose social cohesion and personal disorganization, such as suicide. This generic hypothesis, in modified form, was applied to interpret the onset of schizophrenia. The "lack of group solidarity" as a basis for individual isolation has similarities to the relational criterion, "lack of intimate social contacts." Schizophrenia, then, was interpreted as the percipitate of minimal intimate social relationships for an extended period, such as the prisoner in prolonged solitary confinement, the traveler on the uninhabited island or jungle, or the individual forcibly sequestered in the home. On a community basis, the urban areas which had high rates of specified indices of isolation, also had high rates of schizophrenia, while the urban areas which had low rates for specified indices of isolation also had low rates of schizophrenia (Faris, 1935; Faris, 1952; Jaco, 1954).

Second, this isolation hypothesis has been congenial to interpreting the developmental course of those schizophrenics who had been "shut-in," exclusive persons, and who lacked the empathy to sustain their socialized development. Third, the isolation hypothesis was applied to adolescents who had few or no friendly peers.

The isolation hypothesis, however, has certain qualifications as well. First, it is a sequential redundancy, specifically, that isolation leads to isolation or withdrawal. Second, it does not differentiate adequately between the diverse types of isolation.

Isolation can mean the absence of social stimuli and associations, such as occurs from forced seclusion in prison or from the Robinson Crusoe type of isolation of the solitary figure on an uninhabited island. This type of isolation is not a model for the isolation of urban schizophrenics because they are not isolated by geographic barriers, but by social psychological obstructions. The second and more pertinent type of isolation results from social ostracism or from social rejection. The third type of isolation, which is related to the second, is defensive avoidance or withdrawal against the destructive influences of rejection. The fourth type of isolation, which is constructive, refers to voluntary privacy in order to reorganize oneself and to replenish one's self-esteem. The types of isolation which are relevant to schizophrenic social withdrawal result from social rejection and defensive withdrawal. These types of isolation prevailed among the "shut-in" personalities and among juveniles and adolescents who were in a marginal position with reference to their peers. By remaining isolated from their peers, these persons were not only lonely, but also ignorant of the appropriate responses so necessary for their adaptation and self-defense. Their ignorance frequently became complicated by the disorienting versions of the culture which they acquired from the family (Devereaux, 1939; Dollard, 1934). Sullivan (1935, p. 262) has pointed out:

When, because of deprivations of companionship, one does integrate a situation in spite of more or less intense anxiety, one often shows in the situation evidences of a serious defect of personal orientation. This defective orientation may be due, for instance, to a primary lack of experience which is needed for the correct appraisal of the situation with respect to its significance, aside from its significance as a relief of loneliness.

From the vantage point of meaning, schizophrenic behavior results from private versions of the culture and refers to the person's distorted orientations which he finds necessary to bolster his social position and self-esteem in his relationships. Carothers (1948) has described the life careers of schizophrenics among the Bantu in Africa. These individuals left their tribes for the city, and when they returned to the tribe they were unable to readapt to their village society. They became "de-tribalized" or marginal to the values and mode of life of their tribe, as well as to Western values. Without consistent values or social contacts to sustain themselves, they broke down. This condition has been characterized by Durkheim (1951) as "anomie," which refers to a cultural void in which the individual ceases to have purposeful norms to guide his life career and to sustain his hope.

The schizophrenic's meaningful disorientation results from an inability to shift and to share the perspectives of others because of a disrupting role-taking or empathic facility and, concomitantly, from a lack of ability for self-reference which, in part, spares self-depreciation.

In sum, these hypotheses represent varied perspectives about social influences which pertain to understanding the inner reactions and behavior leading to schizophrenia. These facets of schizophrenia arise from the person's developmental relations with his family, peers, the opposite sex, as well as his relations with co-workers in the business world (Sullivan, 1953). In evaluating these social relations, we emphasize that, except for extreme cases, the schizophrenic reaction is the culmination of the adverse social influences which afflict a person as a bio-social unit. This position differs in accent from that psychobiological view which emphasizes that the schizophrenic's past and present relationships are only symptomatic of deeper organic processes.

THE FAMILY

Family influences upon the schizophrenic person are not restricted to the predispositions which he acquired in early life, but persist through adolescence and young adulthood. These family relations consolidate his immature behavior and his depreciated self-conception by the inferior social role in which he is placed. No single type of family organization or of parent-child relations is evident in the histories of schizophrenics (Weinberg, 1950; Weinberg, 1952). This variety of family organizations would be expected because of the varying constitutional predispositions of persons who become afflicted with schizophrenia and because frequently no one-to-one relationship exists between social organization and personality organization (Weinberg, 1952). In in-grown families, however, we note that the members become so dependent upon and hostile to each other that the most vulnerable members, who are most abused, are forced into inferior roles which, in effect, contribute markedly to schizophrenia (Weinberg, 1952).

The crucial influences of family life inhere in parent-child relations. Despite diversified findings, studies tend to agree that during childhood the schizophrenic has a feeling of being rejected and manipulated (Bateson, et al., 1956). The parents, especially the mother, by subtle or gross domination of his behavior as he passes through adolescence, tend to restrict his emotional growth, his independence for decision-making and his formation of adequate defenses. The schizophrenic reveals pervasive instability during childhood which is not unlike that of the neurotic. The schizophrenic consequences of this childhood instability depend then upon the crises in his later experiences and the measure of his personality growth. McKeown (1950), who compared parental reactions of schizophrenic, neurotic, and normal subjects between the ages of twelve and thirty-two years, found that the parental reactions of the schizophrenic and the neurotic subjects did not differ, although the schizophrenic parents were more "demanding-antagonistic" and "discouraging" than the parents of normal children. Consistent instability characterized the parents of schizophrenics, especially the mothers. Friedlander (1945), Gerard and Siegel (1950), Lidz (1949), Despert (1938), Whitman and Huffman (1944), found that the preponderant proportion of mothers in their samples were unstable, although their expressions of instability varied. They frequently were domineering, aggressive, hostile, or possessively overprotective, or indulgent (R. Lidz and T. Lidz, 1949). Though several studies found that some fathers appeared normal, this outward normality may have been deceptive. Seemingly the fathers affected their children in these ways. They may have disorganized them by their competitive, inconsistent, or demanding relations with them. By their relationships with the mothers they could indirectly sanction the mothers' abusive reactions to the children by not defending the children. Or when they were hostile and abusive to the mothers, the mothers could displace their hostility upon the vulnerable children (Gerard and Siegel, 1950; Tietze, 1949).

The basic familial effects upon the schizophrenics during childhood and adolescence were to suppress their capacity to assert their own needs and instead to direct their behavior towards satisfying parental needs, to inhibit aggression and thereby their capacity for self-defense, to become dependent and yet hostile and competitive, and thereby to lack a capacity for relating effectively with others, especially with persons of their own age.

The family, by the levers of social relations, cultivated a basic lack of self-worth and a diffidence which some schizophrenics manifested by definite trends towards withdrawal, and which others, who were somewhat more competent in their relations, manifested by intense, overcompensatory drives for self-improvement.

PEER RELATIONS

Since the degree of personal stability is influenced markedly by peer relations, especially during adolescence, their effects upon schizophrenics seem significant. Some schizophrenics had friends and companions, and did not lack the sociability for relating with their peers (Weinberg, 1950). Many, however, seemed to operate on the fringe of their peer groups or appeared to be isolated from them. One study (Clausen and Kohn, 1955) found that 34 per cent of forty-five schizophrenic subjects were either solitary or only played occasionally with friends, and merely 4 per cent of the forty-five normal controls were comparably isolated from their associates. On the other extreme, 80 per cent of the normal controls had "close friends" or a "crowd," but only 42 per cent of the schizophrenics had correspondingly close associates.

The systematic inquiry of the influences of one's peers upon schizophrenic behavior was initiated by sociologists whose ecological studies of the residential distribution of schizophrenics revealed that catatonics and some paranoids concentrated in the family slum areas adjacent to the central business district (Faris and Dunham, 1939). Since these catatonics and paranoids were relatively young, that is, under thirty, when they broke down, the neighborhood influences upon their behavior were more suspect and became objects of study. The methods that had been used in studying delinquents, who concentrated in these same areas, were applied to the study of catatonics and paranoids. Juveniles became delinquent, these studies emphasized, by learning their deviant acts from their delinquent associates. By a principle of polarity, the catatonics and paranoids in these slum areas were rejected, estranged, and socially withdrawn from their peers. The results were consistent. Catatonics seldom became delinquents, and the few delinquent paranoids frequently were lone offenders because they could not co-operate with, and remain accepted by, their peers (Dunham, 1944; Weinberg, 1952).

Many of these schizophrenics had histories of being "good boys," that is, "model boys," to their demanding parents; they were obedient to their mothers; the boys hesitated to fight or to engage in rough play. But lower class juvenile and adolescent groups regarded fighting as a means to prestige and even to social acceptance. Since these boys refused to fight or even to participate in body-contact sports, they were victimized by abuse and rejection, and they withdrew. Those who did not develop other friendships became very lonely and sometimes felt that they were "different." These diverse findings suggest that either isolation from peers contributed to their subsequent disorder, or that, in reverse, isolation was an effect of their marked predisposition to solitary behavior.

These inferences vary for different individual subjects. The seclusive individuals who had been isolated and considered strange from childhood, found it difficult and even forbidding to cultivate close friendships of any kind. It was this type of person who Hamilton and Wall (1948) found had "never developed the capacity to make close friends outside the home" and who was the least responsive to treatment. The juveniles' or adolescents' body images also could readily aggravate their isolation. Under-developed ectomorphic boys were more likely to be abused and bullied than the well-developed mesomorphic adolescents. The Gluecks (1950) found that a large percentage of non-delinquents had an ectomorphic body type and, it might be inferred, had difficulty relating with other boys.

Some preschizophrenics were isolated because of the composition of their community. In some neighborhoods they had few companions of a similar age, and in other communities they encountered prejudice from their age mates. Thus, when the members of the majority group in a given area were prejudiced and discriminating in their relationships, the minority group contemporaries became isolated. This explains the observation that members of a minority group in a given area had higher rates of breakdown than the members of the majority group in the same area (Faris and Dunham, 1939). Second, the individuals who acquired parental norms and practices which were incompatible with those norms of their age

mates became relatively isolated. When mothers forbade fighting and participation in rough sports, they created a cultural conflict between parental and peer norms which could isolate their sons. When mothers persuaded their daughters that they were too beautiful or too good for their associates, it aroused a conceit and a false self-image which deterred acceptance by other girls. Furthermore, some preschizophrenics had a childish omnipotence which they had acquired from their unstable parents; while their peers, who identified with more realistic persons, outgrew these omnipotent fantasies (Halmos, 1952).

Finally, some preschizophrenics formed companionable relationships with individuals who tended to exploit them. Seemingly the preschizophrenics preferred this victimized type of companionship to isolation. Other preschizophrenics who had been exploited by their parents, seemed to have somewhat similar relations with their peers.

In brief, some schizophrenics had peer relations which, on one positive extreme, appeared normal, and other schizophrenics, on the negative extreme, were so isolated from their peers that it confirmed their seclusive tendencies. Some schizophrenics, during their juvenile and adolescent periods, while somewhat seclusive were also exploited by their companions and did not know how to cope with these tactics. During adolescence, schizophrenics who were unable to cope with age mates, sought relationships with more protective and benign older persons. In general, peers aggravated personality tendencies which were incipient from family relations, but the effects of isolation from, or exploitation by, peers were usually not so destructive as the rejected relationships incurred from the opposite sex.

SOCIAL RELATIONS WITH THE OPPOSITE SEX

Since preschizophrenics have difficulty with sexual identity, their social relations with the opposite sex tend to be fragmentary and unsatisfying. One index of this difficulty is the proportion of schizophrenics who are single. In an extensive study of 10,575 hospitalized schizophrenics, Faris and Dunham (1939) found that 50.1 per cent were single. Of the 5,435 males, 66.6 per cent were single and only 19.7 per cent were married. Of the 5,140 females, 33.7 per cent were single and 43.2 per cent were married. Of the subtypes of schizophrenics, among males hebephrenics had the lowest (17.4) percentage of married persons, while among the females paranoids had the lowest percentage of marriages (43.7). In rough contrast, over 80 per cent of the people in the United States between the ages twenty-five to thirty-four were married.

The figures on marital status of schizophrenics show that the females tend to foster and sustain martial relations in significantly higher proportions than males. Seemingly, the majority of male schizophrenics were hindered in cultivating relations with the opposite sex because of their personal inadequacies and were relatively isolated from females. On the other hand, female schizophrenics were affected more directly by their relationships with the opposite sex because a significantly larger proportion of married females than of males broke down. These relationships with the opposite sex apparently were crucial to the precipitation of the breakdowns because of the intense self-involvement manifested during dating, courtship, or marriage.

In our studies (Weinberg, 1958d) of 200 normal closest friendships, we found that the cultivation of friendly relations with the opposite sex tended to supersede the close relations with the same sex as determined by degree of idealization, identification, and amount of confiding. Secondly, the capacity to relate effectively with the opposite sex is closely meshed with one's sexual identity and one's personal identity. One prime difficulty noted in the developmental histories of schizophrenics is their inability to relate effectively with the opposite sex. These relationships were so important to them because many had confused notions about their sexual identity from childhood. Since many preschizophrenics were rejected by both parents, they did not identify with either, and hence had no sex role-models whom they followed. Some schizophrenics thought that they were rejected because of their particular sex and hence had latent identifications with the opposite sex. These conflicts concerning their sexual identity came to a manifest climax during adolescence when the sex impulses became more imperative and when age mates compelled association with the opposite sex. Because of their isolation from their peers, they had not acquired the skills and techniques for dating and courtship. They were, therefore, vulnerable because of their inner conflicts about sex and their ignorance of the appropriate manners and practices in dating and courtship relations. Thus female adolescent schizophrenics, whom Hamilton and Wall (1948) observed, were unable "to manage the realities of interpersonal relations, especially with the opposite sex," and sought the protective companionships of older men whom they idealized and upon whom they became very dependent.

Some schizophrenics resolved these conflicts by virtually denying and repressing their sex pursuits or refraining from associating with the opposite sex. Some characteristic statements[1] reflected this attitude:

> I was afraid to go with girls because I had no experience with them.
> I was not fluent in speaking and I was afraid to speak for fear that I would say the wrong thing and she would disapprove.
> I didn't know what to talk about. I was afraid they wouldn't want to go out with me.

The most traumatic experiences result from rejection by the opposite sex, with female schizophrenics more frequently affected by being jilted than males. Males also incurred precipitating reactions as a result of disrupted love affairs. For example, when one male patient found that his mother had ended his prospective marriage with his girl friend, he became very upset, began to lose interest in his former pursuits, was overcome by a feeling of futility, and felt that all his plans which were built around his relationship with this girl, as well as his personal goals, began to crumble. Before his breakdown, he sensed that he "was losing hold of himself and was going to pieces."[2]

WORK AND CAREER RELATIONS

The aspiration for success in one's work directly affects self-esteem. The preschizophrenics who frequently felt unsuccessful in their social relations strived by single means to enhance their status by attending school, reading, or by cultivating some solitary skill (Weinberg, 1952). The male schizophrenic especially was affected by adversities in his career and his work relations because the male's identity generally is so integrated with his occupation. The rates of schizophrenia, as determined by Clark (1949), are highest for the unskilled occupations and decline with the rise in income and occupational prestige. Rates of schizophrenia are influenced by the ages of the subjects in that about two-thirds of the schizophrenics are admitted to the hospital before the age of thirty. The interpretations of these rates, despite the influence of the age factor, are that the unstable personality of the preschizophrenic deters him from getting a better job, but on the other hand, that the conflicts and difficulties of his job relationships may intensify his instability and contribute to his break-down by a process of self-alienation. Some schizophrenics with a compensatory drive were quite competent in school and were diligent workers, at least before their intellectual deterioration. The comparatively high aspirations of middle class male schizophrenics have been noted in the study by Hollingshead and Redlich (1953). They found that middle class schizophrenics had higher occupational aspirations than neurotic and normal subjects of the same class. Some schizophrenics reacted severely to lack of advancement in a job or to their inability to obtain the job of their aspirations as experiences of failure, and these experiences sometimes directly precipitated the breakdown.

One pattern of work behavior consisted in diligent devotion to a job, hoping in vain to be promoted; but the individual's realization of failure became very intense when he saw others surpass him.

In another pattern of career behavior, the parent figure imposed goals upon the schizophrenic which were beyond his intellectual capacities and situational resources. In consequence, the individual became enmeshed in an intolerable conflict which he could not resolve. To illustrate: One male, age twenty-six, who aspired to become an artist, was told by his grandmother, who was his guardian, that he would never succeed. He tried but could not earn enough money by part-time work to support himself and his family. He was then forced to move into a small apartment of a building which his grandmother owned. He became increasingly depressed and irritable because he found the apartment too small for concentrated study and he could not make the grades for which he strived; he considered himself worthless and life not worth living. Because of his depression, he lost his job and could not easily find another except for unskilled work. He worried increasingly because his job interfered with his studying. He began to lose his appetite, to be insomniac, talked of suicide, and put a dog tag on his ankle so that he would be identified if he died. When he went to a company for a prospective job which he hoped to get but did not, he refused to leave the building until the police were called, and he was eventually hospitalized.[3]

Thus preschizophrenics, by their social relations with the family, their peers, the opposite sex, and in work, tended to devaluate their self-esteem, whether by rejection or inability to attain a goal that they aspired to, or to sustain a relationship. Their experiences with these associations and tasks aroused intense anxiety with which they did not know how to cope effectively. The precipitating experience was a fundamental and climactic challenge to their self-esteem and was especially noted when the breakdown was rapid and conflict-ful.

ONSET PROCESS AND SOCIAL DEFINITION OF THE DISORDER

The breakdown experiences cover three interrelated phases: (1) the precipitating situations which immediately preceded the onset, (2) the onset process, and (3) the social definition of the disorder.

Although the precipitating situations may seem relatively unimpressive to an impersonal observer, these situations are extremely threatening to the subjects. Thus, the precipitating situations at best provide external indexes to the inner attitudes leading to the onset. Generally, these situations encompassed conflicts with some family member, the spouse, a friend of the opposite sex, or associates in industry. Although the subjects were usually affected by a series of precipitating situations, which in combination affected their breakdown, the decisive experience—i.e., "the straw that broke the camel's back"—pertinent to the onset showed the following differences for males and females: Fifteen male subjects broke down because of difficulties on the job or in school, but only one female broke down because of these experiences; ten males and nine female subjects were affected by quarrels with the opposite sex; seven males and five females were affected by family quarrels; and four male and two female subjects had other miscellaneous experiences before the breakdown. The female subjects seemed to be primarily affected by their relationships with the opposite sex or the family. The male subjects, though frequently upset by these phenomena, also encountered emotional upheavals from frustration in their careers or jobs.

The onset process concerns the personality changes during the breakdown. In contrast to the chronic schizophrenic, who puts up one or a series of feeble fights as he slowly drifts into disorder, the transient schizophrenic puts up a vigorous struggle in the effort to reorient himself and to regain a more acceptable self-evaluation. His onset brings to a head a vigorous effort at conflict resolution, but one in which no solution is immediately forthcoming (Boisen).

This characterization of the onset is crucial

in differentiating another pattern of development in which the subject seems to be well adjusted externally, and seemingly has an acute breakdown. Yet, on closer inspection his breakdown has been far more gradual than was first apparent. This type does not fight to regain a higher self-esteem, but rather after an acute reaction seems to be resigned to his disorder. In Kraepelinian language, his disorder combines catatonic and hebephrenic defenses.

The transient schizophrenic does not have this deep and persistent withdrawal behavior, but is more emotional and more vigorous in resisting his breakdown.

As a sequential process, the onset begins with somatic and emotional symptoms as in any personal conflict, although the conflicts are, of course, more profound and intense. All patients were harassed and disturbed and some recognized differences in their behavior. Many, however, were not aware that they were breaking down; for they were primarily concerned with isolated symptoms form which they tried to escape. Some also began to disregard some of their needs and to make self-disparaging remarks. When the subjects could no longer contain their tensions they became abruptly explosive or violent in a futile effort to do something about their condition and to reorganize themselves. It was then that the psychotic personality changes set in. Consider the following case:

According to the family, the night before admission the patient started screaming during a thunderstorm, could not be quieted and began to tell the different fears he had in his life. His brother brought him to the Veterans Clinic for examination and arrangements were made for an interview. The next night, however, the patient again awoke and seemed so frightened, screamed so loudly that the family decided to hospitalize him.

According to the patient, he had noticed changes in himself some 5 months before. The home was over-crowded and he felt that he couldn't study. Instead of arguing with the family, he studied as best he could, but was unsuccessful and merely paced the floor. When he could contain himself no longer, he would burst out crying. He became increasingly tense, and to every request that his family made, he said, "I've got to study." In addition, his family wanted him to quit school so he could contribute to the support of the family, which he refused to do. He was worried about his school work. Having taken a pre-medical course, he was in conflict as to whether he would get through and whether he should continue. At this time he was introduced to a Mr. C. who talked to him about the virtues of becoming a vegetarian. This was a vital decision to him, and he decided finally to become one. In this way, although he did not admit it consciously, he absolved himself from having to strive to go to medical school; but in this process he felt very indecisive and felt that he had to lean on someone. He began to neglect his appearance, and when his brother told him to get some clothes he had no patience to do so. He asked his sister about it and she seemed to ignore his question. He then flared into an uncontrollable rage. Finally, he was intensely hostile and guilty about his mother. The mother apparently had periodic seizures and at no time was she to be left alone. One-half year before the onset he was told by the family members to stay home with her, but left against their explicit instructions. While he was away the mother had seizures and was severely hurt. He had feelings of intense self-approach which he repressed. These attitudes were somehow revived at this time by a scene in a motion picture, *Knock on Any Door*, which he saw the week before he had his outburst. In this scene the hero forsook his girl, who became ill and died. This scene terrified him. He felt at that time that there was a force against him which he could not control, and he experienced peculiar sensations through his body. He felt, too, that he was getting smaller and smaller. On the night of the outburst he saw two eyes—his mother's—coming toward him. In terror he indicated that, "I blew my top and started crying, 'Help, Help.'"

The detection and social definition of the psychotic behavior was done usually by the family and usually after the onset. Forty-eight patients were committed by some family member, and five patients were committed by non-family members. It is difficult to ascertain accurately this time differential between the onset and the commitment, but it seemed to range between one month and five months.

The expression of their disorder reflected different periods during or after their breakdowns. The physical complaints which occurred in 9 cases, and the vigorous acting-out of the conflicts, as attempted suicide in 11 cases, or assault upon others in 12 cases, usually happened during or soon after the breakdown. Seclusiveness and withdrawal, as shutting oneself in a room, staying in bed, and refusal to go to work, noted in 7 cases, happened during or after the breakdown. The bizarre behavior which was noted in 14 subjects was reaction to disorientations and to hallucinations.

These discrepancies resulted because the families defined psychotic behavior differently. Some families overlooked or at least sought no medical attention for physical complaints, which they believed would clear up. Other families put up with periodic emotional outbursts. A third group permitted seclusive behavior for a short time until the person became bizarre and uncontrollable. In brief, the family definition of psychotic behavior was not uniform, and was not at all synonymous with the onset.

IDENTITY AND SCHIZOPHRENIC BREAKDOWN

The process of schizophrenic breakdown involves the recasting of selfhood on several levels. The self as adjustive agent is represented by a degree of confidence or diffidence which emerges from the subject's capacity to control or to manipulate his inner and outer environment. The self as identity is an evaluated object of reference which the individual appraises on the basis of his approved or rejected social relations and by the success or failure of his intended tasks (Murphy, 1947; Weinberg, 1952). The crux of an individual's homeostatic or steady state on the level of self-hood is based upon the integrative capacity of his environs and upon the acceptance of self as a symbolic object without obscuring his true identity by false images of himself (Ackerman, 1958; Emerson, 1956; Henry, 1956).

First, when the schizophrenic feels that he is losing hold of himself or even anticipates a disordered reaction in a projected intolerable situation, he frequently reaches for some means to regain control of his capacities, or at least to regain his self-esteem on an acceptable level. This bid for regaining an acceptable self-esteem, without having the defensive techniques for doing so, intensifies his panic reactions. The intensity of this bid for regaining self-acceptance is measured by the degree of explosiveness and conflict during the breakdown. With a gradual, insidious lapse into a disorder, the conflict to regain a former self-esteem is minimal. On the other hand, the schizophrenic with few settled defenses, in a state of panic, may resort to random aggression and abusive declamation as a futile means of self-reclamation.

Second, the normal individual's range of identity is circumscribed subjectively by reactions which he can consciously control or intentionally will. The schizophrenic, however, is beset by uncontrollable impulses, somatic reactions, and inner experiences which challenge the range of his identity. Since he cannot control his inner experiences, he attributes them to forces or agents external to his identity and disrupts his ability to differentiate the self from the outer environs. These reactions and interpretations are exemplified by hallucinatory behavior, which is illustrated by the following "stream-of-consciousness" statement of one patient:

When I first commenced hearing these voices I am hearing and having them unusual feelings in the arms I could tell by them feelings that I was having was caused by electric flashing and drawing through my body and head and them voices I was hearing about everything that I thought and I knew at the time that it was someone communicating with me in the way of having a short wave connected to me; and I knew that the short wave was working on my heart for every time I heard a voice my heart fluttered and pounded; and at night when I went to bed in the army barracks that electric would make me shake all over and I knew it was someone broadcasting to me in the way of having a short wave connected to me, but I could not figure out what they could have to do me them ways or who they was and when they first commenced talking to me. . . .[4]

Third, his continual preoccupation with self and lessened inability to share his experiences intensifies a self-centeredness or narcissism which in its immaturity resembles that of a child. His narcissism obstructs his capacity to relate, magnifies his concern about his symptoms and his conflicts, so that he is less able to "give" of himself emotionally.

Fourth, the social meaning of his aberrant reactions may affect the self in terms of the person's social position. Thus the schizophrenic, when in the upper or upper middle class, may perceive disorder as a "nervous breakdown," and, when he is in the lower class, as "insanity." This categorized stereotype about himself and his new, sometimes strange, role as patient, in turn affects his self-esteem as it is defined in our society, and indirectly contributes to his reactions and to his attitudes towards custody and treatment during his hospital stay (Menninger, 1954; Weinberg, 1958b).

In brief, this social psychological analysis has emphasized the destructive effects of adverse social relationships which pertain to schizophrenic breakdowns. It has described the modes of family relations, peer relations, relations with the opposite sex, and work associations, which have contributed to the schizophrenic disorder, specifically to the weakening of the self-system of the schizophrenic. It has stressed that the reactions of the schizophrenic in the process of breakdown, his withdrawal, his attitudes of low self-worth, his anxiety concerning further social rejection, and his distorted meanings of social reality, emerge from the orbits of his aberrant social relations (Arieti, 1955; Weinberg, 1958).

NOTES

1. Excerpt from case studies on file.

2. *Ibid.*
3. Excerpt from case studies on file.
4. Document on file. Punctuation by the author.

REFERENCES

Ackerman, N. W. *The psychodynamics of family life.* New York: Basic Books, 1958.

Arieti, S. *Interpretation of schizophrenia.* New York: Brunner, 1955.

Appleby, L. Intrusion: a social psychological approach to the treatment of chronic mental patients. *J. Kansas med. Soc.,* 1959, *60*, 173–177.

Bateson, G., Jackson, D. D., Haley, J., and Weakland, J. Toward a theory of schizophrenia. *Behav. Sci.,* 1956, *1*, 251–256.

Bellak, L. *Dementia praecox.* New York: Grune and Stratton, 1948.

Boisen, A. T. *Exploration of the inner world.* Chicago: Willet Clark, 1936.

Cameron, N. Reasoning, regression and communication in schizophrenics. *Psychol. Monogr.,* 1938, *1*, 1–34.

Carothers, J. C. A study of the mental derangement in Africans and an attempt to explain its peculiarities more especially in relation to the African attitude to life. *Psychiatry,* 1948, *11*, 47–86.

Clark, R. E. The relationship of occupation and various psychoses. Unpublished Ph.D. dissertation, University of Chicago, 1947.

Clark, R. E. Psychoses, income, and occupational prestige. *Amer. J. Sociol.,* 1949, *54*, 433–440.

Clausen, J. and Kohn, M. Social isolation and schizophrenia. *Amer. sociol. Rev.,* 1955, *20*, 265–273.

Conn, J. An examination of dementia praecox as a specific disease entity. *Amer. J. Psychiat.,* 1934, *90*, 1039–1082.

Despert, J. Louise. Schizophrenia in children. *Psychiat. Quart.,* 1938, *12*, 366–371.

Devereaux, G. A sociological theory of schizophrenia. *Psychoanal. Rev.,* 1939, *26*, 315–342.

Dollard, J. The psychotic person seen culturally. *Amer. J. Sociol.,* 1934, *39*, 647–649.

Dunham, H. W. The social personality of the catatonic-schizophrenic. *Amer. J. Sociol.,* 1944, *49*, 514–515.

Dunham, H. W. Current status of ecological research in mental disorders. *Social Forces,* 1947, *25*, 321–326.

Durkheim, E. *Suicide.* Glencoe, Ill.: The Free Press, 1951.

Emerson, A. E. Homeostasis and comparison of systems. In R. R. Grinker (Ed.), *Toward a unified theory of human behavior.* New York: Basic Books, 1956.

Faris, R. E. L. Cultural isolation and the schizophrenic personality. *Amer. J. Sociol.,* 1935, *60*, 456–457.

Faris, R. E. L. and Dunham, H. W. *Mental disorders in urban areas.* Chicago: University of Chicago Press, 1939.

Faris, R. E. L. *Social psychology.* New York: The Ronald Press, 1952.

Friedlander, D. Personality development of twenty-seven children who later became psychotic. *J. abnorm. soc. Psychol.,* 1945, *40*, 330–335.

Gerard, D. L. and Siegel, J. The family background of schizophrenia. *Psychiat. Quart.,* 1950, *24*, 47–73.

Glueck, S. and Glueck, Eleanor. *Unraveling juvenile delinquency.* Cambridge: Harvard University Press, 1950.

Gralnick, A. The Carrington family: a psychiatric and social study illustrating the psychoses of association or *folie à deux. Psychiat. Quart.,* 1943, *17*, 32–35.

Grinker, R. R. and Spiegel, J. *Men under stress.* Philadelphia: The Blakiston Co., 1945.

Grinker, R. R. (Ed.) *Toward a unified theory of human behavior.* New York: Basic Books, 1957.

Gross, M., Gross, G. M., and Wortis, S. B. Biochemical studies of schizophrenia: chlorides in plasma and red blood cells. *Psychiat. Quart.,* 1940, *14*, 834–849.

Halmos, P. *Solitude and privacy.* London: Routledge and Kegan Paul, 1952.

Hamilton, D. W. and Wall, J. H. The hospital treatment of dimentia praecox. *Amer. J. Psychiat.,* 1948, *105*, 349–350.

Heath, R. G. *Studies in schizophrenia: a multidisciplinary approach to mind-brain relationships.* Cambridge: Harvard University Press, 1954.

Henry, J. Homeostasis in a special life situation. In R. R. Grinker (Ed.), *Toward a unified theory of human behavior.* New York: Basic Books, 1956.

Hollingshead, A. B. and Redlich, F. C. Social stratification and psychiatric disorders. *Amer. sociol. Rev.,* 1953, *18*, 163–169.

Hoskins, R. G. *The biology of schizophrenia.* New York: W. W. Norton, 1946.

Jaco, E. G. Social isolation hypothesis and schizophrenia. *Amer. sociol. Rev.,* 1954, *19*, 567–577.

Lief, A. (Ed.) *The commonsense psychiatry of Dr. Adolph Meyer.* New York: McGraw-Hill, 1948.

Lidz, Ruth W. and Lidz, T. The family environment of schizophrenic patients. *Amer. J. Psychiat.,* 1949, *106*, 343–344.

Lidz, T., Cornelison, Alice R., Fleck, S., and Terry, Dorothy. The intrafamilial environment of the schizophrenic patient: the father. *Psychiatry,* 1957, *20*, 329–342.

McKeown, J. E. The behavior of parents of schizophrenic, neurotic and normal children. *Amer. J. Sociol.,* 1950, *56*, 175–179.

Masserman, J. *Principles of dynamic psychiatry.* Philadelphia: W. B. Saunders, 1956.

Menninger, K. Regulatory devices of the ego under major stress. *Int. J. Psycho-Anal.,* 1954, *35*, 412–430.

Merton, R. *Social theory and social structure.* Glencoe, Ill.: The Free Press, 1949.

Murphy, G. *Personality: a biosocial approach to origins and structure.* New York: Harper, 1947.

Nielsen, J. N. and Thompson, G. N. *The engrammes of psychiatry.* Springfield, Ill.: Charles C. Thomas, 1947.

Noyes, A. P. *Modern clinical psychiatry.* Philadelphia: W. B. Saunders, 1953.

Parsons, T. *The social system.* Glencoe, Ill.: The Free Press, 1951.

Scott, W. A. Social psychological correlates of mental illness and mental health. *Psychol. Bull.,* 1958, *55*, 65–87.

Sullivan, H. S. *The interpersonal theory of psychiatry.* New York: W. W. Norton, 1953.

Tietze, Trude. A study of mothers of schizophrenic patients. *Psychiatry,* 1949, *12*, 55–65.

U. S. Bureau of the Census. *Patients in mental institutions.* Washington: U. S. Government Printing Office, 1943.

Weinberg, S. K. A sociological analysis of a schizophrenic type. *Amer. sociol. Rev.,* 1950, *15*, 600–610.

Weinberg, S. K. *Society and personality disorders.* Englewood Cliffs, N. J.: Prentice-Hall, 1952.

Weinberg, S. K. *Culture and personality.* New York: Public Affairs Press, 1958. (a)

Weinberg, S. K. Organization, personnel and functions of state and private mental hospitals: a comparative analysis. In E. G. Jaco (Ed.), *Patients, physicians, and illness.* Glencoe, Ill.: The Free Press, 1958. (b) pp. 478–491.

Weinberg, S. K. The pertinence of sociology to psychiatric social work. Paper read at The Society for the Study of Social Problems, Minneapolis, April, 1958. (c)

Weinberg, S. K. Closest friendships of the same sex among male and female adolescents. Paper read at the American Sociological Society, Seattle, September, 1958. (d)

Weinberg, S. K. *Social problems in our time.* Englewood Cliffs, N.J.: Prentice-Hall, 1960.

White, R. R. *The abnormal personality.* New York: Ronald Press, 1948.

Whitehorn, J. C. Psychodynamic approach to the study of psychoses. In F. Alexander and Helen Ross (Eds.) *Dynamic psychiatry.* Chicago: University of Chicago Press, 1952.

Wittman, M. P. and Huffman, A. V. A comparative study of developmental adjusted teen-aged youths. *Elgin State Hospital Papers,* 1944, *5*, 228–237.

SOCIAL PSYCHOLOGICAL ASPECTS OF NEUROTIC ANXIETY

S. Kirson Weinberg

THE ACTION PATTERN OF ANXIETY

NEUROTIC anxiety arises when the subject becomes involved in one or a series of threatening situations with which he strives to cope but is helplessly unable to do so.[1] Beset with these threatening situations, he has the alternative of trying to flee from them or of attempting, however inadequately, to manipulate them. Since he cannot formulate a satisfactory response, he becomes increasingly disorganized and overwhelmed. Anxiety develops in this process of incompleted activity, and involves an inability to define and to respond effectively to a threatening situation which then becomes problematic and leaves the residue of persistent conflict which harasses the subject in the future.

The onset of anxiety may occur quickly or slowly. When one is overcome by sustained physical danger, and/or by threatening social situations, the onset may be relatively quick. When self-confidence is whittled away by certain inconsistent interpersonal relationships which make the individual feel too inadequate to handle certain situations, the onset may be relatively slow. In either case the subject cannot respond effectively, successfully, and completely to a given set of goal-directed stimuli. The actual defensive responses in these given situations, of course, vary: Enforced immobility, flight or avoidance, or compulsive aggression are some alternatives. Whatever the response, the subject becomes defeated and helpless and cannot attain his desired objective or master the particular situation. His responses indicate shock and personal disorganization, persistent conflict, and apprehension.

But not all anxiety is incapacitating. In some instances anxiety may not lead to neurosis. In these instances the anxiety is warranted by the outside danger, but the subject can face the situation and can still manage his behavior without becoming helpless.[2] It is well known that soldiers entering combat are usually scared and apprehensive about

prospective dangers. These attitudes may make them more alert and cautious about getting hurt, and, as long as they can respond effectively to protect themselves from the dangers, they can keep their anxiety under control and remain organized. But it is argued that these are fear reactions which differ upon anxiety; for fear is directed toward an object or set of objects, while anxiety is a vague apprehension of varying intensities which is not limited to a specific object. Yet, in combat, some soldiers may have these vague apprehensions and gnawing doubts about being able to cope with the many and unknown perilous situations that they may face. Despite these attitudes they may still control their behavior, and when they are removed from the battle area their anxiety may disappear. Moreover, anxiety can even lead to constructive achievement.[3]

For example, in a study of adolescents, Symonds found that those adolescents who had anxiety fantasies were able to adjust favorably. He interpreted their favorable adjustment as a reaction against possible failure with its subsequent anxiety.[4] In short, persons in threatening and critical situations may become temporarily apprehensive, but insofar as they do not become defenseless in future threatening situations, their anxiety does not have neurotic consequences.

Neurotic anxiety which persists from past experiences is not warranted by the outside danger. It involves persistent conflicts, lack of confidence, a narrowing of activities and awareness, and the development of neurotic symptoms and defenses.[5]

Yet neurotic anxiety may vary in degrees of severity. This depends upon how severely threatened the individual feels, how vital the threat is to his self-esteem, and how severely disturbed and overwhelmed he becomes. Anxiety may be mild or it may be so malignant and so fraught with intense panic that the individual, as it were, loses control of his behavior, feels completely helpless, and "goes to pieces."

Also, the period when anxiety is experienced may sometimes affect its severity. When an

Part of this paper appeared previously in S. Kirson Weinberg, *Society and Personality Disorders* (Englewood Cliffs, N. J.: Prentice-Hall, 1952).

143

individual is predisposed to neurosis from early childhood and the anxiety becomes an integral part of his personality—sometimes called a character disorder—he would have more difficulty recovering from his anxiety than one who experienced anxiety later in life. This does not mean, however, that the stage of life alone determines the severity of anxiety. It also depends, as we have pointed out, upon the severity of the threat. Hence, an adolescent or an adult can become severely incapacitated by a series of sustained critical experiences.

THE DEVELOPMENT OF ANXIETY IN CHILDHOOD

Developmentally, anxiety arises with the helplessness of the child. How does this helplessness arise? It may result from biological helplessness, but usually it is a function of social relations.

The shocks resulting from biological processes associated with breathing and food absorption are not quite the same as emotionally induced anxiety. It has been shown that sudden startle reactions, such as loss of balance, the crescendo of loud noises, sudden changes in temperature, or any other unexpected stimulus for which the infant is unprepared, may leave him shaky, tense, and with a reaction that has been labeled fearful. But these reactions, however similar to anxiety, are not quite the same. The infant's reaction is a conditioned fear, while the socialized person's reaction would be a symbolic, temporally oriented anxiety.

Of the two forms of relationships in the presymbolic period that may provide the basis for a protoanxiety for the child, one is the mother's intensified overattachment to the child who, in turn, becomes very dependent. The overdependent child finds it difficult to function without the presence of the mother, and this easily leads to conflict in the weaning process and in his general separation from the mother. The other and most pervasive type of protoanxiety-creating relationships inhere in the inconsistent, unstable, and unpredictable relationships between the parents and the child—especially between the mother and the child.[6]

These inconsistent relations become more meaningful to the child when he acquires symbols and self-awareness and when he can compare himself with others. Then his anxieties may arise from anticipated failure and consequent loss of status as defined by the parents.

Horney points to parental hypocrisy as a definite source for disturbed and disrupted relations with the child. These contradictory parental relationships create ambivalent attitudes and conflicts within the youngster who strives to cope with these relationships but often cannot. A wide variety of adverse parent-child relationships can create this helplessness. The parents, directly or indirectly, may dominate the child. They may be erratic or indifferent, or may ridicule the child. They may make him take sides in parental quarrels. The child, in turn, may become so harassed and so fearful that he cannot handle these relations. As a result, he develops improvised techniques and basic anxiety-ridden orientations to the parents and to other people. Horney has referred to these tendencies as neurotic trends.[7]

But these parent-child relationships lead to anxiety only when the child internalizes this ambivalence. For example, a child who sees his parents objectively may play one parent against the other and use each to his own advantage. A child with indifferent parents may cultivate attachments with other persons such as siblings or accessible relatives. Consequently, the child's meaning of parental relations becomes crucial.

The child who identifies with his parents so that his conception of himself is dependent upon their approval and affection cannot easily tolerate their rejection, ridicule, or disapproval. Sullivan has pointed out that the very anxious child does not see his parents as "bad." Instead he cannot decide whether they are "good" or "bad."[8] Fromm indicates that "irrational authority" which is unjust may leave a mark of self-defeat upon the child.[9] The child who is apprehensive about displeasing a parent has his conception of himself tied to the parent's attitude toward him. When his hostile attitudes to the parent do arise, his self-esteem becomes threatened because his hostile expressions will deprive him of the very parental approval by which he evaluates himself. He will tend, therefore, to inhibit his hostility. But, by being unable to "talk back," hit back, or otherwise defend himself, the child feels unprotected and, as we have emphasized, helpless. But this hostility does not disappear; rather, it takes a devious route in dreams and in other vicarious ways. By carrying this hostility the child may behave in antagonistic ways which he cannot control and cannot understand. As a result he may not "trust himself" because he does not know when these hostile attitudes will be expressed. This attitude, in turn, increases his anxiety because he has less confidence in his relationships.

In an intensive study of 13 unwed mothers, May found that nine subjects who experienced varying degrees of anxiety during childhood were involved in a dilemma between their idealized expectations of their parents and the realistic behavior of their parents.[10] They confused the real behavior of their parents with expectations of what the parents should have been or might have become. Since their attitudes toward the parents became internalized, they affected their attitudes toward themselves. It would seem that, by internalizing parental rejection, they began to reject themselves, and they needed and wanted the idealized expectations of their parents in order to accept themselves.

Apparently, the parental pretenses of love, approval, and admiration which are expressed to the child are a means of eliciting his affection and dependency. When these parental attitudes are combined with rejection, cruelty, or punitiveness, the child in turn assumes self-regarding attitudes of self-condemnation. In May's study subjects who were rejected outright by the parents and who did not internalize this rejection did not develop anxiety. Instead, they merely cultivated other relationships. It seems that with the new relationships they began to evaluate themselves from the perspectives of these more favorable relationships and thus could get an integrated and acceptable estimate of themselves.

In a comparative study of children of Polish immigrants and the children of middle-class American families, Green shows that, despite the beatings and harsh parental treatment, the immigrants' children did not become neurotic. These Polish children were accustomed to little parental affection and did not look upon their parents as role models. In a kind of defensive alliance, they avoided them when possible and tolerated or maliciously despised them. This lack of intimate identification, combined with personal and group defenses, deterred or prevented the children from evaluating themselves by their parents' attitudes. Parental beatings, beratings, and depreciation did not affect their self-esteem and did not create attitudes of helplessness with reference to their personal problems.[11]

In contrast, children from middle-class American families are first blanketed with affection. This affection is used by the parents as a lever of control when they threaten to withdraw it. Since these children become attached to the parents, their self-evaluation depends upon parental attitudes. Consequently, parental ridicule, humiliation, belittlement, and abject submission of the children can have an early and very marked effect in predisposing them to anxiety.

Moreover, as these children get older, the parents shift to contradictory demands. They may want implicit obedience in the family and assertive competitiveness outside the family. When these parental relationships are intense enough, they form the typically inconsistent relationships which can predispose middle-class children to anxiety.[12] These children, particularly, are apprehensive that affection may be lost when they are unable to compete successfully outside the family. The need for affection and prestige on the one hand and the need to compete successfully on the other hand constitute one of the typical anxiety conflicts among middle-class children. Since other influences may operate to offset parental demands, these parent-child relationships obtain only in a general sense. The effects of sibling rivalry cannot be discounted in this family context. The parental favoritism of one child over another, as the son over the daughter, the bright child over the dull child, can readily contribute to an anxiety-creating condition.

THE DEVELOPMENTS OF ANXIETY AMONG ADULTS IN DIVERSE SITUATIONS:

Although anxiety is a uniform personal reaction in diverse situations, the modes of social relationships in the cultural context can stimulate anxiety not only as an atypical response among a few individuals but also as a frequent response among many group participants. For this purpose I shall describe the varied social situations in which anxiety can arise as a modal response among adults as well as children. 1. Anxiety can arise among members of the Saulteaux Indian society who by sustained illness would feel threatened as "sinners." 2. It can arise when the basic values and purpose of a society begin to disintegrate, such as in the British mining communities during the economic depression of the 1930s. 3. It can arise in situations of intense stress when personal interests are basically in conflict with group demands, or when the group ceases to be a protective symbol, such as in the combat unit during battle.

The Saulteaux Indians

The normative anxiety toward careeristic failure among competitive personalities in Western industrial society has a parallel anxiety in the morbid appraisal of illness among the Saulteaux Indian tribe. Among the traditions of the Saulteaux

Indians is the belief that severe illness or disease is a penalty for a misdeed.[13] Since the Saulteaux tribe are positively oriented toward health and long life, they invest disease with a meaningful fear beyond its actual physical threat to the afflicted person.

When a Saulteaux does not readily recover from an illness or disease, he attributes his affliction to a penalty for some past misdeed. Not knowing the specific cause of his illness, he is faced with a definite crisis which frightens him. Since his definition of the illness exceeds the actual danger, his response becomes "neurotic." His helpless reaction is also evident when his child, for whom he is responsible, becomes ill; for his child's illness then is attributed to his transgression as a parent. His anxiety specifically begins to mount when medicinal treatment has failed and when the source of the illness remains unknown. Then he no longer can regard the ailment as an impersonal, objective danger; it has become personal and he interprets it as a probable retaliation for something he has done in the past.

This defenseless reaction to illness is typical among the Saulteaux because all members of the society are susceptible to it. It lies midway between objective fear, which is caused by natural dangers, and a unique neurotic anxiety, which is caused by the individual's singular upsetting experiences. Hallowell stated:

Disease may arouse "normal" or objective anxiety, but among the Saulteaux, native theories of disease invest certain disease situations with a traumatic quality which is a function of the beliefs held rather than of the actual danger precipitated by the illness itself. The quality of the anxiety precipitated in the individual affected by such situations suggests neurotic rather than objective anxiety because the ultimate cause of the disease is attributed to the expression of dissocial impulses. The illness is viewed as a punishment for such acts and the anxiety is a danger signal that heralds the imminence of the penalty. Insofar as individuals are motivated to avoid dissocial acts because of the penalty anticipated, the pseudoneurotic anxiety aroused in disease situations has a positive social function. It is a psychic mechanism that acts as a reinforcing agent in upholding the social code.[14]

In this predicament the Saulteaux has one recourse. He can confess his transgressions, almost always in public. Although very reluctant to expose his "sins" in this way, he is confronted by the tribe, who remain suspicious of anything held in privacy or secrecy, for secrecy carries the taint of potential magic or sorcery. Confession presumably relieves the individual of his guilt and reduces his feeling of isolation. Confession then paves the way, psychologically, for recovery from illness.

By these potential anxieties the Saulteaux who places a high value on health and long life is deterred, although not prevented, from practicing forbidden activities. In a society where punitive controls are at a minimum, this anxiety reaction to illness becomes an effective means of social control and of self-control.

The Collapse of Social Values:
The British Mining Communities.

The disintegration of group values in a community is exemplified by periods of mass unemployment. If a minority of individuals is unemployed, people can still believe in the basic values and institutions of the culture, despite their doubts about their abilities and apprehensions about their security. But with mass unemployment, the unemployed individual may no longer have faith in his basic institutions. In a mood of purposelessness, shared with others, he may be seized with panic, hostility, and helplessness.

These pervasive forms of anxiety with their neurotic consequences were clearly illustrated by Halliday in his description of British mining communities. Until about 1916, the mining communities in Great Britain were relatively isolated and self-sufficient settlements.[15] The men dug coal by hand and worked in small cohesive units composed of relatives and close friends. The practice of mining was a definite source of pride to the miner and an integral family tradition. A father imparted to his sons the skills they needed in the mines. In addition, there was a continuity between the work situation and the community, which was culturally homogeneous by its long isolation. Workmates in the mines were friends outside the mines. Despite the many dangers in the pits, the miners knew and shared these dangers, and this intensified their solidarity and social purpose. Since work was done by hand, it afforded a certain personal satisfaction.

Mechanization of the mines began in 1916, and contacts with the outside world increased. Although this transition period stretched to 1936, it began to corrode the very social processes that made for personal stability without providing some means for a needed social reorganization to sustain personal stability. The introduction of machinery for cutting and removing coal reduced the function of the miners "to shoveling coal only." The skills on which miners previously prided themselves were now of no importance. In addition, and perhaps more relevant to personal stability the teams of workers were broken up, and each miner worked alone. Many other personal phases of mining began to disappear; the miner felt part of a gigantic impersonal machine.

Before mechanization, the miner ate his meal in leisure and at his own pace; now he had to eat in an allotted fifteen minutes of a seven-hour shift. Before, he worked at his own time; now he was compelled to become geared to the pace of the machinery. Before, he could detect impending danger by the noises from the cracking of the strata, because the mine was relatively quiet; now the din of the machinery precluded such warnings. Before, he had the determination instilled by the example and support of the other miners who formed part of his work team; now, as an isolated individual, he was without this collective determination, so the prospect of danger mounted by the very fact of his working alone. His work patterns became disrupted; his prestige derived from work skills was removed. These disruptive changes laid the bases for personal disorganization, which was aggravated by the culture conflicts in the community.

The advent of mechanized mediums of transportation, an acculturation process hastened by the miners who returned from the armies after World War I and by workers who lived in the community during the war period, and the economic depression with its consequent mass unemployment precipitated anxiety and other neuroses among many miners. The miners realized that the coal they produced was no longer wanted, but, more significantly, they realized that, as workers, they were no longer useful. Their quest for other types of employment was futile because of economic collapse. Their former status as workers and providers was gone. They condemned themselves, certainly, but they became hostile to the community. Some felt they could no longer give anything useful to the community. At the same time they became dependent upon the community for survival by seeking relief. Then dependency was coupled with feelings of hostility and aggression. They felt their self-respect was compromised by their very predicament.

However, another factor lessened their desire for employment and provided a secondary gain for their neurotic behavior. During the depths of the depression, wages declined, but unemployment insurance, supplemented by local public assistance, went up, particularly for men who were ill. Occasionally some found it possible and feasible to receive more money while they were sick than they did while working. With the incentives for employment reduced, the unemployed miners began to influence those who were employed, by their emotional condition and by their lack of social purpose, because these miners were often relatives and members of the same household.

Under these social conditions, anxiety and other neurotic expressions increased. With a decline in social purpose and social cohesion, members of the community became more individually isolated, and their conflicts and hostility to each other became more manifest. This paved the way for an increase in situational anxieties and in psychosomatic ailments.

Anxiety and the Combat Situation.

The onset of anxiety in the battle situation in war reflects the types of interpersonal relations within the combat unit as well as the personality make-up of the individual combatants. Both contribute to the deterrence of acceleration of this anxiety experience.

The types of relationships within the combat unit are virtually opposite to those of the mining community that has just been discussed. To sustain itself and to prevent the onset of diffusion of anxiety and panic, the combat unit firmly and effectively encourages each member to repress anxiety-ridden frustrations. Since individual hardship and distress are commonplace and death usually imminent, the main protective force for the individual is the cohesion of the combat unit itself. By its social solidarity, the platoon or company acquires a collective pride and determination, instills a protective feeling into the individual, and deters him from disturbing such feelings in others. This individual identification with the other members of the unit, especially with the leaders, anchors the self in the texture of stable relationships and reduces anxiety reactions. In fact, when pride and cohesion in the combat unit decline, neurotic cases correspondingly increase.[16] Thus, the group with high morale can effectively deter neurotic relapses.

In such cohesive units the neurotically anxious person is considered a deviant, although efforts are made to incorporate him into the group. The soldier is made to feel that the group is greater and more important than he, and that individual sacrifices are necessary for its continuance. His courage and resolution reflect the stimulated courage that develops from participating with others. When this solidarity and determination weaken, the soldier then becomes more concerned with himself; the group no longer provides the essential security he seeks. Within this social situation, individual breakdowns are more likely to develop.[17]

The crux of the individual soldier's conflict is between his sense of attachment to his unit and his self-concern for safety within an orbit of danger. When the group is loosely integrated, this individualized self-concern mounts. More breakdowns usually occur in newly and hastily formed units. It has been found that replacements who did not learn to fit into the unit organization also had higher rates of relapse.[18] And as has been mentioned, survivors of platoons or companies that suffered severe losses, despite withstanding past arduous ordeals, eventually became extremely anxious or suffered derivative neuroses.

But what soldiers did break down? Before entering combat nearly all soldiers were apprehensive and tense. Many were uncertain about how they would respond under fire. Though they became more confident after the first few successful battles, they seemed to lose this confidence as the campaign persisted. Some soldiers became fatigued more easily, lacked determination, and had to exert greater effort than formerly to keep pace with the combat unit. Their tensions mounted and they became more anxious and apprehensive. The combat unit tried unsuccessfully to suppress and counteract these feelings. Inadvertently, these soldiers felt that they couldn't "take it any more" and that their "number was up." They found obstacles more formidable than before and they became increasingly preoccupied with their own safety.[19] They felt frightened and overcome by incidents. The unit then was unable to reach them emotionally or to restore their effective identification with the unit. Each potential "breakdownee" felt himself a discrete and isolated individual rather than a member of a combat unit, and his main concern was with his own safety. In this tense, irresolute, and indecisive condition, his main concern was with avoiding or fleeing from the combat situation. Weinstein said:

The main characteristic of the soldier with a combat induced neurosis is that he has become a frightened, lonely, helpless person whose interpersonal relationships have been disrupted. The nature of modern warfare is such that in order to survive in combat, the soldier must function as part of a group, and his resistance to the traumata of combat will vary with the ability to integrate himself with the group.[20]

ANXIETY AND SOCIAL ORGANIZATION

These expressions of anxiety also illustrate certain relationships between the rise and spread of anxiety and its effect on social organization.

The spread of anxiety weakens and disrupts group cohesion and tends to undermine collective determination and social purpose, particularly in critical situations. The individual members become more preoccupied with their own problems, distrustful of and hostile to others, and less integrated within the group; hence, social relations become more distant and less satisfying. This was evident in the mining community during the depression. It was reflected in its low morale, loss of social purpose, and increase of illness. It was evident in the combat unit when anxiety spread and the unit became less effective in battle; the unit ceased to stimulate the individual to collective goals and ceased to be a symbol of protection. In its extreme, the unit disintegrated and each individual became concerned primarily with his own safety. Each individual tended to be encysted almost as a discrete unit because of his distrust of the other members and because of their distrust of him. But among the Saulteaux this did not obtain. The Saulteaux dreaded being isolated from the group and anything held private or in secret was a source of suspicion.

From the opposite perspective, when the group strives to preserve its solidarity, anxiety behavior becomes a threat to the unit and the basis for social disapproval. The neurotic individual becomes a variant and is isolated from the group, and his anxiety is prevented from spreading. This was evident both in the combat unit and in the Saulteaux society. Since the mining community had been disorganized, the spread of anxiety could not be deterred.

But when the unit is well organized and the members more effectively integrated within it, anxiety breakdowns decline. It seems that persons who acquire the support and approval of the group tend to become sustained. Highly integrated military units had less breakdowns than loosely integrated units. The mining work units who were intimate and more solidified also had fewer neurotic breakdowns. The participants of cohesive units are less likely to break down. They find that other participants bolster their self-confidence; they feel less isolated and more protected by identifying with the group; they can reintegrate their behavior more readily by the demonstrated example of others. The Saulteaux Indian who was helplessly isolated from the group had a powerful need to become reaccepted; and hence, he had to confess his "sins," however distasteful this practice might have been to him. Thus, the group used individual anxiety as a means of controlling him.

NOTES

1. See S. Kirson Weinberg "Anxiety", "Neurosis" *A Dictionary of the Social Sciences*, edited by Julius Gould and William L. Kolb, (New York: The Free Press, 1964), pp. 30–32, 466, 467.

2. Rollo May, *The Meaning of Anxiety* (New York: Ronald Press, 1950), pp. 193–95. He regards normal anxiety as being proportionate to the outside danger even if it includes helplessness.

3. Allison Davis and Robert Havighurst, *Father of the Man* (Boston: Houghton Mifflin, 1947), pp. 212–213.

4. Percival M. Symonds, *Adolescent Fantasy* (New York: Columbia University Press, 1949), p. 174.

5. Rollo May, *The Meaning of Anxiety* (New York: Ronald Press, 1950), p. 197.

6. See Arthur T. Jersild, *Child Psychology* (New York: Prentice-Hall, Inc., 1940); also Margaret A. Ribble, "Anxiety in Infants," *Modern Trends in Child Psychiatry*, edited by Nolan D. C. Lewis and Bernhard L. Pacella (New York: International Universities Press, 1945), pp. 17–25.

7. Karen Horney, *Our Inner Conflicts* (New York: W. W. Norton, 1945), pp. 41–42.

8. See in Rollo May, *The Meaning of Anxiety* (New York: Ronald Press, 1950), pp. 341, 342.

9. Erich Fromm, "Individual and Social Origins of Neurosis," *American Sociologial Review* (1944), *IX* 380–384.

10. Rollo May, *The Meaning of Anxiety* (New York: Ronald Press, 1950) pp. 340–343.

11. Arnold W. Green, "The Middle Class Male Child and Neurosis," *American Sociological Review* (February, 1946), *XI* (1), 31–41.

12. *Ibid.*

13. A. Irving Hallowell, "The Social Function of Anxiety in a Primitive Society," *American Sociological Review* (December, 1941), *VI* (6), 869–881; also A. Irving Hallowell, "Fear and Anxiety as Cultural and Individual Variables in a Primitive Society," *The Journal of Social Psychology* (1938), *IX*, 25–47.

14. *Ibid.*, p. 881.

15. From James L. Halliday, *Psychosocial Medicine*, (New York: W. W. Norton, 1948), pp. 184–195.

16. Morton C. Wyatt, "Psychoneurosis and Leadership," *Infantry Journal* (April, 1945), p. 29, S. Kirson Weinberg, "The Combat Neuroses," *American Journal of Sociology*, (March, 1946), *51*: (5) 466–478.

17. Roy R. Grinker and John B. Spiegel, *Men Under Stress* (Philadelphia: Blakiston, 1945), pp. 129, 130.

18. Edwin Weinstein, "The Function of Interpersonal Relations in the Neurosis of Combat," *Psychiatry* (August, 1947), *X*: (3), 307–314.

19. Herbert X. Spiegel, "Psychiatric Observations in the Tunisian Campaign," *American Journal of Orthopsychiatry* (1943), *XIV*: (3), 383; S. Kirson Weinberg, "The Combat Neuroses," *American Journal of Sociology* (March, 1946), 466–478.

20. Edwin Weinstein, "The Function of Interpersonal Relations in the Neurosis of Combat," *Psychiatry* (August, 1947), *X*: (3), 307–314.

SOCIAL PSYCHOLOGICAL ASPECTS OF ACTING-OUT DISORDERS AND DEVIANT BEHAVIOR

S. Kirson Weinberg

INVESTIGATORS often confuse behavior which is acquired in a deviant subculture with behavior which results from psychopathic immaturity. For example, many delinquents who violate the norms of the larger society acquire their behavior in the particular subculture in which they are reared and participate. These delinquents conform to their criminal norms in the same way that conventional persons abide by conventional norms. Nevertheless, these delinquents also may experience guilt feelings and cultivate lasting intimate relationships. Yet, when delinquents are evaluated in terms of the implicit moral norms of the particular clinician, they may be considered psychopathic. Also, some anti-social persons are diagnosed psychopathic because they express very slight guilt feelings, but others who may be guilt-laden after persistent misbehavior also are considered psychopathic. Then again, some investigators contend that psychopaths cannot change; other investigators report that psychopaths have improved.[1] It is not surprising, then, that the category of "psychopathy" is fraught with disagreement and inconsistency.

At the present time, since psychopathy combines a series of loosely related disorders centering about overt, antisocial, or "inadequate" behavior, we refer to this anomalous category as "acting-out disorders." Statistics on psychopathy reflect this inconsistency. For example, Sutherland has shown that more than 75 per cent of the inmates of Illinois state prisons were categorized as psychopathic, but only 10 per cent of the inmates in New York and Massachusetts were so diagnosed.[2] Clearly, this discrepancy resulted from different preconceptions among the psychiatrists rather than from differences in the types of criminals. In a survey of a district in Baltimore, Lemkau found that in 1933, 13 per 10,000 of the population were considered psychopathic. In 1936 only 5.2 per 10,000 of the population were so diagnosed. The figure was revised downward because many unemployed who

Part of this paper appeared previously in S. Kirson Weinberg, *Society and Personality Disorders* (Eaglewood Cliffs, N. J.: Prentice-Hall, 1952).

were considered "psychopathic" in 1933 were not so regarded in 1936 when the lack of job opportunities during the economic depression was considered.[3]

Since the criteria of psychopathy are inconsistent, symptomatic behavior and social evaluations in addition to personality dynamics are usually regarded as the criteria for categorizing psychopathy.[4] Yet these very behavioral reactions and social evaluations can be misleading. By this we mean that psychopathy cannot be ascertained merely by symptomatic reactions such as explosive or eccentric behavior. It cannot be ascertained by traits which characterize prepsychotic and psychotic persons as schizoid or paranoid.[5] It cannot be ascertained by using the norms of the urban, middle-class subculture for gauging the behavior of persons in another subculture with such labels as "inadequate," or "criminal." Indeed, "psychopathic personality" can be ascertained chiefly by the personality structure; and the personality structure can be understood best when traced developmentally.

Approach to Acting-Out Personalities

Sociologists have been interested in acting-out behavior from a developmental viewpoint because of its bearing upon crime. But they have been chiefly concerned with the types of associations and with the subculture which have contributed to criminal behavior and less interested in personality differences among delinquents. Although they have traced the processes by which delinquents and criminals assimilate their deviate forms, they have not pursued the process to its logical extreme by relating defective forms of socialization to criminal behavior. Sutherland and others have studied the relationship between psychopathy and crime,[6] while others have studied the personality structure of delinquents and criminals.[7]

On the other hand, psychoanalysts have emphasized personality differences and the divergent courses of development among individual criminals. Although they often have confused acting-out and antisocial behavior with criminality and have understated the social influences of peer groups upon criminal activity, they have been foremost in trying to classify acting-out persons on a dynamic and developmental level.[8]

In constructing a scheme of acting-out antisocial types which are mutually exclusive we must consider the criteria of personality organization, personality development, and the influence of the subculture. We must omit, however, the so-called marginal acting-out types who have minimal guilt feelings about one particular form of behavior, whether it be stealing, certain sex perversions, or other idiosyncracies; for these behavioral reactions are usually symptoms or expressions of more profound personality differences which often vary with the individual case.

Types of Acting-Out Disorders

From this vantage point we can classify the varied acting-out disorders into the following types: (1) the psychopath, (2) the acting-out neurotic, and (3) the cultural deviant.

Since these types are ideal, particular cases only approximate them, and some acting-out persons may have components of two types. For example, a subcultural deviant, a delinquent, may have certain neurotic characteristics which intensify his acting-out behavior. An acting-out neurotic may be so incorrigible that, despite intense feelings of guilt, he may approximate the psychopath in his hostile behavior, in his distorted social relationships, and in his resistance to treatment.[9] Certain acting-out persons may have guilt feelings about certain matters, and thus be marginal to the psychopath and the acting-out neurotic. Certain immature personalities who have been neglected, then overindulged, in early life may appear as psychopaths by their lack of guilt and resistance to personal change. The vicissitudes of family constellations, parent-child relationships, and personality development are so varied and so complex that marginal and mixed types inevitably arise. The advantage of a classificatory scheme of ideal types is its use as a guide in understanding the personality formation and structure of these types.

THE PSYCHOPATH

Qualifications concerning the Psychopath

Although psychopathy may have specified components that can be isolated and though these components in their patterned whole can be re-lated to personality development, explicit cautions and qualifications concerning this personality type must be emphasized. First, the focus of attention upon the formation of psychopathy in early childhood only, does not sufficiently cover the experiences of the adolescent and adult psychopath. The emotionally deprived child differs from the adult psychopath in somewhat the same way that the autistic child differs from the adult schizophrenic. Second, the attribution of early experiences to psychopathy overlooks the fact that these experiences in somewhat similar form frequently continue during late childhood and adolescence, so that the continuity of these experiences should be emphasized rather than the early experiences only.

Third, the focus of interest upon children of foundling and foster homes as potential psychopaths obscures the overlay of vulnerability of these types of persons who are readily subject to critical disapproval and social condemnation and who may be exposed to a delinquent culture at a relatively early age and hence more apt to act out. The neglected child of an upper-class, self-centered mother may be exposed to a shifting array of governesses unconcerned about his emotional needs. Because of the protection of the family, as he becomes an adult he may frequently be shielded in his deviancies or may have an easier way to express his short-run hedonic desires without a necessary concern for deferred goals.

Fourth, the psychopath frequently is analyzed after he has been detected. In the clinical appraisal, the scrutiny is for antecedent events which sometimes may be judged out of proportion to their significance. Thus in characterizing the psychopath as an extreme type of personality deviant who by the organization of his personality is unable to conform, we must be aware that there are relatively few developmental histories of this type and that these histories accentuate early life without necessarily placing later experiences and social class in proper perspective.

The Development of Psychopathy

The psychopath as a victim of faulty personality development has been emotionally deprived of intimate relationships from early childhood to later in life. Because of this early and later deprivation, he becomes retarded in his facility for intimate role-taking and is less responsive to social disapproval and social control. He seems to lack foresight, has shallow relationships with other persons, and is hard to restrain and hard to change.

As a deviant type, he is defective in his role-taking facilities and seemingly lacks the capacity to anticipate disapproval; when he experiences disapproval, he is surprised and resents it. He prefers immediate goals and short-run hedonism to deferred goals. He ignores the rights and privileges of others when these interfere with personal gratification; he is impulsive and, according to Gough, shows an "apparent incongruity between the strength of the stimulus and the magnitude of the behavioral response."[10] He cannot form deep and persistent attachments with other persons, because he lacks the capacity to identify with another or to share another's viewpoint. He cannot evaluate a situation properly because he cannot anticipate the objections that others will make to his behavior. He lacks guilt for his experiences because he has not internalized the norms and images of others by which to regulate his conduct. Thus he represents a fixated, immature person.

Since the relationships that a child may have with his parents or with other members of the family are so varied, a representation of a static family constellation or parental characteristics is not enough to explain the development of psychopathy. The important influences consist of ways in which the child and parents relate and of ways in which the child internalizes the meanings of these relationships. Even if neglected by his parents, a child may still cultivate intimate relationships with other family members, as Schachtel and Levi have noted.[11] Moreover, if the child is deprived by the parents, he still may remain organized and may be able to abide by the social norms, although he may remain emotionally indifferent to the feelings of others. Hence, no definite and conclusive personality inevitably emerges from a given set of parent-child relationships. Yet within this type of family situation, the child may so develop that he may be unable to cultivate close attachments and respond to social disapproval.

Although the shifting of parent figures, then, may be crucial as emotional deprivation in the formation of the psychopathic personality, the function of shifting children upon deviancy has been tested in some degree by an analysis of children in West Africa who were repeatedly shifted from family to family of close relatives. Seemingly, the shifts *per se* were not crucial in their deviant behavior as were the relationships with the persons and family to whom they were shifted.[3] The shifted child cannot form enduring primary relationships, especially when he lacks affection from his parent figures. Among the settings in which this type of personality may very likely emerge are child institutions such as nurseries or foundling homes and, sometimes, foster families, but crucially in families of emotionally depriving parents.

Although these forms of parent-child relationships may contribute to psychopathic behavior, the content of the interaction cannot be overlooked. Some parents may be so undisciplined emotionally or so perverse sexually that the child, having no other role models, may identify with them and then internalize their perverse forms of behavior. Having received parental sanction from their behavior, he accepts their criteria of right and wrong and he may imitate their behavior with little or no guilt feelings.

The psychopath who emerges from these impersonal relationships is a deprived child and adolescent who differs from the rejected child.[12] The deprived child's and adolescent's relationships with adults are usually meager, barren, and removed. His emotions reflecting these relationships are shallow, simple, and direct, for he does not have the opportunity to acquire and to cultivate intense or complex feelings toward other persons. He does not experience the subtle, continual feelings that come with close attachments to one adult figure, and he does not learn to associate affection with the delights of tactual contact with the mother.

The rejected child, on the other hand, is in continual interaction with his parents, and his emotional development centers about his not being wanted or his being despised. His emotions become complex, indirect, and intense, for he comes to identify with his rejecting parents who may have mixed feelings toward him. He sees them as anchor points with which to interpret his world and himself. In fact, by identifying with his parents in the process of socialization, he internalizes their viewpoints about himself and thus may become disturbed and even disordered. The deprived child does not have any adult figures with whom to identify and to regard as anchor points in interpreting his world and himself; hence, his estimate of himself is somewhat confused and is fixed around body gratification.

By not acquiring gratification from close and binding parental relationships, the deprived child becomes fixated upon his body for satisfaction, whether in thumb sucking or in masturbatory pleasures. Though he may want attention, he is also apathetic to other persons and more concerned with bodily pleasures. He becomes less threatened by the withdrawal and removal of affection because he has not experienced affection sufficiently as a means of self-control. For example, as Goldfarb has pointed out, deprived children who were shifted or who were threatened with being shifted to other families took the chance calmly and without any display of emotion.[13] In addition, the child's estimation of himself is not bound to any single parental figure who can control him. It is therefore questionable whether the deprived child who develops into a psychopath can see himself as a love object and can express affection, for he has not internalized the images of sustained parent figures who see him as a love object. In addition, he has not had the opportunity to cultivate the capacity for intimate role-taking in order to reciprocate a love relationship.

In this condition the deprived child frequently bids for attention. He may revert to negativistic displays such as temper tantrums, illness, or other devices. His bid for attention is indiscriminate and is even displayed to strangers, for whom he shows slight fear.

Moreover, the deprived child does not become disciplined, although he may adjust to a routine if external pressure is very intense. Yet, basically, he finds no purposive rewards that are bound up with postponing and delaying behavior. His delayed behavior would have to be bound up with the approval's and disapprovals of those identifying images who represent the right and wrong of his behavior. But by not internalizing the images of parent figures completely, his norms of approval and disapproval are weak. Although this characterization is extreme, because no child is completely deprived else he would not be human, yet this tendency is the forerunner of a lack of self-restraint and of a stunted conscience.

Freud and Burlingham point out further that, if the parent figures remain distant and impersonal, or if the adults are changed frequently, the children will then show defects in their personality structure and will "be exposed to the danger of all kinds of dissocial development."[14]

It is not surprising, then, that a child, adolescent, or adult with less inner restraints may become restless and hyperactive. Healy and Bronner found that 53 delinquents exhibited overactive tendencies in childhood and adolescence and 25 were overactive and uninhibited before school age. However, Healy and Bronner do not specify what these thwartings and frustrations are, because the neurotic as well as the psychopathic child can be restless.[15]

In a more definitive study of emotional privation, Goldfarb investigated the development of fifteen children who were reared in an institution until about the age of 3 when they were placed in foster homes. He compared these institutional children with children who had been reared by foster parents from early infancy. He found that the institutionalized children showed emotional and mental deficiencies which the foster-family children did not display.[16]

The institutional children were emotionally passive and impoverished and lacked the inhibitory qualities that characterized foster-home children. Of the fifteen cases, fourteen were unmanageable in their classes. Many were subject to temper tantrums, and some were enuretic through the late juvenile and adolescent periods. Frequently, their behavior was random, distractible, and nonpersevering. Their extreme curiosity resulted from an inability to grasp the meaning of their social situations, which left them continually dissatisfied; hence, they were continually moved to test and to try out situations on a trial-and-error basis rather than on a reflective sizing-up process.[17]

Although they were emotionally passive, they continually demanded affection and attention. Their demands for affection were on a physical and sensual level, continual hugging and kissing. Nonetheless, they could not reciprocate these relationships. Despite their insatiable demand for attention, they did not enrich their capacities to form social ties. During adolescence, they were emotionally isolated, socially removed, and cold. They were not responsive to "normal motivation" and could not be appealed to conform, as could other children.

Their capacity for abstraction was also retarded, particularly in terms of time and space. They had difficulty envisioning the consequences of their wayward actions. Because of their poor concept of time, they would come home from school hours late. Because of spatial deficiencies, they would wander away, although they were repeatedly warned against such behavior. Their lessened ability in foresight and their inability to appraise a total situation made them repeat their mistakes again and again. Moreover, their meager emotional reactions were supplemented by the virtual absence of anxiety after acts of cruelty, aggression, or hostility. They were unmoved by failing in school, which sometimes bewildered their foster parents who did not know how to motivate them. Even severe punishment and parental threats of removal from the home were of no avail.

Walter Manson, whose case was so elaborately described by Karpman, was removed from his family at the age of 6, but even at that time he seemingly was unaware of a primary relationship. Manson wrote his autobiography at the age of 36, when he was an opiate addict and had been psychotic. Although Manson's early life is briefly described, it is evident that his deviant behavior became persistent after his departure from the family.[18]

In brief, the psychopath who lacks a capacity for role-taking skills on the primary level develops amid indifferent and changing social relations initially with emotionally depriving parent figures and later with other significant figures.

THE ACTING-OUT NEUROTIC

The acting-out neurotic is often confused with the psychopath because his external behavior seems so similar. Yet the personalities of the two types differ markedly. First, the acting-out neurotic does experience feelings of guilt and has the makings of a conscience. As such, he may feel an unconscious need to be punished for his misdeeds. The psychopath, on the other hand, projects blame onto others and rarely feels guilty. Second, the acting-out neurotic can establish primary relationships, perhaps to a lesser degree than the normal person but far more so than the psychopath. Third, the acting-out neurotic resorts to his hostile behavior as a compensatory defense against anxiety; the psychopath experiences a minimum of anxiety. The style of life of the acting-out neurotic is such that he moves against people and organizes his behavior around overt hostility. Because of his hostility he tends to feel isolated, and this isolation may make him extremely self-centered or self-concerned. Moreover, this may deter him from getting close to people. The psychopath has little need for people except to use them. Fourth, the acting-out neurotic, who can identify with others, may then become amenable to change, particularly under certain conditions of intense identification with the therapist. The "true" psychopath, who cannot identify with others, seems impervious to change or to treatment, at least under present-day techniques.

Yet both have much in common. They are continually in trouble and are maladjusted. Both seem to have no life plan or integrated goals and live for the impulsive moment. Both tend to concentrate upon the present, although the acting-out neurotic may possibly grieve about his past. Both seem to behave in a manner which is essentially self-defeating and erratic. Both may exercise poor judgment, seem not to learn from experience, and seem completely undependable and often irresponsible.

The Development of the Acting-Out Neurotic

The development of the acting-out neurotic is characterized by a very permissive parent, usually the mother, and by a distant or hostile parent, usually the father. The parental constellation occurs in these cases again and again. Greenacre found that the parental constellation consisted of a stern, respected, father who is remote, preoccupied, and fear-inspiring in relation to his children, and an indulgent, pleasure-loving, frequently pretty mother who is often tacitly contemptuous of her husband's importance.[19] ... Though Greenacre's subjects were from upper middle classes, this family constellation is also evident in lower classes.

Generally, the child is either tacitly or overtly approved in his predatory or variant activities, and as a result he feels slight guilt concerning it.[20] "In no instance in which adequate psychiatric therapeutic study of both parent and child has been possible," says Szurek, "has it been difficult to obtain sufficient evidence to reconstruct the chief dynamics of the situation." Frequently, the mother, although the father also is involved in some way, unwittingly encourages the "anti-social behavior of the child."[21] Johnson indicates that the therapy of acting-out children was difficult because the attitudes of guilt developed toward the therapist were counteracted by the unwitting permission of the parents. Consequently, the child became confused, then more fearful of the therapist, and eventually stopped going for treatment to avoid further confusion. Even mild "acting-out" cases could be treated only when the important parent, whether mother or father, was also treated.[22] Some children did not measure up to the perfectionist expectations and hopes of one or both parents. To escape from their anxieties about ever achieving these goals, they reacted by hostile and destructive behavior. Some responded this way, too, as a result of critical experiences in early life.

The neurotic is supposed to limit his aggressions to fantasy. Hence, the "acting-out" neurotic seems to be an anomaly. Actually, however, the neurotic who acts out his hostility has many similarities to the neurotic who limits his aggressions to fantasy. Both react to anxiety; both are overcome by guilt feelings; and, in the last analysis, both are self-defeating in their behavior. The differences are symptomatic rather than basic, and they indicate the kinds of defenses to which different neurotics may resort. In addition, the different social definitions of their symptoms may give them different roles in society, and these divergent roles may affect their self-conceptions and their relationships with other persons.

Why one neurotic expresses his hostility overtly and another neurotic expresses his hostility in fantasy is still not completely known. It seems that some types of neurotics, particularly obsessives, are incapable of acting out their hostile fantasies. As a result, they seldom become acting-out neurotics. Janet has pointed out the following relevant observations:

It is not strange that in so many observations of criminal obsessions bearing upon more than two hundred patients and collected during a dozen years, I could not observe a single real accident? I have never seen any crimes committed, any suicide accomplished by one of these obsessives. It cannot be due only to chance. It must be that in these obsessives, the tendency to act out is very weak.[23]

In some instances the types of approval which the neurotic gets may stimulate him to act out his behavior. The overt hostility may become a compensatory means for social approval from his associates, which he does not get from his parents. It indicates, too, that the neurotic as well as the ordered or stable person, can be introduced into delinquent activities. Another important fact concerns the attitudes of one or both of the parents. In some instances one parent may have such hostility to the other parent that, tacitly, either may want the child to act out his aggressions although he or she may not say so directly. The child may respond to hurt his oppressive parent, whether his father or his mother, by his self-defeating and disgraceful behavior. Thus, the whole problem of the individual's acting out his behavior is involved in a developmental process.

Healy and Bronner, in their comparative study of delinquents and nondelinquents, have described a case in which this acting-out behavior was a direct reaction against the parents.[24] In contrast to his brother, the delinquent subject, who was the youngest child in the family, was healthier and more intelligent. But the control's behavior was uneventful both at home and in school. The delinquent was a difficult problem even in his first year in school. He was hard to control, spoiled, and wanted his own way. By the age of 10 he was studied at the clinic because he displayed many nervous habits and fears. By the age of 14, he had engaged in a long line of delinquencies, some of which were very serious. He admitted that he began his delinquencies at the age of 8. Moreover, he ran away from home at least ten times.

The parents were immigrants who had a shop in front of a house that they owned. The father was a stubborn, tense individual who often got drunk and was very harsh to the boy during his juvenile period. When the subject was 11, the father devoted much of his time in trying "to manage" him. Apparently, because of the father's previous harsh and repressive tactics, an intense antagonism arose between father and son. Although the mother was forgiving and rarely scolded the subject, she was somewhat rejective of him. The other brother also took a hand in punishing him.

The curious result of these parent-child relationships was that the subject could not stand praise. When he was praised, he became uncontrollable; yet when he was punished he engaged in further delinquencies. He seemed to . . . ask for punishment. At one time he gave himself up to a policeman. At other times he claimed that he would have to punish himself if nobody else did, or that he would have to be sent to a reform school. He dreamed frequently of being involved in some disaster. He claimed that he resorted to his delinquencies out of an uncontrollable compulsion.

Although many features of this history are omitted by Healy and Bronner, such as the family constellation and parent-child relationships, the neurotic reactions and self-chastisement indicate the pattern of development of the acting-out neurotic. When he was 18 years old, the subject began to be treated; he also began to behave much better, although his final outcome is not revealed.

THE CULTURAL DEVIANT

The cultural deviant is a product of a particular subculture which sanctions activities that are considered antisocial or inadequate by the larger society. Despite this behavior the cultural deviant may have feelings of guilt, can conform to social controls, is capable of identifying with others in his immediate groups, and can modify his behavior. Yet his antisocial behavior, because it is sanctioned, usually does not create guilt feelings. When two widely disparate cultures exist side by side, this deviant behavior is not unlikely. Carothers calls attention to the fact that the natives of Kenya, when judged by Western standards, would be considered "psychopathic."[25] Some habitual delinquents in our culture exemplify this deviant type. Though considered antisocial by the larger society, stealing is sanctioned in some subcultures, and the individual participant acquires his behavior patterns by participating in these deviant groups. Yet too often this cultural component is overlooked in differentiating between the cultural deviant and the psychopath. The essential problem, then, is one of differentiating between the acquired norms of a subculture and the personality components of the particular deviant. The following case of James Martin describes a person who was a habitual delinquent and who was labeled as a "psychopathic personality" by the prison psychiatrist.[26] This psychopathic label is not unusual in view of the fact that many clinicians regard habitual criminals as psychopaths.[27]

The Case of James Martin

His four brothers were delinquents and criminals. Yet, when he and his brothers were provided with economic opportunities and were treated in a "friendly, informal and confidential" way, they responded to this treatment and became reoriented to conventional and useful pursuits.

At the age of 21, when James wrote his autobiography, he had spent one half of his life in reform schools, jails, prisons, and other state penal institutions. His difficulties with enforcement officers began from the time he was slightly older than 6, and lasted until he was 24.

His parents, Polish immigrants, settled in a typical first-settlement zone near a factory district. As far as is known, none of his ancestors was psychotic or had been committed to a mental hospital.

His father, an unskilled laborer, intermittently worked at odd jobs, but being an alcoholic he dissipated a large share of his salary in drinking. But alcoholism was prevalent among men in the community. Most of the men who worked in the near-by railroad yards and factories customarily gathered in the corner saloon on paydays to squander their money.

James' mother, however, was a hard-working woman who was prudent enough to save what money her husband did earn to bridge the lean days of unemployment and drinking. Pious, self-effacing, she devoted her life to her family and to her children. In retrospect James said, "As I think of all the hardships and troubles my mother went through when I was a small child, I feel ashamed of myself for causing her more trouble by being the kind of boy I was. . . .She was kind to me when I was small. Way back, since I can remember, she was always working, washing clothes, cleaning house, administering to our needs. . . . About the only diversion she took was to go to church." The father, however, was an indifferent figure who seemed too concerned with his own difficulties to bother with the children. Hence, he seemed somewhat distant to the children and they did not become attached to him.

At the age of 6 James began to help the family in obtaining the sheer necessities of life, such as food, clothes, and rent. In fact, begging was a family pattern in which all members at different times participated. When begging with his brother, James' practice was to beg if the residents were at home, but if they were out, he and his brothers would break into the house and steal.

Delinquency was both a family pattern and a neighborhood pattern. The neighborhood boys stole from local fruit stands and from the counters of large department stores. By the age of 8, when James was arrested for burglary, his two older brothers had already been committed to penal institutions. By the age of 9 he had been persuaded by his brother and a friend to help them break into a barbershop.

Conforming to this deviant pattern, he became a truant as well as a thief. When the school reported his chronic truancy to his parents, he lied about his absences. Slightly scared when his mother threatened to spank him, he "wanted to go back to school and behave, but the older fellows always taunted me saying I was a sissy. . . . Then I would go with them to do 'jobs.' " His begging and depredations were mainly from rich people and seldom from poor people. In fact, he seemed to identify with the poor and helpless and considered almsgiving a token of good luck.

By the age of 10, after being arrested for burglary, he was sentenced to St. Charles for three years, at his own request, in order to be with his brother, Michael. In the three years he became much tougher and began to hate the authority he met. After his release he continued burglarizing and stealing cars. But again he was caught and sentenced to St. Charles. While there, his father died, and James was permitted to attend the funeral; but, seemingly, he felt little attachment for his father.

Paroled to a farmer, James escaped and returned to his former associates and to stealing. Caught again, he was returned to St. Charles. Thereafter, he tried to escape at every opportunity. Finally, he was made an officer of a cottage and conformed to the routine.

At this time he had his first sex experience, but he abstained from "gangshags" in which a group of boys would successively have sex relations with a single girl, though it was not uncommon in the neighborhood. After being in and out of St. Charles a few times, he was finally released. Unable to become interested in or to hold a job for long, he worked intermittently. When unemployed, he loafed around the parks, and when the idleness irked him he and some neighborhood companions began stealing cars which they sold to a "fence." A confirmed automobile thief, he finally was caught and sentenced to the Illinois State Reformatory, where he was at the time he wrote his autobiography.

Throughout his life, from childhood to late adolescence, he was embittered and hostile to adult authority figures. " . . . the maltreatments in city and state institutions where I spent most of my childhood, induced me to avenge myself against the city and state officials."

On the other hand, his need for association with other boys and adolescents, and the influence and censure which they exerted, had a sustained effect upon his criminal career. Actually, his intimate friends did not regard him as a successful thief.

"To put it all in one statement, I didn't want to steal or take any chances in stealing but I did it anyway. Down in my heart I hated to go out and steal with other fellows, but I went with them to avoid 'ridicule.' "[28]

COMPARISON OF THE THREE TYPES

The representative three acting-out types, which we have described, were all delinquents and were also diagnosed as psychopathic personalities.[29] Yet, upon closer inspection, we noted that despite certain similarities there were distinct personality differences among them. These differences provided the bases for a more consistent classification, which included (1) the psychopath, (2) the acting-out neurotic, ... and (3) the cultural deviant.

Basic Differences.

The psychopath seems unable to identify with others, has minimal feelings of guilt or anxiety about his misadventures, lives in and for the present, has shallow emotional feelings toward other persons, and is very self-centered because of his indifference to others and because he concentrates upon satisfying his immediate wants. Yet the psychopath does understand the difference between right and wrong, can adjust to others on an impersonal or casual level, and does respond to adverse reprimands for the moment. The basic causes of psychopathy may be either damage to the brain, especially to the frontal lobes, or emotional deprivation in early life, which comes about either from very negligent and/or shifting parent figures. The psychopath who is a victim of emotionally deprived parental relationships tends to be restless and uninhibited even as a child. Hence, this early fixation may make the psychopath impervious to personality change.

The acting-out neurotic does experience feelings of guilt, does have intense feelings of anxiety about his depredations, is ambivalent about his attitudes toward other persons, and may have intense attitudes of hostility toward others. Though self-centered, he is self-preoccupied and fundamentally tends to have a low conception of himself. The acting-out neurotic may have a capacity for identifying with others, but this capacity is usually obscured by his hostility and self-reproach. The acting-out neurotic tends to emerge from a family constellation in which he has a very permissive mother and an aloof and/or hostile father. Under certain conditions of expert therapy, the acting-out neurotic may be amenable to personal change.

The cultural deviant tends to be a normal and accepted person within his immediate milieu. This cultural deviant may be a stable and even mature personality whose norms of behavior differ from those of conventional people. On the one hand, his behavior does not indicate psychopathic immaturity because he can cultivate intimate relations with others and does feel guilty about matters which are considered reprehensible by his immediate group. Like the other acting-out types, he tends to express his hostilities overtly. On the other hand, he is not overcome by undue anxiety and by feelings of guilt. This is manifested in his relationships with the mother and with the father. When the cultural deviant, as in the case of James Martin, feels a definite attachment to the mother and not an undue hostility to the father, the parent-child relations may not create the neurotic constellation that we see in the acting-out neurotic. Hence, under given conditions, the cultural deviant is amenable to personal change.

Similarities and Differences in Delinquent Behavior.

Though all the types we described were delinquents, they acquired their delinquent attitudes and activities in different ways. Walter Manson, the psychopath, stole as an impulsive means of getting what he wanted, even during childhood. Later, however, Manson consorted with different delinquents and criminals and was introduced into a criminal subculture. James Martin, on the other extreme, resorted to crime by conforming to accepted cultural practices in the family and the neighborhood. It was taught to him by his brothers, and by his companions, from a very early age. The acting-out neurotic resorted to delinquency as a means of being accepted socially by his peers. The acting-out neurotic got the social approval in the delinquent group which compensated for the intense disapproval from his father. He resorted to his crimes as a means of least resistance and from the influence of other delinquents in order to avert more responsible behavior in school.

Other similarities in their activities show a general hostility to persons or to "society," an inability to orient themselves around conventional activities, to conform to routine, to work out a life plan that would receive conventional approval. All three types were continually in trouble and continually placing society on the defensive, with respect to their behavior. . . .

NOTES

1. See Robert M. Lindner, *Rebel without a Cause* (New York: Grune and Stratton, 1944).

2. Edwin H. Sutherland, and Donald R. Cressey, *Principles of Criminology* (Philadelphia: J. B. Lippincott, 1966), 7th edition.

3. Paul Lemkau, *Mental Hygiene and Public Health* (New York: McGraw-Hill, 1949), p. 335.

4. See George E. Partridge, "Current Conceptions of Psychopathic Personality," *The American Journal of Psychiatry*, (1930), *X*, 53–99.

5. For example, consider the categories of thinking in the diagnosis of psychopathy in the following: On the basis of the Rorschach tests, Lindner found that psychopaths were qualitatively related to the hebephrenics and the neurotics. Batcheller found a neurotic condition superimposed on "a basic schizophrenic or latent schizoid condition." Kisher and Michael have designated this condition as a "schizoneurosis." Obviously, the substitution of one label for another does not explain anything about psychopathy; it merely leads to confusion. See Robert M. Lindner, "The Rorschach Test and the Diagnosis of Psychopathic Personality," *Journal of Criminal Psychopathology* (July, 1943), *V* (2), 69; Samuel J. Beck, "Introduction to the Rorschach Method," *Research Monographs*, No. 1 (Menasha, Wis.: American Orthopsychiatric Association, 1937); the other citations in W. Rottersman, "The Guardhouse Inmate," *War Medicine* (May, 1944), *V* (5), 276. It must be emphasized, however, that some paranoid persons and some very seclusive persons act out their behavior, but these psychotic tendencies are on a different vector than their acting-out behavior.

6. Edwin H. Sutherland, and Donald R. Cressey, *Principles of Criminology* (Philadelphia: J.B. Lippincott, 1966, pp. 103–117.

7. Ernest W. Burgess, "The Individual Delinquent as a Person," *American Journal of Sociology* (May, 1923), *28*, 657–680.

8. Franz Alexander and Hugo Staub, *The Criminal, the Judge and the Public*, (New York: Macmillan, 1931), pp. 145–152; Otto Fenichel, *The Psychoanalytic Theory of Neurosis*, (New York: W. W. Norton, 1945), pp. 117–139, 324–386, 466–492; Walter Bromberg, *Crime and the Mind* (Philadelphia: J. B. Lippincott, 1948), pp. 54, 55.

9. See, for example, Margaret S. Mahler, "Ego Psychology Applied to Behavior Problems," *Modern Trends in Child Psychiatry*, edited by Nolan D. C. Lewis and Bernard L. Pacella, (New York: International Universities Press, 1945), pp. 53–56.

10. Harrison G. Gough, "A Sociological Theory of Psychopathy," *American Journal of Sociology* (March, 1948), *43*, 359–360.

11. Anna H. Schachtel and Marjorie B. Levi, "Character Structure of Day Nursery Children as Seen through the Rorschach," *American Journal of Orthopsychiatry* (April, 1945), *15* (2), 213–222.

12. William Goldfarb, "Effects of Early Institutional Care on Adolescent Personality," *Journal of Experimental Education* (1943), *12*, 106, 129.

13. *Ibid.*

14. Anna Freud and Dorothy Burlingham, *Infants Without Families* (New York: International Universities Press, Inc., 1944), pp. 124–125.

15. William Healy and Augusta F. Bronner, *New Light on Delinquency and Its Treatment* (New Haven: Yale University Press, 1936), p. 45.

16. William Goldfarb, "Psychological Privation in Infancy and Subsequent Adjustment," *American Journal of Orthopsychiatry* (April, 1945), *15* (2), 249.

17. *Ibid.*, p. 252.

18. Ben Karpman, "The Case of Walter Manson," *Case Studies in the Psychopathology of Crime* (Baltimore: Medical Science Press, 1944), Vol. II, pp. 65–71.

19. Phyllis Greenacre, "Conscience in the Psychopath," *American Journal of Orthopsychiatry* (July, 1945), *15* (3), 498.

20. See Margaret S. Mahler, "Ego Psychology Applied to Behavior Problems," *Modern Trends in Child Psychiatry*, edited by Nolan D. C. Lewis and Bernard L. Pacella (New York: International Universities Press, Inc., 1945), pp. 52–56.

21. Stanislaus Szurek, "Genesis of Psychopathic Personality Trends," *Psychiatry* (February, 1942) *V* (1) 6.

22. Adelaide M. Johnson, "Sanctions for Superego Lacunae of Adolescents," *Searchlights on Delinquency*, edited by K. R. Eissler (New York: International Universities Press, Inc., 1949), pp. 237, 235.

23. Pierre Janet, *Les Observations and La Psychosthenie* (Paris: Alcan Librairie Felix, 1903).

24. Healy and Bronner, *op. cit.,* pp. 81–83.

25. James Carothers, "A Study of Mental Derangement in Africans and an Attempt to Explain Its Peculiarities, More Especially In Relation to the African Attitude To Life," *Psychiatry* (February, 1948), *11* (1), 47–86.

26. Clifford R. Shaw, *et al.*, ed., *Brothers in Crime* (Chicago: University of Chicago Press, 1938), pp. 220–255.

27. L. Kolb, "Types and Characteristics of Drug Addicts," *Mental Hygiene* (1935) *9*, 301.

28. Shaw *et al., op. cit.*, p. 250.

29. Paul William Preu, "The Concept of Psychopathic Personality," in J. McV. Hunt (Ed.), *Personality and the Behavior Disorders* (New York: Ronald Press, 1944), pp. 928–929.

part IV

DISORDERED BEHAVIOR AND SOCIAL DEVIANCE

Disordered persons are confronted by definitions and reactions from both clinicians and laymen. The clinician gauges deviance in terms of its departure from norms of healthy behavior. The layman defines deviance in terms of the person's capacity to participate in society. These clinical and lay definitions of disordered behavior may or may not be consistent, but the manner of definition characterizes the extent of the deviance. Deviant behavior, socially defined, is departure from the expectations of one's social roles and from the ideology and meanings of particular groups of participation.

Disordered behavior as social deviance requires that the group define the behavior and, when the disorder is severe, that the group remove the disordered person from social participation by hospitalizing him. Perhaps, as Kaplan, Reed and Richardson have found, the higher social classes resist hospitalization of their family members more effectively than do the lower classes. This may be because they have the home space and the funds to expedite this resistance or because they view the psychosis differently and without the finality that families in the lower stratum do.[1] Definitions of disorders are relative and vary with the groups in which the individual participates.

Varied definitions of deviance are reflected for different disorders by the ethnic group and by the social class of the persons; these definitions influence whether the afflicted persons receive treatment as well as the type of treatment they receive.

Among the residents of midtown Manhattan, wealthy and educated persons had more positive attitudes toward psychiatrists than, and differed diagnostically from, the poor and less-educated persons. Different diagnostic types are drawn from different class levels, based in parts upon the availability of therapy, attitudes toward such services, subcultural definitions of "illness" and of socially unacceptable behavior, and the very recognition of an attitude toward mental disturbance by the potential patient, his family, and family doctor. Paradoxically, the day laborer is arrested and sent to the emergency ward of a city hospital because he acted out his problems by punching his foreman in the nose, while his wealthier but not necessarily healthier counterpart is encouraged during his psychoanalysis to conquer his neurosis by venting his repressed feelings toward his superior. "One man's 'character disorder' may be another man's therapeutic goal!"[2]

Disordered behavior and deviant behavior may overlap but represent different dimensions of behavior. Disordered behavior is essentially a result of sustained personal conflict and personal disorganization. Deviant behavior is a result of social definitions and social expectations. The extent to which an individual can reorganize his behavior is a criterion of his being ordered or "mentally healthy." But the extent to which an individual fulfills his social roles and abides by the norms of his group determines the degree to which he is socially normal. Although disorders, especially the psychoses, the severe neuroses, and the acting-out disorders, may usually be defined as deviant or abnormal, the two concepts do not necessarily coincide.[3] Persons afflicted with psychosomatic disorders or very anxious persons may conceal their disordered condition by a deep need to conform to the norms of the group, because they consider conformity a necessary defense. Even paranoids who fit the lay conception of disorder more than other diagnostic afflictions do may operate on the social margins of society by self-employed occupations and by structured contacts with others in which their attitudes of persecution and of unreal self-estimation may go relatively undetected.

The papers that follow my own presents first the cultural and clinical conceptions of mental health and normality as well as mental disorder and social deviance. Szasz, in his paper "The Myth of Mental Illness," maintains that mental illness is not a substantive thing but essentially a "myth." It is not a function of a brain disease but a deviation from some implied psychosocial and ethical norm. Hence, Szasz regards mental illness as a form of deviant behavior, not as an illness on the dimension of physical illness.

Nonetheless, psychiatrists with a biomedical orientation traditionally define mental disorders as expressions and dysfunctions of detected or undetected organic pathology. They define mental disorders as biological phenomena even though no physical causes are discerned.

Psychoanalysts view many disorders as basic personality emergents from conflicts and traumas experienced in early life and perceive disorders in terms of formal dynamics removed from the social context.

The lay public has a more diffuse conception of disordered behavior. Star found that the American public is optimistic about the outcome of mental disorder, had faith in and were inclined to use psychiatric facilities to help disordered persons, differentiated between insanity and nervousness, and of six different disorders regarded only paranoid behavior as a mental illness. Since 1950, when this survey was taken, attitudes have become more tolerant to the mentally disordered.[4]

Nunnally, in "An Overview of the Public Conception of Mental Health," discusses a later inquiry into the degree of stigma associated with mental illness, the degree to which laymen trust the experts, the modes of communication about mental disorder and mental health, and the processes affecting changes in attitudes toward problems of mental health.

Manis, Hunt, Brawer, and Kercher who compare the conceptions of mental illness between a group of psychiatrists and a sample of the public from the same locale hypothesized that the public, not the psychiatrists, would tend to consider troublesome behavior more indicative of mental disorder than nontroublesome behavior. The public and the psychiatrists seem to have congruent views about mental disorders, but their views differ about specific disorders. In terms of the agreement of definitions between the clinician and the public, it appears that when the public agrees with the expert they can reinforce his judgment, but when they disagree they can challenge the clinician and ridicule his judgment. They conclude:

The major hypothesis of the study has been that troublesome or disruptive behavior would tend to be identified as mental illness by the public, but not by psychiatrists. On the basis of the present data, *neither* public nor psychiatrists appear to be guided primarily by such interpretations. Also unexpected was the extent of the similarity of public and psychiatric conceptions. Persecutive, bizarre, and emotional behavior are more apt to be considered indicative of mental illness than are manic, conformist, grandiose, or depressive behavior.

Explanation for unpredicted findings is necessarily conjectural. It is quite possible, of course, that the specific questions used in this study may have been lacking in equivalence or pertinence. Other techniques for administering questions and analyzing findings might produce differing results. Furthermore, the representativeness of the present subjects, public and psychiatrists, is not known.

Whatever the influence of specific content, technique, and sampling may have been, it also appears possible that the original hypothesis was oversimplified. It now seems likely that the hypotheses do not take cognizance sufficiently of the "cultural content" of *perceived troubles*. Obviously much of what is considered troublesome in a society is culturally defined. Less obvious is the specific content of cultural definitions. For example, in assuming that "manic" behavior is considered to be disruptive by members of a group, we have ignored some clues to the contrary.

In recent years, there has been a reported decline in the ratio of manic-depressive and paranoid psychotics to the schizophrenics. Is the change a consequence of altered behavioral patterns or of changing diagnoses? The present data suggest the possibility that manic, conformist, depressive, and grandiose behavior are less apt to be defined as mental illness today than they may have been in the past. Indeed, the finding that conformist behavior is slightly *more* likely to be considered a sign of mental illness than manic actions emphasizes the cultural acceptability of the latter. As Weinberg has pointed out, "The mild manic disorder is most consistent with the demands of contemporary society [and] . . . is perhaps far more acceptable in the urban culture of the United States than in other societies." The claim has also been made that "all observers agree that true *manic-depressive* psychoses are rare in technologically backward areas." These reports suggest the hypothesis that modern industrial society not only fosters manic-depressive behavior but also tends to overlook it. This interpretation would appear to be congruent with the present findings.

These considerations suggest the need for further exploration of public and professional (psychiatrists, psychologists, social workers, etc.) conceptions of mental illness. Other aspects of behavior—possibly of a multi-dimensional nature—merit investigation. For example, a revised hypothesis based on the foregoing data and interpretations might be: Non-conformist behavior tends to be interpreted as mental illness by both psychiatrists and the public. Conformist behavior (including manic-depressive and grandiose) is less likely to be so conceived. To test such hypotheses, research is needed in other locales and with differing techniques. Improved understanding of our conceptions of mental illness is a prerequisite to improved accuracy of diagnosis and etiology.[5]

Becoming judged as liable to commitment to the mental hospital is "a socially structured event." Schwartz has shown that the wives of twenty men who had been admitted to the mental hospital for the first time were very reluctant to admit that their husbands were psychotic and tried to show that their aberrant behavior was a result of physical maladies or was a temporary disability. Because of the wives' lack of detachment in appraising their husbands' disorders, the clinical judgment of the psychiatrist was indispensable in this context.[6]

Sampson, Messinger, and Towne have found that when a type of accommodation between family and patient is disrupted, the disturbed person is brought to the psychiatrist; then, if he is disorganized enough, he may be committed to the mental hospital.[7]

The commitment process itself which I discuss represents the path by which the person becomes a mental hospital patient. One persistent problem concerns the person's civil liberties and the other pertains to his adequate and accurate diagnosis. The process by which an individual is hospitalized is critically analyzed in "The Societal Reaction to Deviance" by Scheff, who has pointed out some flimsy pretenses for which some people are hospitalized.

REFERENCES

1. Bert Kaplan, Robert B. Reed, and Wyman Richardson, "A Comparison of the Incidence of Hospitalized and Non-Hospitalized Cases of Psychosis in Two Communities," *American Sociological Review*, 2 (4), 472–479.

2. Thomas S. Langner and Stanley T. Michaels, *Life Stress and Mental Health* (New York: The Free Press of Glencoe, 1963).

3. S. Kirson Weinberg, *Society and Personality Disorders* (Englewood Cliffs, New Jersey: Prentice-Hall, 1952).

4. Shirley A. Star, "Public Conceptions of Mental Illness," unpublished paper.

5. Jerome Manis, Chester L. Hunt, Milton J. Brawer, and Leonard C. Kercher, "Public and Psychiatric Conceptions of Mental Illness" *Journal of Health and Human Behavior* (Spring, 1965), 6, 52–55.

6. Charlotte Schwartz, "Perspective on Deviance—Wives' Definitions of Their Husbands' Mental Illness," *Psychiatry* (1957), 20, 275–291.

7. Harold Sampson, Sheldon L. Messinger, and Robert D. Towne, "Family Processes and Becoming A Mental Patient," *American Journal of Sociology* (1962), pp. 88–96.

A CULTURAL APPROACH TO DISORDERED BEHAVIOR AND SOCIAL DEVIANCE

S. Kirson Weinberg

THE "NORMAL PERSON" AND CULTURE

TO clarify the conception of disorder as deviant behavior, it is first necessary to emphasize the cultural relativity of normality.

If we compare the average persons in different societies the discrepancies in behavior are great. The modal or average Alorese would probably be anxious; the normal Dobuan would be very suspicious; the normal Mundugumor would be very hostile; the Zuñi would be relatively noncompetitive; and the middle-class American would be competitive. In short, the average person in one society develops differently from the average person in another society because of the technology, patterns of relationships, values, social structure, and ethos.

Horney broadly sketched the normal person in the American urban culture as one who is inclined to become more reserved and less inclined to trust people as he reaches adulthood and who is aware that people are not motivated by straightforward actions but are often prompted by expediency and cowardice.[1] Despite his recognition of these shortcomings in others and in himself, he does not become helpless in dealing with them. Moreover, he has some people with whom he can be friendly and in whom he can confide. This normal or healthy person presumably has experienced conflicts that he could usually integrate; by contrast the neurotic who has had traumatic experiences that he could not integrate thus sustains his anxiety. But it is not known how pervasive this normal personality type is. The sketch by Horney is thin and only a means of differentiating the supposedly normal person from the neurotic in our culture.

The so-called average or characteristic personality varies in different cultures. Because each culture, each subculture, and perhaps even each historical epoch may have a recognizable personality type, it becomes misleading to expect

Part of this paper appeared previously in S. Kirson Weinberg, *Society and Personality Disorders* (Englewood Cliffs, N. J., Prentice-Hall, 1952).

the same kind of personality to emerge or thrive in different cultures. For example, the noncompetitive Zuñi would be somewhat out of place in our competitive society, and the aggressive, climbing American "go-getter" would be in complete disfavor among the Zuñis.

DEVIANCE AS SOCIAL DEFINITION

Deviant behavior, as defined by the group, refers to the individual's departure from the norms, standardized practices, and approved outlets for his specific roles in a given society. From this viewpoint, the crucial point of deviation is the group's evaluation of and reaction to individual behavior rather than the degree of personal stability. Each society possesses and transmits a singular configuration of attitudes, gestures, and expressions, which constitute the social expectations and social definitions the members of that society must observe in their social roles. These unique group definitions are used to determine whether a person is socially normal in that society. Two individuals in two distinct societies may behave in somewhat the same way, but their similar behavior may have widely divergent meanings in their separate societies. Kroeber has described in striking fashion how collective superstitions can be mistaken for personal delusions.

An elderly Neapolitan cobbler comes to a hospital clinic with a rambling story told in broken English. His account wanders from headaches and listlessness to an old woman who has made him sick. He is referred to the neuro-psychiatric department with the comment: "Question of psychosis." Examination brings out little more than irrelevant detail about the enemy and how long she wished him ill, and why, and how she makes his head hurt. There is all the more indication of a persecutory delusion. The man is told to come back with an interpreter. He returns with a fluent Italian-American who explains apologetically that the old man is illiterate and he believes the woman is a witch and has cast the evil eye on him. The apparent delusion dissolves into a bit of superstition typical of the lower orders of Neapolitan society. What is normal belief there is a psychotic symptoms in one of our hospitals . . . . the norm of one culture is a sign of nervous pathology in the other.[2]

What appeared as disoriented behavior to the psychiatrist in our culture was indicative of oriented and approved behavior in another society. For this significant reason, behavior cannot be correctly evaluated unless we know how that behavior is defined by the given society or subsociety.

This is true not only for what seems to be disoriented behavior in our culture but also for varied gestures. For instance, although laughter may have many shades of meaning in American society, it is frequently associated with pleasant experiences. But among the Japanese of the nineteenth century, laughter was not necessarily a reaction to amusement but frequently a social duty. The Japanese child was taught to smile just as he was taught to bow or to prostrate himself. He was taught to express a happy appearance so as not to impose his grief upon his friends.

In this light, Klineberg, who used Hearn's materials among others for studying the Japanese, relates the following:

The story is told of a woman servant who smilingly asked her mistress if she might go to her husband's funeral. Later she returned with the ashes in a vase and said, actually laughing, "Here is my husband." Her mistress regarded her as a cynical creature; Hearn suggests that this might have been pure heroism.[3]

The white mistress interpreted her servant's smile as one of joy rather than as a disguise for the intense grief and sorrow that this servant might have felt. Yet the Japanese would have understood her gesture as socially normal.

It is usually necessary, too, for behavior to be overt and manifestly accessible to group evaluation. An individual who silently harbors deviant private beliefs cannot be defined as socially abnormal if he does not allow his actions to be influenced markedly by his views. For example, some mild paranoids in our culture have enough situational insight to suspect that their grandiose ideas of themselves would be denounced by other persons. Consequently, they are usually silent about their private notions unless they have complete confidence in the other person. They may express their ideas in such a way that the listener is not sure whether they are serious or joking.

"Adherence to reality" is sometimes considered a criterion of social normality. But different societies have different versions of reality. What may be real in one society may be clearly false in another society. Reality is a function of communication and agreement rather than objectively demonstrated experiments and refers to the individual's ability to share and evaluate the viewpoints of his immediate groups.

What may be considered deviant on one occasion may be sanctioned on other occasions. The antics of some fraternity pledges or the behavior of anonymous visitors during conventions in large cities, on other occasions, would be considered definitely deviant. If a fraternity pledge is fishing in front of a theater, he is tolerated, but another person without this social role would probably be considered psychotic.

Redlich has pointed out that the motivation of the action is also indicative of disorder. Thus the difference between normal handwashing and compulsive handwashing would not only be frequency and repetition but also the person's conscious and unconscious motives which prompted the actions.[4]

Deviant behavior, then, has a specific group connotation. It challenges, disrupts, or threatens the group. From a functional viewpoint, deviant behavior cannot be used by the society; from the interactional point of view, it is activity the society condemns. Hence, the more threatening the behavior, the more severely it is collectively disapproved and resisted or unwanted.

The disorders that are most frequently recognized cross-culturally are those involving impulsive violence, uncontrollable frenzy, or impulsive attacks upon others. The very presence of such a person constitutes a threat to the society, and the society restrains this individual in some way. A second type of disorder that is recognized in most cultures involves nonritualized incoherence and irrationality. Thus the priest who becomes incoherent in a ritualized dance is not recognized as deviant, but the individual who becomes incoherent and irrational in his usual social role is regarded as disordered. Third, the individual who lacks the capacity for self-care is considered disordered, except for those persons in institutionalized situations who through fasting or some other socially sanctioned procedure become weakened and unable to care for themselves.[5]

NOTES

1. Karen Horney, *The Neurotic Personality of Our Time* (New York: W. W. Norton, 1939), p. 95.

2. Alfred L. Kroeber, "Cultural Anthropology," in Madison Bentley and E. V. Cowdrey (Eds.), *Problems of Mental Disorder* (New York: McGraw-Hill, 1934), p. 347.

3. Otto Klineberg, *Race Differences* (New York: Harper and Brothers, 1935), p. 286.

4. Frederick C. Redlich, "The Concept of Health in Psychiatry," in Alexander Leighton, John A. Clausen, and Robert N. Wilson (Eds.), *Explorations in Social Psychiatry* (New York: Basic Books, 1957), pp. 145–146.

5. *See* Irwin D. Rinder, "New Directions and An Old Problem: The Definition of Normality," *Psychiatry* (May, 1964), **27** (2), 107–115.

DISORDERED BEHAVIOR AND SOCIALLY DEVIANT BEHAVIOR

S. Kirson Weinberg

DISORDERED behavior is essentially a result of sustained personal conflict and personality disorganization. Socially deviant behavior is a result of social definitions and social expectations. The extent to which an individual can reorganize his behavior is a criterion of his being ordered or "mentally healthy." But the extent to which an individual fulfills his social roles and abides by the dictates of the group determines the degree to which he is socially normal. Although the psychoses, the severe neuroses, and the acting-out disorders, may usually be defined as socially deviant, the two concepts do not necessarily coincide.

For example, in analyzing the personality structure of four people in a small town, i.e., Plainsville, Kardiner found that though three persons were severely neurotic, they were able to participate in the community and were considered "normal" by the other residents. Although Kardiner claims that "the distinction between normal and neurotic breaks down completely,"[1] it is apparent that the two terms, normal and neurotic, denote distinct dimensions of behavior. From a clinical point of view these three individuals spoken of by Kardiner lacked personal stability. From the viewpoint of social definition they were normal because they were able to participate in the group within the range of the demands of their prescribed roles. Also, it is not known how far they veered from the empirical norm of stability within this particular community.

Many neurotic persons, who are troubled with severe conflicts, conform in their daily relationships and perform the duties of their roles satisfactorily. Some neurotic are more rigorously conformistic than stable persons because they are more easily threatened by self-assertion and more easily disturbed by social disapproval. Indeed, all their behavior is oriented around being socially accepted. Horney has referred to these neurotic persons as the "compliant type" because

they resort to submission as a defense to allay their anxiety.

Fromm claims, however, that in our competitive society many normal persons who are well adapted and who can satisfactorily fulfill their social roles do so at the expense of their individuality. Insofar as they sacrifice what they want to do in order to be well adapted, these normal persons become emotionally crippled. For their compulsive social efficiency deprives them of the kind of self-realization which can make for optimum development and happiness.[2] Fromm maintains that some neurotics, on the other hand, have not completely surrendered their efforts at self-realization and individuality but strive for it through neurotic symptoms and in fantasy life.

People who cling to the letter of the rule are often highly uncertain of themselves and need external props to remain organized. Benedict regards the Puritans of New England, who persecuted others as "witches," as more disturbed than the people they persecuted. Yet they were the normal persons of their society. In fact,

Few prestige groups in any culture have been allowed such complete intellectual and emotional dictatorship as they were. They were the voice of God. Yet to a modern observer it is they, not the confused and tortured women they put to death as witches who were the psychoneurotics of Puritan New England. A sense of guilt as extreme as they portrayed and demanded both in their own conversion experiences and in those of their converts is found in a slightly saner civilization only in institutions for mental diseases.[3]

An extreme example which clearly points up the difference between disorder and abnormality was observed by the writer over a six-months period. This was in a group of psychotic persons in a hopeful ward of a mental hospital. All these persons were disordered and some were severely disordered, and they were, of course, considered abnormal by conventional society. Nevertheless, in the process of collective participation they evolved standards of "normal" and "abnormal" behavior. The patients usually wanted to be

Part of this paper appeared previously in S. Kirson Weinberg, *Society and Personality Disorders* (Englewood Cliffs, N. J.: Prentice-Hall, 1952).

released from the hospital and wanted to improve as a means of being released. Those few patients who claimed that they were content with the hospital or would never recover were considered atypical or abnormal by the other patients and were often avoided by them. This patient group, like any other group, had norms of approved behavior and strived to retain a collective morale. The few patients who disrupted this morale by their complaints were thus considered "deviant." On the other hand, despite their disordered behavior, the patients were able to maintain a simple informal social organization and to create some value judgments within that organization.

Honigman suggests that, while deviance depends upon the situational cultural context and is gauged by the norms of the particular society, psychiatric disorder is universally recognized and discernible by the criteria of specified symptoms, which are culture free. These criteria of disorders, which are presumably universal or at least cross-cultural, include (1) anxiety; (2) phobias, obsessions, and compulsions that represent defenses against anxiety; (3) emotional disorders ranging from mild to serious depression or manic excitement; (4) regressive behavior to the level of the unsocialized or partly socialized child; (5) psychosomatic illnesses, especially sensory and motor dysfunctions; and (6) an inability to perceive or interpret reality, whether it results from trance, senility, or drunkenness. He also included "reality distortion," but, as we have pointed out, this would involve distortion of the consensus within the society. These disorders would also have to be expressed on nonritualized occasions because culturally approved rituals stimulate trance, manic excitement, and regressive behavior, as well as other types of behavior that can be confused with disordered behavior.[4]

PERSONALITY PATTERNS AND THE DYNAMICS OF DISORDERS

Disordered behavior also cannot be judged apart from the cultural context. Sometimes individual behavior in two different cultures may appear alike, but one type may be ordered and the other disordered. We have shown that what appears as hallucinatory or delusional behavior to us may be accepted as socially normal in other cultures. But what personality dynamics distinguish disordered behavior in one culture from seemingly similar but ordered behavior in another culture?

This point can be clarified by comparing the supposed "paranoidal" behavior of the Kwakiutl Indian with the behavior of the individual paranoid in an American urban society.

The motivational emphasis of the Kwakiutl Indians in the Pacific Northwest was bent upon vindication of insult and upon unrestrained self-glorification. This intense emphasis upon personal superiority made the characteristic Kwakiutl Indian unable to tolerate an affront. The opponent had to be avenged, whether by killing him or by outdoing him in an institutionalized ceremony called the Potlatch. In this ceremonial contest the outraged person distributed gifts to his rival but at the same time glorified himself and berated his opponent. Although this unabated drive toward self-glorification and hypersensitivity to insult seems analogous to paranoidal behavior in our society, the two forms of behavior differ markedly.

The Kwakiutl brave learns his behavioral patterns in a normal process of personal development. He responds as others expect him, and even compel him, to respond. He has no alternative but to fulfill his prescribed role. The chieftain, shaman, or whoever else in the tribe engages in these self-glorifying practices can share the viewpoints of the group and can anticipate the censure of the group should he fail. When he does fail by being defeated in a Potlatch contest, or for some other reason, he may become psychotic, commit suicide, or kill his competitor. For example, a shaman was discovered by other members of the tribe to have performed a feat by a trick rather than by his supposedly supernatural powers. He "withdrew and went crazy within the year."

Hence, this behavior of the Kwakiutl brave is socially normal and ordered in his social context because it fulfills the group's expectations. This does not mean that the Kwakiutl necessarily is a stable person; he may be rather unstable. But his seemingly "paranoidal" behavior is distinctly different from the symptoms of the paranoid in our society.

In our society the paranoid does not pursue an approved course of action but is responding to a defensive and distorted outgrowth of an individual conflict.[5] To retain his self-esteem the paranoid has selected individualized slants to the culture and to himself which others do not share. Only by his distorted evaluations can he retain his self-esteem. The paranoid usually violates the role prescribed by society. He is less amenable to self-control and to social control because he cannot share the views of other persons; and in this respect he isolates himself from the group. This criterion of disordered behavior obtains regardless of the institutionalized patterns within the culture. For example, were a Kwakiutl female to claim that she were a male she would probably be disordered. Moreover, the paranoid does not resolve his conflict by his distorted outlook and activities. On the other hand the Kwakiutl Indian, by resorting to the Potlatch or to some other compensatory means, tends to remove the feeling of being insulted and thus has resolved his conflict.

In discussing the disparate conceptions of mental disorders and of social deviance, we pointed out that criteria of normality vary in different cultures. But what cultural determinants contribute to these different degrees of stability and, more specifically, contribute to disordered behavior? Some determinants which may have a direct bearing upon disordered behavior include the following: (1) technology and rapidity of social change, (2) cultural heterogeneity and social contacts, (3) discipline and frustration of "original drives," such as sex, and (4) early mother-child relationships.

Technology and Social Change.

One of the evils frequently blamed for disordered behavior is the increasing complexity and rapid tempo of modern urban civilization. It is believed that, as civilization becomes more complicated, conflicts multiply, and that some persons unavoidably weaken and break down. On the other hand, some investigators maintain that disorders have not increased. Goldhammer and Marshall, in a study of state hospital commitments for Massachusetts from 1840 to 1860 and for the United States as a whole during 1940, found that the rates of commitment did not increase for persons under 50 years of age.[6] The chief question with respect to this inference is whether Massachusetts at that time was less complex than many communities in contemporary United States as a whole. But the investigators leave this question open by positing two alternative conclusions. Either stress factors have not increased during the past century, or, if stress factors have increased, they are not as directly relevant to psychotic breakdowns as had been supposed.[7] It appears, however, that the differences in technological complexity, degree of urbanization and of social change during the two periods are not so great as would be supposed. Massachusetts was somewhat industrialized, prone to rapid social change and urbanization, and had a large influx of immigrants. For a definitive comparison of the effects of technological complexity upon psychotic disorders, a more rural area would have to be considered. Yet a comparative analysis of this type is difficult, because in rural areas mildly psychotic persons can be cared for at home.

The Hollow Folk.

The past discussion pertained mainly to psychotic behavior. But what effects do technological complexity have upon neurotic behavior? The comparative study, by Sherman and Henry, of five communities in the Blue Ridge Mountains of Virginia may be pertinent in this respect because these communities varied in degrees of technological complexity, rapidity of social change, and social discipline.[8] Neuroses were supposedly more frequent in the more technologically complex communities of Oakton and Rigby than in the technologically simple communities of Colvin and Needles. Only 2 children in Colvin and Needles had nervous symptoms, such as nail biting and excessive blinking of the eyelids. In Oakton and Rigby the investigators found 5 neurotic adults in addition to many children who had conflicts of insecurity and inferiority.

To be sure, few persons in Colvin had the nervous symptoms that we find in urban culture, but this does not mean that they were all stable persons and that few were disordered. They may have expressed their conflicts differently. They accepted sexual indulgence, stealing, and lying; they had slight guilt feelings and shallow, emotional relations. In general, they revealed a stunted emotional development.[9] Their conflicts and hostilities would not have been inhibited as in the urban culture, but probably would have been expressed by stealing, lying, sulking, sexual escapades, fighting, and other acting-out activities. Since the authors searched for symptoms that characterize guilt-laden neurotic behavior in the disciplined urban cultures, they obviously found few persons with those symptoms in the technologically simple communities.

Thus we can infer from this particular study that neuroses which reflect inhibitions and which characterize neurotic persons in an urban community increase with cultural and technological complexity and with rapid social change. Or, conversely, we can infer that acting-out disorders which tend to psychopathy decrease with cultural and technological complexity and rapid social change. Inhabitants of simple communities studied were not more stable but expressed their neurotic aberrations differently from persons in more complex communities.

Of course we cannot infer from this study what

degree or type of personal stability pervades other simple societies. In some simple nonliterate societies neuroses are markedly less frequent than in complex industrial societies. For example, Malinowski claimed that among the Trobriands not a single native had hysteria, nervous tics, compulsions, or obsessive notions.

Cultural Heterogeneity and Social Distance.

The marginal individual who is on the limbo or margin of two cultures may experience acute conflicts and feelings of isolation which he may be unable to resolve. In the position of "outcast" his conflicts may become so severe that a neurosis or psychosis could emerge. Warner has shown that some aspiring Negroes who strive to rise into the white "casteline" may become so severely disturbed that a disorder may result.[10]

Specific studies of nonliterate societies have tried to relate cultural heterogeneity and social distance to psychoses. Ellsworth Faris contends that cultural homogeneity and intimate social contacts deter or prevent the rise of psychotic behavior, especially schizophrenia. In his study of the Congo Forest Bantu in equatorial Africa he found that the natives never heard of anyone with schizophrenia or manic depression. He also visited four hospitals in the region and found no psychotics among these groups. He concluded that psychotic disorders in these tribes must be very rare.[11] Faris' conclusions, however, are based upon a search for symptomatic behavior rather than upon the dynamics of psychotic breakdown. In this society psychoses could have been expressed differently from those in Western societies. It is probable that psychotics could have been treated by native doctors and/or cared for by the society rather than committed to mental hospitals.

Such investigators, as Devereux, Seligman, and Carothers (among others), also have claimed that nonliterate groups which have had minimal contacts with Western peoples rarely have psychotic members in their midst.

On the other hand, the same and other investigators, such as Seligman, Dhunjibhoy, Carothers, and Wulf-Sachs,[12] have shown that nonliterate groups which have had persistent contacts with European peoples do have disordered persons in their midst. . . . According to his view, participants in apparently simple nonliterate societies may experience as many conflicts and become as susceptible to neurotic and psychotic disorders as participants in structurally more complicated societies.

Seemingly, the advocates who maintain that cultural heterogeneity and distant social relationships are the bases for an increase in disordered behavior, especially schizophrenia, have provided more evidence than those investigators who maintain that psychoses are universal. But the claims of the former group are not conclusive. Intensive inquiries, by a team of psychiatrists, social psychologists, and anthropologists, of relatively isolated folk peoples who have had minimal contacts with industrialized Western groups might clarify what psychotic breakdowns occur, what forms these psychoses assume and how the group responds to psychotic persons.

Cultural Suppression of "Original Drives."

We have pointed out that all original drives become channelized into attitudes and motives. The basic attitudes which arise from the sex, hunger, or elementation drive may become laden with guilt. It has sometimes been said that the prohibition of sex attitudes may create repressions and conflicts which can contribute to disordered behavior. Hence, the society which prohibits and frustrates the expression of sex attitudes, by associating these expressions with intense guilt, may provide the situations in which such intense conflicts may arise that disordered behavior on a neurotic level may possibly occur.

Although suppression of sexual attitudes may contribute to disordered behavior, unrestricted sexual activity does not necessarily obviate disordered behavior. For example, Linton and Kardiner have shown that the Marquesan women, who are unrestricted sexually, nonetheless experience sexual frustrations because the sexual act is not accompanied by tenderness.[13] In this society men far outnumber the women. The women, as a result, are in the aggressive and dominant position in this area of activity. They initiate the sexual experience, and the men have to please them. Since the women are so completely outnumbered by the men, the men play down their competitiveness for women and, instead, direct their hostility to them. The women, on the other hand, are very competitive in the sexual area. They regard pregnancy as a source of prestige because they place a high value upon children. Consequently, when they experience intense sexual conflicts, one of their neurotic outlets is pretended pregnancy. Thus Marquesan women do experience neurotic conflicts concerning sex despite their unrestricted sexual freedom.

This instance illustrates that social relationships governing the sex drive rather than the sex drive itself contribute to personal stability or personal instability.

Of course, the more fundamental drive of hunger is intimately bound up with personal stability. Those societies which have definite problems in attaining food and no sex problems will have their anxieties centered upon food. For example, the nomadic Siriono of Eastern Bolivia are very permissive in their sexual activities but have difficult food problems.[14] Thus, if a person is ill and loses his appetite, the Siriono consider this a sign of grave illness. When the person does not eat for several days, they regard this as a sure sign that he is going to die. Hence, the sick person never diets when he is ill, even though it hastens his death. This may indicate that their most intense forms of anxiety center around eating.

Mother-Child Relationships.

The Freudians, Neo-Freudians, and some anthropologists have emphasized the influence of early relationships upon personality formation. In their comparative studies of peoples, they have pursued this emphasis. On this basis Margaret Mead, Kardiner, and Linton, among others, have attempted cross-cultural comparisons of personality types.

Kardiner and his associates, in a detailed and systematic inquiry, have maintained that the early mother-child relationships determine the "modal personality" or the characteristic personality of the particular culture. These mother-child relationships, in turn, are influenced by the socioeconomic organization of the group, and when the socioeconomic organization changes,

these mother-child relationships are revised accordingly.[15] The "basic personality" presumably sustains the given culture by its behavior in adulthood.

Fromm has criticized Kardiner's interpretations on the grounds that Kardiner does not analyze mother-child relationships in terms of feeling tones but tends to concentrate upon the constancy and consistency of mother-child relationships and the influence of these relationships upon erogenous-zone development, particularly in feeding and in toilet training.[16] In addition, the difficulty with appraising the method of mother-child relationships in another culture is that the feeling tones in these relationships are not easy to understand and that ethnocentric value judgments can be made. For example, Gorer and LaBarre have inferred that the compulsive behavior among the Japanese is in part a result of the severe toilet training and the overemphasis upon cleanliness.[17] Sikkema, on the other hand, has shown that what appears to be severe toilet training to the Western person does not reflect the mother's feelings to her child because the mother actually feels kindly disposed to the child. In fact, she found no indication of emotional upset in toilet training.[18]

Despite shortcomings of this Neo-Freudian approach, parent-child relationships are important in personality formation. The characteristic early relationships in a particular society may provide significant clues for finding the comparative stability of persons in different societies, provided the stresses of later age-periods are also considered significant.

NOTES

1. Abram Kardiner et al., Psychological Frontiers of Society (New York: Columbia University Press, 1945), p. 378.
2. Erich Fromm, Escape from Freedom (New York: Rinehart, 1941), pp. 138–141.
3. Ruth Benedict, Patterns of Culture (New York: Penguin Books, 1946), p. 255.
4. John J. Honigman, "Toward A Distinction between Psychiatric and Social Abnormality," Social Forces (1953), 31, 274–277; and Jules H. Masserman, Principles of Dynamic Psychiatry (Philadelphia: W. B. Saunders, 1946).
5. Henry J. Wegrocki, "A Critique of Cultural and Statistical Concepts of Abnormality," Journal of Abnormal and Social Psychology (1939), 50, 166–178.
6. Herbert Goldhammer and Andrew W. Marshall, The Frequency of Mental Disease: Long-term Trends and Present Status (Santa Monica, Calif.: The Rand Corporation, 1949).
7. Ibid., p. 50. (Some investigators who have studied shorter time periods and have found increases of mental disorders have attributed the rise to the greater availability of hospital facilities.) See Henry B. Elkind and Maurice Taylor, "The Alleged Increase in the Incidence of the Major Psychoses,"

The American Journal of Psychiatry (1936), XCII, 817–825; "The Epidemiology of Mental Disease: A Preliminary Discussion," The American Journal of Psychiatry (1927), VI, pp. 623–640; Ellen Winston, "The Assumed Increase of Mental Disease," American Journal of Sociology (1935), XL, 427–439. (Other investigators of trend studies believe that there has been an actual increase of psychotic disorders.) See Benjamin Malzberg, Social and Biological Aspects of Mental Disease (Utica, N. Y.: State Hospital Press, 1940), pp. 38–51.
8. Mandel Sherman and Thomas R. Henry, Hollow Folk (New York: Thomas Y. Crowell, 1933).
9. Sherman and Henry, op. cit., p. 298. The apparent decline in emotional complexity may also have reflected the inability of the investigators to reach emotionally and to communicate intimately with adolescents and adults.
10. W. Lloyd Warner, "The Society, the Individual and His Mental Disorders," The American Journal of Psychiatry (1937), 94, 275–284.
11. Ellsworth Faris, "Culture Among the Forest Bantu," The Nature of Human Nature, (New York: McGraw-Hill, 1937), pp. 287–288.
12. Wulf-Sachs, Black Hamlet (Boston: Little Brown, 1947).
13. Abram Kardiner et al., The Individual and His Society New York: Columbia University Press, 1939), pp. 414–416.

14. Allan R. Holmberg, *Nomads of the Long Bow: The Siriono of Eastern Bolivia* (Washington, D.C.: U.S. Government Printing Office, 1950), pp. 86–87.

15. Abram Kardiner *et al.*, *The Individual and His Society* (New York: Columbia University Press, 1939).

16. Fromm maintains that no convincing relationship has been established between the economic organization and mother-child relationships, at least for the Alorese society. In this society the woman works the fields; hence, she has to desert the child two weeks after his birth, but the very fact that she deserts the child does not completely explain her inconsistent teasing and neglect of the child when she returns from the fields. Erich Fromm, "Psychoanalytic Characterology and Its Application to the Understanding of Culture," *Culture and Personality*, edited by S. Stansfeld Sargent and Marian W. Smith (New York: Viking Fund, 1949), p. 4.

17. Geoffrey Gorer, "Themes in Japanese Culture," *Transactions of New York Academy of Science* (1943), 5, pp. 106–124; Weston LaBarre, "Some Observations on Character Structure in the Orient! The Japanese." *Psychiatry* (August 1945), 8:3, 319–342.

18. Mildred Sikkema, "Observations of Japanese Early Child Training," *Personal Character and Cultural Milieu*, compiled by Douglas G. Haring, (Syracuse: Syracuse University Press, 1949), pp. 500–599.

THE MYTH OF MENTAL ILLNESS

Thomas S. Szasz

MY aim in this essay is to raise the question "Is there such a thing as mental illness?" and to argue that there is not. Since the notion of mental illness is extremely widely used nowadays, inquiry into the ways in which this term is employed would seem to be especially indicated. Mental illness, of course, is not literally a "thing"—or physical object—and hence it can "exist" only in the same sort of way in which other theoretical concepts exist. Yet, familiar theories are in the habit of posing, sooner or later—at least to those who come to believe in them—as "objective truths" (or "facts"). During certain historical periods, explanatory conceptions such as deities, witches, and microorganisms appeared not only as theories but as self-evident *causes* of a vast number of events. I submit that today mental illness is widely regarded in a somewhat similar fashion, that is, as the cause of innumerable diverse happenings. As an antidote to the complacent use of the notion of mental illness—whether as a self-evident phenomenon, theory, or cause—let us ask this question: What is meant when it is asserted that someone is mentally ill?

In what follows I shall describe briefly the main uses to which the concept of mental illness has been put. I shall argue that this notion has outlived whatever usefulness it might have had and that it now functions merely as a convenient myth.

MENTAL ILLNESS AS A SIGN OF BRAIN DISEASE

The notion of mental illness derives its main support from such phenomena as syphilis of the brain or delirious conditions—intoxications, for instance—in which persons are known to manifest various peculiarities or disorders of thinking and behavior. Correctly speaking, however, these are diseases of the brain, not of the mind. According to one school of thought, *all* so-called mental illness is of this type. The assumption is made that some neurological defect, perhaps a very subtle one, will ultimately be found for all the disorders of thinking

Reprinted from *American Psychologist* (February, 1960), *15*, 113–118, by permission of the American Psychological Association.

and behavior. Many contemporary psychiatrists, physicians, and other scientists hold this view. This position implies that people *cannot* have troubles—expressed in what are *now called* "mental illnesses"—because of differences in personal needs, opinions, social aspirations, values, and so on. *All problems in living* are attributed to physicochemical processes which in due time will be discovered by medical research.

"Mental illness" are thus regarded as basically no different than all other diseases (that is, of the body). The only difference, in this view, between mental and bodily diseases is that the former, affecting the brain, manifest themselves by means of mental symptoms; whereas the latter, affecting other organ systems (for example, the skin, liver, etc.), manifest themselves by means of symptoms referable to those parts of the body. This view rests on and expresses what are, in my opinion, two fundamental errors.

In the first place, what central nervous system symptoms would correspond to a skin eruption or a fracture? It would *not* be some emotion or complex bit of behavior. Rather, it would be blindness or a paralysis of some part of the body. The crux of the matter is that a disease of the brain, analogous to a disease of the skin or bone, is a neurological defect, and not a problem in living. For example, a *defect* in a person's visual field may be satisfactorily explained by correlating it with certain definite lesions in the nervous system. On the other hand, a person's *belief*—whether this be a belief in Christianity, in Communism, or in the idea that his internal organs are "rotting" and that his body is, in fact, already "dead"—cannot be explained by a defect or disease of the nervous system. Explanations of this sort of occurrence—assuming that one is interested in the belief itself and does not regard it simply as a "symptom" or expression of something else that is *more interesting*—must be sought along different lines.

The second error in regarding complex psychosocial behavior, consisting of communications about ourselves and the world about us, as mere symptoms of neurological functioning is *epistemological*. In other words, it is an error pertaining not to any mistakes in observation or reasoning, as such, but rather to the way in which we organize and express our knowledge. In the present case, the error lies in making a symmetrical dualism between mental and physical (or bodily) symptoms, a dualism which is merely a habit of speech and to which no known observations can be found to correspond. Let us see if this is so. In medical practice, when we speak of physical disturbances, we mean either signs (for example, a fever) or symptoms (for example, pain). We speak of mental symptoms, on the other hand, when we refer to a patient's *communications about himself, others, and the world about him.* He might state that he is Napoleon or that he is being persecuted by the Communists. These would be considered mental symptoms *only* if the observer believed that the patient was *not* Napoleon or that he was *not* being persecuted by the Communists. This makes it apparent that the statement that "*X* is a mental symptom" involves rendering a judgment. The judgment entails, moreover, a covert comparison or matching of the patient's ideas, concepts, or beliefs with those of the observer and the society in which they live. The notion of mental symptom is therefore inextricably tied to the *social* (including *ethical*) *context* in which it is made in much the same way as the notion of bodily symptom is tied to an *anatomical* and *genetic context* (Szasz, 1957a, 1957b).

To sum up what has been said thus far: I have tried to show that for those who regard mental symptoms as signs of brain disease, the concept of mental illness is unnecessary and misleading. For what they mean is that people so labeled suffer from diseases of the brain; and, if that is what they mean, it would seem better for the sake of clarity to say that and not something else.

MENTAL ILLNESS AS A NAME FOR PROBLEMS IN LIVING

The term "mental illness" is widely used to describe something which is very different than a disease of the brain. Many people today take it for granted that living is an arduous process. Its hardship for modern man, moreover, derives not so much from a struggle for biological survival as from the stresses and strains inherent in the social intercourse of complex human personalities. In this context, the notion of mental illness is used to identify or describe some feature of an individual's so-called personality. Mental illness—as a deformity of the personality, so to speak—is then regarded as the *cause* of the human disharmony. It

is implicit in this view that social intercourse between people is regarded as something *inherently harmonious*, its disturbance being due solely to the presence of "mental illness" in many people. This is obviously fallacious reasoning, for it makes the abstraction "mental illness" into a *cause*, even though this abstraction was created in the first place to serve only as a shorthand expression for certain types of human behavior. It now becomes necessary to ask: "What kinds of behavior are regarded as indicative of mental illness, and by whom?"

The concept of illness, whether bodily or mental, implies *deviation from some clearly defined norm.* In the case of physical illness, the norm is the structural and functional integrity of the human body. Thus, although the desirability of physical health, as such, is an ethical value, what health *is* can be stated in anatomical and physiological terms. What is the norm deviation from which is regarded as mental illness? This question cannot be easily answered. But whatever this norm might be, we can be certain of only one thing: namely, that it is a norm that must be stated in terms of *psychosocial, ethical,* and *legal* concepts. For example, notions such as "excessive repression" or "acting out an unconscious impulse" illustrate the use of psychological concepts for judging (so-called) mental health and illness. The idea that chronic hostility, vengefulness, or divorce are indicative of mental illness would be illustrations of the use of ethical norms (that is, the desirability of love, kindness, and a stable marriage relationship). Finally, the widespread psychiatric opinion that only a mentally ill person would commit homicide illustrates the use of a legal concept as a norm of mental health. The norm from which deviation is measured whenever one speaks of a mental illness is a *psychosocial and ethical one.* Yet, the remedy is sought in terms of *medical* measures which—it is hoped and assumed—are free from wide differences of ethical value. The definition of the disorder and the terms in which its remedy are sought are therefore at serious odds with one another. The practical significance of this covert conflict between the alleged nature of the defect and the remedy can hardly be exaggerated.

Having identified the norms used to measure deviations in cases of mental illness, we will now turn to the question: "Who defines the norms and hence the deviation?" Two basic answers may be offered: (*a*) It may be the person himself (that is, the patient) who decides that he deviates from a norm. For example, an artist may believe that he suffers from a work inhibition; and he may implement this conclusion by seeking help *for* himself from a psychotherapist. (*b*) It may be someone other than the patient who decides that the latter is deviant (for example, relatives, physicians, legal authorities, society generally, etc.). In such a case a psychiatrist may be hired by others to do something *to* the patient in order to correct the deviation.

These considerations underscore the importance of asking the question "Whose agent is the psychiatrist?" and of giving a candid answer to it (Szasz, 1956, 1958). The psychiatrist (psychologist or nonmedical psychotherapist), it now develops, may be the agent of the patient, of the relatives, of the school, of the military services, of a business organization, of a court of law, and so forth. In speaking of the psychiatrist as the agent of these persons or organizations, it is not implied that his values concerning norms, or his ideas and aims concerning the proper nature of remedial action, need to coincide exactly with those of his employer. For example, a patient in individual psychotherapy may believe that his salvation lies in a new marriage; his psychotherapist need not share this hypothesis. As the patient's agent, however, he must abstain from bringing social or legal force to bear on the patient which would prevent him from putting his beliefs into action. If his *contract* is with the patient, the psychiatrist (psychotherapist) may disagree with him or stop his treatment; but he cannot engage others to obstruct the patient's aspirations. Similarly, if a psychiatrist is engaged by a court to determine the sanity of a criminal, he need not fully share the legal authorities' values and intentions in regard to the criminal and the means available for dealing with him. But the psychiatrist is expressly barred from stating, for example, that it is not the criminal who is "insane" but the men who wrote the law on the basis of which the very actions that are being judged are regarded as "criminal." Such an opinion could be voiced, of course, but not in a courtroom, and not by a psychiatrist who makes it his practice to assist the court in performing its daily work.

To recapitulate: In actual contemporary social usage, the finding of a mental illness is made by establishing a deviance in behavior from certain psychosocial, ethical, or legal norms. The judgment may be made, as in medicine, by the patient, the physician (psychiatrist), or others. Remedial action, finally, tends to be sought in a therapeutic— or covertly medical—framework, thus creating a situation in which *psychosocial, ethical*, and/or *legal deviations* are claimed to be correctible by (so-called) *medical action*. Since medical action is designed to correct only medical deviations, it seems logically absurd to expect that it will help solve problems whose very existence had been defined and established on nonmedical grounds. I think that these considerations may be fruitfully applied to the present use of tranquilizers and, more generally, to what might be expected of drugs of whatever type in regard to the amelioration or solution of problems in human living.

THE ROLE OF ETHICS IN PSYCHIATRY

Anything that people *do*—in contrast to things that *happen* to them (Peters, 1958)—takes place in a context of value. In this broad sense, no human activity is devoid of ethical implications. When the values underlying certain activities are widely shared, those who participate in their pursuit may lose sight of them altogether. The discipline of medicine, both as a pure science (for example, research) and as a technology (for example, therapy), contains many ethical considerations and judgments. Unfortunately, these are often denied, minimized, or merely kept out of focus; for the ideal of the medical profession as well as of the people whom it serves seems to be having a system of medicine (allegedly) free of ethical value. This sentimental notion is expressed by such things as the doctor's willingness to treat and help patients irrespective of their religious or political beliefs, whether they are rich or poor, etc. While there may be some grounds for this belief—albeit it is a view that is not impressively true even in these regards— the fact remains that ethical considerations encompass a vast range of human affairs. By making the practice of medicine neutral in regard to some specific issues of value need not, and cannot, mean that it can be kept free from all such values. The practice of medicine is intimately tied to ethics; and the first thing that we must do, it seems to me, is to try to make this clear and explicit. I shall let this matter rest here, for it does not concern us specifically in this essay. Lest there be any vagueness, however, about how or where ethics and medicine meet, let me remind the reader of such issues as birth control, abortion, suicide, and euthanasia as only a few of the major areas of current ethicomedical controversy.

Psychiatry, I submit, is very much more intimately tied to problems of ethics than is medicine. I use the word "psychiatry" here to refer to that contemporary discipline which is concerned with *problems in living* (and not with diseases of the brain, which are problems for neurology).

Problems in human relations can be analyzed, interpreted, and given meaning only within given social and ethical contexts. Accordingly, it *does* make a difference—arguments to the contrary notwithstanding—what the psychiatrist's socio-ethical orientations happen to be; for these will influence his ideas on what is wrong with the patient, what deserves comment or interpretation, in what possible directions change might be desirable, and so forth. Even in medicine proper, these factors play a role, as for instance, in the divergent orientations which physicians, depending on their religious affiliations, have toward such things as birth control and therapeutic abortion. Can anyone really believe that a psychotherapist's ideas concerning religious belief, slavery, or other similar issues play no role in his practical work? If they do make a difference, what are we to infer from it? Does it not seem reasonable that we ought to have different psychiatric therapies—each expressly recognized for the ethical positions which they embody—for, say, Catholics and Jews, religious persons and agnostics, democrats and communists, white supremacists and Negroes, and so on? Indeed, if we look at how psychiatry is actually practiced today (especially in the United States), we find that people do seek psychiatric help in accordance with their social status and ethical beliefs (Hollingshead and Redlich, 1958). This should really not surprise us more than being told that practicing Catholics rarely frequent birth control clinics.

The foregoing position which holds that contemporary psychotherapists deal with problems in living, rather than with mental illnesses and their cures, stands in opposition to a currently prevalent claim, according to which mental illness is just as "real" and "objective" as bodily illness. This is a confusing claim since it is never known exactly what is meant by such words as "real" and "objective." I suspect, however, that what is intended by the proponents of this view is to create the idea in the popular mind that mental illness is some sort of disease entity, like an infection or a malignancy. If this were true, one could *catch* or *get* a "mental illness," one might *have* or *harbor* it, one might *transmit* it to others, and finally one could get *rid* of it. In my opinion, there is not a shred of evidence to support this idea. To the contrary, all the evidence is the other way and supports the view that what people now call mental illnesses are for the most part *communications* expressing unacceptable ideas, often framed, moreover, in an unusual idiom. The scope of this essay allows me to do no more than mention this

alternative theoretical approach to this problem (Szasz, 1957c).

This is not the place to consider in detail the similarities and differences between bodily and mental illnesses. It shall suffice for us here to emphasize only one important difference between them: namely, that whereas bodily disease refers to public, physicochemical occurrences, the notion of mental illness is used to codify relatively more private, sociopsychological happenings of which the observer (diagnostician) forms a part. In other words, the psychiatrist does not stand *apart* from what he observes, but is, in Harry Stack Sullivan's apt words, a "participant observer." This means that he is *committed* to some picture of what he considers reality—and to what he thinks society considers reality—and he observes and judges the patient's behavior in the light of these considerations. This touches on our earlier observation that the notion of mental symptom itself implies a comparison between observer and observed, psychiatrist and patient. This is so obvious that I may be charged with belaboring trivialities. Let me therefore say once more that my aim in presenting this argument was expressly to criticize and counter a prevailing contemporary tendency to deny the moral aspects of psychiatry (and psychotherapy) and to substitute for them allegedly value-free medical considerations. Psychotherapy, for example, is being widely practiced as though it entailed nothing other than restoring the patient from a state of mental sickness to one of mental health. While it is generally accepted that mental illness has something to do with man's social (or interpersonal) relations, it is paradoxically maintained that problems of values (that is, of ethics) do not arise in this process.[1] Yet, in one sense, much of psychotherapy may revolve around nothing other than the elucidation and weighing of goals and values—many of which may be mutually contradictory—and the means whereby they might best be harmonized, realized, or relinquished.

The diversity of human values and the methods by means of which they may be realized is so vast, and many of them remain so unacknowledged, that they cannot fail but lead to conflicts in human relations. Indeed, to say that human relations at all levels—from mother to child, through husband and wife, to nation and nation—are fraught with stress, strain, and disharmony is, once again, making the obvious explicit. Yet, what may be obvious may be also poorly understood. This I think is the case here. For it seems to me that—at least in our scientific theories of behavior—we have failed to *accept* the simple fact that human relations are inherently fraught with difficulties and that to make them even relatively harmonious requires much patience and hard work. I submit that the idea of mental illness is now being put to work to obscure certain difficulties which at present may be inherent—not that they need be unmodifiable—in the social intercourse of persons. If this is true, the concept functions as a disguise; for instead of calling attention to conflicting human needs, aspirations, and values, the notion of mental illness provides an amoral and impersonal "thing" (an "illness") as an explanation for *problems in living* (Szasz, 1959). We may recall in this connection that not so long ago it was devils and witches who were held responsible for men's problems in social living. The belief in mental illness, as something other than man's trouble in getting along with his fellow man, is the proper heir to the belief in demonology and witchcraft. Mental illness exists or is "real" in exactly the same sense in which witches existed or were "real."

CHOICE, RESPONSIBILITY, AND PSYCHIATRY

While I have argued that mental illnesses do not exist, I obviously did not imply that the social and psychological occurrences to which this label is currently being attached also do not exist. Like the personal and social troubles which people had in the Middle Ages, they are real enough. It is the labels we give them that concerns us and, having labelled them, what we do about them. While I cannot go into the ramified implications of this problem here, it is worth noting that a demonologic conception of problems in living gave rise to therapy along theological lines. Today, a belief in mental illness implies—nay, requires—therapy along medical or psychotherapeutic lines.

What is implied in the line of thought set forth here is something quite different. I do not intend to offer a new conception of "psychiatric illness" nor a new form of "therapy." My aim is more modest and yet also more ambitious. It is to suggest that the phenomena now called mental illnesses be looked at afresh and more simply, that they be removed from the category of illnesses, and that they be regarded as the expressions of man's struggle with the problem of *how* he should live. The last mentioned problem is obviously a vast one, its enormity reflecting not only man's inability to cope with his environment, but even more his increasing self-reflectiveness.

By problems in living, then, I refer to that truly explosive chain reaction which began with man's fall from divine grace by partaking of the fruit of the tree of knowledge. Man's awareness of himself and of the world about him seems to be a steadily expanding one, bringing in its wake an ever larger *burden of understanding* (an expression borrowed from Susanne Langer, 1953). *This burden*, then, *is to be expected and must not be misinterpreted.* Our only *rational* means for lightening it is *more understanding*, and appropriate *action* based on such understanding. The main alternative lies in acting as though the burden were not what in fact we perceive it to be and taking refuge in an outmoded theological view of man. In the latter view, man does not fashion his life and much of his world about him, but merely lives out his fate in a world created by superior beings. This may logically lead to pleading nonresponsibility in the face of seemingly unfathomable problems and difficulties. Yet, if man fails to take increasing responsibility for his actions, individually as well as collectively, it seems unlikely that some higher power or being would assume this task and carry this burden for him. Moreover, this seems hardly the proper time in human history for obscuring the issue of man's responsibility for his actions by hiding it behind the skirt of an all-explaining conception of mental illness.

CONCLUSIONS

I have tried to show that the notion of mental illness has outlived whatever usefulness it might have had and that it now functions merely as a convenient myth. As such, it is a true heir to religious myths in general, and to the belief in witchcraft in particular; the role of all these belief-systems was to act as *social tranquilizers*, thus encouraging the hope that mastery of certain specific problems may be achieved by means of substitutive (symbolic-magical) operations. The notion of mental illness thus serves mainly to obscure the everyday fact that life for most people is a continuous struggle, not for biological survival, but for a "place in the sun," "peace of mind," or some other human value. For man aware of himself and of the world about him, once the needs for preserving the body (and perhaps the race) are more or less satisfied, the problem arises as to what he should do with himself. Sustained adherence to the myth of mental illness allows people to avoid facing this problem, believing that mental health, conceived as the absence of mental illness, automatically insures the making of right and safe choices in one's conduct of life. But the facts are all the other way. It is the making of good choices in life that others regard, retrospectively, as good mental health!

The myth of mental illness encourages us, moreover, to believe in its logical corollary: that social intercourse would be harmonious, satisfying, and the secure basis of a "good life" were it not for the disrupting influences of mental illness or "psychopathology." The potentiality for universal human happiness, in this form at least, seems to me but another example of the I-wish-it-were-true type of fantasy. I do believe that human happiness or well-being on a hitherto unimaginably large scale, and not just for a select few, is possible. This, goal could be achieved, however, only at the cost of many men, and not just a few being willing and able to tackle their personal, social, and ethical conflicts. This means having the courage and

integrity to forego waging battles on false fronts, finding solutions for substitute problems—for instance, fighting the battle of stomach acid and chronic fatigue instead of facing up to a marital conflict.

Our adversaries are not demons, witches, fate, or mental illness. We have no enemy whom we can fight, exorcise, or dispel by "cure." What we do have are *problems in living*—whether these be biologic, economic, political, or sociopsychological. In this essay I was concerned only with problems belonging in the last mentioned category, and within this group mainly with those pertaining to moral values. The field to which modern psychiatry addresses itself is vast, and I made no effort to encompass it all. My argument was limited to the proposition that mental illness is a myth, whose function it is to disguise and thus render more palatable the bitter pill of moral conflicts in human relations.

NOTES

1. Freud went so far as to say that: "I consider ethics to be taken for granted. Actually I have never done a mean thing" (Jones, 1957, p. 247). This surely is a strange thing to say for someone who has studied man as a social being as closely as did Freud. I mention it here to show how the notion of "illness" (in the case of psychoanalysis, "psychopathology," or "mental illness") was used by Freud—and by most of his followers—as a means for classifying certain forms of human behavior as falling within the scope of medicine, and hence (by *fiat*) outside that of ethics!

REFERENCES

Hollingshead, A. B., & Redlich, F. C. *Social class and mental illness*. New York: Wiley, 1958.

Jones, E. *The life and work of Sigmund Freud*. Vol. III. New York: Basic Books, 1957.

Langer, S. K. *Philosophy in a new key*. New York: Mentor Books, 1953.

Peters, R. S. *The concept of motivation*. London: Routledge & Kegan Paul, 1958.

Szasz, T. S. Malingering: "Diagnosis" or social condemnation? *AMA Arch Neurol. Psychiat.*, 1956, 76, 432–443.

Szasz, T. S. *Pain and pleasure: A study of bodily feelings*. New York: Basic Books, 1957. (a)

Szasz, T. S. The problem of psychiatric nosology: A contribution to a situational analysis of psychiatric operations. *Amer. J. Psychiat.*, 1957, 114, 405–413. (b)

Szasz, T. S. On the theory of psychoanalytic treatment. *Int. J. Psycho-Anal.*, 1957, 38, 166–182. (c)

Szasz, T. S. Psychiatry, ethics and the criminal law. *Columbia law Rev.*, 1958, 58, 183–198.

Szasz, T. S. Moral conflict and psychiatry, *Yale Rev.*, 1959, in press.

AN OVERVIEW OF THE PUBLIC CONCEPTION OF MENTAL HEALTH

Jum C. Nunnally, Jr.

IN studying what the public knows and thinks about mental-health problems, we could foresee only two possible results: (1) the public is *misinformed*, in the sense that the "average man" holds numerous misconceptions about mental illness, or (2) the public is *uninformed*, in the sense that the average man has little information, correct or incorrect, about many of the problems. It was, and is, inconceivable to us that the average man could be *well informed*. If he were, it would present a curious paradox: because so much is yet to be discovered, even psychologists and psychiatrists are not well informed in the absolute sense.

Our results show clearly that the average man is not grossly misinformed. That is, it is difficult to document specific misconceptions which are widely held by the public. Consequently, the major job in future communication programs will be to fill in the voids where people are uninformed.

Partially because of the anxiety associated with mental-health topics and partially because of the lack of semantic referents for his terms (for example, "neurotic"), the average man does not systematically learn about mental-health phenomena from daily experience. What information he has exists largely as an abstract system. Although the average man swims in a sea of mental-health phenomena, he usually does not catalogue them as such. Consequently, the abstract system is neither confirmed nor denied.

The average man is relatively unsure of his opinions about mental-health phenomena. Consequently, he eagerly looks to experts for "the answers." We found that people do not resist new information, even when that information is plainly incorrect. In general, we found that people will accept almost any seemingly factual and authoritative-sounding information on mental health.

Reprinted from *Popular Conceptions of Mental Health* (New York: Holt, Rinehart, and Winston, 1961), pp. 232–238, by permission.

Attitudes

It is commonly asserted that people attach a stigma to the mentally ill. Our research results leave little doubt that the stigma exists. The most important finding from our studies of public attitudes is that the stigma is very general, both across social groups and across attitude indicators. There is a strong "negative halo" associated with the mentally ill. They are considered, unselectively, as being all things "bad". Some of the "bad" attitudes that people have toward the mentally ill are partially supported by the facts—for example, the mentally ill sometimes *are* unpredictable and dangerous. However, the average man generalizes to the point of considering the mentally ill as dirty, unintelligent, insincere, and worthless. Such unselectively negative attitudes are probably due in part to a lack of information about mental illness and a failure to observe and learn about mental-illness phenomena in daily life.

Our research suggests some of the dynamics of public attitudes toward the mentally ill. One of the cornerstones of public attitudes is the feeling that the mentally ill are highly unpredictable. The mentally ill are thought to be people who do not go by the "rules" and who, because of their erratic behavior, may suddenly embarrass or endanger others. The feeling is like that of sitting next to a temperamental explosive which may detonate without warning. Consequently, most people are very uncomfortable in the presence of someone who is, or is purported to be, mentally ill.

Public attitudes toward psychologists, psychiatrists, and other mental-treatment specialists are evidently not as "bad" as is commonly suspected. The public holds moderately high, favorable attitudes toward mental specialists *as individuals*. What is "wrong" with public attitudes is a moderate distrust and devaluing off mental-treatment methods and institutions. Consequently, the emphasis in information programs should be on improving attitudes toward the tools and methods used by mental specialists.

Interests

Public interest in mental-health topics varies considerably with the topic and with the way in which the topic is treated in communications. Most of the interest is not due to intellectual curiosity, as it is, for example, with information about space flight. Instead, the interest is motivated by a somewhat panicky "need to know." The public is mainly interested in information about mental health of a kind that will relieve immediate personal threats. The public will reject (e.g. not continue to read) messages that raise anxiety and do not supply "solutions." One of the difficulties in preparing a program of public information is designing messages that contain reasonably simple facts about mental-health phenomena and how-to-do-it rules for handling problems; but this is what the public wants.

THE EXPERTS

If experts had a more definitive body of knowledge about mental-health problems, and if they could agree on particular points, the job of communicating with the public would be immensely simplified. We found reasonably good agreement among experts about some things that should be said in a program of public information about mental-health problems. In our studies, however, we dealt only with the relatively narrow range of ideas with which the public is presently familiar. What is needed now is to determine what *new* things can be told to the public. One approach to this problem would be to ask psychiatrists and psychologists to compile a list of facts, or near-facts, that can be communicated to the public about the causes, symptoms, treatment, and social effects of mental-health problems. Such a list might provide many new things to tell the public, or it might prove to be embarrassingly short.

General practitioners of medicine play an important role in the treatment of mental-health problems. They act as "gatekeepers" between the public and the mental specialists. It is often the general practitioner who determines whether or not a patient sees a mental specialist, and if so, what type of specialist he consults. Equally important as the number of referrals that they make are the number of mental cases that general practitioners treat themselves. It remains to be determined what kinds of cases general practitioners treat and what kinds of treatment they give. One of our most important findings was that the younger, better-informed physicians tend to have "better" attitudes toward mental patients; and it is this type of general practitioner who is more likely to treat mental problems instead of referring them to mental specialists.

If the average man uncritically accepted the information contained and implied in mass-media presentations, he would indeed be misinformed. In those cases where media presentations are specifically designed to enlighten the public and where expert advice and cooperation are available, the results are often quite good. Such presentations, however, comprise only a minute proportion of the total "information" relating to mental-health phenomena carried by the media. Most of the information is obliquely woven into dramatic presentations, for example, the suggestion that a healthy person can be driven insane after a rather short exposure to a frustrating or frightening situation.

Evidently, presentations of mental-health problems in the mass media have been stylized to fit the requirements of fiction and drama. The symptoms of mental illness are exaggerated, the causes and treatment are greatly oversimplified and often erroneous, and mental illness usually appears in a context of "horror," sin, and violence. The "cognitive," or informational, implications of such presentations are either so amorphous and contradictory, or so obviously incorrect, that the average man is not particularly affected—he knows better. The affective, or attitudinal, implications may be strong, however, because they closely match the attitudes that the public holds toward the mentally ill.

Mass-media personnel are not to be "blamed" for the nature of presentations relating to mental-health problems. Their primary business is not to educate the public but to entertain, in the broad sense of the word, and that must be done at a profit. Because of the subtle way in which mental-health "information" is woven into programs, and because of the many hands that shape such presentations, even if the media tried to "control" they would find it very difficult. When media personnel try to promote "better" presentations, they often obtain confusing and contradictory advice from mental experts, and the experts are often loathe to cooperate.

We are not sure what should, or could, be done to utilize more effectively the mass media in programs of mental-health information. Because of the faddism that dominates the media, it is doubtful that any sustained drive will be exerted by the media personnel unless they are encouraged and helped by professional societies and other organizations concerned with mental-health problems. We did come up with one solution, though half in jest: Some organization might finance a "good" soap opera, to be produced co-operatively by experts and media personnel and specifically intended to enlighten the public about mental-health problems as well as to be entertaining. Many such programs, in forms suitable to the different media, might go a long way toward providing the public with better information and developing better attitudes toward mental-health phenomena.

The Topic

The topic itself constitutes an important variable in selecting communication strategies. Thus, very different strategies might be needed in order to communicate about labor-management relations than about mental illness. This does not mean that no general science of communication is possible and that communication strategy is chaotically dependent on particular topics. Communication strategy in general consists of promoting interest, satisfying human needs, providing desired information, verbal conditioning, and so on. Before strategies for communicating about a particular topic can be established, it is necessary to determine where that topic presently resides in a nexus of psychological variables. For example, does information about the particular topic supply a pertinent human need? In this section will be summarized some research results which serve to index mental-health information in terms of its communicative properties.

Some of the points relating to this section were mentioned in earlier sections of this chapter. To reiterate: (1) People know very little, and are unsure of what they think; (2) people want to obtain more information about mental health, but their interest is largely restricted to learning ways to meet or avoid threatening situations; (3) people do not systematically gather information from their daily experiences or do not catalogue their experiences as pertaining to mental health; and (4) people want authoritative answers but seldom get them from mass-media presentations, nor do they obtain "closure" from what the experts say.

Another important feature of mental-health topics is that they tend to generate anxiety. People are uneasy when they hear or read about emotional disturbance, neurosis, mental hospitals, hallucinations, psychotherapy, and many other related matters. The reduction of that anxiety is a primary

route to increasing public interest and promoting favorable attitudes.

Mental-health topics are beset by a "language" problem. In Chapter 11 were presented some research results which indicate that a number of things are "wrong" with the available terminology: (1) there is a shortage of terms, (2) the terms bear strong negative connotations, and (3) the terms suggest misleading explanations of mental-health phenomena. These "language" problems limit the effectiveness of some communication strategies. For example, in our experiments we found it nearly impossible to promote more favorable attitudes toward the concept *insane men*. When we translated the term to *mental-hospital patient*, however, we obtained favorable changes in attitudes. Until more is done to develop a suitable terminology, it will be very difficult to undertake effective large-scale programs of public information. We need a lexicon for communicating about mental-health problems, one that is based on agreement among experts and on research evidence concerning the suitability of particular terms.

Information Transmission

Apparently it is very easy to get people to accept new facts about mental-health problems. People will gobble up any seemingly factual and authoritative-sounding information. Indeed, we were surprised to learn the extent to which explanations could be oversimplified and distorted, and still accepted as true. Among high-school students in psychology courses, we were surprised to find huge changes in information (expressed opinions) during the semester. Consequently, for the purpose of transmitting new information, strategy is not an important consideration. In that case, strategy largely concerns rhetorical skill, journalistic niceties, and the maintainance of interest. However, the type of information given to people will very much affect the *attitudes* that they hold, and, consequently, the choice of information to communicate becomes an important aspect of attitude-change strategy.

Attitude Change

In many communication experiments, the effort is to *convince* people to hold opinions (information) that are different from those which they held initially. As was said above, there is little difficulty in convincing people to hold new ideas in the mental-health domain. The widespread "bad" attitudes are not held *because* of existing information, but rather because of the *lack* of it. Early in our research, we hypothesized that to relieve the threat associated with mental-health problems the important ingredient is for people to *think* that they have a valid system of information regardless of its real validity. Our research results tended to bear out this hypothesis. We found that the mere act of *changing* from one set of opinions to another (scrambling information) promoted favorable attitudes toward the mentally ill and toward treatment specialists and methods. This was so even though the new "information" was in many cases less correct than what had been believed initially. Although we do not know how long people can be "fooled" in this way, the results illustrate the comfort that people obtain from having, or thinking they have, mental armament against anxiety-provoking problems.

It should not be implied that *any* communication will have the desired effect. Messages must actually contain information—understandable statements about factual or potentially factual matters. According to this definition, many messages contain little or no information. Instead, they (1) say little that people can understand, (2) ask questions rather than give answers, (3) "destroy" what information people have rather than provide new information, or (4) make exhortative appeals for people to develop better attitudes. Even if messages actually do contain information, that information must have certain optimum properties before it will produce the desired effect. It should usually be related to some problem-solving aspect of mental health. That is, it should help people in some way to cope with mental-health problems. Much of the information currently given to the public does not serve that function; for example, telling people that half the hospital beds in this country are filled with mental patients raises anxiety but does not help them to deal with the problem.

In toto our studies show that the factual content of messages is important largely to the extent that it induces a proper *emotional state*. A message will promote favorable attitudes toward mental-health concepts if (1) the concepts are visible in the message (directly mentioned) or associated with visible concepts (generalization), (2) the message has a high interest-value, (3) the message is thought to come from an authoritative source (e.g., a university or a psychiatrist), and (4) the message makes the reader feel *secure* by sounding certain, by providing solutions, by presenting an understandable explanation, and by reducing anxiety in other ways. If these content characteristics are present, people will develop more favorable attitudes and will be more open to continued learning about mental-health phenomena. If these characteristics are not present, no amount of sermonizing, haranguing, or factual presentation will work; and it would be better not to communicate at all.

THE COMMITMENT OF PATIENTS TO THE

MENTAL HOSPITAL

S. Kirson Weinberg

BECOMING a patient in a state mental hospital represents the final step of a commitment process and varies in different states. In general, the historic issue in commitment has been between safeguarding the patient's civil liberties and protecting the community from possible danger. It has also involved the problem whether the potential patient is receiving an adequate diagnostic examination. Since a normal person conceivably can be "railroaded" into the mental hospital by scheming relatives and a compliant psychiatrist, the state frequently requires a court order for commitment. Some psychiatrists object to this legal step because, they claim, it resembles criminal proceedings and changes a medical procedure into a legal affair. Jurists and others sensitive to civil liberties regard court proceedings as a necessary means to protect the patient's rights.

The movement for legal protection of the legally insane received its momentum during the mid-nineteenth century. In Philadelphia in 1849, a suit was brought by a patient, Hinchman, who had been placed in the Friends' Asylum for the Insane at Frankford. The evidence presumably showed that "he was violently and dangerously insane." He sued everyone connected with his commitment, from his mother to a passing traveler, and obtained heavy damages.

From this case the common law concerning commitment had apparently not been clarified. During the 1860's and 1870's two other events influenced subsequent legislation. One was the sensational and widely read novel *Hard Cash*, by Charles Reade which dealt with the commitment of a sane young man to a private asylum by the intrigues of his business associates, who tried to get his fortune.[2]

The other was the reaction to the commitment of Mrs E. P. W. Packard to the Illinois State Hospital at Jacksonville by Rev. T. Packard, her husband. The hospitalization sparked a crusade. She remained in the hospital for three years. When

Written for this volume.

discharged, she claimed that she had always been sane and that her husband had willfully committed her to a mental hospital. She vigorously pursued her crusade for enacting suitable legislation. She published books on her own "railroading" and went from state to state to address public meetings and legislative bodies. As a result, she influenced the passage of new commitment laws in Illinois, Massachusetts, and Iowa and affected the enactment of new laws in other states. In Illinois and Iowa, her "personal liberty bills" provided that a person could be committed only by a jury trial. In Massachusetts, a number of the patient's nearest relatives had to be notified by the hospital superintendent within two days of the patient's commitment. Thus hasty and secret schemes by one relative would become more difficult. Though failing at the time to have similar laws passed in other states, she influenced the passage of new commitment laws in later years.[3]

At the present time, depending upon the state, a person can be committed by a court order based upon: (1) the findings of an "insanity" commission, (2) the findings of one or more medical examiners, (3) a jury trial, and (4) by an "insanity" commission with lawfully endowed judicial authority.[4]

The specific steps in commitment include (1) a petition or an application for commitment of the designated "insane" person that has been sworn to and filed with the recognized authority, (2) a notice that must be served on the person presumed to be disordered, (3) a certificate of insanity signed by one or more physicians, (4) a hearing by a legally designated appropriate body, whether a court of record or a commission, and (5) a commitment order handed down by an appropriate body, which authorizes the admission of the person into a mental hospital of permanent care.[5]

Good intentions, however, do not always fulfill their expected purposes. The open jury trials of disordered persons, especially in small towns, can humiliate and stigmatize the person. Legal proceedings can create the impression to the disordered person that he has done something wrong and is being "tried" for it. An association of ex-patients in Illinois who vigorously opposed these legal proceedings wrote:[6]

It is now about a year and a half since I broke down. I had what the physicians called a depression. I was weary and tired and slow in action and thought. But withal I understood what went on around me. And when the physician who was called mentioned an "institution" I knew what he meant. I remember how my mother shrank when the word was spoken and how emphatic she refused to consider the proposal. "Institution" meant commitment and court procedure, and my mother was determined that I, her daughter, was not to be stigmatized by the court.[6]

The mother's attitude illustrates that some persons are affected adversely by legal proceedings. On the other hand, one patient threatened to sue a psychiatrist because he committed her to a hospital without legal authority.[7]

Some states have tried to steer a middle course in which the person's civil liberties would be protected while he would not be stigmatized. The temporary care hospitals, "emergency" and tentative commitments, and voluntary admissions are some means toward this middle course. Persons allegedly psychotic can be committed for observation to the temporary care hospital or even to some state hospitals for less than thirty days. Some states permit commitment of patients for a period of ten to thirty days when these persons are violent and potentially harmful. Legal involvements are thus eliminated and the patient is considered a a medical case. In Illinois these voluntary and court-order commitments represented 54.87 per cent and 30.76 per cent respectively. The percentage of voluntary admissions predominated over all other admissions combined.[8]

TABLE 1. Type of Admission to State Mental Health Facilities in Illinois*

Type of Admission	January to June 1965		June to December 1964	
	Number	Percentage (N = 5,546)	Number	Percentage (N = 4,911)
Informal	68	1.23	13	.26
Certified by Physician	417	7.52	524	10.67
Emergency	284	5.12	140	2.85
Needs Mental Treatment by Court Order	1,706	30.76	1,397	28.45
Voluntary	3,043	54.87	2,817	57.36
Detained and Other	28	.50	20	.41
Total	5,546	100.00	4,911	100.00

*From report by Division of Planning and Evaluation Department of Mental Health, State of Illinois, 1965 (Mimeographed).

Another problem of the potential patients concerns perfunctory and biased examinations as the basis of their hospitalization. Kutner found that in the Cook County Mental Health Clinic of Chicago certificates were signed by physicians after "little or no examination."[9] Mechanic observed that in the crowded state and county hospitals in a city in California, the psychiatrist did not have "sufficient time" to diagnose the patient completely.[10] Hence all persons who appeared at the hospital were absorbed into the patient population regardless of their capacity to adapt to outside society. In the following article, Scheff analyzes in detail these processes by which a person is screened for hospitalization and frequently casually examined and inconclusively diagnosed.

NOTES

1. Albert Deutsch, *The Mentally Ill in America* (New York: Columbia University Press, 1949), p. 418.

2. *Ibid.*, pp. 423, 424. See Charles Reade, *Hard Cash*, Parts I and II (New York: P. F. Collier and Son, 1871).

3. *Ibid.*, p. 424.

4. *Ibid.*, p. 428.

5. *Ibid.*, p. 428, 429.

6. *Lost and Found, 1* (3), 73–74.

7. *Chicago Daily News*, April 20, 1949.

8. Report by the Division of Planning and Mental Health, Department of Mental Health, State of Illinois (mimeographed).

9. Luis Kutner, "The Illusion of Due Process in Commitment Proceedings," *Northwestern University Law Review* (September 1962), *57*, 383–399.

10. David Mechanic, "Some Factors in Identifying and Defining Mental Illness," *Mental Hygiene* (January 1962), *46*, 66–75.

THE SOCIETAL REACTION TO DEVIANCE: ASCRIPTIVE ELEMENTS IN THE PSYCHIATRIC SCREENING OF MENTAL PATIENTS IN A MIDWESTERN STATE

Thomas J. Scheff (with the assistance of Daniel M. Culver)

THE case for making the societal reaction to deviance a major independent variable in studies of deviant behavior has been succinctly stated by Kitsuse:

A sociological theory of deviance must focus specifically upon the interactions which not only define behaviors as deviant but also organize and activate the application of sanctions by individuals, groups, or agencies. For in modern society, the socially significant differentiation of deviants from the non-deviant population is increasingly contingent upon circumstances of situation, place, social and personal biography, and the bureaucratically organized activities of agencies of control.[1]

In the case of mental disorder, psychiatric diagnosis is one of the crucial steps which "organizes and activates" the societal reaction, since the state is legally empowered to segregate and isolate those persons whom psychiatrists find to be committable because of mental illness.

Recently, however, it has been argued that mental illness may be more usefully considered to be a social status than a disease, since the symptoms of mental illness are vaguely defined and widely distributed, and the definition of behavior as symptomatic of mental illness is usually dependent upon social rather than medical contingencies.[2] Furthermore, the argument continues, the status of the mental patient is more often an ascribed status, with conditions for status entry external to the patient, than an achieved status with conditions for status entry dependent upon the patient's own behavior. According to this argument, the societal reaction is a fundamentally important variable in all stages of a deviant career.

The actual usefulness of a theory of mental disorder based on the societal reaction is largely an empirical question: to what extent is entry to the status of mental patient independent of the behavior or "condition" of the patient? The present paper will explore this question for one phase of the societal reaction: the legal screening of persons alleged to be mentally ill. This screening represents the official phase of the societal reaction, which occurs after the alleged deviance has been called to the attention of the community by a complainant. This report will make no reference to the initial deviance or other situation which resulted in the complaint, but will deal entirely with procedures used by the courts after the complaint has occurred.

The purpose of the description that follows is to determine the extent of uncertainty that exists concerning new patients' qualifications for involuntary confinement in a mental hospital, and the reactions of the courts to this type of uncertainty. The data presented here indicate that, in the face of uncertainty, there is a strong presumption of illness by the court and the court psychiatrists.[3] In the discussion that follows the presentation of findings, some of the causes, consequences and implications of the presumption of illness are suggested.

The data upon which this report is based were drawn from psychiatrists' ratings of a sample of patients newly admitted to the public mental hospitals in a Midwestern state, official court records, interviews with court officials and psychiatrists, and our observations of psychiatric examinations in four courts. The psychiatrists' ratings of new patients will be considered first.

In order to obtain a rough measure of the incoming patient's qualifications for involuntary confinement, a survey of newly admitted patients was conducted with the cooperation of the hospital psychiatrists. All psychiatrists who made admission examinations in the three large mental hospitals in the state filled out a questionnaire for the first ten consecutive patients they examined in the month of June, 1962. A total of 223 questionnaires were returned by the 25 admission psychiatrists. Although these returns do not constitute a probability sample of all new patients admitted during the year, there were no obvious biases in the

Reprinted from *Social Problems* (Spring, 1964), *II* (4); 401–413.

drawing of the sample. For this reason, this group of patients will be taken to be typical of the newly admitted patients in Midwestern State.

The two principal legal grounds for involuntary confinement in the United States are the police power of the state (the state's right to protect itself from dangerous persons) and *parens patriae* (the State's right to assist those persons who, because of their own incapacity, may not be able to assist themselves.)[4] As a measure of the first ground, the potential dangerousness of the patient, the questionnaire contained this item: "In your opinion, if this patient were released at the present time, is it likely he would harm himself or others?" The psychiatrists were given six options, ranging from Very Likely to Very Unlikely. Their responses were: Very Likely, 5%; Likely, 4%; Somewhat Likely, 14%; Somewhat Unlikely, 20%; Unlikely, 37%; Very Unlikely, 18%. (Three patients were not rated, 1%.)

As a measure of the second ground, *parens patriae*, the questionnaire contained the item: "Based on your observations of the patient's behavior, his present degree of mental impairment is:

None _____ Minimal _____
Mild _____ Moderate _____
Severe _____ " The psychiatrists' responses were: None, 2%; Minimal, 12%; Mild, 25%; Moderate, 42%; Severe, 17%. (Three patients were not rated, 1%.)

To be clearly qualified for involuntary confinement, a patient should be rated as likely to harm self or others (Very Likely, Likely, or Somewhat Likely) and/or as Severely Mentally Impaired. However, voluntary patients should be excluded from this analysis, since the court is not required to assess their qualifications for confinement. Excluding the 59 voluntary admissions (26% of the sample), leaves a sample of 164 involuntary confined patients. Of these patients, 10 were rated as meeting both qualifications for involuntary confinement, 21 were rated as being severely mentally impaired, but not dangerous, 28 were rated as dangerous but not severely mentally impaired, and 102 were rated as not dangerous nor as severely mentally impaired. (Three patients were not rated.)

According to these ratings, there is considerable uncertainty connected with the screening of newly admitted involuntary patients in the state, since a substantial majority (63%) of the patients did not clearly meet the statutory requirements for involuntary confinement. How does the agency responsible for assessing the qualifications for confinement, the court, react in the large numbers of cases involving uncertainity?

On the one hand, the legal rulings on this point by higher courts are quite clear. They have repeatedly held that there should be a presumption of sanity. The burden of proof of insanity is to be on the petitioners, there must be a preponderance of evidence, and the evidence should be of a "clear and unexceptionable" nature.[5]

On the other hand, existing studies suggest that there is a presumption of illness by mental health officials. In a discussion of the "discrediting" of patients by the hospital staff, based on observations at St. Elizabeth's Hospital, Washington, D. C., Goffman states:

[The patient's case record] is apparently not regularly used to record occasions when the patient showed capacity to cope honorably and effectively with difficult life situations. Nor is the case record typically used to provide a rough average or sampling of his past conduct. [Rather, it extracts] from his whole life course a list of those incidents that have or might have had "symptomatic" significance.... I think that most of the information gathered in case records is quite true, although it might seem also to be true that almost anyone's life course could yield up enough denigrating facts to provide grounds for the record's justification of commitment.[6]

Mechanic makes a similar statement in his discussion of two large mental hospitals located in an urban area in California:

In the crowded state or county hospitals, which is the most typical situation, the psychiatrist does not have sufficient time to make a very complete psychiatric diagnosis, nor do his psychiatric tools provide him with the equipment for an expeditious screening of the patient ... In the two mental hospitals studied over a period of three months, the investigator never observed a case where the psychiatrist advised the patient that he did not need treatment. Rather, all persons who appeared at the hospital were absorbed into the patient population regardless of their ability to function adequately outside the hospital.[7]

A comment by Brown suggests that it is a fairly general understanding among mental health workers that state mental hospitals in the U.S. accept all comers.[8]

Kutner, describing commitment procedures in Chicago in 1962, also reports a strong presumption of illness by the staff of the Cook County Mental Health Clinic:

Certificates are signed as a matter of course by staff physicians after little or no examination ... The so-called examinations are made on an assembly-line basis, often being completed in two or three minutes, and never taking more than ten minutes. Although psychiatrists agree that it is practically impossible to determine a person's sanity on the basis of such a short and hurried interview, the doctors recommend confinement in 77% of the cases. It appears in practice that the alleged-mentally-ill is presumed to be insane and bears the burden of proving his sanity in the few minutes allotted to him . . .[9]

These citations suggest that mental health officials handle uncertainty by presuming illness. To ascertain if the presumption of illness occurred in Midwestern State, intensive observations of screening procedures were conducted in the four courts with the largest volume of mental cases in the state. These courts were located in the two most populous cities in the state. Before giving the results of these observations, it is necessary to describe the steps in the legal procedures for hospitalization and commitment.

STEPS IN THE SCREENING OF PERSONS ALLEGED TO BE MENTALLY ILL

The process of screening can be visualized as containing five steps in Midwestern State:

1. The application for judicial inquiry, made by three citizens. This application is heard by deputy clerks in two of the courts (C and D), by a court reporter in the third court, and by a court commissioner in the fourth court.

2. The intake examination, conducted by a hospital psychiatrist.

3. The psychiatric examination, conducted by two psychiatrists appointed by the court.

4. The interview of the patient by the guardian *ad litem*, a lawyer appointed in three of the courts to represent the patient. (Court A did not use guardians *ad litem*.)

5. The judicial hearing, conducted by a judge.

These five steps take place roughly in the order listed, although in many cases (those cases designated as emergencies) step No. 2, the intake examination, may occur before step No. 1. Steps No. 1 and No. 2 usually take place on the same day or the day after hospitalization. Steps No. 3, No. 4, and No. 5 usually take place within a week of hospitalization. (In courts C and D, however, the judicial hearing is held only once a month.)

This series of steps would seem to provide ample opportunity for the presumption of health, and a thorough assessment, therefore, of the patient's qualifications for involuntary confinement, since there are five separate points at which discharge could occur. According to our findings,

however, these procedures usually do not serve the function of screening out persons who do not meet statutory requirements. At most of these decision points, in most of the courts, retention of the patient in the hospital was virtually automatic. A notable exception to this pattern was found in one of the three state hospitals; this hospital attempted to use step No. 2, the intake examination, as a screening point to discharge patients that the superintendent described as "illegitimate," i.e., patients who do not qualify for involuntary confinement.[10] In the other two hospitals, however, this examination was perfunctory and virtually never resulted in a finding of health and a recommendation of discharge. In a similar manner, the other steps were largely ceremonial in character. For example, in court B, we observed twenty-two judicial hearings, all of which were conducted perfunctorily and with lightning rapidity. (The mean time of these hearings was 1.6 minutes.) The judge asked each patient two or three routine questions. Whatever the patient answered, however, the judge always ended the hearings and retained the patient in the hospital.

What appeared to be the key role in justifying these procedures was played by step No. 3, the examination by the court-appointed psychiatrists. In our informal discussions of screening with the judges and other court officials, these officials made it clear that although the statutes give the court the responsibility for the decision to confine or release persons alleged to be mentally ill, they would rarely if ever take the responsibility for releasing a mental patient without a medical recommendation to that effect. The question which is crucial, therefore, for the entire screening process is whether or not the court-appointed psychiatric examiners presume illness. The remainder of the paper will consider this question.

Our observations of 116 judicial hearings raised the question of the adequacy of the psychiatric examination. Eighty-six of the hearings failed to establish that the patients were "mentally ill" (according to the criteria stated by the judges in interviews).[11] Indeed, the behavior and responses of 48 of the patients at the hearings seemed completely unexceptional. Yet the psychiatric examiners had not recommended the release of a single one of these patients. Examining the court records of 80 additional cases, there was still not a single recommendation for release.

Although the recommendation for treatment of 196 out of 196 consecutive cases strongly suggests that the psychiatric examiners were presuming illness, particularly when we observed 48 of these patients to be responding appropriately, it is conceivable that this is not the case. The observer for this study was not a psychiatrist (he was a first year graduate student in social work) and it is possible that he could have missed evidence of disorder which a psychiatrist might have seen. It was therefore arranged for the observer to be present at a series of psychiatric examinations, in order to determine whether the examinations appeared to be merely formalities or whether, on the other hand, through careful examination and interrogation, the psychiatrists were able to establish illness even in patients whose appearance and responses were not obviously disordered The observer was instructed to note the examiner's procedures, the criteria they appeared to use in arriving at their ·decision, and their reaction to uncertainty.

Each of the courts discussed here employs the services of a panel of physicians as medical examiners. The physicians are paid a flat fee of ten dollars per examination, and are usually assigned from three to five patients for each trip to the hospital. In court A, most of the examinations are performed by two psychiatrists, who went to the hospital once a week, seeing from five to ten patients a trip. In court B, C and D, a panel of local physicians was used. These courts seek to arrange the examinations so that one of the examiners is a psychiatrist, the other a general practitioner. Court B has a list of four such pairs, and appoints each pair for a month at a time. Court C and D have a similar list, apparently with some of the same names as court B.

To obtain physicians who were representative of the panel used in these courts, we arranged to observe the examinations of the two psychiatrists employed by court A, and one of the four pairs of physicians used in court B, one a psychiatrist, the other a general practitioner. We observed 13 examinations in court A and 13 examinations in court B. The judges in courts C and D refused to give us the names of the physicians on their panels, and we were unable to observe examinations in these courts. (The judge in court D stated that he did not want these physicians harassed in their work, since it was difficult to obtain their services even under the best of circumstances.) In addition to observing the examinations by four psychiatrists, three other psychiatrists used by these courts were interviewed.

The medical examiners followed two lines of questioning. One line was to inquire about the circumstances which led to the patient's hospitalization, the other was to ask standard questions to test the patient's orientation and his capacity for abstract thinking by asking him the date, the President, Governor, proverbs, and problems requiring arithmetic calculation. These questions were often asked very rapidly, and the patient was usually allowed only a very brief time to answer.

It should be noted that the psychiatrists in these courts had access to the patient's record (which usually contained the Application for Judicial Inquiry and the hospital chart notes on the patient's behavior), and that several of the psychiatrists stated that they almost always familiarized themselves with this record before making the examination. To the extent that they were familiar with the patient's circumstances from such outside information, it is possible that the psychiatrists were basing their diagnoses of illness less on the rapid and peremptory examination than on this other information. Although this was true to some extent, the importance of the record can easily be exaggerated, both because of the deficiencies in the typical record, and because the way it is usually utilized by the examiners.

The deficiencies of the typical record were easily discerned in the approximately one hundred applications and hospital charts which the author read. Both the applications and charts were extremely brief and sometimes garbled. Moreover, in some of the cases where the author and interviewer were familiar with the circumstances involved in the hospitalization, it was not clear that the complainant's testimony was any more accurate than the version presented by the patient. Often the original complaint was so paraphrased and condensed that the application seemed to have little meaning.

The attitude of the examiners toward the record was such that even in those cases where the record was ample, it often did not figure prominently in their decision. Disparaging remarks about the quality and usefulness of the record were made by several of the psychiatrists. One of the examiners was apologetic about his use of the record, giving us the impression that he thought that a good psychiatrist would not need to resort to any information outside his own personal examination of the patient. A casual attitude toward the record was openly displayed in 6 of the 26 examinations we observed. In these 6 examinations, the psychiatrist could not (or in 3 cases, did not bother to) locate the record and conducted the examination without it, with one psychiatrist making it a point of pride that he could easily diagnose most cases "blind."

In his observations of the examinations, the

interviewer was instructed to rate how well the patient responded by noting his behavior during the interview, whether he answered the orientation and concept questions correctly, and whether he denied and explained the allegations which resulted in his hospitalization. If the patient's behavior during the interview obviously departed from conventional social standards (e.g., in one case the patient refused to speak), if he answered the orientation questions incorrectly, or if he did not deny and explain the petitioners' allegations, the case was rated as meeting the statutory requirements for hospitalization. Of the 26 examinations observed, eight were rated as Criteria Met.

If, on the other hand, the patient's behavior was appropriate, his answers correct, and he denied and explained the petitioners' allegations, the interviewer rated the case as not meeting the statutory criteria. Of the 26 cases, seven were rated as Criteria Not Met. Finally, if the examination was inconclusive, but the interviewer felt that more extensive investigation might have established that the criteria were met, he rated the cases as Criteria Possibly Met. Of the 26 examined, 11 were rated in this way. The interviewer's instructions were that whenever he was in doubt he should avoid using the rating Criteria Not Met.

Even giving the examiners the benefit of the doubt, the interviewer's ratings were that in a substantial majority of the cases he observed, the examination failed to establish that the statutory criteria were met. The relationship between the examiners' recommendations and the interviewer's ratings are shown in the following table.

concerning staying or leaving the hospital were: Leave, 14 cases; Indifferent, 1 case; Stay, 9 cases; and Not Ascertained, 2 cases. In only one of the 14 cases in which the patient wished to leave was the interviewer's rating Criteria Met.

The interviews ranged in length from five minutes to 17 minutes, with the mean time being 10.2 minutes. Most of the interviews were hurried, with the questions of the examiners coming so rapidly that the examiner often interrupted the patient, or one examiner interrupted the other. All of the examiners seemed quite hurried. One psychiatrist, after stating in an interview (before we observed his examinations) that he usually took about thirty minutes, stated:

It's not remunerative. I'm taking a hell of a cut. I can't spend 45 minutes with a patient. I don't have the time, it doesn't pay.

In the examinations that we observed, this physician actually spent 8, 10, 5, 8, 8, 7, 17, and 11 minutes with the patients, or an average of 9.2 minutes.

In these short time periods, it is virtually impossible for the examiner to extend his investigation beyond the standard orientation questions, and a short discussion of the circumstances which brought the patient to the hospital. In those cases where the patient answered the orientation questions correctly, behaved appropriately, and explained his presence at the hospital satisfactorily, the examiners did not attempt to assess the reliability of the petitioner's complaints, or to probe further into the patient's answers. Given the fact

TABLE 1. Observer's Ratings and Examiners' Recommendations

Observer's Ratings		Criteria Met	Criteria Possibly Met	Criteria Not Met	Total
Examiners'	Commitment	7	9	2	18
Recommendations	30-day Observation	1	2	3	6
	Release	0	0	2	2
	Total	8	11	7	26

The interviewer's ratings suggest that the examinations established that the statutory criteria were met in only eight cases, but the examiners recommended that the patient be retained in the hospital in 24 cases, leaving 16 cases which the interviewer rated as uncertain, and in which retention was recommended by the examiners. The observer also rated the patient's expressed desires regarding staying in the hospital, and the time taken by the examination. The ratings of the patient's desire

that in most of these instances the examiners were faced with borderline cases, that they took little time in the examinations, and that they usually recommended commitment, we can only conclude that their decisions were based largely on a presumption of illness. Supplementary observations reported by the interviewer support this conclusion.

After each examination, the observer asked the examiner to explain the criteria he used in arriving at his decision. The observer also had access to the examiner's official report, so that he could compare what the examiner said about the case with the record of what actually occurred during the interview. This supplementary information supports the conclusion that the examiner's decisions are based on the presumption of illness, and sheds light on the manner in which these decisions are reached:

1. The "evidence" upon which the examiners based their decision to retain often seemed arbitrary.

2. In some cases, the decision to retain was made even when no evidence could be found.

3. Some of the psychiatrists' remarks suggest   .
prejudgment of the cases.

4. Many of the examinations were characterized by carelessness and haste. The first question, concerning the arbitrariness of the psychiatric evidence, will now be considered.

In the weighing of the patient's responses during the interview, the physician appeared not to give the patient credit for the large number of correct answers he gave. In the typical interview, the examiner might ask the patient fifteen or twenty questions: the date, time, place, who is President, Governor, etc., what is 11×10, 11×11, etc., explain "Don't put all your eggs in one basket," "A rolling stone gathers no moss," etc. The examiners appeared to feel that a wrong answer established lack of orientation, even when it was preceded by a series of correct answers. In other words, the examiners do not establish any standard score on the orientation questions, which would give an objective picture of the degree to which the patient answered the questions correctly, but seem at times to search until they find an incorrect answer.

For those questions which were answered incorrectly, it was not always clear whether the incorrect answers were due to the patient's "mental illness," or to the time pressure in the interview, the patient's lack of education, or other causes. Some of the questions used to establish orientation were sufficiently difficult that persons not mentally ill might have difficulty with them. Thus one of the examiners always asked, in a rapid-fire manner: "What year is it? What year was it seven years ago? Seventeen years before that?" etc. Only two of the five patients who were asked this series of questions were able to answer it correctly. However, it is a moot question whether a higher percentage of persons in a household survey would be able to do any better. To my knowledge, none of the orientation questions that are used have been checked in a normal population.

Finally, the interpretations of some of the evidence as showing mental illness seemed capri-

cious. Thus one of the patients, when asked, "In what way are a banana, an orange, and an apple alike?" answered, "They are all something to eat." This answer was used by the examiner in explaining his recommendation to commit. The observer had noted that the patient's behavior and responses seemed appropriate and asked why the recommendation to commit had been made. The doctor stated that her behavior had been bizarre (possibly referring to her alleged promiscuity), her affect inappropriate ("When she talked about being pregnant, it was without feeling,") and with regard to the question above:

She wasn't able to say a banana and an orange were fruit. She couldn't take it one step further, she had to say it was something to eat.

In other words, this psychiatrist was suggesting that the patient manifested concreteness in her thinking, which is held to be a symptom of mental illness. Yet in her other answers to classification questions, and to proverb interpretations, concreteness was not apparent, suggesting that the examiner's application of this test was arbitrary. In another case, the physician stated that he thought the patient was suspicious and distrustful, because he had asked about the possibility of being represented by counsel at the judicial hearing. The observer felt that these and other similar interpretations might possibly be correct, but that further investigation of the supposedly incorrect responses would be needed to establish that they were manifestations of disorientation.

In several cases where even this type of evidence was not available, the examiners still recommended retention in the hospital. Thus, one examiner, employed by court A stated that he had recommended 30-day observation for a patient whom he had thought *not* to be mentally ill, on the grounds that the patient, a young man, could not get along with his parents, and "might get into trouble." This examiner went on to say:

We always take the conservative side. [Commitment or observation] Suppose a patient should commit suicide. We always make the conservative decision. I had rather play it safe. There's no harm in doing it that way.

It appeared to the observer that "playing safe" meant that even in those cases where the examination established nothing, the psychiatrists did not consider recommending release. Thus in one case the examination had established that the patient had a very good memory, was oriented and spoke quietly and seriously. The observer recorded his discussion with the physician after the examination as follows:

When the doctor told me he was recommending commitment for this patient too (he had also recommended commitment in the two examinations held earlier that day) he laughed because he could see what my next question was going to be. He said, "I already recommended the release of two patients this month." This sounded like it was the maximum amount the way he said it.

Apparently this examiner felt that he had a very limited quota on the number of patients he could recommend for release (less than two percent of those examined).

The language used by these physicians tends to intimate that mental illness was found, even when reporting the opposite. Thus in one case the recommendation stated: "No gross evidence of delusions or hallucinations." This statement is misleading, since not only was there no gross evidence, there was not any evidence, not even the slightest suggestion of delusions or hallucinations, brought out by the interview.

These remarks suggest that the examiners prejudge the cases they examine. Several further comments indicate prejudgment. One physician stated that he thought that most crimes of violence were committed by patients released too early from mental hospitals. (This is an erroneous belief.)[12] He went on to say that he thought that all mental patients should be kept in the hospital at least three months, indicating prejudgment concerning his examinations. Another physician, after a very short interview (8 minutes), told the observer:

On the schizophrenics, I don't bother asking them more questions when I can see they're schizophrenic because *I know what they are going to say*. You could talk to them another half hour and not learn any more.

Another physician, finally, contrasted cases in which the patient's family or others initiated hospitalization ("petition cases," the great majority of cases) with those cases initiated by the court:

The petition cases are pretty *automatic*. If the patient's own family wants to get rid of him you know there is something wrong.

The lack of care which characterized the examinations is evident in the forms on which the examiners make their recommendations. On most of these forms, whole sections have been left unanswered. Others are answered in a peremptory and uninformative way. For example, in the section entitled Physical Examination, the question is asked: "Have you made a physical examination of the patient? State fully what is the present physical condition," a typical answer is "Yes. Fair," or, "Is apparently in good health." Since in none of the examinations we observed was the patient actually physically examined, these answers appear to be mere guesses. One of the examiners used regularly in court B, to the question "On what subject or in what way is derangement now manifested?" always wrote in "Is mentally ill." The omissions, and the almost flippant brevity of these forms, together with the arbitrariness, lack of evidence, and prejudicial character of the examinations, discussed above, all support the observer's conclusion that, except in very unusual cases, the psychiatric examiner's recommendation to retain the patient is virtually automatic.

Lest it be thought that these results are unique to a particularly backward Midwestern State, it should be pointed out that this state is noted for its progressive psychiatric practices. It will be recalled that a number of the psychiatrists employed by the court as examiners had finished their psychiatric residencies, which is not always the case in many other states. A still common practice in other states is to employ, as members of the "Lunacy Panel," partially retired physicians with no psychiatric training whatever. This was the case in Stockton, California, in 1959, where the author observed hundreds of hearings at which these physicians were present. It may be indicative of some of the larger issues underlying the question of civil commitment that, in these hearings, the physicians played very little part; the judge controlled the questioning of the relatives and patients, and the hearings were often a model of impartial and thorough investigation.

DISCUSSION

Ratings of the qualifications for involuntary confinement of patients newly admitted to the public mental hospitals in a Midwestern state, together with observations of judicial hearings and psychiatric examinations by the observer connected with the present study, both suggest that the decision as to the mental condition of a majority of the patients is an uncertain one. The fact that the courts seldom release patients, and the perfunctory manner in which the legal and medical procedures are carried out, suggest that the judicial decision to retain patients in the hospital for treatment is routine and largely based on the presumption of illness. Three reasons for this presumption will be discussed: financial, ideological, and political.

Our discussions with the examiners indicated that one reason that they perform biased "examinations" is that their rate of pay is determined by the length of time spent with the patient. In recommending retention, the examiners are refraining from interrupting the hospitalization and commitment procedures already in progress, and thereby allowing someone else, usually the hospital, to make the effective decision to release or commit. In order to recommend release, however, they would have to build a case showing why these procedures should be interrupted. Building such a case would take much more time than is presently expended by the examiners, thereby reducing their rate of pay.

A more fundamental reason for the presumption of illness by the examiners, and perhaps the reason why this practice is allowed by the courts, is the interpretation of current psychiatric doctrine by the examiners and court officials. These officials make a number of assumptions, which are now thought to be of doubtful validity:

1. The condition of mentally ill persons deteriorates rapidly without psychiatric assistance.
2. Effective psychiatric treatments exist for most mental illnesses.
3. Unlike surgery, there are no risks involved in involuntary psychiatric treatment: it either helps or is neutral, it can't hurt.
4. Exposing a prospective mental patient to questioning, cross-examination, and other screening procedures exposes him to the unnecessary stigma of trial-like procedures, and may do further damage to his mental condition.
5. There is an element of danger to self or others in most mental illness. It is better to risk unnecessary hospitalization than the harm the patient might do himself or others.

Many psychiatrists and others now argue that none of these assumptions are necessarily correct.

1. The assumption that psychiatric disorders usually get worse without treatment rests on very little other than evidence of an anecdotal character. There is just as much evidence that most acute psychological and emotional upsets are self-terminating.[13]
2. It is still not clear, according to systematic studies evaluating psychotherapy, drugs, etc., that most psychiatric interventions are any more effective, on the average, than no treatment at all.[14]

3. There is very good evidence that involuntary hospitalization and social isolation may affect the patient's life: his job, his family affairs, etc. There is some evidence that too hasty exposure to psychiatric treatment may convince the patient that he is "sick," prolonging what might have been an otherwise transitory episode.[15]
4. This assumption is correct, as far as it goes. But it is misleading because it fails to consider what occurs when the patient who does not wish to be hospitalized is forcibly treated. Such patients often become extremely indignant and angry, particularly in the case, as often happens, when they are deceived into coming to the hospital on some pretext.
5. The element of danger is usually exaggerated both in amount and degree. In the psychiatric survey of new patients in state mental hospitals, danger to self or others was mentioned in about a fourth of the cases. Furthermore, in those cases where danger is mentioned, it is not always clear that the risks involved are greater than those encountered in ordinary social life. This issue has been discussed by Ross, an attorney:

> A truck driver with a mild neurosis who is "accident prone" is probably a greater danger to society than most psychotics; yet, he will not be committed for treatment, even if he would be benefited. The community expects a certain amount of dangerous activity. I suspect that as a class, drinking drivers are a greater danger than the mentally ill, and yet the drivers are tolerated or punished with small fines rather than indeterminate imprisonment.[16]

From our observations of the medical examinations and other commitment procedures, we formed a very strong impression that the doctrines of danger to self or others, early treatment, and the avoidance of stigma were invoked partly because the officials believed them to be true, and partly because they provided convenient justification for a pre-existing policy of summary action, minimal investigation, avoidance of responsibility and, after the patient is in the hospital, indecisiveness and delay.

The policy of presuming illness is probably both cause and effect of political pressure on the court from the community. The judge, an elected official, runs the risk of being more heavily penalized for erroneously releasing than for erroneously retaining patients. Since the judge personally appoints the panel of psychiatrists to serve as examiners, he can easily transmit the community pressure to them, by failing to reappoint a psychiatrist whose examinations were inconveniently thorough.

Some of the implications of these findings for the sociology of deviant behavior will be briefly summarized. The discussion above, of the reasons that the psychiatrists tend to presume illness, suggests that the motivations of the key decision-makers in the screening process may be significant in determining the extent and direction of the societal reaction. In the case of psychiatric screening of persons alleged to be mentally ill, the social differentiation of the deviant from the non-deviant population appears to be materially affected by the financial, ideological, and political position of the psychiatrists, who are in this instance the key agents of social control.

Under these circumstances, the character of the societal reaction appears to undergo a marked change from the pattern of denial which occurs in the community. The official societal reaction appears to reverse the presumption of normality reported by the Cummings as a characteristic of informal societal reaction, and instead exaggerates both the amount and degree of deviance.[17] Thus, one extremely important contingency influencing the severity of the societal reaction may be whether or not the original deviance comes to official notice. This paper suggests that in the area of mental disorder, perhaps in contrast to other areas of deviant behavior, if the official societal reaction is invoked, for whatever reason, social differentiation of the deviant from the non-deviant population will usually occur.

CONCLUSION

This paper has described the screening of patients who were admitted to public mental hospitals in early June, 1962, in a Midwestern state. The data presented here suggest that the screening is usually perfunctory, and that in the crucial screening examination by the court-appointed psychiatrists, there is a presumption of illness. Since most court decisions appear to hinge on the recommendation of these psychiatrists, there appears to be a large element of status ascription in the official societal reaction to persons alleged to be mentally ill, as exemplified by the court's actions. This finding points to the importance of lay definitions of mental illness in the community, since the "diagnosis" of mental illness by laymen in the community initiates the official societal reaction, and to the necessity of analyzing social processes connected with the recognition and reaction to the deviant behavior that is called mental illness in our society.

NOTES

1. John I. Kitsuse, "Societal Reaction to Deviant Behavior: Problems of Theory and Method," *Social Problems*, 9 (Winter, 1962), pp. 247–257.

2. Edwin M. Lemert, *Social Pathology*, New York: McGraw-Hill, 1951; Erving Goffman, *Asylums*, Chicago: Aldine, 1962.

3. For a more general discussion of the presumption of illness in medicine, and some of its possible causes and consequences, see the author's "Decision Rules, Types of Error and Their Consequences in Medical Diagnosis," *Behavioral Science*, 8 (April, 1963), pp. 97–107.

4. Hugh Allen Ross, "Commitment of the Mentally Ill: Problems of Law and Policy," *Michigan Law Review*, 57 (May, 1959), pp. 945–1018.

5. This is the typical phrasing in cases in the *Dicennial Legal Digest*, found under the heading "Mental Illness."

6. Goffman, *op. cit.*, pp. 155, 159.

7. David Mechanic, "Some Factors in Identifying and Defining Mental Illness," *Mental Hygiene*, 46 (January, 1962), pp. 66–75.

8. Esther Lucile Brown, *Newer Dimensions of Patient Care*, Part I, New York: Russel Sage, 1961, p. 60, fn.

9. Luis Kutner, "The Illusion of Due Process in Commitment Proceedings," *Northwestern University Law Review*, 57 (September, 1962), pp. 383–399.

10. Other exceptions occurred as follows: the deputy clerks in courts C and D appeared to exercise some discretion in turning away applications they considered improper or incomplete, at step No. 1; the judge in Court D appeared also to perform some screening at step No. 5. For further description of these exceptions see "Rural-Urban Differences in the Judicial Screening of the Mentally Ill in a Midwestern State" (In press).

11. In interviews with the judges, the following criteria were named: Appropriateness of behavior and speech, understanding of the situation, and orientation.

12. The rate of crimes of violence, or any crime, appears to be less among ex-mental patients than in the general population. Henry Brill and Benjamin Maltzberg, "Statistical Report Based on the Arrest Record of 5354 Ex-patients Released from New York State Mental Hospitals During the Period 1946–48." Mimeo available from the authors; Louis H. Cohen and Henry Freeman, "How Dangerous to the Community Are State Hospital Patients?", *Connecticut State Medical Journal*, 9 (September, 1945), pp. 697–700; Donald W. Hastings, "Follow-up Results in Psychiatric Illness," *Amer. Journal of Psychiatry*, 118 (June, 1962), pp. 1078–1086.

13. For a review of epidemiological studies of mental disorder see Richard J. Plunkett and John E. Gordon, *Epidemiology and Mental Illness*. New York: Basic Books, 1960. Most of these studies suggest that at any given point in time, psychiatrists find a substantial proportion of persons in normal populations to be "mentally ill." One interpretation of this finding is that much of the deviance detected in these studies is self-limiting.

14. For an assessment of the evidence regarding the effectiveness of electroshock, drugs, psychotherapy, and other psychiatric treatments, see H. J. Eysenck, *Handbook of Abnormal Psychology*, New York: Basic Books, 1961, Part III.

15. For examples from military psychiatry, see Albert J. Glass, "Psychotherapy in the Combat Zone," in *Symposium on Stress*, Washington, D. C., Army Medical Service Graduate School, 1953, and B. L. Bushard, "The U. S. Army's Mental Hygiene Consultation Service," in *Symposium on Preventive and Social Psychiatry*, 15–17 (April, 1957), Washington, D. C.: Walter Reed Army Institute of Research, pp. 431–43. For a discussion of essentially the same problem in the context of a civilian mental hospital, cf. Kai T. Erikson, "Patient Role and Social Uncertainty—A Dilemma of the Mentally Ill," *Psychiatry*, 20 (August, 1957), pp. 263–275.

16. Ross, *op. cit.*, p. 962.

17. Elaine Cumming and John Cumming, *Closed Ranks*, Cambridge, Mass: Harvard University Press, 1957, 102; for further discussion of the bipolarization of the societal reaction into denial and labeling, see the author's "The Role of the Mentally Ill and the Dynamics of Mental Disorder: A Research Framework," *Sociometry*, 26 (December, 1963), pp. 436–453.

part V

THE MENTAL HOSPITAL

T he state mental hospital is an institution with several functions. It is a treatment center, even though many patients do not respond to treatment. It is custodial, in that it cares for patients and is entrusted with inmates who are involuntarily segregated from the public at large. Finally, it protects these persons from harming themselves. These functions deal mainly with the needs of patients.

But, since the mental hospital is in some measure a self-contained community, it must also provide for the needs and comfort of the staff. It may also serve peripherally as a training and research institution.

American society has committed its very disorganized persons, by designating them insane, to these institutions, many of which are removed from large population centers. As a result, the mental hospital has frequently become a repository for many undesirable persons, where, after a period of time, chronic patients are more or less forgotten.

After World War II, the mental hospital was studied intensively and became the object of considerable reorganization. Brutal instruments for the restraint of patients, such as the strait jacket and iron anklets, were discarded, and forms of outright cruelty by the staff to patients diminished markedly in advanced hospitals. Effective drug and physical therapies supplemented psychotherapeutic techniques and hastened the patients' improvement and discharge.

One positive effect of this multidimensional approach to treatment of patients was a decline in resident patients, beginning in 1956. The discharge of patients has kept pace with and in some years has exceeded admission of patients.

As Table I shows, beginning in 1955, the number of resident patients for all hospitals combined and for state and county mental hospitals in particular tended to decline. The relatively few resident patients in the psychiatric wards of general hospitals tended to increase. The resident patients in veterans and private hospitals, however, remained somewhat stable.

Another pronounced effect of the positive changes by drug therapy was a decline in and even the virtual elimination of the chronically agitated patients. A third effect has been the very challenge to the concept of "chronicity," which heretofore had meant nonresponsiveness to treatment; in some instances, it has been demonstrated that, with new intensive forms of milieu and direct therapy, some "chronic" patients improve and can be discharged. A fourth effect is the increasing recourse to social psychological and psychological approaches to treatment and the increasing success of these measures.

TABLE 1.   PATIENTS RESIDENT IN MENTAL HOSPITALS AND PSYCHIATRIC SERVICES OF
GENERAL HOSPITALS, UNITED STATES* 1954–1964

Year	All Hospitals (excluding clinics and institutions)	Public		Private	General
		State and County Mental Hospitals	Veterans Administration		
1954	629,055	553,979	54,905	13,965	6,206
1955	637,962	558,922	57,991	14,590	6,459
1956	632,804	551,390	60,080	14,096	7,238
1957	628,894	548,626	59,240	13,543	7,485
1958	627,314	545,182	59,855	14,471	7,806
1959	624,402	541,883	60,805	13,696	8,018
1960	617,869	535,540	60,158	13,795	8,376
1961	608,972	527,535	60,108	13,019	8,310
1962	(598,018)	515,700	(60,000)	13,755	8,563
1963	(587,247)	504,947	(60,000)	(13,700)	(8,600)
1964	(577,300)	(495,000)	(60,000)	(13,700)	(8,600)

Number in Parentheses ( ) are estimated.
* Number of facilities reporting data varies from year to year.
SOURCE: U.S. Department of Health, Education, and Welfare, PHS, NIMH, *Patients in Mental Institutions,*
1947–1960, and *Mental Health Statistics: Current Reports, 1961–1963,* and *Veterans with Mental Disorders*
Resident in Veteran Administration Hospitals, U.S. National Institute of Mental Health, *Data on Patients*
of Outpatient Psychiatric Clinics in the United States, 1959–1962.

Other changes pertain to the preference of small hospitals to large hospitals as
more effective and wieldy than large hospitals; the increased continuity between
hospital and the community; the out-patient treatment of some patients; the placement of many elderly patients into nursing homes or special geriatric institutions;
and, more recently, the use of nonmedical clinicians and even relatively untrained
personnel for treatment purposes when necessary.

Certain basic questions concern the structure of the mental hospital and its
impact upon the patients and staff. What type of institution is the mental hospital?
What relevant differences exist between the formal and the informal hospital organization? What relevant differences exist in structure, ideologies, and values between
types of mental hospitals? How do these types of hospitals deter or facilitate the
improvement of patients? What roles do patients acquire while in the hospital? How
do these roles affect their condition? What techniques are used to change the
hospital organization from custodial to therapeutic goals? How do direct social
therapeutic techniques, such as milieu therapy, facilitate the improvement of
patients?

Goffman, in his paper, "The Mental Hospital as a Total Institution," calls the
mental hospital a "twenty-four-hour-a-day institution" because all aspects of life,
including working, eating, and sleeping, are conducted within the institution, and
because the patients are forcibly segregated so that they cannot depart at their own
discretion. He has defined a total institution, from the perspective of the patient, as
"a place of residence and work where a large number of like situated individuals cut
off from the wider society for a period of time together lead an enclosed, formally
administered round of life."[1]

Levinson and Gallagher, however, have criticized this organizational characterization of the hospital as overdrawn and providing too homogeneous an image for
diverse organizational types.[2] The two identifying features of the total institution
are a massive group of inmates whose lives are controlled by a small staff and
segregation from the wider society. But within these broad and inclusive features
there may be considerable variations among total institutions, so that the mental

hospital differs from the prison and the concentration camp. One significant difference is that the mental hospital may change into a treatment center, which would diminish the self-degradation that inmates inevitably experienced in total institutions. In the treatment-oriented hospitals concerned with rehabilitating the patients, this degradation of the patients would be incongruous with their aims.

In his study, "Bureaucratic Structure and Impersonal Experience in Mental Hospitals," Kahne traces the inhibiting processes upon the personal experiences of the patients that accrue from the bureaucratic aspects of the institutional structure itself. "The structure of relations in mental hospitals," Kahne emphasizes, "is such that the forces emanating from its existence operate centrifugally to the efforts of human beings toward personal involvement with each other." He emphasizes the formal, ritualistic and standardized or stereotyped facets of human relations.

The trend away from the custodial to the therapeutic emphasis in the mental hospital has wrought changes in the ideology and social organization in the hospital. Actually, the custodial problems in a 24-hour institution cannot be minimized, but the basic tendency of the contemporary progressive hospital is to perceive the patient as a person who is in the hospital to be rehabilitated if the techniques and knowledge of therapy can realize this goal. Because the constructive changes within the different hospitals in the country vary, some hospitals are more progressive than others in terms of their therapeutic emphasis. Greenblatt pointed out: "Most institutions in this country are at the custodial end of the continuum. Many are in active transition and some are highly developed to the point of approximating a therapeutic community."[3] One basic question concerns the kind of structure that is most conducive to the therapeutic process within the hospital.

Appleby and his associates, in "Institution-Centered and Patient-Centered Mental Hospitals," contrast this bureaucratic, institution-centered, traditional hospital with the emerging ideal, the patient-centered hospital, in terms of their values, organizational structure, and consequences. The patient-centered system aims to affect a personal experience for the patients that would contribute to their improvement and personal fulfillment.

The formal organization, which sets the limits to the informal organization of the mental hospital, contributes directly to the therapeutic effectiveness of the hospital. The formal structure of the hospital is analyzed in terms of the forms of multiple or single subordination. The relationships between the staff and the patients in the two types of hospitals, especially, are different because of the modes of power retention and expression as well as the image and needs of the patients.

In the paper, "A Sociopsychological Conception of Patienthood," Pine and Levinson describe the situation of the patient within the hospital community and formulate some of the role-tasks or problematic issues that confront patients as a consequence of personal needs and organizational requirements, in order to illustrate the conflicting modes of adaptation made by patients in a changing treatment-oriented hospital. The patient's adjustment to problematic issues is characterized from the perspective of the patient and with the aim of developing a conception of the patient and his role.

Schwartz, in his report on "Patient Demands in a Mental Hospital Context," is concerned with the modes of therapeutic intervention by the staff that may contribute to the patient's improvement in the ward of a small private hospital. In sequence, he deals with the patterns of difficulty that characterize a patient's mental disorder, the staff's response to the patient's pattern of difficulty, and the configuration that is stabilized as a consequence of the patient-staff relationships. If the pattern of relations sustains the illness, he indicates how it may be changed. This therapeutic intervention is designed to disrupt this illness-maintaining pattern. Thus he characterizes the conception, content, and mode of introducing this intervention, thereby determining the effects that accrue from it.

The crucial therapeutic problem resides in the large mental hospital, where therapy must be implemented for large numbers of patients. This has been achieved in part by electroshock and drugs. But of more enduring value is the use of the social organization of the hospital toward therapeutic goals and/or the use of staff relationships or interpatient relationships towards the patient's improvement. Patients responsive to improvement and with favorable prospects for improvement are involved in these changes. The means for implementing these changes vary, but they encounter the traditionally resistant attitudes of entrenched personnel, and any large-scale attempt at change must involve a change of attitudes and procedures on the part of the staff.

Two techniques for constructive change of hospital social organization for therapeutic effects, as Clancey has pointed out, are ward staff meetings where nurses express their feelings about the patients and each other[4] and the resolution of interpersonal conflict, which has a therapeutic effect upon the patients because as Dunham and Weinberg and Stanton and Schwartz have pointed out, they respond adversely to staff conflicts.[5]

The final problem is readjusting the patient to the community. This can be accomplished by changing the attitudes of people in the community so that the mentally disordered can enter and leave with greater facility and greater prospect of readjustment. The "halfway house" serves as an intermediary between the hospital and the community, where patients remain after their discharge and are guided more effectively in their adaptation to the community.

REFERENCES

1. Erving Goffman, *Asylums* (Chicago: Aldine, 1962), p. xiii.

2. Daniel J. Levinson and Eugene B. Gallagher, *Patienthood in the Mental Hospital* (Boston: Hughton, Mifflin, 1964), pp. 19–20.

3. Milton Greenblatt, "Implications for Psychiatry and Hospital Practice—The Movement from Custodial Hospital to Therapeutic Community," in Milton Greenblatt, Daniel J. Levinson, and Richard Williams (Eds.), *The patient and the Mental Hospital* (New York: Free Press of Glencoe, 1957), pp. 611–12.

4. I. L. W. Clancey, "Therapeutic Aspects of the Mental Hospital Organization," *Canadian Psychiatric Association Journal* (July, 1959), *4* (3), 153–62.

5. H. Warren Dunham and S. Kirson Weinberg, *The Culture of the State Mental Hospital* (Detroit: Wayne State University Press, 1960), and Alfred H. Stanton and Morris Schwartz, *The Mental Hospital* (New York: Basic Books, 1954).

THE MENTAL HOSPITAL AS A "TOTAL INSTITUTION"

Erving Goffman

EVERY institution captures something of the time and interest of its members and provides something of a world for them; in brief, every institution has encompassing tendencies. When we review the different institutions in our Western society we find some that are encompassing to a degree discontinuously greater than the ones next in line. Their encompassing or total character is symbolized by the barrier to social intercourse with the outside that is often built right into the physical plant, such as locked doors, high walls, barbed wire, cliffs, water, forests, or moors. These I am calling *total institutions*, and it is their general characteristics,[1] especially the characteristics of the inmate world and of the staff world, that I want to explore.

The total institutions of our society can be listed in five rough groupings. First, there are institutions established to care for persons felt to be both incapable and harmless: these are the homes for the blind, the aged, the orphaned and the indigent. Second, there are places established to care for persons felt to be both incapable of looking after themselves and a threat to the community, albeit an unintended one: TB sanitoria, mental hospitals, and leprosoria. A third type of total institution is organized to protect the community against what are felt to be intentional dangers to it, with the welfare of the persons thus sequestered not the immediate issue: jails, penitentiaries, P.O.W. camps and concentration camps. Fourth, there are institutions purportedly established the better to pursue some work-like task, and justifying themselves only on these instrumental grounds: army barracks, ships, boarding schools, work camps, colonial compounds, and the servants' quarters of large mansions. Finally, there are those establishments designed as retreats from the world even while often serving also as training stations for the religious: abbeys, monasteries, convents, and other cloisters. This classification of total institutions is not neat, exhaustive, or of immediate analytical use, but it does provide a purely denotative

definition of the category as a concrete starting point. By anchoring the initial definition of total institutions in this way, I hope to be able to discuss the general characteristics of the type without becoming tautological.

Before I attempt to extract a general profile from this list of establishments, I would like to mention one conceptual problem: none of the elements I will describe seems peculiar to total institutions, and none seems to be shared by every one of them; what is distinctive about total institutions is that each exhibits many items in this family of attributes to an intense degree. In speaking of "common characteristics," then, I will be using this phrase in a way that is restricted but I think logically defensible. At the same time it will become possible to exploit the method of ideal types, so that common features can be established with the hope of highlighting significant differences later.

A basic social arrangement in modern society is that we tend to sleep, play, and work in different places, in each case with a different set of co-participants, under a different authority, and without an over-all rational plan. The central feature of total institutions can be described as a breakdown of the barriers ordinarily separating these three spheres of life. First, all aspects of life are conducted in the same place and under the same single authority. Second, each phase of the member's daily activity is carried on in the immediate company of a large number of others, all of whom are treated alike and required to do the same thing together. Third, all phases of the day's activities are tightly scheduled, with one activity leading at a prearranged time into the next, and the whole sequence of activities being imposed from above through a system of explicit formal rulings and by a body of officials. Finally, the contents of the various enforced activities are brought together as parts of a single over-all rational plan purportedly designed to fulfill the official aims of the institution.

Individually, these totalistic features are found in places other than total institutions. For example, our large commercial, industrial, and educational establishments increasingly provide cafeterias and off-hour recreation for their members; use of these extended facilities remains voluntary in many particulars, however, and special care is taken to see that the ordinary line of authority does not extend to them. Similarly, housewives or farm families can find all their major spheres of life within the same fenced-in area, but these persons are not collectively regimented and do not march through the day's activities in the immediate company of many others like themselves.

The handling of many human needs by the bureaucratic organization of whole blocks of people—whether or not this is a necessary or effective means of social organization in the circumstances—can be taken, then, as the key fact of total institutions. From this follow certain important implications.

When persons are caused to move in blocks, they can be supervised by personnel whose chief activity is not guidance or periodic checking (as in many employer-employee relations) but rather surveillance—a seeing to it that everyone does what he has been clearly told is required of him, under conditions where one person's infraction is likely to stand out in relief against the visible, constantly examined, compliance of the others. Which comes first, the large blocks of managed people or the small supervisory staff, is not here at issue; the point is that each is made for the other.

In total institutions there is a basic split between the large managed group, conveniently called inmates, and the small supervisory staff. Inmates typically live in and have restricted contact with the world outside the walls; staff often operate on an eight-hour day and are socially integrated into the outside world.[2] Each grouping tends to conceive of the other in terms of narrow hostile stereotypes: staff often seeing inmates as bitter, secretive and untrustworthy, while inmates often see staff as condescending, high-handed and mean. Staff tends to feel superior and righteous; inmates tend, in some ways at least, to feel inferior, weak, blameworthy and guilty.[3]

Social mobility between the two strata is grossly restricted; social distance is typically great and often formally prescribed. Even talk across the boundaries may be conducted in a special tone of voice, as illustrated in a fictionalized record of an actual sojourn in a mental hospital:

"I tell you what," said Miss Hart when they were crossing the dayroom. "You do everything Miss Davis says. Don't think about it, just do it. You'll get along all right."

As soon as she heard the name Virginia knew what

was terrible about Ward One. Miss Davis, "Is she the head nurse?"

"And how," muttered Miss Hart. And then she raised her voice. The nurses had a way of acting as if the patients were unable to hear anything that was not shouted. Frequently they said things in normal voices that the ladies were not supposed to hear; if they had not been nurses you would have said they frequently talked to themselves. "A most competent and efficient person, Miss Davis," announced Miss Hart.[4]

Although some communication is necessary between inmates and the staff guarding them, one of the guard's functions is the control of communication from inmates to higher staff levels. A research study of mental hospitals provides an illustration:

Since many of the patients are anxious to see the doctor on his rounds, the attendants must act as mediators between the patients and the physician if the latter is not to be swamped. On Ward 30, it seemed to be generally true that patients without physical symptoms who fell into the two lower privilege groups were almost never permitted to talk to the physician unless Dr. Baker himself asked for them. The persevering, nagging delusional group—who were termed "worry warts," "nuisances," "bird dogs," in the attendants' slang—often tried to break through the attendant-mediator but were always quite summarily dealt with when they tried.[5]

Just as talk across the boundary is restricted, so, too, is the passage of information, especially information about the staff's plans for inmates. An important aspect of the position from which the inmate faces staff is exclusion from knowledge of the decisions taken regarding his fate. Whether the official grounds are military, as in concealing travel destination from the ranks, or medical, as in concealing diagnosis, plan of treatment, and approximate length of stay from tuberculosis patients,[6] such exclusion gives staff a special basis of distance from and control over inmates.

All these restrictions of contact presumably help to maintain the antagonistic stereotypes.[7] Two different social and cultural worlds develop, jogging alongside each other with points of official contact but little mutual penetration. Significantly, the institutional plant and name come to be identified by both staff and inmates as somehow belonging to staff, so that when either grouping refers to the views or interests of "the institution," by implication they are referring (as I shall also) to the views and concerns of the staff.

The staff-inmate split is one major implication of the bureaucratic management of large blocks of persons; a second pertains to work.

In the ordinary arrangements of living in our society, the authority of the work-place stops with the worker's receipt of a money payment; the spending of this in a domestic and recreational setting is the private affair of the worker and a mechanism through which the authority of the work-place is kept within strict bounds. But to say that inmates of total institutions have their full day scheduled for them is to say that all basic needs will have to be planned for, that he institution must guarantee to provide everything essential. Whatever the incentive given for work, then, this incentive will not have the structural significance it has on the outside. There will have to be different motives for work and different attitudes toward it. Here is a basic adjustment required of the inmates and of those who must induce them to work.

Sometimes so little work is required that inmates, often untrained in leisurely pursuits, suffer extremes of boredom. The work that is required is carried on at a very slow pace and may be geared into a system of minor, often ceremonial, payments, such as the weekly tobacco ration and the Christmas presents that lead some mental patients to stay on their jobs. In other cases, of course, more than a full day's work is required, induced not by reward but by threat of physical punishment. In some total institutions, such as logging camps and merchant ships, the practice of forced-saving postpones buying, the usual function of money in the world; all needs are organized by the institution and payment is given only when a work season is over and the men leave the premises. In some institutions there is a kind of slavery, with the inmate's full time placed at the convenience of staff. Here the inmate's sense of self and sense of possession can become alienated from his work capacity. T. E. Lawrence gives an illustration in his record of service in a R.A.F. training depot:

The six-weeks men we meet on fatigues shock our moral sense by their easy-going. "You're silly——, you rookies, to sweat yourselves," they say. Is it our new keenness, or a relic of civility in us? For by the R.A.F. we shall be paid all the twenty-four hours a day, at three halfpence an hour; paid to work, paid to eat, paid to sleep: always those halfpence ara adding up. Impossible, therefore, to dignify a job by doing it well. It must take

as much time as it can for afterwards there is not a fireside waiting, but another job.[8]

Whether there is too much work or too little, the individual who was work-oriented on the outside tends to become demoralized by the work system of the total institution. An example of such demoralization is the practice in state mental hospitals of "bumming" or "working someone for" a nickel or dime to spend in the canteen. Persons do this—often with some defiance—who on the outside would consider such actions beneath their self-respect. (Staff members, interpreting this begging pattern in terms of their own outsider's orientation to earning, tend to see it as a symptom of mental illness and one further bit of evidence that inmates really are unwell.)

There is an incompatibility, then, between total institutions and the basic work-payment structure of our society. Total institutions are also incompatible with another crucial element of our society, the family. Family life is sometimes contrasted with solitary living, but in fact the more pertinent contrast might be with block-living, for those who eat and sleep and work with a group of fellow-workers can hardly sustain a meaningful domestic existence.[9] Correspondingly, maintaining families off the grounds often permits staff members to remain integrated with the outside community and to escape the encompassing tendency of the total institution.

Whether a particular total institution acts as a good or bad force in civil society, force it may well have, and this will depend on the suppression of a whole circle of actual or potential households. Conversely, the formation of households provides a structural guarantee that total institutions will not arise. The incompatibility of these two forms of social organization should tell us something about the wider social functions of them both.

The total institution, then, is a social hybrid, part residential community, part formal organization; therein lies its special sociological interest. There are other reasons for being interested in these establishments, too. They are the forcing houses for changing persons in our society; each is a natural experiment on what can be done to the self. . . .

NOTES

1. The category of total institutions has been pointed out from time to time in sociological literature under a variety of names, and some of the characteristics of the class have been suggested, most notably perhaps in Howard Rowland's neglected paper, "Segregated Communities and Mental Health," in *Mental*

Health Publication of the American Association for the Advancement of Science, No. 9, edited by F. R. Moulton, 1939. A preliminary statement of the present paper is reported in the third (1956) *Group Processes Proceedings*, Josiah Macy, Jr., Foundation, edited by Bertram Schaffner, 1957. The term "total" has also been used in its present context in Amitai Etzioni, "The Organizational Structure of 'Closed' Educational Institutions in Israel," *Harvard Educational Review*, 27 (1957), 115.

2. The binary character of total institutions was pointed out to me by Gregory Bateson, and has been noted in sociological literature. See, for example, Lloyd E. Ohlin, *Sociology and the Field of Corrections* (New York: Russell Sage Foundation, 1956), 14, 20. In situations where staff are also required to live-in, we may expect staff to feel they are suffering special hardships and to have brought home to them a status-dependency on life on the inside which they did not expect. See Jane Cassels Record, "The Marine Radioman's Struggle for Status," *American Journal of Sociology*, 52 (1957), 359.

3. For the prison version, see S. Kirson Weinberg, "Aspects of the Prison's Social Structure," *American Journal of Sociology*, 47 (1942), 717–726.

4. Mary Jane Ward, *The Snake Pit* (New York: Signet Books, 1955), 72.

5. Ivan Belknap, *Human Problems of a State Mental Hospital* (New York: McGraw-Hill, 1956), 177.

6. A very full case report on this matter is provided in a chapter titled "Information and the Control of Treatment," in Julius A. Roth's forthcoming monograph on the tuberculosis hospital. His work promises to be a model study of a total institution. Preliminary statements may be found in his articles, "What is an Activity?" *Etc.*, 14 (Autumn, 1956), 54–56, and "Ritual and Magic in the Control of Contagion," *American Sociological Review*, 22 (June, 1957), 310–314.

7. Suggested in Ohlin, *op. cit.*, p. 20.

8. T. E. Lawrence, *The Mint* (London: Jonathan Cape, 1955), 40.

9. An interesting marginal case here is the Israeli *kibbutz*. See Melford E. Spiro, *Kibbutz: Venture in Utopia* (Cambridge: Harvard University Press, 1956), and Etzioni, *op. cit.*

BUREAUCRATIC STRUCTURE AND IMPERSONAL EXPERIENCE IN MENTAL HOSPITALS

Merton J. Kahne

THE study of the mental hospital as a structured system of social organization is now recognized as a legitimate and fruitful concern of psychiatrists and social scientists. Many recent studies[1] point to the probability that hospital organization has a significant influence on both quantitative and qualitative aspects of patient treatment. It is even suggested that the social structure of the mental hospital materially determines the prevalence and character of certain symptoms,[2] the criteria used in the diagnosis of illness, and perhaps diagnosis itself. Most of the studies have been patient-centered[3]—that is, certain recurrent difficulties of patients were related to various aspects of institutional functioning. Remedial attempts to counteract the observed difficulties were also patient-centered; the mode of hospital functioning was changed where it seemed related to particular difficulties. While I agree with the incremental approach to institutional change as the most desirable—though not utopian—approach, I wish in this paper to focus attention instead upon a major system of hospital organization as such—the bureaucratic system—and to stimulate further interest in its detailed study through a discussion of some of its implications. Virtually all studies of the relationship between institutional structure and patient experience in mental hospitals discuss the degree to which the formal organization promotes or inhibits the emergence of distinctive, subjectively 'personal' experiences in its patients.[4] I hope to show that many of the inhibiting forces can be traced to the bureaucratic aspects of institutional structure.

Statements about structure are descriptions of repetitive patterns of relationships and processes among people. The rules, regulations, chains of command and communication, policies, obligations, expectations, divisions of labor, and other static formalities represent the generalization and systematic codification of the way people will or ought to behave. They describe the possibilities of an event's occurrence and the range of probabilities in the scheduling of choices. Directly or indirectly they cast light on the values and taboos guiding the actions of participants. But however abstract they become, they are always related to events involving human beings, and insofar as a patient occupies a position in the structure, he is involved. That they are shorthand expressions for daily events obscures the impact of the recognition that, in their totality, *they determine the patient's hospital experience.*[5]

This discussion will concentrate on formal institutional structure for many reasons. Formal structure is more stable than informal and as such has more recurrent effects on people hospitalized over a long period of time. It functions more reliably under most circumstances and enables one to predict the consequences of an action more definitively. One can be much more certain about the accuracy of a message and the time it will take to get from a hospital superintendent to a particular patient, if it goes "through channels" rather than via "rumor."

Informal structure is always contingent on the formal, and the number of variables affecting informal structure can usually be specified only within the context of particular events.[6] The study of the informal adds much to an understanding of both the deficiencies and effectiveness of formal structure.[7] However, the influence of informality per se is a separate issue from the influence of bureaucratic form, and I will refer to it only to highlight certain aspects of formal structure.

Bureaucracy, as I understand it, is neither good nor bad; it is a particular organization with certain structural features. It is probably the most universal administrative form in modern social organizations and is certainly the characteristic form of mental hospital organization in the United States at the present time.[8] The connotations of officialism which cling to the term are not the primary area of my interest. I hope to show that it is the subtle, silent, rationally efficient, administratively effective aspects of bureaucracy that inhibit

Reprinted from *Psychiatry* (1959), pp. 363–375. Copyright © 1959 by the William Alanson White Psychiatric Foundation and used by permission.

individualization of patient treatment, *as a common consequence of its functioning.*

The distinction is of particular importance. Because I regard the *normal* functioning of bureaucratic structure as inevitably leading to impersonal relationships, I do not believe it advisable to try to 'personalize' bureaucratic relationships. I advocate instead the elimination of bureaucracy completely in areas where personal relations are shown to be necessary in patient treatment, or, if this is impossible, at least the provision of structural inhibitions to its worst features.

I intend also to discuss the serious lack of safeguards against bureaucratic liabilities in usual hospital administrative structures. I believe that unless the essential nature of the problem is recognized, the gains of the various hospital reforms may easily become engulfed in the system, with the *form* of the changes institutionalized as procedures and the original *purpose* lost in the arid complacency of bureaucratic efficiency.

THE STRUCTURE OF BUREAUCRACY

The wellspring for both theoretical and pragmatic study of bureaucracy is the work of Max Weber.[9] While subsequent students of the subject have altered and delimited his original conception significantly, it still remains the focal point of present-day discussion.[10] The central core of structural characteristics which distinguishes bureaucratic form from other administrative forms consists of: pyramiding chains (a hierarchy) of coordination and control of such aspects of organizational functioning as decision-making, task allocation, communication, and so forth; the use of rules, regulations, or official policies prescribed by the organization's charter to define and limit the alternative choices or actions a person may make when performing his official function; a high degree of specialization of skills and functions, with sharply demarcated division of labor, especially at the top of the hierarchy; organizational ownership of necessary tools, property, and instruments; and a conscious and deliberate attempt by the leaders to organize all of the organization's available means to officially prescribed ends in the most efficient manner through rational planning.[11]

An examination of the usual assumptions underlying the development of such a structure will help focus attention on the relationship of bureaucratic form to the emergence of impersonal patient experience in the mental hospital. Dahl and Lindblom suggest that bureaucracy tends to develop when a situation recurrently requires complex decisions beyond the competence of any one person, when there is need for a relatively small number of people to coordinate the behavior of large numbers, or when there are believed to be advantages to a division of labor to accomplish a particular task. They further suggest that the importance of money as a status symbol is rapidly declining in the United States, and in the absence of an aristocracy or other formalized ways of conferring status, the authority to direct, influence, or exercise control over others is increasingly becoming a significant symbol of status. They believe that the wish for status as an end in itself, coupled with a bias in favor of rational planning—one's behavior at work should at least have the outward appearance of being sensible—further contributes to the cluster of characteristics. Dubin emphasizes that when the size of an organization reaches the point where leaders no longer have time or energy to contact all members personally, intermediaries and lines of authority become necessities.[12] He further stresses that differences in background of personnel—educational, ethnic, social, and so forth—require an organization that can properly select and coordinate personnel and assign them to tasks according to principles of procedure which will be accepted and can be enforced. Dubin also suggests that limitation of purpose and specialization of function of an organization may tend to develop goals which become hard to relate to the more general goals of society. This narrow specialization tends to limit the time employees are willing to devote to their particular organization—other, broader aspects of social living also claim their attention. In such situations, developing an optimum level of output, with minimum friction between the various claims, usually requires marked organization of training and control functions, which fosters bureaucratic form.

These, then, are the characteristics and assumptions surrounding bureaucratic organizational structure. What are some of their effects in the mental hospital?

THE CONCEPT OF "PATIENT NEEDS"

The very conception of what events will 'involve' mental hospital patients is altered by the bureaucratic structure. Specialization and division of labor tend to blind participants to the total picture. The daily experiences of functionally differentiated personnel tend to produce a bias as to the importance of certain events for patient welfare. The more highly specialized the departments, the more difficult it is to secure a consensus; principles acceptable to everyone will necessarily be general formulations which can encompass their biases. Furthermore, hierarchy makes the legitimacy of an opinion mostly a reflection of status, and since control over formal communication rests inevitably with higher echelons, 'official' patient needs usually represent the opinions of upper-level personnel. Because task fragmentation in mental hospitals means that upper-level personnel are most distant from the patient, their formulations about patient needs are invariably based upon the needs of patients in general.

These tendencies toward *generalization* about patient needs are always significantly influenced by additional aspects of bureaucratic organization. For example, decision-makers must continuously strive to maximize use of all available means in the interests of efficiency, and each functional group must promote its own particular service or risk a lower status in the hierarchy. In the mental hospital, as in other bureaucratic structures, busyness and activity are often confused with qualitative values. Patients who do not use available facilities challenge the status interests of personnel and the rationale of the hospital programming; since the fiction of institutional omniscience must be maintained, their behavior is often seen as pathological. Indeed, a great deal of patient ennui is reported incorrectly as depression. Patients are expected to get well, worsen, or remain the same in accordance with a set of rules of social conduct derived from a concept of patient needs which must always be congruent with institutional resources.

Thus, as seen in mental hospitals, patient needs usually turn out to be socially organized rights, obligations, and expectancies required of both patients and personnel. Wishes of patients, if considered important, are acted on in terms of those claims on the services or emotions of others which are considered socially legitimate demands of patients.[13] When personnel recognize that fulfillment of a patient's wishes would cause conflict, they must rationally decide among alternative responses; the maintenance of conflict as such is almost as taboo as are the socially undesirable symptoms of patients, which themselves are classed as against the norms of institutional functioning.

In a bureaucratic structure, behavior, whether intimate or impersonal, is condoned only to the extent that it is socially desirable *within* the hospital system of values, regardless of whether that system does or does not vary from that of society in general. However variant the hospital's value system may be, its structure is rigidly determined and maintained by the bureaucratic system of organization. Any proposed temporary or permanent change in behalf of a patient is immediately caught in such a web of interlocking contingencies, that it will inevitably lose a good deal of its poignancy before it takes its place among the rules and regulations of the established order.

THE LOCUS OF "IMPORTANT" DECISIONS

Because offices in bureaucratic organizations are based upon the presumed *limitations* in competence of participants, "important" decisions tend to drift to the upper echelons. In mental hospitals both functional and scalar status among clinical personnel increase in direct proportion to the distance from patients, and in inverse proportion to the time spent with them. Thus, "important" decision-making, by an official or a committee, tends to be located distantly from the patient. But whether by fiat or consensus, such decisions usually do not include the patient as a participant. In mental hospitals, authority to make "important" decisions involving patients is limited almost entirely to doctors, head nurses, or supervisors of nursing service.[14] The powerful traditions of "doctor knows best," "orders in writing," and "giving" nursing care, coupled with the illusory helplessness of patients, further promotes the upward drift. Events whose significance is unknown are necessarily "important" until proper jurisdiction has been assigned, and the usual policy, for reasons of status as well as conservatism in the face of the unknown, is to delegate downward only after prolonged study and evaluation. And division of labor makes it relatively simple to conceptualize many problems in a way that seemingly does not involve patients at all. Under skilled administrative personnel, events move so silently and effectively, and in such small increments, that many momentous decisions are not even regarded as important. For example, in one institution such intimate matters as personal letters were *routinely* censored by the "next of kin" irrespective of content or the patient's relations with his family—without notification to the patient that this was happening.

The aides themselves are reluctant to make

decisions that might antagonize the patients. Calling attention to the "importance" of a decision is one of the most common ways that lower-echelon personnel can abdicate responsibility—for that matter, it is also one of the most frequent devices for upper-echelon usurpation of authority. The tendency to pass difficult decisions to others—passing the buck—flourishes in bureaucratic structure. Of course, judicious recognition of one's limitations is a necessity if highly specialized or differentially competent staff members are to avoid serious mistakes. However, while buck-passing may have relatively minor or nuisance effects in industry, in the mental hospital it can be devastating in undermining a patient's efforts toward mental health. Often the patient's first resurgence of interest in the world consists of feeble, impulsive requests, demands, and questions which never survive the evanescent moment because they are nipped in the bud by the frost of institutional formality.

And the reverse situation also holds: upper-echelon personnel frequently abdicate responsibility by designating disagreeable decisions as "unimportant," "to be worked out" by lower-level personnel. Also, lower-level personnel commonly usurp authority through quiet minimization of the importance of a decision.

THE AUTOMATION OF BEHAVIOR

The tendency for "important" decisions to be made by upper-echelon personnel does not mean that no significant decisions are made below the level of head nurse; it does mean, however, that there is little opportunity for spontaneity[15] in face-to-face relations between patients and ward nurses, aides, occupational therapists, recreational personnel, and so forth. Plans "have to be cleared" at least with the doctor in charge and usually at higher levels for the most ordinary of everyday events. Aides "have to check and see if passes have been O.K.'d" while patients, or their relatives or friends, fidget in irritation at the locked doors of dismal corridors. Implementation of decisions located distantly from the events they affect requires long and sometimes very complex lines of communication and control, and the enthusiasm accompanying a new idea wilts into listless apathy during the trip "through channels." Furthermore, the tendency to regard lower-level personnel as incompetent to make "important" decisions results in the regulation, codification, and routinization of their activity

to the point where unique behavior with any one patient becomes suspect. Conversely, any patient's behavior which extends beyond the routine is also subject to criticism. At the ward level, routines occupy the center of the stage, and, curiously enough, response to individual needs is regarded as *special treatment*.

The behavior of people functioning within such a structure inevitably is accompanied by concentration on proper action and role. It is critically important that a person's obligations and rights conform with the expectations of others if the evaluation of his interpersonal competence is to be made by persons who are relative strangers to him and to each other. In mental hospitals, the ward is primary unit of social organization, yet in most hospitals the functional and scalar organization seriously interferes with the cohesion in its daily life. Physicians, nurses, aides, housekeepers, and other service personnel such as kitchen help all have independent chains of communication and command. As a result they often find themselves in institutionally induced conflict between responsibility to their own functional group and their obligations to and identification with the ward. The chronic necessity to serve multiple superiors whose aims are frequently tangential to each other tends to reduce their activity to a relatively indifferent, mechanical level,[16] and tends to diminish further the possibilities for closeness in human relations within the ward; such relations as do develop become governed by departmental divisions of labor, scheduled activity, and limited discretion. Doctors, for example, rarely know the names of more than a few "key personnel" on their wards, and are certainly unfamiliar with the daily duties and activities of aides; and nursing personnel are commonly transferred from óne shift to another or from one ward to another by directors of nursing service without consultation with doctors.

In such a setting, 'objective' reporting to be used as a basis for decision-making becomes a necessity. Nursing reports, "mental status evaluations," and case histories are largely a record of performances or opinions about performances, and many momentous decisions involving patients frequently rest upon a few simple behavioral characteristics. In the absence of either a sense of intimate relatedness to the patient or of identification with a social milieu which values investigation of the personal meaning of the patient's behavior, individual motivation cannot seriously be considered except for rather crude evaluations as to suicidal or homocidal intent. It is but a short step to the usually un-mentioned assumption in such decision-making that a person is likely to be "agitated" or "bizarre" in any context. Thus, although the ward is a primary unit, many of the forces acting in and through it are antithetical to its development into a fully social milieu; it remains something akin to a military staging area whose inhabitants vacillate between apathy and tense expectation, while those respons-ible for their management expend a great deal of energy in the promotion of make-work projects designed to keep them busily out of trouble.

But personal needs frequently cannot be adequately handled by the task fragmentation of 'rational' design. Wishes, fears, hopes, guilt, loneliness, grief, and anxieties have little place on the treadmill of compartmentalized and codified relations with people. Preoccupation with matters of personal concern is, in the mental hospital, generally regarded as morbid unless it happens to coincide with institutional standards of approp-riateness, and much time is spent attempting to interest patients in some form of activity, partially on the justifiable assumption that in diversified activity the patient will "get away from" such thoughts and feelings.[17] In the progres-sive fragmentation of patient experience there is small chance for the continuity which is necessary for useful investment in human objects to occur. Change in the mental hospital means a change in ward, associates, and activities. Social values attached to wards make continued relations with friends suspect, and tarrying along the production line can mean a falling out of step, with further serious consequences.

The attitudes that are assumed or the roles that are played in response to the rationalistic bias, a bias which means that even everyday human relations become grist for the mill of increasingly codified and regulated standards of performance, also veer away from consideration of the patient's unique emotional needs. For example, nurses are advised to encourage patient "socializing" but to avoid getting "involved." But in a milieu where participants cannot rely upon shared values resulting from primary group cohesion, simple cautionary suggestions do not provide sufficiently clear distinctions to serve as guides to action. The pyramid of communication itself tends to make personnel increasingly selective about the type of event which they respond to and report. Usually it is disagreeable "incidents" that are brought to the attention of superiors. The many successes that do occur daily, though talked about informally, usually do not appear with any regularity in daily reporting, and those that occasionally are reported cannot be appreciated because they often can be recognized only by intonation of voice or nuance of phrase. Con-sequently, in the mental hospital, social trouble is more easily recognized than psychiatric success, and a telephone call from a superior more often is a request for an explanation rather than recognition for a difficult achievement.

This system of organization, which places a heavy premium on the "uneventful" day and makes the reporting of disagreeable incidents the focus of formal communication, makes role definition and redefinition a tight spiral of increasing complexity, biased heavily in the direction of impersonal participation.

Consider, for example, this advice given in a recent textbook on psychiatric nursing:[18]

Discussion of Personal Relationships and Personal Values Should be Initiated Only by the Patient

In ordinary society, questions relating to family, friends and home are frequently resorted to early in relationships. In caring for mentally ill patients again we have a contrast to accepted practive. Topics to be avoided because of their potential threat to patients are family, politics, and religion. The source of the patients' difficulties may arise from, but are always related to their inter-relationships with those who are closest to them. Feelings of dislike for family members may be increasing a patient's feelings of guilt and conversation where the patient admits his hostility may cause anxiety. In regard to family, their members, occupations, likes and dislikes, always listen when a patient talks but be careful to avoid all judgments or comments that may add to a patient's anxiety. All of the above are "touchy" subjects and should be carefully handled.

When a patient does burst forth with a confession of some feeling or experience about which he obviously feels strongly, care must be exercised not to presume on the revelation. *The patient should be treated exactly as he was previously* [italics mine] and mention of what was revealed should come first from the patient. If he seems standoffish or sarcastic, it should be realized that he may be regretting what he has just said. The same relationship should be held open for him until he can accept it again, and the incident, including the patient's reaction to it, should be brought up only by the patient.

Mental hospital personnel deal daily with matters of intense concern to human beings. The erotic and aggressive preoccupations of patients coupled with regressive modes of expression exercise a continuous drain on the intellectual and particularly on the emotional resources of person-nel. Under such circumstances, where structure makes abdication so easy, detailed rules, regulations, codes of behavior meticulously organized to keep personal feelings at a minimum provide seductive havens for the avoidance of disagreeable yet perhaps desperately needed experience for patients.

Furthermore, hospital personnel are not immune to the general tendency in bureaucratic structure for means to become valued ends in themselves.[19] Mastery of jargon actually enhances one's effectiveness *in the system*. In addition, words, gestures, and the capacity for certain interpersonal performances constitute important tools in the treatment process. Since institutions cannot 'own' these in the classical sense, they must attempt to 'control' them through a codification of the circumstances under which certain events will or will not occur.[20] Like physical tools and property, jurisdiction is assigned on the basis of division of labor, and these become accentuated symbols of prestige and authority. It is not only that "everybody likes to play psychiatrist"; in the mental hospital the "right to interpret" is a hard-fought-for symbol of tremendous social and scalar importance.

The great premium placed on word-mastery has sometimes resulted in patients and personnel talking 'correctly' but with little feeling about matters of great intimacy. Such intimate events as do occur tend to do so along increasingly impersonal lines. Patients "talk" about things according to social role expectations to which they have been indoctrinated and there is a progressive hardening of their defensive positions. Thus what psychiatrists call the "working through" process is short-circuited by blunted affective relations resulting from stereotyped performance.

The clash of rigidly structured rules of relatedness with the *defensive* deviance of mentally ill people means that an enormous potential is thereby lost because daily experiences seldom receive the stamp of "real living" and usually stay at a symbolic level only. Patients have great trouble recognizing what personnel mean, for example, when they express the conviction that what the patient regards as justifiable self-assertiveness is an echo of adolescent rebellion. The arbitrariness of the rules and regulations makes them built-in scapegoats for the expression of unbridled fury—but unfortunately the issue remains continuously befogged. Bureaucratic organization implies systematized preconceptions which must be preserved at all costs. As one administrator put it, "The situation must never be permitted to occur where the patient disorganizes the entire hospital." But it also implies a brittleness

of structure which makes minor deviance a potential hospital catastrophe.

LACK OF SAFEGUARDS AGAINST BUREAUCRATIC LIABILITIES

Possibly nowhere outside the family is power so vaguely defined yet effective as in a mental hospital. There are limitations placed upon the various participants by rules, regulations, and legal codes; but legal safeguards can lull one into a false sense of security, for the powerful traditions and obscurity surrounding the mentally ill serve as bases for espousing almost any theory as to how patients should be managed. Traditionally "doctor knows best," and patients and their families are incompetent to judge what is "good for" a patient.

For example, in one hospital where state law required that commitment recommendations be performed by two physicians not on the hospital staff so as to minimize the possibility of unwarranted hospitalization, the prevailing practice was for the doctors to appear unannounced and unidentified on the ward. They would observe the patient's behavior, ask some questions on the strength of being doctors, and disappear. Patient inquiries as to the reason for the questions would be answered evasively. The nurses and aides on the ward were not clear about either the laws of the state or the doctors' authority to "observe" the patients. This procedure was considered good practice since it was thought to be less upsetting to the patients than a formal interview and supposedly more revealing. Patient suspiciousness regarded as symptomatic of mental illness could be "confirmed" by subsequent patient references to having been railroaded.

The tendency of doctors to justify by-passing social conventions out of a sense of their own good intentions is similar to that of all experts charged with the responsibility to act in the face of the unknown. This is especially so in situations of chronic or recurrent tenseness. Such tendencies are markedly potentiated rather than inhibited by bureaucratic structure. They are of particular concern in mental hospitals because the usual checks on the liabilities of bureaucratic rigidities, disparate values, and impersonalities are ordinarily present only in a limited sense.

Bureaucracies usually attempt to rectify their built-in difficulties by one or more of six methods.[21] Some systems arrange for periodic change in management through automatic mechanisms, such as elections of councils with rotating chairman-ships. Others provide opportunities for the free expression of ideas, and carefully safeguard the rights · of individuals to assemble collectively toward that end. Many attempt to maintain some sort of unified political action potential through the development or encouragement of a single value system. In other cases energetic delegation of responsibility to lower echelons is practiced. Sometimes a sort of automatic mechanism—for example, the stock market—is provided where the relative merits of competing values can be quantified in equivalent terms. Should these methods fail, leaders may *temporarily* attempt to unify the system or overcome the troublesome inflexibilities by narrowing the range of authority and concentrating it in the hands of a few leaders, who are expected to deal with the difficulty and then voluntarily return the authority to the appropriate offices. The last method is usually reserved for situations where forces external to the system are exerting the significant influence.

In the mental hospital, managerial status is achieved primarily through professional affiliation, and it is usually only within the confines of the opportunities set by the functional group that one may move. While there is a certain amount of scalar parallelism between the different functional groups, the "managerial elite" is composed almost entirely of physicians and a limited number of selected departmental heads. In addition to the structurally induced biases which could normally be expected to accentuate differences of opinion, marked differences of economic, educational, religious, and social status between doctors and, for example, aides, support the impression that events will be viewed differently by those at the bottom and those at the top of the hierarchy.

Management, if it changes at all, generally moves only in an upward direction. Competence in task performance usually eventuates in a "promotion." Management is so closely tied to scaler status that a return to the ranks is tant-amount to demotion. The tendency for the most competent to move "up the ladder" and out of the patient's orbit is one of the most devastating structural effects. In addition to lowering the level of social possibilities in the patient's immediate environment, it results in recurrent fluctuation in the integrity of the milieu because of the continuous necessity to indoctrinate and educate new participants.

While freedom to come together and exchange views is not prohibited, it has only recently come to be regarded as a potential tool for maximizing the effectiveness of hospital personnel in relation to patients.[22] But there is no indication that such groups have yet been able to effect a significant counterbalance to institutional rigidities. The acceptance of patient or lower-level personnel opinion in the deliberations of manager-ial councils generally eventuates, in bureaucratic structure, in some sort of formalization of the relatedness of the group to the hierarchy and becomes subject to the same rigidities as all other functional groups.

The characteristic methods used in mental hospitals to achieve some degree of unity of values are sporadic, intensive programs of "in-service education" and recurrent references to the hospital's philosophy of patient care. A great deal of what passes for education in the training of mental hospital personnel, including resident physicians, consists essentially of energetic propagandizing in behalf of a particular system of values made plausible by the self-validating tendencies of closed social structures and reinforced by the rigid protocols of hierarchical status differentiation. Doctors in such organizations usually do not talk about patients with aides as equals, or, if they do, their mutual perspectives are so completely alien that each has the impression that the ideas of the other are by and large irrelevant to the significant problems of the patient.[23] The phenomenon is self-sustaining; when the question of delegation of responsibility to lower levels comes up, upper-level personnel (doctors) justify their assumptions that this must be approached cautiously on the basis that the lower-level personnel (aides) are not competent to make important decisions because they obviously do not see the relevance of the doctors' opinions and must first be educated. Lower-level personnel become more covert in activities which they regard as relevant, since their position in the hierarchy renders hazardous any sustained attempt to go counter to established authority.[24]

Obfuscation of simple observations and common, everyday experience is further stabilized by the mystery surrounding mental illness; the tendency to think of patient behavior as a thing apart is supported both internally, by the residuals of childhood fears and disowned wishes, and externally, by the structure of personnel relations.

Delegation downwards, then, occurs only in the most unusual of circumstances and is main-tained, somewhat precariously, only by the most energetic leadership. Furthermore, although superiors have control over the formal structure of communication, they are special prey to the informal subversion of their official directives by nominal inferiors. The illusion that control is unilateral in hierarchy is one of its more serious handicaps. In mental hospitals formal communication channels are handled so haphazardly and are so lengthy and unwieldy that they are generally useless as agencies for the dissemination of information except perhaps retrospectively. Nursing notes are kept meticulously in most institutions and are rarely if ever read with any regularity by anybody. They are sometimes *scanned* or selectively reported verbally, but even so their stereotype and condensations render them relatively limited as guides to action. Also, the high premium placed on verbal manipulative skill in mental hospitals makes communicative interchange as much an exercise in administrative gamesmanship as in information transfer.

Traditionally, in mental hospitals, when there is recognized difficulty in the enforcement of a particular value, when change in formalities is underway, or when there is a breakdown or excessive rigidity in established modes of performance, the authority to make a decision becomes concentrated in the hands of a particular person, and more often than not such authority is not reassigned. Chronic shortages of personnel believed to have the capacity to assume responsibility, traditions contributing to a feeling of an urgent necessity to take action, legal obstructions to the delegation of responsibility to nonprofessional personnel, and particularly the efficiency of the method, all provide adequate rationalizations for this preferred method of attempting to deal with difficulties. Unfortunately the same rationalizations can be and usually are used as the basis for the maintenance of power in the hands of the few.

THE ARTIFICIAL DIVISION OF LABOR

Finally, although there is a great deal of formal organization of services into various departments in mental hospitals (with marked socioeconomic status differentiation resulting), some of the departmental division of labor seems arbitrary and not supported by clinical necessities.

In a five-day time study of the day shift of three active wards of an intensive treatment psychiatric center,[25] it was found that the roles of aide and staff nurse were usually interchangeable in regard to either the *area* (subject matter) of the activity performed or the *level* (category of personnel to whom the task might most appropriately be assigned) of the task. Both groups

spent approximately 87 to 92 percent of their time in the area of patient care: that is, carrying out a procedure for a patient, assisting a doctor, evaluating patient needs, escorting patients, listening to talk about patients, charting, and so forth. While the amount of time spent in the specific activity varied slightly between staff nurse and aide, almost all of the activities performed by one group were performed by the other.

Except when governed by legal prohibitions, such as preparation of medications, the assignments were largely traditional and varied quantitatively from ward to ward. For example, on Ward A the aides gave more physical care (carrying out a nursing procedure of assisting a doctor with treatments or procedures) than nurses, but on Ward B they gave only about one-third as much physical care as the nurses. On the other hand, in the Insulin and Electric Shock Unit of Ward C, where special conditions prevailed, both the nurses and the aides spent much more time in this activity than either group on Wards A or B. On the other hand, staff nurses usually did not participate in dietary activity except in the insulin unit—ordinarily this was aides' work. (See the accompanying table.)

PERCENTAGE OF STAFF TIME SPENT IN
PHYSICAL NURSING CARE

	Head Nurse	Staff Nurse	Aide	Aide Trainee
Ward A	1.86	8.73	5.10	9.77
Ward B	——	6.90	1.60	.70
Ward C	2.90	32.70	24.00	1.80

The 8 percent to 13 percent of the time not spent in the area of patient care was of interest from the standpoint of status differentiation. Among nurses, about two-thirds of this time was spent in clerical activities, with one-third divided between messenger and dietary activities—almost no housekeeping duty was done by nurses (none recorded in this sample). Aides spent about one-half of this time in housekeeping activities and divided the rest among messenger, dietary, and clerical activities.

The special point is that in all the wards the distribution of labor seemed to be dictated by factors other than one's identity as a nurse or an aide. In my opinion, the only factors which seem consistently to determine the relative numbers of aides or nurses on a ward and their respective task assignments, in the present scarce market for both, are the hospital budget and tradition supported by vested interest.

CONCLUSIONS

In the mental hospital, then, bureaucratic structure provides an important sustaining medium for powerful traditions which favor the development of impersonal experience. Singly, or in combination, the aspects of this administrative form provide a nidus for the development of latent tendencies among its participants toward stereotyped attitudes and procedures in relation to patients. The unspoken but tacitly agreed upon assumptions that these traditional relations between patients and personnel are the preferred relations are actively maintained by rules, regulations, and codes of behavior, so that the sense of having had a 'personal' experience can emerge only under limited and carefully circumscribed circumstances. The determinants for the conditions under which such events will occur are social norms established by administrative decree, despite the fact that there is a marked lack of consensus regarding the importance of 'personal' experiences among the various status groups.

The structure of relations in mental hospitals is such that the forces emenating from its existence operate centrifugally to the efforts of human beings toward personal involvement with each other. It tends to generate generalized conceptions regarding the nature of human aspiration and standardized concepts of individual motivation and behavior. It accentuates the automatic, ritualistic, and formalistic propensities of social structure at the expense of flexibility, individualization, and innovation. It places an exceptional value on what is regarded as rational performance and confuses the socially idiosyncratic with the individually pathological. In addition, in its present form it possesses few of the usual safeguards to bureaucratic liabilities and suffers from repeated distortions of reforms designed to make patient experience more personal.

Perhaps the most striking characteristic emerging from bureaucratic structure in mental hospitals is best described in Weber's terms:

The dominance of a spirit of formalistic impersonality, *"Sine ira et studio,"* without hatred or passion, and hence without affection or enthusiasm. The dominant norms are straightforward duty without regard to personal considerations. Everyone is subject to formal equality of treatment; *that is everyone in the same empirical situation* [italics mine].[26]

A good deal of sophistication has been achieved in understanding the interpersonal determinants of events which effect a material alteration of a person's mental health. One of these, I suggest, is a social setting in which repetitive experience evokes in the patient an active sense of personal involvement with people. While I believe that it is possible to develop such a milieu through deliberate planning, I would caution that the formal structure of the relations among participants is certainly as important as the form of particular events, and, operating through time, exerts a significant effect upon the meaning of such events, often antithetical to the original intent of the planners. My study of bureaucracy in mental hospitals suggests that its context is overwhelmingly impersonal despite particular situations which may have an intimate form. But the study of the details of this particular structure does more than identify a general evil. It suggests another dimension which needs to be mastered if incremental advances are to have a sustained effect upon patients' lives.

NOTES

1. See, for instance, Alfred H. Stanton and Morris S. Schwartz, *The Mental Hospital*; New York, Basic Books, 1954. This excellent model of collaborative activity between a psychiatrist and a social scientist is especially valuable for its critical review of the converging studies of authors from different professional disciplines and of the subsequent development of the emerging field. It also contains an excellent annotated bibliography, and penetrating observations on the relations between specific symptoms of patients and their hospital context. See also Milton Greenblatt, Richard H. York, and Esther Lucile Brown, *From Custodial to Therapeutic Patient Care in Mental Hospitals*; New York, Russell Sage Foundation, 1955; Maxwell Jones, *The Therapeutic Community*; New York, Basic Books, 1953; and Ivan Belknap, *Human Problems of a State Mental Hospital*; New York, McGraw-Hill, 1956.

2. See, for example, the studies of the relation of pathological excitement and incontinence to the hospital setting, in *The Mental Hospital* (footnote 1; pp. 342–377); Edwin A. Weinstein, Robert L. Kahn, and Sidney Malitz, "Confabulation as a Social Process," *Psychiatry* (1956) 19:383–396; and Alfred H. Stanton and Morris S. Schwartz, "Observations on Dissociation as Social Participation," *Psychiatry* (1949) 12:339–354.

3. For a significant exception, see Jules Henry, "Types of Institutional Structure," *Psychiatry* (1957) 20:47–60. In this article the author discusses the properties which emerge as a result of the formal system of task subordination which he has classified around four basic models.

4. 'Personal' experiences result when aspects of a person's personality evoke expectations and responses in others that are not related to one's status within the social system under consideration—in this case, the status of patient. Much of what people regard in themselves as unique is illusory, but it is to this particular *me* which lends the sense of identity to a person that I refer.

5. This concept, of course, carries implications far beyond the aim of this paper. It may be asked, for example: Is this *all* the patient's experience? Patients dream, remember previous experience, and entertain in reverie hopes for the future, all in varying states of consciousness at different times. Also, no system of social organization is perfect in its codification of human experience; and 'social' is not equated with 'mental.' On the other hand, I am persuaded that, at least in adults, all experience is influenced by the person's social reality. A person's current wishes, much of the form taken by the manifest content of his dreams, whether he will consider it important enough to remember, and how and to whom he will report it—all are intimately connected with the daily events of life. It is precisely because

of the continuous interplay between 'social' and 'private' experience that social structure achieves psychiatric importance in the mental hospital.

6. Morale, for example, is unfortunately still considered under informal structure so that its social determinants remain obscure and methods for consciously developing morale are still relatively primitive.

7. There is much to suggest that if the formal structure does not provide opportunities for 'personal' experience, this will develop informally. In bureaucratic structure, however, participation in informal activities is heavily loaded with a sense of illicitness which in turn tends to undermine the social value of an event.

8. While little agreement exists about the necessity for this particular structure and much suggests that other forms might be more desirable, a brief examination of most mental hospitals, however "therapeutic" or "custodial," will convince one that the overwhelming majority of institutions employ this mode of administrative organization. Tables of organization will usually show hierarchical relations organized according to functional divisions of labor, nursing services, medical departments, occupational therapy, and so forth. In fact, the idea that there could be any other method of organization—for example, loosely structured, associational primary groups or confederations—is scarcely ever noted in medical institutions except among so-called public health stations (tuberculosis), research units, or polio wings of general hospitals. Some psychiatrists, Phillip Christiansen, for example, have argued on clinical grounds of the necessity for wards to be organized as loosely structured associational primary groups, but have given little systematic reference beyond the immediate clinical necessities.

It is important to recognize that the rough classification of an institution as "therapeutic" or "custodial" is functional, oriented around a concept of therapeutic activity in which there is one who "gives" and one who "receives"—an illusion which is exploited enormously in the jockeying for position in organizational politics. An aide, for example, supposedly contributes less insight "to" a patient than does a doctor.

9. Max Weber, *The Theory of Social and Economic Organization*, translated by A. M. Henderson and Talcott Parsons and edited by Talcott Parsons; New York, Oxford Univ. Press, 1947.

10. For a comprehensive review of studies of bureaucratic structure, see Robert K. Merton, Ailsa P. Gray, Barbara Hockey, and Hanan C. Selvin, editors, *Reader in Bureaucracy*; Glencoe, Ill., Free Press, 1952.

11. This description of bureaucratic structure leans heavily on a particularly valuable reference covering some of the wider horizons of social science: Robert A. Dahl and Charles E. Lindblom, *Politics, Economics and Welfare: Planning and Politico-Economic Systems Resolved into Basic Social Processes; New York, Harper, 1953.*

12. Robert Dubin, "Technical Characteristics of a Bureaucracy," pp. 156–161; in *Human Relations in Administration*, edited by Robert Dubin; New York, Prentice-Hall, 1951.

13. I do not regard institutional social norms as intrinsically opposed to individual wishes, but I believe that such a structure is especially impervious to the "irrational" whims, preferences, and eccentricities which people value as a mark of so-called individuality. To use an analogy: While pimples constitute a legitimate object of study by the pathologist, skin cancer is of more serious import for survival. Bureaucratic structure as such provides no built-in mechanism for the differentiation of the relative importance of "irrational" events except through involved, hierarchical decision-making.

14. Chronic shortages of personnel, of course, lend a discordant note to the system of values. In most state hospitals, lower-echelon personnel make the majority of decisions and are delegated enormous responsibility. But more often than not official delegation of responsibility to lower levels in the hierarchy is associated with a parallel devaluation of the "importance" of the event.

15. This much abused term needs clarification. Spontaneity in social interaction is often confused with undisciplined indulgence of one's wishes. Personal relations with patients in

no way implies lack of social restraint or abandonment of professional standards of conduct. It connotes removing the woodenness from the formalities and adapting one's performance to individual human needs without compromising one's adherence to technical necessities. I do not advocate abandonment of social responsibility, but wish to make it less awkward.

16. For a more detailed treatment of some of the problems of task-differentiated subordination see Jules Henry, footnote 3.

17. While relief from the press of intense emotional experiences which patients cannot ordinarily handle is a legitimate *temporary* function of mental hospital organization, the structuring of *stable* modes of avoidance can hardly be condoned. The taboo against exposing patients to any experience likely to generate strong emotion is prevalent in most mental hospitals. Yet many thoughtful psychiatrists have increasingly come to recognize that psychotherapeutic procedures which they could not carry out outside the hospital setting can be systematically planned, with the patient, and carried out in the hospital with safety.

Also, the imaginative use of facilities for purposes other than their original intent has often been of considerable value. I am indebted, for example, to Lydia G. Dawes for the observation that the planned use of *somber* music helped evoke illuminating moods in a patient which could be explored usefully and safely within the controlled setting of a hospital.

18. Ruth V. Matheney and Mary Topalis, *Psychiatric Nursing*; St. Louis, C. V. Mosby, 1953; p. 76.

19. If anyone doubts the importance of status in a mental hospital as a valued end in itself, let him seriously propose that Occupational Therapy be changed in name to Hobby Shop, or that Nursing Service be abolished as a department and ward nurses be placed jurisdictionally solely under the doctor on whose ward they work. Or let him note publicly that it is mostly a legal convention to distinguish "psychotherapy" from, for example, "counseling."

20. The myriad ramifications of institutional ownership of all tools involved in the treatment process will not be discussed, although a study of the matter emphasizes the tendency for bureaucratic structure to produce impersonal patient experience. The current literature is replete with references to the importance of maintaining a patient's sense of identity and his interest in life, throughout the difficult period of chronic or seemingly endless hospitalization, by allowing him to retain such mementos of private life as pictures, rings, driver's licenses, and personal clothes. But scant attention has been given to the insidious effects of institutional ownership and departmental distribution of all tools and property necessary to the daily activities of both patients and personnel.

21. After Dahl and Lindblom, footnote 11.

22. I am indebted to Paul Howard for an opportunity to participate in the Patient-Personnel Conference of the McLean Hospital. This unique organization, despite a self-imposed lack of 'official' authority, may be justifiably proud of its many achievements in effecting increased understanding of the needs and aims of patients and staff, to the mutual benefit of both groups.

23. It is curious that persons formulating policies relating to the care and treatment of patients tend to think that their values are or ought to be shared by all personnel, and daily ignore the reality of significant differences of opinion. When differences in values are called to their attention, they rarely consider the possibility that such differences are the inevitable result of institutional structure. I am reminded of the findings of Stouffer and his co-workers of tendency of company commanders to overestimate favorable attitudes among men in their own companies. While these authors considered the phenomenon of projection, they also considered the effect of an officer's attitude on his men, and the possibility of an associational cause: since the men whom the officers knew best shared very similar experiences to those of the officers, and were influenced by the officers' motivations, the commanders tended to assume that the other men in the company were similarly influenced (Samuel Stouffer and others, "Attitudes Toward Leadership and Social Control," pp. 362–429; in *The American*

Soldier, Vol. 1; Princeton, N. J., Princeton Univ. Press, 1949).

24. See, for example, the event described in the Stanton and Schwartz book (footnote 1; pp. 297–298), in which an aide entered into a patient's delusional system, as an emergency measure, contrary to hospital policy. The hospital policy may have been justifiable, but the aide's action may also have been justifiable: he assumed that unless placated by participation in the delusion, the patient would have endangered his entire treatment program by incurring the wrath of the ward. The necessary study of the relative values involved in such instances unfortunately mostly occurs in crises, where the social conventions break down, because the structure of the relations of the various personnel legislates against such study during the usual functioning of the institution.

25. From the Nursing Service of the Veterans Administration Hospital, Boston, Massachusetts, "A Study of Nursing Service on Three Closed Wards on the Neuropsychiatric Service," June, 1955. I am grateful to the Director of Nursing, Bernice Sinclair, R.N., for permission to use this unpublished data. The interpretation of the data is, of course, mine and does not necessarily represent the opinion of the Nursing Service or of the Veterans Administration.

26. Max Weber, See footnote 8.

INSTITUTION-CENTERED AND PATIENT-CENTERED MENTAL HOSPITALS: A COMPARATIVE ANALYSIS OF POLAR TYPES

Lawrence Appleby, Robert Jack Smith, Norman C. Ellis, and Jules Henry

WE aim to present a conceptual framework by which to identify two hospital types that facilitate or impede the rehabilitation of patients: the traditional "institution-centered" or custodial hospital and the emerging "patient-centered" or therapeutic hospital. In our analysis, we shall contrast their values, organizational structure, and consequences.

INSTITUTION-CENTERED HOSPITAL

The "institution-centered" mental hospital is oriented primarily toward protecting the community from the patients and the patients from each other. Underlying an emphasis of organizational efficiency is the aim to resolve the fundamental needs between the individual and his organizational requirements by insisting that man must "fit" the organization.

This type of mental hospital, apart from its emphasis on control, lacks any integrated value system and responds to many situations inconsistently. While its publically stated policies refer to democratic processes, its prevailing philosophy is "authoritarian" (Gilbert and Levinson, 1957). The patient, because of an emphasis on debility and disease, is considered qualitatively different from the normal person. He is expected to be a passive biological recipient of an impersonal treatment process, including electroshock or drugs (Dobson and Ellsworth, 1960; Weinberg, 1960). The doctor alone is considered a therapeutic agent; other personnel are merely ancillary. The institution and the community are distinct worlds and no attempt is made to "bring the outside in."

Written for this volume. Authors' note: This paper was developed as part of a research effort (MH–507), largely supported by the National Institute of Mental Health, U.S. Public Health Service. We would also like to acknowledge the contributions of Dr. Austin DesLauriers and Dr. S. Kirson Weinberg in the early phases of conceptualization.

Maintenance of power or control is the basic theme of the institution-centered hospital, and the *vertical* ordering of personnel into status relations forms the core of its organization. Patients conform primarily because of the threat of physical sanctions, while staff, though technically controlled by wages and other benefits, also respond to the coercive norms of the hospital.

Consistent with these emphases, the highly centralized decision-making process radiates vertically from top to bottom. Hence, ward personnel rarely and patients almost never participate in important decisions. Greenblatt, York and Brown (1955) characterized the administrative function of the custodial institution as:

Governed by the dictates of the organizational chart. Its parallel horizontal lines represent levels of authority and status . . . . Parallel vertical lines represent the several services . . . composed of profession-centered, semi-autonomous groups. Needless to say, there is no line for patients. . . . Within this power structure plans, formulated largely in the form of orders, generally move in one direction—from persons with higher status to those with lower. (p. 420)

This pattern of authority results in a system of multiple dominance and subordination (Henry, 1954) in which lower-echelon employees are confronted with orders from several sources. The patients, as the lowest members of the organization, are very vulnerable to directives from these conflicting authorities (Smith, 1960).

The emphasis is on highly differentiated tasks, which increases the confusion of the lines of authority. Work is carefully categorized and an effort made to bring each distinguishable category under direct supervisory control. Task specialization inevitably leads to "splitting" the patient and to procedure-oriented care (Brown, 1962; Wooden, 1958a). Furthermore, since status is defined so completely by particular task performances, the latter becomes a vested interest. Each staff member closely conforms to a narrowly circumscribed role and avoids encroaching on or overlapping the functions and duties of other personnel (Belknap, 1956). Since the hospital stresses central domination of performance, highly codified rules and regulations are provided that must be followed uncritically. Brown (1962) observed that these rules "can be so detailed that they almost deny the use of common sense even to qualified persons" (p. 72).

Communication is sharply distinguished between the "formal" and legitimate channel and many possible "informal" and illegitimate pathways. The officially prescribed route follows the path in which lower-status personnel have slight access to information. By keeping the official communication process identical with the pattern of decision-making (Caudill, 1958), authority becomes reinforced. This continues down to the lowest level, where ward personnel control the patients (Dunham and Weinberg, 1960). The attrition of information moving downward in the hospital is matched by the tendency for messages to become distorted when moving upward (Greenblatt *et al.*, 1955).

Manifestly, the basic need for rationality in the hospital is frustrated by its own structure. Its emphasis on status and centralized decision-making loses the potential contribution of many lower-status personnel who lack access to intermediaries to whom they could offer suggestions. Plans formulated at such a distance from the experiences affecting patients become highly abstract and stereotyped assessments of situations (Kahne, 1959).

This basic disunity results in "fragmentation," which reflects the failure of bureaucracy (see Argyris, 1962; Etzioni, 1961), and which exists when logically interrelated events become independent. One example is the discrepancy between the explanations emphasizing multiple causation of mental disorders and the stress upon treatment technique such as drugs because it has roots in a medical specialty. Another example is the disparity between intake practices that stress the patient's uniqueness, often described in highly technical jargon, and the discharge practices that simply depend on sufficient conformity with the hospital's procedures for handling patients en masse. One basis for fragmentation is a strategy that creates a definite gap between the community and the hospital. The hospitalized "mental patient" has become discontinuously different from other members of his community and is handled in completely different ways.

The very nature of the social structure in the organization-centered hospital leads to other effects. The "mortification process" (Goffman, 1962) and "herd concept" are intended to sustain order at all costs, including subordinating the patient to hospital requirements (Etzioni, 1961). The authority structure of the ward is legitimized by the facile control it exerts. Admission rites legitimize this power and define clearly the patient's status (Taxel, 1953). The new patient is quickly initiated into a world that demands complete obedience to the rules of the hospital system, "whether that routine is beneficial or harmful to him." (Willoughby, 1953).

The lower echelon staff are affected in about the same manner as the patients. Their initiative, spontaneity, and decision-making potential are lost in this hospital system which demands subservience to impersonal instruction and routine.

The result of the hospital's authoritarian organization ...is a progressive constriction of spontaneity and lowering of job morale as one descends the administrative hierarchy through level II (professionals). Below the barrier, in level III (attendants), the constriction of spontaneity is almost complete.... (Belknap, 1956, p. 218)

Despite formal limitations on their power, attendants exert considerable informal control, which may be unofficially sanctioned (Taxel, 1953). It may be sustained by traditions of the hospital and inadvertently by professionals who "help to perpetuate the notion that the essential feature of dealing with mental patients is their control" (Dunham and Weinberg, 1960, p. 248). In extreme situations, "sabotage" of innovative efforts results (Scheff, 1961). These unofficial acts by attendants do not, however, represent signs of autonomy but rather an abuse of power because they lack constructive direction in working with patients. The lack of regard for attendants is clearly indicated by the failure of professionals to provide guideposts for their behavior and by eventual withdrawal of the professional into other areas. Under such minimal supervision, the attendants' alienation from work increases (Pearlin, 1962) and a rise in "goal displacement" occurs (Scheff, 1962). Kahne (1962) claims in this context that *"usurpation of authority cannot endure without abdication of responsibility"* (p. 239 author's italics).

The route to status in such a system is quite clear. Status will be sought, especially among attendants, by maintaining order, serenity, and physical well-being. Their competence will be determined by their ability to perform these visible skills.

Approval from supervisors is easily won for visible bureaucratic duties.... As a result, the aides have developed a culture whose chief value is to maintain control of the patients, notwithstanding its effects on patient welfare. (Melbin, 1959, p. 89)

Consequently, the most rewarded pattern of behavior in the institution-centered hospital is task-oriented and impersonal. The "ideal" aide-patient relationship is "custody-centered." From the aide's point of view, the relationship is described in terms of power, control, and sustaining order.

In such settings, the patient's role is object-like, something to be acted upon (see Brown, 1961; Dunham and Weinberg, 1960; Goffman, 1962). Passive conformity and deference to the impersonal manipulations must be maintained.

One patient spoke of having learned through her many transfers that it paid to stay on her toes. It was very important, she pointed out, to please everyone and to get along. Otherwise, she would be sent for further shock therapy. She really likes to please people, she added uneasily. Another patient said she would like to get out of the hospital, but when she had asked about timing she had been told, "It's up to you." She watches carefully not to make mistakes and hopes someday she will catch on to what she lacks . . . . (Stone, 1961, p. 20)

Individuality is subjugated to the formal routines and rituals of the institution. Time and space are objectified so that the patient is bound to events and behavior by a rhythmic cycle of predictability (Stone, 1961). The ward to which he is assigned defines his social identity (Dunham and Weinberg, 1960; Goffman, 1962).

Lacking any self-direction or anchorage point, except for the system of privileges, the patient is permitted to drift, although he may contrive "self-saving" devices to preserve semblance of individuality and dignity (Goffman, 1962). The world of the hospital and his part in it are experienced as exceedingly fragmented (see Stone, 1961). Due to the emphasis on restrictions the patient typically views hospitalization as a "sentence " or "time-serving" or "imprisonment" (Goffman, 1962; Willoughby, 1953). Release is facilitated by the patient's adeptness in learning the "rules of the game" so that concealment of symptoms and other avoidances of deviancy can become the quickest routes to discharge (Dunham and Weinberg, 1960).

PATIENT-CENTERED HOSPITAL

The patient-centered system is oriented toward maintaining conditions that can facilitate the personal rehabilitation of the patients, so that the primary focus is up on developing a "therapeutic milieu" (Appleby, Ellis and Smith, 1965). Its premises, in marked contrast to the institution-centered system, are derived from a psychosocial conception of the individual and his relation to the group. There is a basic concern for the individual and his capacity to contribute to the group. The therapeutically organized mental hospital assumes that the psychosocial needs of man can be fulfilled in complex organizations. (see Argyris, 1962). In this sense, the hospital is viewed as an environment that can be manipulated for fostering the personal growth of individuals. Stated slightly differently, "the extent to which the needs of the patients become the focus around which the social structure is built indicates the extent to which the hospital is patient-centered" (Weinberg, 1960, p. 480).

In a patient-centered hospital, a set of beliefs that provides the basis for action to all participants has as its central focus an equalitarian philosophy that emphasizes shared responsibility and the potentially positive therapeutic influence of *all* persons. Consequently, the hospital expresses hope with regard to patient improvement (Von Mering and King, 1957). Therapeutic strategies are developed according to the psychological understanding of the patient's problems or difficulties, and a specific effort is made to integrate these strategies into a program continuous with the patient's habitual pattern of social living. The emphasis is on the patient who, as an active participant, maintains responsibility for assuming the social roles that are as close as possible to his normal, daily routine.

The extent to which the therapeutically derived system is congruent with the professed therapeutic ideology indicates the degree to which a patient-centered hospital exists (see Rapoport, 1960). The efficiency of a total system, ultimately, depends on its interpersonal relations which are largely determined by the social structure. Greenblatt, York, and Brown (1955) articulate this position quite explicitly, and one conclusion is that the social structure should be freed from its "inflexibility." The point of view expressed here, though quite similar, goes a step beyond simply reducing rigidity to advocate a redesign of the social structure.

A patient-centered ideology is most effectively

applied in a system characterized by singular lines of authority ("simple subordination"), by a parallel status structure, and by group decision-making. Rather than being victimized by the contradictions of multiple authority, the staff and patients are responsible to one central figure. This arrangement is readily conducive to integrated functioning and enhances the opportunity for individual self-regulation and reciprocal interaction with formal authority.

Although simple subordination appears as a basic property in a patient-centered hospital, its efficacy is apparently grounded in a system which deemphasizes status differences and maximizes group control. Collapsing of the traditional hierarchy facilitates individual growth and mutual influence (Coser, 1958) and, more important, approximates a performance substantially close to the expected ideal (Barnes, 1960; Seeman and Evans, 1961; Wooden, 1960). Experiments in industrial organizations have also indicated that commitment and performance increased when group participation in decision-making was stressed (Katz, Maccoby, and Morse, 1950).

The evidence is highly suggestive that group participation and minimization of vertical status are essential if the system is to concentrate on the patient. It follows then that they should be built into the structural design from the onset (see Rapoport, 1960). For example, status distance can be informally reduced without modifying the basic authority structure (Wooden, 1960). It is equally apparent, however, that the possibility for strain and ineffectiveness remains. In an ongoing project, we noted increased strain when the institutionalized roles in a decentralized unit were altered in a way inconsistent with the formal practices of the central authority system, despite the latter's sanctioning of the change (Appleby, Ellis, Pack, and Knowles, 1965). Rapoport (1960) observed that discrepancies between the formal and informal systems of authority may involve, "the 'built-in' contradictions between these two sets of role conceptions and their associated expectations (which) give rise to patterned dilemmas for the staff" (p. 276).

Delegation of responsibility is often equated with loss of authority and may lead to an abdication of responsibility for maintaining a highly efficient system. In part, this might explain the high percentage of medication errors found in a well-functioning medical care unit (Seeman and Evans, 1961). Relinquishment of responsibility for direct execution of the therapeutic task necessitates even more attention to the supervisory function (Wooden,

1958b). The amount of time spent in supervision should be proportional to the degree of responsibility delegated (see Brown, 1947). Considerable time must be spent in providing guidance, support, and direction to the personnel. To demand an investment on the part of others is not an opportunity for escape from responsibility; the maintenance of such a system depends on a reciprocal investment. Thus, Artiss (1962), reporting his experience in a milieu therapy program, wrote:

Operationally, I have found that I must spend approximately 40 percent of my time with the staff in order to help it in maintaining a low-enough tension level so as to be useful to the patient-group. This, of course, seems like a huge block of a therapist's time, and as a matter of fact it is. However, I have found it essential to the establishment of such a satisfactory milieu for the patients (p. 17).

Since authority is transferred into supervisory functions, proper execution of these responsibilities will result in the therapist carrying out the required tasks without usurpation of power. Values of the system are expressed in the supervisory relationship; regard for the individual is maintained, but means for guidance exist implying that responsibility, authority, and limits are clearly outlined.

Tasks are relatively undifferentiated in a patient-centered system. The patient is regarded as a whole person and not split up among specialists. One person has major therapeutic responsibility and deals with the patient in a variety of tasks, which may include recreation, hobbies, or discussing family problems. Since therapeutic personnel deal with the total patient, they are not subject to power struggles by supervisors over control of a specialty. The undifferentiated task system commits the person to be responsible for the entire task and assumes in the psychiatric setting "great dedication and energy" (Henry, 1957, p. 79).

Although specialization tends to diminish, there is still recognition of individual skills and achievements. In contrast to the organization centered system, competence is equated not with ascribed status but with demonstrated abilities. In addition, there appears little concern over the protective ownership of these skills so that it is not uncommon to see a mutual exchange of special techniques and knowledge (Barnes, 1960; Kuriloff, 1963). There is a kind of "role permeability" in which people are selected to perform tasks mainly on the basis of demonstrated competence or potential skill rather than on the basis of specialized training. Rapoport (1960) described it as follows:

The Unit advocates an extensive interchangeability and jointness of functions among staff members. Specialized role prescriptions are deemphasized and blurred as much as possible so as to stimulate an equalitarian community with a great deal of joint participation of staff and patients in both therapeutic and administrative affairs. In addition to the elimination of bureaucratic formalities, the Unit seeks through the flattening of the power hierarchy to maximize the use of whatever skills and talents are present in the staff, regardless of anybody's formal position in the authority structure (pp. 275–276).

Routines, rather than becoming rituals, are adapted to the convenience of the patient (for example, Hemmendinger, 1956–57). At the same time, a meaningful organization to events exists so that continuity in daily living is present. This is demonstrated by some patients who have considerable responsibility for arranging their own pattern of living (Jones, 1953). Regulations vary for the patients in terms of therapeutic aims. Rather than ends, they are considered means which the therapist employs in his relationship with patients.

The collapsed status structure reduces the need for formal communication. The preferred mode of communication, on the contrary, is highly informal and likely to be personal (Rosengren, 1964). The opening of channels reduces the possibility of distortion in messages moving either down or up. Since power and status are not linked to the control of communication, there is little reason for distilling messages. In a sense, all have an equal share in an open communication network. The very nature of the structure permits an open communication network making the same message available to all. Sometimes, patients may have direct access to messages (Jones, 1953).

The patient-centered system is characterized by a logical relationship among parts. Its ideology is explicit and therefore available as a criterion for examining and evaluating both the external and internal processes to which the institution is exposed. While the system is "open" to reciprocal influence, there are self-correcting features to cope with strain. Since the system strives to meet the needs of its participants, the gap between formal and informal aspects of the institution is diminished.

The patient-centered system, though aware of the patient's weaknesses, places emphasis on the more positive features of his personality. He is expected to be an active participant in his treatment program and, at some point, to assume his share of responsibility for decisions affecting him. While the patient may initially perceive himself in the role of object, the therapeutic intent is "self-reconstruction" rather than "self-stripping." Furthermore, as self-reconstruction progresses, the patient's role moves toward one of subject (for example, Scher, 1957).

This setting encourages the expression of the subjective side of events; for example, interests, needs, and personal background which markedly influence programming. Tolerance for spontaneity and an encouraging response to individuation represent the norm. The group leader, for instance, who becomes aware of certain needs in the group can offer direct gratification (Appleby, 1960). In this manner, "meaning" forms a significant base for the therapeutic relationship and also contributes to a sense of "subjectification" (Freeman, Cameron, and McGhie, 1958).

In addition to providing a sense of the "personal," the given therapeutic plan has particular objectives. The patient is not allowed to wander aimlessly. Explicit guides are offered, which focus in the relationship between staff and the patient so that, goal-directed experience is continually present.

The feeling of belongingness engendered toward the Section Leader was one of the most important aspects of the situation. The patient no longer need feel that she was just another patient, but rather that she had an adviser on whom she could rely . . . (Von Mering and King, 1957, p. 120).

A stable, on-going relationship enhances the opportunity for experiencing continuity and a stable sense of identity (Appleby, 1963). The emphasis on realistic cultural avenues of expression offers opportunities for social enhancement and for developing personal competence. The group-living programs is a move in this direction (Appleby, 1963; Scher, 1960; Von Mering and King, 1957). Other programs may emphasize education (Bettleheim, 1950), work (Jones, 1953), or even such experiments as admitting infants with their hospitalized mother (Grunebaum and Weiss, 1962). These efforts serve to lessen the experience of "fragmentation" and minimize the gap between hospital and community.

In the patient-centered hospital, the staff, particularly on the ward can be characterized as "therapeutically oriented." As with the patients, emphasis is placed on their creative potential and autonomy. Whatever qualities of "humanness" they possess are used rather than curbed. They have a high degree of self-worth and feel they contribute to the effectiveness of the total program. Morale problems in this setting, are likely to concentrate on the "lack of time" to devote to patients.

Involvement in this system is high. The principal task of the personnel is treating the patients. Their relationships with patients are highly personal, (Henry, 1957), and result in a mutual sharing. They carry the burden of therapeutic success or failure. In a sense, the patient or group becomes the "property" of the therapist, and their problems become his. Status is minimized and reward or acknowledgment is gained only through interpersonal achievement.

Though the conditions for a basic therapeutic program are present, successful operation is possible only to the degree that high involvement can be maintained by personnel. Investment in the patient is accelerated by performance of a wide variety of tasks, yet assumption of this responsibility necessitates an affective appeal (see Etzioni, 1961). Another facet of the involvement is the emotional response on behalf of the supervisors. They must demonstrate an equal interest in the personnel and yet be respected for their competence and leadership, in order for this cycle of high mutual involvement to be an effective process.

REFERENCES

Adams, F. T. Role Accommodation: A study of nurses and attendants in a mental hospital. Unpublished doctoral dissertation, Tulane University, 1958.

Appleby, L. An evaluation of treatment methods for chronic schizophrenia. *Archives of General Psychiatry*, 1963, *8*, 8–21.

Appleby, L., Ellis, N. C., Peck, H. M., and Knowles, J. M. Organizational change: Some observations of an action process in a mental hospital. Paper read at annual meeting of the Society for the Study of Social Problems, Chicago, August, 1965.

Appleby, L., Ellis, N. C., Rogers, G. W., and Zimmerman, Wm. A. A psychological contribution to the study of an hospital social structure. *Journal of Clinical Psychology*, 1961, *17*, 390–393.

Appleby, L., Ellis, N. C., and Smith, R. J. Toward a definition of the therapeutic milieu. *Psychiatry Digest*, 1965, *26*, 31–35.

Appleby, L., Proano, A., and Perry, R. Theoretical vs. empirical treatment models: An exploratory investigation. In L. Appleby, J. Scher, and J. Cumming (Eds.), *Chronic schizophrenia: explorations in theory and treatment*. Glencoe, Ill.: The Free Press, 1960.

Argyris, C. The integration of the individual and the organization. In G. B. Strother (Ed.), *Social science approaches to business behavior*. Homewood, Ill.: Dorsey Press and Richard D. Irwin, 1962.

Artiss, K. L. *Milieu therapy in schizophrenia*. New York: Grune and Stratton, 1962.

Barnes, L. B. *Organizational systems and engineering groups*. Boston: Harvard Business School, Division of Research, 1960.

Belknap, I. *Human problems of a state mental hospital*. New York: McGraw-Hill, 1956.

Bettelheim, B. *Love is not enough*. Glencoe, Ill.: The Free Press, 1950.

Brown, A. *Organization of industry*. New York: Prentice-Hall, 1947.

Brown, Esther Lucille. *Newer dimensions of patient care: Part I. The use of the physical and social environment of the general hospital for therapeutic purposes*. New York: Russell Sage Foundation, 1961.

Brown, Esther Lucille. *Newer dimensions of patient care: Part II. Improving staff motivation and competence in the general hospital*. New York: Russell Sage Foundation, 1962.

Caudill, W. *The psychiatric hospital as a small society*. Cambridge, Mass.: Harvard University Press, 1958.

Cohen, J., and Struening, E. L. Opinions about mental illness in the personnel of two large mental hospitals. *Journal of Abnormal and Social Psychology*, 1962, *64*, 349–360.

Coser, Rose Laub. Authority and decision-making in a hospital: A comparative analysis. *American Sociological Review*, 1958, *23*, 56–63.

Dobson, W. R., and Ellsworth, R. R. Are hospital employees misinformed? *Mental Hospitals*, 1960, *11*, 36–38.

Dunham, H. Warren, and Weinberg, S. Kirson *The culture of the state mental hospital*. Detroit; Wayne State University Press, 1960.

Etzioni, A. Two approaches to organizational effectiveness: A critique and a suggestion. *Administrative Science Quarterly*, 1960, *5*, 257–278.

Etzioni, A. *A comparative analysis of complex organizations*. New York: The Free Press of Glencoe, 1961.

Freeman, T., Cameron, J. L., and McGhie, A. *Chronic schizophrophrenia*. New York: International Universities Press, 1958.

Giedt, H. F. Patterns of attitude similarity among psychiatric hospital staff. *International Journal of Social Psychiatry*, 1959, *4*, 280–290.

Gilbert, Doris C., and Levinson, D. J. "Custodialism" and "humanism" in mental hospital structure and in staff ideology. In M. Greenblatt, D. J. Levinson, and R. H. Williams (Eds.), *The patient and the mental hospital*. Glencoe, Ill.: The Free Press, 1957.

Goffman, E. *Asylums*. Chicago: Aldine, 1962.

Greenblatt, M., York, R. H., and Brown, Esther Lucile. *From custodial to therapeutic patient care in mental hospitals*. New York: Russell Sage Foundation, 1955.

Grunebaum, H. U., and Weiss, J. L. Psychotic mothers and their children: Joint admission to an adult psychiatric hospital. Paper read at annual meeting of the American Psychiatric Association, Toronto, 1962.

Hemmendinger, Miriam. Rx: Admit parents at all times. *Child Study*, 1956–57, *34*, 3–10. Reprinted in Esther Lucile Brown (Ed.), *Newer dimensions of patient care. Part I. The use of the physical and social environment of the general hospital for therapeutic purposes*. New York: Russell Sage Foundation, 1961.

Henry, J. The formal social structure of a psychiatric hospital. *Psychiatry*, 1954, *17*, 139–151.

Henry, J. Types of institutional structure. In M. Greenblatt, D. Levinson, and R. Williams (Eds.), *The patient and the mental hospital*. Glencoe, Ill.: The Free Press, 1957.

Jones, M. *The therapeutic community*. New York: Basic Books, 1953.

Kahne, M. J. Bureaucratic structure and impersonal experience in mental hospitals. *Psychiatry*, 1959, *22*, 363–375.

Kahne, M. J. Some implications of the concept of position for the study of mental hospital organization. *Psychiatry*, 1962, *25*, 227–243.

Katz, D., Maccoby, N., and Morse, Nancy C. *Supervision and morale in an office situation*. Ann Arbor: Survey Research Center, University of Michigan, 1950.

Kuriloff, A. H. An experiment in management—putting theory to the test. *Personnel*, 1963, *40* (6), 8–17.

Melbin, M. Bureaucratic process, personal needs, and turnover among psychiatric aides. Unpublished doctoral dissertation, University of Michigan, 1959.

Morse, Nancy C., and Reimer, E. The experimental change of a major organizational variable. *Journal of Abnormal and Social Psychology*, 1956, *52*, 120–129.

Patchen, M. Supervisory methods and group performance norms. *Administrative Science Quarterly*, 1962, *7*, 275–294.

Pearlin, L. I. Alienation from work. *American Sociological Review*, 1962, *27*, 314–326.

Pratt, S., Scott, G., Treesh, E., Khanna, J., Lesher, T., Khanna, Prabha, Gardiner, G., and Wright, W. The mental hospital and the "treatment-field." *Journal of Psychological Studies*, 1960, *11*, 1–179.

Rapoport, R. N. *Community as doctor: new perspectives on a therapeutic community.* Springfield, Ill.: Charles C. Thomas, 1960.

Rosengren, W. R. Communication, organization, and conduct in the "therapeutic milieu." *Administrative Science Quarterly*, 1964, *9* (1), 70–90.

Scheff, T. J. Control over policy by attendants in a mental hospital. *Journal of Health and Human Behavior*, 1961, *2*, 93–105.

Scheff, T. J. Differential displacement of treatment goals in a mental hospital. *Administrative Science Quarterly*, 1962, *7*, 208–217.

Scher, J. M. Schizophrenia and task orientation: The structured ward setting. *AMA Archives of Neurology and Psychiatry*, 1957, *78*, 531–538.

Scher, J. M. The concept of the self in schizophrenia. In L. Appleby, J. Scher, and J. Cumming (Eds.), *Chronic schizophrenia: Explorations in theory and treatment.* Glencoe, Ill.: The Free Press, 1960.

Schlessinger, A. Schlessinger at the White House; an historian's inside view of Kennedy at work. (A conversation with Henry Brandon.) *Harpers Magazine*, 1964, *229*, 53–60.

Seeman, M., and Evans, J. W. Stratification and hospital care: II. The objective criteria of performance. *American Sociological Review*, 1961, *26*, 193–204.

Smith, Dorothy E. The logic of custodial organization. *Psychiatry*, 1965, *28*, 311–323.

Smith, H. L. Two lines of authority: The hospital's dilemma. In E. Gartley Jaco (Ed.), *Patients, physicians, and illness.* Glencoe, Ill.: The Free Press, 1960.

Stone, Olive M. The three worlds of the back ward. *Mental Hygiene*, 1961, *45*, 18–27.

Taxel, H. Authority structure in a mental hospital ward. Unpublished master's thesis, University of Chicago, 1953.

von Mering, O., and King, S. H. *Remotivating the mental patient.* New York: Russell Sage Foundation, 1957.

Weinberg, S. Kirson. Organization, personnel and functions of state and private mental hospitals: A comparative analysis. In E. Gartley Jaco (Ed.), *Patients, physicians and illness.* Glencoe, Ill.: The Free Press, 1960.

Weinberg, S. Kirson. *Society and Personality Disorders* (Englewood Cliffs, New Jersey: Prentice-Hall Inc., 1952).

Wessen, A. F. Hospital ideology and communication between ward personnel. In E. Gartley Jaco (Ed.), *Patients, physicians and illness.* Glencoe, Ill.: The Free Press, 1960.

Willoughby, R. H. The attendant in the state mental hospital. Unpublished master's thesis, University of Chicago, 1953.

Wooden, H. E. The system may come ahead of the patient. *Modern Hospital*, 1958, *91*, 99–104. (a)

Wooden, H. E. Patient-centered cardiac care. *Hospital Progress*, 1958, *39*, 80ff. (b)

Wooden, H. E. Family-centered maternity care: A summary and analysis of the program. *Hospital Progress*, 1960, *41*, 12ff.

A SOCIOPSYCHOLOGICAL CONCEPTION OF PATIENTHOOD

Fred Pine and Daniel J. Levinson

SCIENCES and professions tend, as is well known, to construct images and myths of men to suit their own purposes. Periods of major change in the character of a given discipline lead to new images of men which serve a historical purpose and are in time outgrown. Economics has its "economic man" and political science its "political man." There is, similarly, a traditional medical image of "patient man." We shall deal here with conceptions of the patient hospitalized for mental illness.

The hospitalized patient has been conceived of as a "case" of a given type of illness treated by the doctor within a supporting hospital facility. In this conception, the crucial features of the patient are his "signs and symptoms" and their origins in a central *pathological process;* the crucial feature of his hospital environment is the *definitive treatment* (shock, drugs, psychotherapy, or the like) it gives the patient; and the crucial feature of his response in his *clinical course* toward (or away from) elimination of pathology.

This view of the mental patient and his hospital environment has been slowly changing. The currently emerging image is more complex and inclusive. The patient's illness, in the sense of a delimited pathology, is only a part of what he brings with him to hospitalization. He brings, as well, conscious and unconscious wishes, fears, values, attitudes, and the like, that will have a crucial influence on his response to hospitalization. Moreover, the specific treatments given by the psychiatrist are only one part of the patient's environment, and often not the most important part. Indeed, the sharp distinction traditionally made between "treatment" and "care" has been seriously questioned.

One of the major theses of recent hospital research is that "the recovery of the mental hospital patient depends not merely upon specific treatment procedures, but, perhaps even more, upon the sociopsychological characteristics of the hospital

Reprinted from *The International Journal of Social Psychiatry* (1961), pp. 106–122, by permission of the Avenue Publishing Company.

community." The available evidence suggests that treatment takes varied and often nonspecific forms, that many facets of the patient's experience in the hospital may have therapeutic relevance. The patient is influenced in varying degrees by the social structure and even the architecture of the hospital. He is sensitive to the emotional climate of the ward, to the peer culture among patients, and to the possibilities of relationships with nurses, aides, and other personnel. Whether he changes, and in what ways, are determined in part by the available opportunities for meaningful work and recreation. He is affected, too, by the reciprocal relation between hospital and outside world and by the situation that awaits him when he leaves the hospital.

This emphasis upon the therapeutic significance of the hospital milieu has been developed largely by social scientists and by socially-oriented psychiatrists. Many of these are psychoanalytically oriented as well. However, there is in some quarters a sense of antithesis between "social" and "psychotherapeutic" approaches. This is reflected in the tendency to make simplified dichotomies as, for example, between psychotherapy and milieu therapy, between psychogenic and sociogenic explanations, between the "proper territory" of the clinician and that of the social scientist. Even those who verbally reject such dichotomies often maintain them in practice. Needless to say, goodwill alone is not enough to bring about a convergence of the two approaches. To do this, and particularly to do it in a systematic, theoretically meaningful way, is a task of great difficulty.

One of the major current needs, we believe, is the development of a sociopsychological conception of patienthood. It requires that the social milieu be regarded in a more psychological manner, in terms of its meaning to and impact upon the individual patient. The analysis of the milieu should be informed by psychodynamic as well as by more purely sociological theory. At the same time, it is essential to conceive of the patient not merely in terms of his unconscious conflicts and defences, but also in terms of his relatedness to the social milieu. In the analysis of the patient's personality, sociological as well as psychodynamic perspectives are needed.[2]

The present paper is a step in this direction. We shall attempt: (a) to characterize the *situation* of the patient within the hospital community; (b) to formulate some of the *role-tasks* or *problematic issues* confronting all patients as a result of both personal need and organizational requirement; and (c) to illustrate the multidetermined and often conflicting *modes of adaptation* made by patients in an intensive treatment hospital which itself is undergoing continual change.

THE SITUATION AND ADAPTIVE TASKS OF THE PATIENT

Our thesis is this. For the patient the mental hospital is not simply a "treatment facility." It is first of all a *community*: a place to live, a new social world, a total life setting within which he pursues his diverse goals. His needs and goals are much like those of any person newly entered into a strange community. He seeks a meaningful identity and social relatedness here as he would elsewhere. He wishes to change in some respects, but he strives as well to achieve continuity with the past. He has a full repertory of human needs. He engages in varied relationships with authorities and peers, with men and women, with persons of various dispositions and social backgrounds. He seeks freedom and security, self-expression and self-control. It is crucial for him to learn what kind of new world he has joined: what it offers him, what it demands of him, what he can contribute to it.

At the same time, the hospital differs in important respects from other communities the patient has known. He has entered it with fear and in most cases under coercion, with a sense of having been ejected from his rightful world. He is not free to leave at will and does not know how or when he can obtain his release. He has lost many of his civil rights as a citizen in the larger society, and his rights within this new community are both limited and ambiguous to him. The thought of living in close contact with mentally ill persons arouses terrifying fantasies about them and about his own probable fate in their company.

If we are to answer the question, "What has the hospital given the patient?" we must comprehend his total engagement with the hospital community. The patient's career and fate in the hospital depend in no small degree upon what it offers and demands, upon its ability as a total

community to meet his needs as a total person.

The encounter of patient with hospital thus involves much more than the "treatment" of "illness." (a) The hospital presents to the patient a complex *environment* of which pathology-specific treatment is a relatively small part. (b) It evokes from him a complex set of *adaptations* (in behaviour, thought and feelings) of which his "clinical course" as usually conceived is but one sector. (c) The patient brings to the hospital within himself a complex system of *personal characteristics* (including more conscious beliefs and values as well as more central fantasies, defences, self-conceptions) of which his psychopathology is but one part. His hospital career can be understood only in the light of the patterning of these multiple forces.

In seeking to analyze the encounter of patient and hospital, we have found it useful to start with the question, "What are the major adaptive tasks confronting the hospitalized patient?" The analysis of such tasks is, we believe, a crucial but frequently neglected step in the investigation of organizational roles generally. Accordingly, we turn first to a list of six tasks or "problematic issues" of patienthood, and the theoretical reasoning used in their derivation. Following this, we shall take up each task in turn, delineating (a) its nature, (b) various modes of adaptation to it, and (c) some intrapersonal and situational determinants of individual adaptation.

The six tasks or issues to be considered are the following.

(1) To develop a conception of self which gives meaning to the fact that he is, in an unavoidable, public sense, a "mentally ill" person.

(2) To orient himself within the hospital community and to come to terms with the social expectations and values governing the position of patient.

(3) To adapt to the expectation that he obey the administrative decisions made by personnel, and particularly by doctors, about his case.

(4) To adapt to the expectation that he get well, in part by achieving insight and control through examination of his problematic feelings and ideas.

(5) To adapt to the expectation that he form friendly relationships with other patients.

(6) To reconcile the antithesis between security and freedom as it appears in each new stage of hospitalization.

Each of these issues, and the resolutions which the patient achieves, have origins within, and significance for, both the individual patient and the hospital structure. For the patient, each issue is problematic and important in at least the following senses. (a) He has a strong personal investment in coming to grips with it; intense needs and feelings are involved. (b) Several alternative modes of adaptation are usually "available" to him (through external example and influence, and as a result of his own varied predilections). It takes considerable time and work to achieve a personally meaningful and socially viable mode of adaptation. (c) The adaptation he makes will have major consequences for his life in the hospital and for his long-term movement toward recovery or toward chronic illness.

In a larger sense, the issues are important to the patient because they are important to the hospital. Every mental hospital has, as it were, an organizational "investment" in them. Of course, hospitals vary in the degree and nature of their investment. A small psychotherapy-oriented hospital and a large custodial one will differ, for example, in the relative emphasis they place on obedience and on insight (issues 3 and 4).

The existence, and the problematic character, of these issues have their origins in fundamental characteristics of hospital organization. First and foremost, the hospital exists for specific purposes and is under pressure to fulfil these purposes. It has *instrumental goals* to carry out. The patient, in turn, is under heavy pressure to play his part in fulfilling the purposes of the hospital. One of its purposes is "custody": to protect the outside community by encapsulating individuals who deviate sharply from its norms, who are presumably dangerous or not self-sufficient. The patient has little choice but to accept the incarcerative aspect of hospitalization. The pressures generated by a second major goal of the hospital—treatment—give patients greater leeway to respond idiosyncratically. The patient is faced with the demand that he accept and make active use of the treatment provided; he is expected, for example, to gain insight and control no matter how painful, threatening, or meaningless the treatment may be for him. Issue 4 deals with this adaptive problem.

To fulfil its instrumental goals, the hospital requires minimally positive *affective relationships* among its member individuals. Patients, like staff, are subjected to pressures for conformity to the "love" needs of the system. The patient is expected to "get along," to be at least minimally co-operative and friendly with staff and other patients, regardless of his personal antipathies and anxieties. While the requirement of "co-operativeness" is usually justified on the grounds of serving the patient's therapeutic progress, it has the additional (implicit) functions of simplifying the work of ward staff and of contributing to communal solidarity. This task (number 5 in our list) is one of the most problematic for patients. The hospital milieu is often not conducive to the formation of positive relationships and social involvements. Also, feelings of mistrust, withdrawal, and resentment are central features of mental illness.

Affective integration is not sufficient to ensure a smoothly functioning system: a large institution requires an administrative hierarchy—a division of responsibility on the basis of competence. Thus, a third aspect of his hospital citizenship is that the patient is subject to pressures to maintain the *administrative integration* of the hospital. He is required to "follow orders," to accept the administrative authority of psychiatrists and ward staff, to take his place in the organizational hierarchy. He must obey numerous "house" rules, maintain a steady schedule of work, sleep, and routine activities, and follow his doctor's administrative decisions. The hand of authority is a heavy one in most hospitals and its workings are rarely made clear to patients. For inner reasons as well, most patients have difficulty in understanding and accepting the demands of a complex organization. It is small wonder, then, that this aspect of hospitalization (issue 3, above) should be problematic.

In short, the patient is under heavy pressure to be a "responsible citizen" in the hospital community: to further the hospital's effective and administrative integration in the service of achievement of instrumental goals. These pressures are, of course, not unique to the mental hospital. Workers and inmates in business, educational, military, and other organizations are faced with problematic tasks stemming from instrumental and integrative requirements of the organization. However, these requirements probably overlap more in the mental hospital than in other settings. Thus, the factory worker's assembly line (instrumental) activities are relatively separate and distinguishable from his relationships with the foreman and other authorities. In mental hospitals like the one studied here, on the other hand, the patient's personal relationships with nurses and other authorities are a more intrinsic feature of his "therapeutic work." Instrumental and integrative tasks are interwoven, and this interweaving has important consequences. If the patient learns, for example, that positive relationships on the ward are taken as a sign of therapeutic progress, he may behave in ways that are superficially "correct" but personally shallow and meaningless. Again, where the doctor has both therapeutic and administrative (e.g., ward assignment) responsibility for the patient, the therapeutic relationship may be impeded.

The problematic role-tasks of the patient arise not merely from structural features of the hospital; to varying degrees they have origins in the needs of the patient himself. There are tasks to be dealt with by anyone who has been taken from his usual social world and transplanted into a new, strange, and encapsulated community. Out of both inner need and external pressure, one is impelled to reshape his conception himself as a member of this community (issue 1), to understand the workings of the community (issue 2), and to evaluate the relative advantages of living here as against returning to his former world (issue 6). These issues are present regardless of the specific character of the hospital or of the patient's illness, although both may influence the severity of the adaptive problems and the ways in which they are handled.

The hospital presents manifold pressures and inducements to adapt to the problematic issues in certain ways rather than others. That is to say, the hospital confronts the patient with a set of *role-requirements*—values, expectations, and accompanying sanctions—that direct and channel his attempts to resolve the problematic issues. At the same time, within a given hospital, patients differ appreciably in their actual modes of adaptation—in the *personal role-definitions* they form. These differences among patients stem from various sources: from being exposed to different sectors of the hospital (different wards, personnel, administrative pressures, and the like); from being treated in differing ways (on the basis of such characteristics as age, sex, and illness), and from differences in personality, which lead patients to think, feel, and act variously in relation to the tasks confronting them.

Hospitals differ greatly in the role-requirements made of patients, and there are differing degrees of congruence or discord between role-requirements and personal role-definitions. However, discord is likely to be softened somewhat by flexibility in what is expected of patients. For example, though patients are expected to relate to one another, they are also permitted to isolate themselves at times. Thus, expectations regarding patient behaviour (as embodied in the socially defined role) are in a sense *ideal* expectations. The patient is expected to live up to them only after a period in the hospital; living up to them

may itself be seen as a sign of therapeutic progress. This characteristic of the patient role—that the expectations represent an ideal to be achieved gradually—may hold for all "correctional" institutions which have the goal of bringing about psychological changes in their members.

In the following pages we shall discuss, in turn, the six problematic issues mentioned above. Our chief concern is to clarify the nature of each issue and its significance for the patient and for the hospital. In formulating this analysis we have in mind a diverse literature as well as our own experience in several private and public hospitals. However, the primary source of material has been fieldwork in one hospital, and the specific examples given are drawn from this source. The usefulness of this analysis for other types of hospital remains to be determined. Before proceeding with the analysis, let us describe briefly the hospital setting and the procedure of data collection.

RESEARCH SETTING AND PROCEDURE

The observational base for the present study was the Massachusetts Mental Health Centre (Boston Psychopathic Hospital), a state hospital closely affiliated with the Harvard Medical School. During the main period of fieldwork, 1945–55, the hospital contained about 120 patients and a somewhat larger number of service, teaching, and research personnel.[3] The patient population was unusually heterogeneous in such characteristics as education, occupation, religion, and age. Patients were admitted for short-term treatment, the average stay being 2–3 months and the maximum stay about a year. Although psychotherapy was a highly valued treatment, various theoretical approaches and modes of treatment were used within the general framework of a "therapeutic community." (For a history and contemporary picture of the hospital, see Greenblatt, York, and Brown (5), and several chapters in Greenblatt, Levinson, and Williams (4).

The primary research material was obtained in the course of several months of intensive fieldwork. A major source of information was participant observation in situations of central importance for patients: electric shock and insulin treatments, group therapy sessions, patient ward meetings, doctors' ward rounds, patient mealtimes, patient government, psychodrama, occupational therapy, and all of the wards. Additional material was obtained through talks with male and female patients and various staff members. These talks ranged from informal chats with patients individually or in groups, to lengthy semi-structural interviews with individual patients about problems of hospital life. Notes on the observations and interviews were transcribed into protocols for later analysis.

PROBLEMATIC ISSUES AND ADAPTIVE RESOLUTIONS

Problem 1: *To develop a conception of self which gives meaning to the fact that he is, in an unavoidable, public sense, a "mentally ill" person.*
Hospitalization formalizes the fact of illness. As one patient put it:

You come here to get well and then find that this leads to more problems. Before you came you could live outside and keep your illness a secret. Once you're in the hospital you can't do this.

Hospitalization brings with it a sense of changed selfhood. It tends to increase fear and disorganization by undermining any remaining sense of stable individuality based upon rootedness in a particular environment.

One of the primary psychosocial tasks of the patient is to reform his conception of self, to acknowledge and assimilate the new reality of being mentally ill. It is no mean problem for any person to acknowledge that he has impulses, fears, and inhibitions that he cannot adequately control. The patient's denial of illness stems in part from a warding-off of disruptive conflicts and anxieties and is an aspect of their psychopathology. However, it is also a reaction against the inferior and deviant social status accorded to the mentally ill. An essential ingredient of the therapeutic task of the hospital is to help the patient to conceive of himself as ill—for only as he acknowledges the elemental fact of being ill can he make active use of the varied therapeutic offerings of the hospital.

Patients use various means of denying illness. Thus some patients divide the patient population into more sick and less sick groups, keeping themselves in the healthier group. Reality factors are utilized here; for example, real differences between patients on the convalescent and the disturbed wards provide a basis for convalescent ward patients to classify themselves as "nervous" in contrast to the "mentally ill."

Other patients readily acknowledge their patient status and conceive themselves to be under the long-term protection of a benevolent hospital

system. Some of these patients have fled to the hospital in order to escape from a difficult situation; for them the hospital is a refuge that they fear to leave. Patients who experience group belongingness and helpful care in the hospital which they have never before experienced may also develop this conception.

Some patients, of course, conceive of themselves as temporarily ill persons needing hospitalization until they are able to return to the community. This, the most realistic and therapeutically useful self-conception, is supported in various informal ways in the hospital under study. Ward personnel not infrequently speak to the patient about his diagnosis and his *previous* behaviour while in an acute state. The temporary nature of hospitalization is brought out to the patient by seeing other patients go home and by talking with personnel about future plans.

Patients also show certain more or less general modes of dealing with the fact of illness and hospitalization. They are, for example, much concerned to maintain some continuity with their past lives. The frequent complaints about everyday details (faulty TV sets, leaky faucets, missing property), though in part realistic, are attempts to make hospital life like outside life. Normalcy in details implies normality in the self, as in this comment by a patient:

The more personal belongings you return, the more normal the patient feels. You restore to him the environment to which he is accustomed by giving him his wallet, his ring. You make him feel less a number. You restore his individuality.

Some patients are able to maintain continuity with their past lives in a deeper sense by achieving some constancy of goals, values, and human relationships. This process is supported by visits from relatives and friends, and by opportunities to pursue serious interests that have meaning in the extra-hospital world.

Humour too is used frequently to deal with anxiety over hospitalization. Patients are highly responsive to jokes about the mentally ill; "this hospital is enough to drive you crazy" is a characteristic joke. Functionally, humour is a way of practising acceptance of illness in an ego-syntonic way until the illness can be acknowledged with greater ease and insight.

We need to know much more about the role of the hospital and the larger social context in the development of the patient's conceptions and values about mental illness. In addition, psychodynamically oriented studies could profitably be made upon the ways in which the fact of having been hospitalized for mental illness alters and is integrated into a person's conception of himself and into his interpersonal relationships.

Problem 2: *To orient himself within the hospital community and come to terms with the social expectations and values governing the position of patient.*

Hospitalization brings with it basic changes in the patterns and details of all aspects of living. Getting oriented to the demands and opportunities of hospital life is not simply a matter of convenience or social necessity for patients. Not to know the rules and procedures of the hospital engenders feelings of fear, of social powerlessness and of being alien. To the extent that these feelings exist, they diminish an already weak initiative in working actively towards one's own cure. They tend to increase the patient's sense of helpless dependence on hospital personnel. Learning the rules, routines, and values—the "reality"—of the hospital gives the patient an essential basis for adequate reality testing and ego functioning. A thorough grasp of the reality materials with which he must work gives him a framework for coping with intrapsychic anxieties and for testing out new modes of relationship in the hospital world.

The problem of orientation cuts across all of the other adaptive problems. The individual patient has to learn what is expected of patients generally as a basis for developing his personal modes of adaptation. Each patient gradually forms his ideas—realistic or otherwise—about the hospital structure and about patients' rights and duties within it. These problems of orientation are especially strong when the patient first enters and must come to terms with patienthood as a whole. They arise anew, in a more differentiated but often no less acute manner, at various stages in hospitalization such as transfer to a new ward or preparation for discharge when many new adjustments are required.

Orientation to specific routines and activities is a more concrete problem, one that most patients accomplish rather quickly. Many facts about the hospital—about daily schedules, patient recreational activities, etc.—are learned through other patients rather than through hospital agencies. However, some patients resist learning about hospital routines and activities as a facet of their tendency to deny their illness. Patients commonly state that they do not care how things work in the hospital since they should not be there anyhow, or

that hospital activities are for the "long-term" patients and not for those, like himself, "here for a short rest."

In the search for orientation, various aspects of hospital life acquire special meaning. For example, patients may infer answers to questions about the degree of their illness from concrete characteristics of their position in the hospital. In the words of one patient:

Once you get locked in the ward you know you must be ill. They strip you of all your possessions . . . you see other sick patients in the ward and you feel "I must be like him" . . . Then you hear about the convalescent ward and about occupational therapy. After six days they asked me if I wanted to go to occupational therapy. That made me feel confident. I thought "I'm not so bad after all" . . . Later on you go to the convalescent ward . . . You know that one more step leads to the door and you will be out of the hospital. To go down to the convalescent ward means that you're getting well.

The special meaning attached to personal property illustrates the new values to which patients become oriented. Property takes on important symbolic meanings. The possessions a patient brings to the hospital are a major connecting link with his past and provide a basis for continuity with his former life. In the communal setting of the hospital, personal possessions may serve as one of the few tangible symbols of individuality. Patients have reported feeling a major loss when some of their possessions were taken away for safe keeping by the hospital at the time of their admission. On the other hand, the break with the past symbolized by this loss of property may provide the patient with an impetus to accept his new position as a patient—to give up his past rights and duties and accept new ones.

The hospital can and does help the patient somewhat in resolving his problems of orientation, especially with regard to rules, time schedules, and physical facilities of the hospitals. However, much of this is done in a formal way only when the patient first enters the hospital—when he is least prepared to benefit from the information he is given. Only little can be done formally in helping the patient in his orientation to the new values and forms of social behaviour expected in the hospital. This is largely a problem in total resocialization involving subtle learning. The ways in which this learning can best be facilitated, especially in patients with impaired ego functioning, is a major problem for research exploration.

Problem 3: *To adapt to the expectation that he*

obey the administrative decisions made by personnel, and particularly by doctors, about his case.

Hierarchical relationships characterize the mental hospital. Patients, incapacitated by their illness, have to follow the prescriptions laid down by others. Doctors and nurses make vital decisions regarding the patients' lives—including such things as kind of treatment, ward or hospital transfer, weekend home visits, and discharge. In many subtle ways, status-cleavages colour the relationships among all groupings within the hospital.

The hierarchical structure inevitably affects the doctor-patient relationship. Patients may withhold therapy-relevant material for fear that the doctor will use it against them. On the other hand, some alert patients complain that doctors avoid assertiveness or disciplinary action on the wards for fear of disrupting their therapeutic relationships with patients.

The patient's administrative subordination on the ward is also important for his intrapsychic functioning. The most striking problem that emerges here is the sense of powerlessness promoted in the patient by the fact that major life-decisions are made for him by others; this will be discussed in more detail below. To accept these decisions and the concomitant feeling of powerlessness may be infantilizing to the already dependent patient. Yet, to rebel against the decisions is to impede one's progress through the hospital. Hospital staff are not always able to distinguish between constructive self-assertion (or self-defence) and impulse-driven rebellion against authority on the part of the patient. To carry out their administrative responsibilities toward patients while minimizing the patients' sense of powerlessness is a continual challenge for staff.

Many forms of influence are used to induce conformity and prevent or punish rebellious behaviour. Disobedience is in the main unrewarding in the hospital setting. More extreme forms of rebellion, such as violence on the wards, lead to such consequences as seclusion, failure to be "promoted" to the convalescent ward, or ultimately, transfer to another hospital. Often, rebellion simply meets with failure, as when a patient resists shock treatment but receives it nonetheless. Rebellion is ordinarily seen as an expression of illness and is opposed by other patients as well as by personnel. Obedience is reinforced by the prestige of the doctor who is conceived of as an omniscient authority in matters of illness. The aura of medical authority is often accentuated by the patient, whose dependency needs are brought to the fore by the incapacitating effects of his illness.

Since rebelliousness is in the end a self-defeating quality, obedience is characteristically the patient's eventual response. This holds not only for his behaviour, but often for his thinking as well. "It's all up to the doctor" is a common attitude. Patients conform more fully to the expectation that they obey hospital decisions than to other hospital expectations. For example, they more often refuse to become engaged in psychotherapy or to relate positively with other patients.

Thus, external pressure plays a larger part than inner preference in determining the patient's resolution of the "obedience" issue. Further problems arise from this. One of these is a frequent sense of powerlessness: a fear of the uncontrollable "administrative" powers and of the absence of self-determination when crucial decisions are being made. From the patient's point of view, the doctor is the judge of what the future will hold and the patient has to live with the unknown until decisions are made. One patient's struggle with this problem comes out in the following remarks:

I'll tell you when I get upset. When my ten days observation were up I thought I'd go home. I hadn't seen a doctor yet. It turned out that my doctor called my husband and said I should stay a month longer . . . One thing was really frightening; it frightened the heck out of me. They have a system where they don't usually ask the patient to sign any papers . . . I suppose they do it for the patient's good. But let's say that your husband tells you that you've got to stay a month longer. You feel he doesn't want you and you get angry. They should explain to the patient why he has to stay another month; most patients are well enough to be able to understand . . . When my husband told me that the doctor advised staying another month, I raised hell. Then he said he hadn't signed yet; he was asking me . . . but I was still upset because they didn't consult me. The doctor should ask me; I'm the one who is in here.

The patient often lives in a state of acute anxiety as to when a major decision will come and how he can influence it. When he is "waiting for the axe to fall"—expecting an unfavourable decision such as transfer to another hospital or being put on a threatening form of treatment—he may live in fear and dread. To combine obedience with a sense of inner initiative is thus a major dilemma.

Problem 4: *To adapt to the expectation that he get well, in part by achieving insight and control through examination of his problematic feelings and ideas.*

Psychotherapy is one of the primary treatment tools of the hospital under study and is utilized with a majority of patients. Though psychotherapy is a complex task, the focal requirement is often regarded by patients as a verbal "opening up"— getting better through talking about one's problems.

Treatment itself constitutes a major adaptive problem since talking about his difficulties is so threatening to the patient. The degree of one's readiness and ability to meet the requirements of psychotherapy are, it would seem, primarily a matter of individual personality. For the hospitalized patient, however, the resolution of the conflict between "talking" and "clamming up" is influenced in varying degrees by diverse pressures within the total hospital system.

Certain features of the hospital facilitate participation in psychotherapy. Perhaps most central is the very existence of psychotherapy (and psychodrama) as a valued therapeutic tool of the hospital. Patients who are in psychotherapy—and, by hearsay, others as well—learn that doctors regard talking about problems as an important step in resolving them. Patients learn that talking about one's illness is not merely "acceptable" but is believed to have therapeutic value. Informal advice from other patients—as, for example, the casual "I've got enough problems of my own; tell yours to your doctor"— provide a stimulus to engagement in psychotherapy. In addition, patients bring with them to the hospital a long-standing conception of the doctor as healer. Whether this conception is based on the reality of the doctor as a trained expert or on the fantasy of the doctor as a magical healer, it is likely to induce compliance with the doctor's expectations. Finally, the immediacy of the patient's own needs—for reassurance, attention, and love—provide a strong inner drive than supports the hospital pressures to become engaged in psychotherapy.

The above influences do not go unopposed. They come into sharp conflict with many of the patient's values, defences, and character traits which produce resistances to communication. Moreover, the patient's reticence or ability to communicate is often fostered by relatives and friends (and some hospital personnel) who tell him to "forget" his problems by "keeping busy" or to solve them on his own through "will power."

The tendency not to talk is supported by a prevalent belief among patients that the patient who says what is on his mind will get into trouble. The immediate fear, often, is that criticism of the hospital will lead to retaliation. The most generalized form of this fear is that *any* communication of personal opinion will lead to retaliation. One patient put it this way:

Patients feel under a compulsion not to be too frank.

Probably this was a problem even before they came to the hospital. Maybe this is just a group phenomenon when two groups get together and one [the doctors] order the other, and the other [the patients] don't sit in on the conferences.

Since, in actuality, patients often do not know the bases for the decisions regarding their fate in the hospital, they can never be sure how their behaviour and conversation affect these decisions. At the same time, their beliefs about the consequences of communication may serve in part to rationalize their inner resistances.

There are other informal (and therefore difficult to control) characteristics of hospital life that play in with the patient's tendency to avoid communicating. Personnel, often short of time on the wards, may find it necessary to cut a patient short when he tries to speak to them—thus providing food for resistance. One patient said that she doesn't talk to her doctor because "he already has a lot on his mind and may become confused if he is asked too many things." It is true that this attitude reflects her way of defending against her own confusion. It is equally true that this defence is facilitated by a *reality* of hospital life, namely, that doctors are overburdened. In addition, the staff are eager for the patient to improve and are likely to reward the patient who says he is "feeling fine" by responding "glad to hear it" or the like. Patients thus find support for their view that normality entails denial of illness. Finally, somatic treatments are cited by some patients who argue that the real treatment comes through medication and not through communication.

Thus, both the communicating and the non-communicating patient are responding to inner needs and to hospital realities. We need to know more about the relationship between a patient's readiness to communicate about private concerns and the likelihood that he will be taken into psychotherapy. Also, too little is known about the fate of the non-communicator in a psychotherapeutically oriented hospital. Finally, the problems of conducting psychotherapy in a hospital context present a major area for systematic research.

Problem 5: *To adapt to the expectation that he form friendly relationships with other patients.*

For any given patient, other patients—individually and as a group—are a crucial part of the hospital setting. His anxieties over human relationships in general and his specific fantasies about "crazy hospital inmates" make the task of relating to other patients a foreboding one. On the other hand, the acceptance and friendship he often gets from other patients may give him a sense of support and security that he has not previously experienced.

Relationships with other patients have great significance in each patient's hospital career. Through his contacts with others the patient can work through the insights he develops in therapy and can learn new modes of relationship. These relationships may affect his relationship with his therapist in various ways. The patient may direct all of his negative feelings against patients rather than his therapist, thus keeping these feelings out of the scrutiny of the therapy situation. Or, he may direct his positive feelings to other patients and find his main gratifications there, keeping the therapy relationship solely a negative one in which little therapeutic progress can be made.

Though patients are expected to be sociable, there is no immediate or strong pressure in this direction. Some patients avoid others for extended periods and some (particularly those who are in the hospital for only ten days of observation) maintain this avoidance throughout their entire stay. There is a flexibility in the norms governing patient-patient relationships which makes it possible for patient to proceed at his own rate.

Over the course of hospitalization most patients undergo marked changes in their relationships with other patients. These relationships begin to develop quite rapidly. As one patient put it, "Like in any other group on the outside, at first you're shy and then you loosen up." A variety of situational factors and inner feelings contribute to the "loosening up" process. One factor is simply the gross amount of time patients spend together. Patients often being relationships over questions of orientation; more experienced patients are sources of information about the hospital for new patients. These contacts tend to reduce the new patient's fear of the hospital and he becomes increasingly more able to relate to others.

Staff members provide additional incentives toward socialization. Ward personnel set a social tone for the ward through their own conversations with patients and through ward meetings. The hospital administration supports activities such as dances and patient government that make for solidarity among patients. One patient complained that he was warned against staying alone and reading; he said the nurse failed to realize that he was reading out of interest rather than out of a wish to avoid other patients. Undoubtedly, pressures to socialize sometimes impose on the patient's normal need for privacy.

Underlying all of the external factors that promote interaction is the patient's own need for others, buried though it may be under tendencies toward withdrawal and isolation. To the extent that the hospital provides a total milieu in which the patient feels understood and accepted, he becomes increasingly free to express his wishes for human contact.

At least two quite different kinds of relationship develop among patients. The first entails personal sharing and mutual aid and seems most characteristic of the admission (disturbed) wards. The second involves more superficial relationships and seems more characteristic of the convalescent wards. One female patient described this difference graphically:

The people [on the female convalescent ward] are not really very friendly. On the disturbed ward, you can't help getting friendly because you're locked in all together. The patients there are sick and get to know each other. On the convalescent ward you mind your own business and you're interested only in yourself. On the disturbed ward, you mind each other's business. You try to help each other. You realize that others may be sicker than you. For example, there is a big cigarette shortage on the disturbed ward. I don't smoke, but I had my husband bring cigarettes for me to give to the other patients. On the disturbed ward, though you're scared of one another, you try to help each other.

Another patient described in sympathetic detail how several patients on the disturbed ward took a young catatonic girl to many hospital activities in order to "bring her out of herself." This patient characterized the convalescent wards as being less tolerant of illness and "more like normal society" in that people are "friendly" but not really concerned with one another. These differences between wards are only relative, however, and a patient may be maternal, isolated, friendly, or autocratic on any ward.

Several features of the convalescent wards contribute to the relatively greater superficiality and distance of relationships among its patients. For one thing, patients spend less time together. The ward doors are not locked and patients disperse around the hospital. Many patients have street privileges and most go home for weekends. The short average stay of 2–3 months, and with it the rapidly-shifting composition of the patient group, contribute to the weakening of emotional involvement in personal relationships. Some patients claimed that it was easier to make close friends in larger state hospitals where patients stayed for more extended periods. The sense of instability in the human environs is most pronounced on the convalescent wards.

Another factor making for changed relationships is the transition from an "illness orientation" on the disturbed wards to a "normality orientation" on the convalescent wards. Patients on the convalescent wards expect that they will soon be discharged from the hospital and they seek a "normal" pattern of polite social conversation rather than sharing of feelings and problems. Ward personnel often contribute to the development of this conception of normality: they speak to patients more often about problems and symptoms on the disturbed wards and about future plans and outside interests on the convalescent wards.

Patients also reinforce the normality orientation in one another. A patient who acts strangely is warned to "watch out or you'll get sent back to the disturbed ward." Deviance is tolerated less. Whereas at the beginning of hospitalization many patients erect a facade to deny that they are as sick as the other patients, they now keep up a front to prove that they are as healthy as the seemingly well patients on the convalescent ward. One female patient said:

If you are sick while on the convalescent ward, it's not very good. You feel apart from the others. The second time I was in the hospital I went to the convalescent ward too soon, before I was ready for it. I felt myself slipping. I really struggled against it. I felt apart from the others. Finally I cracked and went back to the disturbed ward. I felt better there. I felt free to scream if I wanted to.

As they get better, many patients on the convalescent wards are only too happy to "forget" the time of their more serious symptomatology. They gradually withdraw from effective involvement in hospital life. They become more oriented to the future and to their individual lives. The major adaptive problems that emerge during this period centre around the challenge of leaving the hospital and dealing with the community once again.

The patient's relationship to other patients is one of the most vital and pressing aspects of his hospital experience and one that he often feels relatively free to talk about. Research on the meaning and therapeutic relevance of patient-patient relationships is sorely needed and of great potential value.

Problem 6: *To reconcile the antithesis between security and freedom as it appears in each new stage of hospitalization.*

The patient can find care and safety in the hospital when he is ill, but he is expected to assume increasingly greater responsibility and autonomy as he improves. Both security and responsibility have an inner value for him but they are to some degree mutually exclusive. At each stage in his hospitalization (admission, period of initial adjustment, move to convalescent ward, weekend visits home, discharge) the patient must establish anew his inner preference, taking into account the nature and degree of security and freedom offered by hospital and community.

The security offered by the hospital has diverse psychological meanings for patients: as an aid in impulse control, as a restrictive envelope, as a limitless source of gratification for dependent wishes, as an opportunity to express illness without punishment, and so on. Freedom, on the other hand, is not only a source of gratification and a symbol of the return to the status of a normal person but also a source of major threat. One aim of treatment is to induce in the patient a growing readiness to accept and use freedom in ways that are both satisfying and responsible. In pursuing this aim, however, it is well for staff to bear in mind the value of security for the patient as he tries to overcome some of his difficulties, and also to recognize that the security aspects of hospital life may serve as regressive temptations to the already partially infantilized patient.

The disturbed wards provide more security than do the convalescent wards. The doors to the former are generally locked, the boundaries of the patient's world are clearly delineated, and many outside threats are thus cut off. In addition, the larger number of ward personnel on these wards is a guarantee to the patient of protection from himself. However, security on the disturbed wards brings with it a greater dependence on personnel: patients cannot go to occupational therapy until personnel are ready to let them go, they cannot buy cigarettes until personnel will get them, and so on. With security goes a restriction of personal freedom and self-reliance.

The patient's move to the convalescent ward brings an increase in freedom. Doors are open on these wards and patients can come and go relatively unhampered. This provides a transitional step between the security of the disturbed wards and the greater freedom of the outside world. As such it is an important step for patients to take. Like all important steps forward, it poses new problems: the need for effective inner controls once external controls are reduced; fears about going home for weekends; preparing for discharge from the hospital.

Threats associated with the loss of security are greatest at the time of discharge. Though satisfying human relationships in the hospital may contribute to the patient's recovery, they may also leave him unprepared for what comes next. Patients are concerned with the discrepancy between life in and life out of the hospital. As one patient said of another, "I think he's hindered here because he sees the hospital as a salvation. The hospital won't provide a bridge for him back to the reality of life."

Some preparation for discharge is afforded the patient by his weekend visits home before final discharge. Though these visits in themselves may be frightening, they are often less so than the final break from the hospital and can thus serve as an intermediate step. One patient described her experience as follows:

I'm leaving the hospital tomorrow and I'm scared to death. Everyone is when they're leaving. Outside, the everyday frustrations just add up and you're unprotected. I've been going out on weekends for a long time, but the weekends are not so bad. At least you know that you're going back to the hospital, and you feel safe. It's difficult to leave; you fear getting sick again.

The problem of employment confronts many patients at the time of discharge. In speaking to patients who are about to start job hunting, one is struck by the mixture of fear and satisfaction they feel but especially by the unreality of the whole idea of job hunting. Jobs are part of an unreal other world while the patient is still in the protective confines of the hospital.

Along with their fears over resumption of responsibilities and over loss of the safety of the hospital environment, patients often fear the return to a society that may stereotype them as "mentally ill." This fear varies with the patient's own feelings about his illness and with the nature of the social situation to which he is returning. One patient indicated her fear in these words:

I know a lady who said she moved to another city when she left the hospital, to a city where no one knew her. They would accept her. I think of this myself. People are pretty narrow-minded. They can't believe that a person who has been "psycho" can ever recover.

As we have said, the patient's wishes for freedom and security must be re-equilibrated at each step in his hospitalization. The dilemma is a universal one for hospitalized patients and they vary greatly in their tendencies toward the one or the other pole. The manner in which the dilemma is handled depends both on the personality of the individual patient and on the character of the hospital milieu.

CONCLUDING REMARKS

In the foregoing analysis, we have taken as our point of departure the need for a convergence of psychodynamic and sociological perspectives on the hospitalized patient. Psychoanalytically oriented writers have tended to view the patient almost exclusively from the viewpoint of his intrapsychic life. His present symptoms and adjustment difficulties are seen as expressions of more central, unconscious processes which in turn are related to earlier developmental experiences. This conception of the patient is associated with an emphasis upon psychotherapy as the definitive treatment and as the crucial feature of his hospital experience. Questions of management, of "administrative psychiatry," and of the patient's engagement in hospital life are for the most part either ignored or relegated to secondary importance.

Social scientists, on the other hand, have sought to describe the manifold influences brought to bear upon patients by the hospital community. Their work indicates that many aspects of the hospital, in addition to the presumably definitive treatments offered, have crucial effects on the patient population. However, the focus in these studies is usually upon collective events and upon relatively common responses of patients. Their research aims usually have to do with the analysis of hospital social structure, of social process on the wards, of one or other staff role. They seldom take the individual patient as the unit of analysis, and they seldom look at the hospital from the patient's point of view.

We have attempted here to examine the encounter of patient and hospital *from the perspective of the patient*. In seeking to develop a conception of patienthood and the patient's role, we have found it useful, indeed essential, to utilize concepts relating to individual personality and to social structure. Both "psychological" and "social" viewpoints have been incorporated in the analysis of (a) the situation of the patient, (b) his modes of adaptation (ideational—emotional—conative) to it, and (c) the features of the patient and of the hospital world that jointly shape his course of adaptation. Our emphasis in this initial formulation has been on the patient's situation; we have dealt in only the most sketchy way with the various modes of adaptation and their determinants.

The central concept in our analysis of the patient's situation is that of "problematic issues," that is, fundamental tasks or challenges confronting the patient. These issues are, so to say, existential in the sense that they face all hospitalized persons. They have intrapersonal origins in common human proclivities and external origins in the nature of hospitalization in our society.

The patient faces new and problematic tasks as an immediate consequence of hospitalization. The resolution and indeed the very presence of these problems has important implications for the therapeutic purposes of the hospital. Thus, certain problems confront the patient as a direct result of his being transplanted from his home community to the new hospital community—problems of the redefinition of selfhood through membership in a new community, of orientation to that community, and of evaluation of the relative advantages and threats of remaining in the new community or of returning to the old. These problems confront any individual making a shift from one community to another, be it hospital, school, industrial organization, or nation. Additional problems for the patient arise out of the pressures engendered by the organizational requirements of the hospital system. The hospital has instrumental goals (treatment, for example), and in pursuit of these goals, it must have some minimum of affective integration and administrative ordering among the members of the hospital community so that the system can function smoothly. The patient, too, is under heavy pressure to further the hospital's affective and administrative integration—and problematic issues arise out these requirements

We do not propose that the series of six problematic issues delineated here is an exhaustive one; no doubt there are other issues of equal or greater importance and other, perhaps more fruitful ways of conceptualizing the issues. We would suggest, however, that this mode of analysis is a potentially significant one: it leads toward a synthesis of presently divergent theoretical approaches and, what is more important, it leads toward a more complex, many-faceted view of man coming to grips with the demands and opportunities of social reality.

NOTES

1. This research was carried out at the Center for Sociopsychological Research (Massachusetts Mental Health Center and Harvard Medical School). The senior author is now at the Research Center for Mental Health, New York University. The assistance of Drs. Harry C. Solomon, Milton Greenblatt, and Robert W. Hyde is gratefully acknowledged. The research was supported in part by Grants M–687 and M–1000 from the National Institute of Mental Health of the National Institutes of Health, U.S. Public Health Service.

2. The following are a few examples of a slowly developing literature taking a sociopsychological (rather than a purely sociological or a purely psychodynamic) view of patienthood in the mental hospital: Erickson (2), Goffman (3), Jones (7), Caudill (1), Stanton and Schwartz (8), and varied selections in Greenblatt, Levinson, and Williams (4) and Jaco (6).

3. It is to be emphasized that the hospital has grown and changed in many respects in the intervening years. The situation of the patient at the present time is therefore different from that described on these pages.

REFERENCES

1. Caudill, William, *Psychiatric Hospital as a Small Society* (Cambridge; Mass: Harvard University Press, 1958).

2. Erickson, Kai T., "Patient Role and Social Uncertainty," *Psychiatry* (1957), **20**, 263–274.

3. Goffman, Erving, *Asylums* (Chicago: Aldine, 1962).

4. Greenblatt, Milton, Levinson, Daniel, and Williams, Richard (Eds.), *The Patient and the Mental Hospital* (New York: The Free Press, 1957).

5. Greenblatt, Milton, York, Richard H., and Brown, Esther, *From Custodial to Therapeutic Patient Care in Mental Hospitals* (New York: Russell Sage Foundation, Ed. 1955).

6. Jaco, E. Gartly (Ed.), *Patients, Physicians and Illness* (New York: The Free Press, 1958).

7. Jones, Maxwell, *The Therapeutic Community* (New York: Basic Books, 1953).

8. Stanton, Alfred H., and Schwartz, Morris S., *The Mental Hospital* (New York: Basic Books, 1954).

PATIENT DEMANDS IN A MENTAL HOSPITAL CONTEXT

Morris S. Schwartz

THIS paper reports an attempt to investigate a 'sick situation' within a mental hospital in a detailed and systematic sociological way, with the same subtlety and intensity that the psychotherapist uses in investigating the interpersonal process in psychotherapy. The situation concerned a patient whose current pattern of difficulty, as identified by other participants, was excessive demandingness. In describing the situation and the intervention designed to alter various of its aspects, I shall also present a frame of reference for the analysis of the types of processes and structures that contribute to the development, persistence, and elimination of untherapeutic processes.

This paper maintains that much can be gained in mental hospital operation if a strategy of intervention is used that keeps under scrutiny the patient's personality and the social process and structure in both their institutional and small-group forms, and if hospital personnel select for intervention the area that seems to offer the best opportunity for effective change. Through such systematic observation, analysis, and planned interventions, an empirical basis might be developed for the introduction and direction of social change in hospital patterns of interaction and structure—social change which would facilitate the mental health of the patients by removing noxious social situations that virtually predetermine or inevitably elicit sick modes of participation.

The study reported in this paper is part of a larger project[1] in which I observed and analyzed the interaction and social organization of a mental hospital ward in order to suggest modes of intervention. The ward under study[2] ordinarily had fourteen or fifteen patients, three or four nurses or aides, and two or three student nurses on the day shift; the evening shift comprised one less nurse or aide and one less student nurse.

In pursuing the goal, with specific patients, of uncovering social processes that seemed to maintain their mental illness and suggesting ways of interrupting these processes, I formulated the following questions: (1) What patterns of

Reprinted from *Psychiatry: Journal for the Study of Interpersonal Processes* (August, 1957), *20* (3), 249–261. Copyright © 1957 by the William Alanson White Psychiatric Foundation, Inc.

difficulty—modes of participating with others—characterize the patient's mental illness? (2) What is the staff's response to the patient's pattern of difficulty? (3) What is the nature of the configuration that is stabilized as a result of patient-staff interaction? (4) If this configuration is illness-maintaining, how might it be changed? (5) If intervention is to be attempted, how can it be conceptualized, what is to be its nature, and how can it be instituted? (6) What effects follow the intervention?[3]

From a series of transactions that extended over a period of time, those patterns of patient activity were focused upon that seemed to have significance for both patient and personnel. In extracting these modes of patient participation for analysis, I tried not to isolate them from the context of which they were a part, but to view them as emergents from a social process—a process amenable to analysis from a number of perspectives that are relevant to an understanding of the patient's pattern of difficulty. These three independent-interdependent perspectives are: the personality system, the small group system, and the institutional system. These systems are part of each other, are reflected in each other, and, in operating simultaneously, they constitute the social process and structure.

Any system of transactions, seen from the perspectives of personality, the small group, and the institution, can be viewed both in terms of process and structure, for social process and social structure are two aspects of any system of social transactions. In addition, the interrelations of these systems also can be seen in terms of process and structure. The process focus brings into view the changing or continuing flow of events and the connectedness between the past, present, and future aspects of the transactions. Structure is process stopped and fixed at a particular time. It is process assuming persistent patterns that are identifiable; it is process divided into phases that have distinctive and delimitable characteristics. Finally, changes in process—transition events that seem to be influential in guiding or directing the system of transactions from one phase to another or from one structure to another—also can be seen as a series of processes or as a coalescence of structures.

In this paper my interest in the particular patient's pattern of difficulty is two-fold: (1) To analyze the sick mode of behavior in order to show how this type of analysis might contribute to an improvement of the patient's mental health. Thus, it is necessary to examine the kinds of social processes that maintain sick behavior and to indicate ways in which they might be interrupted. (2) To examine the patient's pattern of difficulty in order to develop a framework within which the therapeutic effects of a system of transactions can be evaluated; and conversely, to apply a frame of reference to a system of transactions in order to examine how this system develops from the reciprocal activity of its participants. Therefore, the patient's pattern of difficulty is the reference point around which data from various perspectives have been organized.

In the course of the project a configuration arose on the ward in which for a period of three weeks the patient described here continued to make excessive requests[4] of ward personnel, who responded in a way that contributed to the continuation of these demands. This pattern came into focus as an important issue when it became sufficiently troublesome to be identified as a problem by the staff participants. However, the social process of which this behavior was a part, although just as real and as repetitive in some of its aspects, was not as easily recognizable.[5]

THE PATIENT'S PATTERN OF DIFFICULTY

Mrs. Jay, diagnosed schizophrenic, had been on the ward for approximately two years when she developed a pattern of behavior whose central component was frequent, rapid, and continuous requests for service and attention. The ward personnel experienced these demands as excessive and impossible to fulfill. They labeled her "a demanding patient" because they felt that her demands did not fall within acceptable limits. Conceptualizing her in this way did not help the staff deal with the problem; rather, their responses intensified her demands. After a week of interaction around the patient's demands, this pattern of difficulty became stabilized, and the personnel were at a loss to deal with the patient in a way that did not increase her and their own dissatisfaction and anxiety.

Although the personnel focused almost exclusively on the patient's demandingness, this was not the only mode of behavior she engaged in at this time, nor did it have a long and persistent history. During her residence on the ward she had, at one point, been mute, apathetic, withdrawn, and highly unresponsive to others. At the time the demanding behavior appeared, she was more active but still spent much time alone, autistically preoccupied, hallucinating, and carrying on her fantasy relations in an overt way.

In presenting her demands to the staff, Mrs. Jay would ask fast and furiously for objects and services, frequently making four or five requests a minute—for cigarettes, a light, a glass of water, food, facial tissue, a closet door to be opened, a chair to be moved, and so on. A nurse described her behavior as follows: "Yesterday she asked me for an ash tray; then she asked for more things: the card table, paper to write on, a pencil. First, she wanted the table in her room; then, she wanted it on the hall. She'd say, 'Put the table in front of me.' Then a minute later. 'Put it on the side.' Then she said, 'Get me a cigarette.' It went on like this all day."

The specific object or service Mrs. Jay requested seemed to be less important to her than the process of asking, for sometimes she asked for a cigarette while she was smoking one or did not drink the glass of water she had demanded. She would evidence little interest in the object or service she received and appeared to derive little gratification from having received it. Instead of waiting for a response to her request or attending to the nurse who was responding to her, the patient would return immediately to her autistic preoccupation. If she received no response or if she was refused, she would pursue her request with increased vigor, becoming louder and more upset. Frequently, if her request was fulfilled, she would immediately ask for something else.

Mrs. Jay's requests fell within a restricted range of approaches. She delivered the request curtly and rapidly as if she were commanding the other to serve her; and sometimes she showed irritation, annoyance, and contempt for the person toward whom the request was directed. Ordinarily, her requests were accompanied by anxiety of varying degrees. This anxiety and her intense affect while making her demands were especially noticeable when they were refused, delayed, or ignored. At these times, she berated or derogated the person who refused her, or, when extremely anxious, screamed in a loud, frantic voice, and desperately insisted upon having her request fulfilled. Her requests appeared to be of the utmost urgency, as if life or death were involved.

The pattern of the patient's difficulty can be viewed as an emergent from three systems that include the time dimensions of past, present, and future. It can be seen as action that is contributed to and determined by the convergence of aspects of (1) the patient's personality, (2) a small group configuration, and (3) select institutional values.

From the point of view of her personality as a system of action, the patient's demands can be seen as action oriented toward others that has meaning and intent and serves a function for her. It includes such aspects as her needs, her motivations, her emotional life, her conceptions and attitudes, and the biographical succession and the present operation and organization of her interpersonal relations. The inferences I have made concerning these aspects are based on the information that was available about Mrs. Jay's past, on discussions with staff members who knew the patient well, and on close observation of the patient's interactions with others.

Because Mrs. Jay had suffered considerable deprivation in the past and because she had failed in the maturation process, she maintained an intense dependency on others—a strong covert wish to be taken care of and nurtured. But reality seldom coincided with her wishes, so that she suffered much disappointment in her expectation of gratification from others. As a result, this expecttation had been transformed into an anticipation of pain.[6] In addition, she was distrustful of others and anticipated refusal or misunderstanding from them. With this background of extreme frustration, it was virtually inevitable that situations involving the articulation and recognition of her needs would be fraught with anxiety, and her attempt to have them fulfilled would be accompanied by doubt, internal conflict, fear, and inability to communicate her wants clearly and acceptably.

In the present situation, the content and form of Mrs. Jay's demands were her way of communicating her needs and attempting to have them fulfilled. But her past experiences around these needs crystallized a set of attitudes of regarding herself as an emotionally starved person who would continue to be deprived because others would not recognize or fulfill her needs. Her continued efforts to get them fulfilled were accompanied by a self-image of worthlessness, a self-conception of never getting anything she wanted or needed, and a dread that the past would repeat itself. Driven by the intensity of her needs and a faint hope that it might be different "this time," she tried to reach the personnel through her demands. She revealed her doubts by asking fast and furiously; and, afraid to expose herself to the threat of being ignored, frustrated, or rebuffed, she returned immediately to the protection of her fantasy world. For ignoring her meant to her that she would be annihilated; indifference meant that she did not exist and ought not to exist; refusal she interpreted as a threat of starvation; withholding, that she was doomed to emptiness; and rejection, that nobody cared whether she lived or died. Unsure that she would get anything, she made intense, brief, but continuing efforts. Her demands became her way of indicating her helplessness and desperate need.

One of Mrs. Jay's prominent difficulties in living was her loneliness. She spent most of the time by herself, enclosed in an autistic world. But this existence was not sufficiently satisfying and acceptable to her, and she made intermittent attempts to reach out. Her persistent demands suggested that she very much needed and wanted to be noticed, to be attended to, and to have another's interest invested in her. Her demanding behavior was her means of establishing contact with another and forming some tenuous relationship with him. Because the means she employed to indicate this covert wish were not conventional or direct, they were easily misunderstood by ward personnel.

Presumably because of her past experiences, continued refusal or failure to satisfy her elicited strong affect. Thus, deprivation or frustration was experienced by her as attack, punishment, or annihilation; at these times, feelings of bitterness and despair were quickly evoked in her. She conceptualized her environing others as "bad," for they continued to "make her" experience deprivation and pain. Repeated refusals reaffirmed her belief that she could not expect any satisfaction from "them." Despite the fact that these others were "bad," she felt that she had to depend on them, for they had the power to give or to withhold what she needed. She responded by withdrawing into helpless apathy—a course she had previously pursued in the hospital— or by enraged counterattack, one form of which was her frantic, demanding behavior.

From another perspective, Mrs. Jay's demands were related to and encouraged by certain aspects of the institutional values and ideology. The expectations held by prestigeful figures in the hospital with regard to the role of patient encouraged her to express herself verbally and to make her wishes known. This institutional context also encouraged patients to seek help from the staff and expected the staff to accept and encourage patients' forms of help-seeking. In addition, the organization of the ward was such that many objects were inaccessible to patients; certain items could be obtained only by asking staff members for them.

The patient's demands also were, in part, a product of the staff's responses to her and of the small-group interaction that emerged around her demands, which will be described in the sections that follow.

STAFF RESPONSES

The staff's responses soon became stabilized into quite uniform patterns of interaction. These responses were a product of aspects of: (1) staff personalities—their purposes, needs, motives, affects, and attitudes; (2) the institutional prohibitions, permissions, and facilitations; and

(3) the immediate social configuration in which the patient's behavior had a compelling role in determining staff responses, which, in turn, played an important part in eliciting the patient's behavior.

Because the patient's requests were persistent, the personnel were continuously confronted with the necessity of developing a way of dealing with them. Initial responses were hesitant and indecisive. The personnel floundered about, trying to find an appropriate way of meeting the patient's demands. As the requests persisted, and as the staff continued to fail at a satisfactory solution, they became increasingly rigid and restricted in their response to her. Within a week after the appearance of the problem situation, staff responses were characterized by resistance to recognizing requests, reluctance and withholding in meeting them, and anger and resentment toward the patient for making them. The personnel ignored many requests, acting as if they had not heard them; if they recognized them, they often delayed or refused to fulfill them. They frequently verbalized their anger to each other and at times expressed it to the patient.

While the personnel developed strong impulses "to make her stop her demands," their wishes were in conflict with the institutional ideology, and they felt that direct and aggressive behavior directed toward the patient to inhibit her requests would be untherapeutic. They finally worked out a compromise in the form of an informal agreement among themselves: the patient would have to present her requests in an acceptable manner before they would fulfill them. In actual practice, this requirement applied to many but not all of her requests. They especially required the patient to be more polite about requests which did not involve her physical welfare. For instance, the following comments were made by an aide and a nurse when they were asked about their approach to the patient:

"When she asks me for something, I tell her, 'Do you know what the password is?—it's *please*. If you say *please*, you will get what you want.' If she doesn't say it, I don't give it to her. After all, that's how they do things out in society, and she has to learn how to behave."

"The other night I was walking down the hall and she asked me for a cigarette. I told her that she'd get a cigarette when she asked me in the right way, and I said, 'How about saying *please*?' Then she said that I'm supposed to jump and get her the cigarette when she asks. I told her I wasn't going to do it until she asked me in a more polite way."

When the investigator asked a nurse why she thought the patient should say *please*, the reply was, "My feeling toward these patients is that they are here to learn all over again how to get along with people on the outside. She wouldn't be able to do that on the outside. You can't go and tell just anybody to go and do what you say just like that. You have to keep it [your relationship with her] on a level where you aren't considered a low white-trash servant or something like that. We are here to help them, not to work for them."

This rationalization that requiring her to be polite was for her own benefit—to help her to learn to live outside the hospital—reflected the staff's conflicted feelings about deviating from the institutional expectations by setting up conventional requirements for the patient.

The staff also instituted other means of mild punishment and retaliation against the patient. At times, when Mrs. Jay refused to ask politely for a cigarette and persisted in contemptuously demanding it, personnel took her cigarettes away from her and did not permit her to smoke for a period of time. If she asked for a cigarette while in the hall, the personnel refused to bring it to her and insisted that she come to the nursing office door for it. Such sanctions, designed on the surface to alter the patient's manner and the form of her demands, actually were disguised attempts to prevent her from making the requests at all.

The covert aspects of the staff's attitudes played an important role in molding their overt response to the patient. As their interaction with her remained unsatisfactory, they came more and more to respond selectively to her, seeing her as a demanding patient, and failing to see the rest of her personality and behavior, especially overlooking instances in which she was not demanding. This selective inattention helped them to develop a set of stereotyped attitudes about her and to stabilize a negative emotional response to her which contributed to their withholding and stringent responses. With their restricted focus and perspective, the personnel experienced only the manifest content of the patients's behavior; it seemed that they could not face the anxiety aroused by the patient's desperation, helplessness, and intense dependence. They revealed this by claiming that fulfilling her requests would result only in increasing their frequency, so that the staff eventually would be overwhelmed and exhausted by them. In rejecting the patient's dependency and overlooking her desperation, they rejected her demands—indicators of the dependency and desperation—and the patient herself. Instead of a desperate patient they saw a powerful person who commanded time and attention and assaulted their self-esteem. They experienced her derogatory attitudes as personal affronts designed to make them uncomfortable, and her contemptuousness as an indication of disrespect for each of them personally. Thus, instead of seeing the patient's dependence upon them, they became, in part, dependent upon her for their self-esteem.

As the patient's demands continued, the personnel felt increasingly discouraged and inadequate. The patient contributed to their low self-esteem when she treated them as though they were servants. The nursing role in the hospital also contributed to their feelings of inferiority. Nursing personnel cleaned the ward, handled patients after they had been incontinent, changed soiled linen, served food, and, in general, did the ward housekeeping. Rarely did patients assist in these tasks; for example, patients were neither required nor urged to make their beds. Mrs. Jay, in particular, performed none of these tasks. Thus, she constantly thrust the staff into a servant role, which took on an added reality for them because she was upper-middle class, and, as the staff knew, was accustomed to having servants wait on her, while they came from the lower-middle or upper-lower classes. This real status differential made it difficult for them to see her superior attitudes and approaches as defensive maneuvers. As a result, they retaliated by insisting that she conform to their expectations, and when she refused they retaliated further by refusing to fulfill her demands.

By narrowing their perspective and restricting their perception of the patient, it was easy for the personnel to be moralistic about her. They interpreted her demands as willful and calculated misbehavior, deliberately designed to make them uncomfortable. They assumed she could stop them if she wanted to. Since she continued them, she only had herself to blame for the consequences. They were unable to see their own contribution to the problem situation—the ways in which their own actions were, in part, responsible for her demanding behavior. They proceeded on the assumption that the patient had to change, not that they had to change; that it was her problem, not theirs; and that the problem would be quickly solved "if only she acted differently." This required the patient to do something she could not do at that time and in that situation. At the same time, they neglected to ask of themselves something that had greater probability of being accomplished: changing their responses to her.

Displays of oppositional and resentful affect and behavior toward the patient were accompanied by guilt. Occasionally, in a reflective mood, the staff recognized that their responses were not helping to solve the problem and articulated their discouragement about discovering a solution. As nursing personnel, they felt that they should be able to understand the patient and to fulfill her needs. Yet, in this situation, they did not know what the patient wanted nor how to find out. They knew that her demands were important to her, but this was obscured by the profusion of demands and the staff's feeling of inability to meet them. Although there were realistic limitations on the amount of time they could devote to the patient's requests, they were unable to distinguish situations in which realistic limitations guided their responses from occasions when their negative emotional orientation was the determining factor.

Concerning the contribution of the institutional structure to staff responses, I should add here that the institution afforded much latitude for ward personnel to work out their problems with patients. They were not told what to do in specific problem situations, and the solutions they arrived at among themselves were not interfered with unless they obviously were damaging to the patient. A ward problem situation could persist for a long time before it came to the attention of the institutional authorities. It became an institutional problem only when it had significant ramifications for the rest of the hospital, when the patient's therapist was sufficiently distressed by it, or when an important ward staff member—such as the administrator or charge nurse—raised it as a problem. But at these times, discussion of the problem usually was oriented toward clarification rather than toward the making of a decision for the ward staff.

Although the staff acted with a high degree of consensus on the response patterns described above, there were two conspicuous exceptions to the general approach, one on the day shift and the other on the evening shift. They saw the more desperate, helpless aspect of the patient and were not threatened by her derogatory manner. Each tried to meet the patient's needs and requests, quietly went about fulfilling them, and had very little of the difficulty experienced by other personnel. One of these nurses described her relation with Mrs. Jay as follows:

When I come to see her, she will ask me for six different things: facial tissue, the time, a cigarette, water, a hot water bag. I get them all and then she settles down. All you have to do is about six things when you first come in, and once you have proved to her that you are interested in her, she will settle down and not make any more demands.

THE CONFIGURATION

As a result of the interplay between the patient's pattern of difficulty and the staff's response to it, an identifiable configuration emerged and persisted on the ward. This consisted of a series of reciprocal and complementary processes that were circular and self-reinforcing and were temporarily articulated into a stabilized structure. It was a configuration in which the mode of participation of both patient and staff became automatic, stereotyped, and repetitive and in which each of the participants seemed to reinforce and continue the response of the other. Thus, the configuration can be seen as a small-scale social system maintaining a relatively static equilibrium that tended to perpetuate the same processes that maintained it. The configuration also can be seen as a system of transactions temporarily stabilized in form and direction that emerged as a product of the institutional context, the personalities of the participants, and the immediate social relationships they were having with each other.

Reciprocal Withholding

Each participant in the configuration had specific needs which the other was unable to fill. Each insisted that the other afford him some gratification, by each was unwilling to provide any fulfillment for the other. The frustration of the staff's expectation led them to engage in continuing and oppositional withholding responses. This made the patient even more unable to play the role they required of her. Because she was deprived and frustrated, the patient reacted negativistically, and the staff's withholding evoked the patient's demands as an automatic response—and activity which was a desperate attempt to force fulfillment from the staff.

Reciprocal Negative Affect

Conspicuous in the configuration was the large amount of negative affect and emotional involvement of the participants. On the one hand, the patient elicited negative affect in the personnel, and, on the other, the negative responses of the personnel evoked and maintained the patient's demanding behavior. It is difficult to determine where this reciprocal process started. The reinforcement of reciprocal negative affect and the reflecting back to each other of these disjunctive processes[7] in part stabilized the configuration.

Reciprocal Anxiety

For the patient, demands and anxiety were self-reinforcing as well as being reinforced by the staff. Her demands were, in part, a response to her anxiety, but her anxiety also was a reaction to her demands—to the possibility of deprivation. It seemed that the patient's demands and anxiety reinforced each other—the more anxious she became, the more demanding she was; the more demanding she became, the more anxious she was. In addition, the responses of the staff to both her anxiety and her demands served to validate her fears and led to even more anxiety and demandingness, frantic behavior, agitation, and desperation. For the staff, the patient's increased demands and agitation led to increased anxiety

and to a greater defensiveness and awareness of their own ineffectiveness in solving the problem situation. The more inadequate they felt and the more they failed with the patient, the greater their anxiety became, culminating in feelings of defeat and despair. Thus, through the dynamism of self-reinforcement and other-reinforcement, the patient's anxiety and demands continued.

Demands and Counterdemands

Where the patient saw her requests as legitimate and necessary, the staff, by their counterdemands, first indicated their unacceptance of the form of the requests, then questioned their legitimacy, and finally indicated their lack of acceptance of the patient herself. These counterdemands provoked automatic demanding behavior as a reciprocal response. Thus, each required that the other relinquish his demands and each insisted that the other accede to his wishes. Therefore, an impasse existed in which each became more fixed in his own position and at the same time helped the other become more fixed in his.

Selective Perception

Both patient and personnel selected certain aspects of the other to focus on and interpreted the behavior—or misbehavior—of the other to fit his preconception. Thus, the staff perceived the patient as "bad," not "sick"; and the patient experienced the staff as "bad"—ungratifying. Conceptualizing the patient as "bad" and selectively inattending to the fact that she was sick served a number of functions for the staff; they justified their own punishing behavior; they could insist that she change; and they could expect her to live up to more conventional standards. As a response to the staff's reactions, and in terms of her own selective perceptions, the patient continued her automatic, stereotyped demands. With similar and reciprocal restricted attitudes and stable frames of reference of "other-badness," "self-weakness," and "other-powerfulness," each participant led the other to a virtually preordained pattern of response and, thus, to a continuation of his own response.

Because of these selective perceptions and their affective context, it was difficult for the staff to see the patient's demands as a form of communication and a way of relating. In turn, it was difficult for the patient to see the staff's responses as inadequate and inappropriate ways of meeting a difficult and misunderstood situation.

To summarize, the patient's demanding mode

of participation was, in part, a function of her personality. In part, it was a function of the configuration in which she participated and to which she contributed. And in part, it was a function of what the institution facilitated and positively sanctioned. Viewed in another way, the patient's demanding behavior might be seen as a potential interpersonal activity that was elicited by the social situation and was locked into, and maintained by, the pattern of staff-patient transactions.

It remains to state briefly why the patient's pattern of difficulty could be seen as part of her mental illness and why the continuation of the configuration was illness-maintaining or untherapeutic. First, in this configuration, the patient obtained little satisfaction from her relations with significant others; instead, her anxiety, at times reaching the point of panic or frenzy, was regularly stimulated and provoked without resolution in a constructive way. Second, she maintained disjunctive integrations with others in which her resentment was evoked and her low self-esteem reinforced. Third, in her communication with others there were continued misunderstandings, blocks, and restrictions that prohibited consensus and the working out of the problems associated with her requests. Fourth, her needs were continually frustrated, and she experienced regular deprivation and rejection. Fifth, the patient's suspicions and her expectations that others were "bad" and pain-producing were continued and reinforced. Sixth, her autistic behavior was reinforced and perhaps increased when she was forced to seek more gratification from herself because she could not get it from others.

INTERVENTION

Since the patient's demanding mode of participation was an integral part of the disjunctive configuration and was maintained by certain aspects of the institutional structure and personality of the participants, I hypothesized that, if relevant and significant features of each or all of these systems were altered, a change might result in the patient's behavior. Since both personalities and institutions are notorious for their resistance to change, I decided to try to alter the system of transactions constituting the configuration. Hopefully, a change in the configuration might affect the personalities of the participants as well as the institutional structure, since all were interrelated. While the total configuration could

not be changed directly or immediately, alteration of certain crucial parts might dislodge the stability and the effects of the configuration and result in a reduction in intensity, a subsidence, or an elimination of this aspect of the patient's mental illness.

In initiating the first phase of the process of intervention, I reported to the ward authorities—the administrator and the charge nurse—my findings and analysis and my hypothesis that the patient's demanding behavior continued, in part, because of the staff's pattern of responses to her. I indicated that one staff member on each of the shifts had a conjunctive integration with the patient and, based on the observation of their relations with her, further suggested that the ward leaders try to persuade the staff to approach the patient in an opposite way from their usual approach: that the ward leaders ask the staff to try to meet as many of the patient's requests as they could as soon as possible and that whenever possible they try to anticipate the patient's needs. My other suggestion was that the problem be thoroughly aired at the next staff conference—which was attended by all nursing personnel on both shifts—and that the investigator, administrator, and charge nurse put forth a united effort to influence the staff in the direction suggested. After discussion and exploration of possible alternatives, the ward authorities agreed that the course suggested might be fruitful and that, at the staff conference and in their informal contacts, they would try to persuade the staff to respond differently to the patient.

The transactions during the staff conference—the second phase of intervention—constituted an important, transition process in changing the attitudes and feelings of the staff toward the patient. Encouraged by the administrator, charge nurse, and investigator, the nursing staff openly and forcefully expressed feelings of resentment, antagonism, and anger toward the patient. They focused particularly on the patient's contemptuous and derogatory manner and revealed that the patient had so provoked them that they had informally agreed to deal with her restrictively. They stated their belief that such stringency might force her to give up her demands. They expressed their fear that they would be "spoiling" the patient if they acceded to her requests and that, under these circumstances, her requests would increase and become more unmanageable.

In the course of this frank expression of opinions and feelings, the two staff members who treated the patient differently expressed their disagreement with the dominant attitudes and related their experiences with the patient, pointing out that they had little difficulty with her. As the discussion continued, it was evident that the staff recognized that their approach was not satisfactory, that they felt discouraged about the situation, and that they wanted to be helped to change it.

The ward leaders and the investigator accepted the staff's negative expressions in the spirit of exchange and as an attempt to come to a better understanding of the problem. They stated that the staff's feelings were understandable on the basis of their experiences with the patient, and that the staff was not to be blamed or criticized. Instead, the leaders appealed to the staff to try to develop greater awareness of the patient's experiences with them and to see how their responses might affect her. It was pointed out that the patient was by no means the powerful figure they experienced, but was desperate, frightened, and acutely in need of the staff's help, attention, and approval; the anxiety and agitation accompanying her requests indicated her anticipation that her needs would not be satisfied; and her demands were a way of communicating to the staff how much she needed their help.

It was suggested that the staff's negative and oppositional responses might be contributing to the patient's demands. As long as they frustrated her, she could only resent them and respond more vigorously with her demands; trying to force her to change only seemed to reinforce her demands. It also was indicated that the staff seemed to be asking the patient to change her behavior before they would change theirs, which was unrealistic, since she was sick and this behavior was part of her illness. Since staff and patient seemed at an impasse, the suggestion was advanced that they might consider alternative ways of responding to the patient and then see if their changed approach brought about different responses from her. The concrete suggestions made were that they try to meet the patient's requests promptly and not require her to be polite about them; that when they could not meet a request, they explain the reasons; that they give her direct answers to her questions; and that they try to anticipate her requests whenever possible so that she might feel they really were concerned about her needs.

Initially, the staff resisted these suggestions, reiterating their fear that such indulgence would only increase her demands and that they would be "snowed under" in trying to deal with her while they neglected the rest of the ward. It was pointed out that it would be impossible to meet all of her requests and that it was not necessary to do so in order to help her. The personnel were urged to try the approach suggested, to observe what happened, and to think of other possible approaches if that one did not work. Although there was still much hesitation and skepticism, the conference concluded with a temporary agreement to try to institute the suggestions made.

In the third phase of intervention the personnel, encouraged by the charge nurse, attempted to carry out these suggestions. With tentativeness in their attitude and behavior, some personnel met the patient's requests promptly; others offered her a cigarette or water before she asked for them; still others told her directly the reasons they were unable to accede to her requests. Almost from the beginning, there was a perceptible change in the patient's behavior. As evidence accumulated that this procedure worked, they were encouraged to continue it and to pursue it more actively; as they did so, the patient became less demanding, and at the end of a few days her behavior was dramatically different. At the staff conference a week later, staff members commented that the patient's requests has so diminished that they were no longer a problem. She was beginning to approach the staff for objects instead of commanding them to bring things to her, and she was able to tolerate a delay in having her requests fulfilled without becoming agitated and castigating the personnel. This change occurred without the substitution of another form of symptomatic behavior such as withdrawal. Instead, the patient's anxiety decreased—especially in regard to

the making of requests. She carried on more satisfying relations with the personnel, she became less dependent on them, she responded in a more realistic way in situations involving requests, and in general seemed to be deriving more security from her relations with the staff. In retrospect, some of the personnel regarded this change as one crucial turning point in the patient's illness and as an important contribution to her improvement.

What were some of the conditions that facilitated the initiation of the intervention? First, there was the conviction on the part of the ward leaders that some action was needed to alter the approach of the personnel to the patient, and an agreement was reached between the ward leaders and the investigator as to the course and direction the change might take. Second, the absence of blame helped to alleviate the guilt of the staff; and the latter were encouraged and helped to experience and perceive the patient differently. Third, the personnel's readiness for change because of their dissatisfaction with the present situation was important. Fourth, the concrete proposal put forth and the decision reached to initiate the suggestion also were significant in the process of intervention. Finally, the support and encouragement of the ward leaders in motivating the staff actually to try the suggestion was crucial. Once the interventions showed some success, a circular process came into being in which the staff's success with the patient encouraged them to continue it, and their continuation of it brought about new success.

What happened to the staff, the patient, the configuration, and the institution as a consequence of the intervention? It had the effect of significantly altering the staff's conception of the patient and their feeling about her. They were reoriented toward the patient, and tried to understand her and the reasons for her sick behavior. When they no longer saw her as willfully opposing them, it became unnecessary to continue the power struggle. They changed their values with reference to the patient from control and opposition to therapeutic handling and meeting her needs. They became more sympathetic, less angry at her, and more accepting of her need to be demanding under certain conditions. In addition, as their guilt and anxiety about her decreased, they were able to see her more objectively and less defensively, and to deal with her more appropriately. Finally, the staff experienced a change in their self-conception with reference to the patient. They began to conceive of themselves as being able to act differently toward her; they felt that they had some power in the situation; and they believed that their relations with her could have a therapeutic orientation instead of a retaliatory one.

With the patient and her internal life as the point of reference, it can be said, on the most general level, that different psychological consequences ensued for her in the restructured configuration. Concentrated "giving" on the part of the staff and continuous evidence of their concern for her welfare seemed to modify her conception of these significant others. As her frustration and rejection decreased, she no longer experienced "them" as globally "bad" and responsible for her intense anxiety. As she received gratification and satisfaction from them, she could alter her expectation of continuous pain and suffering. As her tension was reduced and she experienced herself "getting more," she did not have to protest, struggle, and demand fulfillment. When her security increased as she came to feel that others were oriented toward satisfying her needs and that they cared about her, she could become less concerned about forcing these basic satisfactions and less demandingly dependent, and she could relinquish her demand that the staff demonstrate their concern and continually prove themselves to her.

Using the social configuration as the point of reference, one can contrast the pre- and post-intervention configuration. The intervention dislodged the equilibrium of which the demanding behavior was a part and of which the restrictiveness and stereotypy of the interaction were conspicuous aspects. The intervention served to open up the transactions between patient and staff and afforded opportunities for a greater variety of relationships and responses.

The institution served as the broad envelope within which the intervention could occur and facilitated the emergence of the intervention by permitting and encouraging communication between various levels of staff. However, I could discern no noticeable effect on over-all institutional patterns as a consequence of the altered ward configuration.

The intervention itself can be seen as the convergence of a series of successive, simultaneous, and interrelated events. This set of events was introduced into an ongoing but temporarily stabilized social configuration, influencing the structure and direction of the constellation and serving as a transition to a new complex of transactions with different effects on the participants. It occurred at a critical and relevant point in time, and its emergence was characterized by a series of feed-back processes in which the altered response of one participant reinforced the altered response of the other, and vice versa. Thus, by altering one aspect of the configuration, the balance of interactional forces was sufficiently changed to dislodge the social equilibrium that maintained this aspect of the patient's illness.

A few months later, an opportunity arose to obtain partial confirmation of these observations, interpretations, and modes of intervention. Two new personnel arrived on the ward and began to respond to the patient in the mode of the old configuration. For two days, the patient was increasingly demanding with the newcomers. This time, however, intervention was accomplished more quickly. The charge nurse described to the new personnel the previous experience with the patient and suggested that they change their way of approaching her. This they did, and the patient's demands disappeared.

In general, I have found two kinds of patterns of transactions that have appeared to be characteristic of sick situations and tend to maintain patients' sick modes of participation. First, there are parallel or similar transactions in which the participants become reflections of each other—the patient evoking the same responses from staff members that they evoke in him; for example, the patient's demands are met by staff demands or the patient's withdrawal is met by staff withdrawal.[8] In these integrations the disjunctive processes appear to have an imitative quality. Second, there are reciprocal processes in which the participants fit into each other's pattern of transactions so as to prohibit the expansion and development of these transactions in new forms and directions; for example, the patient's demands are met by opposition, moralizing, or requirements that he abide by conventional societal standards, or withdrawal is met with helplessness and guilt. In these situations the disjunctive processes have a static, repetitive quality. I would suggest that, when the above transactions appear either singly or in combination as predominant aspects of a social configuration, they can be used as indicators of an untherapeutic situation and of the need for systematic investigation in order to develop modes of intervention.

In this study an attempt is made to understand a patient's demanding behavior in terms of three systems: (1) the patient's personality—her affective state as influenced by and patterned in the past and as it exists in potential for evocation in the present; and her prevailing needs, motivations, and psychological processes; (2) the network of interpersonal relations that are patterned and persist as her immediate social environment and field of social participation; and (3) the institutional allowances, restrictions, and encouragements that affect and direct the transactions.

Another conceptual perspective used to analyze the patient's pattern of participation is that of social process and structure. I view social process as a series of ongoing transactions and conceptualize it in terms of these three systems. Social process is seen as social structure in formation, crystallization, disintegration, and re-formation, and as divided into subprocesses or phases: prodromal, configurational, intervention, and post-intervention. When the social process has been fixed at a particular time and a distinctive pattern of transactions identified, one is then concerned with attention to the social structure.[9] In this instance, the patient's demanding behavior became part of a stabilized social equilibrium. In this equilibrium, the crystallized forms of transaction recurred and persisted over time and were structured in such a way as to continue, reinforce, and stabilize the patient's mode of participation as well as to perpetuate the structure itself.

I have tried to analyze the structure, changes, and effects of social process in terms of these three interdependent and independent systems. Each is open; is reflected in and is part of the other; and each modifies the other systems.[10] All contribute in different ways and degrees to the nature of the transactions and the pattern shown. Instead of assuming that one system is more basic, fundamental, or real than another, I have assumed that all are necessary constituents of a social process, but that, at a given time in a particular situation, one may predominate and play the major part in shaping the direction, from, and consequences of the social process. Thus I have afforded each system of perspective an independent as well as an interdependent reality.

I hope that this mode of analysis will contribute to the development of a more adequate frame of reference for analyzing the complex phenomena of human relations and mental illness in the mental hospital. This approach also reflects my dissatisfaction with segmental explanatory concepts which elaborate only a single perspective. It seems to me that such partial approaches are insufficient; they introduce a degree of restriction and distortion that occasions unnecessary difficulties in predicting and controlling the social-psychological processes producing and constituting mental illness. What seems to be needed is the application of the same breadth and depth of analysis to at least three systems as is usually applied only to that of the investigator's specialized field. This means, in effect, that in analyzing the phenomena of human relations and mental illness one directs attention both simultaneously and successively to psychodynamics, sociopsychological or small-group dynamics, and institutional or societal dynamics.

NOTES

1. The project, "An Investigation to Determine the Modes of Intervention and the Social Structure Which Will Facilitate the Recovery of Patients on a Disturbed Ward of a Mental Hospital," was supported, in part, by a research grant (M493) made to The Washington School of Psychiatry by the National Institute of Mental Health of the United States Public Health Service. I am indebted to the many staff members of Chestnut Lodge, Inc., who participated actively in the study. I am also much indebted to Charlotte Green Schwartz for her help in the formulation and writing of this paper.

2. This ward is more fully described in Alfred H. Stanton and Morris S. Schwartz, The Mental Hospital, New York, Basic Books, 1954.

3. To answer these questions, I spent a minimum of four hours daily for one year observing interaction on the ward, meeting with ward authorities and personnel, with psychotherapists of patients, and with other hospital staff. My advice and suggestions concerning possible changes in ward functioning were submitted to the ward authorities and staff. Decisions to institute suggested interventions were made by the ward leaders in consultation with the staff, and were effectuated by those who made the decisions.

4. From the patient's point of view approaches to personnel for information, service, or objects, no matter how frequent or constant, may be experienced as legitimate requests. From the staff's point of view, these same approaches may be viewed as excessive demands. In this paper the terms request and demand will be used interchangeably.

5. The phenomena of patient demands could, of course, be pursued with greater depth than is here attempted; aspects I have not considered might be thought equally relevant; the phenomena might be differently approached; other interpretations of the data here presented may be possible. However, the approach used here seemed adequate to explain the problem under consideration, and was useful in enabling constructive change to occur.

6. See the discussion of "malevolent transformation" by Harry Stack Sullivan, in The Interpersonal Theory of Psychiatry, New York, Norton, 1953, pp. 203–216.

7. See for instance Sullivan's definitions of conjunctive and disjunctive processes, reference footnote 6, pp. 350–352.

8. See Morris S. Schwartz and Gwen Tudor Will, "Low Morale and Mutual Withdrawal on a Mental Hospital Ward," PSYCHIATRY (1953) 16:337–353.

9. One thereby indicates recognition of the structuring that occurs in social processes and conversely the fact that social structures are constituted by social processes.

10. For approaches similar to the one here suggested, see Ludwig Von Bertalanffy, "General Systems Theory," Main Currents in Modern Thought (1955) 11:75–83; Roy R. Grinker, editor, Toward a Unified Theory of Human Behavior, New York, Basic Books, 1956; and Talcott Parsons, Family: Socialization and Interaction Process, Glencoe, Ill., Free Press, 1955.

THE MENTAL HOSPITAL AND THE COMMUNITY: CHANGES AND TRENDS

"COMMUNITIES," as used here, are units of population, the members of which share certain values in common, toward which they feel a significant degree of loyalty and identification, and in which they could—but do not necessarily—find all aspects of living. The concept is an abstract one and, in any specific instance of a population in a given territory, it is a matter of degree of "community" present. Local areas (neighborhoods, cities, towns, counties, etc.) are communities in varying degrees. States provide some elements of community life, and the largest effective community in the modern world seems to be the nation. Families tend to be the primary units of communities.

For many patients in mental hospitals as developed in modern society, the hospital itself is the only effective community they know, and the patients are insulated from forms of social participation beyond its confines. For some patients, this state of affairs is probably not alterable, and the modest goals of rehabilitation must be to help such patients achieve an optimal level of social functioning within the community of the hospital. However, the broad public health goals of tertiary prevention, or rehabilitation, must go far beyond such objectives. They are concerned with reducing the "total institution" characteristics of mental hospitals to an absolute minimum and with increasing flexibility in the more open community mental health center.

Important in the accomplishment of these broad goals is greater ease of movement from less to more involved treatment services and in the reverse direction. Far too often in the past, patients have moved from one type of "treatment" situation to another with little if any communication between them. When the path has led into a mental hospital, upon the patient's eventual emergence from this facility, he then has entered a void generally as to continued assistance. It is important also to develop effective and meaningful forms of interaction with such basic institutions

Reprinted from Richard H. Williams (Ed.), *The Prevention of Disability in Mental Disorder*, Public Health Service Publication No. 924 (Washington, D.C.: U.S. Government Printing Office, n.d.), pp. 35–38.

and groups as the family and the school during the treatment process.

Care of the psychotic patient in the past has been achieved by concentrating patients, physical resources and professionals familiar with the field's special problems within institutions. In the period of transition this creates obstacles to the mobility of individuals experienced with these patients that is now felt to be essential. Centralization and hierarchical structuring within the mental institution have led to specialization of roles and overemphasis on specific techniques. The situation has often been molded to fit the technique rather than the technique to fit the situation. The specialists experienced in working with psychotic individuals in institutional settings may find it hard to adapt this special experience in a wider context, including family and community.

The staffs of existing community resources, on the other hand, are likely to be unfamiliar with the special problems of working with the psychotic patient. Where community resources are overextended the convalescent psychotic patient is accepted with hesitation, if at all, and, even if accepted, may not benefit from treatment if guidance from personnel experienced with psychotics is lacking; such experience makes possible anticipation and identification of problems as the first step in supportive intervention. The inevitable lag between recognition of new needs and their implementation means delay in training personnel to meet requirements. Difficulties arise from: (1) an existing trend toward overspecialization and overformalization of roles of professional personnel, (2) the isolation *between* professionals occupying these roles within the hospital, between existing resources in the community, and in "bridging resources," and (3) a lack of balance in the individual professional between working knowledge of the special problems of psychotic personality on one hand and of the community to which the patient will return on the other.

We are thus faced with interlocking problems as the inevitable price of attempting to institute change. The concept of an integrated and community-based program cannot be adequately tested in a piecemeal fashion. Isolated changes at the community level—*or* changes at the hospital level—*or* changes at a level bridging these two defeat the concept. Markedly increased effectiveness of results will surely lag behind expenditure of developmental effort: to recognize this fact seems necessary to prevent overoptimism and premature discouragement as we implement and extend our present knowledge.

Essential is a development of attitudes of tolerance in the community, towards some deviant behavior, and, in particular, of mental illness.

A community with a good hospital is more tolerant. Some general changes in public attitudes have occurred, especially in the past 10 years as people coming from hospitals often are seen to function reasonably well. Deliberate contacts of volunteers with patients are very helpful. Also important is development of close relations with those people in the community who will be emulated. They should know more about the hospital and its patients, and be aware of patients who are leaving the hospital, their needs and problems.

The degree of responsibility of the State and of local communities in care, treatment, and rehabilitation of the mentally ill needs thoughtful definition. The old concept of the State as all-provider with exclusive responsibility for the mentally ill is being supplanted by an inclination to use community agencies and local resources. There are probably many workable relationships between State and local areas which could prove satisfactory though applied differently in different places. However, the most serious problem in the past has been the lack of clarity concerning responsibility. No one assumes responsibility for certain patients and post-hospital care is generally neglected.

We also need to develop the social mechanisms of entering and leaving the hospital. We need to find social techniques for treating the great majority of patients without any loss of their civil status or general position in the social matrix. The idea that the hospital, usually in the person of the superintendent, must *guarantee* the "good behavior" of patients severely handicaps both treatment and discharge planning. The only statement that can ever be made reasonably is that a patient is not believed to be a danger to himself or to others. A doctor can make a judgment that maximum treatment benefit has been reached or the psychiatric situation stabilized, but he is not in a position to decide when patient and community can live together again. As we have emphasized throughout, mental disorders are by nature a social

problem. Traditionally the courts have had a key role in making action determinations; they must apply law developed by representatives of the people and decide that a given person shall or shall not be removed from his present position in the social matrix to another and quite different one. Basically this is a question of social protection and not of health. Psychiatrists brought in as advisors to the court are put in an extremely difficult position. As "alienists" they must make decisions about social risk, for which the data are, to say the least, meager and unsatisfactory. This is quite different from the position of a family doctor concerned primarily with substantive questions of health who has a treatment contract with the patient. Historically, the mental hospital has been used excessively as a place to "put away" people by court order, whether or not it is medically best for patient and family. The position of hospital psychiatrists is shifting; from being humane and respected holders of troublesome people, they are becoming medical practitioners who guide treatment, rehabilitation plans and procedures for essentially medical reasons. The historical roots of the old approach go quite deep and may resist change.

A help in clarifying our thinking would be the recognition that psychosis is not an absolution for crime. Hospitals, further, should not be held responsible for keeping suicide rates below those of free communities, though they are unrealistically expected to do so.

SOME GENERAL TRENDS

We have noted a number of general trends, some just getting started or barely detectable, and some well recognized. All should be encouraged as part of the design of reducing disabilities associated with mental disorders:

(1) Unlocking of wards, removal of other restraints and general development of the open hospital is certainly hopeful. We must remember, however, that the mere removal of some features of hospitalization as developed in the past is not enough. We must make certain that the door does not open onto the edge of a precipice.

(2) There is a growing interest in including families in treatment, especially its rehabilitative phases. Some experimenting has been done with the treatment of whole families as units, certainly a promising field for research, although not yet ready for widespread adoption in practice. In any event, it is now widely recognized that as the

most satisfactory social role for the patient should be sought very early in the illness, the patient's relation to his family is generally crucial in this respect.

(3) Many changes are taking place in relations between the hospital and the wider community. We are learning to use other community resources. There has been the development of day and night hospitals. The "community" is brought into the hospital, through relatives and volunteers. And there is some betterment of public attitudes.

(4) There is a significant new focus on posthospital experience of patients and growth of resources to continue gains made in the hospital. Aftercare programs, halfway houses, clubs for former patients, vocational rehabilitation programs, sheltered workshops, and family care all are potent supportive measures.

(5) Many psychiatrists are becoming genuinely interested in learning to know the social world of the patient and understand the moves which he makes there. They also wish to learn how to make this social world more therapeutic (on the ward, with the family, etc.), and are interested in moving beyond the traditional one-to-one relationship between doctor and patient.

(6) There is general concern about making it easier to enter and leave mental hospitals, and turning mental hospitals into "therapeutic" or "rehabilitative" communities, rather than deprived islands of custodial care. This compels development of therapeutic capabilities of all staff members and removal of restrictive and punitive barriers between staff and patients. It also means harnessing the social environment within the hospital as a therapeutic force to permit patients meaningful social relations and activities while in residence. This is a concept far larger than merely providing "activities" and keeping the patient busy. In some places a strong effort has been made to enlist the patients themselves as a therapeutic force.

MAINTAINING THE GAINS AND MOVING AHEAD

Such new ideas and practices as the open-door policy in mental hospitals are likely to be introduced with a good deal of fervor. People become "converted" to the "cause." To a significant extent, changes thus produced in both staff and patients are probably largely attributable to the enthusiasm generated by the new policy rather than to its intrinsic content; for when initial enthusiasm wanes, the dynamics of the system settle back to their old level within the new formal structure. Considerable study and thought should be given to ways of introducing changes in a more enduring way so that movement continues toward a desired end, that of effecting prevention and reduction of disability. For example, various feedback mechanisms could be built in that would tend to perpetuate the desired movement within the system.

The trends noted and the new ventures described are not the be-all and end-all of tertiary prevention and rehabilitation. We have pointed to some defects in the now traditional handling of mental disorders, and have emphasized those as seeming to cause avoidable disabilities. We have mentioned some methods which show promise in the reduction of disability, particularly when they can affect large numbers of patients and their families and friends. There are many intermediate types of programs, new uses of personnel, new drugs with implications for rehabilitation, developments in psychotherapy and emerging social therapies which we have not described or discussed in detail. Actually, the examples we have given are relatively "conservative," and we have not mentioned some of the more experimental approaches as they are inconclusive. But we do expect many new developments to appear in this period of transition, and we believe the general direction of the changes sketched here is clear and will continue for years to come.

part VI

POSTHOSPITAL ADJUSTMENT

T he patient who is discharged from the mental hospital in effect is confronted with the incipient process of readaptation to the community. Hence his posthospital experiences become crucial in consolidating his improvement. The former patient's posthospital readaptation to the community has been investigated from several perspectives. One viewpoint has emphasized the influences of the posthospital groups, especially the family, upon the patients. Another has stressed the conditions and psychiatric ideologies of the patient. A third has compared mental hospital policies.

The papers in Part VI emphasize the patient's readaptation to the prevailing environment as the former patient encounters it and not the rehabilitative interventions to aid the patient's readaptation. The first, "Familial Expectations and Posthospital Performances of Mental Patients," deals with the influence of tolerance of deviant behavior on posthospital adjustment. According to the reports of Simmons and Freeman, the patient's stay in the community depends not upon his performance and individual traits but upon the "tolerance of deviance" by the interpersonal milieu of family members and the community. This "tolerance of deviance" presumably explains why some patients who behave inadequately remain outside the hospital while other patients who function more adequately by comparison are returned to the hospital.[1] The former patient's adjustment in the community did not depend upon his individual traits but rather upon his posthospital interpersonal milieu, especially the attitudes of key members of his family. But in a subsequent work the authors found that the recurrence of bizarre behavior or a psychiatric symptomatology led to many returns to the mental hospital.[2]

Lefton and his associates, in "Former Mental Patients and Their Neighbors," compare the performance and expectations levels of a group of former female mental patients with those of a similar group of women, with the only difference being that one group has been hospitalized.

In "Social Process and Readmission to the Mental Hospital," Raphael, Howard, and Vernon maintain that readmission is a function of the similarity between the patients' and the experts' conceptions of mental health rather than a function of their adaptation to the hospital. Former patients who are willing to accept the patient role seem to be more inclined to make repeated use of the mental hospital for treatment than those patients who resent the patient role. Those former patients who were readmitted to the mental hospital within one year of release showed greater agreement with the experts' conceptions of mental health than did former patients who remained in the community. Their results suggest that "patients whose initial ideas about mental illness (and mental patients) are relatively expert and humane are more likely to be readmitted at a later time than other patients." This difference implies that chances of readmission into the mental hospital "may be associated with social selection into the hospital society." The influence of the psychiatric ideologies upon the patients' readmissions, however, does not exclude influences upon the patients that result from the judgments of others as well as from those whose recurrence of bizarre behavior from severe crises may have necessitated their return to the mental hospital.

Zolnik and Lantz[3] compared the influences of the policies and procedures of two types of hospitals: a liberal, permissive hospital and a traditional, conservative hospital. They found that more than 50 per cent of the patients returned to the liberal hospital, but that less than 50 per cent returned to the conservative hospital.

Another relevant study made during 1956–57 by Carstairs and his associates[4] evaluated the readjustment of former patients in the community. They noted the records of 240 male subjects between the ages of 20 and 65 who had been patients in seven large London hospitals and were able to follow up 229 of these men with family interviews. Many of these former patients had left the hospital or were withdrawn by relatives against medical judgment, while 23 patients had effected their discharge by escaping from the hospital without being apprehended within the statutory period of fourteen days.

They assessed the posthospital adjustment of these former patients by two criteria. The first was "avoiding readmission into the hospital within twelve months." The second was the relative level of social adjustment, including independence of support, job record, and social relations. By the first criterion, 156 or 68 per cent of 229 cases were successful. By the second, 102 or 44.5 per cent of the total sample had adjusted fairly satisfactory, and 54 or 23.6 per cent had made an unsatisfactory social adjustment.

Although the degree of improvement of the patient at the time of discharge was very significant in his posthospital adjustment, they found that 29 of 58 patients who were discharged contrary to medical advice and 18 of the 23 who escaped from the hospital seemingly succeeded in terms of the first criterion of success.

Of the other items of evaluation, they found that the levels of occupation and social responsibility before the onset of illness were very important in posthospital adjustment. In the posthospital situation itself, they found that if the patient held a job for even part of a year, his chances for success were significantly higher than if he did not, and that the type of group he went to live with affected his adaptation. The attitudes of the patient and the attitudes of those in the patient's immediate social environment were quite important, and the degree of welcome by the members of his group affected his chances for success. Thus, of 78 former patients who were welcomed by all members of the group, 72 or 92 per cent made a successful readjustment, while of 27 who were not welcomed by the group, only 9 or 33 per cent readjusted successfully. The attitude of the key person in the household was also significant to adjustment, but the most surprising finding was that the patients who lived with distant kin or alone were more successfully readjusted than those who lived with their spouses or their parental families.

This study, which *anteceded* the Simmons and Freeman inquiry, also emphasized that the attitudes of the group to which the patient returned were an important criterion in the success of his readaptation to the community. But this study also emphasized that the condition and the confidence of the former patient are important factors in his successful community readaptation.

NOTES

1. Howard D. Freeman and Ozzie G. Simmons, *The Mental Patient Comes Home* (New York: John Wiley and Sons, 1963).

2. See E. Gartly Jaco, a review of *The Mental Patient Comes Home*, in *American Sociological Review* (December, 1965), *30*(6), 952–953.

3. Edwin S. Zolnik and Edna M. Lantz, "A Comparative Study of Return Rates to Two Mental Hospitals," *Community Mental Health Journal* (Fall, 1965), *1*(3), 233–237.

4. G. M. Carstairs, "The Social Limits of Eccentricity: An English Study," in Marvin K. Opler (Ed.), *Culture and Mental Health* (New York: Macmillan, 1959); and G. M. Carstairs *et al.*, "Post-Hospital Adjustment of Chronic Mental Patients," *The Lancet* (September, 1958).

FAMILIAL EXPECTATIONS AND POSTHOSPITAL
PERFORMANCE OF MENTAL PATIENTS[1]

Ozzie G. Simmons and Howard E. Freeman

PARADOXICAL as it may seem, many former mental patients, though actively psychotic and fully as ill as presently hospitalized persons, remain in the community for extended periods instead of being returned to the hospital (2). As we have discussed elsewhere (3, 4), there is considerable evidence that improved functioning or mental health is not necessarily a requisite for "success," i.e. remaining in the community. The continued presence in the community of a large number of patients who are less than well suggests that the process of posthospital experience and the outcome of hospitalization cannot be understood solely in terms of characteristics of patients themselves, and that we must also consider the nature of their interpersonal relations in the posthospital period. Accordingly, tolerance of deviance on the part of family members has been posited as a key factor in the prolonged community tenure of former patients who function at inadequate levels.

This proposition of tolerance of deviance was first advanced to explain the empirical findings of an exploratory study of a small number of patients and their families (3). In that study, patients who remained in the community for a year or more were contrasted with patients released during the same time period but subsequently rehospitalized. Among patients who succeeded in remaining in the community, those with high levels of performance, i.e., those who (i) worked full time or were responsible for the care of the home, (ii) participated regularly and as often as other family members in social activities, and (iii) related well in an interview situation, were found to occupy almost exclusively the kin role of "wife" or "husband" in the family. On the other hand, patients whose kin role was "daughter" or "son" frequently lived so socially isolated that their homes can be fairly described as one-person chronic wards.

The inference that parental families, in comparison with conjugal ones, are more tolerant of

Reprinted by permission from *Human Relations* (August, 1959), pp. 233–241.

deviance was supported by contrasting the family settings of patients with low levels of performance who succeeded in remaining in the community with those of patients who were released during the same time period but were subsequently rehospitalized. Our proposition of tolerance of deviance was strengthened by the finding in that study that, in comparison with patients who perform at low levels in the community, many more "husbands" than "sons" were returned to the hospital (3).

A second, large-scale survey was undertaken both to replicate the empirical relationship between family setting and levels of occupational and social performance among patients who succeed in remaining in the community, and to test other hypotheses derived from the proposition that the tolerance of deviant behavior on the part of family members is critical to the fate of patients in the posthospital period. The informants were female relatives of male patients who succeeded in remaining in the community for at least one year. As before, patients who worked steadily and participated regularly in social activities occupied the kin role of husband rather than son (4).[2] This replication, with its added controls, indicates that the relationship between family settings and performance levels is a stable one.

In addition to this replication, one of the series of hypotheses tested in this study was that patients with low levels of performance reside with female relatives "atypical" in personality, at least with reference to the ideal personality stereotypes in our culture. This hypothesis was based on the premise that tolerance of deviance is associated with reciprocity of needs and/or gratifications between the patient and other relatives in the family. The correlations are in the predicted direction. Patients who remain in the community despite low levels of instrumental performance tend to have female relatives who are anomic, authoritarian, frustrated, rigid, and withdrawn (5).[3] These associations between personality characteristics and performance level are independent of the correlation between family setting and performance level.

In this paper, two further questions are considered:

(i) What is the relationship between patients' posthospital performance levels and familial expectations?

(ii) What is the relationship of patients' posthospital performance levels to family structure?

With regard to the first question, a direct relationship is hypothesized between the performance level of the patient and the expectations of family members. This hypothesis is based on the assumption that congruence between expectations and performance is essential to the stability of an interpersonal system (6); that is, low-level performance on the part of the patient must be complemented by low expectations on the part of his relatives for him to remain in the family. Further, if there is congruence between performance levels of patients and expectations of relatives, then variables identified as correlates of performance levels should also be associated with expectations. Thus, relatives with low expectations will more likely be mothers than wives and will tend to be anomic, authoritarian, frustrated, rigid, and withdrawn.

The primary purpose of investigating the relationship between the expectations of family members and the performance levels of patients is that of providing further support for the proposition that the tolerance shown by family members is of strategic importance for the posthospital fate of the patient. Documentation of this relationship between expectations and performance constitutes as nearly direct a test of the proposition regarding tolerance as is possible in a cross-sectional survey, although the results must be considered tentative owing to the limitation imposed by the retrospective nature of the data.

The second issue examined is the relationship between performance level and family structure. Analysis of this relationship is confined to differences within parental families, since the variability in performance level of patients and in available role alternatives in conjugal families is too limited for such exploration. Our position is that, within parental families, patients with low performance levels will cluster in those households where other actors are available as functional equivalents to occupy, or share the occupancy of, roles normatively prescribed for adult males (4). Thus it is hypothesized that the performance levels of patients are associated with such variations in family structure as group size and the patient's age-sex status in the household.[4]

The primary purpose of describing structural differences among parental families is to improve the prediction of performance levels. Since these hypotheses were derived from the proposition of tolerance of deviance, however, the documentation of relationships between family structure and performance levels can be considered additional evidence that tolerance on the part of family members plays a critical role in the posthospital experience of the patient.

THE STUDY GROUP

The female informants interviewed were all relatives, predominantly wives and mothers, of male patients who had succeeded in remaining in the community since their latest release from a mental hospital sometime between November 1954 and December 1955. Every male patient with the following characteristics was included in the potential study group: between 20 and 60 years of age, white, native born, living in the Boston area at the time of release, hospitalized more than 45 days prior to release, not physically handicapped to the extent of being unemployable, not addicted to narcotics, and not primarily hospitalized for acute alcoholism. By diagnosis, all were psychotics with non-organic disorders, the majority schizophrenic. Patients selected were last hospitalized in one of 13 mental hospitals in the Boston area. Of the 209 interviews attempted, 182 (or 88 per cent) were completed.[5]

FAMILIAL EXPECTATIONS
AND PERFORMANCE LEVEL

A Guttman Scale of five items was employed to assess the expectations of female relatives regarding posthospital performance of the former patients.[6] As indicated in *Table 1*, there is a considerable difference in what relatives reported they expected of patients during the first three months and after six months of community living. In comparison with the earlier time period, almost twice as many informants expected the patient to be working full time at the end of six months.

The Pearsonian correlation between responses for the two time periods is .74. In only three cases do relatives expect less in the later time period than in the earlier. Although expectations do appear to differ markedly from one time period to

TABLE 1.   RELATIVES' EXPECTATIONS OF FORMER MENTAL PATIENTS*

Scale Type	Visit his Relatives	Visit his Friends	Help Entertain at Home	Go to Parties, etc.	Work Full Time	3 months N	3 months %	6 months N	6 months %
I	NO	NO	NO	NO	NO	37	20.3	23	12.6
II	YES	NO	NO	NO	NO	12	6.6	8	4.4
III	YES	YES	NO	NO	NO	12	6.6	5	2.7
IV	YES	YES	YES	NO	NO	5	2.7	4	2.2
V	YES	YES	YES	YES	NO	48	26.4	25	13.7
VI	YES	YES	YES	YES	YES	68	37.4	117	64.4
% yes at 3 months	77	71	60	59	41	Total 182	100.0	182	100.0
% yes at 6 months	79	79	68	69	66	Coef. of reprod. =.94		Coef. of reprod. =.93	

*The exact item was: "Families vary in what they think their relatives should do after they return home from the hospital. Will you tell me if you thought (patient's name) should do these things, say, any time within the first three months after he was home? How about six months after he was home?"

the other, there is a general tendency for informants' expectations regarding performance at six months to vary in accordance with their expectations during the first three months; that is, an informant in Scale Type V is more likely to move to Scale Type VI than is an informant in Scale Type I. Six months after hospitalization, there still remains a "hard core" of female relatives who do not expect the patient to be active, either occupationally or socially. With reference to work alone, one-third of the relatives do not expect instrumental performance even six months after hospitalization.

"Change types" were developed to reflect movement in relatives' scale positions from one time period to another. The relatives' expectations at each time period were first characterized as "high," "moderate," or "low": those in Scale Type VI (who expected the patient to work full time) were considered to have high expectations; those in Scale Types IV and V were regarded as having moderate expectations; and those in Scale Types I, II, and III were viewed as having low expectations. *Table 2* shows the strong relationship between relatives' expectations and patients' performance levels.[7] Patients with the highest performance levels cluster in families where

relatives hold either high or moderate expectations during the first three months and high expectations six months after the patients' return to the family. In contrast, patients with low performance levels reside with relatives whose expectations either change from low to moderate or remain low.

It was hypothesized that if there is congruence between performance levels of patients and expectations of relatives, then variables identified as correlates of the former should also be associated with the latter. The association between the expectations of the relatives and their kin relationship to the patients is shown in *Table 3*. Relatives of patients whose familial role is that of "son" tend to have lower expectations regarding posthospital performance than do relatives of patients whose familial role is "husband." At six months, over one-quarter of the mothers still express minimum expectations compared with approximately one-tenth of the wives.

The assumption of congruence just referred to was also the basis of the hypothesis that the expectations of the relatives would be associated with their personality characteristics. Although the magnitudes of the correlations are low, and therefore the stability of the relationships less

TABLE 2.   CHANGES IN RELATIVES' EXPECTATIONS IN RELATION TO PATIENTS' PERFORMANCE LEVELS

Expectations of Relatives During first three months	At six months	Performance Levels 1 (high) %	2 %	3 %	4 (low) %	Total %	N
Low	Low	19.4	27.8	8.3	44.5	100.0	36
Low moderate	Moderate moderate	17.2	20.7	20.7	41.4	100.0	29
Low	High	22.7	54.6	—	22.7	100.0	22
Moderate	High	44.5	33.3	11.1	11.1	100.0	27
High	High	45.6	27.9	17.7	8.8	100.0	68
	Total	32.9	30.8	13.2	23.1	100.0	182

$r=.33$

TABLE 3.   DIFFERENCES IN MOTHERS' AND WIVES' EXPECTATIONS

Expectations		Kin Affiliation	
During first three months	*At six months*	*Mothers of Patients* %	*Wives of Patients* %
Low	Low	27.0	11.9
Low moderate	Moderate moderate	20.2	10.5
Low	High	12.4	14.9
Moderate	High	10.1	17.9
High	High	30.3	44.8
	Total	100.0	100.0
	N=	89	67*

$r$pbs = .24

*26 cases not included: 14 living with siblings and 12 where informant not mother or wife.

than certain, relatives with low expectations appear to be somewhat more anomic, authoritarian, frustrated, rigid, and withdrawn than those with high expectations. With reference only to expectations regarding work performance at six months, the linkage between the expectations and personality characteristics of relatives and the performance levels of patients is quite evident. In *Table 4* the mean scores on the personality character-istics are presented for three groups: (i) mothers whose expectations are congruent with low performance; (ii) mothers whose expectations are congruent with high performance; and (iii) wives whose expectations are congruent with high performance. Mothers whose expectations are congruent with low performance appear to be more anomic, authoritarian, frustrated, rigid, and withdrawn than the relatives comprising the other two groups. Thus, though the results must be regarded as tentative, it appears that the personality characteristics of the informant, independent of her kin relationship to the patient, are associated with her expectations as well as with the patient's performance levels.[8]

VARIATIONS IN THE STRUCTURE OF PARENTAL FAMILIES

In order to differentiate between parental families of patients with high and low performance levels, a number of variables held to affect the quality of family role relationships were correlated with performance level. One such variable was number of persons in the household. There is a significant relationship between family size and performance level. This finding is clarified when the sex composition of the households is brought into the analysis. There is no relationship between number of females in the household and performance levels. It is the availability of males, rather than the gross number of family members, that is strategic to performance level. Patients who perform at low levels appear to cluster in households where other male actors are available as functional equivalents to occupy, or share the occupancy of, roles normatively pre-scribed for the former patient (see *Table 5*).

Several indexes of family structure were developed to amplify the findings on family size.

TABLE 4.   MEAN SCORES FOR RELATIVES ON PERSONALITY SCALES

	Mothers of Patients		Wives of Patients
Expectations regarding work—six months after hospitalization	*Did not expect to work*	*Expected to work*	*Expected to work*
Performance Level	Low (N=29)	High (N=29)	High (N=50)
Authoritarianism	3.00	3.90*	3.70*
Anomia	2.97	3.24	3.76*
Frustration	4.34	4.96*	5.26*
Rigidity	3.86	4.59*	4.72*
Withdrawal	3.41	3.97*	4.04*

*Significantly different from means of mothers who do not expect patients to work at the $p < .05$ level, one-tailed test.

TABLE 5. PERFORMANCE LEVELS OF PATIENTS AND NUMBER OF
MALE RESIDENTS IN THEIR PARENTAL HOUSEHOLDS

Performance Levels

No. of Male Residents in Household (excluding patient)	1 (high)	2	3	4 (low)	Total	N
	%	%	%	%	%	
0	20.8	37.5	12.5	29.2	100.0	24
1	21.3	27.7	19.1	31.9	100.0	47
2	12.5	12.5	37.5	37.5	100.0	16
3	—	22.2	11.1	66.7	100.0	9
4	25.0	—	—	75.0	100.0	4
Total	12.0	26.0	19.0	37.0	100.0	100
$\overline{X}$	1.00	.88	1.26	1.54	1.22	

$r = .24$

An age index was constructed, for example, whereby persons in the household of ascending generation *vis-à-vis* the patient (i.e., mothers and fathers) were scored "3," those of the same generation (i.e., siblings) "2," and those of descending generation (i.e., nieces and nephews) "1." The total score was divided by the number of household residents. Age-sex indexes were developed by the same scoring procedure. With respect to the index for males, almost twice as many families with means in the same generation range (1.7 to 2.3) have patients who perform at low levels as those families whose means fall within the range of either "ascending generation" or "descending generation" (shown in *Table 6*).

Although the relationship between level of performance and socio-economic status will be the subject of a separate report, it may be noted that the association between family size and performance levels, and the other structural relationships, are not functions of the greater economic capacity of larger families to "afford" the deviant. On the contrary, the more rent paid by the family, or the more money earned by family members, the less likely that a patient with a low performance level resides in the household.[9]

TABLE 6. PATIENTS' PERFORMANCE LEVELS AND
MALE AGE INDEX FOR PARENTAL HOUSEHOLD

Performance Level	Families of ascending or descending generation	Families of same generation
	%	%
1 (high)	21.3	12.8
2	34.4	12.8
3	14.8	25.7
4 (low)	29.5	48.7
Total	100.0	100.0
N =	61	39

$r\text{pbs} = .25$

CONCLUSIONS

The results of this study are consistent with and support the proposition that the tolerance of deviance of family members is critically important in the posthospital experience of mental patients. In studying the relationships between family members' expectations and patients' performance levels, retrospective data were utilized, and we cannot be certain that the same results would have occurred if a two-stage design had been employed. Indeed, in order to answer the vital question of whether or not the expectations are merely post-dictions on the part of relatives, we are presently engaged in a new study in which expectations are elicited from a family member at the time the patient leaves the hospital, while patients' performance levels are assessed one year after return to the community.

We are reasonably confident that the linkage between expectations of family members and performance levels of patients will be supported in this new study, since the limitation of retrospection does not apply either to the family structure variables reported in this paper, or to a number of other relationships indicated in our introductory remarks. The hypotheses are derived from a common conceptual position, and there is consistency of results between variables that do and do not have this retrospective quality.

A number of implications for practice can be drawn from our findings, although further research is clearly desirable before their implementation is attempted. We suggest that hospital personnel who release patients with low performance levels to wives can probably expect to readmit them, which points to the advisability of alternative settings for such "husbands." On the other hand, since there appears to be a large number of parental families likely to retain low-level patients, it is probable that a higher proportion of "sons" presently hospitalized could be released to the community. Although such modifications in release practices might alleviate the shortage of hospital beds, however, it is doubtful if posthospital movement toward higher performance occurs in such settings.

Indeed, family settings most tolerant of the patient with low-level performance may be the least conducive to the development of a high level of performance. Our findings suggest that family milieux characterized by expectations that are high at the time the patient is released, and that remain so, and in which there are no other actors available to occupy or share the occupancy of roles normatively prescribed for the adult male, are most likely to encourage movement toward high performance. The needs of the individual patient and the goals of the hospital thus cannot be viewed independently of the patient's posthospital world. Although practitioners are aware of the importance of posthospital conditions in determining the community tenure of the patient and take them into account, we submit that the systematic documentation of their strategic character may well promote more judicious decisions regarding the release of patients.

NOTES

1. Revised from a paper presented at the 1958 meetings of the American Sociological Society in Seattle, Washington. This research is being undertaken by the Community Health Project, under the direction of Ozzie G. Simmons. The Project is sponsored by the Social Science Program at the Harvard School of Public Health, and is supported by a grant (M 1627) from the National Institute of Mental Health.

2. Actually, the relationship may best be described as conditional rather than direct. Patients with both high and low performance levels reside in parental families, although the latter predominate. However, only a very small proportion of patients who perform at low levels live in conjugal families, "husbands" being almost exclusively high-level performers.

The measurement of performance level is more fully described in (4). Those people rated high work full time and have worked steadily since hospitalization, and participate in formal and informal social activities with considerable frequency and as often as do their families. Those on the low end have not worked since hospitalization and do not participate in any social activities. For each of two ratings, the work and social participation ratings, the distributions were first normalized, then each individual was scored by adding his normal scores together, and finally the group was distributed into four categories. The correlation between the two normalized ratings is .48, indicating that they both measure aspects of a more general mode of performance. The distribution was then split into four categories so that cross-tabular analyses could be undertaken with categories of the same N as used in the correlational computations. Shrinking the distribution has the effect, in general, of lowering the correlation between the dependent variable and the independent ones. The findings reported here also apply to either work or social performance alone, although the magnitudes of the correlations vary.

3. The personality scale items are generally "yes-no" questions of the same type used in Srole's anomia scale. This scale, as well as the five-item authoritarianism scale, has been published by Srole (7). The items comprising the scales on frustration, rigidity, and withdrawal were constructed by Srole and associates for the Midtown Manhattan Mental Health Study, conducted in the Department of Psychiatry, Cornell Medical College, under the direction of the late Dr T. A. C. Rennie. The items and rationale associated with these scales will appear in a forthcoming monograph on the Manhattan study. Our categorization of some of the scales as "personality characteristics" is at variance with the manner in which they were originally conceptualized. Srole postulates anomia, for example, as a phenomenon emerging from the interaction of personality and sociocultural variables, although we have considered it, for our purposes, as a personality characteristic. With respect to anomia in particular, but in terms of all the characteristics discussed, our classification of the scales as individual characteristics makes no reference to their genesis.

4. With respect to group size in particular, but in regard to this entire series of variables, our findings could be integrated with a number of small group studies. Cf. (1).

5. The study group is more fully described in (4).

6. The five items of the Guttman Scale were retained from a set of eight questions originally hypothesized as falling along the same dimension. We anticipated that expectations regarding "dressing himself" and "helping with decisions about money" would also scale. Relatives of almost all the patients expected them to "dress and take care of themselves." This item was, therefore, eliminated since it failed to differentiate between cases. Inclusion of the other two items resulted in considerable scale error and they did not appear to tap the same content area. The unidimensionality of the items must, of course, be regarded as tentative pending replication. Items with other marginals also could be advantageously added to the scale.

7. With the exception of the few cases where an interview was refused, the results are based upon all cases in a population. Differences and relationships are therefore "real" and, strictly speaking, tests of significance are inappropriate. However, as a basis for deciding what is and is not a meaningful magnitude of relationship, we have tended to look upon the study group as a sample. With an N of 182, a Pearsonian correlation value of .12 is generally regarded as significant at the .05 level. In a later part of the analysis, only the 100 families in which the patient occupies the kin role of "son" are considered, and here a coefficient of .16 is significant at the .05 level. These values are for one-tailed tests.

8. We wish to re-emphasize the tentativeness of this analysis. One limitation is that only the data of extreme sub-groups are employed. The small number of cases in other groups based upon a combination of performance level and expectation categories prohibits an analysis utilizing all 182 cases.

9. There is no consistent direction to correlations between the personality characteristics and variables such as family size. The relationships between such variables appear to be expressions of interpersonal differences in families not directly linked to the patient's performance level. For example, although the correlations are very low, in larger families the relatives tend to be less withdrawn though somewhat more rigid and authoritarian. On the other hand, the relationship between family size and expectations is consistent with our assumptions. Families where other actors are available to occupy the roles normatively prescribed for the patient are those in which relatives have low expectations.

REFERENCES

1. Bales, R. F., Hare, A. P., and Borgatta, E. F. 'Structure and Dynamics of Small Groups: A review of four variables.' In J. F. Gittler (Ed.), *Review of Sociology*. New York: John Wiley & Sons, 1957, pp. 391–422.

2. Clausen, J. A. *Sociology and the Field of Mental Health*. New York: Russell Sage Foundation, 1956.

3. Davis J. A., Freeman, H. E., and Simmons, O. G. 'Rehospitalization and Performance Level among Former Mental Patients.' *Soc. Prob.*, 1957, Vol. 5, pp. 37–44.

4. Freeman, H. E., and Simmons, O. G. 'Mental Patients in the Community: Family settings and performance levels.' *Amer. sociol. Rev.*, 1958, Vol. 22, pp. 147–54.

5. Freeman, H. E., and Simmons, O. G. 'Wives, Mothers, and the Posthospital Performance of Mental Patients.' *Soc. Forces*, 1958.

6. Gross, N., Mason, W. S., and McEachern, A. W. *Explorations in Role Analysis*. New York: John Wiley & Sons, 1958.

7. Srole, L. 'Social Integration and Certain Corollaries: An exploratory study.' *Amer, sociol. Rev.*, 1956, Vol. 21, pp. 709–16.

FORMER MENTAL PATIENTS AND THEIR NEIGHBORS:

A COMPARISON OF PERFORMANCE LEVELS

Mark Lefton, Simon Dinitz, Shirley S. Angrist, and

Benjamin Pasamanick

THIS paper compares the performance and expectation levels of a group of former female mental patients with those of a group of women who are similar except for the fact of previous psychiatric hospitalization. That such a comparison is both timely and necessary stems from the following considerations. In the first place, the new drugs are resulting in shorter periods of hospitalization for even the most serious functionally disturbed cases with the effect that increasing numbers of former patients are living in the community with their families. There is consequently an impelling need for more reliable methods by which to evaluate the behavior of such persons.[1] Second, since an evaluative frame of reference for such purposes must be both practically and conceptually compatible with the context in which former patients are functioning, it may be assumed that those aspects of performance which are expected of non-patients are critically relevant to patients as well—e.g., employment, domestic responsibilities. Third, although role performance is a logical and important aspect to be considered in the attempt to evaluate the community experiences of mental patients, a question remains as to its significance for psychiatric purposes—that is, to what extent is role performance a reliable indicator and/or concomitant of adequate or inadequate psychiatric functioning?

The importance of such considerations has recently been emphasized by the findings of two studies of the post-hospital experiences of former patients. In assessing the determinants of prolonged community tenure on the one hand and re-entry into treatment on the other, Simons and Freeman and the present authors have found that

Reprinted by permission of the authors. This investigation was supported by Public Health Service Research Grant M–2953, from the National Institute of Mental Health. The work was undertaken as part of a series of mental health research projects conducted by the Research Division of the Ohio State University Psychiatric Institute and Hospital, directed by Benjamin Pasamanick, M.D. (*Journal of Health and Human Behavior* [Summer, 1966], 7: 106–113.)

patients are re-hospitalized primarily because of disease manifestations rather than because of their failure to perform in accordance with instrumental role responsibilities.[2,3] Furthermore, an earlier report based on an analysis of the interrelationships among social class, expectations and the community performance of 62 married female patients makes it plausible indeed to suggest that their role behavior may be representative of women who have never been the recipients of psychiatric treatment.[4] If such is in fact the case, it would then appear that special concern with role performance as a criterion by which to evaluate the community functioning of mentally ill persons may be less strategic than heretofore presumed.[5]

Notwithstanding the apparent implications of these findings for further concern with such sociological variables as social class, expectations, family type, etc., as potential or actual determinants of post-hospital performance, the fact does remain that the grounds on which to base such judgments are as yet uncertain. Of critical concern in this regard is that virtually all investigations of former mental patients have relied exclusively on internal comparisons—that is, assessments of success or failure, and good or poor functioning, have been based on evaluations of parts of a single sample or cohort. In short, there have been no major efforts to establish a set of normative standards by which to substantiate the qualitative judgments which have been made of the community behavior of former patients. It is our contention that until such standards are available, the task of appropriately evaluating the behavior of patients as well as the associated difficulties in selecting relevant variables for practical or research interests, remains highly problematic.

It is the purpose of this paper, therefore, to contribute toward satisfying this need. In addition to the concern with performance and expectation levels of former patients when compared to non-patients, attention is focused on the similarities and/or differences in the relationships between a set of variables which, on the one hand, were previously postulated as significant concomitants, if not determinants, of role performance (e.g., social class, significant other expectations) and, on the other, performance *per se*.

THE STUDY GROUPS

The Patients

The data employed in this paper were collected as part of a larger investigation of the conditions under which patients succeed in remaining in the community following discharge from a psychiatric hospital.[6] The group which is of concern here consists of 62 married women each of whom met the following criteria: (1) white, (2) functionally as opposed to organically impaired, (3) not addicted to either alcohol or drugs, (4) living with spouse, and (5) both the former patient and her husband were available for interview.[7] These women represent 21.6% of the total number of females discharged during the designated study period; 36.5% of all who were married; and 43.7% of all the married women who had avoided re-entry into treatment and were still living in the community six months after discharge.

The Control Group

The data relevant to this group similarly derive from a larger effort. The original intention was to obtain information which would be comparable in nature and scope to that collected from and about all those former patients who resided within the urban community served by the hospital. This goal was achieved—170 females who had not received any type of psychiatric treatment, and a significant other (SO) for each were interviewed in precisely the same fashion as was the former patient population. The selection procedure involved matching each of the urban patients with a neighbor who resides ten house numbers away. However, for the purposes of this paper the concern is with 60 women who meet those criteria established for the patient group herein considered; they are all married, white, living with spouse, and both marital partners were interviewed. This group represents 35.3% of the total number of females selected for control purposes and 46.9% of all those who were married.

Comparability of the Two Groups

It should be noted that the principal criterion by which the original control group was selected was geographical proximity to the former patients.

It was assumed that this procedure would yield a control group similar to the patient population in terms of social class standing. That this aim was achieved is evidenced by the fact that the critical ratio obtained for the difference between means derived from scores based on the Hollingshead Two Factor Index of Social Position was not significant (CR = .779). But the immediate concern is with that segment of the larger control group which is considered here. Although originally selected because they were married and, in addition, met the other criteria imposed on the patient group herein considered, these women, as a group, are comparable to the latter in a number of other and equally as important respects. First, the two groups are similar in terms of social class (the means for patients and controls based on the Hollingshead Index of Social Position are 45.42 and 48.87, respectively—the resulting t is 1.21, N.S.). Second, they are similar in age (the mean age for patients is 36.47 and for the control group, 38.93—the resulting t is 1.24, N.S.). And third, the two groups are comparable in terms of the percentage of each having school-age children in the household (chi square = .415, N.S.). In short, then, for the purposes at hand, it seems reasonable to assume that these two groups of women are sufficiently similar to warrant the conclusion that the one serves adequately as a control for the other.

METHOD

All of the women, patients and their controls, and their husbands were interviewed by trained psychiatric social workers. The interviews with the former patients were conducted six months after discharge and those with the controls approximately one year following the completion of the patient interviews. These interviews were designed to elicit from each of the husbands an index of his wife's actual performance in three separate areas of functioning—domestic activity (e.g., cooking, shopping, cleaning); social participation (e.g., visiting, entertaining); and psychological behavior (e.g., makes no sense when talking, moves around restlessly, says she hears voices, does not know what goes on around her). These measures consisted of 5, 9, and 32 items respectively.[8]

As noted, the domestic functioning scale contained five items dealing with the performance of routine household tasks. If the patient (or control) was unable to perform a task she received a score of 1. If she needed help from others in performing the task she received a score of 2. A score of 3 on the item indicated that she managed the task on her own. Thus, for the scale as a whole, a score of 5 signified the patient's (or control's) complete inability to function; a score of 15, her complete performance of these household duties.

The social participation index was composed of 9 items with a score range of 1 to 9 per item and a total possible index of 9 to 81. The lower scores indicated that the patient (or control) was participating either less than her spouse or that neither she nor her spouse were participating in the activity. The higher scores signified that both the patient (or control) and her spouse were participating equally or that the patient participated more than her spouse although both were participants. This was an obvious attempt to relate her behavior to that of her husband, using the latter as a referent and thereby controlling for unique social class and family patterns of participation.

The psychological functioning measure consisted of 32 symptoms in terms of which the husband was asked to describe his wife's behavior. The more symptoms manifested by the wife, the lower her psychological functioning. If the husband reported his wife as manifesting a specific symptom "often," she received a score of 1 for that particular behavior, if "sometimes," she received a score of 2, and if "never," the wife received a score of 3 for that symptom. The possible range, therefore, for the psychological functioning index was from 32 to 96.

In addition to the separate scores so obtained, a total performance index was derived as a composite of these three indexes.

A separate section of the interview schedule was designed specifically to elicit the husband's expectations of the role performance of their wives. The twelve items which comprised this index are particularly pertinent to the women's domestic and social behavior and thus parallel, in part, their reports of actual performance. These responses were treated in a manner similar to that discussed above—the higher the score, the greater the expectation for performance.

The measure, "tolerance of bizarre psychological behavior," consists of a series of 19 psychiatric symptoms.[9] All husbands were asked for which symptoms they would consult the hospital (in the case of the control group, psychiatric aid) to seek hospitalization for their wives. The greater the number of symptoms for which the hospital would be consulted, the lower is the husband's tolerance score. In other words, the husband who would not consult professional psychiatric advice for most symptoms is considered tolerant of bizarre psychiatric behavior on the logic that he would be willing to keep his wife at home even though she manifested some abnormal behavior.

While the women were not asked about their actual functioning, they were asked to register their own expectations with respect to performance. The items were identical to those used with their husbands' and were scored in a similar fashion.

As already noted, the social class index used in this report was based on the Hollingshead Two Factor Index of Social Position. The procedure consists of assigning the husband's occupation status a weight of 7 and his educational status a weight of 4.

FINDINGS

The findings to be presented are based on four sets of data: (1) a comparison of the performance levels of the former patient group with those of the controls; (2) a comparison of the role expectations of the former patients and their husbands with those of the control group; (3) an examination of the relationship between expectations and performance; and (4) a factor analysis of eleven variables. Seven of these variables were considered independent (being a former patient or a control, social class standing, self expectations, significant other expectations, tolerance of bizarre psychiatric behavior, age of each woman, having school age children). Four were treated as dependent (domestic performance, social participation, psychological functioning and the Total Performance Index Score).

Performance Levels of Patients and Controls

The data presented in Table 1 show that of the four performance measures utilized, the patients and their controls significantly differ in terms of only one of these—namely, psychological function-

TABLE 1. MEAN PERFORMANCE SCORES FOR PATIENTS AND CONTROLS

Index	Patients (N = 62)	Controls (N = 60)	t	P
Domestic performance	13.15	13.77	1.94	N.S.
Social Participation	58.79	58.15	.55	N.S.
Psychological performance	88.02	91.12	3.65	< .01
Total performance*	159.98	163.03	1.83	N.S.

*Each of the three separate indexes of performance is positively and significantly correlated with the Total Performance Index, for both groups, p < .01 in each case.

ing. These findings are of dual importance. On the one hand, they show that the instrumental role performance level of the former patients is indeed similar to that of a group of women who resemble them except that they have not received psychiatric treatment of any kind. On the other hand, the fact that the two groups of women are reported by their husbands as being significantly different in terms of psychological functioning provides a reasonably sound basis for accepting the former finding as a reliable one. That is to say, the judgments of the husbands regarding the functioning of their wives are clearly reflective of the one major characteristic which distinguishes the groups from each other—namely, the fact of diagnosed psychiatric disorder and hospitalization. Had this not been the case one might be forced to conclude that the reported similarities between the groups are merely a function of instrument insensitivity or response bias, or both.

At the same time, however, it is conceivable that such concordance in terms of reported role performance does not automatically imply concordance in an evaluative sense. We mean by this that the behavioral categories with which this study is concerned are broad enough to permit distinct differences under a common rubric. It seems reasonable, for example, that one's ability to cook or entertain and another's perceptions of such behaviors may vary considerably depending upon custom, situational demands or personal expectations. While it is difficult to understate the importance of such eventualities, it should be emphasized that the concern in this report is with the requisites of the married female role rather than with its options. In a sense, then, our attention is focused upon minimal rather than maximal performance in the two areas considered. Furthermore, given the fact that our original intentions were governed by the assumption that the non-performance of presumably critical role demands was of central importance in determining psychiatric hospitalization, the measures utilized seem justified. Hence, any similarities between the two study groups must be viewed in terms of a performance—non-performance continuum rather than as indexes of relative abilities within and/or across categories.

Instrumental Role Expectations

Whereas these groups of women are similar in terms of domestic performance and level of social participation, the findings with respect to expectations reveal at least one major difference. It can be seen in Table 2, for example, that while the

TABLE 2. MEAN EXPECTATION SCORES FOR PATIENTS, CONTROLS, AND SO's

	Patients (N = 62)	Controls (N = 60)	t	P
Expectations (Total)	32.65	33.60	2.07	< .05
Expectations (domestic)	14.56	14.60	.18	N.S.
Expectations (social)	12.24	13.03	2.19	< .05

	Patient SO's (N = 62)	Control SO's (N = 60)	t	P
Expectations (Total)	32.79	32.57	.43	N.S.
Expectations (domestic)	14.36	14.13	.69	N.S.
Expectations (social)	12.34	12.40	.36	N.S.

expectation levels of both groups of husbands are virtually identical, those expressed by the former patients are significantly lower than that indicated by the controls. The data in Table 2 also show that this difference is accounted for almost exclusively by the fact that the control group registered significantly higher expectations in the area of social participation than did the patients. It should be noted, however, that despite this discrepancy between patients and controls, the relationship between self and significant other expectations for both groups is comparable in that both sets are positively and significantly associated (r = .59 < .01 for controls and .41 < .01 for patients).

Instrumental Role Expectations and Performance

In addition to the question of differences and/or similarities in the levels of expectations and performance of these groups, the issue of the relationship between these variables must be examined. The importance of this issue is virtually self-evident in that it is reflective of one of the most fundamental of sociological propositions and a key conceptual point of departure for outcome studies of the kind reported here—namely, that the expectations held by significant others in one's environmental field are of extreme importance in influencing behavior. Of special interest to this report is that while role performance and expectations levels are quite similar for both groups, the patterning of relationships between these variables was found to be different. An examination of the correlation coefficients presented in Table 3 shows, for example, that although the relationship between the self expectations of the former patients and those of their husbands are positively and

TABLE 3. PEARSONIAN CORRELATIONS BETWEEN
EXPECTATIONS AND PERFORMANCE LEVELS AND
PATIENTS, CONTROLS, AND HUSBANDS

Index	Patients' Expectations		Husbands' Expectations	
	r	p	r	p
Domestic	.25	N.S.	.18	N.S.
Social	.31	<.05	.21	N.S.
Psychological	.38	<.01	.15	N.S.
Total	.48	<.01	.27	<.05

Index	Controls' Expectations		Husbands' Expectations	
	r	p	r	p
Domestic	.49	<.01	.35	<.01
Social	.03	N.S.	.11	N.S.
Psychological	.09	N.S.	.33	<.01
Total	.15	N.S.	.29	<.05

significantly associated, the manner in which each set of expectations relates to the performance indexes is decidedly different. This difference is evidenced not only by the differential magnitude of the coefficients with respect to total performance but especially by those obtained between expectations and psychological behavior and social participation. We have previously reported that these coefficients seem to suggest that the husbands reports of actual performance and their expectations for such performance are to a considerable extent independent of each other and it is, in fact, plausible to suggest further that the expectations held by these men for their wives role performance are dependent upon those registered by their wives.[10] It is also interesting to note that neither the former patients' expectations nor those of their husbands were related to domestic performance. Hence, if the correlation coefficient between patients' expectations and performance is to be attributed to an association between gradients, the source for such a relationship is to be found in the sphere of social participation rather than in the more purely domestic realm.

When we turn from the former patient group to their controls, the data in Table 3 reveal a different pattern. In the first place, unlike the patients and their husbands, the control group and their significant others manifest a strong association between expectations and domestic performance and an extremely weak one between expectations and social participation. Furthermore, a sharp difference is noted between the general way in which the expectations are related to performance. That is to say, whereas the expectations of the patients themselves were far more strongly related to role performance

and psychological functioning than those of their husbands, the reverse appears to be the case for the control group. One is tempted to interpret these latter findings in terms of an argument which is the reverse of the one offered for the relationships between expectations and performance found for the former patient group—namely, that the expectations registered by the husbands of the controls are indeed related to the perceived actual performance of their wives whereas those of the latter are dependent on the expectations of their husbands and relatively independent of their actual performance. In short, given the fact that the two groups of women were reported by their husbands as performing similarly in terms of domestic and social role responsibilities, these data are perhaps more reflective of the subjective dynamics accompanying the return of former mental patients to their families than of any actual differences in overt behavioral patterns.

In summary to this point: The data thus far presented appear partially to substantiate the proposition advanced earlier—that is, the level of role performance of the former patient group is similar to that of a group of women who resemble them but who have not had previous psychiatric treatment of any kind. With respect to expectations, however, several differences were found which, while statistically significant, do not lend themselves to ready interpretation. In an effort, therefore, to examine these findings more closely as well as to discern the relationships between them and the possible influence of several other variables not previously considered, a factor analysis was undertaken.

The Factor Analysis

For the purposes of this analysis both groups were combined (N = 122) but were quantitatively distinguished in such a way so as to represent one of the eleven variables under consideration (O = patient, 1 = control). The remaining ten variables have been noted above. Pearsonian correlations were computed for the eleven variables. A centroid factor analysis[11] was conducted and five factors were extracted from the eleven-item matrix. These factors were graphically rotated, using simple structure for location of axes. The rotated orthogonal factors and their loadings are presented in Table 4.[12]

Five factors emerged in this analysis. Factor A may best be characterized as a *performance factor*. Although the highest loadings occur on Social Participation and the Total Performance Index it is apparent that Domestic Performance and

TABLE 4. FACTORS ROTATED

Variables	A	B	C	D	E	h²
1. Patient vs. Control	10	15	–04	50	–10	.294
2. Social class	08	–30	00	–35	–10	.229
3. Husbands' expectations	13	64	02	–19	–05	.466
4. Self expectations	00	81	01	03	19	.693
5. Tolerance	08	–08	26	–13	–42	.274
6. Age	07	–05	74	19	–04	.593
7. School age children	06	01	–81	–09	–05	.670
8. Domestic performance	42	44	03	00	–10	.381
9. Social participation	85	04	–18	–19	03	.794
10. Psychological performance	43	34	35	40	22	.631
11. Total performance index	74	08	02	11	09	.575
$\frac{\Sigma q^2}{n}$	.153	.137	.130	.062	.028	(.510)

Psychological Performance are also related but to a lesser extent. Obviously, the most interesting factor is that not one of the postulated independent variables loads to any extent which could warrant even an implicit association.

Factor B is most readily interpreted as an *expectation factor*. The highest loadings occur on both husbands' and especially self-expectations. It has moderately positive loadings on Domestic Performance and Psychological Performance and a moderately negative loading on social class. Once again the patient vs. control item failed to load to any extent which would indicate meaningful association. In addition, the failure of Social Participation to load on this factor suggests that of the two dimensions of role performance considered, it is Domestic Performance which is a far better concomitant of expectations than is the former.

Factor C, a *specific factor*, has a high positive loading on age and a high negative on having school-age children in the household. Psychological Performance has a moderately positive loading. No other item loads on this factor in any meaningful fashion.

Factor D is the only factor which was found to distinguish the former patients from their controls. Since the controls were scored 1 and the patients, 0, the relatively high positive loading represents an association between being a control and this factor. A moderately positive loading occurs on Psychological Performance and a moderately negative one on social class.

Factor E emerges as a second specific factor. The variable, "tolerance of psychologically bizarre behavior" loads in a moderately negative fashion. As in the case of Factors A, B and C, no other variable, whether independent or dependent, loads to any meaningful degree.

DISCUSSION

The results of this study, while far from being unequivocal in their implications, nevertheless point to a number of features of the post-hospital functioning of former mental patients which merit special consideration. Of singular importance is the notable similarity in reported role performance between the former patients and their controls. This similarity was very much in evidence in two respects: first, in terms of a straightforward comparison of performance levels, and second, as a result of the factor analysis (see Factor A). The factor analysis also served to confirm the previous finding that the two groups of women are distinguishable in but one of the performance measures utilized—namely, psychological behavior (Factor D). On the other hand, an examination of the manner in which Psychological Performance loads across the five orthogonal factors very clearly suggests that it is indeed a complex variable and any attempt to specify socio-cultural determinants must proceed with caution. It is apparent, for example, that in addition to serving as the major distinguishing characteristic for the two groups herein considered, good psychological functioning is not an exclusive characteristic of the controls: Factor A shows that positive Psychological Performance is associated with high role performance and this association is clearly independent of whether the subject is a patient or control. A further indication of the complexity of Psychological Performance and especially of the concomitant difficulties in readily separating these patients from their controls is offered by the nature of Factor B. This *expectation factor* focuses attention on those variables heretofore regarded as critically influential in affecting the post-hospital performance of mental patients—i.e., instrumental role expectations. There seems little doubt that the expectations of wives and husbands are conspicuously related to each other in both groups.

Somewhat less pronounced but sufficiently high to warrant consideration is the loading which occurs on Domestic Performance. This particular factor makes it possible to entertain the notion that whether expectations be precipitators or reflectors of role behavior, their relevancy as subjective correlates seems most appropriately connected with the performance of the more purely domestic aspects of the married woman's role. The moderately negative loading of social class on this factor suggests that the relationship between expectations and domestic performance may be stronger among the working class subjects than among those of middle class status.

A number of important implications derive from the findings which have been presented. In the first place, they tend to confirm the general proposition which was derived from a previous examination of the patient group—namely, that the role performance of a group of married former female mental patients is in fact very similar to that reported for a control group of never before psychiatrically treated married women. Of equal interest is the finding that the expectations of both groups seem to function in a similar fashion insofar as domestic role performance is concerned. It is of considerable importance to note that these similarities occur despite the fact that the former patients are significantly poorer in terms of their psychological behavior. And, it is precisely because of these findings that role performance may indeed be a poor criterion by which to evaluate the posthospital experiences of mental patients.

It now seems reasonable to argue that the role behavior of these patients as well as their own expectations for such behavior tends to be influenced by circumstances more closely approximating those with which married non-patients must contend than any which are uniquely characteristic of the former patients themselves. In short, the fact of being housewives provides a far better explanation of the role performance and expectations of these former patients than does the fact of previous hospitalization. By the same token, being housewives implies a set of conditions to which all these women must somehow relate and which are clearly independent of the presence or absence of psychiatric disease manifestations. Of particular concern in this regard is that the married state is obviously no guarantee of exceptional or even adequate psychological functioning; this is as true for a number of the controls as it is for the former patients. When it is recalled that psychological functioning is an extremely complex variable which defies simple explanatory relationships with any of the postulated independent variables, this latter assertion appears well founded, if not entirely demonstrable.

In conclusion, this comparative investigation of the community performance of a group of former mental patients with that of a control group of "normal" women fails to provide empirical support for regarding instrumental role performance as a critical dependent variable by which to evaluate the success or failure of discharged mental patients. This assertion rests primarily on the finding that high or low level role performance is not as reliable a concomitant of good or poor psychological functioning as is often assumed. An obvious concern, therefore, is with the difficulties inherently involved in any attempt to examine the experiences of the mentally ill—pre- as well as posthospital—within the context of a frame of reference which either implicitly or explicitly utilizes this assumption as its theoretical point of departure. It must be granted that this point of view enables the sociologist to readily employ a wide array of concepts and hypotheses which he could not otherwise entertain. But it is equally apparent that this approach harbors a very special danger: It may serve to perpetuate a most significant hypothesis in such a manner so as to preclude the examination of variables more appropriately suitable for its testing—namely, that socio-cultural factors are in some way determinative of mental illness. The contribution of this study, therefore, lies in showing that what appears to be the most logical and at the same time the most feasible avenue by which to substantiate our interest in this area may, in the long run, inhibit the very objective it is designed to achieve.

NOTES

1. The Joint Commission on Mental Illness and Health, *Action for Mental Health* (New York: Basic Books, 1961), Chapter 2.

2. Howard E. Freeman and Ozzie G. Simmons, *The Mental Patient Comes Home* (New York: Wiley, 1963), Chapter 4.

3. Shirley Angrist *et al.*, "Rehospitalization of Female Mental Patients," *A.M.A. Archives of General Psychiatry* (April, 1961), *4*, 363–370.

4. Mark Lefton *et al.*, "Social Class, Expectations, and Performance of Mental Patients," *American Journal of Sociology* (July, 1962), *68*, 79–87.

5. Basic to this assertion is the argument that poor role performance is not uniquely characteristic of mentally ill persons. On this point see Freeman and Simmons, *op. cit.*, p. 213.

6. For a description of the original study population see Simon Dinitz *et al.*, "Psychiatric and Social Attributes as Predictors of Case Outcome in Mental Hospitalization" *Social Problems* (Spring, 1961), *8*, 322–328; Angrist *et al.*, *op. cit.*; and Simon Dinitz *et al.*, "The Posthospital Psychological Functioning of Former Mental Hospital Patients," *Mental Hygiene* (October, 1961), *65*, 579–588.

7. The decision to use only these married women for the purposes of this report stems chiefly from the opportunity to control for significant other (SO) reports. The utilization of the reports of SO's other than those of husbands introduces the issue of differential perception, knowledge, and/or concern and their effects upon expectations, tolerance as well as reports of performance.

8. For a complete description of these instruments and a discussion of questions of reliability see Shirley S. Angrist, "Social Factors in the Outcome of Mental Hospitalization" (Ph.D. thesis, Ohio State University, 1960, microfilm). For a specific discussion of the reliability of SO reports of psychological functioning see Benjamin Pasamanick and Leonard Ristine, "Differential Assessment of Posthospital Psychological Functioning: Evaluations by Psychiatrists and Relatives," *American Journal of Psychiatry*, (July, 1961), *118*, 40–46, and Lefton, *et al.*, *op. cit.*, p. 81.

9. See Shirley S. Angrist *et al.*, "Tolerance of Deviant Behavior, Posthospital Performance Levels, and Rehospitalization," *Proceedings of the Third World Congress of Psychiatry* (1961), pp. 238–241.

10. Lefton *et al.*, *op. cit.*, p. 83.

11. L.L. Thurstone, *Multiple-Factor Analysis* (Chicago: University of Chicago Press, 1947).

12. The authors wish to acknowledge with thanks the contribution of Dr. Salomon Rettig of the Research Division in performing this analysis and for his assistance in evaluating the results.

SOCIAL PROCESS AND READMISSION TO THE MENTAL HOSPITAL

Edna E. Raphael, Kenneth I. Howard, and David T. A. Vernon

IN recent years readmission to the mental hospital has been a subject of sociological and other types of inquiry. The possible influence of a number of factors has been studied. Among these are length of continuous hospitalization or institutionalization,[1] socio-economic status,[2] instrumental performance and community participation[3] family attitudes and values,[4] family structure,[5] and tolerance of deviant behavior.[6] The findings of the present paper emphasize the possible influence of still another variable, the psychiatric ideologies of the mental patients. More specifically, the findings suggest that patients whose initial ideas about mental illness (and "mental patients") are relatively expert and humane are more likely to be readmitted at a later time than are other patients.

Two samples of patients were the subjects of this study: 31 first-admission psychiatric patients and 33 readmitted psychiatric patients. Patients were included in these samples on a consecutive admission basis.[7] All were male patients in a 2,000-bed general hospital operated by the Veterans' Administration. The psychiatric section of this hospital is a short-term, intensive-care unit of 120 beds. Although exact figures are not available for the time of the study, the professional staff-patient ratio was considered to be high. Both voluntary and legally committed persons were accepted, but admissions policies dictated that the subjects' conditions be amenable to treatment of six months' duration or less. Among psychiatric facilities of the VA this unit was considered a model for intensive care programs. The therapies offered were varied. A variety of activities to keep the patients socially engaged with others were provided.

The psychiatric ideologies of the patients were measured by a 60-item questionnaire devised by Nunnally and Osgood.[8] For each item, extent of agreement or disagreement is indicated on a 7-point scale. Fifty-six of the items compose ten relatively independent subscales. Each subscale is

Reprinted by permission of the authors.

so constructed that a low score indicates humane or expert opinion (i.e., agreement with the psychiatric ideologies expressed by a sample of psychiatrists and psychologists). For the purposes of this paper the patients' scores on these ten subscales have been averaged, and the resulting average, the Mean Subscale Score for each patient, composes the data. The questionnaire was administered in groups within a day or two, or at the most within two weeks, of admission.

The investigation reported here was prompted by initial observation of a statistically significant difference between the psychiatric ideologies expressed by the two samples of patients on the Nunnally-Osgood questionnaire. The direction of the difference was of interest. Patients in the readmission sample had relatively low scores, more like those already reported for a national sample of mental health experts (t = 3.40, p < .01). Three possible alternative explanations were considered to account for the difference.[9] First, and most obvious, low scores in the readmission sample could be associated with learning or with prior acculturation into the society of the treatment-oriented mental hospital. That is, patients in the readmission sample might have either learned the "right answer" or experienced real attitude change during prior hospitalization. The second explanation is a variant, not strictly independent, of the first one. If patients in the readmission sample were found to be more severely mentally ill than patients in the first admission sample, the difference in sample scores might reasonably be explained. Severely mentally ill persons might be expected to have experienced more extensive hospitalization and thus to be more acculturated, or more familiar with psychiatric thinking.[10] According to a third possible explanation, low scores in the readmission sample might be associated with social selection; that is, patients somehow might select themselves for readmission, or they might be selected by the hospital staff, on the basis of initial rather than acquired (the first alternative explanation) agreement with psychiatric ideologies of professional mental health workers.

In order to test the likelihood of the above alternatives some additional data on the psychiatric patients were considered: 1) "Neuroticism" and "Psychosis" scales derived from subscales scores on the Minnesota Multiphasic Personality Inventory,[11] and 2) information on the incidence of rehospitalization during the year following discharge from the hospital under study.

FINDINGS

Figure 1 schematically summarizes the findings of the study. Table 1 summarizes the Nunnally-Osgood scores, with the critical comparisons among these scores, for relevant classes of patients in the two psychiatric samples. Neither the first nor the second alternative was consonant with the data.

The first of acculturation hypothesis does not account for the following facts:

1. For patients in the readmission sample, expertness of psychiatric ideologies did not vary with number of prior admissions ($F = .03, p < .25$).

2. Even at the beginning of their first hospitalization, those patients in the first admission sample who subsequently were rehospitalized had more expert (and humane) opinions about mental health phenomena than other patients in the first admission sample ($F = 5.56, p < .01$).

3. Even at the beginning of their first hospital-ization, patients in the first admission sample who subsequently were rehospitalized already had psychiatric ideologies similar to those of patients in the readmission sample who had completed a first hospitalization and now were returning to the hospital ($t = .83, p < .40$).

The second hypothesis, a clarification of the acculturation hypothesis—that the relatively expert and humane psychiatric ideologies expressed by patients in the readmission sample were related to greater exposure to psychiatric thinking through more severe mental illness—also finds no support in the data. The differences among patient classes on the "Neuroticism" and "Psychosis" subscales of the MMPI are, in general, small.

The data appear to be more consonant with the third explanation, which purposes that patients are selectively readmitted to the hospital. The facts noted above—namely that new psychiatric patients who subsequently are rehospitalized have on first admission: 1) psychiatric ideologies similar to those patients who have been hospitalized before; but 2) different psychiatric ideologies than new patients who are not subsequently rehospitalized—become intelligible if a bias exists which favors the readmission of patients whose psychiatric ideologies are similar to those of the staff (i.e., are "expert" and humane).

While the data tend to support the hypothesis that readmission to this mental hospital is in some

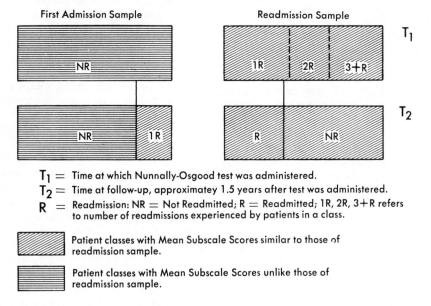

$T_1 =$ Time at which Nunnally-Osgood test was administered.
$T_2 =$ Time at follow-up, approximatey 1.5 years after test was administered.
$R =$ Readmission: NR = Not Readmitted; R = Readmitted; 1R, 2R, 3+R refers to number of readmissions experienced by patients in a class.

Patient classes with Mean Subscale Scores similar to those of readmission sample.

Patient classes with Mean Subscale Scores unlike those of readmission sample.

FIGURE 1. **Psychiatric Ideologies of a Sample of First Admission Patients Compared with Those of a Sample of Readmitted Patients, and Subsequent Careers**

TABLE 1. MEAN SUBSCALE SCORES ON THE NUNNALLY-OSGOOD OPINIONAIRE

PSYCHIATRIC SAMPLE	*NUNNALLY-OSGOOD OPINIONAIRE*	
	N	MEAN SUBSCALE SCORES[a]
Totals:		
1. First admission sample	31	3.88
2. Readmission sample	34	3.43
t-tests		3.40**
2. Readmission sample:		
Patients with		
One prior admission	14	3.45
Two prior admissions	8	3.46
Three or more prior admissions	11	3.41
F-ratios		.03
Careers subsequent to study		
1. First admission patients[b]		
Rehospitalized	7	3.55
Not rehospitalized	14	3.92
No information	9	4.03
F-ratios		5.56**
2. Readmission patients		
Rehospitalized	12	3.30
Not rehospitalized	18	3.53
No information	3	3.42
F-ratios		.56
Rehospitalized patients of		
1. First admission sample	7	3.55
2. Readmission sample	12	3.30
t-tests		1.25
Not rehospitalized patients of		
1. First admission sample	14	3.92
2. Readmission sample	18	3.53
t-tests		2.78**
Rehospitalized patients of		
1. First admission sample	7	3.55
Patients with one prior admissions of		
2. Readmission sample	14	3.45
t-tests		.83

The numbers 1 and 2 refer to first admission sample and readmission sample respectively.

** Statistically significant at .01 per cent level or better.

[a] The "Neuroticism" and "Psychosis" subscale MMPI scores were similarly compared between different patient classes. None of the differences were statistically significant.

[b] Total reduced from 31 to 30 due to death of one patient.

measure influenced by social selection, they do not identify the exact nature of the selection process. That is, it is impossible to determine with these data whether selection is primarily by the patients themselves or primarily by the hospital staff.

There is some indication that selection by the hospital staff was the case on some occasions. According to statements made by the chief of the psychiatric service, a patient is not likely to be readmitted for further hospitalization (at this hospital) if he "did not profit from past hospitalization, was uncooperative, or 'unmotivated' or left the hospital against medical advice." Patients'

psychiatric ideologies, as measured in this study, may have played some part in staff's decisions to readmit or refuse to readmit them.[12]

One model for selection by the patient would involve a tendency to identify oneself as a "mental patient." Patients or other persons who hold a relatively benign humane view of mental illness (i.e., no stigma, "could happen to anyone") might both more easily identify themselves as mental patients and more easily use the facilities available for the treatment of mental patients. On the other hand, patients or other persons who consider the "mentally ill" as subhuman or somehow evil, might both less easily identify themselves as mental patients and less easily use the facilities available for the treatment of mental patients. This model of selection by the patient, is not unlike that already proposed for reentry into the general hospital and some other total institutions.[13] There also is reason to believe that analogous and equivalent influences are operative in any psychiatric setting.[14]

SUMMARY

Exploration of available information, including part of the subsequent careers, of patients newly

admitted to the treatment-oriented psychiatric unit of a large general hospital, suggests the possibility that the chances of readmission may be associated with social selection into the hospital society. The exact nature of the selection process is not clear. However, among new patients, those whose psychiatric ideologies are more expert and humane are more likely to apply for readmission at some later time and to be readmitted than are others.

NOTES

1. J. K. Wing, "Institutionalism in Mental Hospitals," *British Journal of Social and Clinical Psychology*, I (February, 1962), pp. 38–51; Melvin Manis, Peter S. Houts, and Joan B. Blake, "Beliefs about Mental Illness as a Function of Psychiatric Status and Psychiatric Hospitalization," *Journal of Abnormal and Social Psychology*, Vol. 67 (September, 1963), pp. 226–233; Howard H. Freeman and Ozzie G. Simmons, *The Mental Patient Comes Home* (New York: John Wiley and Sons, Inc., 1963), pp. 74–75; Simon Dinitz, Mark Lefton, Shirley Angrist, and Benjamin Pasamanick, "Psychiatric and Social Attributes as Predictors of Case Outcome in Mental Hospitalization," *Social Problems*, VIII (Spring, 1961), pp. 322–328.

2. Freeman and Simmons, *op. cit.*, pp. 125–127; Dinitz, Lefton, Angrist, and Pasamanick, *op. cit.*; August B. Hollingshead and Frederick C. Redlich, *Social Class and Mental Illness* (New York: John Wiley and Sons, Inc., 1958), pp. 294–300; Robert H. Hardt and Sherwin J. Feinhandler, "Social Class and Mental Hospitalization Prognosis, *American Sociological Review*, XXIV (December, 1959), pp. 815–821.

3. Freeman and Simmons, *op. cit.*, pp. 125–127; Dinitz, Lefton, Angrist, and Pasamanick, *op. cit.*; J. S. Bockoven, G. R. Pandiscio, and H. R. Solomon, "Social Adjustment of Patients in the Community Three Years after Commitment to Boston Psychopathic Hospital," *Mental Hygiene*, XL (July, 1956), pp. 353–374.

4. Freeman and Simmons, *op. cit.*, pp. 127–130.

5. Freeman and Simmons, *op. cit.*, pp. 87–103; Dinitz, Lefton, Angrist, and Pasamanick, *op. cit.*?; George W. Brown, "Experiences of Discharged Chronic Schizophrenic Patients in Various Types of Living Groups," *Milbank Memorial Fund Quarterly*, XXXVII (April, 1959), pp. 105–131.

6. Freeman and Simmons, *op. cit.*

7. Since the patients in these two psychiatric samples did not differ in age ($X^2 = 1.82$, df = 2), occupational status ($X^2 = 2.17$, df = 2), or formal educational attainment ($X^2 = 1.42$, df = 2), it was possible to consider socio-economic status as held constant.

8. Jum C. Nunnally and Charles E. Osgood, *The Development and Changes of Popular Conceptions of Mental Health Phenomena*. Final Report, Mental Health Project (Urbana, Ill.: Institute of Communication Research, 1960). This report includes the version of the test instrument which was administered to the patients of this study.

9. The exploration of alternatives was restricted to the data at hand. Other explanations also may be preferred.

10. The authors wish to express their gratitude to Solomon Kobrin, Henry McKay, and Stanton Wheeler who, after reading earlier versions of this paper, drew this alternative version of the data to their attention.

11. The "Neuroticism" score was the sum of the T scores of the *Hs*, *D*, and *Hy* scales. The "Psychosis" score was the sum of the T scores of the *Pt*, *Sc*, and *Ma* scales.

12. However, other policies tended to reduce the effect of the staff's efforts to be selective about patients who were readmitted: (1) patients with service-connected disabilities could not easily be turned away; and (2) sometimes there was a tendency to fill beds in order to maintain the budget. Other informants claim that readmission may occasionally be encouraged by the VA's practice of cutting disability benefits when the patient after release from the hospital has remained in the community for six months.

13. For example, see Rose Laub Coser, "A Home Away From Home," *Social Problems* (July, 1956), pp. 3–17.

14. Edna E. Raphael, "Community Structure and Acceptance of Psychiatric Aide," *American Journal of Sociology*, 69 (January, 1964), pp. 340–358; Charles, Kadushin, "Social Distance between Client and Professional," *American Journal of Sociology*, 67 (March, 1962), pp. 517–531.

part VII
OUT-PATIENT TREATMENT

When troubled by intense conflicts and anxieties, the disturbed person may voluntarily seek or be referred to some professional person or agency for help. Such a mildly afflicted person can participate in society and experience therapeutic or counseling aid as an out-patient. The aim of his therapeutic experiences may be to sustain him in his social role, to resolve his personal conflicts and problems, or to relieve his emotional tension.

In "People Who Have Gone for Help," Gurin, Veroff, and Feld indicate that people seek help primarily from clergymen, physicians, and lawyers, as well as from psychiatrists. The person who searches for help for a mild problem differs from the person who has experienced a psychotic breakdown and whose overwhelming choice for help is the physician. The social process of voluntarily seeking alleviation to one's personal problems as an out-patient contrasts with social reactions to the more severe disorders in which the disturbed person may be considered for voluntary or forcible commitment to a mental hospital.

Although many persons seek some kind of psychiatric aid from the more than 1,800 psychiatric clinics in the United States, one of the remaining contemporary problem is that social selection exists in out-patient treatment. Myers and Schaffer in their paper, "Social Stratification and Psychiatric Practice," point out that since psychotherapy administered in private practice is expensive, people in the lower income levels cannot afford such treatment. In addition, patients in the lower classes define their personality conflicts and emotional discomfort differently from persons in the middle class. They have more difficulty communicating with the middle-class psychiatrists and frequently lack motivation for treatment. However, by reorienting the patient to psychotherapy and by training psychiatrists to understand the problems, orientations, and values of the lower classes, this situation may be altered.

In comparing utilization and fees of the different practitioners Psathas has demonstrated that only the relatively few persons in higher income groups can afford private psychiatric treatment. He found that, in 1960 for St. Louis, the cost of intensive psychotherapy "by a private practitioner is an extremely costly venture which is financially available to only a small segment of the population. If we assume that immediate payment for fees is required, then only families with sufficient earnings or substantial savings can afford treatment. The almost complete unavailability of insurance programs to pay for out-patient psychiatric psychological treatment puts these services out of the reach of those who require them" ("Patients and Fees: A Survey of Private Practitioners," unpublished manuscript).

Miller and Mishler, in "Social Class, Mental Illness, and American Psychiatry," provide a critical analysis of the book, *Social Class and Mental Illness* by A. B. Hollingshead and F. C. Redlich, and point out the relationship between social class and the treated prevalence of mental illness as well as American psychiatry generally.

They concentrate their review on three major hypotheses: (1) The prevalence of treated mental illness is related significantly to an individual's position in the social structure. (2) The types of diagnosed psychiatric disorders are related significantly to the class structure. (3) The kind of psychiatric treatment administered by psychiatrists is associated with the patient's position in the class structure. "Prevalence" as an epidemiological concept refers to the number of given cases of a particular category for a designated period and is distinct from "incidence," which refers to the existence of new cases of a particular category for a designated period. Although a relationship exists between social class and psychosis, it is interesting that Hollingshead and Redlich found no significant difference among classes I through V in the incidence of new cases of neuroses and no significant difference among classes I through IV in the incidence of new or old cases of neuroses or psychoses. Class V has significantly different higher rates of new and old cases of psychoses. This finding is quite consistent with Dunham's findings in "Social Class and Schizophrenia" (see Part II, page 29).

PEOPLE WHO HAVE GONE FOR HELP

Gerald Gurin, Joseph Veroff, and Sheila Feld

SOCIETIES throughout history have set up instit-utions to provide comfort and aid for their troubled members. In the past, this function was usually performed by religious institutions: the oracle, the priest, the witch doctor were often invested with responsibility for the care and healing of the sick in body or spirit. Their approaches to therapy differed, depending upon the nature of their religious doctrines. The persons who sought their help—practicing widely diverse rites and ceremon-ies, trusting in totally different powers—had in common with one another the faith that the counsel of these various religious leaders would be effec-tive in helping them establish personal equilibrium. Such leaders, of course, did not always rise from the ranks of churchmen. At various periods, other kinds of individuals were invested with healing powers. "Expert" insight into human nature has been attributed to politicians, scholars, physicians, and others. These men were often credited with having powers of healing as reliable and effective as those attributed to religious leaders.

Modern society is characterized by the multipli-city of resources that share this therapeutic function and by their growing professionalization. Furthermore, there has been a formal expansion of the functions of more traditional professions to include the psychological counselor role. Thus, included among contemporary professional counselors are clergymen, psychiatrists, psycho-logists, lawyers, marriage counselors, physicians, vocational guidance workers, social workers, and others.

In the present chapter, the discussion centers around the responses to the following set of questions:

Sometimes when people have problems like this, they go someplace for help. Sometimes they go to a doctor or a minister. Sometimes they go to a special place for handling personal problems—like a psychiatrist or a marriage counselor, or a social agency or clinic....

How about you—have you ever gone anywhere like that for advice or help with a personal problem?

Reprinted from *Americans View Their Mental Health* (New York: Basic Books, 1960), pp. 302–315.

What was that about?
Where did you go for help?
How did you happen to go there?
What did they do—how did they try to help you?
How did it turn out—do you think it helped you in any way?

We approached the investigation of the group of people who have used help with several practical and theoretical considerations in mind, expressed in a series of interrelated questions which we ask as we review the data. These questions are listed below to give some perspective on the kinds of issues we are interested in and how we intend to deal with them.

1. *Why did these people go for help?* What kinds of personal problems did they perceive as being serious enough to require formal professional services? What was the specific content of the problems, and from what general cause or locus were they seen to arise? The latter specification will permit us to classify respondents according to whether some personal failing, another person, a situational factor, or an interpersonal relationship was seen as the cause of their difficulty. We were interested in this because we anticipated that a choice among professional sources may be related to what was perceived to be the locus of difficulty.

2. *Whom did these people consult for professional help?* What is the differential use of help resources? Of particular interest was the relative use of the clergy, the psychiatric profession, psychiatric agencies, and the medical profession. We also were interested in relationships between kinds of personal problems and the sources to which people turned for help.

3. *How did these people get to their sources of help?* We dealt with the general issue of referral here by asking such questions as: Are people aware of the means by which they selected a particular source of help? What is the extent to which the selection of a help source is dependent upon particular referral agents—i.e., outside referral agents versus self-referral?

4. *Do respondents feel they received help from the sources they consulted? If so, in what ways do they feel they were helped?* We were interested in what proportion of those who sought help perceived

some benefit from their course of action, and what the nature of that benefit might have been. Did therapy change something about the person, or did it offer comfort and reassurance? Both issues— whether therapy was felt to be beneficial and what kinds of specific gains were perceived—were further related to the kinds of problems our respondents sought to solve and the sources of help they selected.

The issues dealt with by these general questions were further illuminated by a demographic analysis of the help-seeking group, relating demographic characteristics both to the kinds of problems they perceived as serious and the sources of help they selected as relevant. Will age, education, or income, for example, affect the kinds of problems referred to professional help resources? Will different educational or income groups favor certain help sources over others? We are particularly interested in what groups consult psychiatrists.

TABLE 10.1 NATURE OF PERSONAL PROBLEMS FOR WHICH PEOPLE SOUGHT PROFESSIONAL HELP

Problem Area	
Spouse; marriage	42%
Child; relationship with child	12
Other family relationships—parents, in-laws, etc.	5
Other relationship problems; type of relationship problem unspecified	4
Job or school problems; vocational choice	6
Nonjob adjustment problems in the self (general adjustment, specific symptoms, etc.)	18
Situational problems involving other people (e.g., death or illness of a loved one) causing extreme psychological reaction	6
Nonpsychological situational problems	8
Nothing specific; a lot of little things; can't remember	2
Not ascertained	1
Total	**
Number of people	(345)

** Here, and in all subsequent tables, this symbol(**) indicates that percentages total to more than 100 per cent because some respondents gave more than one response.

WHY PEOPLE GO FOR HELP

In our sample, 345 respondents reported that they have gone somewhere for help with a personal problem. In this group there are undoubtedly some for whom this act represented a last resort, a last attempt to forestall despair. Others, of course, may have acted as they did for far less drastic reasons. In either case, we cannot treat this decision as a casual choice among alternatives. A person who goes for help with a personal problem is, in a sense, revealing at least two assumptions that he has made about his situation: first, that he is faced with a personal problem that distresses him; and second, that he cannot solve this problem by himself or by the help and advice of family or friends. We assume that either of the latter choices would be preferable if they were available and were considered as potentially helpful.

It would therefore be important to determine the nature of the perceived difficulties precipitating a decision to give up, even temporarily, one's own coping devices. A tabulation of the particular problems for which help was sought, presented in Table 10.1 discloses that the great majority of them were related to some kind of interpersonal difficulty. Of these, the highest proportion concerned the marriage relationship: 42 per cent went for help because of a problem in the marriage. These problems were either described in terms of the marital relationship—not getting along, sexual difficulties, attempts to forestall divorce or prevent

separation—or as an attempt to gain understanding about a maladjusted spouse.

The impression one gains from the interviews is that these were serious problems, not only the marital problems but the others that brought people to the doctors, psychiatrists, and ministers. A large proportion of them (18 per cent), for example, spoke to some professional about their personal adjustments: not getting along, being unhappy, suffering from peculiar psychological symptoms. Only 8 per cent of the entire group mentioned a problem which was coded as nonpsychological and situational, such as a financial difficulty or poor housing; it is evident that we are, for the most part, investigating truly personal problems.

We find, from the manner in which respondents located the difficulties they perceived as being serious, that mentioning a personal problem does not necessarily imply taking responsibility for having caused that problem. In Table 10.2, we note that 25 per cent of the group who went for help attribute the blame for their personal problems to *another* person; only 23 per cent specifically trace the difficulty to some defect in themselves. In terms of the motivation for therapy, then, it appears that going for help does not necessarily imply any self-insight or readiness to change. In the next section, we shall determine whether help-seeking channels are different for people who attach blame to themselves as opposed to those who perceive the causal defect in another.

TABLE 10.2 NATURE AND LOCUS OF PERSONAL
PROBLEMS FOR WHICH PEOPLE SOUGHT
PROFESSIONAL HELP

Locus of Problem	
Extreme psychological reaction to situational problems	8%
Personal or interpersonal problem involving defect in the self	23
Problem in other person, or interpersonal problem involving defect in the other	25
Interpersonal problem with defect viewed in the relationship, or locus of defect unspecified	32
Problem structured in impersonal, nonpsychological terms	12
Not ascertained	4
Total	**
Number of people	(345)

WHERE PEOPLE GO FOR HELP

Once having recognized a personal problem that cannot be solved by one's own resources, a person in trouble can choose among a number of alternatives if he wishes to seek further help. Some of these, however, may be only potentially, rather than actually, available: the person may not be aware of the existence of certain agents or agencies; he may be skeptical about some or unable to afford or not have ready access to others. We do not know why, ultimately, our respondents chose certain sources of help; we only have reports of the fact that they have done so. But

TABLE 10.3 SOURCE OF HELP USED BY PEOPLE
WHO HAVE SOUGHT PROFESSIONAL HELP FOR A
PERSONAL PROBLEM

Source of Help	
Clergyman	42%
Doctor	29
Psychiatrist (or psychologist): private practitioner or not ascertained whether private or institutional[a]	12
Psychiatrist (or psychologist) in clinic, hospital, other agency; mental hospital	6
Marriage counselor; marriage clinic	3
Other private practitioners or social agencies for handling psychological problems	10
Social service agencies for handling non-psychological problems (e.g., financial problems)	3
Lawyer	6
Other	11
Total	**
Number of people	(345)

[a] Actually only six people specifically mentioned going to a private practitioner. This category should thus be looked upon as representing in the main those people who said "psychiatrist" without specifying that he was part of a mental hygiene agency.

we hope to suggest some of the factors that may have influenced them, by inference from the social characteristics of the groups preferring particular sources and from the kinds of problems for which help was sought.

The professional persons approached for help by our respondents have been listed in the categories outlined in Table 10.3. The most frequently consulted source of help or advice was a clergyman—42 per cent—followed by a doctor—29 per cent (physicians who were not specifically designated as psychiatrists are referred to here as doctors). Thirty-one per cent of the group went to some practitioner or agency subsumed under the heading of "mental health professionals," including psychiatrists, psychologists, marriage counselors, and other private practitioners or institutions that are set up to handle psychological problems. Eighteen per cent specifically mentioned having gone to a psychiatrist or psychologist (6 per cent reported seeing a psychiatrist attached to a clinic, hospital, or other agency; 12 per cent either just referred to a psychiatrist or, in a few instances, specifically mentioned a private psychiatrist). Another 6 per cent mentioned that a lawyer was asked to give help with a personal problem (most of these cases involved counsel associated with divorce proceedings).

Eleven per cent of the responses were coded as using "other sources of help." A content analysis of these "other sources" disclosed that only three responses were directly associated with an agency for mental health rehabilitation, all of these being Alcoholics Anonymous. Five of the remainder referred to consultation with teachers in connection with a child's problems; ten responses referred to nurses or visiting nurses; eight people named policemen or judges as being helpful with personal problems. None of these people, of course, are set up to be psychological counselors. But we feel it is legitimate to include them because, like lawyers, they are associated with situations that may potentially cause intense psychological distress—school problems, health problems, problems with the law—and they have been viewed as having the ability to help with a personal problem and have been asked for such help.

In summary, we find that most of the respondents who went for help in times of personal distress chose a resource that offered, as *one* of its functions, psychological guidance. But it is interesting that those institutions explicitly created for this function alone—such as psychiatry, clinical psychology, social work—were less often consulted than those for which psychological guidance is not a major function—clergymen and physicians in general. It might be contended that clergymen and physicians are more numerous than psychiatric specialists and therefore more available. On the other hand, the greater use of nonpsychiatric specialists may indicate a lack of readiness in the general population to consult mental health professionals in times of crisis, or a lack of knowledge about the availability or effectiveness of such professionals.

To infer what reasons people might have for choosing particular sources of help, we have related the sources of help they chose to the kinds of problems they were interested in solving (Table 10.4). There are slight differences among the kinds of problems that were brought to clergymen, physicians, and psychiatrists. People who consulted clergymen mention marriage problems more often than those who went to physicians or psychiatrists; those who went to psychiatrists were more likely to do so about problems with a child or a personal adjustment problem than those who chose either of the other sources; and physicians are more likely than the other two professions to be confronted with nonpsychological situational problems. In general, however, the three professions seem to be consulted for very

similar reasons and are presented with very similar patterns of personal problems; the differences among them are not so striking as we might have expected.

In attempting to understand why the content of the problems that are referred to physicians, ministers, and psychiatrists are so similar, it should be remembered that we are dealing here with answers to a question that focused on personal problems. We are not dealing, therefore, with all problems that people have faced in their lives that may have had psychological implications and for which they received help. The results—that the contents of the problems for which physicians, ministers, and psychiatrists are consulted are very similar—concern only those problems already defined in personal, psychologically relevant terms. If we were to consider all problems having potential psychological implications, whether or not people defined them in those terms, we might expect to find greater differences in the content of the problems referred to ministers, physicians, and psychiatrists. Specifically, we would expect to find that problems defined in broadly personal or interpersonal terms would be more likely to be handled by psychiatrists than problems not cast in these terms.

This point can be illustrated by comparing the results (on the source of help used) for the

TABLE 10.4 RELATIONSHIP OF SOURCE OF HELP USED TO THE PROBLEM AREA
(FIRST-MENTIONED RESPONSES ONLY)

PROBLEM AREA	SOURCE OF HELP						
	Clergy	Doctor	Psychiatrist[a]	Marriage Counselor	Other Psychological Agencies	Non-psychological Agencies	Lawyer
Spouse; marriage	46%	36%	35%	92%	50%	10%	61%
Child; relationship with child	8	8	20	8	39	10	8
Other family relationships	5	6	4	—	6	—	8
Other relationship problems; type of relationship problem unspecified	8	3	2	—	—	—	8
Job or school	5	2	2	—	—	—	—
Adjustment problems in self (nonjob)	18	22	30	—	5	—	—
Psychological reaction to situational problems	5	6	7	—	—	10	—
Nonpsychological situational problems	2	15	—	—	—	60	15
Nothing specific; can't remember	3	—	—	—	—	—	—
Not ascertained	—	2	—	—	—	10	—
Total	100%	100%	100%	100%	100%	100%	100%
Number of people [b]	(130)	(89)	(46)	(12)	(18)	(10)	(13)

[a] Here and in all subsequent tables this category includes both people who mentioned seeing a "psychiatrist" or a "psychiatrist at a hospital."
[b] Does not include 27 people who mentioned "other" sources of help.

question that dealt with personal problems and the question that asked, "Have you ever felt that you were going to have a nervous breakdown?" It will be recalled that in response to this latter question 19 per cent of the sample answered "Yes," indicating, as they talked of the nature of the problem, that they were defining "nervous breakdown" as an individual collapse in the face of some external stress rather than as a personality problem or a problem in interpersonal relationships. In keeping with this definition, we find, when we asked people what they did about the nervous breakdown problem, that of the 228 people who mentioned going to some professional help resource, only 4 per cent mentioned seeking psychiatric care (Table 10.5). This is in contrast to the 18 per cent of the 345 people reporting having had help for a personal problem who mention a psychiatrist (Table 10.3). As indicated in Table 10.5, the nonpsychiatric physician is the overwhelming choice of people

TABLE 10.5 SOURCES OF PROFESSIONAL HELP USED BY PEOPLE WHO HAD FEELINGS OF IMPENDING NERVOUS BREAKDOWN

Source of Help

Clergyman	3%
Doctor	88
Lawyer and others	4
Social service agencies (psychological and nonpsychological)	12
Psychiatrist (or psychologist)	4
Total	**
Number of people[a]	(228)

[a] Does not include the 235 people who had feelings of impending nervous breakdown but did not refer the problem to any professional help resource.

who go for help for a nervous breakdown—88 per cent of the people who went to any professional resource with the nervous breakdown problem chose a "doctor" (compared to the 29 per cent who chose a physician for help with the personal problem). Not only are psychiatrists seen as inappropriate for handling a nervous breakdown, but clergymen also are largely irrelevant: only 3 per cent of the people went to a clergyman with their nervous breakdown, compared to the 42 per cent who chose this resource when they had a personal problem. Defining tensions and stress as a nervous breakdown apparently emphasizes the physical effects of the experience, making the nonpsychiatric physician the almost inevitable choice when help is sought.

Comparing Tables 10.5 and 10.3—the differences in the professional help resources sought by people defining their problems as a nervous breakdown and those defining them in more psycho-

logical terms—we see that the way the person sees the content of his problem is very important in determining the kind of help he will seek. But it is the *initial* definition that is important, whether he structures the problem initially as a personal or interpersonal psychological problem, or sees it in essentially nonpsychological terms. Once a problem is seen in psychological terms, the findings in Table 10.4 indicate that the specific content of the problem is much less important as determinant of the particular help resource that will be chosen.

These comments are relevant only to the choice of the three major professional help resources—psychiatrists, ministers, and physicians. When we look at the less popular sources of help mentioned in Table 10.4—marriage counselors, psychological agencies, nonpsychological agencies, and lawyers—we see that the particular content of the problem *is* important. These less popular resources were chosen, by and large, for help with specific kinds of problems. To marriage counselors, obviously, were brought problems about marriage; people who chose "other psychological agencies" had marriage problems or problems with their children; those who chose nonpsychological agencies were appropriately troubled by nonpsychological problems; and those who consulted a lawyer, as suggested by the high percentage who mentioned marriage problems, were mostly people who wanted help with divorce proceedings. It is interesting, considering the small number of people in the sample who consulted these less popular sources, how clearly the findings conform to the patterns one would have anticipated.

Table 10.6 presents the relationship between the source of help that was selected and the nature or *locus* of the problem. It will be recalled that respondents were categorized according to whether they localized their difficulties in a personal defect, in the defect of another person, in a particular situation, or in an interpersonal relationship. We find, in Table 10.6, that clergymen were sought to an unusual extent by people who perceived their problems arising either from a defect in a relationship or an unspecified locus, whereas people who consulted a psychiatrist more often connected their problems with defects in themselves. People who asked a physician for advice, however, were as likely to perceive a defect in the self as a defect in another person or a defect in a relationship.

What is the possible significance of these findings? It is reasonable to assume that people who perceive their problems as arising from some

TABLE 10.6 Relationship of Source of Help Used to Nature and Locus of the Problem (First-Mentioned Responses Only)

Nature and Locus of the Problem	Clergy	Doctor	Psychiatrist	Marriage Counselor	Other Psychological Agencies	Non-psychological Agencies	Lawyer
			SOURCE OF HELP				
Problems involving defect in self	21%	22%	41%	—%	6%	—%	—%
Problems involving defect in other person	22	24	26	33	61	—	31
Interpersonal problems involving defect in relationship or locus unspecified	41	26	24	67	33	—	15
Psychological reaction to situational problems	9	9	9	—	—	10	—
Problems structured in impersonal, nonpsychological terms	5	15	—	—	—	70	39
Not ascertained	2	4	—	—	—	20	15
Total	100%	100%	100%	100%	100%	100%	100%
Number of people [a]	(130)	(89)	(46)	(12)	(18)	(10)	(13)

[a] Does not include 27 people who mentioned "other" sources of help.

personal defect and who choose to seek assistance in solving them are the ones most willing to effect some internal personal change in order to alleviate their difficulties. They therefore might be most attuned to seeking the kind of treatment appropriate for personality disorders—i.e., psychiatric treatment. In contrast, people who do not localize their problems in a personal defect or in a defect in another person may be seeking help in order to establish the locus of the defect. They may be looking for a person who could judge and evaluate their difficulties and perhaps recommend the "right" course of behavior rather than prescribe some change in personality organization; religious counsel would be most likely to fulfill this requirement. Finally, the fact that people who have gone to a physician for help are likely to specify their problems as arising from any of three sources suggests that there is some ambiguity in the public mind about the ways a doctor of medicine might be helpful in handling personal problems.

In a comparison of Tables 10.6 and 10.4, it is interesting to note that sharper distinctions appear in the relationship between the source of help that was selected and the nature or *locus* of the problem than in the relationships with the specific *content* of the problem. Choice of a psychiatrist, for example, seems more determined by whether or not a person localizes the cause of the problem in himself than by whether or not he sees the problem as expressing itself in the marital relationship or in some other area of life. It is this self-questioning and probably greater

motivation for self-change that mainly distinguishes the people who choose psychiatric care (although, as Table 10.6 indicates, even the psychiatrists are approached by many people who localize the problem outside of the self).

As a final note about Table 10.6, we may call attention to the strikingly high proportion—61 per cent—of the group who went to "other psychological agencies" with problems related to a defect in another person. This result may be partially explained by the previous finding that 39 per cent of this group consulted specialists about some problem with a child. But there still remains a high percentage who went to these sources with problems attributed to a defect in another and who were not referring to a problem with a child. Although this finding is based on only 18 cases, it is interesting to speculate on what it might mean, assuming that it was confirmed in a larger sample. Most of the people in this category who did not refer to a child were referring to their spouses as the "other" in whom the defect was located. Perhaps this suggests that agencies specializing in social service work appeal to people who are specifically in need of supportive therapy to tide them over some quite tangible difficulty, such as alcoholism, temporary desertion, or illness of the spouse.

HOW PEOPLE CHOOSE HELP RESOURCES

In order to gain some understanding of the motivating factors underlying the choice of a given source, we have looked at the presenting problems with which people came for help in relation to the particular source of help they chose. We also asked people directly how they happened to get to a particular source of help with the question, "How did you happen to go there?" There were two types of responses to this question. Some people answered the question in terms of the outside referral source that sent them to the particular therapeutic resource. And others spoke in terms of their own motivation for choosing a particular resource. Two kinds of motivation were particularly predominant: Many said they chose a particular resource because of a personal relationship with the therapeutic agent; and many said they went to a particular person or agency because they felt that source of help was appropriate for their problems.

Table 10.7 presents the distribution of these responses. Since the interviewers did not specifically probe to determine whether or not there were any referral agents, the fact that only about one

out of four persons mentioned an outside referral source cannot be taken as an indication that no other individuals or agencies were involved in the therapeutic choices of the people in our sample. The lack of specific probing also accounts for the large proportion of responses in the "reason not specified" category. Of special interest in Table 10.7 are the relative figures for the different referral agents. Ministers, for example, apparently see themselves as the final therapeutic agent much more often than physicians do since they do not so often refer the people that come to them to more specialized therapeutic resources. It is also of interest that family and friends were as important as physicians as referral agents, at least among the people to whom the referral sources were so salient that they mentioned them spontaneously in response to our question.

Clear distinctions also appear in the relationships between channels of referral and sources of help. As might be expected, most of the people who sought help from doctors and clergymen mention no specific referral agents, and a very large percentage of the group who saw clergymen did so because of a personal relationship with the priest or minister. The source of help that receives the greatest amount of referral by another outside source falls into the general category of "other psychological agencies." This group included such facilities as psychological clinics, mental hygiene clinics attached to hospitals, and social service agencies; few of them are highly publicized or well known to the public, and we would expect that most of the people going to them would be referred. The majority of the people who went to a psychiatrist were also referred, particularly by a physician, although it is interesting to note that a sizable proportion were also referred by family or friends. . . .

TABLE 10.7 REASONS FOR CHOICE OF PARTICULAR SOURCE OF HELP BY PEOPLE WHO HAVE USED PROFESSIONAL HELP FOR A PERSONAL PROBLEM

Spontaneously Mention Referral from Outside Source

Referred by doctor	8%
Referred by clergyman	1
Referred by family or friends	8
Referred by school, court, other civic agencies	3
Referred by mass media (e.g., "I read about it.")	1
Other referral agent	7

Do not Spontaneously Mention Outside Referral

Personal relationship with help source	19
Help source functionally appropriate for problem	29
Other reasons	7
Reason not specified	41
Total	**
Number of people	(345)

SOCIAL STRATIFICATION AND PSYCHIATRIC PRACTICE:

A STUDY OF AN OUT-PATIENT CLINIC

Jerome K. Myers and Leslie Schaffer

THIS paper is an analysis of the relationship between social class and the selection and treatment of patients in a psychiatric out-patient clinic. It grew out of another research project in which the authors are engaged.[1] In that study a significant relationship was found between the social class background of patients and the type of psychiatric treatment they received.[2] There was a distinctly higher percentage of patients receiving some form of *psychotherapy* in the upper social classes. In contrast, the percentage of persons receiving *custodial care* only or some form of *organic therapy* was greater in the lower social classes.

Because of the significance of these findings, the present authors studied the relationship between social class and psychiatric treatment in more detail, examining a setting where only one type of treatment (psychotherapy) was administered and where most patients had the same disorder (neurosis). In the process was tested an economic explanation offered by many psychiatrists for the findings of the study mentioned above.

Most psychotherapy is administered in private practice and is expensive. It was argued, therefore, that lower class people cannot afford such treatment. There is reason to believe, however that the economic explanation is not wholly satisfactory. Therefore, the authors examined the records of all cases (195 in number)[3] that came to the clinic from October 1, 1950, to September 30, 1951, to determine if social class was related to: (1) acceptance for treatment, and (2) nature of treatment as measured by (a) training and status of the therapist, (b) duration of treatment, and (c) intensity of treatment.

The institution is a training and community clinic where treatment is oriented around expressive psychotherapy. Such therapy is verbal and interpersonal in nature, and based upon fundamental psychoanalytic principles. It requires relatively long and intensive contact between patient and therapist. Anyone with an income of under 5,000 dollars a year and residing within a given geo-graphic area is eligible for care, and the fees charged are nominal and scaled. On theoretical grounds, if ability to pay were the important component in psychotherapy, we would expect that acceptance for therapy and the character of subsequent experience in the clinic would not be related to the patient's social class. This hypothesis was deduced from the economic arguments advanced by psychiatrists to explain the differential association of therapy with social class in the earlier, more comprehensive study.

ANALYSIS OF THE DATA

The clinic's procedure in selecting patients was as follows: If an individual seeking psychiatric help met the clinic's residential and financial requirements, he was referred to an intake interviewer who was either a social worker or a psychiatrist. This interviewer obtained from the patient necessary information to present his case to an intake conference at which all the clinic's psychiatric personnel decided whether or not therapy should be administered. All of the patients accepted by the intake interviewer became the subjects of our study. We classified these individuals operationally according to a method described in a previous paper,[4] using a five-class system developed by Hollingshead, in which the highest status group is labeled class I, with the others following in numerical order, class V being the lowest.[5]

The social class distribution of persons seen by the intake interviewer was as follows: class II—9 per cent, class III—28 per cent, class IV—39 per cent, and class V—23 per cent.[6] It is clear that persons from all social classes, except the highest, sought aid at the clinic. Whether or not an individual was recommended for treatment, however, was directly related to his social class position as can be seen in Table 1. Nearly two-thirds of class V persons were not recommended for therapy, compared to about one-fifth of persons in class IV and only one-tenth of those in classes

Reprinted from *American Sociological Review* (June, 1954), *19*, 307–310, by permission of the American Sociological Association.

TABLE 1. PERCENTAGE DISTRIBUTION OF PATIENTS BY SOCIAL CLASS AND DURATION OF CONTACT WITH CLINIC

Conference Decision	Social Class			
	II	III	IV	V
No treatment recommended	11.8	9.6	22.2	64.3
Assigned to staff	35.3	17.3	2.8	.0
Assigned to resident psychiatrist	29.4	38.5	30.6	2.4
Assigned to medical student	.0	9.6	26.4	23.8
Assigned to other therapist (social workers, psychology students)	5.9	7.7	9.7	7.1
Referred to other agencies	11.8	17.3	4.2	2.4
Unknown*	5.9	.0	4.2	.0
	100.1	100.0	100.1	100.0

Chi-square=81.7924, p less than .001.N=183.

*Unknown cases were not included in the chi-square computation.

II and III. Certainly the economic hypothesis is not supported by these findings.

Just as interesting is the fact that there was a significant difference in the training of the personnel assigned to treat patients in the various social classes. The trained staff psychiatrists treated mainly class II and class III patients; resident psychiatrists in training treated class III and class IV patients; and medical students, taking a four week course, treated class IV and class V patients. The fully trained staff did not treat any patients in class V and only two in class IV. In contrast, medical students with no previous experience in psychotherapy treated no patients in class II and only five in class III.

The third relationship between class position and treatment was that the duration of therapy varied significantly from one class to another. The data in Table 2 show that the higher a patient's social class, the longer his treatment. The percentage of persons receiving treatment for ten or more weeks increased from 14 in class V to 59 in class II. On the other hand, nearly half of all class V patients were seen less than one week, but only 12 per cent of those in class II were seen for such a short period.

The intensity of treatment, as measured by number of contacts with therapist, was also

TABLE 3. PERCENTAGE DISTRIBUTION OF PATIENTS BY SOCIAL CLASS AND TOTAL NUMBER OF TIMES SEEN IN CLINIC

Times Seen	Social Class			
	II	III	IV	V
One	17.6	23.1	38.9	45.2
2–9	29.4	28.8	40.3	42.9
10 or more	52.9	48.1	20.9	11.9
	99.9	100.0	100.1	100.0

Chi-square=22.5410, p less than .001. N=183.

significantly greater in the higher social class. The percentage of persons seen ten or more times rose from 12 in class V to 53 in class II, and the percentage of persons seen only once declined from 45 in class V to 18 in class II.

This relationship between the nature of treatment and the patient's social class is illustrated even more strikingly by analysis of only those cases assigned to a therapist at the intake conference, instead of all cases accepted initially.

As indicated in Table 4, the percentage of patients seen ten or more times declined from 75 in class II to only 29 in class V. These findings indicate clearly that lower class persons did not receive as long and intensive treatment as those higher in the class system.

It must be recognized that factors other than social class may be related to acceptance for treatment and subsequent therapeutic experience. Sex and age of the patient and professional status of the intake interviewer, suggested by psychiatrists as perhaps being relevant, were not. The chi square test was used, and significance was defined at the .05 level. Diagnosis, however, was found to be significantly related to acceptance and subsequent clinical experience. Although most patients were neurotics, approximately one-quarter were suspected of being psychotic and were treated differently. They were not accepted for therapy as frequently as neurotics and did not receive as long and intensive treatment by as highly trained personnel. This did not account for the differential treatment of patients by social class, however, since there was no significant difference in the class distribution of suspected psychotics and neurotics.

TABLE 2. PERCENTAGE DISTRIBUTION OF PATIENTS BY SOCIAL CLASS AND DURATION OF CONTACT WITH CLINIC

Length of Contact	Social Class			
	II	III	IV	V
Less than one week	11.8	26.9	37.5	47.6
1–9 weeks	29.4	26.9	33.3	38.1
10 or more weeks	58.8	46.2	29.2	14.3
	100.0	100.0	100.0	100.0

Chi-square=17.5029, p less than .01. N=183.

TABLE 4. PERCENTAGE DISTRIBUTION OF PATIENTS ACCEPTED AT INTAKE CONFERENCE BY SOCIAL CLASS AND DURATION OF THERAPY

Times Seen	Social Class			
	II	III	IV	V
1–9	25.0	36.8	70.0	71.4
10 or more	75.0	63.2	30.0	28.6
	100.0	100.0	100.0	100.0

Chi-square=15.4446, p less than .01. N=114.

CONCLUSIONS AND INTERPRETATIONS

In summary, it was found that in a situation where the economic factor was held constant, acceptance for therapy and the character of subsequent clinical experience were related significantly to the patient's social class; the higher an individual's social class position, the more likely he was to be accepted for treatment, to be treated by highly trained personnel, and to be treated intensively over a long period.

Although the necessary data to explain these findings are lacking, some tentative explanations which might lead to further research are offered. It may be that differences in the social class backgrounds between psychiatrists, who are mainly from classes I and II, and class IV and V patients are important factors in the differential acceptance rates and subsequent clinic experience. Variations, according to social class, in the conception of the psychiatrist's role and the meaning of therapy seem important. For instance, the psychiatrist's values concerning who should be treated appear to influence the acceptance of patients. Also, lower class persons do not seem to share with psychiatrists the conception of therapy as a process by which the patient gains insight into his problems. Frequently, such patients conceive of the therapist's role in magical terms.

Psychotherapy involves intimate communicative interaction between the patient and therapist. Therefore it may be facilitated if a certain similarity in culturally determined symbols and learned drives exist in both patient and therapist. Differences in value systems and patterns of communication, on the other hand, may hamper the establishment of the therapeutic relationship. At present, it appears possible that lower-class patients need to acquire new symbols and values to participate in expressive psychotherapy. Since this is a difficult process, many of them may be considered unpromising candidates for successful treatment. According to the clinic's staff they often "lack motivation for psychotherapy" or are not "psychologically minded." Perhaps psychiatrists need to acquire new symbols and values in dealing with lower class patients; or perhaps new approaches are necessary to bring psychotherapy to such persons.

NOTES

1. A. B. Hollingshead and F. C. Redlich, "The Relationship of Social Structure to Psychiatric Disorders" aided by U.S.P.H.S. Mental Health Act Grant MH 263 (R).

2. F. C. Redlich, A. B. Hollingshead, *et al.*, "Social Structure and Psychiatric Disorders," *American Journal of Psychiatry*, 109 (April, 1953), pp. 729–34; A. B. Hollingshead and F. C. Redlich, "Social Stratification and Psychiatric Disorders," *American Sociological Review*, 18 (April, 1953), pp. 163–69; H. A. Robinson, F. C. Redlich, and J. K. Myers, "Social Structure and Psychiatric Treatment," in press for *American Journal of Ortho-psychiatry;* B. H. Roberts and J. K. Myers, "Religion, National Origin, Immigration, and Mental Illness," *Americal Journal of Psychiatry*, 110 (April, 1954), pp. 759–64.

3. Twelve cases which could not be class-typed because of paucity of data were omitted from the following analysis.

4. Rodlich, Hollingshead, *et al., op. cit.*

5. A brief description of each class is as follows: *Class I* comprises families of wealth, education, and top social prestige; *class II* consists of families in which the adults for the most part hold college degrees and in which the husbands have executive, high-level managerial, or professional occupations; *Class III* includes proprietors, white-collar workers, and some skilled workers; they are mostly high school graduates; *class IV* consists largely of semi-skilled workers with less than a high school education; *class V* includes unskilled and semi-skilled workers, who have a grade-school education or less, and who live in the poorest areas of the community.

6. The social class distribution of the New Haven population is as fellows: class I—3 per cent, class II—8 per cent, class III—21 per cent, class IV—50 per cent, and class V—18 per cent.

SOCIAL CLASS, MENTAL ILLNESS, AND AMERICAN PSYCHIATRY: AN EXPOSITORY REVIEW*

S. M. Miller and Elliot G. Mishler

THIS book[1] may well have a marked effect upon the future practice of psychiatry. It reports the results of a major investigation by a sociologist-psychiatrist team of the relationships between social class and the appearance and treatment of mental illness. Fragmentary findings had been made available before (twenty-five articles have appeared over the last five years), but a great deal of important material is presented here for the first time and the authors have expanded their forthright interpretations of the study's implications for the treatment of the mentally ill.

The excitement of a pioneering study arises from the freshness of its point of view and the provocativeness of its findings. It poses new questions and places old ones in a new light. This quality of exciting discovery is present in the important and sometimes startling findings of this study. We can give some indication of the significance of the book by quoting the three major hypotheses which are the central concerns of the investigation:

(I) The prevalence of treated mental illness is related significantly to an individual's position in the class structure. (II) The types of diagnosed psychiatric disorders are connected significantly to the class structure. (III) The kind of psychiatric treatment administered by psychiatrists is associated with the patient's position in the class structure.

A major problem of such ground-breaking investigations is that the core discovery overwhelms both authors and readers alike by the brute fact of its existence. In the first wave of response there is often a neglect of fundamental questions concerning the approach, the methodology, and the interpretations placed upon the data. The chapter summaries tend to enter without qualifications into the folklore of the discipline.

The potential importance of this book for theory, research, and practice in the mental illness field is too great to permit such neglect.

Reprinted from *Milbank Memorial Fund Quarterly* (April, 1959), 37 (2), 1–26.

I. EXPOSITION OF FINDINGS

A. The Social Class Structure

The basic data on social class composition is derived from interviews with respondents in a 5 per cent sample of all households in the metropolitan area of New Haven, Connecticut, which had a total population of about 236,940 persons. The New Haven population is divided into five social classes arranged in a hierarchal order. The family's class position is determined by the score of the head of the family on a weighted "Index of Social Position" that is derived from three separate scales measuring the social rank of his (a) area of residence; (b) occupation; and (c) education. The weights used in the formula for computing the summary index and the cutting points used to distinguish between classes were decided on specifically for this study and are not extrapolation from theory or other research. Roughly, occupation receives almost as much weight as the other two scores combined.

Class I, or the *upper class*, constitutes about 3 per cent of the population. It is composed of both "old" and "new" families who live in the most exclusive residential areas; the family head is a college graduate who is either an executive of a large firm or a professional. Class II, the *upper middle class*, is 8.4 per cent of the population and is made up occupationally of the managerial and professional groups. In Class III, the *lower middle class*, who make up 20.4 per cent of the population, about half are in salaried white collar work and the remainder either own small businesses, are semi-professionals, foremen, or skilled workers.

Class IV, the *working class*, is the largest group and accounts for half the households (49.8 per cent). Half of the group is semi-skilled workers, a third is skilled, and about a tenth is white collar employees. The overall educational level is much lower than in the class above it.

The *lower class*, Class V, which is 18.4 per cent of the population of New Haven, is made up of unskilled and semi-skilled workers of low education.

A rich and detailed description is provided of the historical background of the social class structure and of certain cultural characteristics of each of the classes such as their religious, family, ethnic, and leisure time patterns.

B. The Prevalence of Persons in Psychiatric Treatment

A "Psychiatric Census" was carried out in which an attempt was made to enumerate all persons from the New Haven metropolitan area who were "in treatment with a psychiatrist or under the care of a psychiatric clinic or mental hospital between May 31 and December 1, 1950."

The procedure here was remarkably thorough: systematic inquires were made of revelant facilities and practitioners in New England and New York City and to special facilities further afield. The investigators' persistence brought response from every hospital and clinic contact and from 70 per cent of the private practitioners. In all, they believe that they may have missed only about 2 per cent of the community's residents who were receiving treatment. A total of 1,891 cases was enumerated on whom there was sufficient data for analysis. The data thus only permit discussion of *treated* mental illness, not of the total amount of mental illness in the community. To study the latter, a different type of research design with a psychiatric interview or some similar device of a cross-section of the community would be necessary. Thus, in the Hollingshead-Redlich study, there would have had to have been a psychiatric study of all of the individuals included in the 5 per cent sample of New Haven to enable statements to be made about "true" incidence and prevalence.

The major finding—one of the study's core discoveries—is of a systematic relationship between social class and the treated prevalence of mental illness. As can be seen in Table A, classes I through IV are somewhat underrepresented in the patient

population, while Class V, to which 38 per cent of the patient group are assigned by their scores on the Index of Social Position, is greatly overrepresented with twice as many patients as might be expected on the basis of their number in the community. Significant differences are also found in a comparison of treated prevalence rates per 100,000 population (computed so as to adjust for age and sex differences among the classes) which are distributed as follows:

TABLE B.　CLASS STATUS AND RATE OF (TREATED) PSYCHOSIS PER 100,000 POPULATION (AGE AND SEX ADJUSTED)

Class	Adjusted Rate Per 100,000
I–II	523
III	528
IV	665
V	1,668
Total Population	808

SOURCE: Text Table p. 210.

In a more detailed analysis, Hollingshead and Redlich divide the patient group into specific diagnostic categories. A first glance reveals that the differences among the classes in treated prevalence rates are much greater for psychoses than for neuroses. The proportions of patients diagnosed as psychotic increase as one moves from Class I–II through Class V and conversely the proportions diagnosed as neurotic decrease (this reversal of the first relationship is automatic inasmuch as the two general categories make up the whole of the patient group). However, since this is a tempting finding to cite, it is important to point out that the authors discount its general importance and attribute it as possibly arising from the "differential use of psychiatric facilities by the population."

There are interesting differences among the social classes in regard to the specific neurotic disturbance which is modal among those who are in treatment: In Classes I and II the modal disturbance is character neuroses; in III and V, antisocial and immaturity reactions; while phobic-anxiety reactions are frequent in Class IV. Each of the above accounts for about one-third of the neurotic patients in each class as can be seen in Table C.

With regard to specific types of psychoses, much less variation in their percentage importance is found than is the case with the neuroses, as Table D reveals. In particular, for some of the major categories, differences are essentially nonexistent—schizophrenia is the predominant psychotic disorder in all classes and the proportions

TABLE A.　CLASS STATUS AND THE DISTRIBUTION OF PATIENTS AND NONPATIENTS IN THE POPULATION

Class	Population, %	
	Patients	Nonpatients
I	1.0	3.0
II	7.0	8.4
III	13.7	20.4
IV	40.1	49.8
V	38.2	18.4
	n = 1891	236,940

$$\chi^2 = 509.81, 4 \ df, p < .001$$

SOURCE: Hollingshead, A. B., & Redlich, F. C.: *Social Class and Mental Illness*, Table 8, p. 199.

TABLE C. Percentage of Patients in each
Diagnostic Category of [Treated] Neurosis—by
Class (Age and Sex Adjusted)

Diagnostic Category of Neurosis	Class			
	I–II	III	IV	V
Antisocial and Immaturity Reactions	21	32	23	37
Phobic-Anxiety Reactions	16	18	30	16
Character Neuroses	36	23	13	16
Depressive Reactions	12	12	10	8
Psychosomatic Reactions	7	9	13	11
Obsessive-Compulsive Reactions	7	5	5	0
Hysterical Reactions	1	1	6	12
$n =$	98	119	182	65

$$x^2 = 53.62, df\ 18, p < .001$$

Source: Table 13, p. 226.

TABLE E. Class Status and the Rate of
Different Types of [Treated] Psychoses
Per 100,000 of Population (Age and Sex Adjusted)

Type of Disorder	Class			
	I-II	III	IV	V
Affective Psychoses*	40	41	68	105
Psychoses Due to Alcoholism and Drug Addiction†	15	29	32	116
Organic Psychoses‡	9	24	46	254
Schizophrenic Psychoses§	111	168	300	895
Senile Psychoses ‖	21	32	60	175
$n =$	53	142	585	672

* $x^2 = 17.49,\ 3\ df,\ p < .001.$
† $x^2 = 77.14,\ 3\ df,\ p < .001.$
‡ $x^2 = 231.87,\ 3\ df,\ p < .001.$
§ $x^2 = 452.68,\ 3\ df,\ p < .001.$
‖ $x^2 = 88.36,\ 3\ df, p < .001.$
Source: Table 15, p. 232.

of all psychotics who are schizophrenic run from a low of 55 per cent in Class I to 61 per cent in Class IV. This finding is striking since earlier studies have reported a much higher rate of schizophrenia in Class IV and V neighborhoods than in other neighborhoods. Little variation exists among the classes in diagnoses of senile psychoses (11 or 12 per cent in each). Class V is disproportionately low in the affective psychoses with 7 per cent, and the other classes give figures of 14 or 21 per cent. Organic psychoses are highest in Class V (16 per cent) and lowest in Class I (5 per cent), and Class IV with 4 per cent has half the rate of the other classes for psychoses resulting from alcoholism and drug addiction.

The treated prevalence rates for all of the separate neuroses (except hysterical reactions) show statistically significant differences among the classes. However, there is no ordering from a higher to a lower class that is consistent from one diagnostic category to another. The pattern of each neurosis with class must be examined and interpreted separately, as the authors do. Table E on the rates of persons in psychiatric treatment for different types of psychoses by class is the clearest

TABLE D. Percentage of Patients in each
Diagnostic Category of [Treated] Psychosis—
By Class (Age and Sex Adjusted)

Diagnostic Category of Psychosis	Class			
	I–II	III	IV	V
Affective Psychoses	21	14	14	7
Psychoses resulting from Alcoholism and Drug Addiction	8	10	4	8
Organic Psychoses	5	8	9	16
Schizophrenic Psychoses	55	57	61	58
Senile Psychoses	11	11	12	11
$n =$	53	142	584	672

$$x^2 = 48.23, df\ 12, p < .001$$

Source: Table 14, p. 228.

demonstration in the book of an ordered inverse relationship of the type of disorder under treatment and social class. Although the curves for each disorder (affective, organic, schizophrenic, etc.) vary, in *every* case there is an increase in the rates as one moves from Class I–II to Class III, to Class IV, to Class V.

C. The Incidence of Mental Illness

One of the most important tools of epidemiological research and analysis is the distinction between *incidence*, i.e., the occurrence of new cases during some specified time, and *prevalence*, i.e., the total number of active cases in the population during some specified time. Although incidence is one of the components in a total prevalence picture, there is no systematic relation between the two since cases may be active currently that first appeared at any point in the past. In other words, as is generally known, prevalence rates do not directly reflect incidence rates since the former are dependent on rates of recovery and mortality from illness as well as on the occurring of illness.

All the figures reported above, and those in previous articles based on the study are for the prevalence of being in treatment. The most important new material in the volume is the presentation of incidence data for the psychiatric sample. It was derived by separating-out patients who entered or reentered treatment during the interval of observation from those who had been in treatment at the beginning of the interval. It should be emphasized again that both incidence and prevalence rates refer to individuals *in treatment* rather to individuals with a mental disorder whether or not they are in treatment. Consequently, the appropriate definition of incidence data for this investigation might be the numbers or rate of those first coming into treatment and prevalence might be stated as the numbers or rate of those in treatment during the study period.

The rates of coming into treatment for all kinds of mental illness are reported in Table F.

TABLE F. Class Status and Rate of Incidence of [treated] Neurosis and Psychosis per 100,000 Population (Age and Sex Adjusted).

Class	Rate
I–II	97
III	114
IV	89
V	139
Total	104

$x^2 = 8.41, 3\ df, p < .05$
Source: Text Table p. 212.

The table shows that the overall differences remain statistically significant but the differentials are markedly reduced in comparison with the prevalence rates. Class IV now has the lowest rate. The authors summarize by stating: "Classes I and II contribute almost exactly the number of new cases (incidence) as could be expected on the basis of their proportion of the community's population. Class IV had a lower number than could be expected proportionately, whereas Class V had an excess of 36 per cent" (p. 215). In further analyses, Hollingshead and Redlich demonstrate that there is *no* significant statistical difference among the classes in the rate at which persons come under treatment for neuroses and show that the sharpest break in this rate for psychoses as a whole and for schizophrenia (both cases where the overall differences among classes are statistically significant) occurs between Classes IV and V with very little differences appearing among the rates for Classes I through IV (pp. 235–6). (We shall return at a later point to these important findings regarding incidence.)

The data on incidence and prevalence reveal that Classes IV and V comprise two-thirds of the community (68.2 per cent) and provide more than three-fourths (78.3 per cent) of the mental patients. Thus, due to the size of these two classes, the high psychotic incidence rates in Class V, and the long duration of illnesses in both classes, *psychiatry—whether or not it is aware of it—is largely concerned with Class IV and V patients.* Of course, private practitioners have few class IV and V patients, but our calculations of the Hollingshead-Redlich data show that these two sources of treatment work with only 21 per cent of all New Haven mental patients.

D. Paths to Treatment

In an excellent discussion of the paths to psychiatric treatment, the authors make explicit their fundamental orientation that mental illness is a socio-cultural phenomenon as well as a psychological one. Thus, they state " . . . abnormal acts can be evaluated only in terms of their cultural and psychosocial contexts," and "Whether abnormal behavior is judged to be disturbed, delinquent, or merely idiosyncratic depends upon who sees it and how he appraises what he sees."

The sources of referral for treatment, i.e., the agencies or persons who decide that the behavior is that "type" of abnormality for which psychiatric treatment is appropriate, vary systematically by social class. Among neurotics, 55 to 60 per cent of those in Classes I through IV are likely to have been referred by physicians (almost entirely by private practitioners in the first three classes, and about half the time in Class IV by clinic physicians). The proportion of neurotic cases coming from medical referrals drops to 40 per cent in Class V; an equivalent proportion is referred by social agencies; with an additional 14 per cent directed to treatment by the police and courts (p. 186).

The differences are even more striking among psychotics where one-third of the patients in Class I were self-referrals and another 40 per cent came through family and friends. More than three-fifths of the Class III and IV patients were referred by physicians. For Class IV psychotics the police and courts are important, accounting for 19 per cent of the cases, and in Class V these two sources account for 52 per cent while social agencies contribute 20 per cent. The findings for schizophrenia are similar to those for psychosis in general (pp. 187–189).

The brief case reports that are presented to illustrate the different treatment consequences that follow on the same behavior when exhibited by persons of different classes should be required reading in all psychiatric residency programs. The authors note that "there is a definite tendency to induce disturbed persons in Classes I and II to see a psychiatrist in more gentle and 'insightful' ways than is the practice in Class IV and especially in Class V, where direct, authoritative, compulsory, and at times, coercively brutal methods are used."

And, their bitter, concluding epigram to this section is uncomfortably appropriate to their findings: "The goddess of justice may be blind, but she smells differences, and particularly class differences."

E. Patterns of Treatment

At the end of their chapter on the Treatment Process, Hollingshead and Redlich state that "the data presented lead to the conclusion that treatment for mental illness depends not only on medical and psychological considerations, but also on powerful social variables to which psychiatrists have so far given little attention," and that "We have found real differences in *where, how, and how long* persons in the several classes have been cared for by psychiatrists."

These conclusions are based on a large number of detailed analyses of relations among diagnosis, treatment agency, treatment, and social class. We shall cite only a few of the more decisive findings.

First, the patient group as a whole divides into three relatively equal parts according to the principal type of therapy received: psychotherapies, organic therapies, or custodial care. Eighty-four per cent of the psychotic group is in treatment in a state mental hospital; 64 per cent of the neurotics are in the hands of private practitioners and another 23 per cent are being treated in clinics.[2]

Despite the stress placed on diagnosis in psychiatric theory and practice, there is no overall relationship for neurotic patients between type of treatment and the specific diagnostic label attached to the patient. However, treatment is related directly to both social class and the agency in which the patient is treated. Even where treatment is received from the same facility, which is the most stringent test since it eliminates the selective bias that is present in the differential access to and choice of facilities by the different classes, there is a marked relationship between social class and type of treatment. For example, over 85 per cent of the Class IV and V neurotics in treatment with private practitioner receive "directive psychotherapy," while 45 per cent of Class I and II private patients receive "psychoanalysis or analytic psychotherapy." Consistent with this is the inverse relationship between social class and the likelihood of receiving the traditional "50 minute hour." (Ninety-four per cent in Classes I and II, 45 per cent in Class V, Tables 28, and 29, pp. 268–70).

A similar relationship between the "depth" and duration of the therapy and social class is also found in clinics, and there is additional evidence in a separate study of one clinic that the "patient's class status determines the professional level of the therapist who treats him." Public hospitals appear to be more democratic in their assignment of treatment to neurotic patients, inasmuch as there is no overall relationship between social class and treatment in these institutions.

The findings with regard to class bias in the type of treatment given to psychotic patients and to schizophrenics are less clear and less consistent than for the neurotic group. On the other hand, the relations of class to the duration and history of treatment are very significant and very revealing. For example, as one moves down the class ladder, the likelihood for schizophrenics of having been in continuous treatment increases, while moving in the other direction there is an increased likelihood of periods of remission and re-entry into treatment. In other words, once he enters treatment the Class V schizophrenic is likely to be kept under psychiatric care (Table 38, p. 295). Further, for psychotics there is a direct increase from Class I to Class V in the time duration of their present course of treatment; while for a neurotic this relationship is reversed. In other words, while the lower class neurotic is dismissed from treatment much more quickly than patients from higher classes, the lower class psychotic is rarely perceived as "ready" to leave treatment.

In comparing patients of Classes III–V who have been admitted to the hospital for the first time with patients of the same classes who have been hospitalized previously, a striking finding emerges: The new patient is more likely to receive custodial care than the longer time patient! The implication is that patients of these classes are not given custodial care because of the failure of other methods but are somewhat routinely assigned to this very limited care. In Class V, for example, 64 per cent of the patients who are receiving custodial care had not had any previous treatment.

No discussion of treatment is complete that omits mention of expenditures and fees. The chapter dealing with this material contains more detailed comparative information than is available in any other source. One of the most salient findings is that the mean cost per day in private hospitals is higher for Class IV patients than for patients in the higher classes ($31.11 to $23.76 for a Class I person). This result which is contrary to expectation results from the discriminatory discounts granted higher status persons. Further, the higher status persons receive the most expensive therapies which leads the authors to state: "To use a metaphor, private hospitals are designed for the 'carriage trade' but they are supported by the 'shock box.'" A similar relationship is found in clinics where treatment expenditures per patient are strongly related to class status, with the result that "Class II patients receive the most therapy and Class V patients the least." This finding is particularly disturbing since the clinics have presumably been developed to serve the psychiatric needs of lower status persons.

F. Recommendations

In a thoughtful and interpretive summary of the implications of their findings for the problem of the mentally ill in our society, Hollingshead and Redlich point to the gap between the extent of the need and the resources currently available to meet it. While they give proper emphasis to the financial problem (what America needs is a "good five-dollar psychotherapist"), they also point to the difficulties that result from the differences in cultural values and role expectations between psychiatrists and patients from the lower social classes. They note that psychiatrists tend to come from the upper and middle classes and have outlooks which lead many of them to dislike Class IV and V patients and to disapprove of the behavior patterns of Class V individuals.

More than money will be needed. Among the possible partial solutions to the problems that they suggest are proposals that psychiatrists themselves be trained to recognize and deal squarely with the differences between themselves and patients from other classes; that new forms and modes of therapy be developed to reach the "difficult" patients (whose difficulty seems to reflect the difference between his and his therapist's class positions more than his psychological disturbance); and that new non-medical therapists, whose education would be less expensive than psychiatrists', be trained to treat the emotional disorders which do not have medical problems associated with them.

II. DISCUSSION OF FINDINGS

This detailed and complex study touches on a large number of important issues concerning the social context of mental illness and its treatment. It represents a distinct step forward in a number of ways.

Three features of the study are especially notable: (a) The presentation of incidence figures as well as prevalence data is strongly to be commended. (b) The method of estimating the social class of patients and the community, despite the limitations indicated below, is an improve-ment over those employed in previous studies which tended to assume that all who lived in a particular area or paid a similar rent were in the same class. (c) Social class is linked to many more facets of mental illness than just the rate and kind of mental illnesses; in particular, the link of class to the treatment process is innovational.

In our discussion we have restricted ourselves to and organized our comments around three topics that are critical for the study: the concepts of social class and mental illness; the validation of the basic hypotheses; and, the implications of the study for psychiatric treatment.

A. Concepts of Social Class and Mental Illness

Among sociologists, there is a variety of approaches to the problem of social stratification. Hollingshead and Redlich view the different classes as differently primarily in their "styles of life" and use their combined scores on education, occupation, and residence as rough indices of these five different sub-cultures rather than as variables that are important in their own right.

In a study that directs explicit attention to the problems of getting "to" treatment and getting something "out of" treatment, the use of a combined index is unfortunate since it precludes analyses that might help to clarify what is involved in these processes. For example, it would have been of particular interest to be able to examine the relationships of education to the prevalence and treatment data in order to determine if an increase in education is associated with an increase in the propensity to view one's problems in psychological terms and therefore to benefit from psychological modes of treatment. Such a possibility is suggested by results in recent surveys of attitudes toward mental illness.[3] Enough evidence also exists to indicate that educational differences among individuals of the same occupational level are associated with differences in other characteristics, such as attitudes on public issues, so as to make the possibility of such cross-breaks especially desirable.[4]

In the Hollingshead system, some wage-earners are Class IV, others III or V, while white-collar workers are either III or IV. The class groupings thus become overlaps of various kinds, reducing their homogeneity, confusing comparisons and making generalizations difficult. An anomaly is that 18 per cent of New Haven was assigned to Class V in a time of prosperity. This figure seems high even with New Haven's migrant labor situation and may be due to a conceptualization of

Class V which leads to a broad category characterized by widely varying behavior; for example, regular but unskilled workmen are lumped together with irregular but semi-skilled workmen.

Occupation scores correlate .88 with the original criterion on which the weighted index was based, and correlate less highly than this with residence and education (.50 and .72 respectively, p. 394). From this, it would appear that little would have been lost if occupation alone were used as the index of social class. On the other hand, much might have been gained by this procedure since, in addition to permitting potentially revealing analyses, it would have reduced the heterogeneity of the social class groups allowing for more precise interpretations of the results. (If the data for occupation, education, and area of residence have been separately recorded by the researchers, it would be a comparatively simple procedure to see what variations by education exist within levels of occupations as classified, for example, by the Bureau of the Census. Such additional "runs" of the data would extend their usefulness, especially by permitting comparisons with other investigations.)

The importance of the study's findings, and our confidence in them, rests in large part on the fundamental assumption that the two basic variables of social class and mental illness have been measured independently of each other—if not, then the found relationships must be viewed skeptically as possibly spurious. This seems an easy enough assumption to accept. However, the findings in a recent study[5] raise serious doubts as to its validity. In this exceptionally well-controlled study, Haase is able to demonstrate that the same set of presenting symptoms is diagnosed as more severe when the patient is perceived by subtle cues to be a working class person than when he is seen as in the middle class. In the Hollingshead-Redlich study, despite the safeguards, this bias might be reflected in such findings as the relatively higher rates of psychoses as compared to neuroses when one moves down the class hierarchy, and would directly affect the relative sizes of the populations coming into treatment as well as the prevalence rates of persons in treatment for the different classes. One such study, of course, is insufficient grounds for rejecting the findings presented here. The issue, however, is of such crucial importance that the final acceptance of the findings must rest on further investigations of the relationship of class to the diagnostic process itself.

B. The Validation of Hypotheses

Compared to most investigations of complicated areas in social science, this book is a model of clarity with regard to the presentation of its guiding hypotheses and the procedures by which these hypotheses were tested empirically. The assumptions behind each decision in the development of the research design are stated explicitly and the basic instruments are described with sufficient detail so as to permit other researchers to replicate the study with exactitude.

This report is organized around three hypotheses that were formulated explicitly and tested directly. (Findings on two other hypotheses dealing with social mobility and the relation of class to developmental factors in psychiatric disorders will be reported in the forthcoming companion volume by J. K. Myers and B. H. Roberts, *Social Class, Family Dynamics, and Mental Illness*.) Briefly, the hypotheses, which we have quoted earlier, state that the social class structure is related to the treated prevalence of mental illness, the specific types of diagnosed psychiatric disorders, and the types of treatment administered by psychiatrists to patients. The authors conclude that their findings confirm these hypotheses, and we have reported the relevant findings in our expository section above. At this point, we shall re-examine their interpretations of some of the critical tables.

One of the major faults in the authors' approach to their findings is found in the first direct comparison that they present between the proportions of patients and the proportions of persons in the community in each of the five social classes (see Table A). Only *one* class, Class V, has disproportionately more patients than its frequency in the population, and *all* the other classes have less patients than would be expected. (If the data in this table are re-computed with the omission of Class V, the Chi Square test—the statistic used to evaluate all of the major findings—remains statistically significant but is markedly reduced in size, and the disproportionate contribution of Class IV is only 4 per cent more than expected, and of Class III, 3 per cent less than expected.)

While at various points they note that the major difference is between Classes IV and V, they include in their summary of this table the statement that "the lower the class, the greater proportion of patients in the population." The same interpretive tendency is found in their discussion of class differences in adjusted rates of mental illness (p. 210) where they ignore the fact that the Class III rate is actually *lower* than the rate in Class I–II. Again, in commenting on the class differences in incidence rates, they state (p. 212) "In a word, class status is linked to the incidence of treated mental illness." (The rates are shown in Table F.) A re-computation of these data, omitting Class V, reveals Class III and *not* Class IV as having a higher than expected number of patients.

Basing their remarks on the data we have just reviewed, Hollingshead and Redlich conclude their chapter by stating " ... enable us to conclude that Hypothesis I is true. Stated in different terms, a distinct inverse relationship does exist between social class and mental illness. The linkage ... follows a characteristic pattern; Class V, almost invariably, contributes many more patients than its proportion of the population warrants. Among the higher classes there is a more proportionate relationship ... " (p. 217).

What we are attempting to point out by this close review of their data is that the authors' tendency to report that there is a consistent and ordered inverse relationship between social class and mental illness is simply not an accurate interpretation of their findings. It would have been, as a matter of fact, more consistent with their "styles of life" view of social classes to have stressed what we believe is the major finding, namely the consistent differences between Class V and the other classes, with the differences that exist among the latter not clearly and consistently patterned in a hierarchal fashion.

Our attention was first called to this problem by the comments and remarks of other professionals and students who were summarizing the book's findings in seminars and staff meetings by statements like "the lower the class the higher the rates of mental illness." The general tendency in discussions of class differences to group together Classes I–II versus Classes IV and V is another contributor to the misinterpretation of their findings. The book is so notable for its clarity in other respects that it is unfortunate that the interpretive summaries lend themselves so easily to confusion and distortion. (It might also be mentioned that synoptic statements of the order—"The lower the class the higher the rates of mental illness"—ignore the nature of the Hollingshead-Redlich data which are of treated illnesses, not total illnesses. The relation between treated and total illnesses in different social classes is not known and the total rates cannot be assumed to be a standard coefficient of the treated rates.)

In interpreting the relationships between class and specific types of neurosis and psychosis (Hypothesis II) there is a tendency to use an overall significant statistic to report differences for specific disorders when the latter are less systematic and depend on rather small numbers of cases. For example, their two basic tables (Tables C and D) demonstrate that, overall, there are statistically significant associations of the five classes with the seven specific neuroses and with the five specific psychoses. They then refer to an "extreme concentration" of hysterical patients in Class V. Examination reveals there are only eight Class V patients in this category and the reduction of the cell by two or three cases would erase its percentage difference from Class IV. Again, they state, "the higher the class, the larger the proportion of patients who are affective psychotics," yet a reduction of three cases among those in Classes I–II would completely eliminate the differences from Class I through Class IV, leaving only Class V as different from the others.

So far, except for one illustration, we have been concerned in our discussion with the reports and interpretations of prevalence data which permit specific tests of the authors' explicit hypotheses and form the major substantive findings around which the book is organized. We have already remarked on the important distinction between prevalence and incidence and will turn now to the findings on the incidence of specific disorders.

Hollingshead and Redlich separately compute rates for each of the "components" of prevalence: new cases arising during their six months interval of observation (incidence), cases that re-entered treatment during that period (re-entry), and those that had been in treatment at the beginning of the period (continuous). They then proceed to test for significant differences among the classes for each of these rates, separately for neuroses and psychoses. (See data presented in Table G. We consider them to be the most important findings in the book on social class and mental illness.)

They find significant differences among the classes for each of the component rates *except* for the incidence of neurosis. In other words, there is no systematic relationship between social class and the rates of coming into treatment for neurosis.

It appeared to us that the statistical significance of the other relationships of class and incidence rates (both new and old cases) might depend almost entirely on Class V. We recomputed incidence and re-entry rates for neuroses and psychoses, omitting Class V from the calculations. The test showed *no* significant differences among

TABLE G.   Incidence, Re-entry, Continuous, and Prevalence Rates per 100,000 for [Treated] Neuroses and Psychoses—by Class (Sex and Age Adjusted)

Neuroses

Class	Incidence	Re-entry	Continuous	Prevalence
I-II	69	44	251	349
III	78	30	137	250
IV	52	17	82	114
V	66	35	65	97
$x^2 =$	4.40	8.64	69.01	56.05
df	3	3	3	3
p	$> .05$	$< .05$	$< .001$	$< .001$

Psychoses

Class	Incidence	Re-entry	Continuous	Prevalence
I-II	28	44	117	188
III	36	38	217	291
IV	37	42	439	518
V	73	88	1344	1505
$x^2 =$	12.37	15.73	748.47	741.09
df	3	3	3	3
p	$< .01$	$< .01$	$< .001$	$< .001$

SOURCE: Table 16, p. 235.

Classes I through IV. (Chi Square for the incidence and re-entry of neuroses are 1.96 and 3.36; for psychoses, the figures are .28 and .08. None of these is significant at the .05 criterion value.)

To summarize these findings: there are *no* significant differences among social classes I–V in the incidence of new cases of neuroses. There are *no* significant differences among classes I through IV in the incidence of new *or* old cases of neuroses *or* psychoses. Class V has significantly different and higher rates of new and old cases of psychosis (and the inclusion of Class V in the computations suggests that Class IV has a *lower* rate of re-entry of neurotics than the other classes).

The contrast between the significant differences in prevalence and the findings we have just reported of non-significant differences in incidence is extremely important. By concentrating on the prevalence data, an important finding for sociologists and psychiatrists—that Class IV has the lowest overall mental illness rate—is ignored, and some traditional views about the incidence of mental illness are left untouched. There is an implication at many points throughout the book that the prevalence findings may be interpreted as class differences in the likelihood of developing various mental illnesses (the descriptions of class sub-cultures in Chapters 3 and 4, and the discussions of social class and the life cycle in Chapter 12 are presumably given an important place in the book because treated prevalence data are to some extent thought of in these terms). It is also likely that the findings will be discussed in both the lay

and professional literature to some extent as if the prevalence findings did bear on questions of etiology.

Perhaps a recent statement on this by Dr. Redlich himself may serve to minimize such a tendency. "The New Haven study has not really brought out anything which is of etiological significance in explaining differences in prevalence, and prevalence in itself is not a very good measure from an epidemiological viewpoint . . . We found, as far as the accumulation of schizophrenics in the lower classes is concerned, that although not entirely, it is mostly due to the fact that the lower socioeconomic groups get different treatment and have different opportunities for rehabilitation."[6] It is unfortunate that this position was not stated as clearly in the book under review. In addition to these restrictions on the interpretation of the prevalence findings, and the fact that the data deal only with treated prevalence, our re-examination of the incidence data also supports the conclusion that the etiological significance of social classes for mental illness is yet to be demonstrated.

When the spurious issue of etiology is brushed aside, the book's major findings stand out quite clearly and they are of extreme importance. Essentially, these refer to the differential psychiatric treatment given to patients of different classes with the apparent result of an accumulation of cases in the lower classes. Besides the differences between the distributions of incidence and prevalence rates that we have discussed there are other findings that bear on this. The differences among classes on the paths to treatment, the types of treatment received, and the costs of treatment are important contributions to the understanding of the social aspects of medicine.

It should be noted that in many respects the study is an important followup of the Committee on Costs of Medical Care more than two decades ago.[7] By carefully studying how many and what kinds of persons are in psychiatric treatment, the nature and place of treatment, how much medical time is spent with them and the costs of treatment, a baseline is provided for discussion of the most effective social utilization of psychiatric manpower and resources. Coupled with other data, the present study provides an opportunity to define the "psychiatrically indigent" category—undoubtedly a much more inclusive category than that of the "medically indigent."

The authors' conclusions regarding class bias in treatment do not depend on the findings and do not suffer from the weaknesses of method and interpretation that we have discussed above. They are to be commended for their courage in facing this important issue squarely and for their no less courageous attempt to meet the problem by a forthright presentation of a number of proposals that are decidedly controversial in American psychiatric practice.

C. Implications of the Study

In view of the preceding discussion, we shall not take space to discuss the important theoretical issues about the relationship of social factors to the etiology of mental illness.[8] Rather, we shall restrict our remarks in this section to the study's implications for psychiatric practice.

It has been well known before this that the needs of the population for psychiatric treatment were not being met adequately. What this investigation demonstrates beyond this, is that the distribution of available resources is socially discriminatory. We believe that a serious moral question is also involved in this discovery, since the psychiatric profession legitimates its claim to high status and to social and economic rewards on the grounds that it functions in a "universalistic" nondiscriminatory way. Actually, it operates in such a way as to restrict its "best" treatments to persons in the upper social classes.

We agree that the need requires the development of new modes of treatment, better understanding by psychiatrists of social class patterns and their reactions to them, and new types of nonmedical therapists. We wish, however, to point to some of the assumptions involved in these recommendations and raise some questions that deserve further consideration. First, the authors appear to assume that psychoanalysis or some form of analytic psychotherapy is always ideally preferable to a directive or organic mode of treatment, and that therefore Class IV and V patients are being short-changed. At one level this is a value question since the different therapies are associated with different therapeutic goals, and the issues of what goals to select and who is to decide upon them lie in the realm of value. At another level, this is an empirical issue of whether other forms of treatment might not actually be more effective, rather than simply less costly and less demanding for certain groups of patients. Definitive empirical evidence does not yet exist to provide an answer to this question.

There also seems to be the assumption that it is the psychiatrist who relatively completely controls the type of treatment given. It may be that patients search out psychiatrists who will give them their preferred type of treatment and reject nonpreferred treatments, both from private practitioners and within the clinics and hospitals. The selective process and pressures emanating from the patient cannot be ignored in a full account of the biased pattern of psychiatric treatment.

This leads to a related point. There is a tendency to discuss the problem of therapy with working class and lower class persons in a way that implies that the therapist wishes to give the patient "more" than the patient wishes. For example, some practitioners assert that the therapist wants to help the patient come to his own decisions, but the patient only wants to be told what to do; the therapist wants to establish a long term relationship with the patient, but the patient wants a quick remedy; the therapist wants deep and lasting changes, but the patient is satisfied with superficial and transient results. The alternatives may be multiplied beyond this, but what is important is that they seem to imply a rejection of the therapist and the therapeutic process by the patient. We should like to suggest that quite the opposite may be happening. Rather than asking for "less" than he is offered, the working class and lower class patient may actually be asking for "more" in the sense that he wants a fuller, more extensive, and more permanent relationship than is possible either within the traditional definition of the therapeutic relationship or in terms of what the therapist wishes to enter into. In other words, it may be the therapist who drives the patient from treatment because he cannot handle the demands placed upon him, rather than the patient who drops treatment because its demands are too much for him.[9] (With the knowledge we have of working class and ethnic cultures it is difficult to subscribe without qualification to assertions that patients from these groups do not like to talk or have special difficulties entering into relationships. The basic questions are: What kind of relationships, with whom, and under what conditions? In raising these questions we are suggesting that some prevailing interpretations of working class and lower class life may have to be re-evaluated.)

III. RESEARCH PERSPECTIVES IN SOCIAL PSYCHIATRY

Perhaps nothing emerges more clearly from the book viewed as a whole than the need for continued systematic research on the relationships of social factors to mental illness and psychiatric practice. Our critical comments on the Hollingshead-Redlich study have included suggestions as to how future studies of a similar nature might be improved. We should like at this point to note briefly some additional areas and questions for research that have been suggested by both the achievements and shortcomings of this work.

A. The Etiology and Epidemiology of Mental Disorders

The etiological significance of social variables such as social class for various mental disorders remains an open question. Clearly, studies of "true" incidence will be needed before we are able to suggest answers to this question. In design these studies will have to be comparative and longitudinal and they will have to permit the isolation and control of different and changing forms of psychiatric practice. Field investigations of "true" prevalance such as the "Midtown" and "Stirling County" studies, reports from which are now in preparation, will provide a beginning for understanding the relationships between such data and those for treated prevalence as reported by Hollingshead and Redlich. It is to be hoped that future investigations, in addition to including alternative indices of social class, will be concerned with the effects of other social factors such as, for example, community and family structure, and ethnicity.[10]

More attention will have to be paid to the general problems of psychiatric diagnosis and classification. The nomenclature of the clinic is not particularly useful for field studies, but conceptual links must be forged among the different typologies and indices that are being developed. In all of this work it will be of particular importance not to neglect the fact that the process of psychodiagnosis is inherently a social process and full understanding requires the perspectives of sociological theory and analysis. In addition to data on types of disorders, the extension of a public health approach to the control of mental illness will require information on the severity and the extent of disability associated with mental illness so that large-scale social programs in the prevention termination, or reduction of such disabilities may be undertaken.[11]

B. Patterns of Psychiatric Treatment

The findings presented by Hollingshead and Redlich on the different paths to treatment followed by patients from different classes are very important, and this is an area in which we need to know much more. The history of the illness before the point of referral, the factors that enter into seeking help at a particular stage, the relation of time and type of referral to outcome, and the relationships of all of these to social class require exploration in further studies.

What variables and processes are involved in the initial phase of treatment that seems to be such an important determinant of later outcomes? How much choice is available to the patient and how does he exercise his choice? How does the process of class discrimination in assignment and treatment operate in clinics and other treatment facilities? How are the goals of treatment set and how are these goals related to the different values of patients and therapists and to their images of and attitudes toward each other?

The list of important research questions may be expanded easily. We wish to end with a special plea for evaluative studies of the effects of various forms of psychiatric treatment. There is a desparate shortage of systematic evidence in this area, and without such evidence our decisions regarding proper treatment tend to be determined by current fashions in psychiatry or by implicit social values and assumptions.

Although we have been critical of some of the methods and interpretations we should like to stress our respects and admiration for this fascinating and exciting study. It is a book of considerable significance that focuses our attention on a range of important problems which had barely been discussed before. We regard it as a study of psychiatric practice rather than as one of epidemiology, and consider it a great contribution to the study of treatment. If it is not the definitive study that hopefully may be made in the next decade or two, that study will, in part, be possible because of the pioneering work of Hollingshead and Redlich.

NOTES

* A number of persons commented on earlier versions of this paper. In particular, the exposition has benefitted from the detailed comments of Ernest M. Gruenberg, M.D., Matthew Huxley, and Frank Reissman. Only the authors, of course, bear responsibility for the final formulations presented in this paper.

1. Hollingshead, August B., and Redlich, Frederick C., *Social Class and Mental Illness* (New York: John Wiley, 1958).

2. Calculating the data in terms of the psychiatric agency involved reveals some important practices: 30 per cent of the patients treated by private practitioners and by public clinics are suffering from various types of psychotic disorders.

3. See relevant findings in the forthcoming National Opinion Research Center study directed by Shirley Star; *People's Attitudes Concerning Mental Health*. New York: Elmo Roper, 1950; and Elaine and John Cumming, *Closed Ranks*. Cambridge: Harvard University Press, 1957.

4. Stouffer, Samuel: *Communism, Conformity and Civil Liberties*. New York: Doubleday, 1955. Reissman, Frank: "Workers' Attitudes Toward Participation and Leadership," unpublished doctoral dissertation, Columbia University, 1955.

5. Haase, William: "Rorschach Diagnosis, Socio-Economic Class, and Examiner Bias," unpublished Ph. D. dissertation, New York University, 1956. For a general discussion of diagnostic tests and social class, see Riessman, Frank and Miller, S. M.: Social Class and Projective Tests. *Journal of Projective Tests*. December, 1958, 22, pp. 432–439.

6. *Symposium on Preventive and Social Psychiatry*, April 15–17, 1957. Walter Reed Army Institute of Research, Washington, USGPO, 1958. (p. 199).

7. See the report by Lee, Roger I. and Jones, Lewis Webster: *The Fundamentals of Good Medical Care*. Chicago: University of Chicago Press, 1933. They quote Dr. Olin West that "...the outstanding problem before the medical profession today is that involved in the delivery of adequate, scientific medical service to all the people, rich and poor, at a cost which can be reasonably met by them in their respective stations in life." "Adequate medical care" is defined in both quantitative and qualitative terms: "...a sufficient quantity of good medical care to supply the needs of the people according to the standards of good current practice." (p. 3).

8. Nor shall we discuss a problem that we have alluded to several times—how representative the census of patients is of all the mentally ill people in New Haven, especially in regard to the social class distribution of the total. Since individuals of different classes come to clinic and other treatment through different routes, it may not be assumed that the census sampled to the same degree the actual amount of all mental disorders in the different social classes.

9. Some evidence exists that many patients of other classes may have similar sets of expectations and present similar problems to psychiatrists. In a by-product of the study under review, it has been found that Class III and V patients exhibit strong resemblances in their expectations of therapy. Our hypothesis would be that it is the low-educated members of Class III who especially exhibit "non-psychiatric" attitudes. Redlich, F. C., Hollingshead, A. B., and Bellis, E.: Social Class Differences in Attitudes Towards Psychiatry. *American Journal of Orthopsychiatry*, January, 1955, 25, pp. 60–70.

10. For an illustration of the relation of one aspect of community structure, namely, multiple- vs. single-family dwelling units, to cerebral arteriosclerosis and senile psychosis, see, New York State Department of Mental Hygiene, *Fourth Annual Report of the New York State Health Commission*, 1954, pp. 31–33; on the impact of ethnic variations in family structure, see, Barabee, Paul and von Mering, Otto: Ethnic Variations in Mental Stress in Families with Psychotic Children. *Social Problems*, October, 1953, 1, pp. 48–53; and Singer, J. L. and Opler, M. K.: Contrasting Patterns of Fantasy and Motility in Irish and Italian Schizophrenics. *Journal of Abnormal and Social Psychology*, July, 1956, 53, pp. 42–47.

11. Gruenberg, Ernest M.: Application of Control Methods to Mental Illness. *American Journal of Public Health*, August, 1957, 47, pp. 944–952.

part VIII

PREVENTION OF DISORDERED BEHAVIOR AND MENTAL HEALTH: "COMMUNITY PSYCHIATRY"

Psychiatric efforts to cope with and reduce disordered behavior have become an aspect of psychiatry called "community psychiatry," which pertains to the prevention of mental disorders and to therapeutic intervention with both groups and disturbed individuals in the community. This approach to prevention involves a conception of mental health outside the mental hospital that aims to implement community resources and personnel for therapeutic and preventive ends. In effect, it has revised the concept of treatment from the idea of treating individual patients to the idea of changing the community in such a way that the community itself will contribute to the improvement of groups and categories of afflicted persons.

Community psychiatry has been dramatically called the "third revolution in psychiatry." Brimming with promise, it has the potential of rendering many services within the community for rehabilitating mentally disordered persons. It aims to treat patients within their residential habitat and to expand community resources to achieve these objectives. It includes a variety of plans, from facilitating the adjustment of discharged patients to treating mild patients within the community instead of committing them to the remote mental hospital, and depends on the out-patient clinic in great measure for patients' improvement within the community.[1] It means, too, more tolerance of and help for disordered persons on the parts of the family and other persons in the community. To summarize these objectives, Duhl has defined community psychiatry as the aim to increase the adaptive and psychosocial skills of afflicted persons and to decrease the pathology in groups through programs involving "case-finding, care, treatment, and rehabilitation."[2] In this context, the roles of patient and psychiatrist have been considerably redefined. Consistent with this purpose, the Joint Commission on Mental Illness and Health has recommended that contemporary treatment aim to help disordered persons sustain themselves in the community so they will be spared the debilitating effects of hospitalization and that mentally disordered persons who require hospitalization be returned home as rapidly as possible and allowed to remain in the community as long as their conditions warrant. Their aftercare and potential rehabilitation should become vital aspects of generally accessible health services, including day hospitals, night hospitals, aftercare clinics, nursing services, foster-family care, rehabilitation centers, convalescent nursing homes, work services, and former-patient groups. The commission has also recommended demonstration programs for day and night hospitals and more flexible use of hospital facilities for treating chronic and acute patients.[3]

The limited value of treating patients in the quarantined and isolated mental hospitals and the added value of treating some of them in the community was recognized by the Royal Commission on the Law Relating to Mental Illness and Mental Deficiency in 1957. They wrote:

> The recommendations of our witnesses were generally in favor of shift of emphasis from hospital care to community care. In relation to almost all forms of mental disorder, there is increasing medical emphasis on forms of treatment and training and social services which can be given without bringing patients into the hospital as inpatients, or which make it possible to discharge them from the hospital sooner than was usual in the past. The extent to which patients with long term disabilities could live in the future in less isolated residential homes must depend partly on the willingness of the general public to tolerate in their midst some people with mild abnormalities of behavior or appearance. We believe that the increasing public sympathy towards mentally disordered patients will result in a higher degree of tolerance in this regard. But even without this, many of the patients now in hospitals should be immediately acceptable as members of the general community. Whatever form of accomodation is favored in any particular locality we are convinced that the aim should be a deliberate reorientation away from institutional care in its present form and towards residential homes in the community.[4]

Despite the enthusiasm for "community psychiatry," it remains a relatively untried field, especially for the psychiatrist. It involves educating the public to accept out-patient treatment and to tolerate the afflicted person. It means special training for psychiatry students and retraining practicing psychiatrists for a role that is largely sociological in concept and execution. Influenced in part by the community approach to the prevention of delinquency and by the post-hospital care of patients, community psychiatry has been extended to a general orientation to prevention and treatment, an approach of promise rather than of demonstrated effectiveness. Certainly as its minimum, community treatment is preferable for many patients to treatment quarantined in institutions far removed from their homes. The stimulation of public interest in the problem of mental health through the concept of community psychiatry is a constructive endeavor in a therapeutic direction.

The basic aspect of prevention of mental disorders focuses most logically on prevention or treatment of disorders in children. In this sense, the community approach revises the previous approach of restricting treatment of children to the clinic. In this regard, Caplan has written:

> The focus upon the community rather than upon individual children introduces a new viewpoint that transforms some old and rather insignificant side issues into exciting and complicated problems of strategy and tactics in both the research and action fields. For example, as soon as we focus upon the community we can no longer restrict our clinical gaze to those individuals who penetrate the barriers and appear as patients within the walls of our clinics. We must also look outside the walls and we must even go ourselves and work outside the walls. This then upsets our previous equilibrium in regard to the deployment of our specialists resources. We can no longer base our decision on which patients to treat entirely by chance, or upon our

therapeutic predictions, or upon the technical interest of the case. Instead we have to develop priorities based also upon community implications or our treatments. From here it is a short step to realizing the necessity for a careful evaluation of how best to deploy the efforts of our scarce personnel.[5]

Thus the function of the personnel as well as the selection of the types of patients may change. More clinicians may consult in agencies in the community rather than treat patients directly. Children with acute situational disturbances can more readily receive this type of treatment than they could have received treatment within the clinic. The policies and procedures of the child guidance clinic would then be reoriented to the needs of the general community rather than the needs of the tiny segment of people who visit or are referred to the clinic.

This manner of treating persons in the community is not a sudden departure, it is a social trend of long standing. The proliferation of the community clinic, the rise of the halfway house between the mental hospital and the community, and the formation and growth of associations of former patients are established techniques of dealing with persons on an out-patient basis. In addition, both the day hospital and the night hospital treat and care for patients on a part-time basis without removing them from the community. The rise of community psychiatry has given impetus and direction to this trend, and local, state, and federal support and subsidy have intensified and elaborated it. The proliferation of clinics and community-oriented mental health services in the United States is indicated by the increase in the number of psychiatric out-patient clinics from 500 in 1946 to 1600 in 1962. According to Rosen, Bahn, and Kramer, "the next 10 to 20 years will witness still more significant changes in the development of comprehensive community mental health services. Community mental health centers are being planned that will provide for all aspects of mental health care, including preventive, diagnostic, therapeutic, rehabilitative consultative and educational activities."[6]

The sociologist's role in community psychiatry could embrace those of adviser, impartial critic, research analyst, and service participant. Although he may not be part of the clinical team, his knowledge of basic sociological problems and his skills in ascertaining the social processes that contribute to or retard the rehabilitation of the patients will have considerable value to this new scheme of therapeutic intervention.

The sociological function in community psychiatry also encompasses the kinds of research that determine the mental health needs of particular communities as well as the processes that contribute to mental disorders and mental health. For example, the Midtown Manhattan survey showed that the proportion of emotionally impaired persons is very high in the group above the age of 50. As a result of this finding, one general type of therapeutic service could be geared to older persons. On the other hand the community that revealed high rates of disorders among adolescents would expand its services for this age group. The study of a community would aim to determine not only its peculiar problems contributing to mental disorders and personal instability but also the generic social processes that contribute to these problems.

The formulation of programs for mental health within the community raises the question: Is knowledge based on research of the etiology of mental disorders essential to effective action programs in the community? Etiological knowledge is helpful but not essential in effective action programs, as we can see from the effective community programs that were developed for typhoid and scurvy from trial-and-error hunches before basic knowledge about them was obtained. In fact, social action programs may sometimes be the soil in which studies of etiological significance can grow. One chief obstacle to effective programs in community mental health seems to be social inertia rather than lack of knowledge.

Despite this emphasis on public cooperation, the need for basic research in mental disorders and mental health remains a central concern. The Joint Commission on Mental Illness and Health, in its final work, *Action for Mental Health*, recommended the following courses of action, regarding basic research: 1. Congress and state legislatures should subsidize long-term in preference to short-term research projects. 2. More funds should be allocated for basic research to determine the causal workings of mental disorders and rehabilitation. 3. More persons should be supported in mental health research, including young scientists who could be granted ten-year or even life-time appointments. 4. The federal government should support mental health research centers; these could operate independently or in collaboration with educational institutions or training centers. 5. Research facilities should be developed in regions and states that lack such facilities. 6. The federal government should encourage diversification of interest and subject in mental health research.[7]

Although these recommendations accent the crucial role of money in the development of knowledge of disordered behavior, specifically federal and state subsidy, this commission focused particular attention as well on the importance of acquiring basic knowledge through research in mental illness and health.

Part VIII presents some relevant facets of community psychiatry and the prevention and rehabilitation of mental disorders and begins with the late President Kennedy's proposal to the Congress concerning the role of the federal government in promoting and subsidizing research and social action for mental health in the community. The recourse to community resources for rehabilitating the patient rather than to the mental hospital only becomes a prime challenge. This general recommendation is more meaningful when the federal government becomes concerned with the alleviation of mental disorder. As a consequence of the President's message, communities across the United States have been encouraged to create new community mental health centers. A 1964 public health publication manifested this optimism:

> Not since the creation of the National Institute of Mental Health in 1949 has such specific impetus been provided by the Federal Government for the beginning of a new era in treatment of the mentally ill: in the community and by the community. For thousands of disturbed persons, the establishment of this comprehensive community mental health program will have specific and personal meaning, since many persons treated in these community centers need never leave home for the strange and lonely mental hospital which for years has been a world apart. Community mental health centers, in contrast, can remove the shock from that first day of hospitalized treatment and "help the patient help himself." Since the center is situated in the patient's home community, his own family physician may continue to see him and to participate in his treatment. Since the comprehensive centers include several kinds of care and treatment, the patient can receive the sort of treatment he needs in familiar surroundings. Because the patient has not left the community, "he need not return to it."[8]

Of course, implicit in this characterization is the assumption that the community will be benign to the person during and after his disorder. From a social psychological viewpoint, we can inquire to what extent the stresses in the community have contributed to his disorder and if these stresses will be reduced. These questions should be raised because many facets of this community approach remain to be worked out.

In his article, "Community Psychiatry," Gerald Caplan describes the conceptions of community psychiatry as an action program, the changing role of the community psychiatrist, and the issues in training community psychiatrists.

One pertinent effect of community psychiatry as a means of treatment and prevention of mental disorders has been the changing role of the psychiatrist. To train the psychiatrist for this role requires revision in the whole concept of the functions and knowledge of the psychiatrist, which in turn has necessitated a revised curriculum in psychiatric training. According to Ruesch, the broad content of community psychiatry as an aspect of social psychiatry should include: (1) the social determinants of behavior; (2) epidemiology of mental disorders; (3) family, psychodynamics, diagnostics, and treatment; (4) group therapy and the use of group processes for treatment; (5) mental health consultation as distinct from other forms of consultation; (6) preventive aspects of psychiatry such as school and industrial psychiatry; (7) facilities and programs of rehabilitation, such as aftercare and posthospital adjustment; (8) methods in public education about mental disorder and mental health; (9) education in dealing with political representatives and other significant officials; (10) religious aspects of psychiatry; (11) community organization; (12) research methods in appraising community mental health programs; (13) research methods in the study of social problems as well as a general knowledge of social problems; (14) training in the use of matching funds from community mental health programs; and (15) forensic psychiatry.[9] The broad scope of this ambitious program clearly represents a very thorough curriculum and an ideal to be aimed for.

In "An Outline for Community Mental Health Research," Anita K. Bahn describes the relevance and necessity of research in the mental health program for a given community. She points to the effectiveness of research when a psychiatric case register is installed (as in Maryland) that facilitates the recording of uniform data and hence improves the level of the research inquiry. She delineates a model of a comprehensive community mental health research program that would utilize periodic surveys of the demographic, mental health, and attitudinal traits of the population of the community and longitudinal reports on patients from the psychiatric or parapsychiatric case register.

The critical essay, "Community Psychiatry: The Newest Therapeutic Bandwagon" by H. Warren Dunham, indicates some of the theoretical and practical pitfalls that may impede community psychiatry. His critical appraisal, however, though skeptical of the methods and goals of this aspect of psychiatry does not dispense with the significance and potential benefits of community psychiatry. He cautions very enthusiastic advocates against claiming too much by showing the very formidable tasks they have set for themselves.

One of these formidable problems concerns the orientations of the community toward the mentally disordered and the challenge of successfully reorienting the community favorably toward the mentally ill. This difficulty is illustrated in the effort by John and Elaine Cumming to effect a decided change in the attitudes toward the mentally disordered of a small town in Western Canada.[10] Although they used films, pamphlets, articles in local newspapers, radio programs, and group discussions, after a six-month period they found that no significant change was achieved; all that was manifested was definite hostility toward the interviewers. The Cummings attributed their failure to the anxieties aroused in the community when the inhabitants' established beliefs were upset. Although no extensive generalization can be made from one effort that had its imperfections, it still illustrates that changing attitudes toward the mentally disordered can be difficult.

REFERENCES

1. Gerald Caplan (Ed.), *Prevention of Mental Disorders in Children* (New York: Basic Books, 1961).

2. Leonard J. Duhl, cited in Stephen E. Goldston (Ed.), *Concepts of Community Psychiatry*, Public Health Service Publication No. 1319 (Washington, D.C.: U.S. Government Printing Office, 1965), p. 195.

3. Joint Commission on Mental Illness and Health, *Action for Mental Health* (New York: Basic Books, 1961).

4. Report of the Royal Commission on the Law Relating to Mental Illness and Mental Deficiency (London: Her Majesty's Stationery Office, 1957), p. 31.

5. Caplan, *op. cit.*, p. 48.

6. Beatrice M. Rosen, Anita K. Bahn, and Morton Kramer, "Demographic and Diagnostic Characteristics of Psychiatric Clinic Out-Patients in the U.S.A., 1961," *American Journal of Orthopsychiatry* (April, 1964) *34*(3), 455–456.

7. Joint Commission on Mental Illness and Health, *op. cit.*

8. *The Comprehensive Community Mental Health Center: Concept and Challenge*, Public Health Service Publication No. 1137 (Washington, D.C.: U.S. Government Printing Office, 1964), p. 7.

9. Jurgen Ruesch, "Social Psychiatry: An Overview," *Archives of General Psychiatry* (May, 1965), *12*, 501–504.

10. John Cumming and Elaine Cumming, "Mental Health Education in a Canadian Community," in Benjamin D. Paul (Ed.), *Health, Culture, and Community* (New York: Russell Sage Foundation, 1955).

THE ROLE OF THE FEDERAL GOVERNMENT IN THE PREVENTION AND TREATMENT OF MENTAL DISORDERS

John F. Kennedy

I PROPOSE a national mental health program to assist in the inauguration of a wholly new emphasis and approach to care for the mentally ill. This approach relies primarily upon the new knowledge and new drugs acquired and developed in recent years which make it possible for most of the mentally ill to be successfully and quickly treated in their own communities and returned to a useful place in society.

These breakthroughs have rendered obsolete the traditional methods of treatment which imposed upon the mentally ill a social quarantine, a prolonged or permanent confinement in huge, unhappy mental hospitals where they were out of sight and forgotten. I am not unappreciative of the efforts undertaken by many States to improve conditions in these hospitals, or the dedicated work of many hospital staff members. But their task has been staggering and the results too often dismal as the comprehensive study by the Joint Commission on Mental Illness and Health pointed out in 1961. Some States have at times been forced to crowd five, ten, or even fifteen thousand people into one large understaffed institution. Imposed largely for reasons of economy, such practices were costly in human terms, as well as in a real economic sense. The following statistics are illustrative:

Nearly one-fifth of the 279 State mental institutions are fire and health hazards; three-fourth of them were opened prior to World War I.

Nearly half of the 530,000 patients in our State mental hospitals are in institutions with over 3,000 patients, where individual care and consideration are almost impossible.

Many of these institutions have less than half the professional staff required—with less than 1 psychiatrist for every 360 patients.

Forty-five percent of their inmates have been hospitalized continuously for 10 years or more.

But there are hopeful signs. In recent years the increasing trend toward higher and higher concentrations in these institutions has been

From "Mental Illness and Mental Retardation," a Message from the President of the United States, February 5, 1963, to the House of Representatives, 88th Congress, First Session, Document No. 58.

reversed—by the use of new drugs, by the increasing public awareness of the nature of mental illness, and by a trend toward the provision of community facilities, including psychiatric beds in general hospitals, day care centers, and outpatient psychiatric clinics. Community general hospitals in 1961 treated and discharged as cured more than 200,000 psychiatric patients.

I am convinced that, if we apply our medical knowledge and social insights fully, all but a small portion of the mentally ill can eventually achieve a wholesome and constructive social adjustment. It has been demonstrated that two out of three schizophrenics—our largest category of mentally ill—can be treated and released within 6 months, but under the conditions that prevail today the average stay for schizophrenia is 11 years. In 11 States, by the use of modern techniques, 7 out of every 10 schizophrenia patients admitted were discharged within 9 months. In one instance, where a State hospital deliberately sought an alternative to hospitalization in those patients about to be admitted, it was able to treat successfully in the community 50 percent of them. It is clear that a concerted national attack on mental disorders is now both possible and practical.

If we launch a broad new mental health program now, it will be possible within a decade or two to reduce the number of patients now under custodial care by 50 percent or more. Many more mentally ill can be helped to remain in their own homes without hardship to themselves or their families. Those who are hospitalized can be helped to return to their communities. All but a small proportion can be restored to useful life. We can spare them and their families much of the misery which mental illness now entails. We can save public funds and we can conserve our manpower resources.

1. COMPREHENSIVE COMMUNITY MENTAL HEALTH CENTERS

Central to a new mental health program is comprehensive community care. Merely pouring

Federal funds into a continuation of the outmoded type of institutional care which now prevails would make little difference. We need a new type of health facility, one which will return mental health care to the main stream of American medicine, and at the same time upgrade mental health services. I recommend, therefore, that the Congress (1) authorize grants to the States for the construction of comprehensive community mental health centers, beginning in fiscal year 1965, with the Federal Government providing 45 to 75 percent of the project cost; (2) authorize short-term project grants for the initial staffing costs of comprehensive community mental health centers, with the Federal Government providing up to 75 percent of the cost in the early months, on a gradually declining basis, terminating such support for a project within slightly over 4 years; and (3) to facilitate the preparation of community plans for these new facilities as a necessary preliminary to any construction or staffing assistance, appropriate $4.2 million for planning grants under the National Institute of Mental Health. These planning funds, which would be in addition to a similar amount appropriated for fiscal year 1963, have been included in my proposed 1964 budget.

While the essential concept of the comprehensive community mental health center is new, the separate elements which would be combined in it are presently found in many communities: diagnostic and evaluation, services, emergency psychiatric units, outpatient services, inpatient services, day and night care, foster home care, rehabilitation, consultative services to other community agencies, and mental health information and education.

These centers will focus community resources and provide better community facilities for all aspects of mental health care. Prevention as well as treatment will be a major activity. Located in the patient's own environment and community, the center would make possible a better understanding of his needs, a more cordial atmosphere for his recovery, and a continuum of treatment. As his needs change, the patient could move without delay or difficulty to different services—from diagnosis, to cure, to rehabilitation—without need to transfer to different institutions located in different communities.

A comprehensive community mental health center in receipt of Federal aid may be sponsored through a variety of local organizational arrangements. Construction can follow the successful Hill-Burton pattern, under which the Federal Government matches public or voluntary nonprofit funds.

Ideally, the center could be located at an appropriate community general hospital, many of which already have psychiatric units. In such instances, additional services and facilities could be added—either all at once or in several stages—to fill out the comprehensive program. In some instances, an existing outpatient psychiatric clinic might form the nucleus of such a center, its work expanded and integrated with other services in the community. Centers could also function effectively under a variety of other auspices: as affiliates of State mental hospitals, under State or local governments, or under voluntary nonprofit sponsorship.

Private physicians, including general practitioners, psychiatrists, and other medical specialists, would all be able to participate directly and cooperatively in the work of the center. For the first time, a large proportion of our private practitioners will have the opportunity to treat their patients in a mental health facility served by an auxiliary professional staff that is directly and quickly available for outpatient and inpatient care.

While these centers will be primarily designed to serve the mental health needs of the community, the mentally retarded should not be excluded from these centers if emotional problems exist. They should also offer the services of special therapists and consultation services to parents, school systems, health departments, and other public and private agencies concerned with mental retardation.

The services provided by these centers should be financed in the same way as other medical and hospital costs. At one time, this was not feasible in the case of mental illness, where prognosis almost invariably called for long and permanent courses of treatment. But tranquilizers and new therapeutic methods now permit mental illness to be treated successfully in a very high proportion of cases within relatively short periods of time—weeks or months, rather than years.

Consequently, individual fees for services, individual and group insurance, other third-party payments, voluntary and private contributions, and State and local aid can now better bear the continuing burden of these costs to the individual patient after these services are established. Long-range Federal subsidies for operating costs are neither necessary nor desirable. Nevertheless, because this is a new and expensive undertaking for most communities, temporary Federal aid to help them meet the initial burden of establishing and placing centers in operation is desirable. Such assistance would be stimulatory in purpose, granted on a declining basis and terminated in a few years.

The success of this pattern of local and private financing will depend in large part upon the development of appropriate arrangements for health insurance, particularly in the private sector of our economy. Recent studies have indicated that mental health care—particularly the cost of diagnosis and short-term therapy, which would be major components of service in the new centers—is insurable at a moderate cost.

I have directed the Secretary of Health, Education, and Welfare to explore steps for encouraging and stimulating the expansion of private voluntary health insurance to include mental health care. I have also initiated a review of existing Federal programs, such as the health benefits program for Federal personnel, to determine whether further measures may be necessary and desirable to increase their provisions for mental health care.

These comprehensive community mental health centers should become operational at the earliest feasible date. I recommend that we make a major demonstration effort in the early years of the program to be expanded to all major communities as the necessary manpower and facilities become available.

It is to be hoped that within a few years the combination of increased mental health insurance coverage, added State and local support, and the redirection of State resources from State mental institutions will help achieve our goal of having community-centered mental health services readily accessible to all.

2. IMPROVED CARE IN STATE MENTAL INSTITUTIONS

Until the community mental health center program develops fully, it is imperative that the quality of care in existing State mental institutions be improved. By strengthening their therapeutic services; by becoming open institutions serving their local communities, many such institutions can perform a valuable transitional role. The Federal Government can assist materially by encouraging State mental institutions to undertake intensive demonstration and pilot projects, to improve the quality of care, and to provide inservice training for personnel manning these institutions.

This should be done through special grants for demonstration projects for inpatient care and inservice training. I recommend that $10 million be appropriated for such purposes.

3. RESEARCH AND MANPOWER

Although we embark on a major national action program for mental health, there is still much more we need to know. We must not relax our effort to push back the frontiers of knowledge in basic and applied research into the mental processes, in therapy, and in other phases of research with a bearing upon mental illness. More needs to be done also to translate research findings into improved practices. I recommend an expansion of clinical, laboratory, and field research in mental illness and mental health.

Availability of trained manpower is a major factor in the determination of how fast we can expand our research and expand our new action program in the mental health field. At present manpower shortages exist in virtually all of the key professional and auxiliary personnel categories—psychiatrists, clinical psychologists, social workers, and psychiatric nurses. To achieve success, the current supply of professional manpower in these fields must be sharply increased—from the 45,000 in 1960 to approximately 85,000 by 1970. To help move toward this goal I recommend the appropriation of $66 million for training of personnel, and increase of $17 million over the current fiscal year.

I have, in addition, directed that the Manpower Development and Training Act be used to assist in the training of psychiatric aids and other auxiliary personnel for employment in mental institutions and community centers.

Success of these specialized training programs, however, requires that they be undergirded by basic training programs. It is essential to the success of our new national mental health program that Congress enact legislation authorizing aid to train more physicians and related health personnel. I will discuss this measure at greater length in the message on health which I will send to the Congress shortly.

We as a Nation have long neglected the mentally ill and the mentally retarded. This neglect must end, if our Nation is to live up to its own standards of compassion and dignity and achieve the maximum use of its manpower.

This tradition of neglect must be replaced by forceful and far-reaching programs carried out at all levels of government, by private individuals and by state and local agencies in every part of the Union.

We must act—

to bestow the full benefits of our society on those who suffer from mental disabilities;

to prevent the occurrance of mental illness and mental retardation wherever and whenever possible;

to provide for early diagnosis and continuous and comprehensive care, in the community, of those suffering from these disorders;

to stimulate improvements in the level of care given the mentally disabled in our State and private institutions, and to reorient those programs to a community-centered approach;

to reduce, over a number of years, and by hundreds of thousands, the persons confined to these institutions;

to retain in and return to the community the mentally ill and mentally retarded, and there to restore and revitalize their lives through better health programs and strengthened educational and rehabilitation services; and

to reinforce the will and capacity of our communities to meet these problems in order that the communities, in turn, can reinforce the will and capacity of individuals and individual families.

We must promote—to the best of our ability and by all possible and appropriate means—the mental and physical health of all our citizens.

To achieve these important ends, I urge that the Congress favorably act upon the foregoing recommendations.

COMMUNITY PSYCHIATRY: THE CHANGING ROLE OF THE PSYCHIATRIST

Gerald Caplan

OVER the past few years, community leaders have become increasingly interested in people suffering from mental disorders. This interest has arisen partly because of the need to conserve manpower—especially skilled manpower—in a period of rapid technological development; and partly because of the increasing assumption of responsibility by Government for the personal welfare of citizens. In the United States this interest was strikingly manifested by President Kennedy's message to Congress on February 5, 1963. This was a sequel to the Mental Health Study Act of 1955, which established the Joint Commission on Mental Illness and Mental Health, and it followed the publication of the report of that Commission in 1961.

The special significance of the President's message was that it called upon Congress to take the lead and to shoulder responsibility for the prevention and treatment of mental subnormality and mental disorder throughout the country. This is to be accomplished by providing Federal support for community programs which are planned to combat these ills on a wide scale by means of locally coordinated services. The message expresses dissatisfaction with our past ineffectual attack on mental illness through the treatment of individual patients in mental hospitals. It brushes aside some of the major recommendations of the Joint Commission to improve the mental hospital system as the core of a new program, and replaces these by a proposal to establish a series of interlocking community services and facilities. This emphasized the President's demand for a completely new approach. He advocated a focus on the total population of mentally disordered, and the development of services to identify and satisfy the whole range of their needs, rather than the provision, as in the past, of institutions to which certain of them will be admitted in order to remedy particular aspects of their problems.

The President's call to action must evoke a

response not only among legislators but also among psychiatrists. In the past we have operated within the framework of our professional mandate to treat sick individuals. We have looked to the community to provide us with the institutions and other practical resources to allow us to deploy our psychiatric methods and techniques in order to fulfill our mission. Most of us have not been satisfied with these resources, and some of us have also not been satisfied with the restriction of our professional mandate to the treatment of individual patients. We have felt that unless psychiatrists are entrusted with the task of dealing with all the manifestations of mental ill health wherever they exist in the population, and unless we are provided with the necessary sanction and resources to fulfill this task, our efforts to treat those individual casualties, who are referred to us, must always be relatively ineffective in significantly reducing the total load of mental suffering and disability among community members.

The President's message offers us just such an opportunity. It calls for the establishment of co-ordinated programs of community psychiatry in place of facilities for the treatment of sick individuals.

Community Psychiatry is based upon the acceptance by psychiatrists of responsibility for dealing with all the mentally disordered within the confines of a community. This responsibility focuses upon current cases, but also spreads to potential cases through programs of primary prevention.

The psychiatrist in traditional clinical practice accepts responsibility only for his own patients. He restricts his interest to those individuals who come to his office, clinic, or hospital, and who are involved in a personal professional relationship with him. He usually exercises some selection over those whom he accepts for diagnosis, treatment, or management, and he legitimately narrows his practice to particular diagnostic, age, or socio-economic categories. In contrast, the community psychiatrist accepts responsibility for helping those of all ages and classes, who are suffering from

Reprinted from Stephen E. Goldston (Ed.), *Concepts of Community Psychiatry*, Public Health Service Publication No. 1319 (Washington, D.C.: U.S. Government Printing Office, 1965), pp. 3–15.

disorders of all types, wherever they occur in the community. Some will be defined by themselves or others to be suffering from psychiatric disorders and will have been sent or will have come to a psychiatric facility. Others will be under general medical care because their presenting symptoms were defined as physical illness. Others will be defined as maladjusted in the educational, social, occupational, or religious fields and may be struggling on their own, or they may be receiving help from family and friends, or from the professional or administrative workers in those fields. The extent of the population for which the community psychiatrist feels responsible is difficult to determine accurately because mental disorder is arbitrarily differentiated from other forms of deviance and shades off into variations of acceptable patterns of adjustment behavior. Let us not embark on a lengthy debate about the difficult borderline cases. We can define the mentally unhealthy population for practical purposes as all those who manifest abnormalities of behavior or thinking which most psychiatrists would diagnose as being due to mental subnormality, psychosis, neurosis, psychosomatic disorder, personality disorder, and the other illnesses listed in the *A.P.A. Manual of Mental Disorders*, whether or not the individuals concerned, or others, have already defined these people as mentally disordered.

This emphasizes a fundamental problem which confronts the community psychiatrist. He differs from his traditional colleagues in having to provide services for a large number of people with whom he has had no personal contact, and of whose identity and location he has no initial knowledge. He cannot wait for patients to come to him, because he carries equal responsibility for all those who do not come. A significant part of his job consists of finding out who the mentally disordered are and where they are located in his community, and he must deploy his diagnostic and treatment resources in relation to the total group of sufferers rather than restrict them to the select few who ask or are referred for help.

These difficulties are compounded in those programs which also encompass primary prevention. These programs seek to lower the rate of new cases of mental disorder in a community by reducing harmful influences and by increasing the capacity of individuals to adjust and adapt in a reality based way to their life difficulties. Here the community psychiatrist is dealing with those who are not yet sick. He can concentrate his efforts to some extent by giving highest priority to populations at special risk, either because they are the focus of particular harmful forces or because they are especially vulnerable; but despite this, he clearly must deal with numbers of people of a magnitude which far surpasses anything in the experience of the traditional psychiatrist.

The only legitimate limitation of the population focus of the community psychiatrist is the boundary of his community. This may be geographic or functional, i.e., his community may be located within the local limits of a city, region, or State, or it may be a functional community such as an industrial firm, an army unit, a trade union, or the Peace Corps, whose members are bound together by organizational ties and not necessarily by living in one place. Certain types of community have both a geographic and a functional boundary, like colleges, hospitals, or factories. The population of such communities, although sometimes large, is usually relatively easy to investigate and define— as contrasted with the complex situation in a city or county community—because it has been developed by design in relation to stated missions and goals. It seems plausible that lessons learned by psychiatrists in these simpler communities might apply to the more complex ones. Before we proceed to our discussion of the major problems which confront the psychiatrist who accepts responsibility for the community psychiatric program of a city, county, or State, it may be helpful to review briefly some of the experience of psychiatrists working in institutions such as colleges or factories.

The history[1] of college and industrial psychiatric programs is often characterized by a succession of phases. In the beginning it is usual for the psychiatrist to be asked to diagnose and either to treat, or to refer for treatment, individual students or workers whose disordered behavior has aroused attention. The psychiatrist makes use of his traditional methods and skills, and his practice has few special characteristics apart from the more formal structuring of the referral and dispositional channels. Soon, however, the psychiatrist begins to focus more than usual on the social forces and environmental pressures impinging on his patients, because in the relatively closed system of the institution these are more easily visible to him than in the open community. He begins to learn about the conditions of work in different departments, and he finds it easier than in outside practice to identify etiological factors in the patient's current environment. This has more than diagnostic significance. The psychiatrist begins to include in his treatment plan the active manipulation of the organizational aspect of his patient's life. This is aided by his building up collaborative relationships with key figures in the administrative hierarchy of the organization.

The next phase is characterized by the psychiatrist becoming interested in common elements, whether etiological or clinical, among patients coming from certain departments. He becomes sensitive to variations in the numbers of cases referred at different times, and he begins to search for changes in the social and physical milieu of the units of the organization, to which he ascribes pathogenic significance, and which he tries to modify in the interests of groups of his patients.

From this, it is a short step to starting a continuing survey of the flow of patients of varying categories from different units in the organization. He then develops an interest in finding some way of extending the validity of these records by identifying those other disturbed people who do not come to his clinic because of their own low motivation or because their administrators do not refer them. In an organization, such as a factory, which keeps such records of individual performance as quantitative and qualitative productivity figures, punctuality, absenteeism, sick leave, and the like, the psychiatrist soon finds that many criteria are available to him, in addition to the clinical manifestations of referred patients, if he wishes to chart variations in individual performance which are probably related to mental disorder.

By now, it will be seen that the psychiatrist has extended his focus beyond the population of his current patient load. He has begun to investigate the environment of his organization not only as it influences his present patients but also as it may affect now and in the future those disordered people whom he is not seeing.

This widening of focus will probably by now also have been influenced by requests from the administrators of the organization for his help in handling problems of selection and personnel placement and promotion. If he accedes to these requests, he will find that he is using his clinical skills and his knowledge of personality and human relations and needs not only to deal with persons suspected of mental disorder, but also to predict the fitness of healthy persons to deal effectively with particular situations without endangering their mental health. He will also be exercising some influence upon the nature of the population in the organization, and hopefully he will be reducing the risk of mental disorder by excluding vulnerable candidates and by preventing the fitting of round pegs into square holes.

At this stage, if not before, the psychiatrist will be facing the fundamental problem of how best to deploy his own resources, and those of the assistants who have probably been added to his unit as the demands for his services have increased. Although the range of his interests has broadened, his basic concern still remains the reduction of suffering and disability among the mentally disordered in the organization. His awareness of their numbers and condition has increased, as has also his understanding of the environmental forces inimical or conducive to their welfare.

One conclusion should be clear to him by this time. The problem is too big to handle on the traditional basis of the diagnosis and treatment of individuals. No organization can afford to maintain a psychiatric staff big enough to diagnose and treat adequately each of its members who is mentally disturbed. Even with the most effective selection system to screen out disturbed or potentially disturbed candidates for admission, the expectable environmental stresses of any organization, added to the spontaneous incidence of unpredictable disturbances of endogenous or extra-organizational origin, will result in too many patients for such an approach.

If the problem is dealt with by reducing referrals or building waiting lists for intake or treatment, suffering will continue and the productivity of disordered individuals will deteriorate, and also of those other members of the organization who are dependent upon them for support or for the flow of materials and services. Referral to outside treatment resources is no way out, because most private and community agencies are already full, or soon would be if the organization radically increased its volume of referrals. Apart from humanitarian and administrative considerations, the problem cannot be dealt with by discharging a major portion of the sufferers from the organization, because many of them in industry are likely to be skilled employees who are in scarce supply, or in college they are talented students who, apart from their mental difficulties, are of great promise.

This apparent impasse in planning the deployment of psychiatric resources is the turning point in the development of the program. Some psychiatrists are so wedded to their traditional individual-patient diagnosis and treatment approach that they see no way out. Their machine gets clogged up with increasing numbers of patients who are referred from all sides by administrators who have become alerted to problems of mental disorder and who have got to know the psychiatrists and to respect them. At the same time the psychiatrists are exposed to increasing demands for nonclinical help in selection, in personnel management, and in counseling administrators. Lengthening the waiting lists, and interrupting intake—those easy defense mechanisms of psychiatrists in the open community—may be tried, but they lead to the rapid build-up of frustration and resentment in the relatively closed community of an organization. In this setting the visibility of the psychiatrist is greater, as is also the amount of control over him. He may be able to extricate himself by retracing his steps and progressively walling himself off, cutting down his contacts, and narrowing his focus. The alternative is to abandon ship!

The history of psychiatric programs in colleges and industries brings to our attention some psychiatrists who did not reach this sorry state because they interrupted their development at an earlier stage, but also many who have resolved this crisis, or even circumvented it earlier, by a radical shift in orientation which has carried them onto a different plane of professional functioning. These psychiatrists no longer base their programs on the traditional assumption that mental disorder, like any illness, should if at all possible be diagnosed and treated by a medical specialist and on the corollary assumption that a mentally disordered individual who is not personally treated by a psychiatrist is likely to suffer more intensely and for a longer period than if he were. Instead, they begin to operate on the assumption that mental disorder is often caused or aggravated by unhealthy forms of life adjustment, and that when it occurs there are many possibilities available to the sufferer, and the social network of which he is part, to modify their mutual relationships so that a healthier equilibrium will be obtained, which in turn will have a beneficial effect on the disorder.

In a community, a variety of regularly occurring mechanisms exist which may stimulate all concerned in such instances to change the pattern of their relationships. These include social pressures brought into play by alterations in the smooth functioning of the work or social situation. They include the actions of administrators who try to modify the organizational life to produce a better fit between the sufferer and others in order to improve output. They include informal patterns of support by peers, and the operations of a variety of caregiving professionals—personnel and health workers inside the organization, and clergymen, social workers, and counselors in the outside community. Among all these influences the psychiatrist occupies an important position. He has a special contribution to make, which can often be helpful. But he is one among many, and often one or more of the other possibilities might produce as good or better results than if his aid were involved.

The traditional assumptions drive the psychiatrist to see all sufferers personally because he feels that any alternative is second best or even harmful. The second assumption leads to a more leisurely survey of the possibilities. The psychiatrist realizes that as one of the many helpful forces in the community he should evaluate the others and then decide in accordance with each set of circumstances the amount of profit to be gained by his intervention, and whether this should take the form of personal interaction with the sufferer or of supporting the helpful influence of other elements in the system, or of some combination of these. The predicted profit can then be related to the outlay of effort. Since this approach does not necessarily involve a contractual arrangement with the sufferer, whose case may be considered on the basis of information supplied by others, the psychiatrist is free to deploy his efforts in such a way as to benefit the largest number of sufferers in the organization, rather than being forced to deal in a preordained way with each successive case.

From this derives the paradox that the psychiatrist who takes the traditional individual-patient point of view affects less patients than the other and yet is always pressed for time. He is at the mercy of the chance nature of his patient flow. He feels that what he has to do is determined by the number and type of the patients he happens to see. In contrast, the second psychiatrist controls his own operations in the light of explicit judgments of the whole field of forces. He is therefore able to operate at maximum efficiency by choosing the most favorable and opportune moments for his interventions and by utilizing available leverage points so that other helpers in the field of forces multiply his own efforts. This psychiatrist does not feel pressed for time because in his planning he is constantly taking into account the amount of his available resources of time and energy, and the proportions to be deployed in relation to the priority of alternative goals.

His methods include individual diagnostic and treatment contact with certain types of case, and in addition, a whole range of indirect methods which foster the supportive or remedial contributions of the other caregiving persons and services of the institution. The indirect methods consist mainly in offering individual and group consultation to administrators and caregivers on how best to deal with a person currently in crisis or showing signs of disorder. If successful, such consultation has a carryover which will enable similar cases to be handled in the future without having to invoke the aid of the psychiatrist. The effect of this is that gradually more and more cases are handled within the social system of the organization without referral and even without consultation.

The final step for the industrial and college psychiatrist is that he becomes interested in what Dr. O'Dwyer the Principal Medical Adviser of Unilever has called "the health of the firm." By this he means the quality of its organization which affects the well-being of its component parts and ultimately the morale and the health of its workers. The psychiatrist is called in by the administrators for consultation not only in respect to the management of the malfunctioning of an individual or a group of workers, but also in regard to any policy issue which may significantly affect the interrelationships of groups and individuals. Eventually, those who establish the policies which govern the entire structure and functioning of the organization delay major decisions until he has given his views on the probable repercussions of their actions on the mental health of their workers. The administrators may or may not accept his advice, but in any case they take into account the mental health implications of different courses of action before deciding. If their plan involves a hazard for certain individuals and groups they may build into it some additional provisions to counteract the emotional burden or to compensate for it.

At this stage of becoming an adviser on general institutional action, the psychiatrist seems furthest away from his traditional role of diagnosing and treating individual patients, and yet he is now in the position to exercise the most potent preventive and remedial influence on large numbers of actual or potential sufferers among the firm's members. Those psychiatrists who have achieved this role have found that their traditional clinical knowledge and skills, although necessary, are far from sufficient in equiping them to deal effectively with the problems which confront them. The situation of the industrial or college psychiatrist who has reached this level of functioning may help us to understand the community psychiatrist of the future, who may achieve a comparable role in a city or State, and who may be invested with similar responsibilities and offered similar opportunities and challenges. In considering his training needs and the problems he will face, we may perhaps rely on some of the issues already raised, and augment these from the growing experience of those programs in large geographic communities where the collaboration of enlightened citizen leaders and pioneering psychiatrists has produced developments which have progressed through somewhat analogous phases.

The first problem which confronts the community psychiatrist, who wishes to guide his professional operations in a consistent and meaningful way, is the need for new theoretical models. The theoretical systems of psychiatry, psychology, psychodynamics, psychopathology, psychoanalysis, etc., which help him diagnose and treat an individual patient, are still useful when he faces the problems of dealing with many such patients, although he may need to change his focus in order to cope with the large numbers involved. In addition, he requires some theoretical framework for understanding the community in which both he and his patients operate. He also needs a new set of ideas within which to structure and evaluate his own professional role, because this develops additional dimensions in relation to his new responsibilities and opportunities.

A theoretical model is a pattern of organizing our information about a topic in such a way that it can be understood in relation to our professional situation and goals. It provides us with a chart which guides our expectations and our factfinding and which indicates probable lines of undesirable development that help us plan our preventive and remedial action. In this way, our traditional psychiatric models help us understand the manifestations of an individual's mental disorder, chart its probable course, and choose an appropriate form of treatment for him. This takes place within a setting in which he has invoked our medical aid, and in which we accept him as our patient, whose idiosyncratic condition and history we investigate against a background of our general ideas about mental functioning and about the regularly occurring categories of mental disorders and the methods of therapy for dealing with them.

To supplement such a model, the community psychiatrist needs a chart which emphasizes not the individual peculiarities of a single patient, but broad issues of mental disorder and its causation which apply to populations of patients. His task is to investigate widely occurring harmful factors and their pathological consequences, and also to plan programs of intervention which will significantly affect many people not only by his direct interaction with them, but also indirectly through the mediation of other caregivers and by altering social and cultural influences which affect them. He needs, as it were, a small-scale chart of a region rather than a large-scale map of a small area. The lower magnification will blur individual details, but this is exactly what will help him to develop his communitywide picture.

Elsewhere,[2] I have described such a model for understanding communitywide influences on mental health and mental disorder. This is based upon emphasizing and refining a particular dimension of our generally accepted psychiatric ideas. The model uses a long-term focus on the adequacy of the biopsychosocial supplies in a community and the effects of variation in supplies on the mental health of the population; and a short-term focus on the significance for mental health of the nature of the adjustment of members of the community to developmental and accidental life crises. The model guides the psychiatrist in appraising the factors in his community which are conducive or inimical to the mental health of its population, and also suggests leverage points for types of remedial intervention which are likely to have widespread effects.

Some of us have found this model, especially its short-term focus on life-crisis, quite useful in helping us chart a consistent course through the complexities of planning community programs. Much still needs to be done in further refining it. Meanwhile, it is desirable that other workers develop alternative models, so that the advantages of each can be compared, and so that we may eventually have as effective a set of guides for the assessment and remedy of communitywide influences on the mental health of populations as we now have for the diagnosis and treatment of sick individuals.

There need be no incompatibility between the community models and the individual models. They should complement each other, so that the community psychiatrist can use each in its appropriate place, according to whether he is focusing his attention on a particular individual or on a population.

The second topic which demands a new model is the nature of the community. The psychiatrist needs a chart which will guide his appraisal of the forces which influence community members, institutions, and services. A great deal has been written by social scientists about the structure and functioning of communities. Each branch of social science has developed its own models, which order the data with which it commonly deals in accordance with its goals and methods, and with the questions which interest its members. Sociology, anthropology, social psychology, political science, law, and economics each have their distinctive models. Community models have also been developed by workers in the various fields of social action, such as social work, adult education, public administration, politics, and public health. None of these models is completely adequate for community psychiatry, for which they were not designed, but it should be possible for the community psychiatrist to use them in developing a model of community structure and functioning to suit his own needs. Many of the existing models include elements which seem valuable, such as the notion of the community as a social system comprising interrelated and interpenetrating subsystems, concepts of status and role, power and communication networks, patterns of leadership, reference groups, varieties of institutions and organizations, systematic concepts of culture and values, ways of analyzing social change and social action, and the like. We are still, however, in the early stages of welding such concepts together with others drawn from our own profession in order to build a coherent chart which clarifies those particular aspects of community life in which we are interested.

This model should guide us in the collection and interpretation of data on the reverberating relationships among individuals, families, formal and informal groups, organizations, and institutions within the community and outside it, which are conducive to mental disorder, and which affect significantly our efforts to develop and maintain our psychiatric programs. The model should also guide us in gearing our program to the operations of other caregiving agencies and professionals in the health, welfare, educational and religious fields, and also to relevant formal and informal units in the social, political, and economic life of the community. As Leonard Duhl has emphasized,[3] we are faced by an extremely complicated reciprocal relationship among a multitude of factors. Our model must take account of this complexity, but we would like it to provide us with a practical guide for thought and action analogous to the personality system model which guides us in exploring and handling the complexities of individual behavior.

The third area in which the community psychiatrist needs new guidelines is that of his professional role. As we have already seen in industrial and college settings, this is likely to be in a state of change as new opportunities present themselves, and as new demands are successively made upon him. It seems clear that the role model of classical psychiatry—namely the physician who relates to individual patients—can represent no more than one segment of his community functioning. As usual when conditions change and there is a need for a development in concepts, some people have tried to extrapolate the old model in dealing with the changed circumstances, instead of working out a new model. Thus, they have suggested that the community psychiatrist retain the connotations of physician, and that we conceive of his patient as being not an individual but the community. Rapoport has given a wry twist to this oversimplification by calling his recent book on therapeutic communities, *Community as Doctor*.[4] Both variations are nice-sounding catch phrases, but they do not help us much in providing a role model for the community psychiatrist because their oversimplification distorts a complicated situation. This often happens when a model appropriate to one level is extrapolated to a level of greater complexity. The community is not a person and can be neither a patient nor a doctor. The psychiatrist, whose relationship with a patient is easily understood by calling him a doctor, must find some other way of understanding and explaining to others the appropriate patterns of his behavior in his community operations.

One difficulty in developing a valid way of defining conceptually the role of community psychiatrist is that the role itself is both new and changing. Nobody knows to what extent it will continue to change in the relatively near future. Moreover, the psychiatrist in a highly developed program continues to retain functions, and therefore role components, which were developed in previous phases. When he has become a consultant to executives on major policy he probably continues to offer consultation to management on modification of pathogenic situations in certain departments, to consult with foremen on methods of handling particular individuals who are emotionally disturbed, and to diagnose and treat patients. As a staff worker, he may offer advice to the personnel department on its recruitment and selection policies, and concurrently he may be operating as a line worker in interviewing applicants for key jobs. He will also probably be operating as an administrative officer of the organization in managing his own unit and in hiring and firing his subordinates, and he will be competing with other units for what he considers his fair share of the budgetary and other resources of the organization.

From this it appears that the development of an appropriate model for the role of community psychiatrist demands the inclusion of a number of components which are likely to be increased with the passage of time, the growth of his program, and the development of the field as a whole. These components may include physician to patients, counselor to people with problems of adjustment, researcher of community processes, consultant to caregivers and administrators in relation to mentally disturbed clients or subordinates, educator to professionals and the public on mental health matters, administrator of a community agency, consultant to administrators and legislators on mental health aspects of government and social policy, etc.

The development of such a model is far from being a mere academic exercise. It will have important consequences for the guidance of the psychiatrist's professional operations, since it will prescribe modifications in behavior which are appropriate to the various situations that evoke different role components; for instance as a doctor relating to a patient, he is in a position of superior power; as a consultant to a fellow professional he must behave in an egalitarian manner; and as the head of a new community agency trying to establish his position, he is a community servant, who will only by raised by others to a position of equality after he had proved his competence and trustworthiness. A community psychiatrist who did not differentiate these situations and their congruent role components, and who, for instance, related to a colleague, such as a teacher or public health nurse, as though he were a doctor dealing with a patient, would soon come to grief.

The model for the role of community psychiatrist must provide guidance for the operations to be undertaken by him in establishing his role. Clinical psychiatry has inherited hundreds of years of medical tradition in evolving a set of role expectations for its doctors and patients. A clinical psychiatrist relies upon this without even thinking about it. When he moves into community work he must pay explicit attention to the explorations and negotiations with others which are essential in working out appropriate patterns of complementary behavior. This is likely to be rendered more difficult by the tendency on both sides to maintain incongruous expectations derived from the traditional psychiatrist-patient situation. The psychiatrist must therefore be alert to the wishes and fears of fellow professionals and community leaders that he will treat them like patients and uncover their unacceptable fantasies. He must also control his own operations so that while retaining his clinically derived sensitivities and insights into unconscious processes, he interacts with others on the basis of an egalitarian respect for their privacy and adult status, and in a manner which is in keeping with the generally accepted usage of community participation.

The conceptualization of the role of the community psychiatrist must include consideration of his fundamental goals. These must be differentiated from the traditional goals of clinical psychiatry, which they resemble, but from which they differ in important respects. Clinical psychiatrists in this country, especially those with psychoanalytic training, often feel that their fundamental goal is to help their patients alter their personality structure. The more radical the improvement in personality, the more satisfied is the psychiatrist with his psychotherapeutic efforts. The end point of such a process is hard to determine on objective grounds, and in practice the psychiatrist tries to deploy as much treatment effort and time for each patient as seems to lead to continued improvement. Within the framework of the responsibility of the psychiatrist for his individual patients this is legitimate. The number of patients he treats is determined by the character of their disturbance and by his own skill. His merit is manifested not by this number, but by the quality of the therapeutic results in those he treats.

In contrast, the goal of the community psychiatrist is a significant reduction in the number of sufferers and in the amount of disability and defect in the population. The evaluation of his professional efforts must be in these terms. To such a psychiatrist, increasing the amount of personality change in a particular patient is not of supreme importance. His goal is rather to encourage the mentally disturbed in his community, who are faltering or have fallen by the wayside, to stand on their own feet with the support of their social networks, so that they may once more continue their active struggle with the realities of their life situations. This does not mean persuading them to accept their symptoms, but helping them confront the predicaments from which their symptoms represented an escape. In certain cases this may lead to personality modifications. In others, this change will not occur. Instead, there will be a modification of the balance of internal and external forces so that alternative behavior becomes possible. In any case, the community goal demands the smallest possible intervention in each instance, consonant with getting the sufferer back onto the track of adjustment and adaptation in the world of reality.

For the community psychiatrist, numbers are a continual preoccupation, and his concept of his role leads him to concern himself with developing ways of choosing those targets for his professional efforts and those ways of working which will ensure the maximum effect on the community statistic of disorder, disability, and defect. My own analysis of this question has led me to the conclusion that this goal can best be achieved if the psychiatrist approaches all his tasks with a preventive orientation. This is in line with the role model developed by the public health professions, and is based upon the belief that whenever prevention is possible, it is more economic than remedial effort. Primary prevention of mental disorder is, however, often not possible, and cases of mental disorder will always occur in the community. Here again, I believe that economy of effort demands that the treatment and rehabilitation of these cases be planned in terms of the prevention of future disability and defect rather than in terms of the remedy of current ills. The community psychiatrist should approach all his tasks with a preventive orientation. His preventive work at all levels will be improved by an increased understanding not only of the causes of mental disorder, but also of the pathways and influence which lead to mental health. This will allow him to swing the balance in a healthy direction by interventions that support the positive forces.

Such an approach will involve the psychiatrist in explorations which take him far from his traditional clinical haunts. The model of his role must therefore include guidance on how to determine realistically the defined limits of his expertness when he expands his interests to such fields as education, religion, politics, and the like, in which other professions have built up a store of expert knowledge which is superior to his own.

Having developed these charts to guide his operations, the psychiatrist must equip himself with the theoretical and practical tools to deal with the new problems he encounters in the community. There are three major areas of new knowledge and skill which are relevant: epidemiology, biostatistics, and community psychiatric practice.

Both epidemiology and biostatistics are well established public health specialties. They were originally developed to deal with epidemics caused by the infectious diseases, and in recent years their techniques have been further refined to investigate the causative influences of non-infectious and chronic diseases in a community. Their methods can be applied to our field without much modification.

Community psychiatric practice is based in the main on public health practice, which is a body of knowledge and skills developed by public health workers to enable them to plan and carry our organized programs for the control of illness in a population. Over the past few years a number of psychiatrists, working in schools of public health and in State and local health departments, have modified public health theories and practices for application to the special problems of the mental disorders.

We may divide community psychiatric practice into four areas: (*a*) the theory and practice of preventive psychiatry, which is our basic platform, and which derives its fundamental concepts of primary, secondary, and tertiary prevention from public health; (*b*) planning, which deals with ways of developing a rational organizational system at Federal, State, and local levels for achieving the goals of community psychiatry under conditions of scarcity of resources; (*c*) the organization and administration of community programs, which includes methods for building relationships with community representatives and agencies in establishing and maintaining psychiatric programs; (*d*) mental health consultation, which is a method whereby mental health specialists support the efforts of other professionals in promoting mental health, reducing the incidence and prevalence of mental disorders, and combating residual defect.

A basic issue which today confronts many psychiatric educators is that they must build up their own community psychiatric knowledge and skills while they are simultaneously trying to communicate these to their students. This implies that an educational program must be organized within a framework of pioneering practice. It must also be connected with ongoing research, because none of the previously mentioned subject areas can be adequately developed without systematic research. The latter itself introduces significant new problems due to the inherent difficulties of using complex and changing community situations as a research field. The interdigitation of education, practice, and research has obvious value to the student. In a rapidly developing field, where our ignorance is great, it stimulates his creative activity and reduces the risk of his becoming a technician or a conforming disciple. But these three processes make conflicting demands in regard to goal priorities and rhythms of action; and educators in this setting must therefore face the inevitability of strain.

Strain is also likely because many psychiatric educators do not have a well worked out community orientation. The change from an individual-patient focus is no mere cognitive matter which they can achieve by reading the literature and attending meetings. It involves a shift in values and an alteration in professional identity. Happily, there are likely to be many among the most senior educators for whom this broadening of professional identity will be relatively simple. As heads of departments they have much experience in administration and have probably developed skill in building and maintaining relationships within the university and in the outside community with a variety of individuals, groups, and institutions. They have also probably acted as consultants in many different settings. This range of activities and its associated skills has in the past often not been labeled "community psychiatry," but has been a nonformalized part of a professor's role, or has been considered an aspect of administration—a subject which professors are supposed to know, even though they have rarely received systematic training in it. However it has previously been defined, this knowledge is available to be tapped by the new opportunities . . .

NOTES

1. This section has been influenced by recent discussions with Harold Bridger of the Tavistock Institute of Human Relations in London and with Dr. J. J. O'Dwyer, Principal Medical Adviser of Unilever, Ltd.

2. *Principles of Preventive Psychiatry*, Gerald Caplan. Basic Books, New York, 1964.

3. "Conception of Community Medicine and Health—A Background for Training in Comprehensive Community Psychiatry." Leonard J. Duhl, Apr. 24, 1963. Mimeographed paper.

4. *Community as Doctor*, Robert N. Rapoport. Tavistock, London, 1960.

AN OUTLINE FOR COMMUNITY MENTAL HEALTH RESEARCH

Anita K. Bahn

DURING the last several years, with the leadership of key professional persons in the State, Maryland has been a laboratory for the prototype development of an automated research psychiatric case register. Interest in the establishment of community-based mental health services suggests that it is now timely to expand this research laboratory in two additional directions. There is need for a population survey research mechanism to prepare for, and assist in, evaluating the community service programs; and there is need to supplement the psychiatric case register with data from non-psychiatric agencies in order to provide a more complete and earlier identification of psychosocial problems. Because of its success with the psychiatric case register, the professional community of Maryland is in an excellent position to take these next steps.

For purposes of discussion of Maryland's expanded research needs, this working paper presents a conceptual model of a comprehensive community mental health research program. The program is essentially two-pronged, utilizing: (1) periodic surveys of the demographic, mental health and attitudinal characteristics of the community population, and (2) agency reports on patients which have been collated into longitudinal records through a psychiatric or parapsychiatric case register. These two facets of complementary community research—population studies and case register studies—can enrich and reinforce each other and provide the substrata for social psychiatric and epidemiologic investigations of considerable depth.

COMMUNITY POPULATION STUDIES

In order to plan for efficient use of scarce mental health manpower, evaluate programs, and conduct epidemiologic investigations, certain parameters with respect to the community population are needed on a current basis. These parameters may be classified by the nature of the data into three groups: demographic and socio-

Reprinted from *Community Mental Health Journal* (Spring, 1965), *1* (1), 23–28.

cultural dimensions, mental health status and social role functioning, and attitudes and response to mental illness and mental health services.

Demographic, Social, and Cultural Characteristics

The first and most basic description of the population relates to its biosocial and ecological attributes, such as: age, sex, race, religion, and ethnic origin; marital status, household composition, type of household head; socioeconomic level indices such as education, occupation, family income; social and geographic mobility and geographic origin; and housing characteristics, such as extent of overcrowding, owner occupied or rented home, neighborhood density.

These data describe in quantitative terms the social, cultural, and ethnic milieu of the population to which service will be given. For example, how many immigrants are there to the area each year, what are their characteristics, and where do they come from? How many elderly persons are living alone? How many children live with only one parent? These statistics provide pertinent information on some of the life situations with which individuals are coping. Furthermore, these data provide the correlate factors for studying mental illness and mental health functioning in the population, and for investigating differential rates of admission to patient care for various subcultural groups.

While most of these items are collected decennially by the U.S. Census Bureau on a total or sample basis, the dynamics of the population such as migration, birth, marriage, divorce, and death necessitates intercensal updating through sample surveys.

Mental Health Status and Social Role Functioning

Control measures directed toward the reduction of disability in the population through educational, preventive, treatment, and rehabilitative measures require for objective evaluation periodic measurement of the extent of disability in the population (Kramer, 1961). Ideally, such measurements should be taken before and after the community service program has been initiated, and for both the target and appropriate control populations.

A fundamental dimension of interest about the community, therefore, is its prevalence and incidence of mental illness whether or not brought to the attention of professional persons. However, periodic psychiatric examinations of samples of the population in their home to collect data on mental status is not feasible for most communities today because of the shortage of psychiatrists. An additional difficulty is that persons who are not "in crisis" or are not referred for help may be reluctant to participate in a psychiatric home examination or to come to a screening center for such purpose. We know also that in general health surveys conducted in the home, a direct question of the type, "Do you have a chronic nervous condition or a mental illness?", is likely to elicit considerable understatement on the extent of mental illness (Bahn, 1959).

Fortunately in recent years, sociological survey research has greatly increased the potential of home interviewing methods. Through interviews with both structured and indirect (projective) questions, and subsequent application of scaling techniques, the adequacy of individuals in the performance of their social roles can be assessed and the presence or absence of psycho-physiological symptoms estimated. Validated symptom lists and stress scores, such as those used in the Midtown Manhattan Study (Srole, 1962), have provided useful indicators of the level of dysfunctioning in school, work situations, marital and other social relations due to or associated with mental illness. Furthermore, since such interviews can be conducted by trained nonprofessional interviewers, the study of large samples of persons is possible. "Blind" interviews of both patients and nonpatients can assist in the valuation of the interviewing protocol. Data on dysfunctioning collected by survey instruments will not be etiologically precise. Also they may be unsuitable for synthesis into global mental health ratings. Nevertheless, the specific measurements of dysfunctioning—if carefully interpreted—can be of direct interest to control programs and epidemiology. Furthermore, comparisons of these data with information available from a psychiatric case register can yield clues as to the selectivity of the patient population.

Community Perception and Attitudes

The ability to recognize overt signs and symptoms of mental illness in oneself or others, and to seek and accept diagnosis and treatment when indicated, are selective factors which influence the specific pathways to care. Such perceptions affect the rate at which persons enter medical psychiatric channels, for example, as compared with the socio-legal or protective channels—or do not come to the attention of any agency. Differences in the rates of psychiatric care, such as between rural and urban areas, may be due as much to differences in the degree of recognition of mental illness and to modes of dealing with it, as to variation in the extent of disability in the population or to variation in treatment resources. It has been shown also that tolerance and attitudes to deviant behavior may affect the severity of symptoms and the requirements for hospitalization or rehospitalization (Clausen, 1959).

Perception and attitude studies are necessary because those areas with the highest degree of mental disturbance may be characterized by a lesser or greater degree of recognition of signs and symptoms of mental illness than other areas. To some extent, the responsiveness to services possibly might be imputed from other data such as a comparison of psychiatric rates with rates of other psychosocial disturbance and with availability of resources. However, direct attitude studies of the population could help pin-point more precisely why some ill persons become patients and others do not.

This type of research is perhaps the most difficult to validate because it involves motivational aspects. Also putative attitudes and perceptions must be translated to *in vivo* response; these may not be the same. Nevertheless, a fundamental question is: "How do sociocultural modes of defining and dealing with the forms of individual psychiatric disturbance influence the course and consequences of the disease?" (Clausen, 1959). Thus we might restate our goal as that of measuring group response through population research, and tailoring community mental health service programs accordingly (Suchman, 1964).

It is also possible that attitude research can provide the basis for specific goal-oriented mental health education programs. Examples are: programs designed to promote the use of specific mental health facilities by specific population groups such as those of low-income, or to promote acceptance by labor and industry of former hospital patients (Halpert, 1964).

All three dimensions about the community population—demographic and sociocultural data, mental health status and social role functioning, and attitudinal information—would be used conjointly.

CASE REGISTER PATIENT STUDIES

Systematic studies on the characteristics of the psychiatric patient population, the services received, and prognoses should be an integral part of community psychiatric research. Patient studies cannot be carried out efficiently, however, without a case register which links all reports for the same person into cumulative records on psychiatric careers. Such records, if properly maintained, can provide information on long range outcome of treatment and remissions or exacerbations which are brought to the attention of a psychiatric facility. In addition, from a psychiatric case register it is possible to obtain unduplicated accounts of patients treated during any time period (Bahn, Gorwitz, Klee, Kramer, Tuerk, 1965) to identify cases entering psychiatric care for the first time, and to observe flow of patients between facilities. Furthermore, the register can provide a sampling frame for epidemiologic studies of patients; and can be matched with records of various population groups—such as court cases and alcoholics—for exchange of research information.

The various routine and special investigations that can be carried out from case register material have been described elsewhere, particularly in reference to the Maryland Psychiatric Case Register (Gorwitz, Bahn, Chandler, and Martin, 1963; Bahn, 1964). Here, I would like to discuss two areas of concern: the relation of psychiatric case register data to community population survey research and to broader psychosocial parameters.

Relation to Population Research

In the past, community mental health studies, such as in Midtown Manhattan, have made relatively little use of psychiatric patient data. In part, this may be because in such studies patient data were collected for a limited time period such as one year, and the population samples also were relatively small. Valuable retrospective and prospective investigation can be carried out, however, through the matching of population survey data with psychiatric case register material which extends over a long period of time.

We are interested, for example, in answers to such questions as: Are persons rated as with "considerable dysfunctioning" by scaling of interview data more likely than other persons to have received recent psychiatric treatment? Can persons with incipient mental disorder, as evidenced by a subsequent higher risk of entering a psychiatric facility, be detected through home interview methods? Can the present level of functioning of former mental health patients be determined routinely as part of ongoing population survey research? Can assessment of role adequacy as determined by a home interview be validated through subsequent entrance into treatment? Thus, a series of cross validation studies and hypotheses building can be developed through the interplay of these two independent sources of information: the sociologic home interview and the longitudinal case record.

Relation to Psychosocial Parameters

In Maryland—through the excellent cooperation of the psychiatric agencies in the State and nearby District of Columbia facilities—patient data from public and private psychiatric hospitals, general hospitals with psychiatric beds and outpatient clinics are routinely obtained and collated into a psychiatric case register. An obvious next step in community research is the relation of the load of psychiatric patients to the larger parameter of persons with psychosocial or behavior disorders brought to the attention of agencies such as courts, police, welfare departments. It might be hypothesized, for example, that in certain ecological areas of the city the rate of disordered behavior will be higher but the psychiatric treatment rate will be lower than in other areas. Also for certain subcultural groups of the population, the earliest case identification will be made by non-psychiatric agencies concerned with social behavior problems.

It would be desirable to incorporate pertinent psychosocial data from appropriate caretaker community agencies into the psychiatric case register on a routine basis, but the methodology for such register "extension" is far from developed. What types of agencies on facilities should report to a para-psychiatric case register? What types of clients in such caseloads and what information about them can be reported? There is need for a classification of the psychosocial disorders that would permit comparable community-wide data collection from the diverse agencies involved in psychosocial intervention (Bahn, 1965).

Some methodological studies on this problem have been initiated. A committee of the American Orthopsychiatric Association is attempting to begin the development of a standard classification of psychosocial disorders. A study is being considered with the Baltimore Council of Health and Welfare agencies to obtain, for a sample time period, case data from selected social agencies whose primary purpose is to provide services in response to behavioral problems. Included would be correctional services for social control of disorderly behavior, such as delinquency. Psychosocial disorder rates will be computed by census tract and compared with other psychiatric, health and ecological tract data. Also the cases will be matched to the psychiatric case register on both a retrospective and prospective basis. However, the study will be primarily exploratory and methodological. Eventually it may be possible to provide for the inclusion of this broader psychosocial information in the register on a routine basis, thus enriching both the case register and the population studies.

DISCUSSION

The Maryland psychiatric case register has been in operation now for three years. The routine aspects of data collection, and of register maintenance, updating and data retrieval using computer methods have been largely solved (Phillips, Gorwitz and Bahn, 1962). An initial series of annual model tables have been developed and a number of special analyses planned. The exploration of the longitudinal information that is accruing on patients has just begun. Nevertheless, it would seem timely to begin now to develop plans for register extension to para-psychiatric dimensions on at least a sample basis, and for initiating collateral population survey research. Thus, the framework would be laid for a firm matrix of integrated social psychiatric studies.

The interest and excellent relations of the two principal universities and the state and local agencies in Maryland prophesies the eventual success of a cooperative research laboratory of the type outlined. This kind of intensive field laboratory is needed for research training in community psychiatry and for planning for community health service areas. Several one-time population studies have already been carried out in Maryland: for example, the Eastern Health District Studies of Lemkau, Tietze and Cooper (1941, 1942, 1943) in 1936; the study of mental illness and other chronic disability by the Commission on Chronic Illness (1957) in 1952; and the opinion and attitude survey of Lemkau and Crocetti (1962) in 1960 and of Meyer (1964) more recently. In addition a continuous home interview health survey has been conducted during the last several years by the Baltimore City Health Department in connection with the generalized public health nursing program.

Perhaps we are now ready to plan for a continuing total community study of mental illness based on case finding methods applied to the general population, and for data collection from other community agencies—both social and private—that are concerned with psychosocial disorders. Despite methodological and definitional problems and other difficulties, I hope that it will be possible for us to take these next logical steps in the development of Maryland community mental health research. Thus, we would be embarking on the second level of a long-range research design presented to the Maryland Public Health Association five years ago (Bahn, 1960). In summary, we might schematize the community research program outlined here as follows:

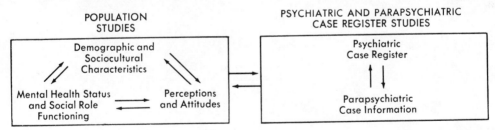

REFERENCES

Bahn, A. K. Epidemiological studies of mental disorders. (Based on Dr. Bahn's presentation for a course on the Epidemiology of Chronic Diseases, at the Graduate School of Hygiene and Public Health of Johns Hopkins University, 1959.) *Mimeographed.*

Bahn, A. K. The development of an effective statistical system in mental illness. *Amer. J. Psychiat.*, 1960, **116**, 798–800.

Bahn, A. K. Need for a classification of the psychosocial disorders. *Public Health Reports*, 1965, **1**, 79–81.

Bahn, A. K. A new psychiatric epidemiology. *Israel Ann. Psychiat. relat. Discipl.*, 1964, **2**, 11–18.

Bahn, A. K., Gorwitz, K., Klee, G. D., Kramer, M. And Tuerk, I. Services received by Maryland residents in facilities directed by a psychiatrist: First year of a state case register. (To be published in *Public Health Reports*, May, 1965.)

Clausen, John A. The sociology of mental illness. In R. K. Merton, L. Broom, and L. S. Cottrell, Jr. Eds.), *Sociology today—problems and prospects*, New York: Basic Books, 1959. Pp. 485–508.

Commission on Chronic Illness. *Chronic Illness in the United*

States, Vol. IV. Chronic Illness in a Large City. Cambridge: Harvard Univer. Press, 1957.

Gorwitz, K., Bahn, A. K., Chandler, C. A. and Martin, W. A. The planned uses of a statewide psychiatric register for aiding mental health in the community. *Amer. J. Orthopsychiat.*, 1963, **33**, 494–500.

Halpert, Harold P. Surveys of public opinions and attitudes about mental illness: Their implications for programming communications activities. (Paper for the First International Congress of Social Psychiatry, August, 1964.)

Kramer, Morton. Special report: Need for data on disability associated with mental disorder. (Prepared as background information for the Director of the National Institute of Mental Health, Public Health Service, U. S. Department of Health, Education and Welfare, in connection with the fiscal year 1962 appropriations hearings in February, 1961.)

Lemkau, P., Tietze, C. and Cooper, M. Mental hygiene problems in an urban district. *Ment. Hyg.*, *N. Y.* (1941), (1942), (1943), **25**: 626–646; **26**: 100–119, 275–288; **27**: 279–295.

Lemkau, P. V. and Crocetti, G. M. An urban population's opinion and knowledge about mental illness. *Amer. J. Psychiat.*, 1962, **118**, 692–700.

Meyer, J. K. Attitudes toward mental illness in a Maryland community. *Public Health Reports*, 1964, **79**, 769–772.

Phillips, W., Jr., Gorwitz, K. and Bahn, A. K. Electronic maintenance of case registers. *Public Health Reports*, 1962, **77**, 503–510.

Srole, L., Langner, T. S., Michael, S. T., Opler, M. K. and Rennie, T. A. C. *Mental health in the metropolis: The Midtown Manhattan Study, Vol. I.* New York: McGraw-Hill, 1962.

Suchman, E. A Health orientation and medical care. (Presented before the Medical Care Section of the American Public Health Association in New York, N. Y., October 6, 1964.)

COMMUNITY PSYCHIATRY:

THE NEWEST THERAPEUTIC BANDWAGON

H. Warren Dunham

THE PROPOSAL to add community psychiatry to the ever-widening list of psychiatric specialties deserves a critical examination. Thus, my purpose in this paper is fourfold. First, I intend to examine the nature of community psychiatry as it is taking shape. Second, I want to consider our continuing uncertainty about mental illness which is manifested in a widening of its definition. Third, I discuss some of the historical landmarks and cultural forces that have brought about the proposal for this new subspecialty of psychiatry. Finally, I examine some of its hidden aspects with respect to the future role of psychiatry.

COMMUNITY PSYCHIATRY: THE NEWEST SUBSPECIALTY

Let us begin by examining the nature of community psychiatry that is apparently emerging as judged by a mounting chorus of voices from those who jump on any bandwagon as long as it is moving. In doing this I will focus first on community psychiatry in relation to community mental health and the various programs, plans, and social actions that are currently getting under way, with emphases that are as varied as the cultural-regional contrasts of American society.

A pattern concerned with maximizing treatment potential for the mentally ill is gradually taking shape. This newest emphasis points to a declining role of the traditional state hospital and the rise of the community mental health center with all of the attendant auxiliary services essential for the treatment of the mentally ill. In its ideal form the community mental health center would provide psychiatric services, both diagnostic and treatment, for all age groups and for both inpatients and outpatients in a particular community. In addition, the center would have attached closely to it day and night hospitals, convalescent homes, rehabilitative programs or, for

Reprinted from *Archives of General Psychiatry* (March, 1965), *12*, 303–313. Copyright © 1965 by the American Medical Association.

that matter, any service that helps toward the maximizing of treatment potential with respect to the characteristics of the population that it is designed to serve. Also attached to this center would be several kinds of research activities aimed at evaluating and experimenting with old and new therapeutic procedures. In the background would still be the state hospital which would, in all likelihood, become the recipient for those patients who seemingly defy all efforts with available therapeutic techniques to fit them back into family and community with an assurance of safety to themselves and others. This reorganization of psychiatric facilities as a community mental health program also implies an increased and workable coordination of the diverse social agencies in the community toward the end of detecting and referring those persons who need psychiatric help.

This ideal structure does appear to be oriented toward the urban community. Therefore, the need arises to clarify the size and type of the population that would be served. Further, a breakdown of the population into the several age and sex categories along with several projected estimates of the number of mentally ill persons that will occur in these population categories would be required. Estimates should be made for the psychoneuroses, the psychoses, the psychopathies, the mentally retarded, and the geriatrics cases that will be found in a community.

Indeed, we should attempt to mobilize and to organize our psychiatric resources in such a manner that they will maximize our existing therapeutic potential for any community. At all events, such a structure seems to suggest to certain professionals at the National Institute of Mental Health that if there comes into existence a realistic community mental health program, there must be a community psychiatry that knows how to use it. While the logic here escapes me, it seems to be quite clear to Viola Bernard who states that, "Recognition of the need to augment the conventional training for mental health personnel to equip them for the newer function of community mental health practice parallels wide-scale trends toward more effective treatment methods at the collective level to augment one-to-one clinical approaches."[1] Dr. Bernard goes on to say that community psychiatry can be regarded as a subspecialty of psychiatry and that it embraces three major subdivisions—social psychiatry, administrative psychiatry, and public health psychiatry.

While Dr. Bernard may see clearly the nature of a community psychiatry that transcends the traditional one-to-one clinical approach, this is not the case with departments of psychiatry in some medical schools as the recent National Institute of Mental Health survey attests.[2] In reviewing the limited literature it is all too clear that different conceptions abound as to what community psychiatry is and while these conceptions are not always inconsistent they nevertheless attest to the fact that the dimensions of the proposed new subspecialty are by no means clear-cut. These conceptions range all the way from the idea that community psychiatry means bringing psychiatric techniques and treatments to the indigent persons in the community to the notion that community psychiatry should involve the education of policemen, teachers, public health nurses, politicians, and junior executives in mental hygiene principles. A mere listing of some of the conceptions of what has been placed under the community psychiatry umbrella will give a further notion of this uncertainty. Community psychiatry has been regarded as encompassing (1) the community base mental hospital, (2) short-term mental hospitalization, (3) attempts to move the chronically hospitalized patient and return him to the community, (4) the integration of various community health services, (5) psychiatric counseling and services to nonpsychiatric institutions such as schools, police departments, industries, and the like, (6) the development of devices for maintaining mental patients in the community, (7) reorganization and administration of community mental health programs, and finally (8) the establishment of auxiliary services to community mental hospitals, such as outpatient clinics, day hospitals, night hospitals, home psychiatric visits, and the utilization of auxiliary psychiatric personnel in treatment programs.[2]

Perhaps we can come close to what someone visualizes as the content of community psychiatry by quoting an announcement of an opening for a fellowship in community psychiatry in Minnesota. In the announcement the program is described as follows: "One year of diversified training and experience, including all aspects of community organization, consultation, and training techniques,

administration, research and mass communication media." Such a psychiatric residency program certainly represents a great difference from the more traditional training program and points to a type of training that might be more fitting for a person who wants to specialize in community organization.

There is no clearer support for this conception than Leonard Duhl's paper[3] where he discusses the training problems for community psychiatry. In this paper he speaks of three contracts that the psychiatrist has, the traditional one with the patient, the more infrequent one with the family, and still more infrequent one with the community. In connection with his community contract, the psychiatrist states, according to Duhl, "I will try to lower the rate of illness and maximize the health of this population." Duhl continues, and I quote, because the direction is most significant.

In preparing psychiatrists for these broadened contracts, a new set of skills must be communicated. For example, he must learn how to be consultant to a community, an institution, or a group without being patient-oriented. Rather, he must have the community's needs in central focus. He must be prepared for situations where he is expected to contribute to planning for services and programs, both in his field and in others, that are related: what information is needed; how it is gathered; what resources are available and so forth. Epidemiology, survey research and planning skills must be passed on to him. He must be prepared to find that people in other fields, such as the legislature often affect a program more than his profession does. He must find himself at home in the world of economics, political science, politics, planning, and all forms of social action.[3]

While these remarks of Bernard and Duhl may not represent any final statement as to what community psychiatry will become, they point to a probable direction that this newest addition to psychiatric subspecialties may take. However, in this conception of the community psychiatrist as a person skilled in the techniques of social action there lie so many uncertainties, unresolved issues, and hidden assumptions that it is difficult to determine where it will be most effective to start the analysis, with the role of the psychiatrist or with the nature of the community.

Perhaps sociologists can garner some small satisfaction in the fact that the psychiatrist finally has discovered the community—something that the sociologist has been studying and reporting on for over half a century in the United States. However, once the psychiatrist makes this discovery he must ask himself what he can do with it in the light of his professional task, how the discovery will affect his traditional professional role, and how working on or in the community structure can improve the mental health level of its people. Now, it seems that those leaders of psychiatry who are proposing this new subspecialty imply several things at the same time and are vague about all of them. They seem to be saying, in one form or another, the following:

1. We, psychiatrists, must know the community and learn how to work with the various groups and social strata composing it so that we can help to secure and organize the necessary psychiatric facilities that will serve to maximize the treatment potential for the mentally ill.

2. We must know the community because the community is composed of families which, through the interaction of their members, evolve those events and processes that in a given context have a pathic effect upon some of the persons who compose them.

3. We must know the community in order to develop more effective methods of treatment at the "collective level," to eliminate mentally disorganizing social relationships, and to achieve a type of community organization that is most conducive to the preservation of mental health.

4. We must know the community if we are ever to make any headway in the prevention of mental illness. For we hold that in the multiple groups, families, and social institutions which compose the community, there are numerous unhealthy interpersonal relationships, pathological attitudes and beliefs, cultural conflicts and tensions, and unhealthy child training practices that make for the development of mental and emotional disturbances in the person.

An analysis of our first implication shows that no new burden is placed upon the psychiatrist but it merely emphasizes his role as a citizen—a role that, like any person in the society, he always has had. It merely emphasizes that the psychiatrist will take a more active part in working with other professionals in the community such as lawyers, teachers, social workers, ministers, labor leaders, and business men in achieving an organization of psychiatric facilities that will maximize the therapeutic potential in a given community. To be sure it means that in working with such persons and groups, he will contribute his own professional knowledge and insights in the attempt to obtain and to organize the psychiatric facilities in such a manner as to achieve a maximum therapeutic potential. Thus, this is hardly a new role for the psychiatrist. It only becomes sharper at this moment in history when a social change in the care and treatment of the mentally ill is impending, namely, a shift from a situation that emphasized the removal of the mental patient from the community to one that attempts to deal with him in the

community and family setting and to keep active and intact his ties with these social structures.

The second implication is routine in the light of the orientation of much of contemporary psychiatry. Here, attention is merely called to the theory that stresses the atypical qualities of the family drama for **providing** an etiological push for the development of the several psychoneuroses, character disorders, adult behavior disturbances and in certain instances, psychotic reactions. Thus, it follows that to change or correct the condition found in the person, some attention must be paid to the family as a collectivity, in order to grasp and then modify those attitudes, behavior patterns, identifications, and emotional attachments that supposedly have a pathogenic effect on the family members. From the focus on the family the concern then extends to the larger community in an attempt to discover the degree to which the family is integrated in or alienated from it.

However, it is in the third implication that many probing questions arise. For here the conception is implicit that the community is the patient and consequently, the necessity arises to develop techniques that can be used in treating the community toward **the end of** supplementing the traditional one-to-one psychiatric relationship. This position also implies a certain etiological view, namely, that within the texture of those institutional arrangements that make up the community there exist dysfunctional processes, subcultures with unhealthy value complexes, specific institutional tensions, various ideological conflicts along age, sex, ethnic, racial and political axes, occasional cultural crises, and an increasing tempo of social change that in their functional interrelationships provide a pathogenic social environment. Thus, when these elements are incorporated into the experience of the persons, especially during their early and adolescent years, they emerge as abnormal forms of traits, attitudes, thought processes, and behavior patterns. In a theoretical vein, this is the Merton[4] paradigm wherein he attempts to show the diverse modes of adaptation that arise as a result of the various patterns of discrepancy between institutional means and cultural goals.

The influence of the social milieu in shaping, organizing, and integrating the personality structure, of course, has been recognized for a long time. What is not so clear, however, is the manner in which such knowledge can be utilized in working at the community level to treat the mental and emotional maladjustments that are continually appearing. In addition, the nature and function of those factors in the social milieu contributing to the production of the bona fide psychotics are by no means established.

These issues point to some very pressing queries. What are the possible techniques that can be developed to treat the "collectivity"? Why do psychiatrists think that it is possible to treat the "collectivity" when there still exists a marked uncertainty with respect to the treatment and cure of the individual case? What causes the **psychiatrist** to think that if he advances certain techniques for treating the "collectivity," they will have community acceptance? If he begins to "treat" a group through discussions in order to develop personal insights, what assurances does he have that the results will be psychologically beneficial to the persons? Does the psychiatrist know how to organize a community along mentally hygienic lines and if he does, what evidence does he have that such an organization will be an improvement over the existing organization? In what institutional setting or in what cultural milieu would the psychiatrist expect to begin in order to move toward more healthy social relationships in the community? These are serious questions and I raise them with reference to the notion that the community is the patient.

If a psychiatrist thinks that he can organize the community to move it toward a more healthy state I suggest that he run for some public office. This would certainly add to his experience and give him some conception as to whether or not the community is ready to be moved in the direction that he regards as mentally hygienic. If he should decide on such a step he will be successful to the extent that he jokingly refers to himself as a "head shrinker" and that he becomes **acceptable** as "one of the boys." But if he does, he functions as an independent citizen, in harmony with our democratic ethos, bringing his professional knowledge to bear on the goal he has set for himself and his constituents. However, successful or not, he will certainly achieve a new insight concerning the complexity involved in treating the community as the patient.

While I have poked at this proposition from the standpoint of politics, let me consider it with respect to education. If this becomes the medium by which the pathology of the community is to be arrested, one can assume that it means adding to and raising the quality of the educational system in the community. The dissemination of psychiatric information with respect to signs and symptoms, the desirability of early treatment, the natural character of mental illness, the therapeutic benefits

of the new drugs, and the correct mental hygiene principles of child training have been going on not only through the usual community lectures and formal educational channels but also by means of the mass media—radio, television, the newspapers, and the slick magazines. I hasten to add, however, that this may not be to the advantage of the community, for it may do nothing else but raise the level of anxiety among certain middle-class persons, who, when they read an article on the correct procedure for bringing up children realize that they have done all the wrong things. Also, the media are frequently sources of misinformation and sometimes imply a promise that psychiatry cannot fulfill.

Further, I observe that in this proposal for a community psychiatry, the psychiatrist seems to be enmeshed in the same cultural vortex as is the professor. For it is becoming fashionable for a professor to measure his success in having hardly any contact with students—he is too busy on larger undertakings, research, consultations, conferences, and the like. Likewise, some psychiatrists think that they have arrived if they have no contact with patients. For example, I have heard of one psychiatrist who has not seen a patient for several years—he spends his time educating teachers, nurses, policemen, businessmen, and the laity in psychiatric principles.

The third and fourth implications of the new focus provided by community psychiatry are closely related because each position partially views the structures and processes of the community as containing certain etiological elements that make for the development of certain types of mental and emotional illness. However, the third implication, as we have shown, point to the development of treatment techniques on the collective level, while the fourth emphasizes that knowledge of the community is essential if mental illness is ever to be prevented.

There is no doubt that the word prevention falling on the ears of well-intentioned Americans, is just what the doctor ordered. It is so hopeful that no one, I am sure, will deny that if we can prevent our pathologies this is far better than sitting back and waiting for them to develop. But, of course, there is a catch. How are we going to take the first preventive actions if we are still uncertain about the causes of mental disorders? How do we know where to even cut into a community's round of life? And if we did cut in, what assurance do we have that the results might not be completely the opposite to those anticipated? Of course, there is always secondary prevention—

that is, directing our efforts to preventing a recurrence of illness in persons who have once been sick. This is a laudable goal but in connection with mental and emotional disturbances we are still uncertain as to the success of our original treatment efforts.

PREVENTION OF BEHAVIORAL PATHOLOGY—SOME PREVIOUS EFFORTS

There is no doubt that the possibility of prevention is something that will continue to intrigue us for years to come. Therefore, it is not without point to take a look at several other programs that, while they have not all been exclusively oriented toward the treatment of the community, have been launched with the hope of preventing the occurrence of certain unacceptable behavior on the part of the members of a community. I cite two experiments which are widely known with respect to the prevention of delinquency.

The first is Kobrin's statement concerning the 25 year assessment of the Chicago Area Project.[5] Kobrin has presented us with a straightforward, modest, and sophisticated account of the accumulated experience provided by this project in the efforts to bring about a greater control of delinquency in certain areas of Chicago. This project has been significant on several counts, but in my judgment its greatest significance was that it helped to initiate various types of community organizational programs that logically proceeded from an empirically developed theory of delinquency. This theory, in general, viewed delinquency as primarily a "breakdown of the machinery of spontaneous social control." The theory stressed that delinquency was adaptive behavior on the part of adolescents in their peer groups in their efforts to achieve meaningful and respected adult roles, "unaided by the older generation and under the influence of criminal models for whom the intercity areas furnish a haven." This theory, in turn, rests upon certain postulates of sociological theory which emphasize that the development and control of conduct are determined by the network of primary relationships in which one's daily existence is embedded.

The significance of this experiment was that this theory of delinquency provided a rationalization for cutting into the community at certain points and seeking persons there who were ready to organize themselves to secure a higher level of welfare for themselves and their children. The results of this experiment are relevant to those advocators of the preventive function of a community psychiatry because there was not only the difficulty of determining what actually had been accomplished in the way of the prevention of delinquency but also a difficulty in assessing the experience in relation to community welfare.

Kobrin, in his opening sentence has stated this problem most cogently.

The Chicago Area Project shares with other delinquency prevention programs the difficulty of measuring its success in a simple and direct manner. At bottom this difficulty rests on the fact that such programs, as efforts to intervene in the life of a person, a group, or a community, cannot by their very nature, constitute more than a subsidiary element in changing the fundamental and sweeping forces which create the problems of groups and of persons or which shape human personality. Decline in rates of delinquents—the only conclusive way to evaluate delinquency prevention—may reflect influences unconnected with those of organized programs and are difficult to define and measure.[6]

The point here is that in a carefully worked out plan based upon an empirically constructed theory it is difficult to determine what has been achieved. One can hazard the observation that if this is true with respect to delinquent behavior where mounting evidence has always supported the idea that its roots are deeply enmeshed in the network of social relationships, how much more difficult it will be in the field of psychiatry to make an assessment in preventive efforts when we are much more uncertain concerning the etiological foundations of those cases which appear in psychiatric offices, clinics, and hospitals.

The well-known Cambridge-Summerville Youth Study[7] provides the second example of a delinquency prevention program. While this study did not focus upon the community as such but rather on certain persons therein, it did proceed from a conception of a relationship between a person's needs and a treatment framework for administering to those needs. In this study an attempt was made to provide a warm, human, and continuing relationship between an assigned counsellor and a sample of delinquents and to withhold this relationship from another comparable matched sample. These relationships with most of the boys in the treatment group lasted for approximately eight years. At the conclusion of the experiment there was an attempt to assess the results. These were mainly negative. The number of boys in the treatment group appearing before the crime prevention bureau of the police department were slightly in excess of the number of boys making such appearances in the control group. The only positive note was that the boys in the control group were somewhat more active as recidivists than were the boys in the treatment group.

Although the results of this study were inconclusive and told us nothing particularly about the communities to which these boys were reacting, they did document the failure of one type of relationship therapy to reduce delinquency. While these results provide no final word they do point up the necessity for the various techniques in psychiatry to first acquire a far greater effectiveness than they now possess befor starting to operate on a community level where there will be a great deal of fumbling in the dark before knowing exactly what to do.

It seems more appropriate in the light of the task envisioned for community psychiatry to call attention to the professional excitement that was engendered when the Commonwealth Fund inaugurated a child-guidance program in 1922. The Child Guidance Clinic was hailed as a step that eventually should have far-reaching consequences. For who saw fit to deny at that time in the light of certain prevailing theories and the optimism

provided by the cultural ethos of the United States that if emotional, mental, and behavioral disturbances were ever to be arrested and prevented at the adult level it would be necessary to arrest these tendencies at their incipient stage, namely, in childhood. This all appears most logical and reasonable. However, 40 years after the opening of the first child guidance clinic we have such clinics in almost every state and they are very much utilized as evidenced by the long waiting lists. Nevertheless, not only does juvenile delinquency remain a continuing community problem but also the adult incidence rates of at least the major psychoses appear to remain approximately constant during this period, especially if the study by Goldhamer and Marshall[8] is accepted as valid.

I cite these three different kinds of experience primarily for the purpose of emphasizing the necessity to review our past efforts in attacking certain behavioral problems at a community level and also to point to some of the difficulties that are inherent in any proposal that emphasizes the development of psychiatric treatment techniques for the "collective level."

NOTES

Thanks for critical comments on the manuscript are extended to the following colleagues at Lafayette Clinic; Jacques Gottlieb, M.D., Director of Lafayette Clinic; Elliott Luby, M.D., Assistant Director in Charge of Clinical Services; Paul Lowinger, M.D., Chief, Adult Out-Patient Services; Garfield Tourney, M.D., Assistant Director in Charge of Education.

REFERENCES

1. Bernard, V., "Some Interrelationships of Training for Community Psychiatry, Community Mental Health Programs and Research in Social Psychiatry," in Proceedings of Third World Congress of Psychiatry, Montreal, Canada: McGill University and University of Toronto Press, 91961, vol. 3, pp. 67–71.

2. Goldston, S. E., "Training in Community Psychiatry: Survey Report of Medical School Departments of Psychiatry," Amer. J. Psychiat., 120:789–792 (Feb.) 1964.

3. Duhl, L. J., "Problems in Training Psychiatric Residents in Community Psychiatry," paper read before the Institute on Training in Community Psychiatry at University of California, Texas, Columbia, and Chicago, mimeographed, Fall-Winter, 1963–1964, p. 6.

4. Merton, R. K., "Social Structures and Anomie," in Social Theory and Social Structure, Glencoe, Ill.: The Free Press, 1949, pp. 125–150.

5. Kobrin, S., "Chicago Area Project—25-Year Assessment," Ann. Amer. Acad. Political Soc. Sci., 322: 20–29 (March) 1959.

6. Kobrin, S.; op. cit.

7. Powers, E., and Witmer, H., Experiment in Prevention of Delinquency, New York: Columbia University Press, 1951.

8. Goldhamer, H., and Marshall, A., Psychoses and Civilization, Glencoe, Ill.: The Free Press, 1953.

part IX

CROSS-CULTURAL ASPECTS OF DISORDERED BEHAVIOR AND TREATMENT

Heretofore we have limited our descriptions of mental disorders largely to a single nation, the United States. The study of disordered behavior in diverse societies provides opportunities for comparing the effects of culture on types of disordered behavior and degrees of personal stability. Some disorders, such as depression, obsessive compulsion, or aggressive frenzy, may be more frequent in some types of cultures than in other types. But other disorders such as schizophrenia may be universal, regardless of the culture's simplicity or complexity. A cross-cultural census of the types of disorders remains to be worked out. This would involve the problems of seeking the common cultural definitions of disorders, uniformity of diagnosis regardless of diverse cultural expressions of a particular diagnostic type, and recognition of the discrepant criteria of hospitalization.

In "Some Problems of Transcultural Psychiatry," Wittkower and Fried introduce this area of inquiry by presenting the results of a cross-cultural survey addressed to psychiatrists and social scientists in 35 countries. They are concerned with the frequency and nature of mental disorders in these countries, the bases for their differences, and the directions for future research.

By comparing the frequencies of the types of disorders and the degree of personal stability among the Yoruba and the people of Stirling County, Nova Scotia, Canada, by age and sex, Leighton and his coinvestigators illustrated the findings, insights, and techniques by which disorders in diverse cultures can be studied. This epidemiological inquiry represents one of the first joint efforts in which non-Western (Nigerian) and Western (Canadian) psychiatric personnel collaborated in a culturally comparative study. In consequence, the cultural barriers which might have biased cross-cultural comparison were reduced to a minimum.[1]

Benedict and Jacks, in "Mental Illness in Primitive Societies," attempt to determine the extent to which the "functional" psychoses including schizophrenia and manic-depression exist among nonliterates, whether different psychiatric symptoms exist between nonliterate and literate peoples, and whether differences in disorders and psychiatric symptoms result from cultural patterns.

But the technological simplicity of a people does not necessarily contribute to the scarcity of depressive disorders among the West African peoples. The rates of depression are low in many village societies of sub-Sahara West Africa and in the South Sea Islands, such as Alor, Samoa, and Truk.[2]

Frenzied anxiety, a somewhat contrasting disorder to depression, exists among nonliterate peoples in different parts of the world. Known as the "latah" in East Asia and "running amuk" among the Dobu, it resembles the frenzied anxiety of a specific disorder among West Africans, an acting-out disorder characterized by random destructive aggression directed against others that in extreme cases may have homicidal consequences.

The psychological treatment of disordered persons in the folk society is consistent with their system of belief in the supernatural and generally is integrated with religio-magical processes. This means that treatment is a process of overcoming malevolent spirits and other intervening forces. Although modes of specific treatment vary, involving the spirits as a means of therapeutic change is one generic treatment process in the folk society.[3]

In my discussion of "Mental Healing and Social Change in West Africa," I characterize the definition and treatment of mental disorders from a folk viewpoint and then trace the meaning of folk therapies by the native doctors whose knowledge and techniques may be regarded as components of a subculture. Under the impact of change, in the urban setting, the therapeutic procedures as well as the occupational status of the native doctors are compared with those of the faith healers and a few Western-trained psychiatrists.

The basic strengths of folk psychotherapy consist of suggestion, reassurance, and emotional support which require dependence upon and trust of the psychotherapist by the patients. This interpersonal relationship that involves basic trust is especially effective for persons in a society that lacks critical individual decision-making. Individual insight resulting from psychotherapy could lead to critical questioning that would detach a member from a folk society and hinder his social participation. Folk psychiatric practices have these common features in diverse folk societies, whether in Ghana, the South Sea Islands, or Latin America.[4] In Ghana, the psychotic who did not molest persons or destroy property remained on the social margin of the village society and was not necessarily committed to a hospital.

For European societies such as Britain and the Netherlands, which have their distinct politico-economic ideologies, the comparative effects of the definition, care, and treatment of disordered behavior are apparent. For example, Willem Meijering describes the mental health program that is part of the social welfare plan of the Dutch government; this program includes hospitalization, family care, and posthospital care.[5] In their paper, "Institutional Framework of Soviet Psychiatry," Field and Aronson analyze the policy and practice of psychiatry within the

TABLE 1. POPULATION, PSYCHIATRIC, AND NONPSYCHIATRIC BEDS: SOVIET UNION AND UNITED STATES (1961)[1]

	Soviet Union	United States
Total population	216,100,000	183,742,000
Nonpsychiatric beds	1,637,600*	895,892
Psychiatric beds	207,800†	775,108
Total number of beds	1,845,400	1,670,000
Percentage, psychiatric beds of all beds	11.2%	46.4%
Proportion, psychiatric to nonpsychiatric beds	1/7.9	1/1.16
Psychiatric beds per 1000 population	.96	4.2
Number of persons per one psychiatric bed	1,040	237

*This figure represents the difference between the total given number of hospital beds (1,845,400) and the sum of given beds for psychotic (175,000) and neurological (32,800) patients—(175,000 + 32,800 = 1,637,600).

† This figure represents the given number of beds for psychotic (175,000) and neurological (32,800) patients.

[1] From Mark G. Field and Jason Aronson, "Institutional Framework of Soviet Psychiatry" *Journal of Nervous and Mental Disease* (April, 1964), *138* (4), 317.

context of a totalitarian ideology. They show that the connotations of disorders and their treatment in an extensive authoritarian society are similar to the Western countries and show that the community-oriented approach to treatment is practised pervasively in the Soviet Union as well as in the United States. One dramatic difference concerns the respective reactions to in-patient therapy and hospitalization: the ratio of psychiatric beds to general medical beds. In the United States almost one out of every two beds is allocated for a psychiatric patient; in the Soviet Union, the ratio is one out of nine. In the United States, the proportion of nonpsychiatric to psychiatric beds is 1.16 to 1, while in the Soviet Union the proportion is 7.9 to 1.

REFERENCES

1. Alexander Leighton et al., *Psychiatric Disorders Among the Yoruba* (Itnaca, New York: Cornell University Press, 1965).

2. S. Kirson Weinberg, "Cultural Aspects of Manic Depression in West Africa," *Journal of Health and Human Behavior* (Winter, 1965), *6*, 247–253.

3. P. M. Yap, "Mental Diseases Peculiar to Certain Cultures," *Journal of Mental Science* (1951).

4. Ari Kiev (Ed.), *Magic, Faith, and Healing* (New York: The Free Press of Glencoe, 1964).

5. Willem L. Meijering, "Social Psychiatry in the Netherlands," *Symposium on Preventive and Social Psychiatry* (Washington, D.C.: Walter Reed Army Institute of Research, 1957), pp. 410–415.

SOME PROBLEMS OF TRANSCULTURAL PSYCHIATRY

E. D. Wittkower and J. Fried

MODERN psychiatry has arrived at a stage of theoretical sophistication where the sociocultural dimension joins with the genetic, biological, and psychological interpretation of human behavior. Valuable contributions to the field of cultural psychiatry, i.e., that branch of psychiatry which deals with the interrelationship of abnormal psychological states and sociocultural milieu, have been made in the past fifteen years. Epidemiological studies related to the ecology of city life (7, 9, 10, 22, 33), to social stratification (15, 16), to occupation (11, 16, 29), and to ethnic groups (2, 6, 18, 19, 23, 31, 36, 38, 39) have been carried out by psychiatrists and social scientists. Another important development has been the careful study of whole communities, such as the Hutterites (8) and the Stirling County [Nova Scotia] project (20, 21), the Yorkville study (28), etc., in which the factors of community social structure and culture were brought into direct relation with mental health. Still another avenue of research has been the study of the beneficial and harmful aspects of the hospital environment in the therapeutic process (4, 5, 37). Most of this literature has been ably surveyed in Arnold M. Rose, *Mental Health and Mental Disorder* (32) and M. K. Opler, *Culture, Psychiatry and Human Values* (26)

Most of the work concerned with the relationship between culture and mental health has been carried out within the boundaries of a single country. Pioneering efforts have been made by such writers as P. K. Benedict and Jacks (1), Lin (23), and Yap (39) to compare the incidence and prevalence of mental illnesses in several cultures. Yet, for reasons which are one of the major concerns of this paper, these efforts have been rather inconclusive.

While some studies have indeed involved samples composed of representatives of different national or cultural groups, these were persons not living in the countries of their origin [cf. Hinkle's study of Chinese in New York City (13, 14), Opler and Singer's studies of Italians and Irish (27, 34), Spiegel's studies of Italians, Irish, and Yankees

(35), and Roberts' and Myers' study of Irish, Italians, Negroes, and Jews (30)]. Thus, for example, a hypothetical study in New York City, contrasting Chinese with Italians or Yankees, is not the same as a comparison of mainland Chinese with Sicilian Italians or Boston Yankees.

What follows is a report on the initial results obtained from a world-wide enquiry addressed to psychiatrists and social scientists in thirty-five countries concerning the frequency and nature of mental illness in their respective countries; a discussion of possible reasons for differences noted; and some theoretical and practical conclusions regarding the possibility of future research.

Our "procedure" for collecting information took the form of a series of communications[1] addressed to scientists strategically placed and qualified to be able to give authoritative information concerning the area of our interest.[2]

To avoid misunderstandings we would like to underline that we are fully aware of the shortcomings of correspondence as a research tool and of the preliminary nature of the observations to be reported. Our aim in presenting our preliminary observations is to stimulate interest in a field of psychiatry which was hitherto been little explored.

PRELIMINARY OBSERVATIONS[3]

Epidemiology

As regards epidemiology, two methods have commonly been used for the estimation of the incidence of mental illness in the population of a given geographical unit: *1*) investigation of a sample population taken as representative of the total population; and *2*) hospital admission statistics. Some authors have combined both methods.

Difficulties which have been encountered in local community surveys include the definition of what is a case, design of reliable sampling procedures, unwillingness of the local population to cooperate, and language handicaps in countries in which the language is incompletely mastered by the investigator.

From *The International Journal of Social Psychiatry* (1958), *3* (4), 245–252.

Hospital admission statistics are easily accessible but cannot be regarded as representative of incidence and prevalence of mental illness in the total culture because composition of institutionalized patients depends to a great extent on the availability of treatment facilities, on the necessity to give priority to grossly disturbed patients in countries in which treatment facilities are scarce, and on the varying degree to which mentally disturbed persons are tolerated and consequently kept in their home environment (26).

While it is difficult enough to make correct estimates regarding the incidence and prevalence of mental illness in a given geographical unit, the difficulties inherent in the task are obviously multiplied if attempts are made to assess the incidence and prevalence of mental illness within the boundaries of a given culture, and even more so on comparison of two or several cultures. Complicating factors in the last case are the introduction of such uncontrollable variables as differences in the quality of the training of psychiatric observers and differences in the clinical concepts, criteria, and labels which they use (26).

Consequently, on methodological grounds, there are no existing statistics which permit valid statistical transcultural comparisons of incidence and prevalence of mental illness. In the light of our present knowledge, approximations and impressions have to be relied upon.

A few gross examples culled from our correspondence must suffice: In contrast to the Western world, a very substantial proportion of patients treated in Indian mental hospitals suffer from psychiatric disturbances associated with nutritional deficiencies. *Cannabis indica* addiction is common in India, and opium addiction in the Far East and in some Arabic countries of the Near East. A high frequency of general paralysis of the insane (G.P.I.) has been observed in Hong Kong and a low frequency on Formosa and in India. Rarity on senile psychoses in the Chinese population has been reported from both Hong Kong and Formosa. Despite some statements to the contrary, the view is generally accepted that schizophrenia is ubiquitous. Manic depressive psychoses seem to be especially frequent in Denmark and rare among African Negroes (3) and in Newfoundland. Obsessional neuroses have been reported as rare on Formosa and as exceedingly rare in Kenya (3) and in Kuwait. Correspondents from Ireland, Greece, and Italy report a high incidence of conversion hysteria. As regards anxiety states and psychosomatic disorders, the writer from Ireland states that, though by no means rare, they are probably fewer and less intractable in Ireland than elsewhere. Immigrants from Iraq into Israel remarkably often develop bronchial asthma. Absence of severe anxiety in clinical pictures and comparative rarity of anxiety states in out-patients have been reported from Hong Kong. Psychoneuroses are said to be rare on Formosa and have not been mentioned at all by Indian correspondents. The correspondent from Hong Kong noted a rarity of homosexuality and of other sexual perversions among the local Chinese population. The rate of perversions and of homosexuality is said to be high in Iran, and there has been "a real epidemic" of sexual crimes in the city of São Paulo in Brazil.

Symptomatology

Any discussion of symptomatology will, regardless of the direction of the approach, run headlong into the problem of the normal-abnormal dichotomy. Both anthropologists and psychiatrists face the astonishingly difficult task of evaluating behaviour in terms of a series of factors, including its relation to accepted norms of behaviour for a given culture and the adequacy of behaviour in its social setting. A principal danger comes from mistaking the culturally defined norms of behaviour in Western culture to be ideal standards. Consequently, numerous Western scientists have been unconsciously guilty of ethnocentric prejudice, and hence of distortion, in evaluating the implications of the psychological organization of non-Western peoples.

A few observations illustrating culture-bound differences in symptomatology may be presented:

1. It has been noted that *schizophrenia* in the more primitive cultures is quieter than in the Western world. Blunting of affect, bizarreness, and other features suggesting deterioration have been described as typical of psychotic populations in Africa (1). It has been said that schizophrenia in primitive cultures is "a poor imitation of European forms" (1). According to a correspondent from India, schizophrenics in India are less aggressive and violent than schizophrenics in the United Kingdom and probably in the United States. On the other hand, it has been reported that states of confused excitement, Carothers' "frenzied anxiety," not infrequently combined with homicidal behaviour, are more common in nonliterate psychotics than in Western patients (2, 26).

2. All observers agree that true *manic-depressive psychoses* are rare in technologically backward areas. For instance, Carothers, working in Kenya, had no case of depression in his series of 558 mentally deranged Africans other than a few involutional

melancholics. In none of these were psychomotor retardation or ideas of sin or unworthiness seen. Nor was there in any of them a previous history of mental disorder. Mania of the acute and chronic form, by contrast, was fairly common (3, 12).

3. A number of *specific syndromes* have been described in various parts of the world under the names of Koro, Imu, Latah, Amok, Arctic hysteria, and Windigo psychosis. Some of these syndromes are characterized by echolalia and echopraxia with or without homicidal behaviour. In the Windigo psychosis of the Ojibway and Cree Indians of Canada, homicidal behaviour is combined with cannibalism.

Reasons for Differences Noted

There are no doubt marked differences in the frequency and nature of mental diseases in various cultures, although no methodology has yet been devised to quantify these differences in a statistically valid manner.

Explanation of some of the differences found is simple. It is obvious that in a country such as India, in which poverty and malnutrition are rampant, mental disorders due to malnutrition and avitaminosis are common; that malarial psychoses do not occur in countries without malaria; and that in countries in which expectation of life is short, senile psychoses are rarely observed.

Errors in Estimation. Open to doubt is the alleged very low incidence of psychoneuroses in African Negroes, Chinese, and Indians. It seems conceivable that the sparsity of trained psychiatrists in these countries is such, and the necessity to deal with psychiatric emergencies is so great, that the problem of psychoneuroses, which looms so large in the Western world, is of minor importance. The observation that obsessional neuroses are nonexistent in African Negroes may be correct; yet it is also possible that many milder cases of obsessive-compulsive psychoneuroses escape detection because their symptoms resemble characteristics of the cultural background itself.

Pseudo differences in incidence, as mentioned before, may come about if different diagnostic criteria and diagnostic labels are applied by psychiatrists in different countries. For instance, the relatively high figures for incidence of the manic form of manic-depressive psychoses in populations of technologically underdeveloped areas have been attributed to the tendency of local psychiatrists to diagnose states of excitement as mania rather than as catatonic excitement or schizo-affective state, as undoubtedly many psychiatrists would (1, 36). P. K. Benedict and

Jacks suggest that the specific syndromes mentioned before, such as Latah, Amok, and Windigo psychosis, are culture-determined schizophrenic variations. Some of the specific syndromes, such as Koro and demoniacal possession, the Hsieh-Ping of the Chinese, have been, rightly or wrongly, regarded as hysterical in origin by local observers (23).

Sociocultural Variables. Beyond this, due consideration for socio-cultural variables alone can account for differences in incidence, type, and content of psychiatric disorders on comparison of various cultures.

Various observers have commented on the paucity of content, the shallowness of affect, the lack of psychogenic precipitating factors, and of gross dilapidation of habits in schizophrenics of primitive cultures. Yap has pointed out that "this is probably true, since the richness of psychiatric symptomatology is dependent on the intellectual and cultural resources of the patient.... The same difference is found," he continues, "between the educated and the uneducated in any culture" (39).

Tooth suggests that the rarity of depressive states in African Negroes is related to the prophylactic catharsis provided by their culture, such as the institutionalized orgies of grief following a death (38), whereas P. K. Benedict and Jacks, contrasting the high incidence of confused excitement (often combined with homicidal behaviour) and the rarity of depressions, suggest that in nonliterates the hostility of the psychotic individual is directed *outward*, whereas in the West this hostility is more often directed *inward*. "Western culture," these writers state, "presents a significant contrast with at least many nonliterate cultures in the mechanisms of conscience (superego) formation and the extent to which supernatural authority figures are incorporated or introjected" (1).

Some cogent remarks have been made by Yap on the depressions of the Chinese. He states: "... there are significant differences in the incidence, intensity, and quality of the depressive illnesses in Chinese as compared with Westerners, and ... the key to the understanding of these differences lies in the investigation of the religious background and the traditional methods of handling guilt, or, for that matter, how the guilt makes its appearance. In Chinese one would have to study specifically the practice of ancestor worship, which is of course very different from Christianity in its concepts of sin and guilt and their absolution" (39).

Various correspondents have suggested social

and cultural factors as either correlated with, or causally connected to, mental illness. These include difficulties arising from the conflict between generations schooled in different values and fundamental attitudes, disturbances in family and community organization which upset traditional systems of security for the individual, dislocations of populations due to migration and attendant adjustment problems, and population pressures combined with poverty. A few examples must suffice:

1. It has been suggested that changes which affect basic cultural values, ideals, or attitudes, traditionally the core of interpersonal relations, adversely affect mental health. Thus, in Japan, Formosa, and India, where powerful traditions of family solidarity are shaken by new economic and political developments, observers are keenly appraising the results. From Japan we learn that in the rural areas the older age groups maintain powerful family solidarity with the twin values of "obligation" and "duty" guiding the relation of the individual to the social world. Such Japanese are typically overanxious and oversensitive to obligation, and this is expressed in the famous "face-saving" concept. However, rapid social and economic changes in Japan, plus the catastrophic defeat in war, have produced a split among generations, especially noticeable among the so-called "lost generation" composed of persons who were between the ages of ten and twenty years during the late war.

2. Evidence is accumulating to substantiate the hypothesis that mental health problems grow in direct relation to the disturbing of traditional bonds that hold families and communities together. It is suggested that individuals socialized under such well-knit family conditions may suffer when they are estranged from traditional systems of security arrangements previously rooted in the family.

Our research in Peru, begun in the summer of 1956 in collaboration with Dr. Seguín of the Hospital Obrero of Lima, is yielding evidence that the migrating individual from the tightly knit family background is especially vulnerable when faced with serious problems in an urban setting, when isolated from the security of his relatives.

3. This raises the extremely significant issue of the relation of migration to mental illness (25). Involved in such movements are all the stresses and difficulties inherent in the tremendous readjustments the immigrants must make to a novel and often hostile sociocultural environment. Again utilizing our Peruvian example, we note that many thousands of the native rural population of the Andean Highlands are flooding in a vast movement toward the coast. The social and economic differences between rural-Indian and urban-coastal culture are so extreme that many migrants are in fact unable to adjust, even assuming there were no serious physiological problems of adaptation to the descent from over 10,000 feet to sea level. Psychiatrically, it appears to produce a distinctive series of psychosomatic symptoms among a high proportion of these migrants.

A startlingly similar picture of the effects of migration is reported from Formosa, where mainland migrant patients show a parallel tendency to develop psychosomatic symptoms as an unconscious defense against anxiety and tension.

4. From the Gold Coast of Africa come excellent examples of the relations between culture change and mental illness. Reports describe how both the incidence and forms of mental illness differ between the more highly Europeanized African urban resident and the more tribal natives. Europeanized Negroes show little significant variation from white European norms in their mental disorders, whereas the more tribal populations undergoing severe acculturation react to stress and anxiety in culturally distinct forms.

5. Few of our correspondents, unfortunately, attempted to delineate the constellation of personality characteristics regarded as typical of the members of a given culture.

Since the shaping of the ego is largely a result of the reciprocal interaction between the human organism and its environment, and since most members of a culture experience a similar childhood environment, there are common features to their ego structures. These shared characteristics have been called "the modal personality type" by Kardiner (17) and Linton (24). It follows that we must understand what forces are responsible for the development of such specific features of character, i.e., every aspect of child-rearing practices must be investigated thoroughly from infancy through childhood.

Given these basic characteristics formed in childhood, which determine values, sentiments, and emotional responses, one can explore to what extent the social and cultural environment provides outlets, expressions, and gratification of needs, or leads to conflicts and frustrations.

This type of approach can be carried out only by workers well-versed in psychoanalytic dynamics and psychopathology. It is only through such an approach that the undoubted effects of culture change, described above, can be understood with any degree of precision.

CONCLUSIONS

The purpose of this paper has been to report preliminary observations obtained in a project concerned with transcultural psychiatric studies.

It becomes apparent that research can advance only when some homogeneity and standardization are introduced into the techniques of diagnosing and evaluating psychological states, and when coordinated and duplicated studies utilizing common methodologies are attempted across national and cultural boundaries.

Suggestive evidence has been submitted to substantiate the hypothesis that cultures differ significantly in incidence and symptomatology of mental illness. The available evidence strongly

suggests that cultures differ *a*) in the amount of aggression, guilt, and anxiety generated within the structure of the life situations faced, and *b*) in the techniques used by the members of these cultures in dealing with aggression, guilt, and anxiety. These areas require further elaboration. Such sociocultural variables as family and community organization, rapid sociocultural changes, migration, population pressure, and political events are undoubtedly related to the etiology of mental illness.

Although examples have been taken predominantly from three continents—Africa, South America, and Asia—to illustrate how social, economic, and other cultural factors adversely affect mental health, it should be emphasized that the principles involved are the same when one considers similar circumstances in dealing with European or North American populations.

NOTES

1. Letters and a brief questionnaire.
2. The information thus received was organized in the form of a number of newsletters (*Newsletter on Transcultural Research in Mental Health Problems*) sent to our correspondents and available to others interested in the subject.
3. With the exception of a few references to published material taken from reprints sent by the authors, all the observations presented are based on personal communications.

REFERENCES

1. Benedict, P. K., and Jacks, I.: "Mental illness in primitive societies." *Psychiatry*, 1954, vol. 17, p. 377.
2. Carothers, J. C.: *The African Mind in Health and Disease*. Geneva: World Health Organization, 1953. Monograph Series No. 17.
3. Carothers, J. C.: "A study of mental derangement in Africans, and an attempt to explain its peculiarities, more especially in relation to the African attitude to life." *Psychiatry*, February 1948, vol. 11, p. 47.
4. Caudill, W.: "Perspectives on administration in psychiatric hospitals." *Administrative Science Quarterly*, 1956, vol. 1, p. 155.
5. Caudill, W.; Redlich, F. C.; Gilmore, H. R.; and Brody, W.: "Social structure and interaction processes on a psychiatric ward." *American Journal of Orthopsychiatry*, 1952, vol. 22, p. 314.
6. Dhunjiboy, J.: "Brief résumé of the types of insanity commonly met with in India." *Journal of Mental Science*, 1920, vol. 16, p. 187.
7. Dunham, H. W.: "The ecology of the functional psychoses in Chicago." *American Sociological Review*, 1937, vol. 2, p. 467.
8. Eaton, J. W., and Weil, R. J.: *Culture and Mental Disorders: A Comparative Study of the Hutterites and Other Populations*. Glencoe, Ill.: Free Press, 1955.
9. Faris, R. E. L.: "Ecological factors in human behavior." In *Personality and the Behavior Disorders* (J. McV. Hunt, ed.). New York: The Ronald Press Company, 1944.
10. Faris, R. E. L., and Dunham, H. W.: *Mental Disorders in Urban Areas*. Chicago: University of Chicago Press, 1939.
11. Frumkin, R. M.: "Occupation and major mental disorders." In *Mental Health and Mental Disorder* (A. M. Rose, ed.). New York: W. W. Norton & Company, 1955.
12. Gordon, H. L.: "Psychiatry in Kenya Colony." *Journal of Mental Science*, 1934, vol. 80, p. 167.
13. Hinkle, L. E., Jr.: "Some Relationships between Health, Personality, and Environmental Factors in a Group of Adult Chinese." Paper read at Annual Meeting of the American Psychosomatic Society, Atlantic City, May 4th and 5th, 1957.
14. Hinkle, L. E., Jr., and Wolff, H. G.: "The nature of man's adaptation to his total environment and the relation of this to illness." *A.M.A. Archives of Internal Medicine*, 1957, vol. 99, p. 442.
15. Hollingshead, A. B., and Redlich, F. C.: "Schizophrenia and social structure." *American Journal of Psychiatry*, 1954, vol. 110, p. 695.
16. ———:"Social stratification and psychiatric disorders." *American Sociological Review*, 1953, vol. 18, p. 163.
17. Kardiner, A.: *Psychological Frontiers of Society*. New York: Columbia University Press, 1945.
18. Lambo, T. A.: "Neuropsychiatric observations in the western region of Nigeria." *British Medical Journal*, 1956, vol. 2, p. 1388.
19. Lambo, T. A.: "The role of cultural factors in paranoid psychosis among the Yoruba tribe." *Journal of Mental Science*, April 1955, vol. 101, p. 239.
20. Leighton, A.: "The Stirling County Study—a brief outline." Cornell University, Ithaca, N.Y., April 1956. (Personal communication.)
21. Leighton, A.: "The Stirling County Study. A research program in social factors related to psychiatric health." In *Interrelations Between the Social Environment and Psychiatric Disorders*. New York: Milbank Memorial Fund, 1953.
22. Lemkau, P.; Tietze, C.; and Cooper, M.: "Mental hygiene problems in an urban district." *Mental Hygiene*, 1942, vol. 26, p. 275.
23. Lin, Tsung-yi: "A study of the incidence of mental disorder in Chinese and other cultures." *Psychiatry*, 1953, vol. 16, p. 313.
24. Linton, R.: *The Cultural Background of Personality*. New York: Appleton-Century-Crofts, 1945.
25. Murphy, H. B. M.: "Einwirkungen von Emigration und Flucht auf die psychische Verfassung." *Geistige Hygiene Forschung und Praxis*, 1955, 253.

26. Opler, M. K.: *Culture, Psychiatry and Human Values.* Springfield, Ill.: Charles C. Thomas, 1956.

27. Opler, M. K., and Singer, J. L.: "Ethnic differences in behavior and psychopathology: Italian and Irish." *International Journal of Social Psychiatry*, 1956, vol. 2, p. 11.

28. Rennie, T. A. C.: "The Yorkville Community Mental Health Research Study." In *Interrelations Between the Social Environment and Psychiatric Disorders.* New York: Milbank Memorial Fund, 1953.

29. Rennie, T. A. C.; Srole, L.; Opler, M. K.; and Langner, T. S.: "Urban life and Mental health. Socio-economic status and mental disorder in the metropolis." *American Journal of Psychiatry*, 1957, vol. 113, p. 831.

30. Roberts, B. H., and Myers, J. K.: "Religion, national origin, immigration, and mental illness." *American Journal of Psychiatry*, 1954, vol. 110, p. 759.

31. Roheim, G. "Racial differences in the neuroses and psychoses." *Psychiatry*, 939, vol. 2–3, p. 375.

32. Rose, Arnold M. (editor): *Mental Health and Mental Disorder.* New York: W. W. Norton & Co., 1955.

33. Schroeder, C. W.: "Mental disorders in cities." *American Journal of Sociology*, 1942, vol. 47, p. 40.

34. Singer, J. L., and Opler, M. K.: "Contrasting patterns of fantasy and motility in Irish and Italian schizophrenics." *Journal of Abnormal and Social Psychology*, 1956. vol. 53, p. 42.

35. Spiegel, J. P.: "The resolution of role conflict within the family." (Personal communication.)

36. Stainbrook, E.: "Some characteristics of the psychopathology of schizophrenic behavior in Bahian society." *American Journal of Psychiatry*, 1952, vol. 109, p. 300.

37. Stanton, A. H., and Schwartz, M. S.: *The Mental Hospital.* New York: Basic Books, 1954.

38. Tooth, G.: *Studies in Mental Illness in the Gold Coast.* London: Her Majesty's Stationery Office, 1950. Colonial Research Publications No. 6.

39. Yap, P. M.: "Mental diseases peculiar to certain cultures: A survey of comparative psychiatry." *Journal of Mental Science*, 1951, vol. 97, p. 313.

PERSONAL COMMUNICATIONS

Africa: Dr. E. F. B. Forster, Dr. G. Jahoda (Ghana); Dr. J. C. Carothers (Kenya); Dr. T. A. Lambo (Nigeria).

Asia: Dr. Luther B. Parhad (Kuwait, Arabia); Dr. Pow Meng Yap (China); Dr. E. K. Yeh, Dr. Tsung-yi Lin, Dr. Hsien Rin (Formosa); Dr. K. R. Masani, Dr. S. C. Srivastava, Dr. N. S. Vahia (India); Dr. Max Valentine (Iran); Dr. Abraham A. Weinberg (Israel); Dr. Tsuneo Muramatsu, Dr. Shogo Terashima (Japan); Dr. H. B. M. Murphy (Malaya).

Europe: Dr. Erik Stromgren (Denmark); Dr. George Spyros Philippopoulos (Greece); Dr. S. D. McGrath (Ireland); Dr. Emilio Servadio (Italy); Dr. Ornulv Odegard (Norway).

North America: Dr. J. Frazier Walsh (Canada).

South America: Dr. A. C. Pacheco e Silva (Brazil); Dr. Carlos A. Seguin (Peru).

MENTAL ILLNESS IN PRIMITIVE SOCIETIES

Paul K. Benedict and Irving Jacks

THE present survey of literature on mental illnesses among primitive (nonliterate) peoples was undertaken in an effort to answer the following questions: (1) Do the major 'functional' psychoses (schizophrenia and the affective psychoses) occur among these peoples—that is, are the specific categories of Western psychiatric nosology applicable? (2) If these psychoses do occur, are there notable differences in form (symptomatology) and/or incidence as compared with the West? (3) If such differences are found, can any significant correlation be shown with cultural patterns?

An earlier survey[1] of the literature was found to be inadequate for answering these questions. Despite some recent note-worthy additions to the literature, the material which is now available and is being surveyed in this article is still inadequate, even in a purely descriptive sense. Many of the writers in this field have had little psychiatric orientation, and even where such orientation is implicit, the suggested diagnoses are often not in keeping with the current psychiatric approach. Statistical analyses, where attempted at all, are frequently faulty in some degree. Refinements such as sampling methods or psychological testing are conspicuously rare. In addition, most of the published material is concerned with one or the other of two large areas of the world (Negro Africa and Indonesia-Oceania), with almost no information on primitive peoples elsewhere. Despite these deficiencies, however, it is felt that certain suggestive findings can be gleaned from a survey of the available material.

Practically all observers report some manifestations of psychotic behavior with schizophrenic or affective features among primitive peoples. Many writers report a low incidence of the major psychoses, but only a few support the view that they are completely absent in nonacculturated natives.[2] One observer, Faris, bases his view of the absence of major psychoses on his study of the Bantu—the same group on which contrary evidence has been reported elsewhere, as discussed below.[3] In view of the overwhelming evidence in support of the ubiquity of psychoses among primitive peoples

Reprinted from *Psychiatry* (1954), *17*, 377–389.

throughout the world, the present writers feel that these negative findings are the result of limited observations or inadequate facilities. In general, then, we believe that one may tentatively conclude that the major functional psychoses occur among all populations, nonliterate and literate alike.

Certain of our sources report cases of psychoses but fail to cite incidence figures.[4] Incidence figures are available for certain populations in Oceania and Negro Africa, but in some instances the samples involved are exceedingly small. Only in one area (Gold Coast)[5] has there been any attempt at a comprehensive census or survey, and this, as indicated below, was admittedly very inadequate. What is available for the most part are mental hospital statistics, which grossly underestimate true incidence, and cases of psychosis brought to the attention of investigators, often in connection with anthropological studies.

SURVEY BY AREAS

Oceania

For Oceania, incidence figures have been calculated by Winston[6] for Samoa (based on data collected by Mead)[7] and by Joseph and Murray[8] for the Chamorro and Carolinians of Saipan. Both studies have the advantage of having been derived from direct observations of populations rather than from hospital statistics. Yet the total cases involved (6 for Samoa and 9 for Saipan) are so few that no great significance can be attached to the cited incidences—Samoa, 100 psychotics per 100,000, and Saipan, 208 per 100,000.

Hawaii

Beaglehole,[9] in analyzing mental hospital admission figures for Hawaii, affords an opportunity to compare the admission rates for native groups with those for part-Hawaiian groups. He studied admissions for the sample years 1930, 1935, and 1936, as well as the relative incidence of insanity in hospital populations. Employing the *insanity ratio* (100 would mean that the group in question has exactly its proportionate share of insanity), he finds that native Hawaiians have a ratio of about 200, while the ratio for part-Hawaiians ranges from about 50 to 75. This would indicate that native Hawaiians have about twice the proportionate amount of psychosis, whereas the part-Hawaiians contribute less than their proportionate share to the total of psychotic individuals.

Both the Hawaiians and part-Hawaiians tended to show extreme variations in the incidences of the different types of psychosis, as compared with groups of other national origins. The Hawaiians had the lowest relative incidence of schizophrenia (30.3 to 43.4 percent of their total incidence of psychoses), but within this relatively small group of schizophrenics the proportion of paranoids (11 out of 27 cases) was higher than for any other group. The Hawaiians also showed an unusually high proportion of manics within the manic-depressive category (16 out of 20 cases), although the over-all relative incidence of manic-depressive psychosis was not remarkable. The part-Hawaiians, on the other hand, had the *highest* relative incidence of schizophrenia (51 to 58 percent of their total incidence of psychoses), with only an average proportion of paranoids. They also showed the *lowest* relative incidence of manic-depressive psychosis with, however, no excess of the manic form.

Beaglehole makes the general point that incidence of psychosis is likely to be higher where the cultural group is struggling to work out a satisfactory adaptation to Western patterns of culture. It is difficult to see, however, how this generalization is applicable, especially in the comparison of the Hawaiians and part-Hawaiians. Assuming that miscegenation is correlated with degree of acculturation, one can conclude only that, in Hawaii, the acculturation process *decreases* the likelihood of hospitalization for mental disorders; *increases* the probability that such mental disorders as occur will be diagnosed as schizophrenia; and *decreases* the likelihood that schizophrenia will be of a paranoid type and that the manic-depressive psychosis will be of a manic type.

New Zealand

In New Zealand, Beaglehole[10] studied mental hospital admissions for a ten-year period (1925–1935), comparing the figures for Europeans and Maori. As he points out, these statistics do not differentiate between acquired and congenital mental disorders (the latter apparently including mental defectives), and so it is uncertain to what extent they reflect incidence of functional psychoses. After making a correction for age differences, he gives the weighted incidence per 10,000 as 8.37 for Europeans and 4.19 for Maori. He concludes that the "incidence of psychosis is definitely lower among the Maoris as compared with the European cultural group in New Zealand." Actually, we can conclude only that Maori are *hospitalized* for mental disorders only about half as often as Europeans in New Zealand. The Maori appear to have a significantly higher relative incidence of manic-depressive psychosis than the Europeans. This is especially true of Maori females, accounting for 52.6 percent of all female first admissions. Unfortunately, no figures are presented on the relative frequency of the manic or depressed forms of this psychosis. The relative incidence of schizophrenia is roughly comparable for the Europeans and Maori.

Fiji

In connection with his New Zealand study, Beaglehole also presents data on Fiji, based on official medical reports and mimeographed material. For the year covered (1936), the Fijians showed an insanity ratio of 40, based on a *hospitalization* rate of 1.6 per 10,000. The figures for Europeans in Fiji—an insanity ratio of 96, based on a hospitalization rate of 4.05 per 10,000—suggest that the European-native ratio regarding hospitalization is comparable with that found in New Zealand.

Negro Africa

For Negro Africa, three major psychiatric studies are available—Laubscher for South Africa (Cape Province),[11] Carothers for East Africa (Kenya),[12] and Tooth for West Africa (Gold Coast).[13] Because of their widely varying approaches, careful evaluation is required in attempting to make any comparison of their findings.

Laubscher describes a population of 555 patients in the Queensland Hospital, but the size of the population from which these patients were drawn is not clear, and so incidence figures can be cited. Carothers presents figures based on 558 Kenya natives admitted to the Mathari Mental Hospital over a five-year period, and cites an *annual admission rate* for mental disorders in general of 3.4 per 100,000. Tooth gives an almost identical figure (3.3 per 100,000) for the Gold Coast (Accra Asylum). Both Carothers and Tooth emphasize the fact that these figures are exceedingly small when compared with those of American or European mental hospitals; for example, Carothers compares it to an annual rate of 161 per 100,000 for American Negroes in Massachusetts.

With respect to *incidence* of mental disorders,

both Carothers and Tooth made an effort to collect data on nonhospitalized cases through surveys conducted by resident officials. Tooth, moreover, travelled about examining as many of these reported cases as he could gain access to. Nevertheless, he considers his material to be inadequate in many respects, partly because of difficulties produced by native resistance, language handicaps, and the like. On the whole, however, his investigation appears to have been more thorough than Carothers'. The incidence figures which Tooth reports (96 per 100,000 according to the surveys conducted by resident officials, and 60 per 100,000 according to Tooth's own examinations) are, not surprisingly, considerably higher than the incidence cited by Carothers (35 per 100,000).

None of these African studies permits of direct comparison with European rates. Carothers does present evidence, however, that the rate of hospitalization (proportion of tribe hospitalized) rises as the proportion of the tribe employed away from home increases. Tooth concludes that there is, for the Gold Coast, no evidence in support of the hypothesis that psychosis is commoner in the Westernized group than in the rest of the population. He handles this point in a peculiarly inconsistent manner, however, and in fact suggests that the literacy rate (which presumably would be correlated with Westernization) is higher than might be anticipated among the psychotics. Moreover, the incidence figures which he cites show a considerably higher value for the one relatively urbanized district—Western Dagomba, with an incidence of 156 per 100,000.

All three investigators present interesting material with respect to types of psychosis and symptomatology encountered among native Africans. Schizophrenia was the most frequent diagnosis for all the populations studied, whether hospitalized or not; for instance, it constituted 60 percent of the Queensland Hospital population. Laubscher states, with reference to the Queensland patients, "The schizophrenics all conform to the classical paranoid, catatonic and hebephrenic types." He does not cite relative incidence figures for these patients, but he does present a breakdown as to type of schizophrenia in a group of 52 schizophrenic patients. These patients were part of a larger group of 78 whose relatives replied to a special questionnaire, and who are described by Laubscher in an appendix. Of the schizophrenics, 27 (52 percent) are described as catatonics, 17 (33 percent) as paranoids, and 8 (15 percent) as hebephrenics. Typical symptoms include auditory and visual hallucinations with predominantly

mythological content, delusions of being poisoned and bewitched, and delusions of grandeur (of being a chief or witch doctor). He states that delusions found in paranoid Europeans involving influences operating from a distance—such as electricity, telepathy, and hypnotism—are not found among native paranoids, who instead complain, for instance, of very concrete acts of poisoning by persons whom they can see. One gains the general impression from the material presented by Laubscher, however, that the bulk of the patients are 'nuclear' schizophrenics—that is, severe schizophrenics in various stages of deterioration, with marked blunting of affect and poorly organized, bizarre, autistic thinking; in short, they are of a type approximating more nearly the hebephrenic than any other category.

Carothers describes the form of schizophrenia commonly encountered among the Kenya natives as "ill-defined" and "primitive," and remarks that most of these patients would be called hebephrenic by conventional standards. He diagnoses only 11 (6.3 percent) of 174 cases of schizophrenia as paranoid. However, he diagnoses another 11 cases as "paranoia" (a category not listed by Laubscher), which he links with stress imposed by the demands of an alien culture. Of these 11 cases of paranoia, 9 had been living in an alien or inimical environment—that is, they were to some degree detribalized. To test further the relation of paranoia to acculturation, he had all the hospital patients rated as to education (which is closely correlated with degree of acculturation) by a native interpreter. These patients were then checked for presence or absence of paranoid features. Of 119 noneducated patients, paranoid features appeared in only 15 (13 percent), whereas they appeared in 15, or one-half, of the 30 educated patients. These findings are highly significant ($x^2 = 21$) and fully support the view that Europeanization contributes to the development or expression of paranoid mechanisms.

Carothers also describes (under the category of psychoneurosis) cases of sudden outbursts of homicidal behavior, usually accompanied by ideas of possession or persecution. To these cases he applied the term "frenzied anxiety" or, later, "psychopathic episode (with hysterical elements)." These appear to be identical with such episodes in other cultures as the classical Malay *amok*, and should probably be regarded as acute paranoid or excited catatonic episodes.

Tooth, who worked with nonhospitalized schizophrenics on the Gold Coast, differentiates between ordinary schizophrenia and "delusional states," which he defines as characterized by "the presence of more or less systematized delusions combined with hallucinosis but, on the whole, a paucity of content and a shallowness of affect; and the lack of psychogenic precipitating factors and of gross dilapidation of habits." Of 38 cases so diagnosed, 31 were from the unsophisticated Northern Territories, while only 7 were from the South, where European influence is marked. These 7 were from small villages where their lives were relatively simple and sheltered. In the South, 24 cases were diagnosed as schizophrenia, as compared with only 9 in the North. In general, however, Tooth stresses the lack of certainty in assigning a schizophrenic patient to one group or another, especially when the patient is not hospitalized: "The schizophrenics under home care did not exhibit the clinical variations as clearly as those seen in the asylum."

A number of valuable case histories are supplied for the Gold Coast natives, and some discussion of symptomatology is also given. According to Tooth, there is a marked contrast in the delusional contents associated with different amounts of acculturation. Among the "bush" people of the North the delusional content is almost invariably concerned with the ramifications of the fetish system, whereas among the sophisticated people of the South and in Accra it includes ideas of influence and control by such means as electricity and wireless, along with Messianic delusions and delusions of grandeur. Hypochondriacal delusions, apart from vague feelings of discomfort localized in the genital organs, are described as rare. Tooth supposes that this may be due to the lack of medical knowledge and the preoccupation with spiritual matters.

As in Kenya, paranoid forms of schizophrenia appear to be relatively uncommon on the Gold Coast. If we combine the figures for delusional states and schizophrenia, we find that of a total of 71 such cases only 10 (14 percent) were diagnosed as paranoid in type. This figure closely agrees with that for Kenya (combining paranoia with paranoid schizophrenia), while both are considerably below the figure (33 percent) indicated by Laubscher for South Africa. On the Gold Coast, the proportions of paranoids are roughly comparable for the North (6 out of 40 cases) and the South (4 out of 31 cases). In view of the findings for Kenya, where the paranoid form could definitely be correlated with the degree of acculturation or detribalization, it is somewhat surprising that this relationship does not appear to hold here. It must be recalled, however, that

these figures are for nonhospitalized schizophrenics, whereas Carothers' findings for Kenya were with institutionalized patients.

Tooth, like Laubscher, does not recognize any special group of cases comparable with the "frenzied anxiety" category of Carothers. He does, however, apply the term "psychopath" to 4 cases, and the illustrative case that he presents would appear to have many of the characteristics of this category (the patient abused and attacked strangers in the market, and murdered a child by beating its head on the ground). It is apparent that many of the "psychopaths" mentioned here and in other reports on primitive peoples are schizophrenic, frequently fitting into the "pseudo-psychopathic schizophrenia" type described by one of the present writers.[14]

All three African sources emphasize the relative rarity of the affective disorders, especially of psychotic depressions. Laubscher states, "A true manic-depressive psychosis is indeed rare among the Cape colored and native races." He cites a relative frequency, in his hospitalized population, for this psychosis of 6.7 percent for males and 6.0 percent for females; however, his tabulated figures for the Queensland Hospital population show only 10 males (2.8 percent) with this diagnosis out of a total of 359 male patients. Apparently most of the cases which Laubscher includes are of the manic variety, without depression. He states that some of the female cases diagnosed as manic-depressive may later be found to be catatonic schizophrenics.

In Kenya, for the period 1939–1943, Carothers found only 3.8 percent of the hospitalized patients to be manic-depressives, but for the next 5-year period (1944–1948) he gives an incidence of 55 manic cases (6.1 percent), comparable with that found by Laubscher in South Africa. Carothers observes, however, that these cases "often show schizophrenic features" (grimacing, posturing, and the like), and it is apparent that many of these would more accurately be diagnosed as schizoaffectives or excited catatonics. Carothers remarks that the classical cases of mania, with such symptoms as sustained elation, and of depression seldom occur except with a background of education and sophistication; he also comments that "many abortive cases, not previously recognized as manic-depressive, occur in the more unsophisticated."

Tooth, studying nonhospitalized psychotics on the Gold Coast, reports a relatively high proportion of manic-depressive cases: 29 out of a total of 173 examined (16.8 percent). However, these are diagnosed as "mania" (14 cases) or "hypomania" (14 cases), with only one case showing mood swings to depression. The descriptions offered of some of these cases suggest that here too a diagnosis of schizophrenia would frequently be more acceptable; for example, some of the patients with "mania" were said to "hear voices."

The rarity of depression among native Africans has impressed all three investigators. Laubscher states that "severe depressions and depressions with agitation are hardly ever seen among the natives." He made a special investigation of suicides and found only 14 cases (4 attempts) over a two-year period in a population of about 870,000. These statistics indicate a suicide rate of less than 1 per 100,000, which is almost unbelievably low by Western norms. Lamont,[15] who studied a similar population of South African natives in Valkenburg Mental Hospital, reports that the natives showed much less depression than the Europeans, showed much less guilt about such matters as sex, and generally were volatile, emotional, and carefree.

Carothers found only 24 cases (1.6 percent) of "depressive psychosis of any sort" among native hospital patients in Kenya over a 10-year period. Of these, 6 "might be classed" as involutional melancholia, 2 as agitated depressions (ages 30 and 40), while 16 (ages 25 to 60) were cases of retarded depression "mostly exhibiting hypochondriacal or persecutory delusions." Certainly a number of cases in the last-named group, at any rate, were primarily schizophrenic rather than affective disorders. By way of contrast, Carothers reports that out of 222 European admissions to the same hospital (Mathari) for the same period of years, 22 percent were depressed.

The data for the Gold Coast presented by Tooth is in close agreement with the material from elsewhere in Africa. Out of a total of 173 patients examined, he found no cases of "pure, reactive depression," only 3 cases of involutional depression (with agitation), and 2 other cases of depression (with hysteria). All of these depressed patients were female. He, too, notes the rarity of suicide among natives, and reports that in the Accra Hospital, with a total population of 680, there were no successful suicides and only 3 instances of self-inflicted wounds for the year studied (1947). The ratio of wounds inflicted by patients on their fellows to self-inflicted wounds was 117:1.

Other Areas

Most of the available material on areas outside Oceania and Negro Africa is limited to reports of individual cases of psychosis. For Eurasia, Sklar and Stankowa,[16] working in the district of Astrachow (Russia), report that schizophrenia is rare among the Kalmuck (2.6 percent of the total mental disorder for this group) and the Kirghiz (1.9 percent), as compared with the Russians (6.4 percent) and Armenians (20 percent). However, these figures are for hospitalized cases and do not necessarily represent true incidence.

For the American Indian, Hummer[17] provides data for the year 1911. Of an estimated American Indian population of 300,000 for that year, he lists 150 known cases and 150 reported cases of mental disorders of all kinds, yielding an incidence of 100 per 100,000. The 58 patients in the Canton (South Dakota) hospital that year included 15 cases of schizophrenia, 5 of manic-depressive psychosis, 2 of hysteria, and 1 of paranoia. An analysis of 126 admissions to this hospital revealed that two-thirds (84) of the Indian patients were full-blooded and one-third were half-blooded or less. This statistic is difficult to evaluate, however, since by that date (1911) acculturation was already far advanced, even among full-blooded Indians.

From this review of the material relating to incidence and symptomatology, we feel that certain general conclusions may be drawn:

INCIDENCE OF PSYCHOSIS

The annual hospital admission rates for mental disorders cited for primitive groups are extremely low by Western norms. It must be noted, however, that even among Western countries these rates vary widely, reflecting as they do a host of sociocultural factors. In Italy, for example, the general rate is 59 to 62 per 100,000, or about one-third that of the United States and one-quarter that of Switzerland; moreover, even within Italy, the rate for the northern part of the country is about twice that for the southern part. Lemkau and de Sanctis,[18] who present these statistics, doubt that this difference within Italy represents any variation in actual incidence of psychoses, and explain the relatively low rate in the south by the greater family cohesion in that part of Italy (for example, the aged are kept home); by the stigma attached to mental disease (cases are kept secret so that the daughter in the family can get married); and by other factors. The ideal yardstick for comparison of European with primitive rates would be provided by an area in which a settled (not colonial) European population lived side by side under comparable conditions with a native population. The closest approach to this ideal is furnished by New Zealand, where Beaglehole found that the Maori were hospitalized only about one-half as frequently as were the Europeans. Beaglehole, although aware of some of the complicating factors, regards this as reflecting a true difference in incidence, and he also feels that a defference in incidence is reflected by the figures for Fiji. When one recalls, however, that the Maori are predominantly a rural population, and then considers that in the United States the rates of first admissions with schizophrenia vary directly with density of population, the New Zealand material loses much of its apparent significance. Actually, the standardized ratio of urban to rural admissions in the United States for schizophrenia, as worked out by Malzberg,[19] is 1.8 to 1, thus being comparable to the 2 to 1 ratio for the urban Europeans as opposed to the rural Maori of New Zealand.

There is some evidence that the rate of hospitalization tends to increase with increase in detribalization and acculturation. This is best seen in Kenya, where the problem received special attention from Carothers. There may also be a comparable increase in incidence apart from hospitalization, as suggested by the Gold Coast figures cited by Tooth. Many other observers have made generalizations to this effect without citing incidence figures. Joseph and Murray,[20] working in Saipan, gained the impression that the more acculturated Chamorro show a higher incidence of psychosis than the less acculturated Carolinians, although the series was too small to show significant differences. In observations on the natives of New Guinea,[21] India,[22] and Brazil,[23] Western influence was specifically held accountable for the development of psychoses. Devereux[24] also emphasizes the relative rarity of schizophrenia among primitives; however, he notes that among the Ha[rhn]de:a[ng] with whom he worked in Indochina, at least 5 percent of the population were neurotic or psychotic. Only the Hawaiian data, as noted above, stand in opposition to the general trend reported from most sources, and here special local factors may be operative.

It is apparent that two general types of interpretation can be offered in explanation of the general trend of the data. One can argue that in incidence is actually low in primitive societies and that the unusual stresses involved in acculturation are truly *causal* factors. Carothers follows this general line of interpretation in analyzing his Kenya material. Devereux has even developed a

"sociological theory of schizophrenia" on this basis, suggesting that schizophrenia results when the culture becomes so complex that the individual becomes disoriented as to his role in it. On the other hand, one can argue that psychotic individuals living in simple surroundings are able to effect a better superficial adjustment and thus are less likely to be hospitalized; moreover, schizophrenia, especially, is likely to escape detection in the magico-religious world of the primitive. Sachs, a psychoanalyst familiar with South African native culture, remarks in this connection: "Investigation of deeper motivations meets with almost insurmountable difficulties. It is hard to determine where the primitive spiritual world ends and the pathological spiritual structures begin."[25] Laubscher, who emphasizes this general point, goes so far as to suggest that the former has to some degree been shaped in eons past by the latter.

The general problem raised above is also encountered when one considers the epidemiology of a single psychosis within a single cultural area—for example, schizophrenia within the United States. The incidence of this psychosis shows a high degree of correlation with density of population[26]; with occupation[27]; and with nativity, nationality, and race (for instance, the standardized rate for Negroes is twice that for whites).[28] Carothers and Laubscher make use of a single finding— the high rate for Negroes in the United States—to support fundamentally opposed views. For Carothers it is a reflection of the acculturation process; for Laubscher, on the contrary, it is still another indication that Negroes have an unusual predilection for psychosis even when living under conditions like those of whites (he neglects the matter of social pressures to which American Negroes are subjected). Psychiatric writers in general adopt a somewhat intermediate position.[29] Hallowell,[30] in a Rorschach study of two groups of Berens River Salteaux Indians, found that 81 percent of the best adjusted, as well as 75 percent of the maladjusted, came from the more acculturated "Lakeside" group. While his study serves as a correction to the impressionistic view that acculturation must inevitably give rise to destructive intrapsychic conflicts, it suggests at the same time that acculturation may precipitate such conflicts, conceivably reaching psychotic levels, in susceptible individuals.

INCIDENCE OF DEPRESSION

Depressive states, in any form (including reactive depressions, involutional depressions, schizophrenic depressions, and manic-depressive states), are relatively rare in the native populations studied. This is especially well documented for Negro Africa, where it is reflected in extremely low suicide rates (under 1 per 100,000, as compared with rates of 10 to 16 in the United States, and rates as high as 255 per 100,000 in Denmark).[31] While the reported incidence of manic-depressive psychoses is often rather high (in Hawaii, New Zealand, and the Gold Coast), whenever a breakdown is given, the manic type seems always to predominate (for instance, in 16 out of 20 Hawaiian cases, and 28 out of 29 Gold Coast cases). Many of the cases labeled "manic" would probably be diagnosed by many psychiatrists as excited catatonic schizophrenic or schizo-affective cases. In any event, the depressive form of manic-depressive psychosis is infrequently seen among primitives, in keeping with the rarity of depressive reactions in general. Carothers states that the more classical varieties of mania or depression are encountered only with a background of Europeanization. This observation, not confirmed elsewhere, suggests a parallelism with the situation that obtains with schizophrenia, which we shall discuss later. Carothers also points out that many "abortive" depressions occur but escape psychiatric attention—a statement which would also be applicable to Western psychiatry.

Tooth discusses this problem with considerable insight, explaining the rarity of psychotic depressions in terms of (a) the prophylactic catharsis provided by the culture, such as the institutionalized orgies of grief following a death, and (b) the lack of self-reproach, which is seldom encountered in African psychotics. The latter in turn he relates to basic cultural attitudes in which all responsibility is shifted to supernatural powers, to the virtual exclusion of ideas of free will and personal responsibility. Carothers, approaching the problem somewhat differently, discusses it in terms of failure of repression mechanisms; but he likewise stresses the point that basic guilt is less severe, less overwhelming than in the Judeo-Christian world of the West.

There also appears to be a virtual absence among native Africans of obsessive-compulsive psychoneuroses, at least of the classical type. None were reported from Kenya (Carothers) and Nigeria (Cunyngham Brown)[32]; Tooth cites three cases from the Gold Coast, at least two of which were probably cases of pseudoneurotic schizophrenia ("severe reactions amounting to a psychosis"). Many milder cases of obsessive-compulsive psychoneurosis are probably unrecognized because

their symptoms resemble characteristics of the cultural background itself, as suggested by Tooth. Hallowell,[33] in a similar connection, describes a case of zoophobia which approached paranoid proportions, but which long went unnoticed by a community of Berens River Indians, who normally feel a great fear of animals.

SYMPTOMATOLOGY

Schizophrenia among primitive peoples, *as reported in our sources*, tends to be poorly defined in terms of Western nosology. This is especially evident in Negro Africa, where Carothers writes of "ill-defined" and "primitive" psychoses, and Tooth feels compelled to set up a special category of "delusional states." Several different factors appear to be involved here. We have been impressed by the 'nuclear' nature of the bulk of the cases, with blunting of affect, bizarreness, and other features suggesting deterioration. The relatively 'intact' forms of schizophrenia, in other words, appear to be underrepresented in these native psychotic populations. States of excitement and confusion, on the other hand, seem to be unusually prevalent, and are often misdiagnosed as manic states, as suggested by Joseph and Murray[34] for the six Alorese cases described by Du Bois.[35] This diagnostic error probably explains in part the unusually high incidence figures cited for manic-depressive psychosis for some groups. Support for this view comes from a recent paper by Tsung-yi Lin[36] based on a *census* study of the incidence of mental disorder in three communities in Formosa. He reports the incidence of schizophrenia (2.1 per 1000) to be higher than that of any other class of mental disorder, and contrasts this finding with earlier studies suggesting a predominance of manic-depressive psychosis in this area. It seems that, in general, only the more disturbed or severely deteriorated schizophrenics have come to the attention of the observers, whether working with hospitalized or nonhospitalized patients.

A number of acute, apparently psychotic, states have been reported from various parts of the world.[37] Malay *latah* and *amok* are the classical examples of two forms that have been reported. *Latah* is characterized by echolalia and echopraxia, and appears to conform closely to a type of catatonic schizophrenia commonly seen in the West. *Amok* refers to a violent homicidal outburst of maiming and killing with hand weapons; ideas of possession or persecution are often in evidence, and the aggression is usually directed initially toward a specific victim but may radiate outward to include various victims indiscriminately. Cases of this type again are familiar to every Western psychiatrist and are chronicled frequently in Western newspapers. These cases are usually diagnosed as either catatonic or paranoid schizophrenia, depending on the over-all clinical picture. The "frenzied anxiety" of the Kenya natives described by Carothers is of this general type, as is the "running wild" of Fuegian tribes.[38] The *windigo* psychosis of the Ojibwa and Cree of Canada[39] combines homicidal behavior with marked oral sadistic (cannibalistic) features. Finally, the "Arctic hysteria" of the Eskimo[40] seems to be closer to the *latah* type of psychosis, with echolalia and echopraxia predominating, but may also exhibit other features such as trances, convulsions, coprolalia, and even, at times, violent aggression.

We suggest that these states of excitement are, in general, acute schizophrenic episodes (catatonic or paranoid), although some of them— such as the Greenland Eskimo *piblokto*, in which women run about naked[41]—present a problem of differentiation from the true manias and severe hysterias. The view that these states of excitement are schizophrenic reflects the growing recognition of the atypical forms of schizophrenia, notably the pseudoneurotic[42] and pseudoaffective (schizoaffective) varieties. Incidence figures for these acute states are not available, apart from the figure of 2 percent (of total hospital admissions) cited by Carothers for "frenzied anxiety" among the Kenya natives. It is our impression, however, that these states occur more frequently, at least in certain nonliterate societies, than in the West. Van Loon,[43] for example, states that "dementia praecox announces itself amongst Malays very often by aggressive confusion," and Berne,[44] in a survey of Oriental mental hospitals, reports that the Malay are unusual in that schizophrenia is not the predominant mental illness, being replaced by an "unusually high percentage of toxic confusional psychoses." Also of interest in this connection is the high proportion of manic-depressive psychosis and catatonic schizophrenia among the Filipinos hospitalized in Hawaii.[45] Even Seligman,[46] who favors the view that mental disease is the product of acculturation, admits the existence of "brief maniacal attacks" among nonacculturated natives in New Guinea. The very fact that so many cases of *windigo* and the like have been noted in the very small populations of many nonliterate groups strongly suggests a higher incidence of such acute states than among Western societies. The relatively high figures cited for incidence of the manic form of manic-depressive psychosis, which we have already discussed, also point in this direction.

It will be noted that the relatively high incidence of these states of confused excitement, frequently accompanied by homicidal behavior, contrasts with the relatively low incidence of depressed and suicidal states among nonliterate peoples in general. Interpreted in psychodynamic terms, this suggests that in these groups the hostility of the psychotic individual tends to be directed *outward*, whereas in the West this hostility is more often directed *inward*. The writers suggest that Western culture presents a significant contrast with *at least many* nonliterate cultures in the mechanisms of conscience (superego) formation and the extent to which supernatural authority figures are incorporated or introjected.

PARANOID REACTIONS

Paranoid schizophrenia and paranoid forms of mental illness in general appear to be relatively infrequent among primitive peoples—or, at any rate, they are *less frequently recognized as such*. This generalization is consistent with the impression already presented—that the relatively 'intact' forms of schizophrenia appear to be underrepresented in native psychotic populations. Faris[47] writes of paranoid mechanisms as peculiarly characteristic of Western civilization, and this opinion appears to be widely prevalent in current psychiatric thinking. It is quite clear, however, that typical paranoid psychoses are encountered in nonliterate societies even under conditions of little or no acculturation. It is nevertheless apparent that the impact of Western civilization (or its equivalent) tends to increase the *manifest* paranoid behavior, as clearly shown by Carothers' study of hospitalized natives in Kenya. Also to be noted are the observations of Spiro[48] in Ifaluk (Carolines) on violent paranoid outbursts which appeared only after Japanese occupation, and the emphasis placed by Slotkin[49] on paranoid schizophrenic phenomena among the Menomini, a strongly acculturated American Indian tribe. There is also a change in delusional content and configuration, as we have already pointed out, with a tendency toward abstraction and complex systematization. This process can be viewed as a *nonspecific* form of conditioning.

CULTURE AND ACCULTURATION

We have already presented evidence to show that literate and nonliterate societies show differences in both incidence and symptomatology of mental disorders. Similar observations have been reported elsewhere; for example, Partridge[50] notes that different racial or national groups in military service in the Levant are peculiarly liable to different psychiatric disorders (apathy states among British, anxiety-depression among Balkan groups, intractable hysterical states among Indians, bizarre bodily sensations in connection with primitive superstitious beliefs among African natives, and so on). In India, Williams[51] reports marked differences in the incidence of various psychiatric disorders, especially schizophrenia, among native troops from different parts of India, and in Indian as compared with British troops. The question arises: Are certain mental disorders *sui generis* or are they specific for certain cultures? While psychiatric observers of nonliterate societies often stress the "primitive" or "confusional" aspects of the cases they encounter, they are in general agreement that these cases are only varieties of the same nosological entities described in Western textbooks, and that the predominance of schizophrenic psychoses is similar to that in the West. However, just as many Western patients are said to have their "own psychosis"—that is, to have an individually mediated symptom-complex— so certain cultures appear to develop distinctive varieties of the basic mental disorders. In other words, the psychotic deviations themselves are subject to the total cultural configuration and become highly specialized. The *windigo* psychosis of the Cree and Ojibwa, with its marked oral-sadistic component related to severe oral deprivation, illustrates this kind of cultural shaping; yet Hallowell[52] suggests that if enough cases of *wingido* were collected, it might become apparent that they fall along a continuum of states comparable to those seen in other cultures, and that only the content of the delusions is specific to the Cree and Ojibwa. Wegrocki[53] expresses a similar belief about *amok, latah,* and the like. Devereux[54] has given an excellent, dynamically oriented account of *hiwa:itik* among the Mohave, a state of depression usually found among elderly men who have been deserted by their younger wives; it is generally followed by spontaneous remission, although it occasionally terminates in suicide. This also is a highly specialized cultural entity; yet the cases described appear to fit without undue difficulty into the conventional categories of reactive or involutional depressions. The more penetrating the analysis of the individual dynamics— along with a subtle awareness of the cultural context—the more apparent become the underlying similarities of these mental disorders among primitive peoples to those seen in the West. Tsung-yi Lin[55] writes, "In psychiatric experience in Formosa, Japan, and the United States, the author has perceived little difference in the signs and symptoms of schizophrenic patients." This general congruency extends not only to the pathological processes per se but to their dynamics as well, as is borne out by psychoanalytical observations on nonpsychotic patients from such scattered cultures as Plains Indian,[56] South African Bantu,[57] and Batak (Indonesian).[58]

The knotty problem of what is normal and what is abnormal—of evaluating behavior in one culture by the normative standards of another—has engaged the attention of numerous observers, especially those with an anthropological orientation. Mackay[59] protests as follows: "Consider the essence of mental disorder. It is all a question of abnormality, of the bizarre, the out-of-place. But what, when we have no Normal? Then truly we have chaos. And we in Africa have not got a Normal for our basis, because we have never taken the trouble to study African Normality. The published attempts to produce an African Normal for psychiatry are so ridiculously inadequate as to be almost funny. We have so far judged our mental cases on their departure from European Normal, if we have judged them at all. Or else we have judged them on their departure from a Normal which we do not know. Therefore our only psychiatry has been among the obviously lunatic...."

Mackay actually oversimplifies the problem by the implied assumption of a readily recognized and accepted European or Western 'normal.' Even within Western culture there is a large reservoir of magico-religious ideation and wide variation in its acceptance, so that the same general belief expressed by two different patients may be of no special psychiatric significance in the one case, but pathognomic of delusional thinking in the other. In considering primitive societies, one simply encounters an exaggeration of this fundamental difficulty. Moreover, as pointed out above, primitive cultures in general tend to mask latent delusional thinking because of their over-all magical configuration. In a witchcraft-ridden culture such as that of the Aivilik Eskimo described by Carpenter,[60] for example, the cited cases of paranoid psychosis appear to have been recognized as such only when the behavior became utterly bizarre. As another example, on a different level, in the Fatshan society (South China), male patients recovering from a somatic disease regularly develop acute castration anxiety, in conformity with the cultural concept that the penis is at such times in danger of disappearance[61]; in this society it would be exceedingly difficult to recognize castration fears arising on an individual psychodynamic basis. Western culture, as it abandons the supernaturalism of the past and drives almost compulsively toward goals of objectivity and rationality, is making it progressively more difficult for the psychotic person to adjust— and this is especially true for the schizophrenic.[62]

The emphasis on cultural relativism, especially among anthropologically oriented writers,[63] has sometimes led to implied assumptions regarding etiology of mental disorders that appear to be unjustified. Ackerknecht[64] who makes a formal distinction between "autonormal" and "autopathological" states, and "heteronormal" and "heteropathological" states, despairs of finding any "universal" criteria for mental disorders.

We feel, however, that it has been amply demonstrated by trained observers that the mental disorders known to Western psychiatry do occur among primitive peoples throughout the world, despite the differences in incidence and symptomatology discussed above. This universality of occurrence does not per se point to any particular etiological hypothesis, constitutional or cultural. The need exists for further investigations of non-Western societies, more systematic and detailed than any hitherto conducted, with careful surveys of the type now being made in Denmark[65] to determine actual incidence of the various mental disorders, supplemented by additional psychological studies,[66] all within the appropriate culturological framework. Only with this interdisciplinary approach will it be possible to arrive at a proper evaluation of the role of constitutional and cultural factors in personality formation, and to understand the genesis of psychotic and other personality disturbances.

REFERENCES

1. N. J. Demerath, "Schizophrenia Among Primitives: The Present Status of Sociological Research," *Amer. J. Psychiatry* (1942) 98:703–707.

2. C. G. Seligman, "Temperament, Conflict and Psychosis in a Stone Age Population," *Brit. J. Med. Psychol.* (1929) 9:187–202. E. Faris, "Culture and Personality Among the Forest Bantu"; in *The Nature of Human Nature;* New York, McGraw, 1937. J. Dhunjiboy, "A Brief Résumé of the Types of Insanity Commonly Met With in India," *J. Ment. Sci.* (1930) 16:254–264. C. Lopez, "Ethnographische Betrachtungen uber Schizophrenie," *Ztschr. Gesamte Neurol. Psychiat.* (1932) 142:706–711.

3. B. J. F. Laubscher, *Sex, Custom and Psychopathology;* London, Routledge & Sons Ltd., 1937.

4. E. S. Carpenter, "Witch-Fear Among the Aivilik Eskimos," *Amer. J. Psychiatry* (1935) 110:194–199. R. M. Berndt and C. H. Berndt, "The Concept of Abnormality in an Australian Aboriginal Society", in *Psychoanalysis and Culture: Essays in Honor of Géze Róheim*, edited by G. B. Wilbur and W. Muensterberger; New York, Internat. Univ. Press, 1951.

5. G. Tooth, *Studies in Mental Illness in the Gold Coast;* London, His Majesty's Stationery Office, 1950 (Colonial Research Publications, no. 6).

6. E. Winston, "The Alleged Lack of Mental Disease Among Primitive Groups," *Amer. Anthropol.* (1934) 36:234–238.

7. M. Mead, *Coming of Age in Samoa;* New York, William Morrow, 1928; Appendix IV.

8. A. Joseph and V. F. Murray, *Chamorros and Carolinians of Saipan: Personality Studies;* Cambridge, Harvard Univ. Press, 1951.

9. E. Beaglehole, *Some Modern Hawaiians: Culture and Psychosis in Hawaii;* Univ. of Hawaii Research Publication No. 19, 1939; Appendix B.

10. E. Beaglehole, "Culture and Psychosis in New Zealand," *J. Polynesian Soc.* (1939) 48:144–155.

11. Reference footnote 3.

12. J. C. Carothers, "A Study of Mental Derangement in Africans and an Attempt to Explain Its Peculiarities, More Especially in Relation to the African Attitude to Life," PSYCHIATRY (1948) 11:47–85. Carothers, "Frontal Lobe Function and the African," *J. Ment. Sci.* (1951) 97:12–47.

13. Reference footnote 5.

14. P. K. Benedict and S. Connell, "Pseudopsychopathic Schizophrenia: With a Case Study" (unpublished).

15. A. M. Lamont, "Affective Types of Psychotic Reactions in Cape Colored Persons," *South African Med. J.* (1941) 25:40.

16. N. Sklar and K. Stankowa, "Zur vergleichenden Psychiatrie," *Arch. f. Psychiat. und Nervkrkh.* (1929) 88:554–585.

17. H. R. Hummer, "Insanity Among the Indians at the Asylum for Insane Indians, Canton, S. Dak."; in *The Institutional Care of the Insane in the United States and Canada*, edited by H. M. Hurd; Baltimore, Johns Hopkins Press, 1916; vol. 1.

18. P. V. Lemkau and G. de Sanctis, "A Survey of Italian Psychiatry, 1949," *Amer. J. Psychiatry* (1950) 170:401.

19. B. Malzberg, *Social and Biological Aspects of Mental Disease;* Utica, N. Y., State Hospitals Press, 1940.

20. Reference footnote 8.

21. Seligman, reference footnote 2.

22. Dhunjiboy, reference footnote 2.

23. Lopez, reference footnote 2.

24. G. Devereux, "A Sociological Theory of Schizophrenia," *Psychoanalytic Rev.* (1934) 26:315–342.

25. W. Sachs, "Psychoses Among South African Natives," *Amer. J. Psychotherapy* (1948) 2:123.

26. Reference footnote 19.

27. R. E. Clark, "The Relationship of Schizophrenia to Occupational Income and Occupational Prestige," *Amer. Sociological Rev.* (1948) 13:325.

28. Reference footnote 19.

29. L. Bellak, *Dementia Praecox;* New York, Grune & Stratton, 1948.

30. A. J. Hallowell, "Acculturation Processes and Personality Change as Indicated by Rorschach Technique," *Rorschach Rsc. Exch.* (1942) 6:42–50.

31. V. Vekko, "Suicide in Europe and Especially in the Northern Countries," *Menneske og Miljo* (1946) 1:215.

32. R. Cunyngham Brown, *On the Care and Treatment of*

Lunatics in the Northern Countries; Nigeria, 1938; Report 3; cited in Tooth, reference footnote 5.

33. A. I. Hallowell, "Culture and Mental Disorder," *J. Abnormal and Social Psychol.* (1934) 29:1–9.

34. Reference footnote 8.

35. C. Du Bois, *The People of Alor;* Minneapolis, Univ. of Minnesota Press, 1944.

36. Tsung-yi Lin, "A Study of the Incidence of Mental Disorder in Chinese and Other Cultures," PSYCHIATRY (1953) 16:313–336.

37. E. H. Ackerknecht, "Psychopathology, Primitive Medicine and Primitive Culture," *Bull. Hist. Med.* (1943) 14:30–67. J. M. Cooper, "Mental Disease Situations in Certain Cultures," *J. Abnormal and Social Psychol.* (1934) 29:10–17. P. M. Yap, "The Latah Reaction: Its Pathodynamics and Nosological Position," *J. Ment. Sci.* (1952) 98:515. Yap, "Mental Diseases Peculiar to Certain Cultures: A Survey of Comparative Psychiatry," *J. Ment. Sci.* (1951) 97:313–327.

38. Cooper, reference footnote 37.

39. Cooper, reference footnote 37. R. Landis, "The Abnormal Among the Ojibwa Indians," *J. Abnormal and Social Psychol.* (1938) 33:14–33.

40. Cooper, reference footnote 37.

41. Cooper, reference footnote 37.

42. P. Hoch and P. Polatin, "Pseudoneurotic Forms of Schizophrenia," *Psychiatric Quart.* (1949) 23:248–276.

43. F. H. G. Van Loon, "Protopathic Instinctive Phenomena in Normal and Pathological Malay Life," *British J. Med. Psychol.* (1928) 8:264–276.

44. E. Berne, "Some Oriental Mental Hospitals," *Amer. J. Psychiatry* (1949) 106:376.

45. Reference footnote 9.

46. Seligman, reference footnote 2.

47. Reference footnote 2.

48. M. E. Spiro, "A Psychotic Personality in the South Seas," PSYCHIATRY (1950) 13:189–204.

49. J. S. Slotkin, "Social Psychiatry of a Menomini Community," *J. Abnormal and Social Psychol.* (1953) 48:10–16.

50. M. A. Partridge, "Psychiatry in the Levant," *J. Royal Nav. Med. Serv.* (1946) 32:115.

51. A. H. Williams, "A Psychiatric Study of Indian Soldiers in the Arakan," *British J. Med. Psychol.* (1950) 23:130.

52. Reference footnote 33.

53. H. S. Wegrocki, "A Critique of Cultural and Statistical Concepts of Abnormality"; in *Personality in Nature, Society and Culture,* edited by C. Kluckhohn and H. A. Murray; New York, Knopf, 1948.

54. G. Devereux, "Primitive Psychiatry," *Bull. Hist. Med.* (1940) 8:1194–1213.

55. Reference footnote 36.

56. G. Devereux, *Reality and Dream: The Psychotherapy of a Plains Indian*; New York, Internat. Univ. Press, 1951.

57. W. Sachs, *Black Anger*; Boston, Little, Brown, 1947.

58. W. Oesterreicher, "Sadomasochistic Obsessions in an Indonesian," *Amer. J. Psychotherapy* (1948) 2:264.

59. D. Mackay, "A Background for African Psychiatry," *East African Med. J.* (1948) 25:1.

60. Reference footnote 4.

61. F. Kobler, "Description of an Acute Castration Fear, Based on Superstition," *Psychoanalytic Rev.* (1948) 35:285.

62. R. A. Clark, "Cosmic Consciousness in Catatonic Schizophrenia," *Psychoanalytic Rev.* (1946) 33:460.

63. R. Benedict, *Patterns of Culture*; New York, Houghton Mifflin, 1934. A. L. Kroeber, "Psychosis or Social Sanction," *Character and Personality* (1940) 8:204–215.

64. Ackerknecht, reference footnote 37.

65. E. Stromgren, "Social Surveys," *J. Ment. Sci.* (1948) 94:266.

66. Du Bois, reference footnote 35. P. H. Cook, "The Application of the Rorschach Test to a Samoan Group," *Rorschach Rsc. Exch.* (1942) 6:51–60. J. Henry, "Rorschach Technique in Primitive Cultures," *Amer. J. Orthopsychiatry* (1941) 11:230–234. H. Lantz, "Rorschach Testing in Preliterate Cultures," *Amer. J. Orthopsychiatry* (1948) 18:287–291.

"MENTAL HEALING" AND SOCIAL CHANGE IN

WEST AFRICA

S. Kirson Weinberg

THE indigenous treatment of mental disorders in Ghana, West Africa, despite its continuity with a tribal past, is in process of change by the pressures of urbanization. Although retaining a dominant position in the therapy of mental disorders, it is challenged increasingly by Christian faith healing and Western psychiatry. Our aim in this paper is to analyze 1) the meaning of illness from perspective of the patients, 2) the diagnostic and therapeutic procedures of the native doctor as components of a sub-culture, and 3) the mode of change in the position of this profession as compared with that of Christian faith healing and Western psychiatry.[1]

I. RATIONALE OF METHOD

This sociological study of a changing occupational culture in a non-Western, urban society differs from the characteristic anthropological study of the traditional heritage of a static, territorially contiguous tribe into which the individual is born and becomes socialized.[2] This study investigates instead the changing culture of dispersed urban practitioners into which a socialized novice is recruited and becomes acculturated. From this perspective it aims specifically to ascertain not only the diagnostic and therapeutic orientations and techniques of the native doctors and the effectiveness of their skills, but also the extent to which they enforced standards of practice, communicated and shared their professional lore, and selected competent recruits to sustain their craft. Since these native doctors were members of several groups, we had to sift their professional ideas and techniques from those which are idiosyncratic or peculiar to their tribe. Although we emphasized the shared facets of this occupation, we recognized too that manifest differences existed in the professional knowledge and skills of the members. Some native doctors had knowledge of herb mixtures which others lacked; some doctors were more effective than others in

their psychotherapeutic procedures and in their handling of patients.

This inquiry emerged from a study of hospitalized schizophrenics in the state hospital in Accra.[3] We found that the characteristic lower class, non-violent schizophrenics, who were so numerous in state hospitals in the United States, were relatively scarce in this hospital. From further inquiry we found that some persons whose symptoms were those of schizophrenics were treated by native doctors or faith healers, and other persons with these symptoms were in the villages and in the marketplaces of the city. As we continued this tangential search we realized that these native doctors were the indigenous psychiatrists in this society and that their orientations and procedures differed somewhat from those of their counterparts in the villages as described by Rattray and Field.[4] We then concentrated upon the characteristics and direction of this changing occupational culture.

Our first informants were two native doctors and one college student who described in detail the orientation and theoretical framework of the medicine man. These informants presented us to sixteen native doctors and five faith healers whom we interviewed at length. For validating information concerning this occupational culture we interviewed mental hospital patients and other persons who had been treated by native doctors or faith healers.

We gathered information concerning the official characteristics of the native doctors from the records at two towns near Accra, Amasaman and Prampram, where the doctors were licensed. Information about the mental hospital was obtained from our interviews with the staff and patients, from direct observation and from hospital records. Although our findings concerning the workings of the diverse forms of healings are circumscribed to and around Accra, Ghana, the relative similarity of conditions to other parts of West Africa means that our conclusions could pertain with minor variations to the urban sectors of West Africa generally.

Reprinted from *Social Problems* (Winter, 1964), *11* (3), 257–269.

II. CONCEPTIONS OF ILLNESS AND THE TYPES OF PATIENTS

Since the native doctor treats psychological and organic difficulties, his role approximates that of the Western physician and psychiatrist. His dual therapeutic role results from the African's conception of illness and health. In a holistic sense he considers illness or ill-being in polarity to well-being, so that it connotes not only 1) physical ailments but also (on a temporal and psychological dimension) 2) present and 3) future personal misfortune, and finally, 4) social deviation. The African interprets deviant behavior both as a symptom and cause of illness, because deviant behavior can weaken the kra or kla, the vital spiritual source of well-being.[5] Since the patient does not distinguish between organic and personality difficulties, he may seek treatment from a native doctor because of an organic ailment such as a stomach-ache or sexual impotency, or because of a personal problem such as marital difficulties or unemployment. He regards physical illness and emotional disturbances as supernaturally caused and as manifestations of his personal destiny. He does not consider infection by germs or agitation by conflict as the bases of his malady or misfortune.

The African consistently regards healing as a religio-psychological process, involving the spiritual triumph of the idol, i.e., the "juju," and/or the medicine or the spirit of the native doctor over the spirit of the illness. The patient defines treatment as symptom-removal and as an invocation to spirits who can remove the supernatural sources of the symptom. Some doctors and faith healers do not consider the removal of symptoms possible without placating or vanquishing the proper spirits. When confronted with personal difficulties, the patient, lacking a developmental perspective, does not attribute past influences in childhood to his present condition. Instead he perceives his condition as a result of animistic influences.[6] Nonetheless, he may also have a trial and success empirical naturalism so that, for example, he can relate his recovery to specific herbs.

Personality and mental disorders range in severity from minor situational and personality difficulties to chronic psychoses. For example, an individual who seeks a job or a promotion or who strives to avert future misfortune visits the native doctor to correct his condition. When he incurs a physical ailment which resists medication, or when he is gripped by compulsive addictions such as alcoholism, and drug addiction, he believes that he is influenced by witches, by black magic or juju, by ancestral or other spirits which obscure his will and obstruct his destiny, and he believes that only the native doctor can help him. Why does the African interpret his condition in this way?

Apart from the concepts of well-being or ill-being, of spirit possession or spirit-relief, his thought categories of personality and for introspective analysis are simple and few. His conception of himself is simpler than his knowledge and his skills in mechanical, political and clerical pursuits.

Even though an urbanized person becomes relatively individualized and in the process of detribalization changes his value scheme from family-centered status to bureaucratic-centered status, he still may interpret his tensions and interpersonal conflicts as well as his misfortunes in terms of spirits, juju and witchcraft. His conceptions used in introspective analysis of his predicament are not those of Western psychology. Instead he resorts to folk beliefs to appraise his behavior, beliefs which seem to be compartmentalized from his rational orientation towards his work and mechanical pursuits.

From this supernatural vantage point, the African believes that a witch or literally a released spirit—in Twi, called oba-yi—can harm him.[7] By thinking harmful thoughts a witch can project her spirit onto his destiny and thereby affect his present or future fortunes. An idol or the black magic of juju also can affect his personal condition. Consequently, when an African with this perspective encounters misfortune, he does not seek explanations in terms of natural causes but rather contemplates the intervention of supernatural forces which contributed to his particular misfortune. With this frame of mind he would seek help from the native doctor who shares his frame of reference and the idiomatic aspects of his personal expressions.

Hence persons in nearly all strata of society would visit the native doctor when personal stress impelled psychological help. According to one survey, however, the proportion of persons in a given social stratum declined with the amount of schooling. Of those persons who "had no schooling," 20.3 per cent admittedly visited the native doctor, 13.8 per cent of those who attended primary school, 2.9 per cent of those who attended middle school and 1.2 per cent of those who had commercial and technical training or higher visit the native doctor.[8] Although these figures demonstrate that as people acquired more education fewer of them visited the native doctor, these figures must be viewed in a more complete social perspective. First, the majority of people in Accra (especially women), had little or no schooling. Hence most sick or emotionally distressed people would visit the native doctor or a faith healer. Second, some educated people would visit the native doctor furtively and would hesitate to divulge their visits. Third, some people who were treated by the Western-trained doctor for physical maladies would prefer the native doctor for help in their personal problems. Thus it appears that more people would use the services of the native doctor than the results of this survey imply.

The widespread visits of people to the native doctor are consistent with the beliefs of the people towards supernatural processes. In an exploratory survey of 40 college students, we asked them to estimate the percentage of people in their range of contacts who believed in spirits, juju and witchcraft. Their estimates of the persons in their scope of social relations who believed in the influence of supernatural forces upon personality ranged from 65 to 99 per cent, with an average of 85 per cent. The native doctor who could communicate with these people in their frame of reference could provide the kinds of psychotherapy and its resultant emotional security which many Africans in nearly all strata of Ghanaian society would appreciate and seek.

III. THE ORIENTATIONS AND TECHNIQUES OF THE NATIVE DOCTOR AS "MENTAL HEALER"

The African's holistic, bio-psychological conception of illness permits the native doctor to apply two broad points of departure to therapy. The first is bio-medical, emphasizes the healing properties of herbs, veers towards a quasi-naturalism and represents the specialty of the herbalist. The second is religio-psychological, emphasizes the therapeutic force of prayer, sacrifice and incantation, is supernaturalistic and is the specialty of the fetish priest.[9] In an analysis of 108 records of native doctors who applied for licenses from 1951 to 1960, we found that 49 per cent regarded themselves primarily as herbalists, 43.5 per cent considered themselves herbalist-soothsayers, and 7.5 per cent regarded themselves as fetish priests (including individual and cultistic priests, such as the Tigare).[10] These records from the local councils where the licenses are granted

reveal the marked decline of the fetish priests who were cult leaders, and the marked increase of individual practitioners who combined herbalist and priest-like functions in their adaptation to the shifting needs of the urban populace. This meant that the native doctor tended to perform religious rituals as well as to administer herbs. Although a few herbalists confined their practice to those with physical maladies mainly, most native doctors did attempt to treat mental disorders and emotional disturbances.

The native doctor, whether predominantly herbalist or fetish priest, used a sequence of therapeutic procedures to remedy personality disorders. When the native doctor initially encountered the patient, he found it incumbent upon himself to diagnose the illness as well as to prescribe the remedy in so impressively convincing a manner that the patient would return for additional treatment. For example, one native doctor claimed that his intuitive judgment had an empathic basis for his diagnosis. When he shook hands with the patient he noted the firmness of his grasp, observed his appearance, modes of expression, and quality of speech. He pursued his observations by asking pointed questions until he felt that he had discerned the patient's condition.[11]

The native doctor usually had a particular diagnostic procedure which became virtually a trademark and which was sometimes quite flamboyant. One doctor deciphered handwriting which he claimed to have learned from Spanish Morrocans. Another used what he called "Jacob's stone pillow," which he supposedly acquired in Egypt. A third looked into a mirror as if he were peering into the patient's present and future condition. A fourth used Egyptian sand-writing by counting the strung beads flung into a designated space of sand by the patient. A fifth doctor shook cowry shells and made squealling noises. All the doctors seemed to emphasize a certain mystery in their techniques and strived to impress the patient as well as to diagnose his condition.

The knowledgeable medicine man or fetish priest could apply the following characteristic psychotherapeutic techniques in handling his patient. First, the doctor could impress the patient that he had the spiritual power to protect him from witches, juju and other hostile spirits. Second, he could "immunize" the patient from future injury or misfortune by a given protective medicine; this protective medicine was effective presumably as long as the patient himself conformed so he was motivated not to deviate. On the other hand, the patient felt secure in the belief that the culprit who tried to harm him would get "caught" by the medicine and become sick. Third, the medicine man could persuade a guilt-ridden person to relieve himself by confession and to become "purified" by the sacrifice of an animal. For example, in one ritual, he could cut the throat of a chicken and fling it towards the shrine. If the bird died breast upward, it signified that the gift was accepted by the gods and the patient had been purified. If the bird died breast downward, it meant that that patient had sins which he must confess. But some medicine men did not ask the patient to confess when the bird died breast downward, but merely repeated the ritual until the bird died breast upward. Apparently they felt that the ritual was sufficient. Fourth, the medicine man could resort to exorcism to dispel an evil spirit from a disturbed patient who felt that an intruding spirit compelled him to behave bizarrely. Fifth, he could try to offset by suggestive techniques the influence of a supposed witch when a person's illness was very sudden, resisted medication or recurred. On this level, he recognized and emphasized a psychosomatic view of illness. Sixth, he could apply various devices to test a person charged with witchcraft with the intent of either accusing or clearing him of the charge. If the patient did admit witchcraft, the medicine man could use exorcism and other suggestive techniques in an effort to rid the patient from the alien or perverse spirit. Seventh, the medicine man who treated a psychotic had the knowledge and means to restrain him—usually by chains or rope—and to quiet him by sedation.[12] His treatment consisted of making incisions on the patient's arm or shoulders to emit the evil spirits, to prescribe emetics and to inject varied substances in the patient's nose in order to clear his brain. Eighth, some medicine men had private hospitals where they kept patients on an in-treatment and custody basis and, in effect, were administrators of small hospitals.

When evaluated from a social-psychological viewpoint, how meaningful and effective were these modes of therapy? Since many techniques of therapy were learned by rote and in blind conformity to traditional belief, the effective workability of the techniques and the medicines were not tested and were of dubious value—except perhaps to impress the patient. For example, one patient recounted his experience with a medicine man as follows:

My mother took me to one herbalist and I followed like a sheep because I did not know what was the matter with me. I stayed at this herbalist's place for six months and wasn't helped at all. He made cuts on my arm and chest. He put an awful mixture of eggs and herbs over my body and that didn't help. He put some stuff in my nose and later poured a libation of schnapps on a stone while praying in a loud voice. I left after six months and was not improved.

Since the medicine man and the patient shared a supernatural orientation to illness, they could communicate and the medicine man could reach and influence the patient. On a psychological level, the medicine man could provide emotional security and reassurance to the anxious and harassed patient who was troubled by supposedly hostile spirits and people who might harm him. He could relieve the guilt-ridden by permitting confession and by the purification of a designated sacrifice. He could reduce the intensity of an enraged person by permitting the confessional, and he could reduce the tension within a family by testing whether a person was or was not a witch, which could mean that this person may be harming others. On the other hand, the native doctor could actually harm a person by labelling him a witch and, in effect, condemning the person in the eyes of the family. He could enhance a person's confidence by protective reassurance and encouragement; and he could arouse diffidence in a person by the knowledge that black magic or juju is being practised on him. Although the medicine man might deny that he would try to harm a person by juju, he would claim that other medicine men did practice this type of juju for a suitable fee.

Since the medicine man was concerned more with the pragmatic workability of his procedures and medicines than with the rationale of his techniques, his capacity to explain the reasons behind his practices was very inadequate. In general, his theories of mental disorder represented a composite of superstitious animism, mystical and biological ideas of personality from the West which sometimes were as antiquated as those from the 18th century. For example, he believed that piles affect the veins of the brain and cause emotional disorders. His recourse to incisions for bleeding and his use of emetics were medical procedures of the 19th century. Since he seemed to lack the knowledge of even the traditional lore of psychodynamics of personality, he seemed unaware of the traditional recognition and practice of confession as was institutionalized in the Apo ceremony of the Ashanti. Rattray has reported an account of a high priest concerning the rationale of this eight day holiday, the name of which means "to speak harshly to":

You know that every one has a sunsum (soul) that may get hurt or knocked about or become sick, and so make the body ill. Very often, although there may be other causes, e.g., witchcraft, ill-health is caused by the evil and the hate that another has in his head. Again you may have hatred in your head against another because of something that person has done to you, and that causes your sunsum to fret and become sick. Our forebears knew this to be the case and so they ordained a time once every year when every man and woman, free and slave, should have the freedom to speak out just what was in his head, to tell the neighbors just what they thought of them, and of their actions and not only their neighbors but also the king or chief. When a man has spoken freely his sunsum is cool and quieted, and the sunsum of the other person against whom he has spoken openly will be quieted also.[13]

Since the native doctor appraised his therapeutic prowess by the improvement of the patient, he tended to rely upon this criterion as the rationale for his techniques and as the basis for his spiritual "power" in coping with the patient's illness. Furthermore, he might publicize his successes and overlook his failures in treatment. Although some doctors were discreet and modest about their successes, others promoted their successes in treatment by written testimonials from the patient or his relatives. For example, one doctor publicized the following letter:

I have known Mr. O. as Divine Healer and Herbalist of no mean order. In support of my recommendation I would like to mention that my niece had a complete mental breakdown and after having failed to her normal state of health, I approached Mr. O. who was able to cure her within a couple of months which is really a remarkable achievement on his part.

These testimonials were used by the native doctor as evidence of his prowess and as means to convince other and prospective patients of his spiritual "power."

These native doctors varied considerably in their knowledge, procedural effectiveness and scope of their practice. On the one extreme, some doctors had a very extensive practice, owned several offices, a shrine and a hospital and were known for their "power." On the other extreme, many doctors hardly earned a living and were forced to turn to other occupations for supplementary income, or to abandon the profession entirely. Their mobility away from the practice of native medicine was indicative of a more profound disorganization within the occupation itself.

IV. THE DECLINING POSITION OF THE NATIVE DOCTOR AS "MENTAL HEALER"

The native doctor's declining if still dominant role of "mental healer" was influenced by the indifferent and discouraging attitude of the government, by the lack of professional authority to control the practitioners and to enforce standards of practice, by the adverse reaction of the people to the abuses of some practitioners and by the spread of competing therapies.

Although the government has encouraged the rise of Western medicine, it has either ignored or discouraged native medicine. The government has required examinations for licensing Western-trained doctors but it has permitted the regional councils to grant licenses to native doctors on the recommendation of a chief herbalist and without an examination. The government has hoped that eventually the indigenous medicinal and psychotherapeutic practices would become extinct and be replaced and its best features incorporated by Western practices. The implicit contrast between the two forms of therapy was noted unwittingly by a native doctor who referred to a Western-trained doctor as a "qualified doctor," implying that the other type was not.

But the profession itself because of its inability to authoritatively set and maintain standards and to control its members has become disorganized or even unorganized. In 1946, the Ga Medical Association was formed and in 1955 had 155 members, but its founders and leaders were unable to sustain standards.[14] When it lapsed, the profession had no controls over the activities of its members. The traditional controls which existed for the native doctor in the villages were reduced amidst the anonymity of the urban community, and by the changing and tribally diverse clientele. In addition, the native doctor had no formal standards for recruiting and training novices. Traditionally, and in the present, he strived to interest a son or nephew or an enthusiastic youth in his craft and then to train him. But the native doctor found that few competent youths were attracted to his occupation and instead wanted more modern jobs, such as clerking in the ministries. A successful practitioner could induce a son or relative to be trained as a partner and eventual successor, but in this instance the entreprenurial as well as the therapeutic interests become rewarding considerations. With the decrease in the recruitment of competent novices the continuity of the profession was being disrupted.

Furthermore, the ease with which the aspirant for native doctorhood secured a license not only lessened the need for training but also reduced the standards of practice. In the past, the apprentice to the native doctor was trained for about three years and thus acquired the lore for his specialty.[15] But some native doctors who claimed to have been inspired by the "call" to become native doctors evidently lacked this training and were not competent even in terms of folk standards.

The native doctor lacked the formal means for acquiring new formulas and techniques from other native doctors unless he solicited formulas from them for a given payment or for herb formulas of his own. Although some friendly native doctors exchanged formulas and ideas, the profession lacked any institutionalized means for such exchange. Moreover, the native doctor seemed to distrust and avoid many of his colleagues some of whom he regarded as scoundrels.

Furthermore, because they dealt with an unknown clientele of diverse tribes in a changing urban society and aspired for monetary success, some native doctors were not bound by professional restraints and resorted to sharp practices. Intermittently, a few native doctors were charged with criminal practices, such as in an extreme instance conspiring to murder a given victim by black magic or juju. These practices, of course, adversely affected the image of and confidence in the whole profession.

But the native doctor encountered a crucial conflict from the competing therapies. On the one hand he saw that Western medicines and techniques were more effective than his. On the other hand, he perceived that Christian faith-healing frequently was more attractive in the realm of faith than his appeals to jujus and deities. He noted that patients were being drawn increasingly to these other therapies. But his dominant role as mental healer was sustained by the inherent weaknesses of the competing therapies. Western psychiatry lacked the supernatural orientation which would enable the psychiatrist to share the patient's conflicts in his own idiom, which the native doctor understood. Christian faith-healing lacked any knowledge of medicines which the patient frequently wanted and which the native doctor could provide. Thus the native doctor's combined supernatural orientation and knowledge of herbs sustained him against the intensified competition of the two other therapies.

V. THE EFFECTIVE BUT LIMITED ROLE OF THE WESTERN-TRAINED PSYCHIATRIST

Psychiatric therapy was limited almost exclusively to the in-patient treatment of the state mental hospital and was largely organic in orientation. The three psychiatrists in this hospital used drugs and electric shock as their modes of therapy although they did practice some form of group therapy for the educated, volunteer patients. Out-patient treatment was negligible or virtually non-existent. But the spreading acceptance of Western psychiatry was evidenced by the increasing number of resident patients in the hospital. Thus in 1955, the state mental hospital had an excess of 8.1 per cent over capacity of 1100 patients.[16] In 1960, the excess rose to 54.5 per cent (see Table 1).

TABLE 1. EXCESS OF RESIDENT PATIENTS OVER HOSPITAL CAPACITY IN STATE MENTAL HOSPITALS ACCRA GHANA: 1955–1960*

Year	Resident Patients	Excess of Capacity Per cent.†
1955	1189	8.1
1956	1287	17.0
1957	1362	23.8
1958	1495	35.9
1959	1555	41.3
1960	1700	54.5

*Data from auditing office of State Mental Hospital, Accra Ghana.

† Capacity equals 1100 patients.

The two major types of hospitalized patients were 1) the volunteer "paying" patients and 2) the violently insane. The "paying" patients were the educated persons who tired of or discarded native treatments and sought Western therapies. These paying patients were frequently detribalized and Western-oriented. By contrast, the tribally and animistically oriented African suspected the mental hospital. In fact, Field observed that rural patients were rarely committed to the mental hospital because mental illness was considered supernaturally determined and outside the scope of the hospital.[17]

On the other hand, news of the successful treatment of patients spread so that increasingly people began to accept the hospital as an institution to which they could commit their psychotic relatives for custody as well as therapy. But the hospitalization of patients became complicated by the stigma of defective heredity which was associated with insanity. In this respect, the family of the patient also became suspect of the hereditary "taint." Educated persons were especially sensitive about this point. When psychotics were reluctant to be sent to the mental hospital, their relatives felt a similar hesitation. Thus they were caught in the dilemma of seeking effective treatment and of being stigmatized. Some sought out the native doctor for initial treatment as a way out, but soon recognized the futility of this procedure and as a last recourse turned to the state mental hospital.

Western psychiatry, despite its effective modes of physical therapy for the several types of psychoses, was a very circumscribed form of therapy in Ghana. It was limited mainly to in-patient treatment and to psychotics. Biological in its emphasis, it also lacked the frame of reference for treating on a psychological level the supernaturally oriented African. But news of its effectiveness in treating psychotic cases spread so that more people sent relatives to the hospital for treatment, although these people encountered the complicating fact of prejudice towards the insane by many urban people.

VI. THE SPREADING INFLUENCE OF THE CHRISTIAN FAITH HEALER

The Christian faith healer's influence has spread because of the declining influence of the native doctor, the decline of tribal animism as manifested in fetish cults, and the search for more powerful gods. As a central facet of an indigenous religion, Christian faith healing has been consistent with the African's form of orgiastic and emotional worship and with his version of the function of religion in healing. Its central tenets have been expressed by one of the Christian cults, "The Lord is There," as follows: "Jesus Christ is not only the Savior of the soul but the Healer of the body, the great and perfect Physician." Because of this emphasis upon healing, indigenous Christianity thus differed from missionary Christianity which is more restrained and rational in its method of worship and far more concentrated upon education and social service.

The African's acceptance of indigenous Christianity contributed to his sense of social purpose while his reaction to its faith healing sustained his emotional security. Some followers of healing cults lived in colonies so that their religious credo was the basis for a complete way of life, not just a response to a mode of therapy.

But the faith healer also used specific forms of psychotherapy many of which were similar to and perhaps imitations of the native doctor. But he incorporated these techniques within the general framework of his belief system. One prevalent form of crude group psychotherapy which was peculiar to the faith healer's technique was the revival. During a revival, the faith healer could arouse the audience to pitches of emotional intensity which would lead to deep emotional catharses and to seizures. These revivals were not only verbal but had the deep rhythmic pulse of the drumming, the effects of which were unavoidable. These revivals were especially effective for hysterical persons and for suggestible, social marginal followers.

Since the faith healer compelled his followers to manifest their belief in Christ, he could also demand that they disavow their belief in witchcraft and juju as spiritual forces, and even surrender their idols. He could elicit confessions or restrain them. Sometimes, his inadequate training in psychotherapy led to strange uses of these techniques. For example, one faith healer restrained his followers from uninhibited confessions, perhaps not to arouse his own anxieties. His rationalization was the following:

Confessing disease is like signing for a package that the Express Company has delivered. Don't accept anything that Satan brings. A spiritual law that few recognize is that our confession rules us. It is what we confess with our lips that really dominates our inner being. Make your lips do their duty.[18]

The faith healer also forbade the use of medicines for physical ailments, and the newer cult leader proscribed medicine even for serious physical diseases. Instead, he advocated the use of "holy water" as a healing potion for emotional as well as physical disorders. He also distributed a protective symbol such as the "holy handkerchief" to avert misfortune from evil persons and spirits.

The faith healer in the established cult seemed more trained, more responsible and milder in manner than the faith healer from the newer and "wilder" cults. The faith healer in the newer cults frequently felt that a "divine call" was almost enough for his vocation. Hence he relied upon informal training, inspirational improvising and copying from other healers for his psychotherapeutic procedures. Since these indigenous faith-healing cults lacked an association, the faith healer had no professional restraints upon his practices. The extreme type of faith healer was both flamboyant and unscrupulous. His chief emphasis in his varied healing procedures was faith in God and faith in his own prowess, which from his claims approached omnipotence. His exaggerated emphasis upon his healing prowess was presumably "verified" by testimonial letters and statements from his patients and their relatives. Even the faith healer of the more established cult presented an exaggerated version of his healing prowess, as can be seen from the following account by the Pastor-prophet James K. Nkansah.

At Teppa in Ashanti I prayed and 50 blind persons, 693 devil-possessed persons were healed on Sunday the 26th of March, 1961. At Kukuom, I prayed and 47 blind persons, 592 devil-possessed persons were healed on the 2nd day of April, 1961. Last Sunday when you came here and departed 9 blind persons got their sight.[19]

As head of a religious movement the faith healer solicited gifts and money from his followers and his patients, which sometimes left room for unscrupulous practices.

The faith healer had a widespread appeal for many persons who, in the anomie of the urban community, were in search of new gods for spiritual protection and craved the social purpose that a cohesive religious movement provided. Although his repertoire of psychotherapeutic techniques did not differ markedly from that of the native doctor, and included counseling, exorcism and even environmental manipulation, the faith healer also had the impetus of a social movement to reinforce his individual forms of therapy. Thus the cathartic expressions in the revivals and drummings and the emotionally supportive therapy of group approval were implicit psychotherapeutic processes which the native doctor lacked. But just as there were no enforced standards of treatment for the native doctor, the faith healer also had no associational restraints upon his practices, so that the unscrupulous and deceptive practitioner diminished the confidence and aroused the suspicions of initially trusting followers. Nonetheless, his aggressive recruiting practices and a flamboyant manner have continued to attract many followers, especially women. These followers have turned to the faith healer not only for religious guidance but for counsel and psychotherapy when in distress over their personal problems.

VII. CONCLUSIONS AND IMPLICATIONS

The native doctor in Ghana, West Africa has a heritage of orientations, practices and rituals for the diagnosis and treatment of mental disorders as components of an occupational culture. This culture is suitable peculiarly to the treatment of the African's disordered behavior because it provides a frame of reference and perspective to illness generally and mental disorders particularly which the patient and native doctor, as indigenous psychiatrist, share. Both conceive of disordered behavior as a supernatural phenomenon and as determined by spirits, black magic or juju and witches and not as naturalistic products of conflicts or germs. Hence the native doctor can communicate with and influence the patient. Although ineffectual in treating many mental disorders as well as physical ailments, the competent native doctor can provide reassurance to the anxious patient who fears harm or misfortune from spirits or witches, can reduce the intensity of the guilt-ridden patient, can soften the individual afflicted with silent rage and can quiet the agitated psychotic by restraints, sedation and relevant conversation.

But amidst the rapid changes of the urban community, his profession, though conforming superficially to the needs of the urban populace, has become disorganized and its prestige has begun to decline. This decline has been facilitated by the pressures within the urban community and has been focused mainly in the lack of enforcement of standards, the inadequate communication and exchange of ideas and techniques, the inability to recruit competent personnel to sustain the profession, the ease of obtaining a license from the regional council, and the increase of untrained, incompetent and unscrupulous practitioners who have damaged the confidence which the people have had in the native doctor. The outward forces which have contributed to the declining influence of the native doctor are the negative attitude of the government towards this profession as an instance of tribalism and the challenge of competing therapists such as the Western psychiatrist and the Christian faith healer. In spite of these pressures, the native doctor remains the dominant healer of mental disorders because of the limitations underlying the strengths of the competing therapists.

The Western psychiatrist has confined his practice largely to the in-patient treatment in the state mental hospital, so that out-patient treatment is definitely negligible. In addition, his emphasis on organic and physical therapies and his naturalistic orientation to behavior would deter him from effective and therapeutic communication with his supernaturally oriented patients. Although his physical therapies within the hospital have been successful and have attracted an increasing number of people who are becoming agreeable to committing their psychotic relatives to this institution, his influence as therapist remains circumscribed, and on an out-patient, psycho-therapeutic basis would be effective mainly with Western-oriented, educated Africans.

The Christian faith healer, however, represents a formidable, but not necessarily enduring, challenge to the native doctor as counselor and improvised psychotherapist. His widespread appeal as a religious leader provides him with the impetus of a social movement to bolster his individual psychotherapy as well as his crude group therapy in the revivals and the drummings. But the faith healer, like the medicine man, lacks professional restraints upon his behavior and his exaggerated claims; this lack of inherent pro-fessional controls enables the new and "wild" faith healers to indulge in grandiose pretensions and in unscrupulous practices. In this light, it remains to be seen whether the indigenous Christian cult with its central tenet of healing is not a tentative recourse resulting from the declining prestige of the native doctor and the retardation in the training of Western trained doctors and Western trained psychiatrists.

The trend of the future is revealed partly by the increasingly educated youth who are turning away from supernatural versions of healing and relying increasingly upon the naturalistic practices of the Western doctor. For example, in a survey of 100 primary and middle school children we found that 92 per cent preferred Western-trained doctors to the indigenous doctor for treatment.

Although some may have concealed their attitudes and preferences for the native doctor, still the evidence showing changed attitudes towards healing is definite. On the other hand, we do not know whether this trust in the Western-trained doctor will carry over into the amelioration of their personal difficulties.

In view of the urgent mental health needs of the people amidst the rapidly changing position of the native doctor in the urban context, the following implications suggest themselves from this inquiry. First, on the level of social action, it means that a concerted program is necessary to fulfill the urgent mental health needs of the people and that this program can be facilitated by training competent native doctors as well as educated youth who can implement the treatment of disordered behavior within the supernatural framework of their patients but by the use of modern psychotherapeutic techniques. Second, on the level of social control, it indicates that more effective vigilance by the government is necessary to deter unscrupulous practitioners (whether native doctors or Christian faith healers) from harming unsuspecting patients. Third, on the level of social change, it means that a trans-planted occupational group from a rural to an urban environment can become quickly disor-ganized by the pressures of urban processes. Fourth, and finally, it reveals on the level of historiography the need to record and document these and other facets of change in the transition from village tribalism to urban nationalism before these facets of urban life in West Africa dissipate and are lost to further inquiry.

NOTES

1. See S. Kirson Weinberg, "The Occupational Culture of the Boxer," *American Journal of Sociology* (1952) 57, pp. 460–469.

2. See E. Evans-Pritchard, *The Nuer* (Oxford: Clarendon Press, 1940) M. Fortes, *The Web of Kinship Among the Tallensi*, London: Oxford University Press, 1949.

3. S. Kirson Weinberg, "Social Psychiatry in West Africa," paper presented at the Fifth World Congress of the International Sociological Association, Washington, D.C., September 7, 1962. Tooth maintains that the person afflicted with trypanosomiasis, a sickness resulting from the tsetse fly had symptoms similar to schizophrenia. See G. Tooth, *Studies in Mental Illness in the Gold Coast* (London H.M.S., 1950).

4. Robert S. Rattray, *Religion and Art in Ashanti*, London: Oxford University Press, 1959. Margaret J. Field, *Search for Security*, London: Faber and Faber, 1960.

5. See Margaret J. Field, *Religion and Medicine of the Ga People*, London: Oxford University Press, 1937.

6. Kofi A. Busia, *"Ashanti of the Gold Coast" African*

Worlds, edited by Daryll Forde, London: Oxford University Press, 1955, pp. 190–209.

7. Rev. H. Debrunner, *Witchcraft in Ghana*, Kumasi: Presbyterian Book Depot, 1959.

8. Ione Acquah, *Accra Survey*, London: London University Press, 1959.

9. See H. J. Simans, "Tribal Medicine, Diviners and Herbalists," *African Studies*, (1957) 16:2 pp. 85–92.

10. In her survey of Accra, Acquah found 258 native doctors or medicine men and fetish priests, 6 Western trained doctors in private practice and 22 Western trained doctors and 1 psych-iatric specialist. In 1962, the estimate was that between 500 and 600 Western doctors in Ghana and 50 Western-trained doctors in Accra as compared with about 500 native doctors. Of the Western-trained doctors in Accra, 3 were psychiatric specialists. See Ione Acquah, *Accra Survey*, London: University of London Press, 1958, pp. 122–125.

11. See Wulf-Sachs, *Black Hamlet*, Boston: Little Brown and Company, 1947, pp. 149–152.

12. In Ghana, there are over 500 varieties of herbs and trees with medicinal properties. See Fred Irvine, *Woody Plants*

of Ghana, London: Oxford University Press, 1961. Supplemental information derived from interviews with Dr. Irvine.

13. Robert S. Rattray, *Ashanti*, Oxford: The Clarendon Press, 1923, p. 153.

14. Ione Acquah, *Accra Survey* p. 125.

15. The folklore concerning the locating of herbs and the preparing, mixing, brewing and administering of herbs is considerable. The herbs which seem to be plentiful and effective are those which remedy stomach disorders; other herbs and woody plants which are effective are those which reduce swelling and quiet agitation. Even in the 19th century, it was noted that "in every village (of Ghana) there are professors of the healing art though ignorant of every ology that goes to make up medical science their empirical knowledge leads to very creditable measure of success for milder forms of diseases." Charles A. Gordon, *Life on the Gold Coast*, London: Balliere, Tindall and Cox, 1874, pp. 39, 40.

16. Data obtained from auditing office of the State Mental Hospital. Accra, Ghana.

17. Margaret J. Field, *Search For Security*, p. 14.

18. *Divine Healer's Magazine* (Spring) 3:1.

19. Letter to the author.

20. Revised version of paper presented at the annual meeting of the Society For The Study of Social Problems, Washington, D.C., August 29, 1962.

THE INSTITUTIONAL FRAMEWORK OF SOVIET PSYCHIATRY

Mark G. Field and Jason Aronson

AN IMPORTANT element of the psychiatric system of any society are the facilities established for the treatment and/or custodial care of psychiatric patients. These reflect, in turn, the prevalent therapeutic commitments of the time and by their nature tend to determine the kind and locus of treatment available to the population. In the United States, for example, there is still a heavy nineteenth-century legacy of large, geographically isolated mental hospitals, built with a clinically pessimistic, and a custodial, if not punitive, view of the psychiatric patient. The availability of these large state mental hospitals has deflected attention from alternative facilities and thus contributed to long-term hospitalization of patients who might otherwise fare better in other types of treatment institutions or even in the community. The Soviet Union is fortunate in that it has escaped the pattern of large mental hospitals. In the Soviet institutional framework, outpatient treatment is central; inpatient care plays an accessory rather than primary role.

OUTPATIENT FACILITIES

In the Soviet Union, the keystone of the psychiatric system is the outpatient psychoneurological clinic (*psikhonevrologicheskii dispanser*). There are, broadly speaking, three types of such clinics: the first, and presumably the model for further development, is the independent clinic. It is a purely psychiatric installation in the community, administratively separate from the district polyclinic. It is open to the individuals who live in the territory served by it, although it is sometimes possible for patients from other areas to be treated there also.

The second type is the outpatient department of a regular mental hospital, and the third is simply a part of a regular district polyclinic. Apparently the independent clinic is most favored in contemporary Soviet psychiatric thinking and is the model (because of its comprehensiveness) for further

Reprinted from *Journal of Nervous and Mental Disease* (April, 1964), *138* (4). Copyright © 1964 by The Williams and Williams Co.

development. In 1956, according to data released by the Health Ministry, there were 2,327 PN clinics in the Soviet Union, 119 of which were of the first or independent type (35). In 1959, the number of independent clinics was reported as 146 (32); in 1961, it was 167 (37).

Since Soviet psychiatric thinking places so much emphasis on the independent clinic and since it seems to point to the direction of future development, we shall emphasize in our description this type of facility, bearing in mind that the other two types are, in essence, similar in concept although perhaps not so comprehensive in functions and services.

The psychoneurological clinic is seen as a psychiatric installation *in the community*, whose mandate it is to provide for the comprehensive handling of psychiatric patients in the different phases of their disability, with the exception of long-term hospitalization. Clinics may be placed directly under the administrative jurisdiction of five different types of health organizations: republican, provincial, regional, municipal and district. In each of these cases, the dispensary is subordinate to one of these health organizations, and the clinic head is appointed on a competitive basis.

The functions of the psychiatric clinic are broad and comprehensive; they can be subsumed under four major categories:

1) *Medical:* Diagnosis, treatment, rehabilitation and consultation;

2) *Social:* Supportive assistance such as vocational placement, welfare benefits, legal assistance, certification of illness and disability, guardianship, financial support;

3) *Prevention and education:* Measures to prevent illness or to avoid irreversibility or chronicity of pathological processes, education of psychiatric personnel and of the lay population;

4) *Accounting:* A dynamic record of morbidity in the area served by clinic.

The typical clinic consists of several divisions (*otdelenia*), each one providing a specific range of services. A large, well-equipped, model clinic should have all or most of the following divisions:

1) *Clinical-diagnostic:* This is, of course, the major service offered by the clinic staff, usually

to the adult population of the area served by the clinic. The allocation of personnel to population follows norms established by the Health Ministry, and the district psychiatrist carries responsibility for psychiatric services to the district population. He arranges for treatment either at the clinic, or when necessary, at the patient's home (see below), refers patients to a mental hospital and provides after-care when the patient is released from the hospital (26). The standard treatment procedures are chemotherapy (treatment of choice), psychotherapy (directive rather than analytical),narcotherapy, hypnosis, speech therapy and adjunct procedures such as physiotherapy and injections.

When he refers a patient to a mental hospital, the psychiatrist is expected to provide the hospital with a summary of the case history (diagnosis, course of illness, treatment provided), and when the patient is released, the hospital is expected to do the same for the psychiatrist. If the patient fails to report to the clinic, the initiative then passes to the clinic staff, who must send for the patient or visit him at home.

Home treatment is indicated for those patients who do not need hospitalization either in a mental hospital or psychiatric colony, or for whom such hospitalization might impose unnecessary hardship, but who nonetheless need special supervision, treatment and material assistance at home. Non-agitated patients with long-standing psychoses, living in the area serviced by the clinic, are registered and taken under home-care treatment. The decision to take, or discharge, a patient in home treatment is the responsibility of a permanent commission chaired by the clinic chief, and including the head of the local health department and the patient's treating physician. There are two aspects to home treatment: the medical or clinical measures prescribed by the district psychiatrist who must visit the patient at home at regular intervals, check on the patient's health and material surroundings and arrange, when the need arises, for his transfer to a mental or a general hospital; the other aspect of home treatment includes the non-clinical but supportive measures designed to help the patient in his general social adjustments. While these tend to be initiated by the district psychiatrist, they are carried out in the main by visiting nurses working from another special department of the clinic described in greater detail below (25).

2) *Child and adolescent:* This service caters to the needs of the child and adolescent population of the district, providing clinical, remedial and preventive treatment. A speech clinic is sometimes combined with a day hospital. A most important function expected of this service is the establishment and maintenance of liaison with the educational and occupational institutions of the district. This permits the staff of the clinic to engage in preventive work by examining and observing children and adolescents who exhibit pathological behavior and psychic insufficiency in kindergartens, schools, vocational schools, technicums and in enterprises employing adolescents.

3) *Inpatient (statsionar):* Traditionally, outpatient psychiatry has developed as an extension of services provided by the mental hospital. The Soviet clinic seems to reverse this process by establishing psychiatric beds as a community extension of its outpatient services. These beds are not intended to replace mental hospitals. Rather, they permit the psychiatric clinic to carry out certain functions and procedures it otherwise could not do. Naturally, in isolated settlements or in the face of great distances and transportation difficulties, these beds will tend to assume, temporarily at least, some of the functions of a mental hospital. The number of beds in a clinic may vary from 15 to 100, depending on local conditions and the availability of an easily accessible mental hospital. As such, this service performs one or more of the following functions: a) a receiving center for patients awaiting transfer to a mental hospital; b) a place where violent or agitated patients can be kept under medical supervision; c) a facility where diagnostic workups can be performed; d) a clinical base for those cases requiring only short periods of hospitalization; and e) a temporary haven for psychiatric patients who need to be removed from a disturbed home environment (19). According to regulations of the Health Ministry, the limit of an inpatient stay is 15 days in communities where mental hospitals are available, more in other cases. It may be said that this service is the functional equivalent of the psychopathic hospital, the receiving hospital and the psychiatric department or ward of the general hospital, as these terms are understood in the United States.

4) *Work-therapy and day hospital:* Work therapy (as distinct from occupational therapy) occupies an important position in the Soviet psychiatric system; it is, further, reinforced by the Marxist ideology which holds work and production to be central elements in social life, in the formation of personality and of motives and behavior. The aim of work therapy is thus not so much to keep the patient occupied in such economically sterile activities as basket-weaving, but to train or re-train him to assume a productive role in society. Work

therapy is often carried out as part of day-hospital care, and has the following facilities: a) Therapeutic work-shops *(lechebnoproizvoditel'nie masterski):* These are placed under the supervision both of medical (and psychiatric) personnel and production experts, provide different types of activities to psychiatric patients, graded (as to their complexity) to patients' capacities and abilities, but resembling work under normal conditions as much as possible. The aim of the workshop is not only to teach the patient a trade, but also to imbue him with the values and attitudes necessary for work in a factory (discipline, punctuality, accuracy, diligence). The maximum workday is six hours; patients receive payment on a scale comparable to that of regular industry. Those patients who, once released from the work-shop, are still unable to assume regular employment may join an invalid cooperative. This is a work group consisting of disabled or otherwise incapacitated individuals who produce small consumer items primarily. The income from their sale is divided among the members of the cooperative. b) Day hospitals *(dnevnii statsionar).* These resemble our own day hospitals in that they provide hospital-type psychiatric and medical treatment without the "hotel" functions. Patients who have been released from a mental hospital (and some others) who are as yet unable to live by themselves in the community may attend the day hospital, where they receive medical and psychiatric treatment, food, and where they usually spend their time in the workshops. It also may assume the position of a half-way station between the hospital and community.

5) *Social assistance, prevention and mental hygiene*: A comprehensive concept of mental illness and of the position of the patient in his social milieu leads to the conclusion that psychiatric treatment given, so to speak, in a vacuum may contribute little to improving his condition. The individual is enmeshed in a variety of social relationships that are related, to some degree, to his adjustment or maladjustment. And insofar as the Soviet treatment commitment is to attempt to maintain the patient in the community and to hospitalize him only when no other management is feasible or safe (for himself and those around him), the psychiatric clinic undertakes a series of supportive services aimed at making his environment as favorable as possible for him. The following are examples of these services: a) Improvement of the patient's living conditions: it has been noted, at least by one observer (4) that the problem with respect to mental illness in our times may be less an actual increase in the number of the mentally

ill as the decrease in the tolerance of our (urban) society for them. While about half of the Soviet population still lives in the country where mental patients are much less disturbing to people around them than in the town, the rest live under incredibly crowded conditions in urban areas. Indeed, the housing shortage caused by the very rapid increase in the size of urban population and the almost total lack of a housing program to keep pace with this increase until recently is one of the salient aspects of the round of daily living in Soviet society (2, 27). In the typical situation, one family lives in each room of an apartment, all sharing the kitchen and bathroom. These conditions, bad enough as they are for the average individual, are much worse for a mental patient and his family, particularly if the patient is frankly psychotic. Recognition of this problem led, as early as thirty years ago, to measures aimed at providing private rooms for mental patients living in the community (3). These clinics provide certificates that help patients secure such single rooms. In addition, the clinic may provide the patient (or his family) with some financial and other assistance to improve his living conditions. b) Social and welfare assistance: Aid is provided in solving family conflicts and quarrels occasioned by the patient's condition, in applying for social welfare benefits to which the patient (or his family) may be entitled, in placing children in crèches and kindergartens, and in referring the patient, when indicated, to the other medical institutions of the area. For this purpose, liaison is maintained both with the organs of Social Welfare and of Education. c) Vocational assistance: Since work is considered of therapeutic value, the clinic attempts to arrange in the community a working situation best suited to the patient's condition. This may take two forms: help (primarily through the labor union organization) in finding a job the patient can easily perform (arranging, for example, a transfer to a different type of work, or shift from the night to the day shift). Thus, whenever possible, an attempt is made to maintain the patient at work in the community, even if he has only partial or residual work capacity. Soviet experience has shown that this facilitates the preservation of a certain "tone of life" for many years, tends to prevent chronicity in the course of illness, and the deterioration that almost inevitably accompanies long-term hospitalization.

Arranging for the vocational placement of the patient is not as difficult as it would be in the West, particularly in the United States. For one thing, the Soviet Union is suffering, in a period of industrial expansion, from a manpower shortage aggravated by the very high losses (both in terms of excess mortality and deficits in births) from the second World War (5, 16). There is, therefore, a constant demand for manpower which patients, under treatment or supervision by the clinic, can fill. Second, clinic personnel, because of the very nature of psychiatric organization, are expected to know the territory they serve and its occupational resources. This is reinforced by the fact that personnel turnover is small since salaries are standard for the entire country and there is no private practice to exercise a strong pull away from public facilities. Third, since all economic organizations are owned and operated by the state, there is probably less resistance to the employment of mental patients (or ex-mental patients) than there might be in private organizations in a highly competitive situation. An important role, in these matters, is also played by the so-called social insurance delegates who are appointed by the trade unions precisely to help arrange such matters, as well as sick pay, pension benefits and so on (20). The clinic may also act to protect the patient in his relationship with his employing organization. For example, an individual may be penalized if he has not gone to work and has not obtained an illness certificate from a physician to excuse him. Often, psychiatric patients (or those close to him) do not realize he is sick and in need of medical attention. The role of the clinic in such cases would be to certify the patient's right to an illness certificate and to re-establish the individual's seniority, a step that is important for receiving social welfare and other benefits. d) legal assistance: There may be instances in which a patient may require legal assistance; in addition to the problems that may arise under conditions outlined in (a) and (b) above, arrangements must sometimes be made to establish guardianship over the mentally incompetent; in other cases, patients (or relatives) need someone to appear on their behalf or represent them in court. This assistance may be provided by someone from the clinic who has legal experience (though there is no indication that this person must have had formal legal training) or by referring (or facilitating the referral of) the patient to what is called a legal consultation. e) Certification and forensic psychiatry: An important function performed by the medical system in any society is that of the certification, on the part of physicians, of the health or the degree of disability of patients. It is on the strength of such certification that an individual may be excused from his ordinary social obligations or duties (army service, for example) or, on the contrary, be held accountable or responsible for what he does or fails to do (in committing a crime, for example). This is a particularly critical area in the Soviet Union, with its shortage of manpower and its complicated system of social welfare, and with the possibilities for abuses and evasions that the medical certificate presents (9, 12). Every medical institution has a special commission whose duty is to certify the degree of disability and residual work capacity of each patient who comes before the commission. The psychiatric clinic must, thus, also provide certification of the health and illness of patients and, in addition, play a role in the provision of expert psychiatric knowledge in cases that come before the courts of law (15).

f) Home visiting (*patronazh*): We have seen that home care is an important element of the work of the clinic personnel. While the clinic psychiatrist has as his primary function the giving of treatment to patients at home, a great many of the supportive services in home care are given by the visiting nurse (*patronazhnaia sestra*) who combines, in this respect, the roles of doctor's assistant and social worker. The physician might, for example, order injections or other modes of treatment to be administered by the visiting nurse; in addition, she must gather, for the psychiatrist's use, information about the life situation and family conditions of the patient to guide the psychiatrist in his work. Soviet literature on the subject stresses that the nurses "must be carefully instructed so that while they gather information about the patient, particularly from those who are close to the patient, it is indispensable to be careful and show the maximum amount of tact" (30, Vol. 2, pp. 265–269). It is often on the basis of the visiting nurses' reports that measures are undertaken to improve the living arrangements of the patient, to provide material assistance, to settle family conflicts and other similar problems. The visiting nurse, thus, to a greater extent than the psychiatrist, establishes a link between the patient in the community and the psychiatric clinic, and stands ready to assist him in most non-clinical aspects of his life situation.

g) Mental hygiene and prevention: In accordance with the preventive emphasis that is so much a part of Soviet medical philosophy, every person in the medical field is required to engage in some preventive work. In the psychiatric field, and particularly at the clinic, this emphasis expresses itself in programs to educate the population on mental illness, and early detection and early treatment. The assumption is that these efforts will prevent incipient conditions from becoming either chronic or irreversible. This is accomplished through the following programs. Health propaganda: Like all other physicians, the psychiatrist is expected to devote a few hours each month (a minimum of four hours) to educational talks in his area of competence. These are given either at the clinic or outside it and may take the form of evenings of questions and answers, consultations, group work with patients, sanitary (hygiene) instruction, radio talks, distribution of printed materials, and similar activities (30, p. 573). Education of personnel: Health propaganda, in the Soviet design, is not limited to the lay population, but is also addressed to other medical personnel either in the form of training for junior medical personnel in the psychiatric field, or in teaching non-psychiatric medical personnel to recognize psychiatric illness and to refer patients to psychiatric facilities when necessary. The educational program of the clinic, on paper at least, is extensive and impressive and is facilitated by the fact that often the clinic itself constitutes a sizeable aggregation of personnel under one roof. For example, the clinic of the Kiev district in Moscow, which has 47.5 positions budgeted (13.5 for physicians, 20.5 for nurses, 9.5 for attendants and four for others), has the following intramural educational program: Twice a month, special educational conferences held with the aim of improving the professional skill of the physicians and the nurses; problems of medical treatment and preventive work as well as brief case histories are discussed at the conferences; every second month, conferences devoted to the theoretical and practical problems of psychiatry are held under the supervision of a professor (presumably not one permanently attached to the clinic); at these conferences (called "practice and research conferences") reports and brief accounts are delivered by psychiatrists; once a week, furthermore, the professor sees patients in a consulting room to verify diagnoses and to

improve the quality of treatment; the clinic physicians, in addition to attending meetings of the Scientific Society of Psychiatrists and Neuropathologists, also give lectures on topical problems at least six times a year for the nurses and workshop personnel (examples of the topics are the following: "Care of Patients Who Have Undergone Aminasin (chlorpromazine) Treatment," "Treatment of Alcoholism" and "Management of Psychotic Patients"); once a year, in addition, one of the psychiatrists gives a short course on the care and supervision of psychiatric out-patients.

Again, while it is impossible to determine how typical this program is, the fact, however, that practically every textbook on medical organization refers to the importance of education indicates that it is a significant part of the official blueprint. Preventive measures: The psychiatrist must (or may) be consulted on all measures that might affect the mental health of the population in his area, particularly new industrial construction. A psychiatrist might, for example, state that the noise level in a plant was too high and that this would tend to fatigue the workers' nervous systems unnecessarily. Whether this would lead to remedial action is, however, an open question. h) Dispensarization: Dispensarization is a Soviet term denoting frequent examinations of groups of the population, and instituting treatment and constant observation over those who need it. In the area of mental illness, the clinic is expected to provide this service to the following four categories of individuals: chronically and acutely ill patients; war invalids; workers in shops and plants where conditions are a hazard to (mental) health (nervous system); and to chronic (long-term) and frequently ill patients and war invalids residing in *Sovkhozes* (state farms) and *Kolkhozes* (collective farms). . . .

REFERENCES

1. Albee, G. W. *Mental Health Manpower Needs*, p. 294. Basic Books, New York, 1959.

2. Bauer, R. A. and Inkeles, A. *The Soviet Citizen*, pp. 123–124. Harvard Univ. Press, Cambridge, 1959.

3. Decision of the Central Executive Committee (Party) and the Council of Peoples' Commissars, Dated: February 28, 1930.

4. Dubos, R. *Mirage of Health*, p. 173. Harper, New York, 1959.

5. Eason, W. The Soviet population today. J. Foreign Affairs, *37*: 598–607, 1959.

6. Eckstein, H. *The English Health Service*. Harvard Univ. Press, Cambridge, 1958.

7. *Encyclopedia of Russia and the Soviet Union*, pp. 341–343. McGraw-Hill, New York, 1961.

8. Fainsod, M. *How Russia is Ruled*. Harvard Univ. Press, Cambridge, 1963.

9. Field, M. G. Some problems of Soviet medical practice: A sociological approach. New Engl. J. Med., *248*: 919–926, 1953.

10. Field, M. G. Health services in the USSR. Soviet Survey, *35*: 100–105, 1961.

11. Field, M. G. Soviet society and science: The paradox of the service concept. Presented at the Midwestern Conference of the American Association for the Advancement of Slavic Studies, Madison, Wisconsin, 1962. Mimeographed.

12. Field, M. G. Structured strain in the role of the Soviet physician. Amer. J. Sociol., *58*: 493–502, 1953.

13. Field, M. G. Approaches to mental illness in Soviet society. Some comparisons and conjectures. Soc. Problems, *7*: 277–297, 1960.

14. *Health, Education and Welfare Trends, 1962*, p. 33. Department of Health, Education and Welfare, Washington, D.C.

15. *Instruction on Carrying out Forensic Psychiatric Certification in the USSR*. Confirmed by Health Ministry USSR on May 31, 1954, with agreement of the Ministry of Justice USSR, Ministry of Internal Affairs USSR, and the Procuracy USSR. In Russian.

16. Kantner, J. A comparison of the current population in the USSR and USA. In *Soviet Society: A Book of Readings*, pp. 15–28. Houghton Mifflin, Boston, 1961.

17. Kerbikov, O. V. et al. *Uchebnik Psikhiatrii*, p. 331. Medgiz, Moscow, 1958.

18. Kline, N. S. The organization of psychiatric care and psychiatric research in the Union of Soviet Socialist Republics. Ann. N. Y. Acad. Sci., *84*: 147–224, 1960.

19. Lesse, S. Current clinical and research trends in Soviet Psychiatry. Amer. J. Psychiat., *114*: 1018, 1958.

20. Madison, B. Welfare personnel in the Soviet Union. Social Work, *7*: 57–68, 1962.

21. *Ministerstvo zdravookhranenia RSFSR, Katalog pasportov tipovikh proektov kurortnosanatornikh, lechebno-profilaktichaskikh i detskikh uchrezhdenii*, pp. 406–413. Meduchposobi, Moscow, 1960.

22. *Narodnoe Khoziaistvo SSR v 1961 godu*, pp. 8 and 747. Gosstatizdat, Moscow, 1962.

23. Psikhonevrologicheskaia bol'nitsa. *Large Medical Encyclopaedia* (in Russian). 2nd ed. Vol. 4, Columns 145–148.

24. Querido, A. Early diagnosis and treatment services. In *Elements of a Community Mental Health Program*, pp. 138–169. Milbank Memorial Fund, New York, 1956.

25. *Regulations on the Psychiatric Clinic Under Republican, Provincial, Regional, Municipal and District Jurisdiction.* Confirmed by Health Ministry, USSR, December 4, 1953. In Russian.

26. Snezhnevskii, A. V. Dispensary method of registering psychiatric morbidity and the Soviet system of psychiatric services. I. *Living Conditions and Health.* No. 4, 236–241, 1959.

27. Sosnovy, T. *The Housing Problem in the USSR.* Research Program on the USSR, New York, 1954.

28. *Statistical Abstract of the United States, 1963*, p. 5. Bureau of the Census, Washington, D. C., 1963.

29. U.S. Dept. of Health, Education & Welfare. *Report of the United States Public Health Mission to the Union of Soviet Socialist Republics*, p. 15. Public Health Service Publication No. 649, chart No. 4, 1959.

30. Vinogradov, N. A. *Organizatsia zdravookhranenia v SSR* (Organization of Health Protection in the USSR) Vols. 1 & 2. Medigz, Moscow, 1958.

31. World Health Organization. Expert Committee on Mental Health, Table I. p. 3.

32. World Health Organization. Guide line for panel consultations on mental health. Persons, Plans and Priorities, 1960, annex.

33. World Health Organization. Health services in the USSR. WHO/PHA 27, 4 May 1959, Geneva, p. 49.

34. Wortis, J. The thaw in Soviet psychiatry. Amer. J. Psychiat., *119*: 586–588, 1962.

35. *Zdravookhranenie v. SSR*, p. 103. Medgiz, Moscow, 1957.

36. *Zdravookhranenie v SSR*. Gosstatizdat, Moscow, 1960.

37. *Large Medical Encyclopedia*, 2nd ed., Vol. 30, Cols. 1111 and 1112, Table 71. Moscow, 1963. In Russian.

CONTRIBUTORS

SHIRLEY ANGRIST, M.A., Assistant Professor of Psychiatric Nursing, University of Pittsburgh.

LAWRENCE APPLEBY, Ph.D., Assistant Professor of Psychology, University of Michigan, and Chief Psychologist, Ypsilanti State Hospital.

JASON ARONSON, M.D., Editor, *International Journal of Psychiatry*, and Assistant Clinical Professor of Psychiatry, Cornell Medical College.

ANITA K. BAHN, D.Sc., Chief, Outpatient Studies Section, Office of Biometry, National Institute of Mental Health, U.S. Public Health Service, and Lecturer in Epidemiology, Johns Hopkins University School of Hygiene and Public Health.

PAUL BENEDICT, M.D., Director, Alcoholism Research and Treatment Center, Home Term Court, New York.

GERALD CAPLAN, M.D., Clinical Professor of Psychiatry and Director, Laboratory of Community Psychiatry, Harvard Medical School.

JOHN CLAUSEN, Ph.D., Professor of Sociology, University of California, Berkeley.

SIMON DINITZ, Ph.D., Professor of Sociology, University of Texas.

H. WARREN DUNHAM, Ph.D., Professor of Sociology, Wayne State University, and Research Director, Lafayette Clinic, Detroit.

NORMAN C. ELLIS, Ph.D., Research Psychologist, Social Systems Project, Osawatomie State Hospital, Kansas.

R. A. ELLIS, Ph.D., Associate Professor of Sociology, University of Oregon.

SHEILA FELD, Ph.D., Psychologist, Mental Health Study Center, National Institute of Mental Health, U.S. Public Health Service.

MARK G. FIELD, Ph.D., Professor of Sociology, Boston University.

LAWRENCE Z. FREEDMAN, M.D., Research Professor of Psychiatry, University of Chicago Medical School.

HOWARD E. FREEMAN, Ph.D., Professor of Social Work, Brandeis University.

J. FRIED, Ph.D., Department of Sociology and Anthropology, McGill University.

ERVING GOFFMAN, Ph.D., Professor of Sociology, University of California, Berkeley.

GERALD GURIN, Ph.D., Department of Psychology, University of Michigan.

JULES HENRY, Ph.D., Professor of Anthropology, Washington University.

A. B. HOLLINGSHEAD, Ph.D. Professor of Sociology, Yale University.

KENNETH I. HOWARD, Ph.D., Chief, Division of Measurement and Evaluation, Department of Research, Institute for Juvenile Research, Chicago.

IRVING JACKS, Ph.D., Assistant Professor of Psychology, Temple University Medical School.

MERTON J. KAHNE, M.D., Assistant Professor of Psychiatry, Harvard Medical School.

E. C. KIRBY, M.D., Psychiatrist, St. Elizabeth's Hospital, Washington, D.C.

ROBERT KLEINER, Ph.D., Associate Professor of Sociology, Temple University.

MELVIN KOHN, Ph.D., Head, Division of Population Studies, National Institute of Mental Health, U.S. Public Health Service.

THOMAS LANGNER, Ph.D., Assistant Professor of Social Psychiatry (Sociology), Cornell University.

STANLEY A. LEAVY, M.D., Assistant Clinical Professor of Psychiatry, Yale University, and Attending Assistant and Psychiatrist, Grace–New Haven Hospital.

MARK LEFTON, Ph.D., Associate Professor of Sociology, Western Reserve University.

DANIEL J. LEVINSON, Ph.D., Assistant Professor of Psychology, Harvard Medical School, and Director, Center for Sociopsychological Research, Massachusetts Mental Health Center.

MARJORIE FISKE LOWENTHAL, Ph.D., Langley Porter Clinic, University of California, Berkeley.

YI-CHUANG LU, Ph.D., Director of Sociological Research, Manteno State Hospital, Illinois State Department of Mental Health.

S. M. MILLER, Ph.D., Professor of Sociology, New York University.

ELLIOT G. MISHLER, Ph.D., Director of Psychological Research, Massachusetts Mental Health Center, and Assistant Clinical Professor of Psychology, Harvard Medical School.

JEROME K. MYERS, Ph.D., Professor of Sociology, Yale University.

357

JUM C. NUNNALLY, JR., Ph.D., Professor of Psychology, Vanderbilt University.

SEYMOUR PARKER, Ph.D., Associate Professor of Sociology, Michigan State University.

BENJAMIN PASAMANICK, M.D., Assistant Director of Research, Illinois State Psychiatric Institute.

FRED PINE, Ph.D., Research Scientist, New York State University Medical College.

EDNA RAPHAEL, Ph.D., Supervising Sociologist, Institute for Juvenile Research, Chicago, and Associate Professor of Labor Studies and Sociology, Pennsylvania State College.

BERTRAM H. ROBERTS, M.D., Assistant Professor of Psychiatry, Yale University.

LESLIE SCHAFFER, B.S. (Med.), National Institute of Mental Health, U.S. Public Health Service.

THOMAS SCHEFF, Ph.D., Associate Professor of Sociology, University of California, Santa Barbara.

MORRIS S. SCHWARTZ, Ph.D., Professor of Sociology, Brandeis University.

WILLIAM SCOTT, Ph.D., Professor of Psychology, University of Colorado.

OZZIE G. SIMMONS, Ph.D., Professor of Sociology, University of Colorado.

ROBERT J. SMITH, Ph.D., Associate Professor of Anthropology, Western Michigan University.

LEO SROLE, Ph.D, Professor of Sociology, College of Physicians and Surgeons, Columbia University.

THOMAS S. SZASZ, M.D., Professor of Psychiatry, State University of New York, Upstate Medical Center, Syracuse.

DAVID T. A. VERNON, M.A., Associate Director of Field Foundation Project, Child Guidance Clinic, Children's Memorial Hospital, Chicago.

JOSEPH VEROFF, Ph.D., Study Director, Survey Research Center, University of Michigan.

S. KIRSON WEINBERG, Ph.D., Professor of Sociology, Portland State College and Roosevelt University, and Consulting Research Sociologist, Institute for Juvenile Research, Chicago.

E. D. WITTKOWER, M.D., Professor of Psychiatry, McGill University.

NAME INDEX

359

⁹SUBJECT INDEX